DEFINING SHINTO

This book provides key official documents alongside political, religious-philosophical, and historical essays, illustrating how the term "Shinto" has metamorphosed terminologically from Japan's emergence as a modern nation state in the late 19th century to the postmodern Japan of today.

"Shinto" is one of the most contested categories in the field of Japanese religious studies. While the term "Shinto" has a long history in the pre-modern period, this volume focuses on how the term has evolved in modern Japan. Divided into five parts, the book covers:

- Shinto and the modern Japanese nation state
- Pre-war Japanese intellectuals on Shinto
- Shinto and ultra-nationalism of the 1930s and 1940s
- Post-war reforms and reformulations
- Contemporary ways of defining Shinto

Presenting a wealth of documents, most of which have been translated here for the first time, the book is an invaluable resource for scholars and students of Japanese religion.

Mark W. MacWilliams is Professor of Religious Studies at St. Lawrence University, USA, and has published widely in the field of Japanese religions.

Okuyama Michiaki is Research Fellow at the Nanzan Institute of Religion and Culture and Professor at the Faculty of Humanities at Nanzan University, Japan. He has written extensively on the concept of Shinto in the light of studies on comparative religion.

D1789553

CRITICAL CATEGORIES IN THE STUDY OF RELIGION

Series editors:

Russell T. McCutcheon, University of Alabama, USA
Steffen Führding, Leibniz Universität Hannover, Germany

Critical Categories in the Study of Religion aims to present the pivotal articles that best represent the most important trends in how scholars have gone about the task of describing, interpreting, and explaining the place of religion in human life. The series focuses on the development of categories and the terminology of scholarship that make possible knowledge about human beliefs, behaviours, and institutions. Each volume in the series is intended as both an introductory survey of the issues that surround the use of various key terms as well as an opportunity for a thorough retooling of the concept under study, making clear to readers that the cognitive categories of scholarship are themselves historical artefacts that change over time.

RELIGION AND COGNITION
Edited by D. Jason Slone

DEFINING ISLAM
Edited by Andrew Rippin

DEFINING BUDDHISM(S)
Edited by Karen Derris and Natalie Gummer

MYTHS AND MYTHOLOGIES
Edited by Jeppe Sinding Jensen

DEFINING JUDAISM
Edited by Aaron W. Hughes

RELIGIOUS EXPERIENCE
Edited by Craig Martin and Russell T. McCutcheon, with Leslie Dorrough Smith

DEFINING MAGIC
Edited by Bernd-Christian Otto and Michael Stausberg

DEFINING SHINTO
Edited by Mark W. MacWilliams and Okuyama Michiaki

For more information about this series, please visit: https://www.routledge.com/Critical-Categories-in-the-Study-of-Religion/book-series/TFSE00054

DEFINING SHINTO

A Reader

Edited by Mark W. MacWilliams and Okuyama Michiaki

Routledge
Taylor & Francis Group

LONDON AND NEW YORK

First published 2020
by Routledge
2 Park Square, Milton Park, Abingdon, Oxon OX14 4RN

and by Routledge
52 Vanderbilt Avenue, New York, NY 10017

Routledge is an imprint of the Taylor & Francis Group, an informa business

British Library Cataloguing-in-Publication Data
A catalogue record for this book is available from the British Library

Library of Congress Cataloging-in-Publication Data
Names: Macwilliams, Mark Wheeler, 1952- editor. | Okuyama, Michiaki,
1963- editor.
Title: Defining Shinto : a reader / edited by Mark W. MacWilliams and
Okuyama Michiaki.
Description: New York : Routledge, 2019. | Series: Critical categories in the study
of religion | Includes bibliographical references and index. |
Identifiers: LCCN 2019036223 | ISBN 9781844658374 (hardback) |
ISBN 9781844658381 (paperback)
Subjects: LCSH: Shinto—History—1945- | Shinto—History—1868-1945.
Classification: LCC BL2218.5 .D45 2019 | DDC 299.5/61—dc23
LC record available at https://lccn.loc.gov/2019036223

ISBN: 978-1-84465-837-4 (hbk)
ISBN: 978-1-84465-838-1 (pbk)

Typeset in Times New Roman
by Swales & Willis Ltd, Exeter, Devon, UK

CONTENTS

CONTENTS

CONTENTS

CONVENTIONS

In this book, we have generally followed the *Monumenta Nipponica* manual of style for translating Japanese terms, names, administrative offices, and so on. We also have followed the standard practice of putting Japanese names in Japanese word order with surname first and first name last. We have preserved macrons for indicating long vowels for Japanese words except when the word has become common parlance in English. Thus, for example, "*Shintō*" is not italicized and without a macron and is transposed into "Shinto" throughout the text, except for cases where technical linguistic issues are discussed and the macron in "Shintō" specifies or clarifies the argument. Some changes in orthography should be noted. Words often romanized as *tc* are spelled *cc*, for example, *itchi* is *icchi*, and *m* is spelled with an *n*, for example, *shimbun* is spelled *shinbun*.

We always include the romanized Japanese original in parenthesis after translated Japanese terms when they first appear in an essay or when it is necessary to clarify a point. While exceptions do occur, they are rare (for example, we generally leave Ise Jingū as it is rather than translating it as Ise Grand Shine or Ise Shrine).

One great confusion when dealing with Shinto is that key terms for governmental bureaus, offices, ordinances, and so on have been translated variously overtime. We perhaps have added to this confusion by having our own translations for these key terms. However, we have tried to achieve accuracy and consistency throughout the text and have attempted to mitigate confusion by including a glossary at the back of this book. So, for example, we translate Jingiin as "Board of Divinities" as opposed to other previous translations of this governmental office, such as the "Institute of Divinities" (*Encyclopedia of Shinto*) or the "Institute of Shinto Ceremonies" (Helen Hardacre).

All translations from Japanese sources are our own except in cases where we have indicated the original translated source. In cases where we used an existing English translation, we have made only minor changes for stylistic consistency in this volume.

ACKNOWLEDGEMENTS

Many people have devoted time, energy and inspiration to make this book, long in the making, possible. At the outset, Professor Watanabe Manabu, former director of Nanzan Institute of Religion and Culture, was instrumental in encouraging our collaboration. A JUSEC Fulbright Research Fellowship in 2010 allowed Dr. MacWilliams to work with Dr. Okuyama in Japan. Dr. Richard Gardner graciously helped secure his affiliation with Sophia University. That free time from teaching made it possible to explore what was a new area of research for him. A JSPS grant in 2011–13 also allowed him to affiliate with Nanzan University as an associate research fellow, which greatly facilitated the work. Major and small grants from St. Lawrence University also helped financially to pay for editorial work, indexing, and copyright permission fees. We would also like to thank the Suntory Foundation for their generous support in making the publication of this book possible.

People we would also like to thank are Victoria Esposito for her careful work improving our crabbed prose, Jim Heisig for being such a gracious host at the Paulus Heim house at Nanzan University. Others who really assisted us along the way include Mark Mullins, Katja Fersti, Melek Ortabasi, Gary Ebersole, Matsumura Kazuo, Russell McCutcheon, Zhenjun Zhang, Elisabetta Porcu, Miyasaka Kai, Michaela Mross, Hayashi Nanako, Russell Kirkland, Sarah Gore, Sarah Thal, and Kilmeny MacBride. We also want to give special thanks to Kaori Takashima MacWilliams whose photograph of the Torii gate of Hie Shrine in Tokyo adorns the paperback cover of this book.

SOURCES

Part 1

#1 to #10 Miyachi Masato. Ed. "Shūkyō kankei hōrei ichiran," In *Shūkyō to kokka* Nihon Kindai Shisō Taikei. Eds. Yasumaru Yoshio and Miyachi Masato, 423–88. Tokyo: Iwanami Shoten, 1998.

#11 Ito Miyoji. Trans. The Constitution of the Empire of Japan (1889), https://history.hanover.edu/texts/1889con.html

#12 Umeda Yoshihiko. *Kaitei zōho Nihon shūkyō seidoshi: kindai hen.* Tokyo: Tōsen Shuppan, 472, 1971.

#13 Jinja shinpō seikyō kenkyūshitsu ed., *Zōho kaitei, Kindai jinja Shintōshi.* Tokyo: Jinja Shinpōsha, 137–38, 1986.

#14 Jingiin kansei, goshomei genpon, https://www.digital.archives.go.jp/das/image/F000000000000 0038414

Part 2

Kume Kunitake. "Shintō wa saiten no kozoku" (Shinto as an Ancient Custom of Worshiping Heaven). In *Meiji shisōshū* 2, vol. 31 of *Kindai Nihon shisō taikei,* 117–36. Tokyo: Chikuma Shobō, 1977.

Kawakami Hajime. "Nihon dokutoku no kokkashugi" (Japan's Unique Form of Nationalism). In *Kawakami Hajime shū,* vol. 18 of *Kindai Nihon shisō taikei,* 131–50. Tokyo: Chikuma Shobō, 1977.

Yanagita Kunio. "Shintō shiken" (My View of Shinto). In vol. 13 of *Yanagita Kunio zenshū,* 587–626. Tokyo: Chikuma Shobō, 1990.

Katō Genchi. Chapter 4 "Shintō, A Religion of the Theanthropic Type, as Distinguished from a Religion of the Theocratic Type" and Chapter 5 "Shintō as a National Religion, Not Entirely Devoid of a Universal Aspect, and Remarkably Tolerant." In *What is Shintō?* Tourist Library 8, 53–72. Tokyo: Japanese Tourist Bureau, 1935.

Tsuda Sōkichi. "Shintō no go no shuju no igi" (The Various Meanings of the Word Shintō). In *Nihon no Shintō,* 1–18, vol. 9 of Tsuda Sōkichi zenshū. Tokyo: Iwanami Shoten, 1964.

Part 3

Kōno Seizō. "Kannagara no Michi" (The Way of *Kannagara*). *Monumenta Nipponica* 3 (July, 1940): 369–91.

King, Robert. Ed. Chapter 3 "The Inherent Character of the People," Chapter 4 "Ceremonial Rites and Morality." In *Kokutai No Hongi: Cardinal Principles of the National Entity of Japan.* Translated by John Owen Gauntlett, 129–50. Cambridge, MA: Harvard University Press, 1949.

Monbushō (Ministry of Education). "Shinmin no michi no jissen—1 kōkoku shinmin toshite no shūren" (Practicing the Way of Imperial Subjects—The Discipline of Imperial Subjects). In *Sengo dōtoku*

kyōiku bunken shiryōshū, series 1, no. 2, *Kokutai no hongi/ Shinmin no michi,* 59–70. Tokyo: Nihon Tosho Sentā, 2003.
Jingiin (Board of Divinities). 1 "Kokutai to jinja" (National Polity and Shrines), 2 "Kokushi to jinja" (National History and Shrines), 3 "Kokka to jinja" (State and Shrines), 23–45.

Part 4

General Headquarters of the Supreme Commander for the Allied Powers. "The Shinto Directive." *Contemporary Religions of Japan* 1 (June, 1960): 85–89.
Orikuchi Shinobu. "Shintō no atarashii hōkō" (A New Direction for Shinto). *Orikuchi Shinobu zenshū,* vol. 20, 304–14. Tokyo: Chūō Kōronsha, 1996).
Watsuji Tetsurō. "Hōken shisō to Shintō no kyōgi"(Feudal Thought and Shinto Doctrine) and "Kokumin zentaisei no hyōgensha" (Representative of the Whole People). In *Watsuji Tetsurō zenshū,* vol. 14, 319–54. Tokyo: Iwanami Shoten, 1962.
Ashizu Uzuhiko. "Gendai jinja no shomondai" (The Various Issues Related to Contemporary Shrines). In *Ashizu Uzuhiko zenshū,* vol. 1 (Tennō, Shintō, Kenpō), 421–40. Tokyo: Jinja Shinpōsha, 1996.
Murakami Shigeyoshi. 3 *Arahitogami toshiteno tennō*—4 *Tennōken no kakuritsu— kōshitsu tempan, teikoku kenpō, kyōiku chokugo* (Chapter 3: The Emperor as a Deity in Human Form—Part 4: The Establishment of Imperial Authority—the Imperial House Law, Imperial Constitution, and Imperial Rescript on Education) and 4 *Kōshitsu saishi no tenkai* —1 *kōshitsu saishirei to tōkyokurei*—2 *kōshitsu gisei no seibi* (Chapter 4: The Development of Imperial House Rites—Part 1: Regulations for Imperial House Rites and the Emperor's Enthronement—Part 2: The Formation of The Imperial House's Ceremonial System). In *Tennō no saishi,* 144–64,169–70, 172–73, 182–84. Tokyo: Iwanami Shoten, 1999.
Kuroda Toshio, "Shinto in the History of Japanese Religion." Translated by James C. Dobbins and Suzanne Gay. *Journal of Japanese Studies* 7 (Winter, 1981):1–21.

Part 5

Miyata Noboru. "Kokka Shintō" (State Shinto). In *Shūkyō to seikatsu,* Kindai Nihon Bunkaron 9. Eds. Aoki Tamotsu, Kawamoto Saburō, Yamaori Tetsuo, et al., 39–54. Tokyo: Iwanami Shoten, 1996.
Ueda Kenji. 3 "Shintō shinkō no kōzō"—1 Shintō: Sono sonzaironteki rikai eno kokoromi (Chapter 3: The Structure of Shinto Faith—Part 1: Shinto, an Attempt to Understand it Ontologically). In *Shintō shingaku: soshiki shingaku e no joshō,* 143–64. Tokyo: Taimeidō, 1995.
Sonoda Minoru. Joshō "Wagamichi no jinja to Shintō" (Forward: Our Way of Shrines and Shinto), "Jinja Shintō no shōraizō o tou" (Asking about What Shrine Shinto will Look Like in the Future), 2 "Shintō no kodaisei to genzai"—"Chinju no mori: Kakyō no Shintōteki zōkei" (Chapter 2: Archaism and the Present in Shinto, The Local Shrine Grove—A Shinto Model of One's Home), and 5 "Kōzō shingaku to kankyō mondai"— "Shintō no seimeikan": Jinja to Shintō (Chapter 5: Structural Theology and Environmental Issues—Shrines and Shinto in Shinto Views of Life). In *Daredemo no Shintō—shūkyō no Nihonteki kanōsei* (Shinto for Everyone: A Possibility for Religion in Japan) 2–15, 40–46. Tokyo: Kōbundō, 1998.
Kamata Tōji. 1 "Shintō to wa nanika" (Chapter 1: What is Shinto). In *Shintō yōgo no kiso chishiki* (Basics on Shinto Terms),12–34. Tokyo: Kadokawa Shoten, 1999.
Inoue Hiroshi. "Hajime ni" and 2 "Kakuri ni motozuku shūgō—'Shintō' no seiritsu," (Introduction and Chapter 2: A Syncretism Based Upon Differentiation: The Formation of "Shinto"). In *'Shintō' no kyozō to jitsuzō* (Shinto's False and True Image), 7–19, 68–103, 112–16. Tokyo: Kōdansha, 2011).

INTRODUCTION
Defining Shinto in modern Japan

Defining Shinto is an anthology that wrestles with a seemingly simple question: What is Shinto? While the term "Shinto" has a long history in the pre-modern period, this volume deals with how the term has evolved in modern Japan. From the late nineteenth century to the present day, the Japanese have confronted modernity institutionally, economically, politically, and intellectually. A related part of this process has been their struggle to define what Shinto is and what its spiritual, moral, and political role is in Japanese society.

This is especially true today as Japan faces a new uncertainties, given the problems of a shrinking population, the gradual loss of national pride due to its stagnant economy, and the clearly visible loss of its status in global politics. Emperor Heisei (Akihito), the 125th of his line according to traditional reckoning, has recently abdicated for reasons of health and old age (he is 85). The ascension of his son, Crown Prince Naruhito, to the Chrysanthemum Throne on May 1, 2019, marks the beginning of a new Japanese era, the Reiwa period,[1] where questions about the emperor's ritual and symbolic roles will rise to prominence again.

Shinto, especially within conservative right-wing circles, is playing an important role in the debate over national identity. The current Japanese prime minister, Abe Shinzō, for example, also supports the Shinto Association of Spiritual Leadership (Shintō Seiji Renmei), the powerful political wing of the Association of Shinto Shrines (Jinja Honchō), which aspires for Shinto to again attain a central public role in government as it had prior to the Second World War. Abe agrees with the organization's view that Shinto embodies "Japanese spiritual values." It was Abe who, on May 26, 2016 during the G-7 Summit at Ise Shima, led world leaders on a tour of Ise Jingū, the central imperial shrine enshrining the sun goddess Amaterasu. He did so in order that they could feel those spiritual values directly in "Japan's natural beauty, rich culture and traditions."[2] As Mark Mullins has described this, "There is this sense that Japan needs to get back what it lost after World War II and that this will be good for the nation."[3] Defining Shinto will most definitely be high on Japan's political and cultural agenda in the years ahead.

The anthology is designed as a compact collection of key official documents and essays by Japanese intellectuals who try to define Shinto. We have chosen important works dating from the Meiji period (1868–1912) to the present, most of which have never before been translated. The major sections of *Defining Shinto* include: (1) Shinto and the modern nation state, (2) Pre-war Japanese intellectuals on Shinto, (3) Shinto and ultra-nationalism in the 1930s and 1940s, (4) Recasting Shinto—Post-war reforms and reformulations, (5) Contemporary ways of defining Shinto. Each section begins with a short overview of the time period with brief biographies of individual authors. This helps to contextualize them within the social, political, and intellectual milieu of the period in which they lived. Our overarching goal is to show that the Japanese have interpreted Shinto in myriad ways. There is no single way to define Shinto.

Definitions of Shinto in these readings are not just descriptive or "academic." They can be prescriptive, inspiring official policy as well as new political, social and religious movements. They can also be enormously influential in debates over Japanese national identity, polity, civil rights, and religious freedom. The well-known Shinto scholar of the 1930s, Kōno Seizō, for example, defines a "way of the *kami*" highlighting the sacred character of the imperial state and way of being a loyal Japanese subject. Kōno, a professor at Kokugakuin University,[4] helped shape official moral education in pre-war secondary and post-secondary schools. His view reflects the fundamental dogmas of the State Shinto later promoted in government propaganda tracts like the *Kokutai no hongi* (The Cardinal Principles of the National Polity, Reading #21) and *Shinmin no michi* (The Way of Subjects, Reading #22). Therefore, ways of defining Shinto such as his are not just creations of the scholar's study for academic purposes; they can also exist outside the classroom and have a profound effect on the wider popular discourse and, by extension, alter history itself. Definitions of Shinto matter.[5]

By focusing exclusively on Japanese writings, we have had to make significant sacrifices in content. A key lacuna in the anthology is early Western scholars who defined Shinto, including founders in the field of Japanese studies such as William Elliot Griffis, William George Aston, Basil Hall Chamberlain, Lafcadio Hearn, and Daniel Clarence Holtom.[6] We also chose to omit more contemporary Western scholars like Mark Teeuwen, John Breen, and Helen Hardacre, as their work on Shinto is readily accessible in English (see the suggested readings provided at the end of each part).

Given these omissions, it is important to be aware that definitions of Shinto do not develop in isolation. First, they are often reactions to other religions, particularly Christianity. The term religion is also itself, of course, a Western category which entered Japan together with Christian missionaries during the Meiji Period. As scholars like Isomae Jun'ichi, Helen Hardacre, and Jason Ānanda Josephson have explained in detail, the influence of the Western category of religion on defining Shinto is palpable. How should Shinto be classified in reference to the category of religion? Is Shinto a religion? If so, what kind of a religion is it? If not, how should it be classified?

The anthology shows the fascinating ways Western theories of religion have significantly impacted defining Shinto. Of course, Western scholars were the first to try to do so. A good example is W.G. Aston (1841–1911), the British scholar diplomat of the Meiji period and famed linguist and translator of the *Nihongi* (*Nihonshoki*), who penned one of the first Western studies, *Shinto—The Way of the Gods* (1905). This became a basic text for understanding Shinto in the West, regularly quoted in world religion textbooks through the 1950s. He defines Shinto as "essentially a religion of gratitude and love. The great Gods, such as the Sun Goddess and the Deity of Food are beneficent beings. They are addressed as parents or dear divine ancestors, and their festivals have a joyous character."[7] Aston's approach reflects nineteenth century evolutionary theories of religion popularized by British sociologist and social Darwinist Herbert Spencer (1820–1903) in his *Principles of Sociology* (1897–98). In his preface, Aston also explicitly cites his indebtedness to the works of anthropologists E.B. Tylor (*Primitive Culture*, 1871) and James G. Frazer (*The Golden Bough*, 1890, 1900). Shinto, according to Aston, occupies stages one and two in his four-part model of religious evolution—(1) the sun, moon, and wind are alive (that is, animism) and (2) the sun (for instance) is a man, a father, a chief, or a king (that is, anthropomorphism). In Aston's view, Shinto reveals the early stages in the history of religions of an evolutionary process of increasing "personification" and the "humanization of nature." It occupies a relatively low evolutionary rung on the ladder or "phases of conception" that mark religion's progressive rise toward a higher notion of deity of "infinite power and absolute humanity"—such as we find in Christianity. Indeed, Aston concludes, "in the stage of religious progress represented by Shinto, we are far indeed from such a result."[8]

Many questioned Western conceptions of Shinto like Aston's. They do not accept that Shinto is either "primitive" or inferior to Christianity. The famous founder of Japanese folklore studies, Yanagita Kunio (1875–1962), for example, in his lecture, "My view of Shinto" (*Shintō shiken*, 1918), discounts Aston's definition. Japanese students relying on Western authors like Aston for "the gist of the subject" of Shinto, Yanagita complains, is "problematic" (Reading #17).[9]

Overall, our anthology reveals that Shinto is a contested category. During the rise, fall, and post-war rebirth of Japan as a powerful nation state, Shinto has been viewed variously as a national religion, a non-religious patriotic cult, a moral way, a suprareligious entity, a "private religion" of Shinto shrines (*jinja Shintō*), an ancient form of animism offering a contemporary ecological ethic, and in many other ways. But no matter how it is defined, throughout the modern period Shinto has consistently provided a powerful model of and for the Japanese people's sense of reality. The anthology's selections show the ways Shinto has shaped Japanese identity, politics, society, and Japanese life.

What does "Shinto" mean?

Broadly speaking, Shinto refers to a disparate and diffuse set of beliefs, ritual practices, sacred cults, sects, and political movements related to the *kami* at the local, regional, and national levels. Often, when people talk about Shinto today, they think of it as having four major forms: Shinto of the imperial house (*kōshitsu Shintō*), shrine Shinto (*jinja Shintō*), sect Shinto (*kyōha Shintō*), and folk Shinto (*minkan Shintō*).[10]

But if this tells us anything, it points to the fact, noted by the sociologist of religion Inoue Nobutaka, that Shinto is "notoriously vague and difficult to define. A brief look at the term's history confuses more than it enlightens."[11] Joseph M. Kitagawa, a pioneer of Japanese religious studies in the West, concurs, noting that Shinto's inherent "terminological ambiguity" reveals "a very loose and a very broad range of meaning."[12] More recently, Mark Teeuwen and Bernhard Scheid have observed that "[t]here is a fundamental uncertainty about central questions relating to Shinto" that give it "an elusive, and, in the minds of many, an outright dubious character."[13] Especially in light of the seminal work of Japanese medieval historian Kuroda Toshio (Reading #29), many Shinto scholars today take what Norman Havens calls an "onion strategy," arguing that when you peel the historical overlays away "little remains of an immutable entity worthy of the name 'Shinto'—at least not until the creation of Shrine Shinto in the modern period."[14]

As a term, "Shintō" is composed of two characters literally meaning the "*kami*" (Chinese, *shen*, Japanese, *shin* or *kami*—often translated as "gods" or "divinities") and "the way" (Chinese, *dao*, Japanese, *dō*, *tō* or *michi*). But even the terms are uncertain, as it is unclear (1) whether this is the definitive term for the phenomenon we are discussing, and (2) what it really means.

As for the former, it is important to note that "Shintō" is not always the preferred term for talking about the way of the *kami*. The pre-modern national learning scholar, Motoori

Norinaga (1730–1801), calls it the "ancient way" (*kodō*). His famous self-proclaimed disciple, Hirata Atsutane (1776–1843), uses the term the "original teaching" (*honkyō*) instead of Shinto in his *Honkyō gaihen* and other major works. Pre-World War II nationalists like Kōno Seizō prefer an indigenous Japanese rendering, *kannagara no michi* ("the way as it is with the gods") to the Sinicized "Shintō." He believed it was the earliest appellation for an ancient national faith pre-dating Chinese influence, indicating "the quintessence of Shinto." In the 1941 government tract, *Shinmin no michi* (The Way of Subjects, Reading #22) the word Shinto is not even mentioned. The authors use the term solely to denote sectarian Shinto religious groups (*kyōha Shintō*) as opposed to a "way" extolled in the text. Shinto, therefore, is one of a number of labels used in pre-war texts. By contrast, in post-war Japan, Shinto becomes the preferred word for designating the "way of the *kami*." The most important instance of this is the Occupation GHQ's Shinto Directive (Reading #24) issued December 15, 1945, four months after the armistice marking the end of the Second World War.

However, the term itself has its own mysteries: What does "Shintō," which appears initially in the early eighth-century Japanese chronicle, the *Nihonshoki*, really mean? The great Japanese historian Tsuda Sōkichi (1873–1961; Reading #19) caused great controversy in 1939 by arguing that in the earliest Japanese documents the word had nothing to do with the "way of the gods" (*kami no michi*). Tsuda argues that such a reading—understood to mean the "established teachings of Japan's *kami*, which also includes the politics and ethical standards special to Japan"—is in fact a recent rather than the original meaning. This definition of Shinto is first advanced by National Learning (*kokugaku*) and Restoration Shinto (*fukko Shintō*) scholars like Motoori Norinaga and Hirata Atsutane in the eighteenth and nineteenth centuries. Drawing from antiquarian and philological work, they construct what Sarah Thal has described as a "style of worship of the *kami* based on ancient texts based on naturalness, sincerity, emotionality, and the sacred power of the Japanese language as Russian and American ships encroached on Japanese waters."[15] Thus Shinto develops as a nativist response to European imperialism in East Asia as well as to the threatening re-entry of Christianity into Japan from the middle of the nineteenth century; it ultimately becomes the basis of the Meiji Restoration's early policy of making Shinto into a nationally unifying state religion. By contrast, Tsuda argues that in the earliest documents Shinto simply refers to non-Buddhist folk religion and customs; as we shall see, that definition has itself been dismissed as anachronistic by Japanese historians like Kuroda Toshio (Reading #29) and Inoue Hiroshi (Reading #34).

In contemporary Japan, Shinto remains elusive. People regularly call themselves Buddhists, Christians, and Muslims, identifying themselves in terms of their specific religious affiliation and faith. But this is not what usually happens in the case of Shinto. As Breen and Teeuwen have noted, while recent official statistics from the Association of Shinto Shrines, for example, identify 90% of the population as shrine parishioners, ordinary Japanese would never identify themselves as "Shintoist," nor find much meaning in the term.[16] Moreover, although there are Shinto affiliated new religions and sects, few Japanese belong to these groups.[17] Many might go to a shrine during New Year (*hatsumōde*) or participate in festivals (*matsuri*) at local Shinto shrines (*jinja*). But most Japanese consider themselves non-religious, without affiliation to a particular sect or denomination. They do not self-consciously identify themselves as "Shintoist" in the way that most Americans (over 70.6%) readily identify themselves as Christian.[18] Shinto, therefore, is not an "emic" label that Japanese people usually use to describe themselves. As Kitagawa observes, the word Shinto refers to "communal and cultural features beyond normal academic definitions of religion."[19]

Most Japanese today find it difficult to distinguish Shinto either as an identifiable religion or a specific customary or cultural set of beliefs and practices. Recently, a puzzled Japanese friend asked us this question: Is worshipping one of the seven gods of fortune (*shichifuku-jin*) a form of Shinto? These seven gods of fortune, often depicted on their "treasure ship" (*takarabune*), are found enshrined in both Buddhist temples and Shinto shrines. All except one originally came from India and China. At New Year, Shichifukujin mini-pilgrimages are a popular pastime for some Japanese people. There are dozens of pilgrimage circuits, for example, within metropolitan Tokyo, attracting thousands of pilgrims over the holidays. The Shichifukujin are gods, to be sure, but are they Shinto gods? Are they *kami*? Our friend really had no idea, and we were also left sputtering trying to explain. For how does one draw the line between what is and is not a *kami*? What is "Shinto" and what is "Buddhist"? What is "Japanese" and what is not? Most younger Japanese today do not see any difference between a *kami* and a *buddha*, nor can they readily distinguish a Shinto shrine (*jinja*) from a Buddhist temple (*otera*).[20] There are good historical reasons for this. Until the modern period, Shinto was not an independent religion, but was fused with Buddhism; *kami* and buddhas were combined together (*shinbutsu shūgō*) into one complex religious system.

In any case, Shinto remains hard to define. And yet, many intellectuals, governmental officials, and Shinto scholars have tried to define it clearly and unambiguously. Noted Japanese historian Kuroda Toshio (Reading #29) groups these definitions into two types.

The first, which he calls the common person's or conventional view, defines Shinto as an unchanging religion "continuing in an unbroken line from prehistoric times down to the present." Such a view is also clearly expressed, for example, by 1930s Japanese nationalists like Kōno Seizō (Reading #20), who explains that the origin of Shinto, in his terminology, the *kannagara no michi* or the "way as it is with the gods," begins from "the age of the gods," —that is, at the beginning of the creation of the cosmos as conveyed in early texts like the *Kojiki.* Of course, this faith was revitalized in the Meiji Restoration. By that time, it had officially become, in Kōno's words, "the fundamental principle and guiding power of rising Japan." Kōno's Shinto has always existed in Japan, focusing on reverence for the imperial ancestress, Amaterasu Ōmikami, and undivided loyalty to the emperor who has a divine character as her direct descendent.

Kuroda's second definition assumes "Shinto-like beliefs or customs (*shinkō*) have always existed." This is a standard feature of the work of folklorists and historians like Yanagita Kunio (Reading #17), Hori Ichirō (see Miyata Noboru, Reading #30), Maruyama Masao, and so on. Here Shinto is conceived as an "underlying will" existing as an essential element within Japan's changing religious diversity or as an "ancient stratum," remaining the same no matter what changes and subsequent ideas are layered on top of it.[21]

A good example of this second approach to defining Shinto may be found in Japanese intellectual historian Ishida Ichirō's (1913–2006) book, *Kami to Nihon bunka* (Kami and Japanese Culture, 1983). In this work (not included in this anthology), Ishida contends that Shinto,

> formed its original essence in primeval times in the Yayoi period when wet rice agriculture first began in our country. Since then, it appears that this original essence has been preserved until today. Throughout the course of Japan's historical development, it has transformed into various forms of Shinto that are tied to different religions and ideologies from period to period. In one era, it is tied to religions (like Buddhism and Confucianism) originally transmitted from China; in another era, it is connected to systems of thought that have arisen from within the country

(like national learning and nationalistic thought that regards a nation as a family). Roughly speaking, in ancient times, it was connected to early Confucianism from China, and developed into the clan-based ancestor worship that helped form the basis of the ancient Japanese state. Next, it became connected to ancient Chinese Buddhism, developing into Ryōbu (Dual) and *honji suijaku* Shinto, and, following that, in the early modern period, it was connected to Sung and Ming Neo-Confucianism developing into various Confucian Shinto schools. On one hand, it was also connected to national learning developing into "ancient learning" (*kogaku*) Shinto, while on the other, it was connected to modern Japanese nationalism that compares nation to family and became State Shinto (*kokka Shintō*) characterized by emperor worship. When I make this point, I am sure there are some who think that in every religion's history you can find influences from other religions and systems of thought. However, in the history of Shinto there is something that cannot be found in the histories of other religions.[22]

The difference Ishida identifies is this: Other religious traditions change by accumulating new spiritual and intellectual layers while preserving some of their heritage from the past. Shinto, however, changes its "guise" (*henshin*) by completely sweeping away older influences borrowed from earlier periods and seamlessly fitting new religions and ideologies around its core. Ishida calls this unique capability "functionism" and compares Shinto to a children's doll with a body that remains the same while dressed up in different costumes over time. Scholars tend to explore the different costumes—that is, the guise Shinto takes in certain periods—rather than its true essence. But that true "essence" or "natural form" of Shinto beneath its protean guise remains frustratingly unclear. Ishida argues that Shinto is ultimately about the worship of *kami*—divinities whose key quality is their spiritually creative power (*musubi*) to bring positive this worldly benefits. "That Shinto is about searching for prosperity in daily living and affirming one's existence"[23] is a definition advanced by others as well, such as the writings of the famous folklorist and literary esthete, Orikuchi Shinobu (1887–1953) (Reading #24) and the contemporary scholar of Shinto studies, Sonoda Minoru (1936–) (Reading #32).

Kuroda picks up Tsuda's critique of the ahistorical readings of Shinto. Terminologically, he exposes the false assumptions that have obscured the historical processes which formed Shinto as we know it today. However, despite his critique, such approaches nevertheless remain the *de facto* definition of Shinto, even in the West where it commonly appears in chapters on "Japanese religion" in "world religions" textbooks. In these texts, Shinto usually merits its own special chapter alongside Christianity, Islam, and Judaism and is essentially defined as Japan's "ancient indigenous religion" or the "national faith of Japan."[24] Such simplistic discourse about Shinto's "essence" and "uniqueness" is a major reason why this anthology is important. A more nuanced critical perspective requires an awareness of the multitude of ways Shinto has been defined.

Defining Shinto as a "historical product of discursive processes"

We often take textbook or dictionary definitions for granted. We all crave a solid foundation on which to build our understanding of things. When first-year college students write essays for a class, many begin with a definition from Webster's because they believe it will ensure their readers have a clear, unassailably true and objective basis from which to learn. However, such seemingly generic definitions can be deeply misleading or just plain wrong.

Dictionaries and textbooks are not handed down from heaven, however; nor do they contain some objective truth about what something is and does. In fact, definitions are human fabrications—imagined, created and advanced by people who, in turn, are products of their own times. This is just as true when defining religion. In his seminal work, *Genealogies of Religion* (1993), Talad Asad makes an important methodological point that historical forces are at work in every act of naming and defining something; definitions are deeply colored by their authors' personal history, ideological interests, ties to power, historical moment in which they arise, and so on. Looked at this way, definitions seem anything but universal, eternal, objective, and innocent, even if their authors think otherwise.[25]

Defining Shinto is no different from defining religion in this respect. Its definitions are molded by a complex set of historical, political, social, and cultural forces forming the backdrop of the intellectual labor that created them. We must attend to this backdrop to fully understand why people define Shinto the way they do. And additionally, we must attend to how these definitions, in turn, have the power to shape people's specific worldviews and the political arena in which they live.

A good example is Watsuji Tetsurō. In his essay, "Representative of the whole people" (1948, Reading #26), Watsuji defines Shinto by reinterpreting the nature of the emperor as its central component. His essay appears after Japan's defeat in World War II. The pre-war militarism centered on the emperor's person was repudiated, as he had been described in the 1889 Meiji Constitution as "sacred and inviolable." It is important to note that in the pre-war period Watsuji was involved as a member of the Ministry of Education's board of specialists who helped create the infamous propaganda tract, *Kokutai no hongi* (The Cardinal Principles of National Polity, 1937). However, Watsuji found himself in a new world after 1945. What was to happen to the emperor in the post-war period? Did he continue to be a *kami* manifest in human form (*arahitogami, akitsumikami*) as the direct imperial descendent of the sun goddess Amaterasu?

Watsuji's post-war take on these questions completely aligns with the Occupation authorities, as expressed in the GHQ's Shinto Directive (Reading #24). The Directive states unequivocally that there had been "perversion of Shinto theory and beliefs into militaristic and ultra-nationalistic propaganda" in pre-war Japan. Watsuji completely agrees with this view; the military control of the government and its warrior ethos were a medieval invention and had nothing to do at all with the earlier imperial political system. Watsuji's views are also in accord with the emperor's 1946 New Year's rescript, "The Humanity Declaration" (Ningen Sengen) and the "MacArthur Constitution," both inspired by the GHQ, that refashioned the emperor from a manifest *kami* (*akitsumikami*) into "the symbol of state and the unity of the people."

According to Watsuji, the emperor is a fitting symbol of a newly democratized Japan because he always expresses the will of the people. His role of representing the collective will of the people is the source of his sacredness, not any mistaken belief of him as a living god. That role has its mythological charter in the "assembly at Kawara," in the "Age of the Gods" section of the *Kojiki*. The emperor is simply idealized as someone who expresses the sacred will of the people, just as defined in the new Constitution. Watsuji's definition of Shinto, therefore, directly speaks to the times in which he lives by refashioning the emperor's new symbolic role that preserves the imperial system while supporting the new democratic government. Definitions of Shinto do reflect the historical conditions within which they emerge. But they also mold those conditions as well: Watsuji's essays are important for redefining the emperor's new symbolic role in the post-war period.

One of the goals of the anthology, therefore, is to situate each essay in terms of its historical context. What are the particular historical, political, and social conditions within which writers developed their own understanding of Shinto? In this way, our book can assist readers in comprehending the diverse ways —from Kume Kunitake's "Shinto as an ancient custom of worshiping heaven," published in 1891 (Reading #15), to Inoue Hiroshi's *Shintō' no kyozō to jitsuzō* (Shinto's False and True Image, Reading #34) in 2011—that Japanese in modern times have tried to define Shinto.

Monothetic approaches to defining Shinto

The anthology has another goal as well—to give readers the opportunity to compare and contrast definitions of Shinto synchronically. Comparison can reveal a bigger picture by clarifying some of the basic strategies Japanese scholars, officials, and intellectuals have used to define what Shinto is and does. In his book, *Imagining Religion*, Jonathan Z. Smith makes the case that different strategies are used when defining religions (including Shinto). First are what Smith calls monothetic taxonomies, which are also employed in the classical Linnaean classification system in the biological sciences. A monothetic approach defines by classifying all members of a species by a *single definitive trait* shared in common—a unique quality without which they would belong to another taxon. A walnut tree, Smith notes, is unique; it is distinguished in the Linnaean classification system as a distinct species because it has petals while, for example, a pecan tree does not.[26]

Religions are often defined monothetically as well—by finding that single trait that is *sui generis*, an essence that essentially differentiates it from other religions or cultural activities. Christianity, for example, is the "religion of love," Judaism is the "observance of law," and so on. Monothetic definitions like these, Smith observes, are crudely superficial because they rely on a single feature to define their terms. In Smith's estimation an "inappropriate notion of 'essence'" is a poor strategy for constructing a proper classificatory scheme for religions in general.[27]

A monothetic approach is often used for defining Shinto as well. As we have seen, Aston defines Shinto monothetically when he describes it as "essentially a religion of gratitude and love." Writing in the 1930s, for example, Katō Genchi (Reading #18), who lived during a time of increasing ultranationalism in Japan, defines Shinto (by which he means the national faith as opposed to sectarian Shinto) as the "religion of loyalty," a phrase, incidentally, that he borrows from the Western Japanophile, Lafcadio Hearn (Koizumi Yakumo).[28]

In the post-war period, monothetic definitions are often tied to theories of being Japanese (*Nihonjinron*), a chauvinistic discourse that often highlights Shinto as the source of the uniqueness at the heart of the Japanese soul, national character, and race. A good example is Kamata Tōji's "What is Shinto? (1999, Reading #33). Kamata, like Katō, takes his cue from Lafcadio Hearn to define Shinto's essence. Hearn himself championed a form of cultural nationalism by emphasizing the ancient folk tradition as the locus of the "Soul of Old Japan," his translation for the eighteenth- and nineteenth-century Japanese national learning ideal of *Yamatodamashii*. In his books, such as *Japan: An Attempt at Interpretation*, Hearn believes "the influence of Shinto accomplished wonderful things . . . [it] evolved a national type of character worthy, in many ways, of earnest admiration."[29]

Developing Hearn's idea that the way of the *kami* is the soul of Japan, Kamata asserts that a deep "sense of Shinto" has been central to the spiritual experience of the Japanese people from the earliest prehistoric Jōmon period:

[A]ctual Shinto does not live inside books. Nor is it even found in rituals or religious precepts. It lives and breathes in people's hearts. And the purest expression of that faith lying in people's hearts, the expression that never dies, and never grows old is Shinto. Beneath antiquated superstitions, simple myths, strange incantations growing on the surface above, Shinto lies far below, as the vital living pulse beating deep within the soul of the Japanese folk. This folk's instinctive nature, intuition, and vitality also find their origin here as well.

As this anthology will show, interpreters of Shinto often choose different notions of "essence" to define Shinto monothetically. These monothetic definitions are often tied to a larger discourse on Japanese national polity (*kokutai*) in pre-war Japan and identity politics in post-war Japan.

Defining Shinto polythetically

Is there another way of defining Shinto? It may well be a fool's errand according to Talad Asad. Asad rejects the whole project of defining religion "not only because its constituent elements and relationships are historically specific, but because that definition is itself the historic product of discursive processes."[30] Trying to come up with a universal definition of religion is a futile enterprise because one can never grasp "essences" of religion by definitions that, as historian of religions Bruce Lincoln summarizes it, are themselves "culturally bound, historically recent, and discursively loaded."[31]

However, historians of religions like Lincoln and Jonathan Z. Smith disagree with Asad on this very point. Universal definitions of religion can have a heuristic value for fathoming one's field of study more deeply. Defining can help us to raise significant questions, to become aware of similarities and differences, and to challenge the assumptions of received models. Scholars can construct universal definitions of religion if they serve as "provisional attempts to clarify one's thought, not to capture the innate essence of things."[32]

The same is true for a provisional definition of Shinto. It can serve a valuable purpose by clarifying our thoughts about Shinto and reveal how it is changing in the modern world. For our purposes, what we need is a definition that helps us better comprehend the multifarious ways Shinto has been defined—a definition that helps to compare and contrast the work of scholars, intellectuals, and officials advancing their own ideas on the nature of Shinto.

The proper way to do this is to take what Smith calls a "polythetic" approach. Polythetic definitions are used today in the biological sciences. Basically, biologists use multiple criteria to define something; the possession of any one of these criteria is enough to bring something within that grouping. For example, in virology the old Latinized Linnaean system was replaced in the 1990s with a new polythetic taxonomy. Virus species are now classed by possessing "a consensus set of statistically covariant properties but not a single common property that is necessary and sufficient for membership in a class."[33] A virus that shares a replicating lineage and an ecological niche may be classed as a particular species, but there is no single defining property that distinguishes one virus from others. Viruses may be identified by a host of characteristics, including the natural and experimental host range, pathogenicity, vector specificity, antigenic type, cell and tissue tropism, and many others.[34] A virus may still be included in a species even if it lacks certain properties commonly shared by the type. The key to polythetic definitions, therefore, is that each member of a species shares a combination of properties and is not reduced to a single property. Since viruses are genetically variable and constantly undergoing evolutionary change, with different strains appearing rapidly, this type of definition is particularly useful in virology.

As our anthology clearly shows, Shinto is also variable and has changed significantly over time. A polythetic approach seeks a general set of characteristics that Japanese officials, Shinto scholars, and intellectuals have used when describing what Shinto is and does. This catalog of characteristics of Shinto can be divided into several "dichotomous divisions" or binaries, which Smith explains is a typical classificatory strategy. That is, most works in this anthology define Shinto in terms of one or more dyads of either/or classifications. Some of the key dyads often used to define Shinto are the following:

Secular/Religious

Ancient/Modern

Indigenous/Foreign

Ritual/Doctrinal

Experiential/Textual

Immanent/Transcendent

Maximalist/Minimalist

Collective/Individual

Local/National

Given the sheer volume of discourse on Shinto in the modern period, this catalog of binary traits is necessarily incomplete and fragmentary. However, such a delimited list can be insightful for analyzing how a given author or text goes about defining Shinto. For example, one particular definition might classify Shinto as indigenous, not foreign, collective, not a private faith, and experiential, not textual, while another definition, while sharing the first two traits, differs on the third, describing Shinto as primarily textual rather than experiential in nature. A polythetic definition of Shinto is useful academically because it offers what Lincoln calls a "provisional attempt to clarify one's thought, not to capture the innate essence of things."[35] Such a catalog of traits can help raise significant questions, create a deeper awareness of complexity and differences, and challenge assumptions of received models. It has a heuristic value for more deeply fathoming the large variety of different ways people define Shinto, and how their understanding of Shinto changes in the modern world. In what follows, we will briefly explain each binary that lies at the heart of the Shinto definitions found in this anthology.

Secular/Religious

Shinto is often defined using this binary. But it is important here to acknowledge that it is originally a Western cultural import. Helen Hardacre, Isomae Jun'ichi, and, most recently, Jason Ānanda Josephson have traced the emergence of the secular/sacred dichotomy in the bureaucratic, diplomatic, and intellectual discourse of modern Japan. The category of religion has a complex history; the word was first translated from English to Japanese in 1853 during treaty negotiations with American and European envoys, but the agreed term for religion (translated as *shūkyō*) was not settled until 1873.[36] This is not the place to delve into that history. What is important, as Josephson notes, is that religion was intrinsically tied to the notion of the secular—it is the opposite side of the binary that was exported globally, and in particular to Japan, by Western Christianity and the Enlightenment. His point is that the categories of the religious and the secular are "fundamentally entangled" with each other—secularization is potentially religious, and the construction of religions is potentially secularizing. This helps us to understand why Meiji officialdom places Shinto outside the category of religion as a non-religious state cult.[37] While the thirteen Shinto sects are defined as religions and thus fell under Article 28 of the Meiji Constitution's protection of "freedom of belief," shrine Shinto is not classified as a private religion. Instead, it consists of the institutions responsible for state-sponsored rites for the veneration of Amaterasu Ōmikami, the sun goddess, and of the emperor as the head of the imperial state. It is conceived as a patriotic cult promoting civic moral virtues such as love of country, loyalty, and self-sacrifice to the state. By guaranteeing religious freedom while labeling Shinto shrines as non-religious, Meiji officials therefore give Shinto a vital role as a unifying state set of rituals and ideology.[38] Many of the readings from the 1930s and 1940s in this volume reflect this secularized view of shrine Shinto. A classic example is the chapter on "Ceremonial rites and morality," in *Kokutai no hongi* (1937, Reading #21): "As Shinto shrines have their basic significance in being national existences, they have, since the establishment of the Council of Divinities in the Code of Laws, come down to us as national organs and institutions; so that they are differently treated from all the Shinto sects[39] and other religions of a general nature."

What was behind this distinction between shrine Shinto and religion? As Helen Hardacre has pointed out, Japanese scholars and officials had absorbed Protestant-influenced views of religion that emphasized the essential role of doctrines, faith, and personal religious experience, as opposed to rituals and festivals. Shrine Shinto, understood essentially as a set of national rituals of the state, was officially relegated to a category separate from religion.[40]

However, even in the pre-war period, there was some dispute over whether shrine Shinto was truly secular in nature. In his 1918 work (Reading #17), for example, Yanagita Kunio directly challenges the government's attempt to define Shinto as a state cult, bluntly arguing that it makes "absolutely no sense." A case in point, he notes, is the administrative division between shrines and religion, which is accomplished by creating separate administrative bureaus—the Bureau of Shrines (Jinjakyoku) for Shinto and the Bureau of Religion (Shūkyōkyoku) for religions. At that time, one of the head priests at Izumo shrine also served as the leader of one of the officially recognized Shinto religious sects. Yanagita asks, can ordinary people worshipping at Izumo "really distinguish between state shrine worship that occurs before eleven in the morning and the commencement of Shinto sectarian religious activities after eleven?" The bureaucratic distinction is superficial and ignores the parishioners' religious piety toward the shrine. National morality and patriotic reverence for the emperor at shrines may be ideologically prescribed by the state, but ordinary people often come for their own heartfelt reasons to pray to the *kami* for spiritual blessings.

Contemporary Shinto scholar Sonoda Minoru (Reading #32) also defines Shinto as a religion. However, Sonoda takes issue with defining it solely as a private set of beliefs held by individuals. A shrine, he argues, is actually "not a place for the private practice of religion." Understanding people's faith at shrines requires us to abandon defining Shinto as a public secular practice as opposed to a personal matter of privately held beliefs. He proposes instead a broader concept of "cultural religion" (*bunkateki shūkyō*) that transcends religion conceived as one's personal individual faith. Shrines, according to Sonoda, offer a public cultural symbolic system that is "the source for a local village's sense of order, and, above all, inspires a collective sense of belonging to one's native home (*kokoro no furusato*) among local people."[41] In all the essays found in this anthology, readers must pay special attention to the different ways the category of religion is used to either include or exclude Shinto.

Ancient/Modern

Shinto has often been defined as an ancient or eternally existing "Japanese religion." As we have discussed above, Kuroda finds that most definitions of Shinto take this side of the binary. The idea of "the way of the gods" as an archaic religion or an unchanging essential will or spirit has its origin in pre-modern national learning scholars like Motoori Norinaga who calls it the "ancient way" (*kodō*).

Norinaga explains this in *Naobi no mitama* ("Spirit of the *Naobi* God"), a part of his magnum opus, the *Kojikiden*. The term "way of the gods" appears initially early on in the *Nihonshoki*. As a way, though, its origin is archaic, *in illo tempore*, in that time of creation of the world by the deities Izanagi and Izanami. The way of the gods therefore antedates human history before the arrival in Japan of human-founded foreign religions, such as Confucianism and Buddhism. According to Norinaga, "[t]he meaning of the way can be known now by studying *Kojiki* and other ancient texts."[42] As we have seen, this corresponds with the view of later nationalists like Kōno Seizō (Reading #20), who parrots Norinaga's position on the archaicism of the way of the gods: "*Kannagara* was an ancient expression implying the sanctity of the reign of the emperor, thence signifying that the emperor is the reincarnation of Amaterasu Ōmikami and that he rules the empire of Japan according to the divine message of this ancestral deity." According to Kōno, from the very beginning Shinto was an imperial faith devoted to worshipping the emperor as a divine figure and the living descendent of the sun goddess, Amaterasu.

Others also accept that Shinto is ancient, in one form or another. Kume Kunitake (Reading #15) calls Shinto the "ancient custom of worshiping heaven." Tsuda Sōkichi (Reading #19) criticizes those who, like Kōno, prefer mythical to critical historical analysis—but he still defines Shinto as "the religious faith (which also includes magic) passed down from old as part of Japanese folk custom." He goes on to explain that the term "was devised to distinguish the old faith from Buddhism." Kamata Tōji (Reading #33) calls it "the life pulse of an ancient faith." Shinto's hoary antiquity is a given for many interpreters of Shinto.

But others contest Shinto's archaic nature. One important example is Basil Hall Chamberlain (1850–1935), the pioneering British philologist, translator, and interpreter of Japan. In his essay, "The Invention of a New Religion" (which is not included in this anthology), published as a pamphlet in 1912 one year after he had returned to Europe, Chamberlain offers his critique. Unlike his close friend, Lafcadio Hearn, Chamberlain had become disillusioned with Japan, particularly given the assault on human rights and intellectual freedom by the autocratic Meiji government of which he was highly critical. Chamberlain dismisses the Shinto of his time as an "invented religion." It is a mishmash of ideas and practices based upon a now discredited "primitive nature cult." The Meiji government transformed it into a new religion of "Mikado-worship and Japan-worship" supported by a modern Bushido ethic of loyalty and filial piety.[43] But Meiji officialdom's claims that this Shinto was Japan's ancient religion is anachronistic, flying in the face of historical facts. They insist that the emperor is a living god descending from the sun goddess with "supreme—one might say supernatural—authority," and that the foundation of the monarchy dates from Emperor

Jinmu in 660 BCE. However, Chamblerlain shows that, in fact, "the origins of Japanese history are recent compared with that of European countries. The first glimmer of Japanese history dates from the fifth century after Christ."[44] Meiji era Shinto is, therefore, a patently absurd modern invention that Japanese believe in, although they know it is not true.[45] Post-war Shinto intellectual Ashizu Uzuhiko (1909–92; Reading #27) shares Chamberlain's view insofar as he agrees that the pre-war State Shinto was largely a creation of Emperor Meiji. Nonetheless, he sees this invented Shinto tradition positively. He cautions that "[m]atters of faith should not be valued just because they are old. Shinto is by no means an ancient cultural asset, but that does not lessen its value."

In this anthology, we have included the works of key Japanese historians who have relentlessly attacked the view of Shinto as Japan's ancient religion. All would accept Isomae Jun'ichi's definition of Shinto as a "native tradition in reaction to influences from abroad, such as Sinification during the ancient and medieval eras and Westernization in the modern era."[46] Murakami Shigeyoshi (1928–91; Reading #26), for example, examines how State Shinto emerged in the pre-war period as a modern ritual and ideological construct of the modern Japanese nation state. Kuroda Toshio (Reading #29) builds on Tsuda's historical analysis of the term Shinto and advances his argument that it emerged as an independent religion only in modern times.[47] Kuroda argues that rather than running in a continuous line, the meaning of Shinto changes over time. In part, this is in reaction to the highly syncretic esoteric/exoteric (*kenmitsu*) Buddhism, the longstanding tradition which enveloped Shinto in pre-modern times. Inoue Hiroshi (1941– ; Reading #34) places Shinto's religious origins in the medieval period. The distinctive *ichinomiya* shrine system that originated during the medieval period formed the framework for what we know as Shinto today.

Indigenous/Foreign

As we have seen, Shinto is often defined as the indigenous Japanese religion. Not surprisingly this idea, as we have seen, can also be traced back to national learning scholars like Motoori Norinaga, who sought a "pure Shinto" that could be distinguished from the "foreign" Buddhist practices that were introduced later on and were associated with the declining Tokugawa regime of his time. Indeed, Kuroda has demonstrated that the notion of an indigenous Shinto, existing independently from Buddhism, is directly tied to the rise of Japanese nationalism, which culminated with the establishment of State Shinto in the Meiji period. The idea also persists in the post-war period.[48] As Kuroda concludes, Shinto's indigenousness "has remained the basis for defining Shinto down to the present."

This anthology, if anything, corroborates Kuroda's point. What is interesting, however, is how Shinto's indigenous character is variously interpreted. For example, the folklorist Yanagita Kunio strictly divides what is indigenous from what is foreign with his notion of the common people *jōmin*. His abiding interest in the ordinary life of the Japanese folk (see Miyata, Reading #30) emphasizes a common, local form of Shinto (*koyū shinkō*) of ancestor worship, occurring at village shrines and local festivals. This common faith, for Yanagita, transcends the official state supported shrine Shinto of the Meiji period, which borrows heavily from foreign Western notions of religion. By contrast, prominent Shinto scholar Ashizu Uzuhiko (1909–92; Reading #27) is highly critical of folkloric approaches that, like Yanagita's, deemphasize the deep imperial connections with shrines. For him, "each shrine's faith retains a national and ethnic consciousness. This is due to their tendency to maintain close ties to the Grand Shrine." Shinto is an indigenous faith for the

Japanese people, Ashizu argues, because of Emperor Meiji's genius in creating the ritual observances, the institutional system, and the spiritual quality (*seishin*) of Ise-centered shrine Shinto, a religion particular to Japan.

Ritual/Doctrinal

This binary is concerned with whether Shinto emphasizes action and practices or is primarily doctrinal in nature. This division is sometimes used more generally in defining Japanese religions as a whole. For example, Ian Reader in his classic *Religion in Contemporary Japan* draws on this distinction, noting that the major theme of religion in Japan is "the primacy of action" tied to specific situations, etiquette, and customary practices.[49] Buddhist scholar Richard Payne also makes much the same point in his recent essay, "The Ritual Culture of Japan." By "ritual culture," Payne means the broadest range of social and religious practices that are "of primary importance for our understanding of the actualities of Japanese religion as it is practiced by the vast majority of people . . . It is practice which makes it possible for one to attain one's goals whether those be defined as liberation, awakening, harmony, longevity, purification, or protection."[50]

An example of "the primacy of action" would be *omiyamairi*, the shrine visit to present a family's newborn child for the blessing of the *kami*. Such a rite of passage is a popular customary practice in Japan. The family visits a shrine one month after birth, wearing formal attire with the infant dressed in special *kimono* or white clothing. They also pray before the main sanctuary of the shrine, take a commemorative photo with the grandmother holding the child, and perform various other ritualistic activities. Similarly, the same primacy of action is also evident in the rituals to the dead before a family's Buddhist home altar (*butsudan*).[51] In this view, traditional rites and practices are central and doctrines the least important element of religious life in Japan.

Indeed, Shinto is often distinguished from religions like Christianity because of its purported lack of specific doctrines, dogmas, or theological beliefs. In Article 28 of the 1889 Meiji Constitution, for example, Japanese subjects were guaranteed freedom of religious belief "within limits not prejudicial to peace and order, and not antagonistic to their duties as subjects." Bernard Schied, Helen Hardacre and others explain that embedded in this article is a nineteenth-century "Eurocentric" or "Protestant" definition of religion as a form of inward personal piety and spiritual belief. Indeed, the word for religion itself in this sense, *shūkyō*, as we have seen, dates from the Meiji period. In Meiji Japan, then, Shinto is officially defined either as customary local practices or a system of national rites performed at shrines and the imperial household, distinguished from religion as defined in Article 28.[52] State-supported shrine Shinto revolving around emperor (*tennō*) worship is treated as non-religious in character from 1882.[53] For many in the Shinto priesthood and as official governmental policy at the time, personal religious beliefs and doctrines have no place within Shinto.

Even after its disestablishment in the post-war period, this characterization continues. The major Shinto organization of the post-war period, which represents the interests of over 80 percent of shrines, the Association of Shinto Shrines (Jinja Honchō), rejects any central authority which would determine doctrine. Ashizu Uzuhiko asserts in his essay, "The various issues about contemporary Shinto shrines" (1956, Reading #27), that the Association was intentionally created without any definitive credo or dogmas. Given the unique history of each shrine, Ashizu notes, establishing any doctrinal uniformity "both organizationally and spiritually is neither possible nor even desirable."[54] The Association, therefore, as a general matter of principle, refrains from any formal teachings and doctrines.[55]

And yet, efforts have been made to identify fundamental Shinto beliefs, teachings, or doctrines. The important pre-war example is the Meiji government's early experiment of organizing a major Institute (Daikyōin) for the "Dissemination of the Great Teachings" (taikyō senpu) Campaign from 1870 onwards. A host of proselytizers called kyōdōshoku (priests, Buddhist clergy, and storytellers) were dispatched throughout the country to spread a simple government-sanctioned faith highlighting such principles as respect for the kami, patriotism, and reverence to the emperor. The campaign ended in 1884, riven by internal disputes, financial problems, and infighting.[56]

Mark Teeuwen has argued that in pre-war Japan attempts were made to transform Shinto from a non-religious ritual cult into a "'supra-religious entity,' and to transform it into a state religion with a better-defined theology and more universally observed practice."[57] Nationalists like Kōno Seizō (Reading #20) writing in the 1930s and 1940s, are an excellent example of this. What Kōno called "the way of kannagara" which he characterizes as "the essence and life blood of the Nation," had a doctrine that "was the moral and practical code of the people." Its key tenet is the divine character of the emperor, who, "being the son of the heavenly gods . . . rules according to the will of his ancestors." Kōno's "universal principles" hearken back to the "Great Teachings" (taikyō) of the early Meiji period: revering the heavenly gods, love of country, living according to the way of man, worshipping the ancestors, doing one's duty, and avoiding doing evil. Here Shinto is a national supra-religious faith—with a basic set of beliefs and an explicit moral code.

Post-war, the Association of Shinto Shrines has also ventured into doctrinal-like pronouncements. In 1956, it issued an important document, "General Principles for a Life of Reverence toward Deities" (Keishin seikatsu no kōryō). These principles include being grateful for the blessing of the kami and ancestors, serving society according to the wishes of the kami, and respecting the emperor as mediator of the wishes of the kami. Ashizu Uzuhiko himself favors the creation of a theology to revive the Shinto tradition.

Other luminaries in the Shinto orbit have shown an interest in theology. Famed literary esthete and folklorist Orikuchi Shinobu (Reading #25) is known for his desire for a post-war revitalization of shrine Shinto. Orikuchi rejects the bland patriotic credo of pre-war State Shinto for the hope that a new charismatic leader would appear, bringing a vibrant new spiritual direction for Shinto. During the war, he was struck by the fervor of true Christian believers and wondered why Japan could not generate a similar spiritual fervor through a renewed faith in the kami. Orikuchi avers that Japanese have typically a deep faith in ancestral kami. In the Meiji era, these are replaced by government-approved paragons of imperial loyalty like the famous warrior Kusonoki Masashige, who sacrificed himself for Emperor Godaigo. Minatogawa shrine in Kobe, where he is enshrined as a kami, became a prominent state-supported shrine. But for Orikuchi, at the heart of Shinto are kami who are worshipped because of their power to bestow the life force into all of nature, including human beings. Some examples are the famous gods of creation, Takamimusubi no Kami and Kamimusubi no Kami. "The belief in kami who provide élan vital, animating the soul and the body, is a basic tenet of Shinto teaching." Therein, in that basic belief, lies the true origin of Shinto religiosity.

Another major example is the post-war Shinto scholar Ueda Kenji (1927–2003). In his "The structure of Shinto faith" (Reading #31), he declares that it is wrong to distinguish Shinto from religions like Christianity because of its seemingly exclusive focus on ritual. Ueda's essay identifies a basic conceptual framework underlying Shinto faith that could be

the foundation for a coherent theology. He defines Shinto as "Japan's unique value orientation, formed in reaction to the stimulus of foreign cultures."

Experiential/Textual

This binary distinguishes between understanding Shinto to be primarily rooted in a non-
rational spiritual experience as opposed to being essentially textual in nature. This binary
has its roots in the work of Motoori Norinaga. Norinaga is famous as the great eighteenth-
century philologist who was able to decipher the ancient hybrid Chinese-Japanese script of
the *Kojiki* (Records of Ancient Matters, 712) that had been largely impenetrable to readers
for centuries. His brilliant commentary on it, the forty-four volume *Kojikiden* completed
in 1822, unlocked the text's meaning and made it accessible to a wide audience. Norinaga
believed that, as the oldest extant book in Japan predating the *Nihonshoki*, the *Kojiki* with its
account of the age of the gods, revealed the true history of the creation of the world to the
early Japanese emperors beginning with Jinmu. His commentary was written to reveal this
ancient true way, which revealed Japan's divine destiny as a land of the gods most properly
ruled by the emperor who embodied the will of the sun goddess, Amaterasu.[58]

In *Naobi no mitama*, Norinaga clearly states that "[t]he meaning of the way can be known
by studying *Kojiki* and other ancient texts."[59] Ancient texts reveal the "way of the gods,"
which has been transmitted unchanged from the age of the gods. The Chinese classics, such
as the *Analects*, which rely on a "way of the sages," are not worth studying; it is the *Kojiki*,
unadulterated by Chinese teachings, that reveals the true way of the gods of Japan. It is
essential to interpret the *Kojiki* correctly in order to understand the will of the *kami*, imperial
rule, and the natural way of the human heart in order to be a good subject.[60] This is the way
of sincerity, where the subject selflessly identifies, respects, and obeys imperial rule.[61] The
Kojiki is foundational, therefore, for defining Shinto as a set of principles, as an ideology and
an ethical way.

In our anthology, there are several examples of defining Shinto as a set of principles, as an
ethical way, or as an ideology deriving from the *Kojiki*. For example, the 1941 government
tract *Shinmin no michi* (The Way of Subjects, Reading #22) relies heavily on Norinaga's
gloss. Like Norinaga, it defines that way as originating from the age of the gods as recorded
in the *Kojiki*. It highlights the importance of the imperial ancestress, Amaterasu Ōmikami;
the imperial unity of ritual and governance (*saisei icchi*); worshipping the *kami* and reverencing the ancestors (*keishinsūso*); and upholding one's duties as a subject to the emperor by
following the "imperial way" (*kōdō*). Other examples that depend on text-based definitions
of Shinto include Kōno Seizō (Reading #20), *Kokutai no hongi* (Reading #21), and Watsuji
Tetsurō (Reading #26).

As Isomae Jun'ichi and Jason Ânanda Josephson have recently argued, the Shinto set
forth in these texts defined it as national rituals and patriotic ethical duty. It is a rationalized
civil practice organized by the state to produce loyal subjects who would, in turn, dedicate
themselves to producing a strong, unified nation. As we have seen, Shinto is therefore differentiated from religions understood as a personal and intuitive "psychological towardness to
unlimited beings" or irrational superstitions (*meishin*).[62]

On the other hand, Norinaga is also a source for seeing Shinto as essentially based in non-
rational experience. Here we are not talking about Norinaga's important aesthetics of *mono no
aware* ("the pathos of things"), which he identifies as the deeply powerful "true human feeling" palpable in the *Kojiki* and other classic Japanese texts.[63] Rather, it stems from his famous

passage explaining that "[a]ny form of being whatsoever which possesses some unique and eminent quality, and is awe inspiring may be called *kami*." Norinaga identifies a number of amazing and awe-inspiring *kami*, including thunder, foxes and *tengu* (mountain goblins), the sea, and mountains. Stuart Picken, in his commentary on this passage, notes that Norinaga's description resembles German theologian Rudolf Otto's notion of numinous experience in his famous book, *Das Heilige*.[64] Numinous experiences evoke a powerful sense of awe, mystery, and fascination that are fundamental for apprehending divinity. Norinaga does not only source Shinto in texts but also in direct, powerful non-ordinary experiences of the natural world.

In our anthology, a good example of defining Shinto experientially comes from Kamata Tōji (1951–). In his introduction to his book, *Shintō yōgo no kiso chishiki* (Fundamental Knowledge of Shinto Terminology, 1999, Reading #33), Kamata answers the question "What is Shinto?" by drawing on Lafcadio Hearn's account of his first visit to Izumo shrine in his 1891 travelogue *Kitzuki*. He describes the beautiful environs of Izumo as having a "sense of divine magic in the very atmosphere . . . [a] sense of Shinto."[65]

Kamata suggests that Hearn's "sense of Shinto" points beyond typical definitions based on "world religions" like Christianity. While Christianity has a founder, fixed doctrines and beliefs, and an organization, Shinto's religiousness comes from "discovering the *kami* within the very nature and atmosphere," a physical/psychological feeling that cannot be fully expressed conceptually. Shinto, Kamata argues, is not found in any "scripture." He dismisses attempts to grasp Shinto through exegesis of the *Kojiki* or other ancient texts. Shinto "does not live inside books" but "lives and breathes in people's hearts." This is the essential characteristic that differentiates it from dogmatic and doctrinal Western Christianity. Kamata defines Shinto monothetically as a powerful experience of the *kami* in the natural world.

Transcendent/Immanent

This is yet another important binary for defining Shinto. As Isomae Jun'ichi has recently observed, the term "religion" comes from the West imbued with a notion of transcendence— a notion associated with Western Christianity. What is sacred ultimately lies outside or beyond the natural and human social-political world. The perceived transcendental character of Christianity thus becomes a point of contrast with Shinto.[66]

Katō Genchi (Reading #18) offers a good example of this type of classification. Katō, ever the comparativist, draws a key distinction between Western and Eastern conceptions of divinity. Western notions of the sacred, which include not only Christianity but also Judaism and Islamic religions "born of the practical mind of the Semites" are theocratic in nature. In defining "theocratic," Katō explains that in these religions, "Divinity stands high above man and nature; with its formula 'god is above us.'" By contrast, Eastern religions are "theanthropic," which Katō explains as "divinity in man and nature; it is immanent or inherent in man and the universe, and its language proclaims, 'god is in us.'" Western religions are monotheistic. Eastern religions involve nature, ancestors, heroes, and emperor worship. Christianity is theocratic; for Katō, Shinto is "in its salient features" a classical instance of a theanthropic religion. It focuses on nature and ancestor worship; Katō notes, for instance, that according to the *Nihonshoki*, Jinmu, the legendary first emperor, was deified early on as Ame no Oshigami [Ame osu no kami] or "Heaven Conquering God." In documents of olden times, each emperor is described as a visible deity or a god incarnate.

Katō wrote in the mid-1930s, and his theanthropic definition of Shinto closely parallels those nationalists who, like Kōno Seizō, elaborated upon the Meiji Constitution definition of the emperor as "sacred and inviolable." According to Kōno, Amaterasu Ōmikami is a heavenly deity (*amatsukami*) at the center of Shinto as a religion (which Kōno calls the "way of *kannagara*"), but she is not a transcendent figure. Her essence

> signifies the sublime and mightiest power of the nation, namely the throne, and the great-august-heart or the soul of the ruler, which is embodied in the throne. In other words, it represents the divine soul of the ruler of the empire, the emperor. The emperor is the divine manifestation of Amaterasu Ōmikami and rules the empire in accordance with her will. Thus the emperor and the imperial throne, transmitted in an unbroken line, are sacred and inviolable.

That is, the sacred is immanent in the person of the emperor, who is Amaterasu's "divine manifestation." Not only that, but Kōno goes on to say that "the spirit of the nation, in its essential form, is known as the 'great way of *kannagara*.'" This association of divinity with "national spirit" points to other binaries for defining Shinto such as nationalism versus universalism and collectivism versus individual piety and morality.

Minimalist/Maximalist

Historian of religions Bruce Lincoln developed this binary for distinguishing two common models of religion. Minimalism is a view which restricts "religion to an important set of (chiefly metaphysical) concerns, protects its privileges against state intrusion, and restricts its activity and influence to this specialized sphere." By contrast, a maximalist position sees religion as permeating "all aspects of human existence."[67]

As discussed above, from the Meiji period onward, many Japanese intellectuals, priests, and government officials had the minimalist view as their default view of religion. We have also seen that religion was defined as something confined to the private sphere of individual faith, prayer, and religious experience. Shinto, on the other hand, was considered nonreligious in character *because* it was maximalist. Rites were unified with the government; it involved public rites and ceremonies; and its ethic was supposed to permeate every aspect of Japanese lives. While sectarian forms of Shinto with their doctrines and private religious organizations fit the minimalist definition, shrine Shinto, imperial household rites, and the national polity (*kokutai*) ideology were something else entirely. We can see such a maximalist orientation in texts such as *Kokutai no hongi* (Reading #21) and *Shinmin no michi* (Reading #22)

This distinction was, if anything, reinforced by the Supreme Commander of the Allied Powers' (SCAP) 1945 Shinto Directive and Article 20 of the New "MacArthur" Constitution (1946), which guaranteed freedom of religion by separating religious organizations from the state. In the Directive, shrine Shinto is redefined as private religious organizations in contrast to pre-war "State Shinto," which is described as a perverted form of militaristic and ultranationalist ideology rather than a religion. As a legal matter, the Constitution guarantees freedom of religion. Private religious organizations do not receive "any privileges from the state, nor exercise any political authority."

Some authors in our anthology wrestle with Shinto in light of minimalist definitions of religion. For Yanagita Kunio and others, as we have seen, folk or village Shinto is not secular but religious in character. But religion is conceived here in the broadest sense—as maximalist rather than minimalist in orientation. They define Shinto as a religion not because it is

18

linked to an underlying national polity but because it permeates the folk culture. "Culture" here, as Bruce Lincoln has noted, is a very ambiguous category. On the one hand, it can stand for a group or community to which one belongs; on the other hand, it refers to specific habits, customs, and ways of life practiced by that group or community. So, it refers both to a particular community of belonging and a specific cultural identity.[68]

Sonoda Minoru (Reading #32) draws on this division most conspicuously when discussing "how to foster awareness of Shinto as a 'religion'?" As previously noted, Sonoda defines Shinto as a "cultural religion" (*bunkateki shūkyō*), arguing that "[w]e need to understand the concept of religion more broadly signifying how religion can give intrinsic meaning to a traditional culture and collectivity as a symbolic system." As part of Japanese folk culture, it provides a "spiritual outlook" for "the indigenous peoples who settled in this mountainous archipelago and is openly practiced in their cultural life." Thus, Shinto is the customs and beliefs of ordinary daily Japanese life but also a religion for the Japanese people who live within its spiritual world.

Collective/Individual

We have already noted that in the pre-war period the Japanese state's view of religion was shaped by Protestantism. Religion meant, to borrow Isomae's words, a "psychological towardness to unlimited beings."[69] This is at the heart of Article 28 of the Meiji Constitution allowing the individual's right to have a personal faith. Religion in this sense is essentially an affair of the heart—tolerated so long as it remains essentially a matter of personal piety. Government tracts on Shinto, such as the Board of Divinities' (Jingiin) 1944 educational guide, *Jinja hongi* (The Cardinal Principles of Shrines, Reading #23) reflect this view of religion. Shrine Shinto was a public and collective faith that lay outside the limits of this legally prescribed definition of religion as private belief:

> Shrine ceremonies are core state rituals. Of course they should not be the private affairs of an individual or a family. This makes it clear that shrines are not the focus of private faith, but are for the state to revere and worship. This is fundamentally different from the thirteen sects of sect Shinto, which are based on a religious faith and are treated as religions.

It is interesting that the Occupation's Shinto Directive generally reaffirms this definition to achieve its political aim of separating Shinto from state support and control. In a GHQ Civil Information and Education Section memorandum, dated December 3, 1945 (before SCAP's issuance of the Shinto Directive on December 15) religious freedom is conceived as an individual right. State Shinto is to be proscribed because it is an aberration: "It does not, like a universal religion such as Christianity or Buddhism, center on the individual and thus transcend national boundaries. Of necessity it is racialistic and nationalistic." Occupation policy should abolish "[a]ll government support, direction, or control over the shrines, their priests, ceremonies, or rituals" so that shrine Shinto can "continue as a religion of individuals."[70]

Shinto is often viewed as a collective phenomenon. However, official and scholarly writings have different conceptions of the nature of that collectivity. For example, the famous pre-war Marxist economist Kawakami Hajime (1879–1946; Reading #16) was deeply critical of Western capitalism with its individualistic ethic of personal self-interest. For him, "[t]he state is our god, and the emperor is the representative of god." The greatness of Japan lies in its religion of nationalism, and the emperor as a *kami* embodies the absolute sacredness of the nation. He is "the concrete embodiment of the state's abstract divinity." This faith in the state and in the emperor as the embodiment of the supreme goodness and power of Japan's national polity (*kokutai*) should be central to every Japanese citizen's ethic of self-sacrifice.

Yanagita Kunio (Reading #17) offers a different take on Shinto as a collective "national faith." He never used the phrase "State Shinto" and dismissed the Shinto Directive because he believed it misinterpreted shrine Shinto. Shrine Shinto has nothing to do with the state-supported national cult. Shrines did not serve the artificially imposed emperor-centered state nationalism of the Meiji period; rather they answered to a collectivity which comes from a folk Shinto practiced at the local village and regional levels. It is essentially the folk traditions and observances associated with *uji* shrines. In post-war Japan, Yanagita sought to revive this village-based popular Shinto (*minshū no Shintō*) of ordinary citizens, which lay hidden beneath the ruins of State Shinto. Shrines are objects of reverence giving people a place to pray to the *kami*. This local-shrine-centered, rather than state-centered Shinto is the true national faith of Japan. Yanagita sees the Shinto of the family, village, and regional collectivities, rather than the family-state with the emperor at its head, as the Shinto that "completely depends upon the natural tendencies of the people's hearts."

Local/National

This binary is closely related to the above dyad. Like Yanagita Kunio above, Shinto priest and scholar Sonoda Minoru, in his *Daredemo no shintō—shūkyō no Nihonteki kanōsei* (Shinto for Everyone: A Possibility for Religion in Japan, 1998, Reading #32), defines Shinto as a religion tied directly to local shrines. A key to his definition is that shrines function as sanctified places for festivals (*matsuri*). Sonoda also emphasizes the "socio-ecological" character of Shinto shrines, particularly at the local level, in what he calls "climatic" (*fūdo*) cults.[71] Local shrines, situated as they are within their local landscapes and socio-ecosystems, are key in Shinto. He thinks that the common, community-based character of a shrine is different from Western religious institutions, which emphasize the private practice of religion. Indeed, Sonoda argues that defining Shinto as a religion in the Western sense is incorrect; he believes that we should redefine "religion" more broadly and should think of it as an intrinsic part of local traditional culture and people. The ancient local shrine grove is what offers a place to find one's home. Even in modern urban Japan, Shinto's rich public, collectively shared culture that is found in its local festivals can ground human life.

This can be contrasted with Kawakami, Kōno, Katō Genchi, and what we find in government propaganda tracts before World War II, all of which stress Shinto's national character as a state cult. Katō (Reading #18), for example, describes the state cult as a national faith. "It is, in fact, a Japanese patriotism suffused with religious emotion; or, in other words, a peculiar enthusiastic patriotic sentiment, often soaring into the plane of adoration or religious worship, towards the emperor." "It is a religion *a priori* of the heart and life of every Japanese subject, male and female, high and low, old and young, educated or illiterate." This same national focus can also be found in the *Jinja hongi* (Reading #23) issued by the government Board of Divinities:

> In our country, a succession of emperors has always been united as one with the imperial ancestor, and has ruled as manifest *kami* (*akitsumikami*), just as in the age of the gods. They have broad, unlimited and unsurpassed virtues. The people bask

in this compassionate imperial kindness, and they put the emperors' divine commands into effect by wholeheartedly and unconditionally respecting the ancestral will, serving generations of emperors, and exhibiting the fine virtues of loyalty and filial piety. This brings about an incomparable unity of the sovereign and his people that form one great family state. The life of this eternally undying state continues to develop vigorously.

In this tract "the great way of the gods" (*kannagara no michi*) is revealed in its "most sublime and venerable form" in Japanese shrines, beginning with Ise Jingū. The close connection between shrines, the Japanese imperial state, and the national destiny can be seen in the number of new shrines being established in Japan's foreign territories under its control in pre-war Taiwan, Sakhalin, Korea, and elsewhere. Although these shrines are local, they symbolize Japan's imperial expansion and are based in Japan's unique national polity (*kokutai*) which is closely tied to the state. This same idea also appears in another famous government text for teaching students moral education, the *Kokutai no hongi*: "Thus, all functions of the Shinto shrines ultimately unite in the services rendered by the emperor to the imperial ancestors; and it is in this that we find the basis of our national reverence for the deities."

Conclusion

The above list of binaries is by no means comprehensive. Definitions of Shinto can also be classified using other binaries as well, such as tutelary *kami* / heavenly *kami*, folk/emperor, sacred place (*seichi*) / divine land (*shinkoku*), public/private, and so on, an exercise that can be quite useful. Each one of the essays in our anthology, therefore, can be characterized by a set of binaries situating its definition of Shinto polythetically, and this offers a useful lens to compare different definitions of Shinto (though the reader should bear in mind that not all authors define their terms in the same way). This anthology, therefore, looks at the range of different definitions Shinto scholars and officials have devised in modernity. Our goal is to define the field of features that they have identified so that we can have a general model for clarifying our thinking. Each of the writings presents a definition of Shinto at a given historical moment, and this allows us to see how the authors' approaches and selected characteristics have changed over time. The goal is to have readers reflect upon the following: What characteristics are selected? What characteristics are deemphasized or rejected? And how do authors go about interpreting Shinto at their particular historical moment?

Suggested readings

Aston, W.G. *Nihongi: Chronicles of Japan from the Earliest Times to A.D. 697.* Rutland, VT: Charles E. Tuttle Co., 1972.

Bocking, Brian. *A Popular Dictionary of Shinto.* Richmond, UK: Curzon Press, 1996.

Buruma, Ian. *Inventing Japan 1853–1964.* New York: Modern Library, 2003.

Breen, John and Mark Teeuwen eds. *Shinto in History—Ways of the Kami.* Honolulu, Hawai'i: The University of Hawai'i Press, 2000.

———. *A New History of Shinto.* Chichester, UK: Wiley-Blackwell, 2010.

Grapard, Allan G. "The Shinto of Yoshida Kanetomo." *Monumenta Nipponica* 47:27–58.

Hardacre, Helen. *Shinto: A History.* Oxford: Oxford University Press, 2017.

Havens, Norman. "Shinto." In *Nanzan Guide to Japanese Religions*, edited by Paul L. Swanson and Clark Chilson. Honolulu, Hawai'i: University of Hawai'i Press, 2006.

Holtom, Daniel. *The National Faith of Japan.* London: Kegan Paul, Trench, Trubner & Co., 1938.

Inoue Nobutaka ed., Itō Satoshi, Endō Jun, and Mori Mizue. *Shinto: A Short History.* Translated by Mark Teeuwen and John Breen. London: RoutledgeCurzon, 1998.

Itō Satoshi. *Shintō to wa nani ka—kami to hotoke no Nihonshi.* Tokyo: Chūōkōron shinsha, 2012.

Isomae Jun'ichi. *Religious Discourse in Modern Japan.* Translated by Galen Amstutz and Lynne E. Riggs. Leiden: Brill, 2014.

Kasulis, Thomas. *Shinto: The Way Home.* Honolulu, Hawai'i: University of Hawai'i Press. 2004.

Kokugakuin University. *Encyclopedia of Shinto,* http://k-amc.kokugakuin.ac.jp/DM/dbTop.do?class_name=col_eos.

Picken, Stuart, D.B. *Essentials of Shinto: An Analytical Guide to Principal Teachings.* Westport, CN: Greenwood Press, 1994.

———. *A Historical Dictionary of Shinto.* Lanham, MD: Scarecrow Press, 2002.

———. *Sourcebook in Shinto: Selected Documents.* Westport, CN: Praeger, 2004.

———. *The A to Z of Shinto.* Lanham, MD: Scarecrow Press, 2006.

Phillippi, Donald, trans. *Kojiki.* Tokyo: The University of Tokyo Press, 1968.

Plutschow, Herbert. *Matsuri: The Festivals of Japan.* Richmond, UK: Japan Library, 1996.

Reader, Ian. *Shinto.* London: Simple Guides, 2007.

Scheid, Bernard. "Shintō Shrines: Traditions and Transformations," In *Handbook of Contemporary Japanese Religions,* edited by Inken Prohl and John Nelson. Leiden: Brill, 2012.

Teeuwen, Mark. "From *jindō* to Shinto: A Concept Takes Shape." *Japanese Journal of Religious Studies* 29 (Fall, 2002):233–64

Teeuwen, Mark, and Fabio Rambelli eds. *Buddhas and Kami in Japan: Honji Suijaku as a Combinatory Paradigm.* London: RoutledgeCurzon, 2002.

Ueda Kenji. "Shinto." In *Japanese Religion: A Survey by the Agency for Cultural Affairs,* edited by Hori Ichirō et al. Tokyo: Kodansha International, 1972.

Notes

1 According to the Japanese Foreign Ministry, this official imperial era (*gengō*) name translates as "beautiful harmony." However, some critics were quick to point out that an alternative reading could be "strict command or control peace," stirring up associations with Japan's militaristic past.

2 "Shushō 'Nihon no dentō jikkan'," *Nihon Keizai shinbun* May 5, 2015, http://www.nikkei.com/article/DGXLASFS05H8P_V00C15A6MM8000/.

3 Michael Holtz, "Reviving Shinto: Prime Minister Abe Tends Special place in Japan's Soul," *The Christian Science Monitor,* October 5, 2015, https://www.csmonitor.com/World/Asia-Pacific/2015/1005/Reviving-Shinto-Prime-Minister-Abe-tends-special-place-in-Japan-s-soul-video.

4 Kokugakuin University was established through the government supported Office of Japanese Classics Research (Kōten Kyōkūjo) in 1890, originally with the intention to train Shinto priests and to study Japanese classic texts.

5 That does not mean, however, that the scholar's act of imagining religion is not valuable. As Jonathan Z. Smith points out, defining religion is done "for the scholar's analytical purposes by his imaginative acts of comparison and generalization" (*xi*). See his *Imagining Religion: From Babylon to Jonestown* (Chicago: The University of Chicago Press, 1982).

6 See for example, William Elliot Griffis, *The Religions of Japan: From the Dawn of History to the Era of Meiji* (New York: Charles Scribner's Sons, 1907); Lafcadio Hearn, *Japan: An Attempt at Interpretation* (New York: The Macmillan Co, 1928); W.G. Aston, *Shinto: The Way of the Gods* (New York: Longmans, Green, and Co., 1905); and Basil Hall Chamberlain, "The Invention of a New Religion" (London: Watts and Co, 1912).

7 Aston, *Shinto,* 6.

8 Ibid., 10.

9 Others draw on Western theories for their own definitions of Shinto as a religion. Katō Genchi (1873–1965; Reading #18) draws on the classificatory systems of Dutch scholar of *Religionswissenschaft,*

C.P. Tiele (1830–1902), Watsuji Tetsurō (1889–1960; Reading #26) uses Polish anthropologist Bronisław Malinowski's (1884–1942) ideas on myth in primitive society, and Kamata Tōji (1951–) is inspired by Lafcadio Hearn (Koizumi Yakumo, 1850–1904).

10 See Ueda Kenji's "Shinto," in *Japanese Religion: A Survey by the Agency for Cultural Affairs,* eds. Hori Ichirō et al. (Tokyo: Kodansha International, 1972), 29.

11 Inoue Nobutaka ed., *Shinto: A Short History* (London: RoutledgeCurzon, 2003), 1.

12 Joseph M. Kitagawa, "History of Religions in America," in *The History of Religions: Essays in Methodology*, eds. Mircea Eliade and Joseph M. Kitagawa (Chicago: The University of Chicago Press, 1959), 22.

13 Mark Teeuwen and Bernard Scheid, "Tracing Shinto in the History of Kami Worship—Editors' Introduction," *Japanese Journal of Religious Studies* 29 (2002):195.

14 Norman Havens, "Shinto," in *Nanzan Guide to Japanese Religions*, eds. Paul L. Swanson and Clark Chilson (Honolulu: University of Hawai'i Press, 2006), 18.

15 Sarah Thal, "Redefining the Gods: Politics and Survival in the Creation of Modern Kami," *Japanese Journal of Religious Studies* 29 (Fall, 2002):401.

16 John Breen and Mark Teeuwen eds., *Shinto in History: Ways of the Kami* (University of Hawai'i Press, 2000), 3.

17 Toshimaro Ama, *Why are the Japanese Non-Religious?* (New York: University Press of America, 2005), 1–2.

18 Pew Research Center, "America's Changing Religious Landscape," May 12, 2015, http://www.pew forum.org/2015/05/12/americas-changing-religious-landscape/. As Ian Reader notes, Japanese tend to see religious belonging as multiple in nature. See *Religion in Contemporary Japan* (Honolulu: University of Hawai'i Press, 1991), 6.

19 Kitagawa, "History of Religions," 22.

20 This is also indicated in a recent 2015–16 survey where Gunma University students were asked to write down the differences between Buddhism and Shinto. Over 64 percent either wrote nothing or said directly they did not know. Of the 36 percent of respondents who responded, it was clear to the researcher that most simply guessed given the question—Buddha or *kami*? Buddhist teachings versus Shinto way? See Flavia Bartellone, "Nihonjin no wakamono ni okeru shūkyōkan—Gunma Daigaku de okonawatta ankeeto chōsa to sono kekka" (GUIC Gunma University International Center, 2015–16), http://www.guic.gunma-u.ac.jp/wp/wp-content/uploads/2017/03/論文フラヴィア.pdf.

21 Motoori Norinaga talks about the underlying will of the heavenly gods which the emperor takes as his own. See Sey Nishimura, trans., "The Way of the Gods Motoori Norinaga's *Naobi no Mitama*," *Monumenta Nipponica* 46 (1) (1991):28.

22 Ishida Ichirō, *Kami to Nihon bunka* (Tokyo, Perikansha, 1983), 10–11.

23 Ibid., 158.

24 See Mark MacWilliams, "Manufacturing Shintō as a 'World Religion'—An Analysis of Anglo-American Textbooks," *Journal of Religion in Japan* 6 (2017):171–207.

25 Talal Asad, *Genealogies of Religion: Discipline and Reasons of Power in Christianity and Islam* (Baltimore, MD: The Johns Hopkins University Press, 1993), 29.

26 Smith, *Imagining Religion, 3.*

27 Ibid., 7.

28 Hearn (1850–1904), a well-known international man of letters, who lived in Japan from 1890 until his death, wrote prolifically about Japanese literature, culture, and religion.

29 Lafcadio Hearn, *Japan An Attempt at Interpretation* (New York: Grosset and Dunlap, 1904):159–61; Roy Starrs, "Lafcadio Hearn as a Japanese Nationalist," *Japan Review* 18 (2006):195. Hearn, himself, was influenced by Romanticism, particularly its emphasis on an intuitive spiritual experience of the sublime in nature. He also shared German Romantic Johann Herder's nostalgic vision of an organic nationalism: a theory that the state owes its legitimacy to a pure "spirit of the folk" (*volkgeist*) or cultural-ethnically based national character.

30 Asad, *Genealogies,* 29.

31 Bruce Lincoln, *Holy Terrors: Thinking about Religion after September 11* (Chicago: The University of Chicago Press, 2003), 2.

32 Ibid., 2.

33 Michel Tibayrenc ed., *Genetics and Evolution of Infectious Diseases* (Amsterdam, Netherlands: Elsevier, 2010), 7.

34 Jonathan Pevsner, *Bioinformatics and Functional Genomics* (Oxford, UK: Wiley-Blackwell, 2015), 756.
35 Lincoln, *Holy Terrors,* 2.
36 See Jason Ānanda Josephson provocative study, *The Invention of Religion in Japan* (Chicago, The University of Chicago Press, 2012), Chapter 3, 71–93.
37 Ibid., 135.
38 Ibid., 96.
39 Of these, there were thirteen sects officially recognized by the Meiji government from the late nineteenth to early twentieth centuries. See Inoue Nobutaka, "The Formation of Sect Shinto in Modernizing Japan," *Japanese Journal of Religious Studies* 29 (2002):405–27.
40 Helen Hardacre, *Shintō and the State 1868–1988* (Princeton: Princeton University Press, 1989), 65.
41 This is exactly the kind of approach that John K. Nelson takes, for example, in his analysis of the Okunchi Festival of Suwa Shrine in Nagasaki. In that analysis, he takes a cultural semiotic approach relying on the work of anthropologist Clifford Geertz. See *A Day in the Life of a Shinto Shrine* (Seattle, WA: University of Washington Press, 1996), 133–59.
42 Nishimura, "The Way of the Gods," 35–36.
43 Basil H. Chamberlain, "The Invention of a New Religion" (London: Watts & Co, 1912), 6.
44 Ibid., 10.
45 Ibid., 27. Chamberlain has high disdain for the Meiji state because it unhesitatingly attacked scholars who had the audacity to note the errors of historical fact in the ideology. As his biographer Yuzo Ota aptly notes, Chamberlain is a worthy predecessor of Tsuda Sōkichi in this respect. See Yuzo Ota, *Basil Hall Chamberlain: Portrait of a Japanologist* (Richmond, UK: The Japan Library, 1998).
46 Isomae, Jun'ichi, "Deconstructing 'Japanese Religion'—A Historical Survey," *Japanese Journal of Religious Studies* 32 (2005):240.
47 As Mark Teeuwen points out, however, Kuroda nowhere denies the long continuous tradition of *kami* worship in Japan that existed throughout Japanese history. See his "State Shinto: An 'Independent Religion'?" *Monumenta Nipponica* 54 (Spring, 1999):111–21.
48 The influential University of Tokyo religious studies scholar Kishimoto Hideo (1903–64) (not included in this anthology) offers a classic example. He continued to emphasize Shinto's indigenous character by categorizing Shinto as an ethnic or national religion like Judaism, as opposed to universal religions like Christianity and Buddhism. Kishimoto served as a key advisor to the Civil Information and Education Section of GHQ and SCAP during the Occupation as it designed the post-war religious reforms. See Okuyama Michiaki, "Shinto in the Japanese Religious System and the Western Influences," *Revue Roumaine de Philosophie* 48 (2004):183–90.
49 Reader, *Religion in Contemporary Japan,* 15.
50 Richard Payne, "The Ritual Culture of Japan," in *Nanzan Guide to Japanese Religions,* eds. Paul L. Swanson and Clark Chilson (Honolulu: University of Hawai'i Press, 2006), 235–36.
51 Reader, *Religion in Contemporary Japan,* 1.
52 Hardacre, *Shintō and the State,* 65. Bernard Schied, "Shintō Shrines: Traditions and Transformations," in *Handbook of Contemporary Japanese Religions,* eds. Inken Prohl and John Nelson. (Leiden: Brill, 2012), 97.
53 Ueda Kenji has noted that this period marks a "vacuum as regards the development of a modern theology." See his "Contemporary Social Change and Shinto Tradition," *Japanese Journal of Religious Studies* 6 (March/June, 1979), 308.
54 By contrast, the Kyoto-based Shrine Organization of the Fundamental Teachings (Jinja Honkyō), established in 1946 and continuing this day with seventy-six shrines as members (as of 2015), stipulated a "head administrator" who had authority to decide over acceptable doctrines.
55 Mark Teeuwen, "Jinja Honchō and Shrine Shintō Policy," *Japan Forum* 8 (2) (1996):184.
56 Hardacre, *Shintō and State,* 42–48. In a 1966 survey of priests, for example, when asked if it was advisable to create a Shinto orthodox of doctrine, only 39.8% thought it would be probably advisable. Opponents often noted that Shinto has never relied on doctrines and creeds. Ueda, "Contemporary Social Change," 309.
57 Mark Teeuwen, "State Shinto: An Independent Religion," *Monumenta Nipponica* 54 (Spring, 1999):117.
58 Nishimura, "The Way of the Gods," 22.

59 Ibid., 36.

60 Ibid., 39.

61 Isomae Jun'ichi, "Reappropriating the Japanese Myths Motoori Norinaga and the Creation Myths of the *Kojiki* and *Nihonshoki*," *Japanese Journal of Religious Studies* 27 (2000): 18.

62 Isomae, "Deconstructing," 240.

63 *Mono no aware* is any deep emotion that arises when something goes against one's desires. Norinaga cites as a classical instance the poignant scene in the *Kojiki* when the creator gods Izanagi and Izanami sadly part ways when Izanami must go to the land of the dead, Yomi. As Isomae Jun'ichi has argued, this emotional power to be moved by things (*aware*) undergirded the way of sincerity by giving people the sensitivity to feel sympathy towards others and work for harmony. Nishimura, "The Way of the Gods," 22.

64 Stuart Picken, *Sourcebook in Shinto: Selected Documents* (London: Praeger, 2004), 200–1.

65 On Hearn, see Roy Starrs, "Lafcadio Hearn as Japanese Nationalist," *Japan Review* 18 (2006): 181–213.

66 Isomae, "Deconstructing," 236–40

67 Lincoln, *Holy Terrors*, 5.

68 Ibid., 51.

69 Isomae, "Deconstructing," 236.

70 General Headquarters Supreme Commander for the Allied Powers, Civil Information and Education Section, "Memorandum," (December 3, 1945), 328, 336.

71 See Sonoda, "Shinto and the Natural Environment," 32–46.

PART 1: SHINTO AND THE MODERN JAPANESE NATION STATE AND PART 2: PRE-WAR JAPANESE INTELLECTUALS ON SHINTO

INTRODUCTION

This section offers readings primarily from the Meiji (1868–1912) through the Taishō (1912–26) periods. Part 1 contains key administrative edicts, notifications, ordinances and selections from the Meiji Constitution, all of which cover the rise of what is called State Shinto. State Shinto is a term originally dating from the post-war period, initially appearing in SCAP's famous Shinto Directive issued on December 15, 1945.[1] Later, it became popularized by the great scholar of modern Japanese religions, Murakami Shigeyoshi, in his seminal book, *Kokka shintō* (State Shinto 1970).[2] State Shinto is a form of government-supported religious nationalism with a central focus on reverence to the emperor. It was put into practice through a bureaucratically organized system of shrines, priesthood-officials, and civil rituals, and through fostering a spirit of loyalty and self-sacrifice for the emperor among his subjects. The term often used for it during this period was the imperial way (*kōdō*).[3]

Part 2 is a selection of essays by Japanese intellectuals extending to the 1930s. They are from very different academic fields and political persuasions: for example, Kawakami Hajime was a leftist Marxist economist, and Yanagita Kunio founded Japanese folklore studies. However, all these authors defined Shinto in response to the spiritual and political realities of the age in which they lived. During this period, State Shinto played a powerful ritual, ethical, and ideological role in legitimizing the modern Japanese imperial state. As we shall see, these authors offer something new—redefining Shinto in different ways that transcend the State Shinto orthodoxy.

Historical overview

The Meiji and Taishō eras were a remarkable time of comprehensive change for the Japanese. In just half a century, Japan metamorphosed from an isolated feudal society, technologically and industrially backward, into a modern nation state that competed on the world stage.

It began with the decline of the Tokugawa *ancien regime*. The Tokugawa military government (*bakufu*) had dominated Japan's disparate feudal domains (*han*) for over 250 years. But that hegemony had gradually weakened over time. By the second half of the nineteenth century, it had reached a crisis. Several factors combined to undermine Tokugawa rule during the *bakumatsu* (or end of military government) period. First came several devastating natural and human disasters—catastrophic crop failures, earthquakes, famines, epidemics, and peasant rural and urban rebellions—that broke out during the Tenpō (1830–44) and Ansei (1855–60) periods. The country also underwent massive social and economic changes as a market economy was established and as cities like Edo (the center of Tokugawa rule) grew and flourished with economic expansion. Inveterate rural poverty and famine, however, intensified, leading to a series of revolts by the heavily taxed peasant farmers on whom the samurai depended for their rice stipends. Just as destabilizing was a widening gap in wealth between the samurai, whose real income through stipends largely declined during this period, and an increasingly powerful merchant (*shōnin*) class, who profited commercially as middlemen and purveyors of goods. The *bakufu*, despite its attempts at fiscal reform, failed to effectively address these alarming economic and social problems.

A third factor was external foreign threats that undermined Tokugawa fiscal health and civil authority. The American Commodore Matthew Perry's black ships, which steamed into Edo Bay in July 1853, revealed that the *bakufu* was outgunned and unable to repel them. Tokugawa resistance ultimately proved futile. A series of "peace and amity" treaties led to the inevitable opening of Japan (*kaikoku*) to the West; the first of these being the Treaty of Kanagawa, negotiated with the United States in 1854, and soon followed by treaties with the UK, Russia, and the Netherlands. The humiliating terms of these treaties clearly showed the shogunate's weakness in its new trade and diplomatic relations with the West.

Internal opponents, particularly an alliance between the samurai of Satsuma and Chōshū domains (*Saccho dōmei*), increasingly agitated for the overthrow of the Tokugawa. The cry of insurgents, the "men of spirit" (*shishi*), was "revere the emperor and expel the barbarians" (*sonnō jōi*). This ultimately led to the Boshin War (1868–69) culminating in the defeat of the *bakufu*, a momentous event known as the Meiji Restoration (*Meiji ishin*). The new Meiji government that restored imperial rule was led by a clique of talented young bureaucrats who were predominantly samurai from the victorious domains, leaders such as Ōkubo Toshimichi (1830–78), Saigō Takamori (1827–77), Kido Takayoshi (1833–77), and Iwakura Tomomi (1825–83), all of whom were deeply influenced by national learning thought. With the young Emperor Meiji (1852–1912) installed at his new palace (originally the Tokugawa's castle in Edo (now Tokyo)), they consolidated their power behind the throne. The young samurai officials occupied powerful governmental posts as they set their sights on establishing a new, strong, and stable Japanese state.

Although the Meiji Restoration was officially portrayed as a return to the idyllic reign of the legendary first Emperor Jinmu, the reality is far more complex. The Restoration was truly revolutionary, radically transforming Japan in every sense.[4] This was best expressed by no less a figure than Emperor Meiji, whose April 6, 1868 Charter Oath boldly outlined the progressive course set by the new government. To modernize Japan, knowledge must "be sought throughout the world so as to strengthen the foundations of the imperial rule."[5] The motivation for this is not hard to find. As historian Jackson Bailey has noted, Japan at this time saw itself as a "poor country struggling to survive," which was a "pragmatic response to the realities of the world in the 19th century" given it was a "world dominated by Western imperialism and an emerging 'social Darwinist' mentality that the Japanese took seriously and some took literally."[6]

The Meiji era national slogans of "enrich the country and strengthen the army" (*fukoku kyōhei*) and "civilization and enlightenment" (*bunmei kaika*) pointed to the ultimate goal of the new government. It encouraged the adoption of Western technology, industry, institutions, and culture in order to build a powerful modern Japan that would rival Western powers.

Rapid political, social, and economic transformations soon followed. First came the destruction of the old political order with the end of the *baku-han* system in 1871. The *han* were converted into seventy-two prefectures and three municipalities; with the creation of the Home Ministry in 1873, the old *daimyō* lords and their former retainers were pensioned off and the former *han* placed under the direct control of the central government.[7] The government also effectively eliminated the Tokugawa four-tiered hierarchical class system, replacing it with a society where both nobility (*kazoku*) and commoners should all equally be loyal subjects (*shinmin*) of the emperor. As Emperor Meiji pledged in the Charter Oath, all classes could now fulfill their "just aspirations," and "evil customs of the past" would be eliminated. A key symbol of the latter was the 1876 ban on samurai wearing their two swords in public.

A host of administrative reforms and innovations soon followed. These included adopting the internationally recognized gold standard with the yen as Japan's national currency (the New Currency Act of 1871);[8] establishing a national banking system, with the Bank of Japan incorporated by 1882; creating a uniform land taxation system for funding the government; forming a modern military based upon universal conscription of all male subjects (The Conscription Law of 1873); and putting in place a compulsory elementary school system, which was promulgated by the new Ministry of Education (Monbushō) in 1872. (The Ministry, taking its cue from the American system, extended elementary education to six years in 1907.) These are just a few examples of the early Meiji government's drive toward modernization and the ways in which it was deeply indebted to Western models.

Not all changes were government-inspired. The Japanese people were genuinely fascinated with all things Western. For example, the famous popularizer of the Occident, Fukuzawa Yukichi (1835–1901), published numerous influential essays and books touting the advantages of Western civilization—such as his *Things Western* (*Seiyō jijō*, published three times from 1866 to 1870) and his magnum opus, *An Outline of the Theory of Civilization* (*Bunmeiron no gairyaku*, 1875). Fukuzawa believed that modernization could best be accomplished by educating the general public about the West. This did not just mean studying practical subjects like the military arts, bookkeeping, business, and education; it even included adopting everyday Western customs. For example, in his 1870 essay, "On Meat Eating," part of an advertising campaign for a new dairy company, Fukuzawa argued that meat and milk consumption would make people so strong that, "for the first time we will not feel ashamed to be called Japanese."[9] Eating beef became quite fashionable, particularly after the Edo period ban on it was abolished, and the trend-setting Emperor Meiji himself ate beef during an 1872 New Year celebration.[10] In this and other ways the emperor symbolized this time of revolutionary change. For his 1888 official imperial portrait (*goshin'ei*), he wore a Prussian-style military uniform rather than traditional court robes.[11] Copies of the photograph, which was treated as a sacred object in public schools throughout Japan, made this modern image of the Japanese potentate visible to his subjects.[12]

Meiji Japan also experienced dramatic industrial and economic growth from the 1870s to the 1900s.[13] This was made possible through the new banking system together with other farsighted government policies such as industrial promotion (*shokusan kōgyō*),[14] investment in basic infrastructure like rail and road systems, hiring foreign experts and studying abroad (one famous example of this was the Iwakura Mission to the West in 1871), building model factories, and large-scale electrification projects in the 1920s.[15] Textiles, particularly cotton and silk, were a major success story in Japan's burgeoning industrial revolution by becoming its key commodity export until World War II.

But heavy industries such as iron and steel, chemicals, construction, and shipbuilding also developed rapidly. Japan's transformation to a manufacturing economy is clearly indicated by the rapid decline in agriculture's percentage of net domestic product (NDP), from 42% in the late 1880s to only 18% by the 1930s.[16] Large financial cliques (*zaibatsu*) that arose at the end of the nineteenth century and ultimately, taking the form of huge industrial conglomerates, soon became an increasingly dominant force in the economy. From 1887 to 1938, economic growth averaged 6.34% annually, and the share of industry increased from 20% of NDP in 1887 to 51.7% in 1938.[17] Japan's rapid economic rise helped it become a formidable actor on the world stage.

Another major development was political reform after the promulgation of the Meiji Constitution in 1889. The emperor, after all, had promised the creation of "deliberative assemblies" in his Charter Oath. The Iwakura Mission to the West in 1871–73 was commissioned to study Western governments as well as to acquire knowledge of culture and technology. Itō Hirobumi, who was a member of the mission, modeled the new Constitution on the Prussian-German form of constitutional monarchy. The Meiji oligarchs (*genrō*) believed a new constitution was vital for Japan. It strengthened national unity by creating a more rationalized and centralized government; it also silenced the criticism of those Japanese liberals who, like Itagaki Taisuke (1837–1919) of the Freedom and People's Rights Movement (Jiyū Minken Undō), agitated for liberal democratic reforms. The new Constitution boosted Japan's diplomatic stature as a civilized nation, giving the country the leverage it needed to renegotiate the unequal treaties that had marked Japan's relations with the West from the outset.

Historian Elise Tipton has argued that the 1880s and 1890s saw a reaction against this initial embrace of wholesale Westernization. By this time, the Japanese had become more selective in their borrowing from foreign sources, as they came to believe that Japan had its own unique spiritual, cultural, and political identity central to its national unity.[18] The Meiji Constitution, despite its Western influence, created a distinctive Japanese style of governance. The first four articles of the document made crystal clear that sovereignty did not arise from the natural rights of the people. Rather, since the emperor is sacred and the empire ruled by the imperial house "for ages eternal," it is the emperor himself who has sovereignty as the head of the state. As declared in the Imperial Oath (Reading #11), the emperor issued his Constitution for "the stability of the country and [to] promote the welfare of the people's life." This allowed the imperial subjects to enjoy such rights as an elected national assembly, the Imperial Diet, freedom of religion (Article 28), a judiciary, and limited suffrage and elections. The Meiji constitutional framework allowed the emergence of political parties and—after the last of the Meiji oligarchs had died in the 1920s—the transition to party-based rule. Civil administrative government, however, proved unstable and fragile, even later during the Taishō period with democratically elected political parties. While these parties appointed prime ministers to lead the government, parliamentary-based party rule was significantly circumscribed by the entrenched power of the Japanese military. Army and Navy cabinet ministers were appointed by their own respective services and often acted independently of the will of civil authorities.

By the late Meiji period, Japan's strong economy and military allowed for a reversal of its second-class status in foreign affairs. By the early Taishō period, Japan had renegotiated its unequal treaties with the West and began to pursue an aggressive expansionist policy abroad to acquire its own colonies and to secure vital access to raw materials for industrial development. This put the Japanese Empire on the path to a direct conflict with rival Western imperial powers. An early example of this occurred in the Korean peninsula, which while having great strategic value for Japan, was threatened by Chinese and Russian domination. In 1873, high officials like Saigō Takamori and Itagaki Taisuke wanted to start a war with Korea.[19] Although this plan was ultimately shelved, the drive to turn Korea into a Japanese satellite continued apace. In 1875 the Japanese used a military show of force to establish their own unequal treaty with the Korean kingdom. From 1894 to 1895, Japan went to war over Korea with China, ultimately forcing the Chinese to make significant concessions. They permitted Korea to be independent from their control and ceded Formosa and other territories to Japan in the Treaty of Shimonoseki (1895). Japan's next imperialist military venture was the Russo-Japanese War of 1904–5, which ended with another hard-fought Japanese victory against a powerful foreign competitor. In the Portsmouth Treaty, signed on September 5, 1905, the Russians ceded control over Korea and much of Southern Manchuria to Japan. After becoming a protectorate, Korea was eventually formally annexed and occupied by Japan in 1910. Japan's great successes on the world stage signaled its new international status: It was now a member of the club of great imperial powers. The country's successes abroad, however, had disturbing consequences domestically. The patriotic fervor whipped up by Japan's foreign policy success was leading the country toward an increasingly bellicose ultranationalism.[20]

With the onset of the "Taishō Democracy," Japan was now led by its first full-fledged party-led civil government, with Hara Takashi's ascension as prime minister from 1918 until his assassination in 1921. Changing domestic political realities led to changes in Japan's foreign policy, abandoning an aggressive militarism in favor of a more diplomatic approach advocating peaceful accommodation.[21] For example, Japan joined the League of Nations in 1920, and its more conciliatory posture can be seen in agreements such as the Washington Conference of 1921, in which Japan agreed to abide by its existing defensive measures in the Pacific, and the 1928 Kellogg-Briand Pact in which the country renounced war. This approach did not please the military factions in government, who feared losing Japan's vital strategic interests in Manchuria, Korea, and elsewhere.

The Taishō period posted mixed results for Japan's economy, domestic policy, and foreign policy. By the 1920s, Japan had transformed itself into an urbanized industrialized society of fifty-five million, with a population double that of the Tokugawa era. But modernization brought with it enormous social and political costs with which the government had to wrestle. Horrific working conditions and low wages in the factories led to a vigorous labor movement and calls for unionization. Poverty— particularly among tenant farmers in rural Japan—and rampant unemployment led to political and social turmoil, with grave incidents like the 1918 rice riots, that caused the downfall of the Terauchi Masatake administration. Mass protests, in some cases influenced by socialist and Marxist ideas, challenged the status quo and were met with harsh repressive measures by the government in response. The state, for example, used a 1925 Public Security Preservation Law (Chian Ijihō) to ruthlessly suppress any organization, including the Japan Communist Party, which was formed in 1922, that was perceived to be dangerous to Japan's national polity (*kokutai*) and private property.[22]

Shinto developments

State Shinto originated as a system of thought developed by native intellectuals in the eighteenth and nineteenth centuries; it was subsequently institutionalized by the modern Meiji imperial state. This was a nativist response to European imperialism in East Asia as well as the threatening re-entry of Christianity into Japan around the middle of the nineteenth century. National learning scholars like Motoori Norinaga (1730–1801) and Hirata Atsutane (1776–1843) sought to find a "pure Shinto" that could be distinguished from the "foreign" Buddhist practices associated with the declining Tokugawa regime. They drew on antiquarian and philological studies to construct a "style of worship of the *kami* based on ancient texts based on naturalness, sincerity, emotionality, and the sacred power of the Japanese language as Russian and American ships encroached on Japanese waters."[23]

Shinto, in the sense of an independent set of religious institutions, is very much a modern phenomenon dating from the Meiji period (1868–1912). B.H. Chamberlain, a former professor at Tokyo Imperial University, was first to observe that State Shinto was a manufactured religion, "still [in 1912] in the process of being . . . put together by the official class, in order to serve the interests of that class, and the interests of the nation at large."[24] As Okuyama Michiaki has recently argued, part of the Meiji policy for "civilization and enlightenment" included adopting the modern Western institution of the nation state in addition to advancing commercially, industrially, and technologically. The nation state in the West was originally conceived as a secular nationalism that unified a people based upon their common ancestral or adopted homeland. However, by the nineteenth and twentieth centuries, France and America had blended Christian symbols with secular nationalism to create a powerful civil religion unifying the state and fostering patriotism.[25] Meiji officials and priests adapted this idea to create their own unique form of Japanese civil religion; their version centered around worship of the emperor at state-supported shrines and using the story of his descent from the sun goddess Amaterasu to invoke the weight and stateliness of his throne and person. State Shinto was a way to unify a country facing immense economic and political changes because of Japan's rapid industrialization and the imminent threats from abroad. State-sponsored Shinto became a symbol of the polity or essence of the Japanese nation (*kokutai*) and inculcated a "national morality" (*kokumin dōtoku*) of "submissiveness, loyalty to the state, and unquestioned acceptance of the official views of the proper nature of society and of political and social morality" and an ideal of good citizenship "identified with the acceptance of Shinto mythology."[26] Moreover, as historian of Japanese religions Sarah Thal has argued, the goal was to create a national cult which was centered on the divine emperor and imperial *kami* that was superior to Christianity. The Meiji political elite saw the individual-centered religion (*shūkyō*) of Christianity as a potentially dangerous and corrosive influence, with its doctrines emphasizing personal salvation and faith in a transcendent God rather than unswerving loyalty to Japanese state.[27] The Meiji government found its ritual, institutional, moral, and symbolic framework for national homogeneity in Shinto, which they initially defined as a religion and then redefined as something separate from religion. It was a development that caused a momentous change in Japan's spiritual tradition.[28]

State Shinto was legally instituted by an imperial edict of 1868 that formally separated Shinto from Buddhism (*shinbutsu bunri*); it forced the creation of Shinto shrines (*jinja*), priests, and ritual practices that were distinct from Buddhism.[29] By 1871, the Meiji government had brought shrines under state control. From 1870 to 1884, the government sponsored the Great Promulgation Campaign (Taikyō Senpu Undō), an attempt to create its own state religion. It featured a "Great Teaching" Institute (Daikyōin), a central agency that was housed in a shrine-like building with altars to worship its state pantheon of deities, with the imperial sun goddess Amaterasu featured prominently. The institute organized a large cadre of proselytizers (*kyōdōshoku*) who were posted throughout the country spreading the Great Teachings of respect for the gods, love of country, and reverencing the emperor.

These teachings were intended to transcend religious and sectarian division and thus to unify all Japanese subjects. The movement was finally dissolved after Shin Pure Land Buddhists opposed to dominance of Shinto in the Great Promulgation Campaign. Helen Hardacre notes that the lesson learned by Shinto priests and Meiji officialdom was that Shinto should have nothing to do with doctrines. State Shinto seemed best conceived as something non-religious or supra-religious in character.[30]

Another key date for State Shinto is 1882, when the government first distinguished between shrine priests and religious instructors. This juridical classification allowed the government to make a distinction between shrines and Shinto and other religious groups. Shrines were officially characterized as sites presided over by priests for the civic veneration of the imperial ancestors and military heroes who had died for the greater glory of the empire. An example is the Tōkyō Shōkonsha ("Shrine to beckon the souls"), later known as Yasukuni Shrine, which the Meiji emperor himself founded in 1869 after the Boshin War to commemorate the loyalists who sacrificed their lives for restoration of imperial rule.

Shrine Shinto was declared as an obligatory "way of practice" for all loyal imperial subjects. The Imperial Rescript on Education (Kyōiku Chokugo,1890) added an official pronouncement which detailed a Confucian-infused national morality of filial piety, loyalty, and reverence to the emperor whose imperial ancestors had founded the empire "on a basis broad and everlasting, and have deeply and firmly implanted virtue." Government decree, therefore, distinguished a now non-religious or supra-religious shrine Shinto from the doctrinally based Shinto groups who were now classified officially as "sect" (kyōha) Shinto.[31]

Another milestone for the emergence of State Shinto was the Meiji Constitution of 1889. Article 28 guaranteed freedom of "religious belief" to all Japanese insofar as it was "not antagonistic to their duties as subjects." It made great political sense, given external foreign pressures, to guarantee religious freedom. Churches (kyōkai), which included Buddhist and Christian denominations as well as Shinto sects, now had constitutional protections for freedom of belief.[32] For the new Japanese religious movements that had emerged in the nineteenth and early twentieth centuries it was a different story. Groups like Tenrikyō and Ōmotokyō were often criticized in the popular media as pseudo-religions (ruiji shūkyō) or heresies (jakyō), which put them in an ambiguous position given that they not guaranteed any protections as bona fide religions. Government authorities were quick to suppress any groups which appeared to challenge the central state orthodoxy, the emperor's sacred nature, and the preeminence of the sun goddess Amaterasu.[33]

By the turn of the century, the emperor had become head priest, and imperial kami were venerated as national deities, uniting the Japanese as loyal subjects through their civic duty to participate in the rites. Institutionally, the government organized this state cult through an officially sanctioned shrine hierarchy, an appointment system for priests as civil servants, national holidays, a cult of the war dead, and a systematized liturgy and set of calendrical rites supported through state funding, all spread to the masses through official propaganda campaigns.[34]

By 1900, this distinction between public shrine Shinto and private religion was firmly established bureaucratically and the Bureau of Shrines (Jinjakyoku), a new government agency solely in charge of shrine supervision, was created. Sect Shinto—together with other officially recognized religious organizations like Buddhism and Christianity—fell under the purview of a different government office, the Bureau of Religion (Shūkyōkyoku). By bureaucratic legerdemain, shrine Shinto was administratively defined as a system of government-supported shrines, with patriotic rituals, and a civil morality that was non-religious or supra-religious in character.[35]

Shimazono Susumu, a historian of Japanese religions, argues that this legal and institutional distinction between shrines and sect Shinto was itself based on a narrow definition of religion (*shūkyō*). Religion only signified voluntary organizations to which individuals belong as a matter of personal private faith.[36] Shrine worship, by contrast, was considered to be based on a public patriotic faith in "the glory of the fundamental character of Our Empire" (*waga kokutai no seika*) as described in the Imperial Rescript on Education. As such, there was a "dual structure," creating a system that sanctified imperial rule even as it allowed religious freedom for privately held beliefs.[37]

To sum up: What is fascinating is how Meiji officials and priests initially tried to invent Shinto in the vein of Western religions, as a national religion with its own cult, beliefs, and institutions. After the Meiji Constitution of 1889, which guaranteed religious freedom, Shinto was re-invented as a non-religious patriotic cult which did not rely on exclusive faith, doctrine, or numinous experience.[38] State Shinto, in this sense, continued until 1945, when SCAP's Shinto Directive abolished the Board of Divinities (Jingiin), the last governmental agency in charge of shrines, which had replaced the Bureau of Shrines in 1940.

What is State Shinto? Academic controversies

The brief historical overview above omits the fact that there is considerable controversy over exactly what State Shinto is. Shimazono has argued that two approaches are typically taken to define the relationship between Shinto and state—a narrow definition and the broader one which he himself prefers.[39] The narrow definition limits State Shinto to shrine Shinto (*jinja Shintō*) in the pre-war period.[40] Under this definition, State Shinto is equated with the official shrine system constructed and controlled by the Japanese imperial state. Shrine Shinto, in this narrow sense, was a bureaucratic system that directly organized, administered and, in some cases, financially supported shrines until the end of World War II. This narrow definition is favored by post-war Shinto scholars like Ashizu Uzuhiko and Sakamoto Koremaru.

However, Shimazono also points to the broader definition of State Shinto, which was first proposed by Murakami Shigeyoshi in his book, *Kokka shintō*:

> State Shinto is the state religion created by the modern imperial state, and it held sway spiritually over the Japanese people for almost eighty years, from the Meiji Restoration until Japan's defeat in the Pacific War. This new Japanese state religion, which came into being in the latter half of the nineteenth century, was established by fusing shrine Shinto (*jinja Shintō*) and imperial Shinto (*kōshitsu Shintō*) together and by amalgamating rituals at shrines (*jingū* and *jinja*) based on court rituals.[41]

Murakami sees shrine Shinto as part of a larger whole that he calls State Shinto. It incorporated Imperial Household Shinto, the Imperial Palace rites under the auspices of the emperor as stipulated by the Imperial House Law (Kōshitsu Tenpan). Together with the new Meiji Constitution, also established in 1889, this "signified the establishment of imperial authority in the modern state . . . [and] also created the legal foundation of the Japanese empire as a religious state."[42] A third component of Murakami's model of State Shinto is the doctrine of national polity (*kokutai*). This refers to the system of ideas which emphasizes reverence for the emperor as a living divinity (*akitsumikami* or *arahitogami*). Identifying the emperor and his ancestors as direct descendants of the sun goddess Amaterasu meant that, as set forth in Article 1 of the Meiji Constitution, the rule of Japan had been "unbroken for ages eternal." *Kokutai* ideology touted a Japanese exceptionalism with a sacred emperor who presided over both national rites and governance (*saisei icchi*).[43] Also part of Japan's "fundamental character" was the "[u]nique relationship between the Imperial House and the people, which is not simply a relation between the present Emperor and the people but one that has existed between the people for generations, through more than twenty centuries."[44] "Good and faithful subjects," who obeyed laws, respected the Constitution and courageously sacrificed themselves for the good and prosperity of the imperial throne, were the core of Japanese national polity. This belief, spelled out in the Imperial Rescript on Education among other documents, formed the basis of moral teaching in Japanese middle schools in the pre-war period.[45]

Shimazono agrees with Murakami, arguing that "Shinto concepts and practices connected to the state and the Emperor were spread among and accepted by the nation, and eventually [were] closely related to the establishment of the modern Japanese nation-state."[46] In the pre-war period, State Shinto's influence was pervasive. It was propagated through the mass media, celebrated on national holidays and at imperial marriages and funerals, and particularly propagated through the nation's educational system. Schools in particular played a major role in indoctrination (*chikyō*), placing sacred icons of the emperor (*goshin'ei*) reverently on school altars and intoning the Imperial Rescript of Education in solemn rites.[47]

Redefining Shinto

All the authors in Part 2, "Pre-War Japanese Intellectuals on Shinto," wrestle with State Shinto—in some cases criticizing it, in other cases refashioning it in ways that Meiji officialdom had not initially characterized it.

Some, like Tokyo Imperial University historian of religions scholar Katō Genchi (Reading #18), define Shinto in ways that are compatible with the imperial way. Katō borrows the words of Lafcadio Hearn by defining it as the Japanese "religion of loyalty"—"Japanese patriotism suffused with religious emotion." And yet, Katō uses the tools of the Western understanding of religion—particularly the work of the Dutch scholar C.P. Tiele—to argue that Shinto is an original religion of Japan.

Others are critics. The earliest of these is Tokyo Imperial University historian Kume Kunitake, His 1891 essay, "Shinto as an ancient custom of worshipping heaven" (Reading #15), got him into trouble with right-wing nationalists and the authorities. Accused of *lèse-majesté* (*fukeizai*), he was forced to resign his professorship in disgrace. In his essay, Kume denies Shinto is a religion, relegates it to a primitive cult of heaven worship, and ties it to other Eastern customs of revering heaven. Yanagita Kunio, writing in 1918 (Reading #17), also criticizes State Shinto as an "artificial" construct, a blatant attempt to have it both ways—establishing a state religion on the one hand while maintaining freedom of belief on the other. From his folklorist's perspective, the official view of shrines made absolutely no sense. If true, Yanagita asks, who is it that "accepts the petitions, distributes charms and talismans, receives offerings, and hears the prayers of the priests and parishioners?" After all, local villagers clearly worshipped their local tutelary *kami* without making the bureaucratic distinction that the government had foisted upon them.

Others, like Waseda University historian Tsuda Sōkichi (Reading #19), define Shinto in ways that challenge official state orthodoxy. In particular, Tsuda famously points out the weaknesses, historical inaccuracies, and outright impossibilities undermining the legitimacy of State Shinto, which got him into deep trouble with the authorities. Tsuda, in particular, shows that there are multiple ways of defining Shinto throughout Japanese history and that these definitions are deeply indebted to Chinese thought. The imperial way advanced by the Meiji government Tsuda places late historically as his fifth definition of Shinto. This version of the "way of *kami*" (*kami no michi*) was deeply influenced by Confucianism and widely utilized by national learning scholars in the Tokugawa period. This definition of Shinto refers to the "established teachings of Japan's *kami,* and also includes the politics and ethical standards unique to Japan."

Kawakami Hajime (Reading #16), a Marxist economist at Kyoto University who was arrested in 1933 for violating the Public Security Preservation Law, is another critic. While he whole-heartedly believed that the emperor embodied the sacred national polity, Kawakami criticized Japan's wholesale acceptance of Western capitalism, with its emphasis on individual self-interest, the profit motive, and private property. Kawakami believed that Japan had its own unique brand of nationalism (*kokkashugi*), where the state and the collectivity take precedence over the individual. In his view, the emperor "possesses the most perfect national character and regards the national interests as his own, and he does not have any personal and individual interests outside the public interests of the state." This view of the emperor as a sacred figure who promoted collective well-being over individual self-interest was considered dangerous by the authorities. It promoted a portrait of the emperor opposed to the entrenched classes and corporate interests of the *zaibatsu.* Such a view had revolutionary implications, setting the emperor up as a champion of the people against corporate greed and wealthy landowners, and it "contested orthodox state nationalism, which stressed loyalty, obedience, and sacrifice in the name of the state, instead favoring communitarian visions of social and economic justice."[48] This was a powerful symbol for radical left- and right-wing groups who directly threatened the state by calling for the revival of the Japanese spirit against the evils of the status quo in the late 1920s and 1930s.

Of course, the readings in Parts 1 and 2 of this anthology represent only a small slice of the numerous official documents and writings on Shinto during this time period. One key area missing in this volume is Japanese new religions. Some defined themselves against State Shinto orthodoxy. This was a fraught enterprise, given the government's anxiety over anything they thought "antagonistic to their duties as subjects," violating Article 28 of the Constitution. Deguchi Onisaburō (1871–1948), for example, the leader of the new religious group Ōmotokyō, avoided affiliating his group with sect Shinto. He eschewed gaining official status because "the teachings of the *kami* should not be something supervised or dependent on man-made laws created by men."[49] In essays such as his 1917 "The Fate of the Ancient Gods"(*Taiko no kami no innen*), Onisaburō attacked State Shinto dogma by offering a counter-mythology in which Oomoto's key deity, Ushitora no Konjin, was the supreme deity and superior to Amaterasu. While the government had its "national teachings," Onisaburō's version of the way of the *kami* was based on his own personal insights after being spiritually possessed by powerful deities.[50] New religious movements and their ways of defining Shinto unfortunately remain beyond the scope of this anthology.

Notes

1 See Susumu Shimazono, "State Shinto and the Religious Structure of Modern Japan," *Journal of the American Academy of Religion* 73 (December, 2005):1077–98, especially 1079–81.
2 See Okuyama Michiaki, "State Shinto in Recent Japanese Scholarship," *Monumenta Nipponica*, 66 (1) (2011):123–45.

3 On the history of this term, see Shimazono, "State Shinto and Emperor Veneration," in *The Emperors of Modern Japan*, ed. Ben-Ami Shillony (Leiden: Brill, 2008), 66–72.
4 See, for example, Hiroshi Mitani's essay, "Meiji Revolution," *Oxford Research Encyclopedia—Asian History* (April, 2017), http://oxfordre.com/asianhistory/view/10.1093/acrefore/9780190277 727.001.0001/acrefore-9780190277727-e-84.
5 William Theodore de Bary, Ryusaku Tsunoda, and Donald Keene eds. *Sources of Japanese Tradition*, Vol. 2 (New York: Columbia University Press, 1964), 137.
6 Jackson H. Bailey, "Japan on the World Scene: Reflections on Uniqueness and Commonality," Occasional Papers Vol. 1 No. 2 (Earlham College: Institute for Education on Japan, 1989), 11.
7 John Whitney Hall, *Japan from Prehistory to Modern Times* (New York: Dell Publishing, 1970), 276.
8 Ibid., 278
9 Fukuzawa Yukichi (Michael Bourdaghs, trans.), "On Meat Eating," https://www.bourdaghs.com/fukuzawa.htm.
10 Zenjiro Watanabe, "The Meat Eating Culture at the Beginning of Westernization," *Food Culture* 9 (Tokyo: Kikkoman Institute for International Food Culture, 2005), 8, https://www.kikkoman.co.jp/kiifc/foodculture/pdf_09/e_002_008.pdf.
11 The photograph was based on a sketch of the emperor's face by the Italian artist Edoardo Chiossone (1833–98), who had to peep through the door of an adjacent room to make the likeness. The imperial court photographer, Maruki Riyō (1854–1925) made a photograph from Chiossone's final portrait. See Ono Masaaki, *Goshin'ei to gakkō — "hōgo" no henyō* (Tokyo: Tōkyō Daigaku Shuppankai, 2014).
12 Makiko Hirayama, "The Emperor's New Clothes: Japanese Visuality and Imperial Portrait Photography," *History of Photography* 33 (2009):165–84.
13 W.J. Macpherson, *The Economic Development of Japan 1868–1941* (Cambridge: Cambridge University Press, 1987), 2.
14 One example is the Tomioka Silk Mill, the first mechanized silk-reeling model factory that the Meiji government established in 1872. Using Western silk reeling technology and employing cheap female workers, the factory produced high-quality raw silk that was a major export for Japan during this period. See "World Heritage Site Tomioka Silk Mill," http://www.tomioka-silk.jp.e.wv.hp.transer.com/tomioka-silk-mill/?_ga=2.36332706.324328020.1549549828-2035259406.1549549828.
15 Elise Tipton, *Modern Japan: A Social and Political History* (New York: Routledge, 2002), 55
16 Macpherson, *The Economic Development of Japan*, 45.
17 Ibid., 9.
18 See Tipton, *Modern Japan*, Ch. 4 "The 1880s and 1890s Defining a Japanese National Identity," 59–92.
19 Hall, *Japan from Prehistory to Modern Times*, 283
20 Tipton, *Modern Japan*, 79–84.
21 Ibid., 95.
22 Ibid., 101.
23 Sarah Thal, "A Religion that Was Not a Religion: The Creation of Modern Shintō in 19th Century Japan," in *Inventing Religion: Rethinking Belief in Politics and History*, eds. Derek R. Peterson and Darren R. Walhof (New Brunswick, NJ: Rutgers University Press, 2002), 101.
24 Basil Hall Chamberlain, *The Invention of a New Religion* (London: Watts & Co., 1912), 6.
25 See Mark Juergensmeyer, *The New Cold War?: Religious Nationalism Confronts the Secular State* (Berkeley: University of California Press, 1993), 27–28; Okuyama Michiaki, "Religious Nationalism in the Modernization Process: State Shintō and Nichirenism in Japan," *Nanzan Bulletin* 26:19–21.
26 Robert King Hall ed., *Kokutai no hongi* (Cambridge, MA: Harvard University Press, 1949), 84. On the modernist search for order in the Meiji Restoration, see Bernard Silberman, "The Politics of Modernism: Once Again the Problem of Fascism," in *Japan in the World, The World in Japan*, ed. Center for Japanese Studies (Ann Arbor, MI: The University of Michigan, 2001), 159–68.
27 Thal, "Religion," 101.
28 See Yasumaro Yoshio, *Kamigami no Meiji ishin—Shinbutsu bunri to haibutsu kishaku* (Tokyo: Iwanami Shoten, 1979).

29 In terms of the development of State Shinto over time, scholars have offered varying chronologies. Murakami divides the history of State Shinto until 1945 into four periods: 1868–80 the formative period; 1889–1905 the period of completion of doctrine (from the Imperial Constitution of 1889 to the Russo-Japanese War 1905); 1900s–1930s the period of completion of system;1931–45 the period of fascist state religion (from the Manchurian Incident of 1931 until the end of World War II in 1945). See Shimazono Susumu, "State Shinto in the Lives of the People: The Establishment of Emperor Worship, Modern Nationalism, and Shrine Shinto in Late Meiji," *Japanese Journal of Religious Studies* 36 (2009):94–95. Helen Hardacre's chronology closely matches Murakami's but emphasizes different points: 1868–80 "Experimentation and Disillusion"; 1880–1905 "Declining State Support"; 1905–30 "Expansion and Increased Influence"; 1930–45 "Maximized Influence." See Helen Hardacre, Shintō and the State *1868–1988* (Princeton, NJ: Princeton University Press, 1989), 23–26. Jun'ichi Isomae has three historical stages: 1868–82 the period of Shinto national indoctrination policies when the government advocated a state emperor-centered religious nationalism; 1889–1906 the period where the government in the Meiji Constitution separated church from state and emphasized a secular imperial nationalism in line with Western modernity; 1906–45, when the state actively developed a system of state-supported national shrines, which were seen as secular institutions for indoctrinating subjects in an imperial-centered state nationalism. See Jun'ichi Isomae, "The Formative Process of State Shinto in Relation to the Westernization of Japan: The Concept of 'Religion' and 'Shinto'" in *Religion and the Secular: Historical and Colonial Formations,* ed. Timothy Fitzgerald (London: Routledge, 2016), 93–101; Okuyama Michiaki, "'State Shinto' in Recent Japanese Scholarship," *Monumenta Nipponica* 66 (2011):123–45.
30 Ibid., 42–50.
31 Thal, "Religion," 107–11. Hardacre also notes that this was not just governmental policy but had the full support of many in the Shinto priesthood. See Shintō and the State,128–29.
32 Inoue Nobutaka, trans. by Mark Teeuwen, "The Formation of Sect Shinto in Modernizing Japan," *Japanese Journal of Religious Studies* 29 (2002):404–8. This happened at a moment when Japan was attempting to revise the unequal treaties it had been forced to accept when it opened itself to the West in the *bakumatsu* period. It placated the Western powers who saw it as a basic right for civilized peoples and a safeguard protecting Christianity in Japan.
33 The popular press played a central role in defining this state orthodoxy to its mass audience. See Erica Baffelli, *Media and New Religions in Japan* (New York: Routledge, 2016), 17. Some groups, like Tenrikyō, Konkōkyō, and Kurozumikyō sought protection by affiliating with one of the thirteen officially approved Shinto sects. However, that protection came at a price by putting them under strict controls of the state. See Nancy K. Stalker, *Prophet Motive: Deguchi Onisaburō, Oomoto, and the Rise of New Religions in Imperial Japan* (Honolulu: The University of Hawai'i Press, 2008), 52–53.
34 Hardacre, Shintō and the State,32–33, 79–85, 100–6.
35 On national teaching, see Hardacre, Shintō and the State, 66–68.
36 Shimazono, "State Shinto," 1085. Shimazono notes that it is this same narrow definition of religion as *shūkyō* that also underlies SCAP's Shinto Directive of 1945.
37 Ibid., 1096.
38 Hardacre, Shintō and the State, 65.
39 Shimazono Susumu, "State Shinto and Religion in Post-War Japan," in *The Sage Handbook of the Sociology of Religion*, eds. James Beckford and N.J. Demarath III (Los Angeles: Sage Publications, 2007), 697–709.
40 Shimazono, "State Shinto," 1081–82. See also Sakamoto Koremaru, "The Structure of State Shinto: Its Creation, Development, and Demise," in *Shinto in History Ways of the Kami,* eds. John Breen and Mark Teeuwen (Honolulu: University of Hawai'i Press 2000), 272–94; Ashizu Uzuhiko, "The Various Issues Related to Contemporary Shrines" (Reading #27 in this volume).
41 Murakami Shigeyoshi, *Kokka shintō* (Tokyo: Iwanami Shoten, 1970), 1.
42 See Murakami Shigeyoshi, "The Emperor as a Deity in Human Form; The Development of Imperial House Rites," (Reading #28).
43 Shimazono Susumu, "State Shinto and Emperor Veneration," 51–78.
44 Baron Dairoku Kikuchi, *Japanese Education: Lectures Delivered in the University of London* (London: John Murray, 1909), 4.

45 Shimazono's point is that elements of this broader notion of State Shinto persisted even after it was abolished by the Shinto Directive. A good example is the *kokutai* belief in a special bond that has always existed between the emperor and his people. Even after defeat in World War II, it appears in the Shōwa emperor's so called "Humanity Declaration" (Ningen sengen, in fact entitled, Imperial Rescript on the Construction of a New Japan (Shin Nippon Kensetsu ni kansuru Shōsho)), a document dated January 1, 1946, that Occupation authorities forced the emperor to produce, formally denying his divinity. In it, the emperor claims that, "[t]he ties between Us and Our people have always stood upon mutual trust and affection. They do not depend upon mere legends and myths. They are not predicated on the false conception that the Emperor is divine, and that the Japanese people are superior to other races and fated to rule the world." While denying divinity, the rescript preserves the special nature of Japan's *kokutai* that depends on an everlasting bond (*chūtai*) between sovereign and subject based upon love and respect (*keiai*). See National Diet Library, "Birth of the Constitution of Japan"—3-1 Emperor, Imperial Rescript, Denying His Divinity (Professing His Humanity)," http://www.ndl. go.jp/constitution/e/shiryo/03/056shoshi.html.

46 Shimazono, "State Shinto," 1084.

47 Shimazono, along with many others, also points to problems with Murakami's classical model of State Shinto. First, he argues that Murakami was wrong to claim that it is unique to Japan. There are many other examples of religious nationalism that can be found throughout the world (1093). Second, he takes issue with Murakami's top-down model which assumes that State Shinto was aggressively imposed by officialdom on a passive population. Shimazono has argued that, in fact, ordinary people were the principal agents in spreading State Shinto and "actively embraced it." See Shimazono Susumu, "State Shinto and Emperor Veneration," 54–55; "State Shinto in the Lives of the People: The Establishment of Emperor Worship, Modern Nationalism, and Shrine Shinto in Late Meiji," *Japanese Journal of Religious Studies* 36 (2009):93–124. Others question Murakami's reliance on the *Jinja hongi,* a work of propaganda from 1941, for his understanding of *kokutai* doctrine, arguing that this is not really representative of what was occurring in the Meiji period. Even in the 1940s, according to Sakamoto Koremaru, the government lacked "the fascist capacity" to enforce mandatory shrine attendance, let alone the power to compel subjects to reverence the *kami*. See Sakamoto Koremaru, "The Structure of State Shinto," 286.

48 Nancy Stalker, *Prophet Motive,* 172.

49 Quoted in Nancy Stalker, *Prophet Motive,* 53.

50 Ibid., 59.

Part 1

SHINTO AND THE MODERN JAPANESE NATION STATE

Official documents concerning Shinto and
shrine administration

1

PROCLAMATION CONCERNING THE RESTORATION OF THE COUNCIL OF DIVINITIES

(March 13, 1868)

The following orders concern restoring the unity of rituals and governance (*saisei icchi*), reestablishing the Council of Divinities (Jingikan), abolishing priestly lineages as conduits between the emperor and the people, and affiliating shrines and priests with the Council of Divinities.

This restoration of imperial rule is based upon the founding acts of Emperor Jinmu. It renews everything restoring institutionally the unity of rituals and governance. In this regard, first, most noteworthy is that, after the reestablishment of the Council of Divinities, various rituals and ceremonies are to be established in due course. This proclamation should be promulgated throughout Japan, the *gokishichidō* [five districts of Kinki region, and seven circuits], to restore the ancient institutions and to terminate the priestly lineages as conduits between the emperor and the people. All the shrines under the heavens, all levels of priests—*kannushi, negi, hafuri* as well as *kanbe*—are to be affiliated with the above-mentioned Council of Divinities. In due course, it should be noted that all inquiries over these matters and details starting with the shrine ranking and priestly ranks should be directed to the Council.

Accordingly, in due course as the background of the shrines are examined, the details of the rituals and ceremonies shall be announced, but in the case of urgent circumstances, inquiries will be allowed to be made.

2

ORDINANCE DISTINGUISHING DIVINE AND BUDDHIST MATTERS, PROCLAMATION ISSUED BY THE COUNCIL OF STATE

(March 28, 1868)

The following orders shrines that venerate a deity with a Buddhist name should report the reasons why this is so. Also, shrines that have a Buddhist statue as an enshrined object of devotion (*shintai*) should reform themselves, and shrines that store Buddhist images and paraphernalia should discard them.

(1) Since the middle ages there have been many shrines that enshrine a certain *gongen, gozutennō* and the like, or use a Buddhist term for its enshrined deity. These shrines are required to report in writing the detailed history of this immediately.

   If the shrines are those that perform their festivals according to emperor's order and have an imperial letter or frame to that effect, they are allowed to make inquiries. On request, directions will be delivered. All the other shrines are required to report to the court, the army, the officers, or the head in control in the locality.

(2) Shrines that enshrine a Buddhist statue as a divine entity are required to reform this situation hitherto. If shrines venerate a Buddha statue as its true object, present a Buddha image in front of a shrine, or keep metal instruments, gong, or any other Buddhist paraphernalia, they should get rid of them immediately.

The above mentioned should be followed.

3

IMPERIAL RESCRIPT FOR THE PROMULGATION OF THE GREAT TEACHINGS

(January 3, 1870)

I deferentially consider that the heavenly deities and the heavenly ancestors established the foundations and left directions, which each of later emperors in succession have proclaimed. As for the unification between rituals and governance and billions and trillions of people, whose hearts are one, governance and teachings clarify it on a higher level, while folk customs ornament it on a lower one. After the middle ages, however, through occasional ups and downs, lightness and darkness have in turn prevailed. Now the heavenly destiny returns full circle, bringing about the restoration of the hundred institutions. Now we should clarify the governance and teachings, thus upholding the great divine way. We order anew missionaries to go forth to propagate [the Great Teachings (*taikyō*)] under the heaven. You, my subjects and commoners, be convinced of their significance.

4

OFFICIAL NOTICE ISSUED BY THE COUNCIL OF STATE—SHRINE RITUALS AS A STATE RELIGIOUS PRACTICE

(May 14, 1871)

For the revised appointment of official priests in the family lineages of the two Great Shrines of Ise, and of the other priests at all levels

It is a clear fact that rituals at shrines are fundamental rites of the state (*kokka no sōshi*) that should not be privatized by anyone nor any family. Since the middle ages, however, as the Great Way of the state experienced a decline, certain segments of official priests and their families have transmitted their own special family histories from the ancient mythological ages. Yet most of them gained their role as priests, for which they were only temporarily appointed, or as landlords and land stewards, who, through some happenstance, ended up taking complete control over a shrine. Other lower priests of small shrines in villages and communities have also inherited their roles as priests. Thus, they have taken the shrine income as their family income, with the understanding that shrine management was a private family matter. This has been a chronic problem associated with shrines in general. Official priests, therefore, have naturally moved beyond the ordinary social classes both high and low. This contradicts a polity for unifying rituals and governance. Since the resulting evil effects cannot be ignored, a reformation should now be realized so that not only the official priests of the two Great Shrines of Ise, who have inherited their offices, but also other priests of major or minor shrines should undergo a rigorous selection for reappointment. Thus issued and announced.

5

NOTIFICATION ISSUED BY THE COUNCIL OF STATE—THE PRINCIPAL AIM OF THE GREAT TEACHINGS

(July 4, 1871)

The essence of the Great Teachings (*taikyō*) consists in reverence toward deities, elucidation of human ethics, leading people to justice, and having them work effectively. Through these activities, the teachings guide people to serve the imperial court. If the teachings should fail to provide this guidance, they cannot lead people to righteousness. If the government should fail to govern people, it cannot make people work effectively. This is the reason why the teachings and governance should be conducted side by side. Now is a time of renovation.

Based on the great achievements of Emperor Jinmu, who started this great enterprise of creating [the imperial state], and of [the tenth] Emperor Sujin, who extended the dominion of its jurisdiction in all directions, the current emperor is also exerting his benevolent administration at the appropriate time, bringing about great transformations and renovations.

The Great Teachings, on the other hand, have not prevailed yet, and people's minds and hearts cannot become united, straying in their way. Because of this situation, the propagation of the teachings is urgently needed. Human beings are the highest spiritually and, among all things, beings whom the deities most favor.

Since the grandson of Amaterasu descended to the earth, conveying Amaterasu's original intention, all successive emperors have without exception followed her will to care for the people.

That said, however, occasionally there have been changes in our political institutions because of vicissitudes over time. All saints throughout history have followed the same path by freeing the people from their confusion, leading them to justice, and making them work effectively, while simultaneously convincing them whom they should revere. Those who propagate the Great Teachings should become sincerely convinced of their true meaning. They should reflect on the people's mind and feelings so that they can harmonize them, and observe folk customs so that they can educate people.

Accordingly, they should enlighten and enliven the people, educating them in the divine knowledge and ethical ways. Always respectful to the deities and without disregarding the magnitude of divine favor, they should obey the imperial principles, engaging people in political efforts for reformation. This is the plan for the unification between governance and teachings.

6

THREE ARTICLES FOR TEACHING ISSUED BY THE MINISTRY OF PUBLIC INSTRUCTION

(April 28, 1872)

For public instructors

Article 1. Learn the meaning of reverence to the deities and love of country.

Article 2. Clarify the natural principles of heaven and the human way of morality.

Article 3. Guide people to respectfully uphold the emperor and to follow the imperial way.

7

NOTIFICATION [REGARDING YASUKUNI SHRINE] ISSUED BY THE COUNCIL OF STATE. ISSUED WITH THE HOME MINISTRY AND THE MINISTRIES OF THE ARMY, NAVY, AND TOKYO PREFECTURE

(June 4, 1879)

The Tokyo Shōkonsha should be renamed as Yasukuni Shrine and be ranked as a *bekkaku kanpeisha* (shrines in a special grade financed by the state). It will be under the administration of three ministries, Home, Army and Navy. The division of the regular management including ceremonies is regulated as below.

Tokyo Shōkonsha

It should be notified that the above mentioned is renamed Yasukuni Shrine, and given the rank of a *bekkaku kanpeisha*.

Accordingly, along with the renaming of Tokyo Shōkonsha as Yasukuni Shrine, given its rank as a *bekkaku kanpeisha,* the Home, Army, and Navy Ministries will administer the shrine hitherto. It should be also announced that ceremonies and other regular management will be conducted as follows:

(1) Ceremonies should be performed according to the liturgical documents for shrines and attended by the bureaucrats of the Ministries of the Army and Navy.
(2) Smaller or lower level customary events, other than the ceremonies conducted in the shrine, should follow the ongoing rules.
(3) Promotions and demotions of the priests should exclusively be administered by the Home Ministry.
(4) Increasing priests on the staff or increasing their salary, should be discussed among the three ministries of Home, Army, and Navy, and be reported to the government.
(5) Constructions, renovations, and all the other budget-related items should exclusively be administered by the Ministry of Army. Note that resituating the main sanctuary and the worship hall should be discussed among the three ministries.

8

NOTIFICATION (NO.1 IN THE FOURTH CATEGORY) ISSUED BY THE HOME MINISTRY
(January 24, 1882)

Official statements about the administration of Jingū priests and shrines, particularly on religious matters that are forbidden, issued to the Jingū priests and the priests of state-supported shrines and national-supported shrines

Official priests have been able to hold positions as public instructors concurrently, which should be abolished hereafter. Official priests should no longer engage in performing funerals. The above mentioned should be followed.

But priests who work for shrines in prefectures or at smaller administrative units can continue serving as public instructors for the time being.

9

NOTIFICATION (NO. 30 IN THE SECOND CATEGORY) ISSUED BY THE HOME MINISTRY

(May 15, 1882)

Permission for Shinto church groups to operate as independent religious organizations
    The following churches (*kyōkai*) of Shinto are allowed to have their own denominational names and to be independent hereafter.

Shinto Jingū group, Jingū Church

Shinto Taisha group, Izumo Ōyashiro Church

Shinto Fusō group, Fusō Church

Shinto Jikkō group, Jikkō Church

Shinto Taisei group, Honkyō Taisei Church

Shinto Shinshū group, Shinshū Church

10

NOTIFICATION (NO. 19) ISSUED BY THE COUNCIL OF STATE

(August 11, 1884)

Abolishment of the nomination of teachers of Shinto and Buddhism as public instructors

The nomination of teachers of Shinto [sect Shinto] and Buddhism as public instructors should be abolished hereafter. The nominating of a head priest of a temple, as well as the promotion and the grading of teachers should be totally the responsibility of a chief managing priest (*kanchō*) from each organization. The conditions are as follows [in what follows there is also a detailed list of conditions that regulate the scope of authority of the mangers of the religious organization].[1]

Note

1 The above (Readings #1–10) are translations based on texts found in Yasumaru Yoshio and Miyachi Masato eds., *Shūkyō to kokka—Nihon kindai shisō taikei* (Tokyo: Iwanami Shoten, 1988).

11

THE CONSTITUTION OF THE EMPIRE OF JAPAN

Imperial oath at the sanctuary of the Imperial Palace, and Articles 1–3, and 28[1] (February 11, 1889)

Translated by Ito Miyoji

Imperial oath at the sanctuary of the Imperial Palace

I do humbly and solemnly swear to the divine spirits of the imperial founder and the other imperial ancestors that, following their eternal and great plans, I have succeeded to and secured the divine throne of the emperor, and I will be true to their ancient intentions and preserve them from corruption.

In consideration of human progress in the course of its affairs and with the advance of civilization, I deem it expedient to give clarity and distinctness to the instructions that have been bequeathed by the imperial founder and the other imperial ancestors. I shall establish the Imperial House Law and the Constitution, with the formulation of specific provisions, so that, on the one hand, we may possess an explicit guide for the course we are to follow for posterity, and that, on the other, our subjects shall thereby enjoy a broader means of giving us their support, and that these means shall continue to the end of time.

We will thereby ensure greater stability of the country and promote the welfare of the people's life within the boundaries of the Japanese islands.

We now establish the Imperial House Law and the Constitution. These laws amount to only a model for the rule of government, bequeathed by the imperial founder and by the other imperial ancestors. That I have been so fortunate, in keeping with the tendency of the times, as to accomplish this work, I owe to the glorious spirits of the imperial founder and of the other imperial ancestors.

I now reverently make my prayers for divine help from them and from my father, and also make a solemn oath to them that neither now nor in the future will I fail to be an example to our subjects in the observance of the laws hereby established.

May the divine spirits witness this solemn oath.

Chapter I: The Emperor

(1) The empire of Japan shall be reigned over and governed by a line of emperors unbroken for ages eternal.

(2) The imperial throne shall be succeeded to by imperial male descendants, according to the provisions of the Imperial House Law.

(3) The emperor is sacred and inviolable.

Chapter II: Rights and Duties of Subjects

(28) Japanese subjects shall, within limits not prejudicial to peace and order, and not antagonistic to their duties as subjects, enjoy freedom of religious belief.

Note

1 A full official translation by Itō Miyoji can be referenced at the National Diet Library, http://www.ndl.go.jp/constitution/e/etc/c02.html.

12

IMPERIAL EDICT (NO. 220) ON THE DISPOSITION OF VACANT PROPERTIES AFTER THE CONSOLIDATION OF SHRINES, TEMPLES, OR BUDDHIST HALLS

(August 10, 1906)

Precincts in public lots that have become unnecessary after the consolidation of shrines, temples, or Buddhist halls can be transferred under the responsibility of the Home Minister to consolidated shrines, temples, or Buddhist halls unless they are necessary to maintain the public property. [Editors' note: This concerns the reorganizing, reducing, and the merging of Shinto shrines (*jinja gōshi*).]

13

DATES OF IMPORTANT SUBSEQUENT ORDINANCES ISSUED BY THE JAPANESE IMPERIAL STATE

Ordinance of the Rituals in the Imperial Household: September 19, 1908

Ordinance on the Enthronement: February 11, 1909

Ordinance on the Rituals of Jingū [of Ise]: January 26, 1914

Ordinance on the Rituals of National and Regional Shrines and Other Shrines of Lower Levels: January 26, 1914

Religious Organizations Law: April, 1939

14

IMPERIAL EDICT (NO. 736) ON THE OFFICIAL INSTITUTIONALIZATION OF THE BOARD OF DIVINITIES (JINGIIN)

(November 9, 1940)

(1) The Board of Divinities is under the charge of the Home Minister and is responsible for the following administrations:

1) Issues related to Jingū [of Ise]
2) Issues related to national and regional shrines and other shrines of lower levels
3) Issues related to official priests and other professional priests
4) Issues related to promoting interest in revering deities

Part 2

PRE-WAR JAPANESE
INTELLECTUALS ON SHINTO

15

KUME KUNITAKE

Shinto as the ancient custom of
worshipping heaven (1891)

Kume Kunitake (1839–1931) was a noted historian whose writings on Shinto got him into deep trouble with the authorities, forcing him to resign his professorship at Tokyo Imperial University. Born the third son of Kume Kunisato, a Hizen samurai-official of the Saga Domain, he distinguished himself academically early on and, in 1863, went on to study in Edo at the Shōheikō, the shogunal-sponsored school where he pursued Chinese studies (*kangaku*).[1]

His scholarly abilities served him well as the official recorder of the famous Iwakura Embassy to the United States and Europe in 1871–73. After his return to Japan, he cemented his reputation as a historian with his record of the trip, the *Beiō kairan jikki* (Account of the Embassy's Tour of America and Europe), which was published in 1878. He was subsequently appointed to the government's History Compilation Office in 1879 where he assisted in creating the official imperial history of Japan. After this office was transferred to Tokyo Imperial University in 1888, Kume was appointed professor there in the faculty of literature and was instrumental in creating the history department the following year.

The Kume affair begins in 1891 when his essay, "Shinto as the ancient custom of worshipping heaven" (*Shintō wa saiten no kozoku*) was published in the new academic journal in history, the *Shigakukai zasshi* (*Journal of the Historical Society of Japan*). The essay stirred great controversy among conservative Shintoists and right-wing monarchists, who found its content offensive. In his essay, Kume denies Shinto is a religion and relegates it to being nothing more than an ancient cult of heaven worship without the rationally developed doctrines and moral codes present in established religions like Buddhism.

His angry critics brought a complaint against him to the Imperial Household, Home, and Education Ministries. They charged him with failing to uphold his academic integrity as a public official by committing *lèse-majesté* (*fukeizai*). In addition, they accused him of dismissing the gods as imaginary, of claiming that Amaterasu was not only worshipped at Ise, and that Buddhism, not only Shinto, was the spiritual foundation of Japan, etc.

Kume was forced to print a retraction soon afterward.[2] *Shigakukai zasshi* and another journal that printed the essay were forced to suspend operations. And, on March 4, 1892, Kume was formally dismissed, eventually moving on to Waseda University, a private college where he obtained a professorship finally in 1907.

Kume was a historian who was molded by both Confucian rationalism and a Western Enlightenment-inspired faith in scientific historical criticism. His downfall occurred because he offered his critique of Shinto at a time of rising conservatism in Japan. His essay challenged the basic officially sanctioned historical views that underpinned the emperor system, which had been firmly politically established by the Meiji Constitution of 1889. His offense was joined by another famous incident in 1891, when the Christian high school teacher Uchimura Kanzô refused to bow before a copy of the Imperial Rescript on Education at a school ceremony.[3]

It is interesting to note that Kume's critique of Shinto was also echoed by Western interpreters of the time. Famous pioneers like Basil Chamberlain, Kume's colleague at Tokyo Imperial University, and W.G. Aston, the British consular official and master linguist who translated the *Nihonshoki*, also criticized Shinto. Unlike Kume, however, both printed their views of Shinto as a primitive faith only after they had returned to Europe.

The following is a partial translation of Kume's controversial essay.

SHINTO AS THE ANCIENT CUSTOM OF WORSHIPING HEAVEN (1891)

Japan is a country where the gods are revered and buddhas are worshipped. Japanese history has developed under these conditions, but historians have not paid enough attention to this, and they therefore cannot fully understand our reality. That is why I am outlining it in this essay.

Reverence toward the gods is indigenous to Japan. Buddhism was introduced from abroad and went on to become the foundation of our politics as well as the divine reverence. This began with the Constitution promulgated by Prince Shōtoku and established by the Ordinances of Taika (646). Its main intention is exemplified in one of Empress Kōken's rescripts, issued in July of the second year of Jingo (766), that states: "Expelling misfortunes and inviting fortunes inevitably depends on a subtle dark world. Revering gods and respecting buddhas comes after purifications." As Emperor Kanmu's rescript, issued in January of the twenty-fifth year of Enryaku (806), states: "In expelling misfortunes and increasing fortunes, Buddhism excels most. In inviting goodness and benefiting the living, nothing is superior to this way of Buddhism." This draws a clear distinction between gods and buddhas. In my understanding, *Shinto is not a religion*. Thus it does not contain any intent of inviting goodness and benefiting the living. As long as it *only performs rituals for the heaven and purifications for expelling misfortunes and inviting fortunes, Shinto has been performed along with Buddhism without any problem*. And, therefore, the royal politics has established the way the gods are revered and buddhas are worshipped as the basis of governance until today. *This custom is tied to the imperial subjects and has become fixed as part of the national polity (kokutai)*.

But there are a number of confusing fallacies in relation to gods. History must carefully consider Shinto, Buddhism, and Confucianism impartially, avoiding imbalanced devotion toward any of them. Here, in this essay, I begin by studying the present national reverence toward gods; I will look at the ancient Eastern customs of revering heaven, as well as the origin of the New Tasting Festival (Niinamesai), Autumn First Fruits Festival (Kan'namesai), and the Great Harvest Festival (Daijōsai), the three great festivals of the imperial court. Then I will argue that both Inner and Outer Shrines at Ise, as well as the Kashikodokoro, are shrines for revering heaven. I will base my interpretation in history and in the fact that various shrines enshrine mirrors, *magatama* (curved beads), and swords as divine entities. Then I will discuss Shinto's emphasis on avoiding the impurity of death and of respecting purity, rather than worshipping indigenous deities or humanlike powerful spirits. There are some bad customs, which are byproducts of the legalized enforcement of purification, however, and we will review the results, both good and ill. As this was happening, belief systems like Confucianism, Buddhism, and Onmyōdō were introduced into Japan, which I believe was necessary to supplement our national wisdom. Thus, over the past thousand years or so, Japan has become a country of revering gods and worshipping buddhas. Up until the present, the way of revering gods and worshipping buddhas have been conducted side by side without any particular preference between them. I will also discuss this.

National customs of reverence toward gods

Seen from the outside, Japan appears to be a country of buddha worship, but observing customs in both cities and rural areas will soon show that this is not the case. For example, people living in Tokyo perform the Sannō festival in some wards and the Kanda festival in others. They also have festivals of Tenjin, Inari, or many other *ujigami*, making them big festivals every year. These wards do not correspond to the contemporary administrative wards, but rather derive from older divisions of these places as agricultural localities. As the present urban areas are no longer agricultural, they have lost the true meaning of these festivals. But in any village in the countryside, people continue to celebrate the *ujigami,* originally ancestral gods of a clan, in their festivals. The precincts for *ujigami* were more often than not different from the present contours of these villages, and the customs differ from one area to another. All share, however, the customs of *fermenting newly harvested rice to make unrefined sake, and of steaming rice, both as nectar and ambrosia to offer, observing older traditions of each locality*. The date of such a festival is called also an offertory day. *Since the sake and steamed rice are traditional foods from of old, the festival is an occasion to offer prayers of gratitude for the good life that the gods had provided in the past*. The common people have customarily served heaven every year, and in times of hardships such as flood, drought, storm, or plague, they would pray ceremonially to expel misfortune.

Now watch these common people work and act in their everyday life. If you walk in a field, a village, or a back street in the early morning, you will see and hear men and women washing their faces and gargling with water from a river or well, and then bow and pray to the god by clapping. This is *the scene seen from the mythological "Age of the Gods."* If you observe closely, you will see that the bow and prayer are performed in a great variety of ways, including placing hands together, chanting a Buddhist sutra, bowing toward the cardinal points as well as heaven and earth, facing toward the sunrise, standing, kneeling, worshipping buddhas, and devoting themselves as if they were Muslims. It all depends on in which tradition they are taught their way of bowing and praying; for example, people who receive formal Buddhist instruction will face the Buddhist altar. Here, in this manner, people show their own sense of sincerity. The truth is that all these show *the surviving customs of purification and of revering heaven, to which they all pray for fortune. This is the true way in which Japanese people are.*

Generally speaking, Japanese people feel pleasure in purity and cleanliness while hating impurity. This custom is greatly different from those in China or Korea. Westerners say the East is characterized by cleanliness, but this cleanliness comes from reverence towards gods rather than from personal hygiene. This is the main difference between Japanese cleanliness and hygienic cleanliness. Either way, it is a beautiful custom. China and Korea both had customs of purification and revering heaven, but over the course of time they lost them, thus changing their national character and becoming unstable countries. Only Japan has kept the ancient tradition and built its nation upon it, starting at the beginning of the country when the offspring of the heavenly goddess was upheld as the monarch descended from the sun. Even today, the emperor, as an offspring of the sun, never fails to perform everyday worship at the site known as the Takamikura.[4] in the imperial court. When the new harvest is reaped, he performs Kan'namesai and Niinamesai as the main festivals in the year, and likewise people celebrate the fall festivals nationwide. At the enthronement, the emperor performs the Daijōsai, the most important ceremony of Shinto, only once in his or her life.

The ceremony of serving heaven offering gratitude for the origin of all things is conducted every day and every year by everyone, from the heavenly respected one [the emperor] down to the ignorant people living in the field, village, or the backstreet. Since national polity is firm and unwavering, there is no need for commands from above and the monarch and his subjects are united and merged as one. This unwavering unity of our national polity is so impressive that, deeply moved, I feel almost inclined to cry. If, as we like to say, this is the country that respects the unitary descent of the imperial family for tens of thousands of generations and excels all the other countries, *isn't this because these beautiful customs have spread all over the nation and remained stable?* These points should be considered particularly notable in our national history.

The origin of revering heaven in the East

If we review the development of nations around the world, we could assume that reverence toward heaven began from a simple thought early on for humanity. The earliest human beings lived in groups in the mountains or plains where bushes were thick and animals flocked together, as Liu Tsung-yuán [柳宗元 a Chinese writer in the eighth–ninth century] wrote. People depended on natural resources in this kind of life, and they owed their life to the blessings of nature. When they feared changes in the weather, from cold to hot, to windy, and to rainy, they most probably believed that there was a lord who inhabited the lofty heaven and presided over this world, giving us both fortunes and misfortunes. They must *have imagined a god-like being, which they worshipped*, praying that misfortune be expelled and good fortune be reaped from it. After they took in their all-important harvest every year, they must have begun festivals to give thanks for these original blessings. *If you think about it, it is notable that what most countries call god is heaven, a heavenly god.* In Japanese, the word *kami* sounds the same as god, above, chief, head, and hair. All are something one holds up above oneself. In Japan, the *kami* that is specified is Amenominakanushi. In China, it is called Huang T'ien Shang Ti [皇天上帝 Supreme Sovereign God of Heaven]; in India, the Heavenly Palace [of the gods] or Tathatā [真如]; and in the West, God. They all have the same meaning, but the customs of revering and expressing gratitude to heaven differ from country to country.

Gods, therefore, emerged from ancient people's imagination. And as the human mind gradually developed and customs became more complex with the addition of various impure elements, the types and variety of gods increased, including formidable spirits like cattle, or deities like snakes or worms in some countries. These differences are due to highly specific developments; however, if we focus on the main line of development, we can assume that indigenous deities emerged from a heavenly god, from these gods and deities emerged awe-inspiring spirits, and from these emerged monsters, which people came finally to believe in. Early on, when the human mind was beginning to develop, such aberrations were unavoidable.

In India, the human mind developed very early historically. Before the birth of Gautama Buddha around 2,500 years ago, there had been six preceding buddhas who preached the doctrine of cause and effect over the course of three rebirths from the past, to the present, and future. When [the historical Buddha] Gautama Buddha began preaching, believers looked up to him as the savior of the world who would replace heaven. Buddha, who is full of virtues, stands for the human capacity for compassion, and provides a way to save people as a whole. *Here we see the beginning of religion.* Then around six hundred years afterward, Rome encountered Jesus, who was also considered a savior descended from heaven. I would suppose that both Moses and Jesus established a religion that was actually based on Indian Buddhism, which had traveled westward. Around the same time of Jesus' birth, Buddhism had traveled eastward as well. *Shinto existed in Japan even before the introduction of Buddhism, and lacks a savior and a doctrine of cause and effect. It only started as a custom of revering and offering gratitude to the heavens and of treating the offspring of a heavenly goddess as the emperor of the nation.* With the assistance of aristocratic houses like the Nakatomi or Inbe, emperors conveyed how to do divination and properly treat the gods, judged and decided things in accordance with divine will, and established rule through the unity of rituals and government. *This marks the establishment of the national polity and the source of the imperial lineage. Before then, there had been only simple reverence toward heaven, lacking indigenous deities.* The entry of Empress Suiko in the *Nihonshoki* reads, "The Kings of the two countries of Silla and Imna [both supposedly located in the Korean peninsula] sent envoys with tribute, and delivered a memorial to the empress, saying: 'In heaven above there are gods; on earth below there are emperors. Besides these two classes of deities, what else is there that we should fear?'"[5] Reading this passage shows us both what our national character is and what Shinto is.

Since Gautama Buddha, Confucius, and Jesus all originated [from cultures that had] the custom of revering heaven, they do not contradict either Japan's national polity or Shinto. Here I would like to briefly give an outline of the ancient custom of revering heaven that is common throughout the East generally. In the East, the Chinese mind developed early historically. In a commentary on the *Book of Changes* (*I ching*), Confucius wrote: "When Fu Hsi [庖犧] looked up to the heavens he saw solar phenomena. When he looked down to the ground he saw the law at work in the world. When he looked at the colors and patterns of the birds and animals and the local peculiarities, he began to draw the eight trigrams (*pa kua*[八卦])." This is the beginning of philosophical speculation in China at least 5,000 years ago. I would imagine that both in Japan and Korea around that period people were already living in communities and *establishing their own customs of revering heaven.* Around 500 to 600 years later, during the declining years of Emperor Shao-hao [少昊], the custom of revering heaven went out of style. A book of *Marquis Lü on Punishments* in *the Classic of History* [書経、呂刑], contains the following passage:

> The mass of the people became dark and disorderly. Their hearts were no longer set on good faith, and they violated their oaths and covenants. The multitudes, who suffered from oppressive terrors, and were in danger of being murdered, declared their innocence to heaven. God surveyed his people, and there was no fragrance of virtue arising from them, but rather the rank odor of their cruelty. The great emperor felt compassion toward those innocent multitudes in danger of being murdered and made their oppressors feel the terrors of his majesty. Then he commissioned Chung [重] and Le [黎] to terminate the connection between earth and heaven, and the descent of the spirits ceased.[6]

An interpretation by Kuan she-fu of Ch'u [楚観射父], compiled in the *Chiao ssu chih* [Treatise on Sacrifies] of the *Book of Han* [漢書、郊祀志], states:

> When the rule of Shao-hao was declining, the people lost their morality, confused over the people's way and the divine way, forgetting the right way of doing things. Every family had its own shamans and chroniclers, causing disorder in the rituals, profaning the offering, and blocking the purification for gods. Blessed harvests were not received, disasters continued, and people could not fulfill their own destiny. When Ch'uan-hsü (顓頊) succeeded to the throne in this disordered time, he commissioned the head of the southern Chung to preside over heaven and gods, and the head of the Fire Le to preside over the earth and people. This meant the end of the interchanges between earth and heaven.

These passages show that people who had sincerely revered heaven came to neglect or despise god gradually, as they grew in experience. *We know that people worshipped a sole heavenly god until this period.* In time, however, Chung began to offer service to heaven whereas Le began to offer service to the earth. This is where we see the beginning of reverence to a heavenly god and also to indigenous deities; it is also where we begin to see heaven characterized either as an emperor or a father and the earth as an empress or a mother.

Around 300 to 400 years later, in the *Canon of Shun,* of *the Books of Yu, The Book of Documents* [書経、虞書、舜典], one reads: "Shun [舜] took pains making sacrifices in the nomal way to God; sacrificed purely to the six Honored Ones; offered their appropriate sacrifices to the hills and rivers; and extended his worship to a host of spirits."[7] Thus already here, the land was ritually attended to. Services to the gods of the sun, moon, stars, winds, and rains followed. Services were done for hills and rivers, and therefore services would be done at hillsides and riversides. *Thus came the custom of worshipping many gods, and it was to be followed also by worship of humanlike awe-inspiring spirits.* One part of *the Canon of Shun* reads: "When he returned to the capital, he went to the temple of the enlightened ancestor,"[8] and another in *the Speech at Kan* of *the Book of Hsia* [夏書、甘誓] reads: "You who obey my orders shall be rewarded before my ancestors; and you who disobey my orders shall be put to death before the spirits of the land."[9] For the ancestors, the hall should be built in the Imperial Palace, where ancestors of the country should be enshrined and be transferred to heaven. Thus, what is called a worship hall for ancestors is, in reality, a hall for revering heaven. The spirits of the land means indigenous deities.

Some parts of *Chiao ssu chih* narrate:

> Kung-kung [共工] spread his hegemony over the land of China. His son, Kou lung [勾竜], governed the land and waters ably, and after his death he was enshrined as a local god. After Lieh-Shan [烈山] became the king, his son Chu [柱] grew a hundred kinds of grain, and after his death he was enshrined as a grain god. And, therefore, enshrinement of gods of the locality and grain in the suburbs can be traced far back in the early history. [. . .] King T'ang [湯] of the Shang dynasty defeated King Chieh [桀] of Hsia. Some wanted to move the local gods of Hsia, but T'ang did not approve it, and instead compiled the book of local gods of Hsia. Then he moved away Ch'u of Lieh-Shan, enshrining instead Ch'i [棄], the ancestral god of the Chou dynasty, as a grain god of Shang.

In later years, when questions arose as to whether humanlike awe-inspiring spirits were enshrined as local gods and grain gods, as the *Classic of Filial Piety* (*Hsiao ching* [孝経]) states "*She* [社] is the lord of the locality, and *Ch'i* [稷] is the head of grain," and as Cheng Hsüan [鄭玄], a Confucian scholar of the Late Han Dynasty, states "In early years, the governors made great contributions, by serving meals to their gods. Thus Kou lung served meals to a shrine called *she*, Ch'i to *Chi*." This became the standard explanation. In summary, the ancestral hall used to be a place for revering heaven, the shrine for the lord of the locality, but changes in custom later generated the idea of "the ancestral mausoleum and local shrines [宗廟社稷]." *Now enshrined at the ancestral mausoleum were ancestors of the kings of the country, for whom solemn service was held every five years. In this case the service is dedicated to humanlike fearsome spirits.* At local shrines in prefectures and villages, festivals were performed in spring and autumn, which could be regarded as times for offerings. Festivals mean presenting offerings, as illustrated by a poem from the T'ang dynasty: "Bits of mulberry shadows appear on the autumn shrine, / people go home in twos and threes, / one can imagine the customs associated with shrines." In this case, the shrine is dedicated to local deities. In rural Japan, on the other hand, the offering day is dedicated to the heavenly god, which is different from Chinese gods. We need to be careful when considering Japanese and Chinese forms of worship; they look similar, but they are in fact different, and we must think about these customs clearly in order to avoid any confusion.

The Niinamesai, Kan'namesai, and Daijōsai

In regard to ancient Japan, a section on Chi-Ch'ou [冀州] in *the Tribute of Yu* in the *Book of Hsia* [夏書、禹貢] states that "the wild people of the islands brought dresses of skins," or the section on Yang-Chow [揚州] states that "the wild people of the islands brought garments of grass."[10] The island people of the K'o-Ch'ou, Koreans, dealt in leathers, whereas the island people of the Yang-Ch'ou dealt in fabrics of linen and cotton. Thus, since about 4,000 years ago, these three areas, China, Korea, and Japan, have traded with one another, and accordingly we can assume that they imported and exported their customs too. As for their gods, however, *Japan and Korea were not different from each other, and both similarly revere heaven.* About one thousand years later, at the beginning of the Chou dynasty, even the Su-shen [肅慎], the most violent and illiterate people residing in the fields and mountains along the Amur River, dealt in stone arrowheads and red wooden arrows. Around the same period, Japanese and Korean development probably approximated with that of Shao-hao [少昊], which was in a period of decline.

If we calculate how long the imperial lineage has existed, we can estimate that the grandson of Amaterasu, Ninigi, descended from heaven around 2,400 or 2,500 years ago, which corresponds to the mid-Chou. Even before this period, Amenokoyane (offspring of Kamimusubi) and Futotama (offspring of Takamimusubi) each guarded the Nakatomi and Inbe clans respectively. The Nakatomi served the gods by preserving *futomani* divination and the methods of purification, while the Inbe served by preparing the offerings. This division of labor seems rather similar to the different services to the heaven and the earth performed by the Chung [重] and Le [黎] clans in China.

The great ritual of revering heaven is none other than Niinamesai (the New Tasting Festival or Festival of First Crops). *The Niinamesai is not the festival for Amaterasu Ōmikami but an ancient ritual for revering heaven.* We can see this in the "Age of the Gods" section of the *Nihonshoki*:

When he [Susanoo] saw that Amaterasu no Ōkami was about to celebrate the feast of first-fruits [Niinamesai], he secretly voided excrement in the New Palace. Moreover, when he saw that Amaterasu no Ōkami was in her sacred weaving hall, engaged in weaving the garments of the gods, he flayed a piebald colt of heaven, and breaking a hole in the roof-tiles of the hall, flung it in.[11]

This is why Amaterasu hid herself in the Rock Cave of Heaven, and it is clear that *Amaterasu herself performed the Niinamesai and Kanmisosai* (the Festival of Weaving Divine Garments). We can also see that the taboo against touching dirt and impurities must have existed before this period. The festivals of first crops were also performed in China, as illustrated in the *Sh'ih T'ien* of the *Erh-ya* [爾雅、釈天]: "Spring festivals are called Tz'u [祠], summer festivals Yüeh [礿], autumn festivals Ch'ang [嘗], winter festivals Cheng [蒸]." Tung Chung-shu [董仲舒] explains:

Tz'u is held in the new year when one begins to eat leeks. Yüeh is in April when one eats wheat. Ch'ang is in July when one tastes millet. Cheng is in October when one offers new crops of rice.

Kuo P'u [郭璞], on the other hand, annotates that Ch'ang means tasting new crops, and Cheng means offering some produce. If so, Ch'ang and Cheng both mean offering new crops, which look similar to our festivals of Kan'name and Niiname. But I am wondering when the division began that puts Kan'name for September, and Niiname for October. Book 29 of the *Nihonshoki* chronicles that on September of the fifth year of Emperor Tenmu, "We [the Department of Shinto religion] have ascertained by divination that the provinces and districts supplying rice for the Festival of the First Fruits," and, in October, "Offerings of cloth were made to all the various gods of heaven and earth, meaning the regular offering of Kan'name."[12] The entry for the first of November that year reads: "On account of the New Tasting Festival, the ceremony of announcing the first day of the month was omitted," which is the first reference to Niiname in the Japanese history.[13]

Niinamesai is an ancient custom of the East, and it appeared in Korea too. The *Book of Later Han* states that in Goryeo, "in October one reveres heaven. The whole nation holds a big ceremony. This festival is named Dong Myeong [東盟]." Dong Myeong is the same as Tung ming [東明], and probably the same as Toyono Akari no Sechie [豊明節会, the feast held on the last day of Niinamesai]. Among the Yeh people [濊] too, "always in October one reveres heaven, drinking alcohol, singing, and dancing. This is named the dancing king." Among Mahan [馬韓], on the other hand,

always in May around the borders of the rice field, one enshrines powerful spirits. Day and night the crowd sings and dances. Dozens of people gather, stamping the ground and marking the season. When one reaps the harvest in October, people repeat the same thing.

These show that there were big festivals in summer and winter, when the feast was held in a similar way. In Puyŏ [夫余], "people revere heaven in December, when they enjoy big events everyday, with drinking, eating, singing, and dancing. This is named Greetings by Drumming [迎鼓]." Thus, in Puyŏ the festival was held in December, but the meaning was the same.

The *name* (tasting) festival in our country was originally held once, not twice, a year. In the *Engishiki,* Kan'name, held in September, appears in the entry on Ise Jingū, while Niiname, in October, is written in the entry on the festivals of four seasons (Shijisai). An annotation to the Codes for the Official Rituals (*jingiryô*) states: "The Kan'namesai is the festival that the messenger celebrates on the same day as the festival for *Kanmiso,*" and it is held at Ise Jingū. This is the reason why the emperor visits the Jingikan (Council of Divinities) and sends a messenger to make offerings for the festival. A passage of the *Gōkeshidai* [江家次第] reads: "The Emperor always says that he makes offerings at Kan'name in September. You, Nakatomi, convey this to heaven, and with a deep bow, the Nakatomi only withdraws making a slight sound." This offering is called a regular offering [例幣]. Niiname in November is the festival that the emperor performs at the office of Jingikan, which the *Codes for the Official Rituals* refers to as the Daijōsai of the day of (the second) U [卯, a day in the Chinese calendar] in November. It is stated in *Shokuinryō no gige* [職員令義解] that

tasting new crops will be called a celebration for the deities. In the morning is held an Ainame no Matsuri, a feast for various deities, while in the evening there is the offering of the new crops to the sovereignty.

After the celebration, the Toyono Akari no Sechie was held. One of the Emperor Uda's occasional rescripts, issued in March of the fifth year of Kanpei (893), states:

In February, a yearly festival is held. In June and December, Tsukinami festivals are held. In November, events like a Niiname are important for the state. On every occasion, one wishes that no calamities occur. In this festival, deities participate at 558 shrines in total, both small and big, in the nine regions of Kyoto and Kinki,

which illustrates the outline of Niiname. In earlier times, Niinamesai was called the Daijō, but there is an explanation in the code (*ryō* [令]): "at the enthronement of an emperor, all enshrine heavenly and indigenous deities," whereas "Daijō is the event to be held once every year, as performed by the head of every country." The festival held every year came to be called Niiname so that this Daijō would not be mistaken for the big festival which the emperor held only once in a lifetime. In the Daijō Festival, new buildings called the Yuki and Suki (悠紀主基) are constructed at the Jingikan, and the emperor performs the rite in heavenly garments of feather. Nijō Yoshimoto wrote his observations about Daijōsai in the Bunwa years (1352–54), which is written in *kana* easy enough to be grasped clearly.

The present emperor performed the Daijōsai in November 1871. A number of people may remember this festival. While I was accompanying the Ambassador Plenipotentiary Iwakura who sailed to the United States, Mr. De Long, the U.S. Minister to Japan, delivered his address and offered a toast on this highest festival of the emperor to be held only once in his life. As all the subjects should know, *Niiname and Daijōsai are official occasions when the emperor performs the ritual himself or herself* and are the most important festivals in Shinto that *keep their traditions with the imperial lineage.*

Revering heaven also at Ise Jingū

As is well known, a divine mirror and a sword (which was later transferred to Atsuta Jingū) were enshrined among the three imperial regalia. This mirror is described in *Kojiki* as follows:

Amaterasu Ōmikami said, "This mirror—have [it with you] as my spirit and worship it just as you would worship in my very presence."[14] It may lead one to think that Amaterasu should be enshrined, but *in reality it is heaven that is enshrined. Pay attention to the words "my spirit."* Another example is the following reference in the *Nihonshoki* to Ōmiwa shrine:

> Then said Oho-na-muchi no Kami: "True, I know, therefore, that thou art my guardian spirit. Where dost thou now wish to dwell?" The spirit answered and said: "I wish to dwell on Mount Mimuro, in the province of Yamato." Accordingly, he built a shrine in that place and made the spirit to go and dwell there. This is the God of Ohmiwa.[15]

Thus the Ōmiwa Shrine is the place where Ōnamuchi no Kami is enshrined as its own guarding and wondrous spirit. *Spirits are spiritual manifestations of heaven. Otherwise, it would be unreasonable for one to worship one's own spirit. This is also true in Amaterasu Ōmikami's description of the mirror as her spirit.* In addition, remember that the chapter on Emperor Suinin in *Nihonshoki* reads:

> In compliance with the instruction of the great goddess, a shrine was erected to her in the province of Ise. Accordingly, an Abstinence Palace was built at Kaha-kami [along the upper waters] in [the river of] Isuzu. This was called the Palace of Iso. It was there that Amaterasu Ōmikami first descended from heaven.[16]

If we compare this passage with Sarutahiko's words when the grandson of Amaterasu, Ninigi, descended from the heaven, "I will go to the upper waters of the River Isuzu at Sanada in Ise," we could assume that at this moment Amaterasu Ōmikami moved the capital from Takamagahara, actually Yamato, to Ise to rule the Eastern country. *The Palace of Iso should be the remains of the old palace. Before the rule of Emperor Sujin, it must have been a rule that when Ōmikami was present, the halls for niiname and imihata [weaving garments] were built to revere heaven, where the administration was conducted.*

Gekū [the outer palace] is, on the other hand, the detached shrine of the palace. Motoori Norinaga wrote in his *Kojikiden*:

> In *Norito kō*, the Master (Kamo no Mabuchi) referring to an example of Totsumiya in the *Manyōshū*, wrote that Totsumiya (an outer palace) is always built separately outside of the Grand Palace as another imperial palace where the emperors stop by, adding that there are no other owners. In the same manner, Totsumiya of Ise [Gekū] is the Outer Shrine revering Amaterasu Ōmikami, with the Inner Shrine beside Isuzu river as its counterpart. This explanation shows his incomparable thinking, which I sincerely agree with. And therefore, there originally was an Outer Shrine for Amaterasu Ōmikami, where a great deity, Toyouke, was enshrined.[17]

Among a number of Motoori's ideas, this is the most valuable. Gekū is, therefore, not originally a shrine to revere Toyoukebime, but an Outer Shrine for the Palace of Iso. And the Palace of Iso was not the shrine to revere Amaterasu Ōmikami, but a place to enshrine a divine mirror at the remains of the Great Palace of Iso. The Ōmiwa Shrine was not built as a hall for treasures, but only as a hall for worship. This is because the shrine is a place to revere Mount Mimuro as a place where a guarding and wondrous spirit dwells, without enshrining any other divine entities to revere. *The Ise Grand Shrine and Ōmiwa originated in this way, and both revere heaven.* When we say that Ise has the spirit of Amaterasu Ōmikami to revere, while Ōmiwa has the spirit of Ōkunidama [another name of Ōnamuchi], it may sound as if they revere such divine figures, leading to the split between Ise for revering the heavenly gods and Ōmiwa for revering the indigenous gods. It may also suggest that they should be the halls to worship humanlike awe-inspiring spirits, causing someone to mistake Ise Shrine for a great mausoleum. I will clarify the reasons for this mistake now.

Compared to the sun, Amaterasu Ōmikami's virtue is thought of as the heaven that shines and is also known as Ōhirumenomuchi. Emperor Jinmu said: "I am the descendant of the sun goddess, and if I proceed against the sun to attack the enemy, I shall act contrary to the way of heaven."[18] When Emperor Shōmu decided to have a statue of Great Buddha cast to be set at Tōdaiji, he believed that Amaterasu Ōmikami was the avatar of Vairocana Buddha, which he thought of as the great sun. In heaven, there is nothing more important to human beings than the sun, and thus this is a way to praise the virtue of this great goddess. I would argue, however, that the great goddess is not the sun itself nor was the sun meant to represent heaven. Rather, the great goddess is believed to be the representative of heaven, comparable to the sun. Ise Grand Shrine is the place where the spirit of Amaterasu should be worshipped, just as the divine prescript orders to worship the mirror as though it were the great goddess. This is different from the Chinese custom that the ancestors of the country should be enshrined in the mausoleum and then be transferred to heaven.

Kashikodokoro and the three divine treasures

The Kashikodokoro, also called Naishidokoro, is the place where a substitute is enshrined for the mirror that is treasured at Ise as the divine entity. In the ancient period, the three imperial regalia were treasured at the imperial court, where the emperor kept the same bedroom and led the administration. Under the rule of Emperor Sujin, the copies of the mirror and the sword were manufactured, and the originals were enshrined in a Kasanui village of the Yamato region, which is the origin of the Ise Grand Shrine. Since then, the copies of the mirror and sword have been stored in the imperial court, which was the beginning of the Kashikodokoro. An entry for Emperor Jinmu in the *Kogoshūi* reads: "Following the prescripts of the two imperial and celestial ancestors [Amaterasu and Takamimusubi], a divine tree of *himorogi* is erected for Takamimusubi, Kamimusubi, etc.," but it actually refers to the so-called Palace for the Eight Gods (Hasshinden). This palace was built by the Jingikan, and it existed until the northern and southern court period. This must be emphasized because recently, some people have mistaken the Kashikodokoro for a place for revering a series of imperial spirits, something like a storage place for the memorial tablets for these ancestors. This mistake has arisen because the festivals for imperial spirits are held in spring and autumn in the Imperial Palace.

The custom of building a hall for revering heaven in the Imperial Palace had a parallel in ancient Goryeo. In the *Book of Wei* [魏志], one reads "Goguryeo likes to rule the royal court. There at both right and left of the court were established the grand halls to revere the powerful spirits." As mentioned above, an enlightened founder of the Chinese mythological period was to be enshrined later at a main mausoleum, which in turn changed into a divine hall where people worshipped humanlike awesome spirits. In Goryeo, the old customs became obsolete after some revolutionary changes. Only in Japan have old customs been maintained, and a single imperial lineage has been preserved and respected. Thus we should consider Japan to be a very blissful country.

Since Amaterasu Ōmikami granted the mirror, sword, and *magatama* (curved beads) to her grandson Ninigi no Mikoto, these three treasures, called the three imperial regalia, have been transmitted as the imperial symbols. The mirror is called "Yata no kagami," and the beads "Yasaka no magatama." Both are hung as decorations on a branch of Sakaki tree, in front of the Rock Cave of Heaven where Amaterasu hid herself. The sword is the one that Susanoo gained when he conquered the *Yamata no orochi* (the eight-branched giant snake) at the upper part of Hino river in Izumo. Susanoo offered this sword called *Amano murakumo no tsurugi* to Amaterasu; it was later called *Kusanagi no tsurugi*.

Although we know that this sword has been enshrined at Atsuta Shrine, we do not know the original use for each of these regalia. I would argue that *these should be considered decorations for the divine site of revering heaven*. In the section on Emperor Keikō of the *Nihonshoki*, Kamunatsusohime in the country of Buzen (northern Kyushu) is described as follows:

> She broke off branches of the hard wood of Mount Shitsu. On the upper branch she hung an eight-span sword, on the middle branch she hung an eight-hand mirror, and on the lower branch a Yasaka jewel. She also hoisted a white flag on the bow of her ship.[19]

On the other hand, in the section on Emperor Chūai, the ancestor of the Agatanushi of Oka of Tsukushi (northern Kyushu)

> pulled up beforehand a 500-branched sakaki tree, which he set up on the bows of a nine-fathom ship. On the upper branches he hung a white-copper mirror, on the middle branches he hung a ten-span sword, and on the lower branches he hung Yasaka jewels.[20]

And the ancestor of the Agata-nushi of Ito in Tsukushi

> pulled up sakaki trees of 500 branches, which he set up in the bow and stern of his ship. On the upper branches he hung Yasaka jewels, on the middle branches white-copper mirrors, and on the lower branches ten-span swords, and coming to meet the Emperor [. . .] he addressed the emperor, saying: "As to these things which thy servant dares to offer, mayst thou govern the universe with an intricate subtlety like the curvings of the Yasaka jewels; may thy glance survey mountains, streams and sea-plains bright like the mirror of white copper; mayst thou, wielding this ten-span sword, maintain peace in the Empire."[21]

The *Jinnō shōtōki* compares the three imperial regalia to wisdom (智), compassion (仁), and courage (勇), based on these episodes. *The three regalia are, therefore, symbols of the spiritual virtue of the heavenly goddess*, and the mirror is considered divine. When Yamatotakeru attacked Hidakami no kuni [northeastern part of Japan], he took only the mirror with him. We know this because the *Nihonshoki* tells us that: "at this time a great mirror was hung upon the Prince's ship."[22] This is one backdrop for enshrining the mirror in divine shrines even today.

In other cases, the beads can be enshrined as the divine entity of shrines. A part of *Chikuzen fudoki* reads:

The Munakata goddesses descended from heaven. When they were at Mount Sakito, they put a blue flowery jewel to stand for Okitsu Shrine, a purple Yasaka jewel for Nakatsu Shrine, and the Yata mirror for Hetsu Shrine. They had these three symbols as divine entities enshrined at these three shrines.

It is also clear that the Munakata three shrines, where the three goddesses' jewels and swords are enshrined, are the place to revere heaven. In the wartime code, the sword signifies the so-called violent souls. Thus the sword was not hung on the branch of Sakaki tree in front of the Rock Cave of Heaven. Also, in later years, people usually have not had a sword enshrined as an emblem of divinity. If we consider all these cases together, *decorating the divine throne with three treasures did not start with the gathering of the gods at the Yasu river of the heaven when Amaterasu hid herself.* This custom had begun long before this as an old way of revering heaven.

*　　*　　*

Notes

1 Graham Healey and Chishiki Tsuzuki eds., "Introduction," in *The Iwakura Embassy 1871–73, A True Account of the Ambassador Extraordinary & Plenipotentiary's Journey of Observation through the United States of America and Europe,* trans. Martin Collcutt, Vol. 1 (Tokyo: The Japan Documents, 2002), xxi.
2 John S. Brownlee, *Japanese Historians and the Nationalist Myths, 1600–1945; The Age of the Gods and Emperor Jinmu* (Tokyo: The University of Tokyo Press, 1997), 99–100.
3 Margaret Mehl, "Scholarship and Ideology in Conflict: The Kume Affair, 1892," *Monumenta Nipponica* 48 (Autumn, 1993): 337–39.
4 Takamikura means "the lofty site" where the emperor's throne is located in the imperial court.
5 W.G Aston, trans., *Nihongi: Chronicles of Japan from the Earliest Times to A.D 697,* Vol. 2 (Rutland, VT, Charles E. Tuttle Co., 1972), 125.
6 James Legge, *The Chinese Classics,* Vol. 3 (Taipei: SMC Publishing, 1991), 592–93.
7 Ibid., 33–34.
8 Ibid., 37.
9 Ibid., 155.
10 Ibid., 98, 111.
11 Aston, *Nihongi,* Vol. 1, 40–41.
12 Ibid., Vol.2, 334–35.
13 Ibid., Vol. 2, 335.
14 Donald L. Phiippi, trans., *Kojiki* (Tokyo: The University of Tokyo Press, 1968), 140.
15 Aston, *Nihongi,* Vol. 1, 61.
16 Ibid., Vol. 1, 176.
17 Motoori Norinaga, *Kojikiden,* Vol. 13 (Tokyo: Chikuma Shobo, 1968), 172.
18 Aston, *Nihongi,* Vol. 1, 113.
19 Ibid., Vol. 1, 113.
20 Ibid., Vol. 1, 219–220.
21 Ibid., Vol 1, 221.
22 Ibid., Vol 1, 206.

16

KAWAKAMI HAJIME

Japan's unique form of nationalism
(1911)

Kawakami Hajime (1879–1946), one of early leaders of Marxist economics in Japan, was a major intellectual of the pre-war period until his imprisonment in 1933 for violating the anti-socialist Public Security Preservation Law of 1925. Kawakami was son of a Chōshū samurai who was inspired by Yoshida Shōin (1830–59), his hero from his own domain, who combined a passion to learn about the West with an ethic of absolute self-sacrifice for the emperor and Japan. In 1898 Kawakami began his studies of political science and economics at the faculty of law at Tokyo Imperial University and grew deeply interested in Christianity and socialism. He taught at the School of Agriculture of Tokyo Imperial University from 1903 to 1905, and, in 1908, moved to Kyoto Imperial University, becoming a full professor in 1915 and teaching until 1928, when he had to resign his professorship because of his Marxist affiliation.

In the 1910s, Kawakami, like many intellectuals of his time, was obsessed with cultural identity. What was it that made the Japanese unique? This question arose in 1913–15, during his travels in Europe, which had heightened his awareness of the gulf that existed between Japan and the West.

Kawakami was deeply critical of Western individualism. It emphasized an ethic of selfishness and materialism that ignored the common good. The rapid industrialization and modernization of Japan along Western lines had produced not just goods, but horrific poverty, gross economic inequality, and great human misery. A key question was whether it was possible to be moral by abandoning the profit motive behind modern capitalism. Initially, Kawakami saw a solution in a new universal ethic of absolute selflessness. This was inspired by traditional Confucian mores of his youth, an eye-opening reading of the New Testament, and his own deeply religiously inspired meditative experience of no self. But he increasingly realized that it was institutional change along Marxist lines not moral reform that would ultimately transform the suffering of the proletariat. He spoke out against the harsh economic realities of modernity by publishing *Binbō monogatari* (A Tale of Poverty) in 1917, which began as a popular series of articles in the *Osaka Asahi shinbun*.

For Kawakami, the Japanese spirit is dedicated to revering the emperor, not the spirit of capitalism and individual-centered self-interest. For him, "[t]he god of Japan is the nation. Thus the emperor is the one who represents this sacred national polity" (*kokutai*).[1] The emperor as a *kami* embodied the absolute sacredness of Japan in his person. His sacredness, as proclaimed in the Meiji Constitution, meant that patriotism, the spirit of loyalty to the emperor, was the Japanese way. Yet Kawakami still had doubts about the official ideology of the Meiji state, based as it was on a Shinto nationalism centered on Amaterasu that accepted a capitalistic system of private property.[2] Amaterasu for him was not the deity for all Japanese

74

from ages eternal, but an imperial clan god that had existed along other *kami* in ancient times. With the political ascendancy of the emperor, however, Amaterasu became a common god of the people.

After the Russian Revolution of 1917 and the rice riots of 1918 in Japan, Kawakami finally abandoned his faith in a personal religious morality to fully embrace true Marxism. By the mid-1920s his left-wing political activities increasingly got him into trouble with the thought police (*tokkō*). He publicly joined the Communist Party in 1932, fully espousing Marxist teachings that he never recanted even after his imprisonment (1933–37) until his death. The following essay, "Japan's unique form of nationalism" (*Nihon dokutoku no kokkashugi*) appeared in the monthly literary magazine *Chūōkōron* (Central Review) on February 14, 1911.

JAPAN'S UNIQUE FORM OF NATIONALISM
(1911)

Our country's current world of thought

More than three years have passed rather quickly since I left Tokyo. I have wondered how Nihonbashi Avenue in Ginza and the Komagome and Yodobashi areas, where I lived for a while, have changed. But while I do occasionally visit the city, I have been unable to stay for very long, and nowadays I have almost forgotten the grand spectacle of the imperial capital with its many intoxications. However, I sometimes go to Osaka, and when I get off at my stop and go right, there is a high-class pay toilet. On a white signboard it is posted, "two *sen* for a number #1 and three *sen* for a number #2." So, has it become a world where money is essential even for going to the bathroom? That is remarkably shocking for me, since it is really rare to see such a social change in Japanese civilization. Ordinarily, I spend much of my time quietly in my study, reading about the debates of the ancients and searching for remnants of antiquity. It is not unusual for me to not even look at a newspaper for days. Even on occasions when I do leave my house, I find myself doing such things as fondly reminiscing over Shunkan Sōzu at Shishigadani[3] and longing for Hōnen Shōnin at Kurodani.[4]

Although I remain isolated from the air of modernity—air that abides far, far away—eventually, the sound of the waves from Japan's currents of thought reverberate even on the window of my own retreat. At times, it causes ripples in the sea of my own heart. Occasionally, my sentences flow together. Am I not responding to its insistence by filling this article with what pours from my heart?

A time of national pride, a time of reaction against the importation of Western civilization

Based on what I have seen and felt, it seems that in the period from 1907 onwards, at the end of the Meiji period, the Japanese completely changed their thinking.

To my mind, it is undeniable that my fellow citizens' feelings of national pride greatly intensified after the victory of the 1894–95 Sino-Japanese War. And yet, these Chinese are the same as us. Not only are they also Easterners, but the one instance when we defeated them is no cause for celebration since large parts of our own culture come directly from them, and that victory did not satisfy our own pride as an Eastern people. What we should think about is that we won because of our country's ability to be one step ahead of China by

75

importing Western civilization. However, the aftermath of the 1904–5 Russo-Japanese War[5] victory is something very different altogether. This is because the Russians are Westerners not Easterners. In fact, that we had defeated Westerners very much boosted Japanese people's pride, particularly as Easterners. Until then we thought such a victory was completely unattainable. But with it, we, who had so eagerly imported Western civilization, no longer had anything to fear. As a result, we realized that there was something in our own civilization worthy of respect. After we defeated China, we thought that it was probably the result of adopting Western civilization, but beating Russia sparked the idea in Japan that we must have some great strength which does not exist in other Eastern countries, nor even in Western countries. The worship of Western civilization had definitely dominated Japanese thinking after the Meiji Restoration, and it suffused high and low, urban and rural classes. But now things had changed; the worship of Western civilization was now scorned and rejected. The welcome it had received when first introduced to Japan changed to an air of caution, and some efforts were made to prohibit it. Should not this great conceptual shift be surprising, since it goes against all expectations?

The Japanese people have already begun to realize that there are some great strengths to their own civilization. One brash group of people have started making nativist comments and have begun campaigns based on whatever pops into their heads and whatever partisan thing that comes their way. They do not consider it carefully by doing good research, nor do they care about the historic value of anything; they care insofar as it is not Western and only Japanese. They call for the revival of Chinese classics, they call for the revival of the family system,[6] they call for restoring filial piety, they call for restoring Bushidō, they call for restoring social welfare teachings (*hōtokushū*),[7] they say this and that. Although each call is different, all demand trying only to protect what's old and not to promote anything new. Besides this, the striking general tendency academically is research into the nature of the Japanese people. Ethicists, historians, constitutional scholars, and economists alike often focus on this in their research, and some of them are extremely enthusiastic about the distinctive qualities of the Japanese people. It seems as though they are raising their voices in praise over contemporary Japan. Additionally, any tone of worship towards the West is rare, even among those who have traveled abroad for pleasure or for study. Instead, it seems that many abruptly accent Japan's strengths while noting only the weaknesses of the West.

To sum up, we are in a period of reaction against the importation of Western civilization. This is a time that requires us eagerly to try to clarify the unique character of our people, as well as to preserve it. Given the force and appeal of this reaction, I cannot see it as a temporary phenomenon coming from just one segment of the society. Rather, it should be viewed as an enduring phenomenon arising from deep down within people. As I have stated above, this has arisen because of the victory of 1904–5. To my mind, this war was truly a national war, and because it was a great war where all parts of society, whether high or low, worried about defeat and celebrated victory, both in public and in private, that victory produced a truly national pride. In other words, our pride manifests itself among the high and the low, among those inside and outside the government, and it has restored harmony in the country.

Therefore, today's reactionism is both broad and deep. It is in no way the product of just one group of intellectuals or writers. (The reactionary movement in the Meiji twenties (1887–96) was such a thing). Moreover, the introduction of Western civilization after the Meiji Restoration happened extremely rapidly; now, forty years later, so-called Western civilization has reached a point where it has already percolated down to the lowest levels of society. Western-style hats, clothes, and shoes can be seen in villages everywhere, on civilians as well as on the police and the military. And, along with such forms of attire, a Western-style air fills the villages, to the point of arousing even the dullest sensibilities of the countryside. It is apparent, for example, in the attitudes towards parents whose children have received a lower and middle school education [who have lost traditional Confucian family values and so on]. Thus, I see this era's pride as a nationalistic self-pride, and I consider this era's reactionary movements to be nationalistic as well as reactionary. And thus, I also think it could certainly be a powerful long-lasting force. We may regard the period right after the Meiji forties as a new chapter in the history of Meiji thought.

Following this line of thought, it is enough for us to understand that we are in a period that is very important ideologically but that is also very dangerous. Because of our national pride, things are being done that we should not be proud of; likewise, we are supporting things that should not be supported and not changing things that should be changed. And we may have fallen prey to erroneous ethnocentric thinking, straying too far from reason and superstitiously believing in divine help from above. The development of our Japanese civilization could become completely arrested because of it. We as the reading public, at least, probably need to see it as our duty to work toward developing our thought not by accepting the other's ideas unquestioningly but by sharing what each believes. Allow me, if I may, to state a few of my thoughts.

The distinctive features of the Japanese folk are most clearly developed at this time

From what I see, it seems there are many points of similarity if you go back to Japanese and Western antiquity. However, evolution immediately means differentiation. That is, if you compare the Japanese with today's Westerners, they are conspicuously marked with distinctive features as a people. I will try to thoroughly discuss this difference in their fundamental characteristics as they exist today. I consider the Japanese of today rather than those in the past as advanced. Thus, I believe that our distinctive national features are more obvious today than they were in the Japanese people of the past. We should therefore seek the reasons for Japan's greatness not in the past, but in the present. —(I know that the present is a product of history. However, milk, which is beneficial for growth during infancy, may not be necessarily sufficient as food in one's prime, and the exercise which is suitable for development in one's prime may not necessarily be sufficient in one's old age. Likewise, I believe that we need to search for the cause of Japan's greatness now, rather than looking to the past. I will not try to make Japan great in the future by studying the reasons why it is great today. Instead, I want to seek the cause of our present illustriousness so that we can use that to determine future national policy. I know that I am speaking in the abstract and have not made my position clear, but I will explain further throughout this essay.)

Japanese nationalism and Western individualism

As I see it, the biggest feature of contemporary Japan is its nationalism. To begin with, the word nationalism "*kokkashugi*" is a term unique to Japan, and since there is no exact equivalent word in Europe, Europeans cannot comprehend the spirit behind its ideology at all. After all, according to contemporary Japanese nationalism, the state is the goal and the individual is the means. The state is first in importance, and the individual is second. The individual is only valuable as a tool or agent to advance the state. Thus, let us take the most extreme hypothetical case. Imagine a situation where it was necessary to kill every individual in order to preserve the state, and sacrificing every individual also spared the nation. That is the inevitable logical conclusion of nationalism, and contemporary Japanese people's ethical outlook has no reservations about such an outcome. However, Western people's ideology is not nationalism but individualism. Thus, according to their ideology, the individual is the goal and the state is its means. The individual is first in importance, and the state is second. The state exists only insofar as it is a tool or agent for fulfiling an individual's life. Thus, if we take the most extreme hypothetical example again, what if the state had to be destroyed to satisfy an individual's life? Doing away with the state system is the inevitable logical conclusion of individualism, and contemporary Westerners' ethical outlook has no reservations about such an outcome.

Western natural human rights and popular sovereignty and Japan's state-based human rights and natural state sovereignty– Westerners' individuality and Japanese national character

In this way, the West and Japan have a completely different rationale for the foundation of their countries. And this distinction in fundamental aims, on both sides, leads to a number of differences in the national situations between them. Here are some that come to mind.

Western ideology is based on individualism. Thus, in the West you regard individuals as having intrinsic value and having a purpose. Thus, you have the idea of natural human rights. Holding human life in high esteem and respecting individual personality lie beyond Japanese people's imagination. The ideology of the Japanese people is not individualism, but nationalism. Thus, in Japan we cannot think of individuals as having intrinsic value and their own self-interest. Only the state has value and self-interest. Thus, Japanese people have no idea of natural human rights, but they do have the idea of the natural rights of the state. The individual's rights exist by the state's consent, and the state permits limited rights to the individual only as a means for achieving its own objectives. The rights that individuals have are not intended for their own personal goals but to make the individual a useful tool of the state. Thus, in the West, human rights are natural, and the power of the state is the consent of the people, whereas in Japan the power of the state is innate, and human rights are allotted by the state. The respect for individuality and high value of human life in the West seems to transcend Japanese people's imagination.

In turn, Westerners cannot comprehend the high value placed on the state and the respect for the nation in Japan. Here the notion that each person has a unique individuality is extremely rare. To put it baldly, the Japanese have no concept of an individual personality. However, even though they do not have this Western type of individuality, each person respectively represents the national character. Representing the national character means that the people realize their significance as agents of the state. In the West, the highest and most noble person is one who possesses the greatest individual character, but, in Japan, the highest and most noble person is one who most fully represents the national character. With all due respect, His Majesty, Japan's emperor, possesses the most perfect national character and regards the national interests as his own, and he does not have any personal and individual interests outside the public interests of the state. Thus, the emperor is the highest and most revered figure in Japan. No one under His Majesty's rule can possess the perfect national character that he does. Each subject has individual interests over and above the state's public interests. And from a Japanese perspective, the more self-interest a person has, or to put it differently, the less national character a person has, the more he or she accordingly slips lower in people's estimation—viewed as part of a vulgar class.

Western countries are all democratic; only Japan is a statist country

As we have seen, in the West, the individual is primary and the state is secondary. Thus, the national polity (*kokutai*) of the West is an entirely democratic system. Whether the state in its political form has a monarch or chooses a president, the fundamental spirit of the state is completely democratic. That is to say, it is an ideology that treats the state lightly and deeply esteems the people. However, since the nation is primary and the individual is secondary in Japan, our national polity has its own peculiarities that we should think of as a statist system. Thus, in so far as this fundamental spirit does not change [censored] Japan will never be a democratic country and, further, could never be a democratic country. To state it more baldly still, in the West the state is the slave of the people, and in Japan the people are the slaves of the state.

Japan is the land of the gods (*shinkoku*)—Westerners' idea of rights and the Japanese people's idea of the state—Western nations are based on individual rights, Japan is a nation of duty (*gimu*)

Japan is the land of the gods. In other words, the country is divine. This is the common faith of Japanese people. This may not be a consciously conceived belief, but, if pressed, it is something ordinary Japanese people would certainly agree with. After all, according to Japanese thought, not only is the state the supreme good, but it is almighty. The state is not something that causes harm to its citizens—no, it can never do that. The state should demand that its citizens do everything; there is no reason it should not be able to make these demands. Why? Just as we stated before, the Japanese belief is that citizens are all agents of the state, and individuals never have their own goals. Thus, if there is a goal which is beneficial for the state, it should always be able to command its citizens to make specific sacrifices to that end, at any time and to any degree. And because individuals take it on faith that they exist only as agents of the state, they naturally cannot disobey a command for this kind of sacrifice; there is no room in the world view for ethical criticisms of this kind of edict. This may not be actually happening in all circumstances today, but, at the very least, it is a popular ideal and belief. In the West, the individual has the right to insist on his own personal gain. What we call *kenri* is rendered as "right" in English. This word, "right" originally meant the right path and justice, and it is the opposite of the word "wrong," which means sin and injustice. After all, when a national character is centered upon the individual, like the West, then, when those individuals insist on their own personal benefit, it is equivalent to justice and the right path, and not asserting it is rather a sin and unjust. However, for a state-centered national character, like that of Japan, asserting one's rights never has this moral force. Thus, the word "right" in Britain translated into Japanese is construed as *kenri*. The *ken* (power, authority, right) is the *ken* of *kendō* (meaning expediency), and *ri* (profit) is the *ri* of *shiri* (personal profit, self interest). Therefore, in the word *kenri* itself there is no ethical meaning originally. Although, if it were literally translated, the Western word would have the exact meaning of "justice," in Japan such a moral sense is never just. Rather, loyalty and courageous service are the highest morality. Thus, if we call the West a place of countries with rights, Japan is a country of duty. And although Western rights arise from their origin in the relations between individuals, the Japanese duty arises from the relations between the state and the individual. In the heart, mind, and vision of the Japanese people, the state is the most noble thing, above all else. Thus, while they strive to sacrifice anything and everything for the state, they are unable to sacrifice the state for anything and everything. The state is their one and only god, to which they offer all their sacrifices. They cannot dream of other gods to whom they should sacrifice. For them, the state has the highest, loftiest, greatest authority. They could never imagine any greater authority than that of the state. Thus, scholars sacrifice what is true for them to the state, and monks sacrifice their faith to the state. This is the reason why no great intellectual and religious figures have appeared in Japan, but one could also argue that since the Japanese have no need to appreciate thought and religion that would contradict the existence of the state, they don't regret, or rather they are pleased with, the absence of great intellectual and religious figures.

In Japan the emperor is the state; in the West, an emperor is an agent of the state—in Japan, loyalty to the sovereign and love of country are identical—what is not suitable for the times are arguments for a unity of loyalty and filial piety as well as ancestor worship

As such, the deity of the Japanese is the state, and the emperor represents the national polity that comes from this divinity. In a word, the emperor is the concrete embodiment of the state's abstract divinity. Thus, according to the Japanese belief, the imperial throne has the status of a *kami*. The emperor is a godlike person. This is the reason why the Imperial Constitution clearly states that the emperor is sacred and inviolable, and therefore this article is the most important part of the Constitution and of the creed of the Japanese citizens. After all, as stated earlier, our country's emperor upholds our national character entirely flawlessly; his only concern in national politics is the official interests of the state, and he does not have any interests of his own. Thus, in Japan, the emperor and state are one and the same and indivisible. The state is our god, and the emperor is the representative of god. Thus, in our country, while love of country is the highest virtue, it is ultimately the same as loyalty to the sovereign. The distinctive feature of the Japanese people is not being united in loyalty and filial piety but being united in patriotism and loyalty toward the emperor. That is the reason I regard those who try to use filial piety as a vehicle to encourage loyalty as foolish.

In the West, all people possess personality based on their own individual standpoint. Thus, the sovereign is also an individual person with the same status and rank as the people. In their way of thinking, each person is noble for retaining his or her individuality. Thus, the sovereign also retains his own personal identity, and has his own private self-interest. Thus, according to this Western view, since he can never be united with the state and has an individuality independent and apart from it, the sovereign is in essence an organ of the state.[8] Western jurisprudence uniformly explains sovereignty in this way. However, in Japan, the sovereign is united with the state, and all individuals are tools and organs of either that sovereign or the state. In any case, since the emperor is perfectly representative of the state, Japanese people regard him as sacred and the imperial status as divine, based on the presumption that the state is divine.

Some try to use ancestor worship and a common racial ancestor to explain how the Japanese treat the emperor as a representative of the *kami*. But from my perspective, this is a glaring misunderstanding as well as extremely dangerous. We can understand that a religion of ancestor worship, which should never be confused with the fine custom of venerating the ancestors, comes from the most primitive of religions from an uncivilized age, if we think not only about antiquity but also about the way savages still live. That is to say, it derives from the superstitions and ignorance of savages; it is based on their superstition that the spirits of the dead continue to exist after death and that they protect their descendants from disaster and allow them to gain good fortune. Thus, they worship the spirits of the dead and show respect for them as *kami*. This type of religion is in no way unique to the Japanese people; it is found in every society in its infancy. The only characteristic that is uniquely Japanese about it is the way in which it gradually developed into the religion of state worship we see today. The Japanese people today treat the emperor as a representative of the *kami*. It is not that they regard the imperial household with its divine ancestry as central because they believe their own ancestors are *kami*. They do so because they only regard the state as divine and because they respect the present emperor as a representative of the state which in turn represents the *kami*.

Japan's principle of collective cooperation and the West's principle of the division of labor—a high level of patriotic ethics and a low level of business ethics—Western people have a special individuality; Japanese people are endowed with a monochromatic national character

In Japan, the mysterious effect of nationalism appears when people combine their power together collectively, and in the West the mysterious effect of individualism appears on the side of the division of labor.

The division of labor also has a kind of collective co-operation. However, what I mean here by "collective co-operation" is a simple combination of power, excluding the more complex division of labor. For example, in order to try to move a huge rock that weighs hundreds of pounds, lots of people need to combine their strength to move it in the same direction. We can think that this is a simple form of collective co-operation. However, when you are making wooden clogs, you work together in a different way. You divide up the work respectively; one person planes the wood, another polishes it, another makes the cord, and yet another assembles all these materials together to make a pair of clogs. Working like this is the division of labor. Collective co-operation is a strong point for Japanese people, and the division of labor is the strong point of Western people.

When collective co-operation develops, it will naturally become something more complex to the point where it realizes the division of labor. The division of labor depends on combining efforts collectively, and it is where this is seen most effectively. The ideal situation would be to progress by aligning collective co-operation and the division of labor from the outset, like the two wheels of a cart. However, the undeniable strong point of Japanese people is our tendency toward collective co-operation, and the strong point of Westerners is their tendency toward the division of labor. And this is after all the natural result of nationalism and individualism.

In these times, war is a good example of how collective co-operation is most effective, while economics is a sphere where the division of labor is most effective. Is it not quite natural then that among today's civilized nations the one strongest in war and most backward economically is our own Japan?

Recently, there are two phenomena that Westerners have considered extremely strange about Japanese moral attributes. The first is that Japanese people are spiritually rich in their loyalty to the emperor and love of country. On this point, as ever, Westerners should defer to us. However, the Japanese, whose moral nature is so elevated in this respect, are nonetheless not immune from a variety of ethical shortcomings in terms of business ethics, beginning with making things crudely and then over-producing them. This is the second phenomenon that Westerners regard as strange. After all, patriotic ethics and business ethics are both forms of ethics. While we consider that Westerners cannot possibly match the Japanese in patriotic virtue, almost no one talks about Japanese people's virtue in business. This must seem very odd for Westerners reflecting on it. But, from my point of view, there is nothing at all strange about it. Why? When there is war, Japan's peculiar form of nationalism achieves its highest pitch. Although Japanese collective co-operation is most obvious when the whole country is united, its effects are largely invisible in ordinary peaceful conditions when people are doing everyday business transactions. These are the very times to trust every person's personal character and not to interfere with their own autonomy.

To my mind, both war and trade involve an element of contact and negotiation with foreigners. Thus, foreigners' doubts arise given the different ways we display our moral character in these two areas. We see moral deficiencies in the Japanese not only in business ethics but also at a park where someone picks flowers without permission, or in a station where we fight over who gets on a train first, or at a buffet dinner where someone behaves in an ungentlemanly fashion—actually a number of things clearly reveal Japanese people's individual ethical shortcomings. In normal peaceful times, when nationalism has not reached a fever pitch, Japanese moral character is something that should be suspect—even in the case of national duties like paying unpleasant taxes.

To move a large rock hundreds of kilograms in size, everyone needs to go in the same direction, combining their power into a unified whole. The biggest problem in these situations comes when their strength is not channeled in the same direction. If one person pushes east, another west, another pulls north, another south, and so on, there is no way to effectively combine their energy. Japanese ideology today is one of unified collective co-operation. Thus, the idea of respecting individuals' character and honoring their distinctiveness is extremely rare in Japan and the power of conformism and uniformism is very strong. Thus, it is rare for Japanese people to have distinctive characters, and almost all of those who are so acclaimed are cut from the same cloth. All people have this power to face the same direction, directly for the nation. And persons great and small are quickly judged by how great or small the level of their contribution to the nation is. In other words, in Japan, the amount one contributes for the country's sake is the criterion for evaluating a person, whereas in the West the so-called superiority or inferiority of a person's own character is the criterion for evaluating that person. Thus, in contrast to those in the West, who have their own separate, distinctive personal character, in Japan, people who are respected publicly all individually exhibit a monochromatic national character.

In Japan, people who are respected are those who have contributed directly to the state. Here we have a great respect for officialdom but lack respect for civilians; we have great respect for the military but lack respect for the literary world. Because of this, even those who produce tobacco or alcohol aver that they benefit the country, using this as the rationale for their own self-serving undertakings.

The reason for rejecting anarchism and socialism in Japan— in Japan, Western style socialism, social policies, constitutional politics, political party government cannot exist

In short, the Japanese people acknowledge that the state has the greatest value. Therefore, the greatest fear of contemporary Japan and of those common people who hold power here is the destruction of this faith in the state's supremacy, and so-called anarchism is particularly worrisome. In the West, anarchists are feared because some of them cause violence;

this is no different from the reason people fear murderers and robbers. However, in Japan, anarchists are dreaded for an entirely different reason. Even if viewed as extremely peaceful, their ideology would be feared, hated, and disliked. It should be remembered here that anarchism is not spread only through violence. Some anarchists, like the American Sophie Tucker,[9] only proselytize through speeches and the press. Violence could be a last resort if they were deprived of the ability to express themselves peacefully; however, a large number of Japanese are completely against letting ideologues like this obtain that very thing— freedom of speech. At the very least, many Japanese support the suppression of this group's speech. The Japanese people abhor anarchists not only because they think of them as robbers, murderers, and lunatics but simply because their ideology is directly opposed to the lofty Japanese faith in state supremacy.

Socialism is deplored in Japan for similar reasons. At a glance, nationalism and socialism are similar in nature. Both seem to go against individualism. How so? What we call socialism is something that insists that all land and capital should be publicly owned and that all industry should be under public management; therefore, it seems quite incompatible with individualism. However, their similarity is really just skin deep. In essence, what we call socialism is completely based on individualism. Land and capital should be publicly owned, and industry should be publicly managed, not for the good of the state but for the good of the individual. Although this individualism may occasionally resemble nationalism as it strives to reach its goals, its fundamental spirit, its original starting point, and its end goal is individualism. And this foundation of individualism is the very reason why socialism is vigorously rejected in our country. To state it even more baldly, we are not really rejecting socialism, but individualism. Starting with the national ownership of the railroads, we already accept that many industries and forms of capital are publicly owned, and we also agree that many types of enterprises should be publicly managed. Even though this is in fact a partial realization of socialism, the power elite (both in and out of the government) have no reservations about it. That is because they do not consider the reason for public management and ownership to be for the benefit of the individual but for the benefit of the state. It is reminiscent of groups that, even as they advocate for the revival of Chinese, wear Western hats and clothes. If one rejects something, what is rejected will not be something superficial but close to their heart. They do not reject the public ownership of industry but rather the public ownership of industry in the service of individualism. I once read Satō Nobuhiro's noteworthy book and was surprised.[10] Why? He asserts that all land and capital should be publicly owned and that all industries should be publicly managed—his arguments seem to completely reflect the principles of socialism. This is particularly noteworthy because he was a contemporary of the pioneers of modern socialism, the clique of the Frenchmen Fourier and Comte de Saint-Simon. Two or three years ago, I commented upon this fact in an article titled, "Satō Nobuhiro—a *bakumatsu* era socialist," in the *Kyoto Law Society Magazine*. Afterward, Professor Fukuda [Tokuzō] commented on my manuscript saying, "Through this article, I could understand for the first time why there were no socialists in our country." It is a phrase that says everything about the flaws in my argument. After all, even if Satō Nobuhiro was insisting on the public ownership of land and capital, as well as public management of all industries, his fundamental focus was on nationalism rather than individualism. His beliefs, therefore, are totally different from what we call socialism in the West.

However, it is important to note that even with this understanding of socialism, social policy has not been put into practice in our country. Why? Even factory laws, for example, are not intended to respect the workers as individuals and increase the class interests of the working class. In the final analysis, workers are regarded as tools for state industry. Therefore, other than their importance for the robust industrial development of the state, there is no reason to deeply reflect upon the spiritual and physical development of these tools. This is really a production policy not a modern social policy. Where Western economic theory focuses on theories of distribution, Japanese economic theory stresses the theory of production. This is only natural, since an individual standpoint will lead to a focus on distribution and a nationalistic standpoint will lead to a focus on production. The state began when a group of individuals came together to form it; since the state is not independent from individuals, its form will often result in the same, whether the beginning was individualistic or nationalistic. So, if we are talking about its form, we can say that even from the *bakumatsu* period in Japan the social policies came from a superb socialism. Even though the Diet was founded after the Meiji Restoration with the establishment of constitutional politics, can we not argue that because of Japan's fundamental spirit, there is no socialism, no social policies, no constitutional politics, and no party politics? Or rather, it is not a mistake to say that there cannot be socialism, social policies, constitutional politics, and party politics as yet in Japan.

The difference between freedom and no freedom of speech in Japan and the West—Western Christianity and Japanese state religion

In a certain sense, there is no country with as much freedom of speech as Japan. But in another sense, no country has as little freedom of speech as Japan. Why is that?

As many of you well know, the theory of evolution was spread throughout the world by Darwin's writings. However, this type of thinking was entertained by early modern scholars long before Darwin (setting aside ancient Greece for the time being). For example, in Buffon's *Natural History* there is a paragraph that clearly recognizes the fact of biological evolution.[11]

However, right after Buffon wrote, he offered a contrary statement, saying, "Yes it's exactly so, but no!," adding the explanation, "Based on what the Bible indicates, God created all living things immediately, and the first pair of all animal species was created perfectly in the beginning by the hand of God." This, of course, agrees with Christian doctrine as it existed at that time. The Christianity of that time had enormous power, and expressing an opinion that contradicted it meant that you were endangering your life. Thus, Buffon hypothesized about a biological evolution and then, on the next page, immediately nullified it by regarding what the Bible reveals as authoritative.

Lamarck[12] who worked about forty years after Buffon, was the first person to offer the world a theory of biological evolution, around fifty years earlier than Darwin. Because of this, however, "he was attacked and persecuted with detestable mockery from all sides. For a longtime he was dismissed in this way by everyone and lived a life that was both poor and blind" (in his friend's words). However, Cuvier,[13] who was a biologist of the same period, flirted with the conventional view and fully opposed Lamarck; therefore, he far surpassed him, ultimately becoming president of the Council of Public Instruction and being awarded the title of baron.

While this is a bit of a digression, it should help us understand how Western society lacks freedom of speech about religion. Granted that this story is a century old and one should not judge the present by the past, it is still generally taboo to criticize Christianity in Western society. In this area, our country has far and away more freedom of speech. On the other hand, if you look at socialism (for example), you will see that Western socialists can publicize their views in speeches, books, magazines, and newspapers; they can even assume important positions in government, such as ministers or bureau chiefs. However, in our country, those who call themselves socialists cannot even find work in the private sector. In this area, therefore, our country has far less freedom of speech than others.

It is thus difficult to make any sweeping generalizations, either saying that our country has more or less freedom of speech than others. The main point, however, is that the restrictions on freedom of speech differ from country to country. While we could say that other countries are more restrictive on the religious side and we are more restrictive on the political side, that is quite superficial and not at all interesting. Indeed, if we go one step further, we will see that our societies are equally restrictive where free speech about religion is concerned.

Perhaps this applies more to talking about societal religions than to talking about truly religious religions (*shin no shūkyōtekina shūkyō*). Thus, if we accept that certain items represent the common feelings and faiths of the people, and if these come to have the highest and greatest authority in society, I would consider this religion. And, in this sense, just as Christianity in Western society is a form of national religion, ultranationalism is a form of national religion in Japanese society. Thus, just as criticizing Christianity is taboo in the West, it is taboo to criticize ultranationalism in our country. Under the present circumstances, that ideology has reached its highest pitch; it is treated as the highest faith and sentiment to which the common people should aspire. Attempting to confront and attack it now, of course, is really the greatest taboo, or even just trying to judge it will be impossible.

Considering these situations, it will be easy to understand why free speech in certain areas is so restricted in Japan. And to regard these restrictions as coming from the arbitrary decisions of officials or the prejudices of hardheaded members of a certain part of society does not acknowledge reality. It seems to me that severe restrictions on free speech in certain areas exist because they are demanded by the people and by public opinion. On this point, government policy is endorsed by many magazine and newspaper reporters, and by many party members in the Diet—or in other words, a majority of our citizens completely endorse it. For me as a writer, it is completely unavoidable to endorse it here as well.

The revolt of the new science against traditional faith—compromise and contradiction are characteristic of the present day

In my understanding, unifying people can become enduring only when they share a common faith and a common sentiment that permeates all social classes. Thus, either finding or supporting such a unifying faith and sentiment becomes the most urgent political objective.

Ancient knowledge accumulates and condenses into faith and sentiment, and new knowledge helps develop that faith and sentiment into progress. However, when new knowledge completely differing from what is traditionally accepted suddenly appears, the unity of faith is destroyed because the old knowledge is not able to adopt, assimilate, and incorporate that new knowledge into the national faith. That will definitely end up violently disturbing a nation's foundations. In order to avoid this, present-day Japan has gradually moved toward a policy that strictly curtails speech. It is for that very reason that we live in an age of contradictions.

As I have argued in somewhat greater detail in the latest issue of *Changing Times,* we live in an age of unprecedented material progress, not just in Japan but throughout the world. (The causes of this, as I have stated before, are inventions and the technological development of machinery.) However, along with this material progress, we are also seeing unprecedented intellectual progress. As our new knowledge, the product of science and learning, flourishes, it threatens to destroy the old knowledge, which is at the core of traditional faith. In other words, we are living through a violent collision between science and faith, such as we have already seen in the West. Under these circumstances, it is inevitable that our country—which very rapidly imported a new civilization that is completely different from Japan's traditional civilization—will experience a far more violent clash between science and tradition. In this respect, the Japan of today is beset by the most extreme contradictions. How so? Insofar as we do not want to lose to other nations, we must work tirelessly to promote the rapid development and spread of science. Simultaneously, however, we must devote all our energy to impede the rapid rise and spread of the new knowledge, in order to prevent turmoil in our country's internal faith. Isn't this the height of contradiction? And aren't these inconsistencies felt most keenly by those intellectuals who have offered their services to the government?[14]

After all, while, on the one hand, we are mandated not to fall behind the rapid advances in knowledge of the Occident, on the other hand, we are ordered not to budge even the slightest bit from the sentiments our country has handed down to us. Nonetheless, knowledge alters sentiment. The stronger the convictions about the new knowledge, the more difficult it is to quell a stirring of faith that originates from the old knowledge. Under these circumstances, it is not necessarily an exaggeration to say that we are trying to keep on going by following the extremely contradictory dictate for progress while remaining exactly the same. However, we are not necessarily the only people in this type of situation. For example, even among the government authorities there are those who will always protect science—it would be impossible for them not to be its supporters. And yet, the very science which they are ardently supporting destroys the faith which they are trying to support fervently. Their biggest problem politically, then, is how they can compromise with these scientific rebels. We need to know that contradictions and compromises profoundly impact contemporary Japan.

Not able to explain the reasons for faith, Japanese people are not irreligious—Japanese are people without anxieties

I have already stated that ultranationalism is the faith and religion of our citizens. However, please do not ask why people are following this type of ideology. (It seems that most Westerners generally would raise this kind of question.) It is important to note here that this is already our nation's faith; thus, it is not a conclusion but rather the assumed premise for a deduction. We can give an account of that faith and the results of its history, but we cannot prove anything at all, whether inductively or deductively, about why we consider nationalism superior to individualism.

If ultranationalism is the common faith and religion of Japanese people, many already have a form of religion. Westerners hear many educated Japanese gentlemen declare openly that they are completely unreligious and have said that they think that is quite strange. However, doubt no more! Not religious (*mushūkyō*) means only not believing in Confucianism and Christianity. These men are generally believers in the state religion—or at least, no one can admit openly to not being a devotee of the state religion.

Moreover, modern Japanese people do not experience intense religious anxieties, even though we live in an age of turmoil that should cause anxiety, and particularly religious anxiety. This is because the majority are firm believers in the state religion. For them, the purpose of human life lies in the state, and they take it as their ideal to live and die for the state. Therefore, even though countless adult men died in the two great wars—the Sino-Japanese war and the Russo-Japanese war—we Japanese did not and could not fall victim to anguish and skepticism. From the outset, a few skeptical and worried voices complained; however, these all belonged to young people who were not yet believers in the state religion. They will also be destined to become devotees of the state religion.

Nationalism has already become religion for the Japanese people. Let us look, therefore, at the people who gave their lives to nationalism. After their deaths, they were all worshipped as *kami*. Yasukuni shrine became one of those places of worship. What is more, one of my predecessors in my home village, master Yoshida Shōin,[15] was worshipped as a *kami* for this reason, as is Duke Itō Hirobumi[16] also coming to be.

The plus and minus of nationalism—a strong state and a weak individual

I already regard nationalism as the Japanese people's religion, and in such a public essay I prefer not to make a value judgment, which would be based on my own standards, against this religion. Considering the current situation, I should be prudent enough to avoid making a value judgement, and for that reason I have refrained from doing so by recounting only the facts, intending that any commentary be entirely omitted. However, if readers kindly permit, I would like to add just a few comments.

In my opinion, this nationalism is the quintessence of our country Japan. The ability to make this poor small country into a strong country is entirely the reward of this nationalism. Look at ants; other than our own, no other society has reached the high level of their civilization. However, this is completely due to their society's extreme nationalism. If we compare individuals to individuals, we Japanese cannot match Westerners at all in wealth, knowledge, or even in physical strength. But do we not create the Japanese state by combining all of these? The spirit of that nationalism allows us to make a really great and strong state a reality.

Thus, I will keep longing for the healthy development of this nationalism in the future. However, I am against all editorials, movements, policies, or systems that try to offer unnecessarily harmful praise of this nationalism as a trait of the Japanese people. Because I ardently hope to guide this nationalism in the right direction, I ardently oppose those who want to have it fall prey to evil ways. However, in the present circumstances, I do not want to risk subjecting this argument to deeply serious misunderstandings. For that reason, I will stop with these comments and will postpone my further remarks to a later date.

As I have already stated, except for humans, ants have developed the highest level of civilization of any living creature. (Cf. another essay of mine *The Division of Labor and Sharing Pleasure*.[17]) However, ants as individual organisms are very small and weak. If circumstances made animals like lions and tigers adopt the same social system as ants, imagine how much more frightening they would be. Japan as a country is very strong, but the Japanese are certainly weak. My heart's desire is to see us assimilate Western individualism—it is not necessary to be hostile toward it, and it will help give the Japanese people a double advantage. In my view, in order to assimilate that individualism (and in order to support my argument here) it would be valuable to argue about the type of policy we should adopt. But tonight it's a little past one in the morning, so, given the late hour, shall I postpone finishing my argument to a later date? (The above article is from February 10, 1911 (Meiji 44).)

(Completed Meiji 44 (1911) February 14, and published in *Chūōkōron*)

[Postscript omitted]

87

Notes

1 Gail Lee Bernstein, *Japanese Marxist: A Portrait of Kawakami Hajime 1879–1946* (Cambridge, MA: Harvard University Press, 1976), 73.
2 Yūshi Itō, "Kawakami Hajime and Inoue Tetsujirō's Conflicting Views of Religion and State," in *Japan in Crisis: Essays on Taishō Democracy,* eds., Bernard Silberman and H.D. Harootunian (New York: Routledge, 1974), 182.
3 Japanese monk (1143–1179) of the Ninnaji Buddhist temple in Kyoto and member of the Minamoto clan who took part in the plot to overthrow Taira Kiyomori and whose story is found in the *Heike monogatari.* Shishigatani was the mountain villa where the conspirators made their plans. Shunkan was exiled for his role.
4 Hōnen (1133–1212) is the famous founder of the Pure Land school (Jōdoshū). At thirteen, he left Mount Hiei, the center of the Tendai School, to seek universal religious salvation. He eventually found the key in the Pure Land teachings, which he studied in a hermitage in the Kurodani valley outside Kyoto.
5 This was the Russo-Japanese War where Japan prevailed over Czarist Russia for power over Manchuria and Korea.
6 Kawakami is referring to the traditional patriarchal multigenerational household system (*ie*).
7 Credit unions and voluntary mutual-aid confraternities designed to help farmers financially manage their long-term resources and budgeting to stave off misfortunes advocated by the Tokugawa era agronomist Ninomiya Sontoku (1787–1856).
8 Kawakami's point here is similar to Minobe Tatsukichi's controversial interpretation of the monarchy, which posited the emperor as merely an organ of the state.
9 She was a famous entertainer, vaudeville singer, and comedian in the early twentieth century (1887–1963).
10 Satō Nobuhiro (1769–1850) was a political economist of the late Tokugawa period and an early advocate of Westernization for economic and military expansion so that Japan could contend with the threat posed by Western powers.
11 Georges-Louis Leclerc, Comte de Buffon (1707–88) was a French naturalist whose thirty-six volume work established the field of natural history.
12 Jean-Baptiste Lamarck (1744–1829) was a French naturalist and early proponent of natural evolution best known for his theory of adaptation or the inheritance of acquired characteristics as proposed in his 1809 work, *Philosophie Zoologique.*
13 Georges Cuvier (1769–1832) was a renowned French scientist specializing in comparative anatomy and paleontology who strongly opposed Lamarckism, favoring a theory that successive creations follow catastrophic events rather than evolutionism.
14 Kawakami is referring here to the fact that scholars at Japanese public universities at the time were in fact serving as government officials.
15 Yoshida Shōin (1830–59) was a famous ex-samurai and intellectual and political activist who helped spur the Meiji Restoration. He is enshrined at two *Shōin jinja,* one at his grave in Tokyo, and the other his birthplace in Hagi, Yamaguchi Prefecture.
16 Itō Hirobumi (1841–1909) was a former prime minister of Japan and elder statesman who played a crucial political role in the early Meiji state, including the drafting of its key political document, the Meiji Constitution.
17 Published in 1911 in a book called *Keizai to jinsei.*

17

YANAGITA KUNIO
My view of Shinto
(1918)

Yanagita Kunio (1875–1962) was the famous scholar credited with founding folklore studies (*minzokugaku*) in Japan. Born in 1875 in Hyōgo Prefecture, he was the sixth son of Matsuoka Misao, a physician who also followed the Hirata school of national learning before retiring to become a Shinto priest. At twelve, Yanagita traveled to Kantō to live with his older brothers, eventually matriculating to Tokyo Imperial University, graduating from the Department of Politics of its prestigious Faculty of Law in 1900.

In the early years, Yanagita's career trajectory lay working as a bureaucrat in the Ministry of Agriculture and Commerce, which reflected his passion for social reform for impoverished farmers whose plight had so moved him in his childhood. In the years that followed, Yanagita occupied a number of important civil posts: in 1902, councilor of the Legislation Bureau; in 1908, secretary of the Imperial Household Office; and, in 1914, secretary general of the House of Peers until resigning in 1919. He resigned in order to devote himself fulltime to his ongoing literary and scholarly pursuits, and while working as an editor of the *Asahi shinbun* until 1930, his scholarly output was prodigious, amounting to over 130 volumes of material by his death in 1962.

Yanagita displayed great literary talent as well as being a seminal figure in folklore studies. In his methods of research, Yanagita was influenced by intellectual currents outside Japan, being widely read in Western literature and, in particular, the classic Western works in anthropology and folklore that relied on the comparative method such as J.G. Frazer's *The Golden Bough* (1890) and E.B. Tylor's *Primitive Culture* (1871).[1]

Yanagita believed the real faith of the Japanese was to be found in the study of the folklore and folkways of the "*jōmin*," his term for ordinary people. In his life's work, his abiding interest lay in the everyday life of the Japanese people.

Yanagita is perhaps best known for his famous short collection of local legends and folktales, *The Tales of Tōno* (1910). However, the writings that are most directly connected to Shinto date from later in Yanagita's life. These include *Shintō to minzokugaku* (Shinto and Folklore Studies, 1943), *Nihon no matsuri* (Japanese Festivals, 1942), and *Senzo no hanashi* (Stories of Our Ancestors, 1946).

The following short essay, "My view of Shinto" ("Shintō shiken")—only nearly the first half of the whole essay is included here—dating from much earlier (1918), outlines his view that folklore reveals a Shinto that exists in Japanese village life outside the doctrinal and theological forms of Shinto that have appeared over time. In other studies, Yanagita called this a common, local, and indigenous form of faith (*koyū shinkō*) based upon ancestor worship at village shrines and local festivals. Because this was so deeply connected to family and local communities, it was a source for the spiritual unification of the Japanese people.

Yanagita never directly challenges the emperor system that lay at the heart of Taishō-Shōwa national polity, but he is highly critical of the state's policies toward local shrines. Particularly egregious for him was the shrine merger plan from 1906 onwards, which recognized only one shrine per village as legitimate, while abolishing and merging thousands of unranked village shrines. Yanagita is also critical of the state's officially sanctioned definition of Shinto as non-religious in character. The state-supported national morality cult, he argued, was a fabrication developed by national learning scholars and state officials who had ignored the authentic ancient religion of Shinto based in local villages. As one biographer, Kawada Minoru, has argued, Yanagita's concern, echoed in this essay, is over Japan's rapid modernization and industrialization. With the erosion of the traditional village-centered lifestyle of Japan's agrarian communities, modern Japan was losing the ancient village centered core of spiritual beliefs and practices that Yanagita found so central to Japanese identity.[2]

MY VIEW OF SHINTO
(1918)

I would like to offer a few opinions about how what we now call Shinto has a much more superficial connection with ordinary people's lives than you might imagine. Needless to say, given my perhaps superficial reading of the materials, what I say may be off-base, so please feel free to correct any mistakes I have made as you see fit.

What has made a most singular impression on me recently was the very spirited debate that took place this spring in our neighbor China's national assembly over the pros and cons of making Confucianism its state religion (*kokkyō*). When I visited Tsinghua University in Peking in May, there were several Confucian banners in the lecture hall that had been pushed into the corner without yet being put away. It spoke volumes about the course of the country's political debates. From a purely dispassionate point of view, I think that using the teachings of Confucius, which are an organized set of morals, as a national religion illustrates China's tendency of either affecting a European manner or a failure of reason.

By contrast, in Japan we have deliberately left the big issue of "whether shrine reverence is a religion" unresolved for the last thirty or forty years. I am saying this with the full knowledge that people at the Home Ministry have implied that it has not been left unresolved at all and that offering reverence at shrines is not a religion. If that is true, however, who then accepts the petitions, distributes charms and talismans, receives offerings, and hears the prayers of the priests and parishioners? While examples abound in any age where logic alone cannot make sense of things, I nonetheless think that facts speak for themselves. When the outcome of the Russo-Japanese War was uncertain, the only way villagers who had sent their young to the battlefield could alleviate their fear was by facing their local *kami* and offering prayers for the defeat of the enemy before their tutelary shrines. District heads and other conscientious government officials who attended these services took the lead and deeply moved people's hearts. There were also numerous examples of loving mothers, virtuous wives, and the like who frequently fasted, did water purification rites, and performed the austerity of going to a shrine one hundred times. These acts of faith were counted retrospectively among the examples of good and beneficial deeds done in wartime. Taking such things into account, I think there is little support to conclude that shrines are just places to show respect to the ancestors or great men. And, however much shrine officials may view shrines as places for veneration, this is simply not what ordinary people believe. Although it is true that the cult of worshipping snakes and foxes has almost disappeared nowadays, I think it is nonetheless dangerous academically to conclude that the shrine cult is, therefore, all about the veneration of people who lived at a certain period.

However, from my perspective, the situation in Japan is also a result of a state religion problem common to many East Asian countries. While its specific effects (both positive and negative) may be different, I think the cause of the present situation in Japan resembles our neighboring country of China. In Japan, to say that the cult of the great shrines to our imperial ancestors is the same as acts of faith at Buddhist temples or at Christian chapels contradicts great principles dating from the Restoration. However, if the government had tried to make the shrine cult Japan's state religion, establishing equal treaties with European countries that did not know much about Japan would have been difficult. I think there was no other way than to treat shrines as something completely different from religion. It is difficult to freely criticize this development because it involves people who are still alive today. However, if we disregard the historical origins of this particular policy and base our reflections on villagers' attitudes toward their own tutelary shrines, it is clear that the official view of shrines today makes absolutely no sense. This is why even those who subscribe to these beliefs about shrines try not to reflect upon it too deeply; there is an inclination to try to stop the debate at a certain point. I believe, however, that allowing this issue to remain unresolved will cause problems over the long term.

In June 1913, the Home Ministry kept the Bureau of Shrines (Jinjakyoku) under its own purview and transferred just the Bureau of Religion (Shūkyōkyoku) to the Ministry of Education. The Bureau of Religion ended up having jurisdiction over each of what are now called the Shinto sects along with Buddhism and Christianity, but the affairs of all shrines above unranked shrines (*mukakusha*) came under the supervision of the Bureau of Shrines. Considered in the cool light of reason, this is an unusual phenomenon. If official priests at any given shrine have the deepest piety and, accordingly, increase their deity's prestige and promote its worship so that even people from outside the locality are attracted, in this case, the priests' actions would theoretically fall under the purview of the Ministry of Education. This would be because they have done something above and beyond their ordinary duties. Indeed, if you visit Izumo shrine, you will see that this is more than just theoretical. The two baronial families, the Senge and the Kitajima, have established two Shinto sects in the small locale of Kizuki. These are known respectively as the Taisha (or Izumo Ōyashiro-kyōkai) sect and the Izumo sect. In addition, the Senge family head serves as the shrine's priest.[3]

That is to say, he serves as the head of one of these Shinto sects while having the status as shrine priest. However, while a learned person can probably understand the distinction, can local people who come there for daily worship do so? Can they really distinguish between shrine worship that occurs before eleven in the morning and the commencement of Shinto sectarian religious activities after eleven? Likewise, at great shrines such as Fushimi Inari, Kotohira in Sanuki, Tenjin at Dazaifu, Usa Hachiman, Nishinomiya of Settsu, it is difficult to split priests' duties because for hundreds of years they have actively proselytized their faith beyond their local shrines.

No matter what new Shinto sects there are, they all ultimately preach worshipping the *kami*. So, even the Shinto that an old woman began in the rice fields like Tenrikyō, also had to construct a shrine building afterwards. There are no distinctions apparent even in their respective forms of service, so I think that drawing lines between what are so deeply intertwined—between shrines and Shinto, for example, or between the administration of the Bureau of Shrines and the Bureau of Religion—is very artificial. Sometime in the autumn of last year, as I recall, the son of the Senge lineage published a magazine in Kizuki called, *Shintoizumu (Shintoism)*, which was written in *katakana*. Even I was initially more than a little surprised by this. However, upon reflection I realized that this word "Shintoism" was used early on by foreigners. It is not at all a term that entertains the distinction instituted by the present government. If it were only foreigners who made a definition differing at present from Japan's policy, then I think it would be fine at this point to ignore it. But there are no good introductory works written by Japanese scholars, so there is a possibility, I fear, that it might be relatively easy for Japanese students, seeking the gist of the subject, to focus their studies of Japan's Shinto by only using the works of Aston and Griffis. This is problematic, and makes you wonder what the outcome will be, but that is the situation at present.

The Shinto of the Bureau of Religion [that is sect Shinto] is early modern—I do not care how you take this at all—and additionally, I think it is hard to accept that, even today, scholarship has not clarified the character of our village and provincial shrines; since the beginning of the nation, these places of worship have helped to preserve the most important ties to the lives of the people. It is undeniable that that lack of clarity will become increasingly problematic as time goes by. I want you to please kindly attend to this point. It may be true that religions like Japan's, with as many as eight million gods, are considered inferior in the eyes of Western missionaries and their books on the study of religion. But we should be careful before adopting views like this. Even for the Japanese, it seems, those who try to relegate so-called Shinto under the jurisdiction of the Bureau of Religion have their own quiet misgivings. Given that shrines have no systematic doctrines, many regional differences in beliefs, and offer no unity on a national level, some might possibly have a good reason, even if it is not apparently clear, in treating only sectarian Shinto as a religion, given that it has what shrines lack.

My response is as follows. The beliefs of any religion become dogmatized and systematized only after a certain period of time. While religions that appear systematically organized from the very beginning might exist in Japan, they do not exist in other countries. It is something that occurs later after a first gathering of believers takes place. So, in such cases, both Buddhism and Christianity exerted a great amount of power to rid themselves of heterodox views when they had their assemblies and councils. Thus, they had to, in effect, discard many old things in order to unify themselves. This does not just occur in the history of ancient and distant foreign countries but even in Japan, if you look at the history of Honganji. This temple's most serious undertaking was to defeat what is known as the Pure Land heresy (*ianjin*).[4] My understanding may be limited, but I think that it is extremely doubtful that what the head temple now accepts as orthodoxy remained unchanged for five to six hundred years while those on the *ianjin* side of the controversy made heretical statements that were mostly later fabrications. It is much more likely that they finally achieved unity by drawing on the wisdom of later generations and also by using power other than religion. It suggests that unification is not necessarily that wonderful or valuable. To go a bit further, I not only think that such regional differences in shrine worship have no direct bearing on whether shrines are religious but also that these so-called differences are not as extreme as imagined. For example, to the best of our knowledge, not one single shrine festival or ritual existing today is actually unique or distinctive to a single place. You will most definitely find examples of somewhat similar things elsewhere. So, the attempt of some trying to argue that shrine worship is not a religion is quite unconvincing, even when they shed light on it through the so-called discipline of religious studies.

If I may be so bold, what seems lacking specifically in Japanese religions is the power of hierarchy. However, as you are all quite well aware, in early modern times, it was the

Yoshida family in Kyoto and, before that, the Council of Divinities who extended their control to some degree throughout the country. And, with all due respect, this has always had the imperial household in the background. From ancient times right up to the present day, the imperial household has provided the model for *kami* rituals throughout the country. Whether we look at large court rituals [of the recent enthronement] or everyday rituals contained in the regulations for imperial household rites, many of these go beyond ancestor worship or the veneration of great people. For example, the rite of spirit pacification (*chinkonsai*) conducted before the New Tasting Festival (Niinamesai) is more than just an event for pacifying the spirits. Before the rite takes place, they build a shrine fence enclosure for worship (*kamigaki*) and welcome the deities[5] who have descended from heaven. Also in the divination ceremonies for the divine rice fields (*saiden*), the deities are first implored ritually to descend to the earth; at the end of the rite, they are asked to once again ascend to heaven. At the risk of piling on examples, many of these imperial household rites have become models for divine rites for the gods throughout the country. Because of the great number of *kami* and the room that remains for further research, it may appear today that there is no unity—and yet I believe that even this should not encourage people to ignore the ancient faith of the nation.

From a different angle, it is also a big mistake to regard today's so-called Shinto [that is, sect Shinto] as encompassing the religious side of shrine worship. Granted, this is a fairly common explanation across all sects of Shinto. However, if you try to analyze the gist of this argument, the material that is there is a real mishmash. It is difficult to consider it rooted in native Japanese thought unless you are first of all one of the parties who stubbornly believe in your sect's teaching. The word Shinto, of course, existed from extremely ancient times. But its meaning seems to have changed remarkably over time. The first use of this term was close to what we think it must mean. Yet, it is certainly a fact that its usage was naive. Those who have tried to explain it to some degree systematically and academically, even if they doubt arguments that it comes from Saichō or Kūkai, are still convinced that it initially originated from Esoteric Buddhist (*mikkyō*) thought on mandalas. No matter what nation it entered, this school of Buddhism had enormous power to accept and assimilate existing local faiths. Before too long, Japanese *kami* became transformed into Buddhist divinities. Although the blessings our ancestors received from Buddhism are considerable, we disapprove of the matter of treating Japanese gods as heavenly Buddhist divinities. Our intellectually inferior ancestors were also spineless, and, besides that, mandala doctrines had a formidable assimilative power, and, no matter what the *kami*, these deities soon became part of the lower Buddhist pantheon of guardian deities.

One example of this is Wakasa's two deities, Wakasahiko and Wakasahime. They once gave oracles to their priests who had served them for generations, asking for a taste of the Buddhist law since they wanted to quickly escape their suffering along the *kami* way as related in the *Ruijū kokushi*,[6] Priests often recited scriptures before the *kami* on festival days, calling it a blessing of the Dharma (*hōraku*) or a taste of the Dharma (*hōmi*). In many instances, the *kami* were considered to be guardians of the Dharma. In other words, they were venerated as powerful beings of the spirit world who protected the teachings of Buddhism. Their status was higher than that of the monks, but not as high as that of the buddhas. They were placed in the middle between monks and buddhas. I think that this belief that the native *kami* wanted blessings and a taste of the Dharma and that they wanted to be freed from the suffering of the way of the *kami* spread broadly among ordinary people, and this ultimately caused Buddhist priests to hold Buddhist ceremonies at shrines. The natural result of this was that people tried to use Buddhist teachings to explain the virtues of the *kami*. In other words, this is the origin of the theory known as *honji suijaku* ("original substance, manifest traces").

Since this is still being debated in various arenas, I can never conclude this for certain, but I think that Sannō Ichijitsu Shinto is probably the oldest and most influential form of what we mean by Shinto today. However, I think that it was limited to the *kami* of the Hakurei Hie lineage, and there were definitely other forms of Shinto opposed to it. Nara had the Shinto of the monks of Kōfukuji, which was connected to Kasuga Shrine, and, at Kōya, there was the Shinto of the Kōya monks which had Ama no Myōjin as their object of worship. (While I could go into details distinguishing each one, I will refrain from doing so here.) Ise had the status to be the first to oppose these forms of Shinto originating from Buddhism and to stand up against them. But the tide of the times proved irresistible; over a long period, things drifted along with the general trend of *honji suijaku* thought, and people say that even at Ise, temples were built when the *kami* expressed a desire for them, and these have remained until quite recently. Some later scholars, such as Watarai Nobuyoshi,[7] were privately disconsolate about it. However, a closer look reveals that remarkably, scholars like him were all influenced by Buddhist teachings. As far as we can see, the school of Yamazaki Ansai, for example, reacted against the trend.[8] There were various branches of Shinto at the beginning of the Tokugawa period, but they were under the influence of the beliefs of Onmyō practitioners if they were not associated with the Shingon Buddhist lineage. Under the circumstances, I think that of these, Ansai's school, insofar that their argument was somewhat pure, exemplified one form of opposition to Buddhism. They were exasperated with Shinto being explained Buddhistically. The Yoshida school of Shinto also was extensively influenced by external elements, although they called themselves Sōgen Shinto,[9] which they always explained as something unique to Japan but whose thought and style contained many impurities. Fortunately, we do not do scholarship as a whimsical pastime and do not have extra energy to expend on this kind of triviality.

The timing was fortuitous, as public sentiment turned against the half-hearted, formalistic, and threadbare arguments which supported the harmony of Shinto, Buddhism, and Confucianism. It happened for the first time through the efforts of the national learning scholars known as the four great men,[10] which came to fruition in the work of Hirata Atsutane.[11] While this trend had gradually developed since Kada Azumamaro, it was argued systematically for the first time in Hirata's books. Hirata Shinto not only removed as many foreign elements as possible but took a very aggressive attitude towards foreign influences, saying that the Indian gods were Ōnamuchi[12] and Sukunabikona,[13] and that the Chinese deity, Taitsu, was also equivalent to Takamimusubi no Mikoto. Thus, the Hirata school was pleased by those who argued for the unity of the world however baseless their arguments. This school of scholars selected only ancient ideas found in books before the *Engishiki* and expended great effort to try to establish a new variety of Shinto. Of course, they probably deserve the notoriety they have today; in the final analysis, however, they were part of a reactionary movement against the muddled Shinto theories of the Tokugawa period that occurred after Ansai. Going one step further, they fell into the same errors as many other forms of Shinto, both ancient and modern. They privileged old writings and other extraneous materials and made light of genuine folk beliefs, and they did not adequately represent the actual thinking about the *kami* found in the villages. Therefore, I find it especially difficult to think of this school as the only true Shinto. I think this is where their work differs remarkably from Christian theology, for example, of Mary and the saints. This was the case not only for Ansai's school but for the many Shintoists in Osaka and Edo who always denounced ordinary shrine priests and in turn were resented by these priests as enemies. But, occasionally, some among these shrine priests also came knocking at the door of the Shintoists to learn their doctrines. These were ambitious priests, and their studiousness brought them a warm welcome into one Shinto school or another. However, this also benefited them as well, much like those monks who had converted from the Zen and Tendai schools and were therefore ranked among the wise and virtuous prelates in True Pure Land Buddhism. This also means that those who retrace the history by using documents about disputes between scholars and non-scholars find that these arguments typically end with the defeat of the non-scholars. It seems that these Shinto scholars suffocated a whole generation by espousing an unnatural new theory rather than trying to represent the faith that was actually found in Japan's shrines. As a result, the various forms of Shinto that had competed so intensely together disappeared at the onset of the new era, scarcely leaving any traces. No one read their books even though they remained on the shelves. And although the Hirata school of Shinto eventually prevailed, being influential within the Council of Divinities in Meiji (or the Shinto associated with Kokugakuin), it is quite possible that even this well-established school of today could disappear at some point in the future. It is built upon a bureaucratic appointment system for priests (*shinkan kansen*)[14] that is, in short, artificial. Other competitors have appeared within Shinto, such as Tenrikyō, which worships a deity not written about in the ancient books, and Konkōkyō, which has Konjin as its sole deity for worship. These would really be reluctant to accept the Hirata school's control. There are several faiths other than these that are growing in strength and already have begun to call into question the Hirata school's special supremacy.

Trying to explain folk deities by means of writings such as the "Age of the Gods" section of the *Nihonshoki,* the *Kojiki,* and *Kujiki* did not necessarily originate in what we call the Hirata school. It appears that it was historically the policy to say that the names of all the enshrined *kami* should be mentioned at least once in the classics. This is exemplified in the *Jinmeichō kōshō* or in the *Jingi hōten*[15] of Watarai Nobuyoshi[16] in Owari Province and also by priests affiliated with the Yoshida house in Kyoto who traveled throughout the provinces explaining to people that their local *kami* were such and such a divinity. In fact, as early on as the *Jinmeichō* (Roster of Deity Names) in the *Engishiki,* if an enshrined deity was unknown, only the place as such and such a divinity of such and such a place would be mentioned. On the other hand, if a name bore even a faint resemblance to one in the roster, the deity enshrined there was immediately included in the family tree of the *kami* as such and such a deity and such and such a child of the *kami.* This had been a common practice from the time even before the *Jingi hōten.* However, many of these forced sophistries came about simply because scholars of old did not know any better. It is just like presuming that, because a certain Japanese word resembles a certain Greek word, the Japanese are the descendants of the Persians [who must have transmitted it]. *Kami* were identified with deities from the "Age of the Gods" section due to some faint resemblance since those not found in the ancient histories were treated with disrespect. Similarly, many of the Hirata school were scholars, and, because many were skilled in reading ancient texts, they frequently corrected past mistakes in their study of old documents. They excelled in belittling those who made silly claims, which allowed them gradually to perfect their way of explaining things. On this point, too, they deserve a measure of respect. Their achievement was such that they made improvements in their scholastic methods and in the materials for academic study. The explanation that all Japanese *kami,* whether they were enshrined under the shade of a pine tree on a solitary island or on top of a rock deep within the mountains, were all to be venerated and respected as great figures from the age of the gods both pleased the conservative nationalists and helped carry out the work of the Meiji Restoration—even if no one pragmatically asked whether it was really true or not academically. One could say the Hirata school was definitely successful in defining the truth at one level.

However, when we note this Shinto school's achievements, we must also inquire into its scholarly offenses as well. From our viewpoint, what we call the Hirata school of Shinto based itself on two very dangerous assumptions. The first of these assumptions is that until the time of the *Engishiki*, Japanese Shinto had not changed for over fifteen hundred years. The second is that after that time, there has been extreme confusion for eight to nine hundred years. Hirata Shinto bases its views on these two assumptions. The custom of worshipping *kami* in buildings—that is to say, in today's shrines, gradually became more popular from around the Nara period. There is no trouble inferring this even from the plain lines of the *Rikkokushi*. Nevertheless, the Hirata school considers that the shrines of the *kami* in the *Engishiki* worshipped chiefly *kami* found within the "Age of the Gods" section of the chronicle literature, and they understood that around Enchō 5 (927) people served the *kami* by thinking of them just as they appeared in the *Kojiki* and *Nihongi*. The Hirata school assumed that, up to that point, people did not think about *kami* unless they had appeared more than once in the myths, and, at the same time, they seemed to have believed that for eight to nine hundred years—from the *Engishiki* until today—ordinary shrine parishioners were influenced by Buddhist and Confucian books they could not read. So, for them, ordinary shrine parishioners had almost forgotten the original meaning and were, in fact, practicing newly imported beliefs and rituals that had been substituted for the originals.

Actually, my father was a priest who was a middle-aged convert [to Hirata Shinto]. As he was a devoted follower of ancient learning (*kogaku*), at a young age, I was forced to listen to plenty of talk about how we absolutely had to reform our foreign ways and the ways of life introduced later on in our history. But as I later learned, it is indeed a fact that foreign influences have swept over Japan, and perhaps we must consider that this peaked far before even the *Engishiki* or in the period prior even to the compilation of the *Nihonshoki*. If it was the case that Kyoto's civilization was carried even to distant provinces by the work of government officials who were dispatched to their new provincial posts, then we must regard its spread and transmission as slower and narrower in scope in the era after the *Engishiki*. This was when power had become decentralized with provincial officials, in name only, not leaving Kyoto to go into the hinterlands. Therefore, we should doubt any assumption that foreign influence was particularly strong in the times after the *Engishiki*. Even regarding the second point about the ways of life that were introduced later in Japan, the new school of Shinto has neglected two types of preliminary research that ought to be done. One is whether folk customs really can be influenced by the scholarship of older times that was knowledge without a complete means of dissemination. The other is research into whether really extremely little or a lot can be discovered in the postmedieval ideas that have persisted in today's local annual events and oral traditions that have their original or common form in the ancient records.

I think that it is quite dishonest that our predecessors neglected this but still concluded that folk customs were too deeply contaminated by foreign ideas for posterity. However, having said that, even if this has not been fully studied in Japan, the first subject is an issue that can be contemplated in any country of this day and age; therefore, we can all learn from others' examples. For example, there is extensive evidence that earlier paganism before Christianity has survived to the present day. By incorporating various rationales, customs, and thought patterns from pre-Christian pagan times, Christianity has preserved older elements. It is therefore generally recognized that folk customs are very resilient; this phenomenon is not at all unique to just one country or to Christian Europe. This being the case, I think nothing prevents us from adopting some, if not all of these conclusions and explanations. On the other hand, regarding the second subject, it is unfortunate that before now no one has tried to study the origins of early modern thought in Japan. Here the person to whom I have to express my feelings of deep respect is Ban Nobutomo.[17] Ban became famous around the same time as Hirata but, while immersed in the same scholarly traditions, nevertheless had a different attitude toward research. He preferred to collect materials for study rather than to draw firm conclusions, with an attitude that can be described as, "I do not understand the reason for it, but here is a fact that is inexplicable," or "this point perhaps goes like this, but I cannot say for sure." Ban's approach was possible because his work did not help spread the new faith and he was therefore not a Shintoist as we understand that term today. Like the Shintoists who followed Ansai, those who through the force of their own strong wills tried to make people believe in their own new doctrines believed that success was not achieved if you deliberate and treat materials contrary to your viewpoint as important in the way that Ban did. Therefore, even those rare scholars from the Hirata lineage who paid careful attention to folk traditions would immediately conclude that something was a fabrication of medieval Buddhism or probably some misunderstanding of the villagers when they came up against materials that clashed even a little with Hirata school doctrine. They typically dismissed other views with phrases such as "Doubtless they were pretending to be clever as per usual" and tossed these folk traditions aside as though they were worthless. Although many of these legends and customs were forgotten, nonetheless, thanks to the efforts of influential scholars like Nobutomo and Kurokawa Harumura[18] among others, some of these materials collected locally prior to the beginning of the Meiji period remain in the archives of Shintoists from the latter half of the Edo period. While some have vanished and some have been greatly altered, even just the small number that have been preserved offer good evidence for those asserting that today's faith has acquired its original form from ancient times and that it is not a fabrication from later influences. For example, I think that the custom of offering things like uncooked rice, raw fish, and radishes (which were more a nuisance than anything else for the recipients) clearly began in the early Meiji period. Nonetheless, after fifty years, people will really believe it could be an ancient custom. In such a case, at the very least, there should be a long debate about it that musters lots of different evidence to convince people that it was not the ancient custom. At this point, however, there is fortunately much evidence and many documents in the archives mentioned above that tell us that, from ancient times until recently, the special Japanese way of doing things has always been to offer cooked food to the *kami*.

Notes

1 Mori Kōichi, "Yanagita Kunio: An Interpretative Study," *Japanese Journal of Religious Studies* 7 (June–September, 1980): 93–99.

2 Minoru Kawada, *The Origin of Ethnography in Japan: Yanagita Kunio and His Times,* trans. Toshiko Kishida-Ellis (New York: Kegan Paul, 1993), 2–44.

3 Kitajima Naganori (1834–93) used to be a head of Izumo Taisha until 1873, together with Senge Takatomi. In 1873, only the Senge was appointed as the head of Izumo Taisha. In 1882, Kitajima established Izumo Kitajima kyōkai, under the administration of Shintō Jimukyoku (one branch of sect Shinto), and Izumo Kitajima kyōkai was renamed as Shinto Izumo kyōkai in 1883.

4 Hongan-ji is a famous True Pure Land (Jōdo Shinshū) Buddhist temple in Kyoto that faced competition from other temples that claimed to preserve the true teachings of the founder, Shinran. Abbots of the temple such as Kakunyo and Rennyo in the fourteenth and fifteenth centuries were notable for

their successful struggles against what they saw as these temples' distortions of Shinran's teachings. See Mark Blum and Shin'ya Yasutomi, eds., *Rennyo and the Roots of Modern Japanese Buddhism* (Oxford University Press, 2005), 52.

5 Literally the one and eight deities. The *hasshin* were the eight protective deities of the imperial family. The Shrine to the Eight Deities (Hasshinden), in ancient times, was located in the Western hall of the Jingikan. The additional deity is called Ōnaobinokami.

6 *Assorted National Histories* edited by Sugawara Michizane was an early Heian period compendium containing entries from the six national histories (including the *Nihonshoki*). Originally in 200 volumes, it was intended as a practical sourcebook on court procedures and precedents. See Robert Borgon, *Sugawara No Michizane and the Early Heian Court* (Cambridge: Harvard University Press, 1986), 220.

7 Watarai Nobuyoshi was a Shinto scholar of the early Tokugawa period.

8 He was an early Tokugawa period scholar of Confucianism and Shinto (1618–82). Learning the esoteric teachings of Ise and Yoshida Shinto, Ansai founded his own branch of Shinto, Suika Shinto, named after his own shrine where he worshipped his own spirit. Influenced by Neo-Confucian teachings, he identified the *kami* with Principle (*ri*), the key cosmic and ethical way inherent in all things including humankind, and tried to systematize the Shinto teachings of his day with Neo-Confucian thought. The disciple groups to which Yanagita refers are Hoshina Masayuki and others from the Aizu Domain, hereditary priestly shrine families from the Kyoto area, and others. See Inoue Nobutaka, *Shinto—A Short History,* trans. by Mark Teeuwen and John Breen (London: RoutledgeCurzon, 2003), 132–38.

9 This is also referred to as Yuiitsu Shinto and Yoshida Shinto.

10 They are also called the four great national learning scholars (*kokugaku no shidaijin*); alongside Hirata, they are Kada (no) Azumamaro (1669–1736), Kamo no Mabuchi, and Motoori Norinaga.

11 Hirata Atsutane (1776–1843) was a famous national learning scholar and self-declared disciple of Motoori Norinaga. Author of several influential studies on ancient Japanese traditions and Shinto, including works such as *Kodō taii* (True Meaning of the Ancient Way), *Zoku Shintō taii* (True Meaning of Common Shinto), and *Tenchō mukyūreki* (Chronicle of the Perpetual Rule of the Emperor), a work published in 1841 that incurred the wrath of the Tokugawa *bakufu.* See *Encyclopedia of Shinto,* Vol. 3, ed. by Norman Havens (Kokugakuin University, Institute for Japanese Culture and Classics, 2006), 140–41.

12 Another name for the deity Ōkuninushi no Mikoto.

13 This deity is described as one of the three *kami* of creation (*zōka sanshin*) in the *Kojiki.*

14 Before the Meiji restoration, shrine priests gained their posts primarily through hereditary succession. This was banned by the government in 1871 and replaced with a government system of appointing priests to government-administered shrines and assigning them a requisite priestly rank.

15 Written in 1646 by Tokugawa Yoshinao, feudal lord of Nagoya and the ninth son of Tokugawa Ieyasu who excelled in Confucian studies, this is a nine-volume work.

16 Watarai Nobuyoshi (1615–90) was a Shinto scholar of the early Tokugawa period from the noted Watarai priestly family, hereditary officiants in charge of the outer shrine at Ise Jingū. His works largely revived the fortunes of the Watarai school. His eight-volume work is a historical study of the Register of Deities in the *Engishiki.*

17 Ban Nobutomo (1773–1846) was a national learning scholar who was a posthumous disciple of Motoori Norinaga and famous for his historical scholarship and intellectual integrity. Ranked with Hirata as one of the great national learning scholars after Norinaga, his work often stood in direct conflict with Hirata's.

18 Kurokawa Harumura (1799–1866), a national learning scholar and philologist of the late Tokugawa period.

18

KATŌ GENCHI

Shinto, a religion of the theanthropic type, as distinguished from a religion of the theocratic type and Shinto as a national religion, not entirely devoid of a universal aspect and remarkably tolerant
(1935)

Katō Genchi (1873–1965) was a major Shinto scholar of the Taishō and early Shōwa periods who was deeply interested in the comparative "science" of religion. Born in 1873 to a True Pure Land family ministering Shōnen-ji temple in Asakusa in Tokyo, he forsook the priestly life to attend Tokyo Imperial University, where he learned the newly imported Western discipline of the science of religion. He was appointed as a professor of English at the Military Academy in Tokyo in 1906, and in that same year he began to lecture widely in Shinto and comparative religions at Tokyo Imperial University. When the university established a Chair of Shinto Studies in 1921, he became an associate professor in that field and taught both at the Military Academy and the university until 1933. After retiring, he continued to teach at several private universities including Kokugakuin University.

In 1912, he had a central role in establishing the Meiji Japan Society (Meiji Seitoku Kinen Gakkai), where he met some of the most famous Western Japanologists of his day, including D.C. Holtom and R. Ponsonby-Fane. Although purged from public office in 1945 by the Occupation, he eventually regained his international reputation as a noted Shinto scholar until his death in 1965.

Katō authored several important works on Shinto both in Japanese and English. In English, his book *A Study of Shinto* (1926) ranks with Aston's work as a groundbreaking attempt to explain Shinto, and his jointly edited *Bibliography of Shinto in Western Languages from Oldest Times till 1952,* remains a valuable scholarly resource studying Shinto in the West.

The selection below comes from a small volume he wrote for the Japanese Tourist Library, *What is Shinto?* (1935). This essay reveals Katō's passion to explain Shinto to a Western audience by situating it comparatively by drawing on the work of the Dutch savant of the science of religion, C.P. Tiele. Katō argues that Shinto is indeed "the original religion of Japan."[1] He also is highly critical of Western interpreters who dismissed Shinto as a lowly primitive nature religion. Using Tiele's classifications of religions, Katō argues that Shinto is not inferior but a different type of religion; it is "theanthropic" (emphasizing the divine in man) rather than theocratic, and a national rather than proselytizing global faith. Katō points to flaws within Tiele's classificatory system and offers a new category of religion that transcends Tiele's most basic distinction between natural and ethical religions. Shinto is anything but primitive, containing an ethical and intellectual complexity in its modern guise that rivals Christianity.[2]

SHINTO, A RELIGION OF THE THEANTHROPIC TYPE, AS DISTINGUISHED FROM A RELIGION OF THE THEOCRATIC TYPE AND SHINTO AS A NATIONAL RELIGION, NOT ENTIRELY DEVOID OF A UNIVERSAL ASPECT AND REMARKABLY TOLERANT
(1935)

Shinto, a religion of the theanthropic type, as distinguished from a religion of the theocratic type

As a comparative study of religions now shows, there are two main trends of the world's religious thought, that is to say, there are two fundamentally different ways of conceiving divinity. One is, Westerners might say, a mode of the Near Eastern type and the other that of the Far Eastern type. The former may be styled as belonging to the theocratic type or creative type of religion and the latter as of the theanthropic or genealogical or generative type. The religion of the Hebrews (Judaism), Islam or Mohammedanism, and Christianity, born of the practical mind of the Semites, belong as a rule to the theocratic type; while Buddhism or the Indian religions in general, and the ancient Greek religion, along with the Roman religion, all of which perhaps with the exception of the last-named are products of the speculative mind of the Aryan or Indo-European race, and the religious consciousness of the Japanese, and that of the Chinese also, belong to the theanthropic category. In theocratic religion divinity stands high above man and nature; with its formula "God is above us," it is transcendent of man and the world. Theanthropic religion, contrarily, sees divinity in man and nature; it is immanent or inherent in man and the universe, and its language proclaims, "God is in us." According to the religious consciousness of the theanthropic type, it is a matter of course that man ascends to God, and God descends to man. The philosophy of theocratic religion is monotheism, rising from monolatry, while pantheism is the natural outcome of theanthropic religion originated from nature worship in its primitive stage. In theocratic religion, there is the creation of man and nature by the One Supreme God, and in the theanthropic religion, not creation but emanation of the world from the Divine. According to the theanthropic religious consciousness, heaven and earth, God or gods beget man and nature, or, broadly speaking, organic and inorganic objects of the universe just as men are born of their parents. Nature worship, ancestor worship, necrolatry, hero worship, emperor worship, generally speaking, are religious expressions of the theanthropic type. Hero worship of the ancient Greeks, emperor worship among the Romans of old, the deification of the Gautama Buddha, the founder of Buddhism, all appear in the history of religions of the theanthropic type.

Now, I am going to consider Shinto, with the distinction of both types of religion, theocratic and theanthropic, in view. Throughout both stages of religious development, natural and cultural or ethico-intellectualistic, Shinto in its salient features is theanthropic; it does not belong to the theocratic type. In Shinto at the stage of nature religion, we have several personages deified, as, for instance, emperors, empresses, imperial princes, heroes, one's ancestors, and so on. Emperor Jinmu was called Ame no Oshigami or "Heaven Conquering God," according to the *Nihongi,* and in documents of olden times each emperor is described as a visible deity or a god incarnate. Minamoto no Yoshiie, a brave warrior and skillful archer of the eleventh century, is revered as a god because in the skill of his archery he had no equal, he stood aloof above any man; in short, he is superhuman, i.e., he is a deity in flesh and blood, according to the *Fusōryakki,* an old Japanese history. The Empress Jingō was also a deity, according to the *Kojiki.* Therefore, Motoori Norinaga of the eighteenth century, a famous commentator of the *Kojiki,* says: "True household gods we in our parents see; Revere and honor them whole-heartedly!"

In a Buddhist canon, entitled the *Forty-Two Chapter Sutra,* anthropolatry of the same kind is taught as regards one's parents, thus: "To be obedient to one's parents with filial piety is better than to worship all the deities in Heaven and Earth: for one's parents are for each the supreme deities."

The development of Shinto did not stop here; theanthropic Shinto has grown into a religion of a higher order, i.e., a religion of the ethico-intellectualistic stage. In 718, when a high government official, kindhearted towards his people, Michi no Kimi no Obina by name, died, he was at once deified and a shrine was erected to his memory because he did his utmost to promote the people's welfare by means of improving their way of life and making them happy: in short, he was indeed a man of a godlike character, and the result was his apotheosis after death, in the religious consciousness of the theanthropic type of the Japanese. In the same way, to Kusunoki Masashige (1294–1336),[3] an incarnation of loyalty to the emperor, and to the late General Nogi (1849–1912),[4] another type of loyalty to the Imperial Ruler, Shinto shrines are dedicated, to the former at Minatogawa [Minatogawa Jinja] in Kobe and to the latter at Akasaka [Nogi Jinja] in Tokyo. The worship of the emperor came to be conducted in the ethico-religious sense of the term. Therefore, in the fourteenth century, the royalist Kitabatake Chikafusa saw the essence of the theanthropic nature of higher Shinto in the worship of the emperor in this ethico-religious sense, when he says: "Since a righteous man, pure in mind and just in conduct, is himself a deity, we understand a visible deity (*akitsukami*)—so often mentioned in the imperial edicts—in this ethico-religious meaning of the words" (*Nijūissha no ki*).

In the same spirit, the Buddhist priest Jihen[*] of the fourteenth century says:

> Heaven's grace enlivens different grasses in an impartial manner, and Mother Earth justly and benevolently offers to all beings in her bosom equal opportunity to enjoy uninterrupted natural growth. The virtuous sovereign may well be compared to Heaven and Earth for his justice and equity, so that we call him not the son of man, but the son of Heaven or the son quite akin to Heaven, because of his righteous government. (*Kujihongi gengi*)

According to the *Buke kandan,* Tokugawa Hidetada (1579–1632), the second of the Tokugawa shoguns, is quoted as saying that he could not consent to the project of the Buddhist Abbot Tenkai to worship him after death by erecting a Shinto shrine in his honor, because he was not conscious of having acted in the virtuous manner of a deity, and so he did not, unlike his father, Ieyasu (1542–1616), deserve a shrine. Foreigners who have visited Nikkō may surely be aware of the beautiful shrine in which Ieyasu, the first of the Tokugawa shoguns, was eventually canonized with the name of Tōshōdaigongen or "East-Shining-Great-Incarnate-Deity."

A noble character laying down his life on the battlefield for his sovereign and his country is canonized, so to speak, as a *kami*, or deity, in the Yasukuni Shrine in Tokyo or in the Kenkō Shrine in Taiwan (Formosa) because such noble self-sacrifice suggests something divine to the Japanese religious consciousness of the theanthropic type, even when the religious consciousness of the theocratic type might be so affected. Such being the case, the theanthropic religious mind of the Japanese makes a visible deity of the emperor himself on the stage of ethico-intellectualistic religion and calls him a divine ruler (*jinnō*), and Shinto in its cultural or ethico-intellectualistic stage culminates in the faith of the divine ruler of the nation, and herein lies the life and essence of Shinto, the national religion of the Japanese people, past and present, throughout all stages, natural and cultural alike, completely in accord with the Japanese mind of the present age of enlightenment, as it has always been in the past.

In this respect, Shinto—I mean the national Shinto faith as distinguished from sectarian Shinto—is the Japanese "religion of loyalty," as Lafcadio Hearn characterizes it. It is, in fact, a Japanese patriotism suffused with religious emotion, or, in other words, a peculiar enthusiastic patriotic sentiment, often soaring into the plane of adoration or religious worship, towards the emperor or mikado, a manifest deity in the sense of theanthropic religion. I should, indeed, call it a form of emperor worship of mikadoism, a faith in the divine ruler; a manifestation, coupled with religious zeal of *Yamatodamashii* or "the soul of Japan." This peculiar religious sentiment or belief in the *jinnō* or divine ruler of the nation is manifested in the people's paying tribute to the memory of the Emperor Meiji by erecting, immediately after his death, a shrine on a grand scale at Yoyogi, a suburb of Tokyo. Yoyogi is now, indeed, a second Ise. And the same devotional feeling of overwhelming gratitude towards their august godly sovereign is equally evidenced by the existence of shrines dedicated to the same emperor during his lifetime. For instance, one is at Ono Village of Shinano Province; another at the port of Ishinomaki, near Matsushima, one of the three loveliest sights of Japan; a third at Kusatsu-machi in Hiroshima city, etc. Thus Shinto, strictly speaking, from the beginning down to the present time, through each and every stage of its gradual evolution, has existed unmistakably as the national religion of the Japanese people.

In the fourteenth century, Saka Shibutsu, in *The Diary of My Pilgrimage to the Ise Shine*, happily expresses this moral and religious sentiment of the devotional Japanese people towards the Ancestral Sun-Goddess and her imperial descendants as the successive divine rulers in the following words;

> In Japan the reigning emperor is a legitimate descendant of divine lineage while the Imperial Ancestress is revered as a Great Deity at Ise, so that the divine gace of the Ancestral Goddess pledges to bestow tranquility and welfare upon the Empire.

Hence, I can summarize this brief survey of Shinto by defining or rather describing it as follows:

> The vital essence of Shinto manifests itself in an expression of that unique spirit of the national service of the Japanese people, which comprehends not only their morality but their religion culminating in centripetal mikadoism or their own peculiar form of loyalty or patriotism towards the divine ruler, the united head, both political and religious, in a governmental theocratico-patriarchal as well as constitutional [way].

Shinto as a national religion, not entirely devoid of a universal aspect, and remarkably tolerant

I have tried to show that Shinto is a thoroughgoing national religion throughout each and every phase of its long development, from the stage of nature religion to that of culture religion. It has the *jinnō* or divine ruler of the nation at the center of worship, keeping pace with the progress of Japanese civilization in general, so that in the mental texture of the people their religious faith and national consciousness have been so closely interwoven as now to be incapable of separation. The consciousness of the Japanese or their attitude of patriotic reverence towards the Jinnō has been raised to the extent of intensely religious fervor. Lafcadio Hearn calls it the "religion of loyalty," but he confesses that so trite an English word as loyalty cannot cover all the connotation of the original Japanese and that the word loyalty is an utterly dead rendering; he wishes to call it "mystical exaltation" or "a sense of uttermost devotion" to the *jinnō* or divine ruler of the nation.

Shinto, characterized as faith in the *jinnō* or divine ruler of the nation, is not a religion *a posteriori* adopted purposely by the state as in the case of the state religion in a Western country, but the religion *a priori* of the heart and life of every Japanese subject, male and female, high and low, old and young, educated or illiterate. This is the reason why a Japanese never ceases to be a Shintoist, i.e., an inborn steadfast holder of the national faith, or one who embraces the national faith or the way of the gods as a group of folk religion, as distinguished from a personal or individual religion, even though he may accept the tenets of Buddhism or Confucianism—probably Christianity here in Japan not being excepted—as his personal or individual religion. In effect, this amounts to saying that abjuration by a Japanese of the national Shinto faith would mean treachery to the empire and disloyalty to its divine ruler. Professor Royce of Harvard University very happily explains in his book, *Sources of Religious Insight,* how this national Shinto faith, vehemently alive, and constantly stimulating the sentiment of every Japanese towards the heaven-descended sovereign of his native land, is a characteristic phase of national religion, when he says:

> However far you go in loyalty, you will never regard loyalty as a mere morality. It will also be in essence a religion. Loyalty is a source not only of moral but also of religious insight. The spirit of true loyalty is of its very essence a complete synthesis of the moral and of the religious interests. The cause is a religious object, it points out to you the way of salvation.

As demonstrated above, Shinto is truly the faith of the Japanese people from of old. It is thus a national religion and so has an aspect of particularism or separatism or exclusionism like Judaism, but at the same time it is by no means devoid of a noble spirit of religious universalism. Religious tolerance, to my mind, is in the main one of the remarkable features of theanthropic religion.

Accordingly, Buddhism is very tolerant in character; whereas Judaism and Mohammedanism—Christianity is not an exception—are rather intolerant, because each of these shares more or less the common character of a theocratic religion. As Shinto is characteristically theanthropic and *ipso facto* tolerant, there has resulted the *rapproachement* between Shinto and Buddhism, which actually took place quite easily, immediately after the introduction of Buddhism into Japan. The earliest consequence of this reconciling tendency, harmonization and syncretism in both religions, was to be seen at the time of Imperial Prince Regent Shōtoku (574–621), and afterwards thanks to the genius of the celebrated Buddhist priests Dengyō (767–822), Kōbō (744–835), Jikaku (794–864), Chishō (814–90), and many other religious leaders both Buddhist and Shintoist, in Japan; Shinto was by degrees formulated as Ryōbu or Dual Shinto—a syncretism of Shinto and Buddhism—at about the beginning of the thirteenth century.

By way of illustrating this strikingly reconciling religious spirit of the Japanese, I wish here to quote one instance out of many.

The renowned Daibutsu or colossal bronze statue of the Buddha Birushana (Sanskrit, Vairocana) at Nara, familiar to every foreign tourist, is a statue of a Buddhist god in name, but in fact it represents Amaterasu Ōmikami, the Ancestral Sun Goddess of Ise, according to the Siren of the fourteenth century, a celebrated biographer of Japanese Buddhist priests (*Genkō syakusho*). So the colossal image of worldwide fame may appropriately be called a pious monument erected by the Emperor Shōmu in 752, materially symbolizing that noble spirit of religious tolerance—one of the essential characteristics alike of Shinto and Buddhism, both belonging to the theanthropic trend of religious thought.

As the Japanese history *Azumakagami* tells, in 1195 the statue of Birushana at Ōba in Matano village, Kanagawa prefecture, was made of the wooden material which had been the august central pillar of the Ise Shrine sacred to the Ancestral Sun Goddess. This shows that, to the Japanese religious consciousness, Shinto and Buddhism were by that time perfectly reconciled and completely amalgamated, and the people took it as a matter of course that buddhas and Shinto gods were one and the same thing in essence, only in a different manifestation. To such an extent were the foreign religion and national faith on amicable terms by the beginning of the thirteenth century, they knew no more conflict between them. This is nothing but a manifestation of the tolerant spirit, which is characteristically theanthropic. Thus, Isonokami no Yakatsugu (729–81), as early as the eighth century, said:

> The esoteric teachings of the Buddhism and the tenets of the outsiders are after all one and the same in essence. At a cursory glance, the latter many seem strange and incompatible with the former; yet, tactfully utilized, there is no conflicting difference at all between them. (*Shoku Nihongi*)

In the same strain the reputed author Kitabatake Chikafusa also says: "If examined carefully, there is no antagonistic difference at all between foreign teachings and our own" (*Tōkehiden*).

And in a similar manner, the learned court noble Ichijō Kaneyoshi declares: "Buddhism never differs from the original teachings of our country and thus there is perfect coincidence of the teachings of the foreign texts and our own."—*Shōdan chiyō*

Lastly, let us add a few words on the universalistic phase of Shinto. Sectarian or denominational Shinto reveals an aspect of universalism much more than the Shinto of the national faith, because the former is rather less closely connected than the latter with the nation, and, in consequence, some of the Shinto sects have a *kami* or Shinto god who has no reference to the history of the country. For instance, the *kami* or god which the Konkō sect worships has little or no connection with the *Kojiki* or the *Nihongi*, the time-honored historical chronicles of Japan, and, so far, it is not national but universal, fairly free from national tradition. The god of this sect is called Tenchi Kane no Kami, which means "Heaven-and-Earth-Including-Deity," i.e., the Absolute Divinity, the Boundless One, with Heaven and Earth within its own Divine Self. Such a god, like the God of Christianity, transcends the boundaries of any particular nation or country, so it is quite natural that the Shinto sect, with such a universal god at its centre of faith, is also of a universal nature. The same may hold good in some other Shinto sects, the Kurozumi sect, for instance. Kurozumi Munetada (1779–1849), the founder of the sect, preaches that the Sun Goddess, Divine Ancestress of the imperial house, is nothing but a manifestation of the ethico-cosmic principle of sincerity, once taught in Chinese classics of olden times and introduced into this country long before the days of Kurozumi Munetada, although the sect says that Kurozumi Munetada promulgated it without any apparently traceable connection with any Chinese philosophical system then prevalent in Japan, as, for instance, the philosophy of Ōyōmei or Wang-Yang-Ming (1472–1528), of which Nakae Tōju (1608–48) and Kumazawa Banzan (1619–91), as the latter is popularly called, were two great professed advocates in this country. If Kurozumi Munetada sees the Shinto deity in the spiritual light of ethics, it hardly needs mentioning that the Kurozumi sect preaches in some way or other moral universalism in the Shinto religion, like the prophetism of Israel, whose essence is religious moralism, which naturally led it to universalism in ancient Israel. So, Kurozumi Munetada declares:

> Blest be Sincerity, of virtues chief!
>   Along in it the world shall seek relief
> From doubt and fear—till men of every land
>   In universal brotherhood do stand.

Nearly the same religious universalism appears in the Misogi sect, founded by Inoue Masakane (1790–1849).

An oracular utterance of the Shinto deity of Suminoe, the modern Sumiyoshi, breathes the same spirit, thus:

> The Deity of Suminoe Shrine
>   Free aid doth promise both to friend and foe
> Who do with reverence their hearts incline
>   And to this holy place for guidance go. (*Jinja injin*)

These references recall the world-renowned poem from the pen of the Emperor Meiji, with the quotation of which these pages may appropriately close:

> Whereas I deem this as an age
> Wherein the world in brotherhood is bound:
> How is it that the fierce winds rage,
> And dash and spread wild waves around?

Notes

1 Katō Genchi, *What is Shinto?* (Tokyo: Japanese Tourist Library, 1935), 11.
2 *Encyclopedia of Shinto,* "Katō Genchi," http://eos.kokugakuin.ac.jp/modules/xwords/entry.php?entryID=474.
3 A famous warrior known for his fealty toward Emperor Godaigo (1288–1339) during the Genkō War (1331–33).
4 A famous general famous for his loyalty to Emperor Meiji, who committed ritual suicide by *seppuku* in order to follow his emperor into death in 1912.
* In order to understand the Japanese mind correctly, foreigners must bear in mind the fact that a Japanese Buddhist is, because he is Japanese, a Shintoist, meaning an inborn partaker of, or an unprofessed believer in, the national faith of Shintō. He knows nothing of inward discordance [an original note added by Katō].

19

TSUDA SŌKICHI

The various meanings of the word Shinto
(1937–39)

Tsuda Sōkichi (1873–1961) was a noted Japanese historian who in the early 1940s became embroiled in a great controversy over his academic conclusions that were seen as offensive to the imperial family. Tsuda graduated from the politics department at the private university Tōkyō Senmon Gakkō (later Waseda Univesity) in 1891. After teaching as a high school instructor, Tsuda became a researcher for the Tokyo Branch of the South Manchuria Railway Company in 1908. In 1918 he obtained a professorship at Waseda University, where he taught until forced to resign in 1940.

Influenced by the positivist historian Shiratori Kurakichi (1865–1942) who rejected literalist minded interpretations of national learning scholars like Motoori Norinaga, Tsuda argued that early myths like those in the "Age of the Gods" section of the *Kojiki* and *Nihonshoki* were not historically factual. Despite that, such myths gave insight into the thoughts of the ancient peoples. Therefore, the proper object of historical research is to uncover what these myths meant to those who recorded them. The "Age of the Gods" and the histories of the early emperors were best understood as self-serving legends of Yamato court officials who insisted that the emperor was divine and whose primary goal was to politically legitimize the ancient centralized imperial state.[1] This approach forms the basis of Tsuda's pre-war works, beginning with his *Jindaishi no atarashii kenkyū* (New Research on the Age of the Gods, 1913).[2]

On March 8, 1940, after four books of his had been banned by the government, Tsuda was prosecuted for *lèse-majesté* (*fukeizai*) under article 26 of the Publication Law, which made it illegal for anyone to publish books profaning the dignity of the imperial house.[3] His crime was challenging in print the historical existence of the first emperor of Japan, Jinmu, as well as the next thirteen emperors of the imperial line, as described in the *Kojiki* and other early Japanese sources. Tsuda also questioned the government-approved date for the founding of the empire from the time of the first legendary Yamato Emperor Jinmu, who ascended the throne supposedly in 660 BCE. Tsuda's views were considered offensive by the government and rightist groups. But more importantly, they struck at the ideological heart of the Japanese imperial state. The bedrock of the Japanese state's notion of national polity (*kokutai*) was that Jinmu was the first Japanese emperor with a line of imperial succession that was "unbroken for ages eternal." Tsuda's conclusions cast grave doubt about the historicity of the officially sanctioned dates and eternal sovereignty of the imperial system (*tennōsei*). His work explicitly challenged the official creed that these claims were historically true.[4] Tsuda called into question whether early texts like the *Kojiki, Nihonshoki*, etc. could be treated as infallible sacred texts teaching the Japanese people about their true spiritual essence as a people and the imperial way to be an obedient subject.[5] These texts formed the basis of compulsory moral education courses (*shūshin*) in the public education system of the time.

106

Although Tsuda was found guilty as charged on May 21, 1942, his prison sentence was never carried out. Nonetheless, his trial underscored the government's determination to suppress academic freedom if it contradicted imperial ideology.

The following essay is Tsuda's seminal first chapter on the origin of the term Shinto from his *Nihon no Shintō* (Japanese Shinto, 1937–39). In this essay, Tsuda uses the historical critical method to show that Shinto in the earliest Japanese documents refers to generally to non-Buddhist folk customs and has nothing to do with later meanings of the term. The meaning of Shinto, he argues, evolves over time. It is only among national learning scholars that it becomes something of "national significance," as a term referring to the organized ritual-ideological Tennō system of the modern Japanese state.

THE VARIOUS MEANINGS OF THE WORD SHINTO
(1937–39)

The goal of this short work is to try to consider the ways in which Chinese thought operates within what is called Shinto in Japan. It is well known that in the past, Chinese thought permeated every facet of Japanese thought. It is a mistake, however, to think that this means that Japanese and Chinese thought are the same; this simply does not recognize the originality of Japanese spiritual life. Rather, it is important to understand the conditions under which Chinese thought was adopted and how it functioned within the spiritual life of the Japanese. As this is an important question within Shinto, there has already been research done about it, but I would like to outline my own views here. I will be glad if this helps some to uncover one side of Japanese spiritual life.

First, we must elucidate what the word Shinto means, since it is used to mean various things. It means the religious faith (which also includes magic) passed down from old as part of Japanese folk custom, and we see "Shinto" used this way in the oldest documents. For example, in the chronicle of Emperor Yōmei[6] in the *Nihonshoki,* we find the word "Shinto" used in contrast to the teachings of Buddhism. There had originally been no name for the religious faith that was part of folk custom, but the name Shinto was devised to distinguish the old faith from Buddhism, which had come to Japan from outside by spreading throughout the world (as I will discuss later, this word is a Chinese compound).

Although Confucianism and Taoism were both foreign systems of thought brought to Japan, they were not considered to be religions. Confucianism was taught as a political practice, but its concrete social and ritual expressions and their practical meaning were not cultivated; it was no more than a system of thought that was known through books. Likewise, although knowledge and texts about Taoism were also transmitted, it did not enter Japan as a religion. Thus, the word "Shinto" was needed to distinguish the religion of the folk from Buddhism, since Buddhism was the only religious system in existence. Although it is difficult to determine exactly when this occurred, it was probably after Buddhism had already grown powerful. As I will discuss in more detail later, at the time Buddhism first spread, the Buddha was called a *kami,* and perhaps such an identification simply occurred naturally to the compilers of the *Nihonshoki.* From the extent to which these compilers included information both about Shinto's rites and festivals in the fifteenth year of Empress Suiko's reign, as well as records about Buddhism's prosperity, it is probably safe to assume that they intended to contrast Shinto with Buddhism. This same spirit also seems present in the above-mentioned chronicles of Emperors Yōmei and Kōtoku.[7] This same trend of thought also carries on in the chronicles of Emperors Kinmei and Bidatsu; without question, its story of the struggle over the adoption or rejection of Buddhism by clan factions was powerfully depicted by the compilers of the *Nihonshoki*, even if they were not necessarily the original sources. It is also of note that the forger of the so-called "Seventeen Article Constitution" held Buddhism in high esteem without making an issue of the traditional religion of the folk; although he was riding the wave of Buddhism's popularity, it seems that this same trend both approved of the Buddhist faith and its prosperity while simultaneously trying to clearly distinguish Buddhism from the existing religion of the folk.[8] (On these matters, please refer to the fourth chapter of the fourth edition of my *Nihon koten no kenkyū*. Although not noted there, the forged constitution probably dates from the reign of Emperor Tenmu).[9] It is therefore conceivable that these circumstances brought the word Shinto into the world. Since "Shinto" continued to be used in this sense, it became the only way to contrast the religion of the Japanese folk with Buddhism; the word's later variety of meanings all spring from this source.

There are also cases where the word Shinto refers to such things as a deity's authority, power, functions, deeds, divine status, spirit, or even the divinity itself. Examples of this usage can be found in quotes like "the false accusations against Shinto," in the memorial to the throne in the first year of Enryaku (782) in the *Shoku Nihongi*;[10] "Shinto's benefits to the world," found in an official government document dating from Enryaku 17 (798) in the *Ruiju sandai kyaku*;[11] "enjoy offering one's respect to Shinto and reap a very great and bountiful harvest," recorded in an imperial rescript dating from Kōnin 7 (816) in the *Ruijū kokushi*.[12] It is also seen in an imperial rescript from Tenchō 5 (796), "Did this [landslide and flood] happen possibly because there had been a lack in the everyday political practices? Or possibly because there had been some obstruction of Shinto?"; in "Ordinary people should always act the same way and Shinto should also remain the same too"; in "As a rule, when there are differences Shinto works to mediate them perfectly," from an anonymous entry quoted in the *Shoku Nihongi*. Finally, we see this usage in "Amusing oneself writing flowery words can have no benefit at all in Shinto," from a prayer request of Yoshishige no Yasutane[13] in the *Honchōmonzui*;[14] in "Although it is the final age, really, what one should really be worried about is Shinto," as recorded in the Kanji 8 (1094) *Chūyūki*;[15] and in, "Having no concern for Shinto, will make people compete for other's praise," in a poem by Ōe Masafusa[16] from a poetry competition found in the *Chōyagunsai*.[17] Although some seem to be referring to worshipping a deity or its ceremony among these examples, it is difficult to draw any sweeping conclusions.

Secondly, some juxtapose Shinto with Buddhism. For example, the chapter on miscellaneous temples in the Buddhism section of the *Ruijū kokushi*, contains an entry recorded for Tenchō 6 (829) as an oracle of the deity Wakasahiko, "Converting to the Buddhist teachings, therefore frees you from Shinto." Similarly, in an imperial rescript dated Jōwa 3 (836) in the *Shoku kōki*,[18] it is said that "To defend and maintain Shinto, the power of the One Vehicle is the best." In the biography of Kūkai Sōzu, we can find in the words of the deity Niu Myōjin, "The servant is Shinto," and in the *Fusōryakki*[19] in the prayer made before the deity in the fifth year of Enkyū (1073), "Thankfully, Shinto has appeared solely for the protection of those Buddhist teachings." If we grant that the word "Shinto" has this sense, we are also assuming that its meaning has changed from its original meaning. However, because this usage appears more and more frequently in later documents, it is appropriate to include these examples in the second sense of the word Shinto. Moreover, in certain contexts, such as entries in the "Age of the Gods" section of the *Nihonshoki*, people regard the tales as having a religious meaning; there, they use the word "Shinto" to refer not only to the actions of the *kami* who are described there but also to humans who are called *kami*. Similar references can also be found in the private documents quoted in the *Shoku Nihongi*,[20] and they should also be considered as examples of Shinto in the second sense described here.

A third meaning of Shinto refers to a system of thought which has added an intellectual interpretation, and thus a further meaning, to tales from the "Age of the Gods." This usage is seen in such examples as Ryōbu Shinto, Yuiitsu Shinto, and Suika Shinto, and it goes beyond the first and even the second meanings of Shinto. These are really more like theologies or dogmas, and various traditions of Shinto arise from these distinct intellectual views. However, Shinto in this sense does not just encompass the formation of a simple system of thought, such as Ryōbu Shinto, but also puts into practice distinctive forms of worship and rituals that accompany it. Even in these cases, however, this third usage of Shinto can mean simply a system of thought without reference to a ritual side.

The fourth sense of Shinto is distinctive because the shrine becomes the principal object of propaganda, such as Ise Shinto and Sannō Shinto. These types of Shinto do have their own respective theologies and dogmas, so in some sense this is the same as the third sense of the term. However, those theologies and dogmas are connected with specific shrines, and therefore this meaning of "Shinto" is distinct because the authority of the shrine permeates that system of thought.

The fifth meaning of Shinto refers to the established teachings of Japan's *kami,* which also includes the politics and ethical standards unique to Japan. This was mainly influenced by Confucianism; it came from the attempt to construct a "way of Shinto" (*kami no michi*) that was distinct from the ways sages or previous rulers had conceived of Shinto. This usage was most frequently used among scholars in the Tokugawa period; it also includes the Shinto that the so-called national learning scholars referred to as the way of the *kami* or the way of *Sumegami*.

The third and fourth meanings of Shinto have directly inherited the religious sense of the term. The Chinese characters used for Shinto should be interpreted to mean a way of worshipping the *kami* or, even more broadly, a way related to the *kami*. Shinto in the fifth sense of the term is different from these, as it is not a way that the *kami* established or taught. It is safe to say that this fifth form of Shinto only exists conceptually and that the worship of the *kami* as a folk custom has almost no connection with it. Further, it is separate even from the material recorded in the classics, and, in several respects, it twists these to fit into its own interpretation. Therefore, it is difficult to clearly distinguish this from "Shinto" in the third sense of the term. The next and sixth meaning of the term is sect Shinto.

It is important to understand that there has been a recent movement to understand "Shinto" in the first sense of the term to symbolize national authority. Conceptually this is included in the third, fourth, and fifth senses of the term and originates from them. Therefore, while national authority does not have to be treated as something separate from these senses, we must be wary of the unprecedented character of such an assertion, particularly when it directly ties that authority to national institutions or policies. This seems to be an attempt to imbue national authority with religious significance by placing it upon the foundation of Shinto, and therefore it requires that Shinto have a national significance. Using the word "Shinto" in this case may be informal, but it should be accepted as one claim about Shinto as long as we can use that term in the first sense.

However, this is not inherent in Shinto as the religion of the folk. Indeed, even though the rites of the *kami,* which are still practiced today, are called Shinto, this understanding of

Shinto excludes its religious character and replaces it with ethical and political meanings. This notion has its historical origin in the fifth sense of the word "Shinto"; however, in not considering *kami* rites at shrines and the worship of the *kami* as having a religious character, it clearly ignores existing facts. Although there has been a tendency recently to use the word "Shinto" to describe the spirit of the Japanese folk (*minzoku seishin*), this should be considered a misuse of the term.

Recently, the term "primitive Shinto" has been used to describe the Shinto of the first sense in ancient times. However, if "primitive Shinto" refers to Shinto in its third or fifth sense, then this term is not appropriate. This is because these two types of Shinto have a completely different character. Similarly, what national learning scholars like Motoori Norinaga called their "way of the *kami*" referred to Restoration Shinto (*fukko Shintō*, literally, "Shinto that restores the ancient" (*ko*)).[21] This usage can also already be found in Oyamada Tomokiyo's *Matsunoya hikki*.[22] If we understand "ancient conditions" to mean Shinto in its original or first sense, then this term is invalid. If the explanations of Norinaga and others can be called Shinto, it is only because it is in the fifth sense of the term and has absolutely nothing to do with religious belief as in the folk customs of ancient times. Even Shinto in its first sense has historically transformed itself. In later ages it might have been influenced by Shinto in its third, fourth, or fifth senses. There are also cases where the latter is explained by its particular relationship to the former. However, there are several points where Shinto as a folk custom, and most especially as a folk belief, has been passed down—even if it has perhaps changed superficially, it is inherently and essentially the same as it was in the past. The Shinto that scholars seem to expound upon has very little relationship with it.

Scholarly interpretations are not based on the systemization of actual folk belief. Their work mainly interprets the classic literature, especially the "Age of the Gods" section of the chronicles. In the "Age of the Gods" section, as I will mention later, there are very few religious elements, and there are no free-standing folk beliefs. Nevertheless, their interpretations do not clarify the ideas inherent within the classics. Instead, they forcibly combine them with unrelated ideas that are completely disconnected from the entries in the classics. This is due to the influence of Chinese and Indian ideas. Thus, it is natural that there is no connection between Shinto as an actual religion of the folk and the third through fifth senses of Shinto that developed afterward. In the first half of this short work, I have attempted to clarify these matters. Put simply, not enough attention has been given to the various meanings of the word "Shinto," which must have resulted in the labels of primitive Shinto or Restoration Shinto.

It is rare that an ancient religion of the folk like this one has continued to exist throughout so many eras. In Japan, there came a time when intellectual and cultural pursuits developed. Scholars of those periods have created various theories about Shinto to satisfy their intellectual curiosity. Is not this one of the reasons for the recent efforts to interpret and propagandize the meanings of Shinto that diverge from its original nature and to forcibly admix various ideas in it? Of course, propagandists have their own purposes. However, we should also remember that Shinto as a religion of the folk, if transmitted from the past as it was, would be set apart from the intellectual desires of modern people.

The term "Shinto" carries a wide variety of meanings. The reasons for this will become clearer as research advances. In this essay, I have tried to focus on Shinto in its third, fourth, and fifth senses; this springs naturally from the subject of my investigation itself. Shinto in the first sense is properly considered by the sociology of religion and by folklore studies. It is completely different from any dogmas that Shinto in the third through fifth sense had developed through scholarly thought; it is the latter, not the former, that includes elements of Chinese thought. That said, even the tales from the "Age of Gods", which we have used as an example of Shinto in the second sense, contain Chinese elements. Therefore, we must be careful about generalizing. Since I had several occasions to discuss this point, as long as it is necessary to explain conceptually the origin of Shinto thought in the third through fourth senses, I will try to refer to Shinto in the second sense.

As discussed previously, the term for this Shinto is originally a Chinese compound; it carried a variety of meanings in China. I have already discussed this in chapter three of the fourth section of *Nihon koten no kenkyū*, and will therefore refrain from repeating it here. However, since the elements of Chinese thought are an essential part of thinking about Shinto, I do want to supplement those thoughts with a discussion of the Chinese word *shen* (神). There are various meanings, even in Chinese, recorded for the character *shen*. The entries in the classics suggest that, when it is used as a noun, its religious and magical meaning should be considered initially. It means that there are various types of spiritual beings or entities which have power beyond human powers and affect human life; examples of this would be heaven and earth, mountains and streams, animals, plants, and even stones. All these spiritual entities either inherently exist within such things or exist outside them. These spiritual beings are considered to have magical powers or are objects of magic and worship. Human spirits or souls that exist after death, generally called *kuei* (鬼), are also are called *shen* (according to contemporary usage) in cases where they become the objects of devotion in religious rites of ancestor worship. Some *shen* that appear in later periods show a degree of cultural development and arose later in the thought of the literate classes. For example, millet was considered to be an agricultural deity, and local tutelary deities were envisioned as old men. (Presumably millet as a *shen* originally was the power inherent in the grain and the grain itself. But one can speculate that after a certain period it developed into an agricultural deity.) In addition, in the stories that were created by the literati, certain types of *shen* had a human form and, in some cases, human personalities. But, generally, this was not the case, even for *shen* who were tied to human culture.

It is important to note that *shen* can also be considered as mysterious powers or functions in the universe, or of the universe itself. The *shen* of the *Hsiang chuan* in the *I ching*[23] is described as follows: "Spirit (*shen*) has no limitations and change has no form," or "Someone who knows the way of Tranformationality (regarding) his knowledge of Spirit, what does it come to?" Another example of the *shen* indicating something unfathomable is "The immeasurability/immensity of *yin/yang* is called spirit (*shen*)." The *shen* of *the Lao Tzu*'s "Spirit obtained the One and became divine"[24] also seems to have this meaning, especially since the passage also refers to heaven, earth, and all things. This has changed from the *shen* in the first sense of the term. We can see that the religious meaning has given way to a metaphysical sensibility, which indicates that this probably developed from the thought of the intelligentsia.

For the third, there is the *shen* or spirit that exists within human beings; this is the source for the concept ordinarily expressed today by the word *seishin* (精神). This sense of the word *shen* can be used in opposition to the form, or the form and feeling (*ch'i*), or to the form and heart and mind (*hsin*). An example of the first is seen in the *Chuang tzu*'s "Heaven and Earth" and "Ingrained Thinking" chapters; the second may be seen in the *Huai-nan tzu*'s "Searching out the Tao" chapter, "Form is the place of life, breath fills up life and the spirit controls life"; and the last appears most often, in the "Seminal Breath and Spirit" chapter, "The heart is the head of form, and spirit is the treasure of the heart-mind."[25]

Form is the body, breath is that which physiologically gives life to the body, and the heart-mind is that which has a psychological function. But spirit seems to be thought of as mysteriously existing inside the heart-mind, presiding over it and the living body. However, spirit may also be interpreted as something similar to the heart-mind; while there is an example of this in the *Chuang tzu*'s "Heaven and Earth" chapter, it probably is not the original meaning of *shen* as something existing in humans. This seems to be the case because the chapter uses the special term *shen*. This *shen* has no religious meaning, but it does have a cosmic and mysterious power or function; we can assume that this *shen*, which exerts its power in human beings, derives from *shen* in the religious sense. (The *Chi i* [Meaning of the Sacrifices] volume from the *Li chi*, says, "That which has life force (*ch'i*) is full of spirit," but also "that which has a soul is full of troublesome spirits" (*kuei*); these examples explain ghosts and spirits in a religious sense, but while they call *shen* something that is within a living body, it has a different meaning than the *shen* in these passages. Here *ch'i* appears to either refer to or become confused with the ethereal soul (*hun* [魂]), which becomes a term generally contrasting with the corporeal soul (*po* [魄]), and, therefore, *shen* probably carries a similar meaning. The opposition between *kuei* and *shen* is analogous to that between *po* and *hun*.[26] However, this way of thinking is far-fetched insofar as it links these opposing concepts. Moreover, regarding *hun* as *shen* probably comes from cases where the dead are worshipped at the ancestral mausoleum. The *shen* that is mentioned in these passages and that is contrasted with form, vital force (*ch'i*) and heart-mind does not refer to *hun* in its religious sense. Of course, the meaning of the word changes and the meanings are mixed together, so such a word is used in various ways. However, while this spirit in human beings does not have a religious meaning, it has an ethical meaning of sorts instead. Form and spirit are considered opposed to each other, and either spirit controls form or form controls spirit. What emerges conceptually here is spirit's important function in controlling one's bodily needs. However, we have the expression *yang shen* ([養神], "nurturing the spirit") since the spirit is thought of as something attached to the body, and it is explained as a method for *yang sheng* ([養生], "nurturing life"), together with *yang hsing* (養形) "nurturing the form." Moreover, many in the Taoist school explained spirit as a mental state of tranquilly and non-action (*wu wei*). The *Chuang tzu*'s "Ingrained Thinking" chapter says, "The simple way through purity, only the spirit protects it, if you protect and do not lose it, you become one with the spirit."

We should also be aware that the word *shen* is sometimes used as an adjective. The *shen* of the Taoist term *shen jen* ([神人], an immortal) is an adjective for a person who has attained the Tao. Naming China *shen chou* ([神州], divine land) and calling the realm or the imperial throne ([神器], *shen chi*, divine treasures) are similar examples of the way this term is used. It does not carry a religious meaning here either; rather, it seems to be used to accent the superiority of their divine power or operation. Since in classical Chinese separate parts of speech do not appear as inflections, such a thing is possible. The *shen* of "The immeasurability/immensity of *yin/yang* is called spirit" quoted above can also be regarded as an example of *shen* referring to immeasurability/immensity.

Although all these meanings of the word *shen* appear in the classics, these were generally handed down even in later periods. However, changes and development in thought brought new content to the religious sense of "spirit." Although one example of spirit is worshipped in Taoism as something that furnishes a human form, this was influenced by Indian knowledge about the deities that accompanied Buddhism and the Buddha. The Buddha himself was called a spiritual being and is said to be so even in the opening of the *Sutra of Forty-Two Chapters*.[27] Although this was because the Buddha was seen as an object of religious worship, it is a well-known fact that names like *Hu shen* or *Jung shen*[28] were invented to distinguish the Buddha from spiritual beings originally from China. Or, when we look at the debate over the immortality of the spirit, which was emphasized by the Buddhists in the Six Dynasties period,[29] this spirit is the opposite of form and seems to have been given a character much like the soul (*reikon*) (in our modern use of the term). This also is another change in the meaning of *shen*.

If *shen* has various meanings such as this, it would also be natural for the label Shinto to be like this as well. Given that the term *shin* in its religious sense was used especially to refer to an object of worship, and that worship and prayer, or more broadly, religion itself was naturally called Shinto, many examples exist as a matter of course. Buddhism itself was called Shinto in this sense. Although in terms of its linguistic structure, it probably means the way of worshipping the *kami* (*shin*), or the way concerning the *kami,* we may see *shin* used as an adjective modifying *tō* (the way). While *shin* is used as a modifier, there are also not a few cases of naming things Shinto even though they have no religious sense. The oldest of these is the *shen tao* in the famous *T'uan chuan*[30] on the divinatory signs (*kua*) for divination (in the *Book of Changes*), "For the spiritual way of observing the heavens, no matter what season, the holy person provides his teaching by means of his spiritual way and the realm will obey." It praises the mystery of the way (the law of nature) and describes it as spiritual. The *Tao* of the Taoist school, which was also called the spiritual way, is another example of this. If the Taoists interpreted the spirit that exists in human beings as a mental state of tranquility and non-action, it does seem in this sense that this *shen tao* means a way that expounds upon the spirit. Since calling the *tao* of the Taoists *shen* seems to be from the Chin dynasty period (265–420) when many considered that divination and Taoist thought were connected, interpreting it this way is probably valid. Further, such things as magic or the magical arts of Taoist immortals are called *shen tao,* which describes that way (arts) together with the word *shen*, which refers to mysterious functions. There are many other examples of these usages of the term *shen tao,* but I will limit myself to these (I will not treat *shen tao* in cemeteries because it is a separate problem).

In the *Nihonshoki*, the worship of *kami* as a Japanese folk custom called Shinto was a Japanese example of "Shinto" being used in a religious sense. That said, given that in China the Buddha was called a *shen,* that the prevalent practice of Buddhism was called a spiritual way, and even that in Japan the Buddha was sometimes called a *kami*, it seems odd that traditional religion of the folk was called Shinto in order to set it apart from Buddhism. But, for a long time before that, the character of *shen/shin* had been assigned for the Japanese word *kami*, and, in the period of the compilation of the *Nihonshoki*, the practice of calling the Buddha a *kami* had become outdated. Therefore, the traditional religion of the Japanese folk came to be called Shinto in the *Nihonshoki*.

The name Shinto, used in this way, was eventually translated in Japanese as the "way of the *kami.*" However, it is clear that the term "the way of the *kami*" did not exist in Japanese originally; this meaning of the word *tao* was limited to China. *tao* originally meant the path on which people walk, but it also came to mean, among other things, a standard of human action, the law of things or a fixed teaching about these, a doctrine (in the modern sense of the term) or a special knowledge or art. As the meaning of *tao* shifted, so did the "way" of Shinto's meaning. This can be seen in the terms *Judō* (the way of Confucius) *Butsudō* (the way of the Buddha). This Chinese usage is also seen in such Japanese terms as Jihen's[31] "imperial way" (*kōdō*), Mabuchi's[32] "the way of the age of the gods" (*kamiyo no michi*), and "the way of the imperial *kami*" (*sumekami no michi*). It is also apparent in Norinaga's "way of the *kami*" (*kami no michi*), "way of the great sun *kami*" (*hi no ōkami no michi*), "the way handed down only by the sun" (*hinomiko uketsutaemasu michi*), and "the way only of a divine country" (*kami no mikuni no michi*). Mabuchi and Norinaga, in particular, used this form as a specifically Japanese expression for what was called "the way." There was no real reason for them not to use the old word Shinto, but these coinages go hand in glove with their attitude as national learning scholars. Even their referring to *michi* in that sense comes from Chinese thought. National learning scholars created these words in order to criticize old Shinto and to differentiate the so-called contemporary Shinto from it. Even so, we must look carefully at the way they used the word "Shinto."

In particular, I would like to consider the term, "the way in accordance with the will of the *kami*" (*kannagara no michi*). This term does not appear in ancient documents and was first introduced in the modern period. In the first volume of his *Commentary of Ancient History* (*Koshichō, Kaidaiki*), among other writings,[33] Atsutane spoke of *Kaminagara naru michi* (惟神なる道, 神随なる道). Considering that these terms have a reading of *kaminagara*, can we not assume that he was the origin of this word? Popular opinion claims that it is an ancient word. Norinaga does not seem to have used the term "*kaminagara naru michi*," but he states that "the will of the *kami* revealing itself under heaven" (*kannagara ama no shita shiroshimesu*) is "*kami no michi*." So perhaps the origin of this word can be traced back to him. Norinaga also uses the words "the way in accordance with the way of the *kami*" (*kami no michi no mama naru michi*). If so, then those who had inherited Norinaga's thought prior to Atsutane might already have been using the expression *kaminagara naru michi*. The Shirakawa house seems to have been influenced by Norinaga in a number of ways, and the term *kaminagara no Shintō* (惟神の神道, 神随の神道) is used in their *Jingihakke gakus-oku*.[34] The Shirakawa House were Shintoists, so they used the term Shinto rather than *michi*. It is also conceivable that Atsutane added his own words to this document. However, the term *kaminagara naru michi* is mentioned in Yoshida Noriyo's[35] *Seimonshigen* in regard to the study of imperially ruled states; it appears to be a reference to Norinaga's work, without reference to Atsutane. The origin of the phrase must be carefully investigated, but it does seem that it was one of Norinaga's disciples.

Of course, the term *kaminagara* has existed since ancient times. It is used in poems of the *Manyō* and in imperial decrees found in the *Shoku Nihongi*, but these do not have the word *michi*, nor should they be regarded as "ways." "*Kannagara naru michi*" is not a term that is found in the classics. And yet, Atsutane created that reading because he understood the characters 惟神, 神随 to correspond to *kaminagara*. It is because the character 惟神, in the entry Taika 3 (647) of Emperor Kōtoku in the *Nihonshoki*, was customarily pronounced as "*kannagara*" and the commentary for that says, "The phrase 惟神 means to follow the way of the gods or again to possess in oneself the way of the gods."[36] It is therefore speculated that there is some relationship between Shinto and the term *kannagara*, or even that the term expressed a key idea of Shinto, and from this the term "*kaminagara naru michi*" occurred to Atsutane. (Norinaga's "*kami no michi no mama naru michi*" uses the exact words from the annotation quoted above, and he seems to have regarded it as naming the way, but its meaning is different from what the word in the annotation signifies.) And once such a word was proposed, it became mistakenly understood by the public as something ancient that is the same as the word Shinto or perhaps something even older—and thus the term "*kaminagara no michi*" also came into use. (Since this term was adopted officially at the beginning of Meiji, (the term "*kannagara no daidō*" appears even in official documents like the imperial decree proclaiming the Great Teaching (*taikyō*).

However, as noted in my detailed explanation in the fifth edition of *Nihon koten no ken-kyū*, the two Chinese characters 惟神 originally did not represent the term *kannagara* and do not express a single concept in and of themselves. 惟 is a prefix that is commonly used in Chinese, and 神 *shen* is the subject of a sentence grammatically for "*agamiko shirasamu to koto yosashiki*" ("My children shall rule it"), which follows these two characters. Therefore, the above annotation, which tries to explain the passage exclusively in terms of the single term 惟神 was never part of the original text but had to have been added later carelessly by someone. Clearly, one cannot assume, on the basis of the Chinese character alone, that the word *nagara* corresponds to the character 惟. Although it is unclear at what time 惟神 was read as *kaminagara*, in the Heian period when the *Nihonshoki* was often the subject of lectures at the imperial court, the incorrect and made-up reading became common as is illustrated by the fragments of private writings from the time. And, therefore, the reading of *kaminagara* must have begun around the Heian period. First, the reading *kaminagara* was added, and the annotation may have been created as a consequence.

These words combined with the reading *kami nagara* ("in their capacity as deities") after *agamiko* ("my children") are understood by anyone as Japanese phrasing. So, the two Chinese characters 惟神 in the quote above, although they seem to be a little different from the Japanese language, became a Japanese word with a definite meaning following the use of the Japanese *agamiko*. Placing the discourse marker 惟 first and attaching the word 神 *shen* after it as the grammatical subject in cases when saying something about the acts of the *kami*, for example, like "Only the god looked" or "Only the deities looked") (惟神鑒矣, 惟祇鑑矣) in the *Lyrics of Ch'i* appearing in the *Records of Music in the Book of Sui*,[37] is not unusual in Chinese sentences, so the compilers of the *Nihonshoki* followed this and wrote it that way. This kind of misunderstanding occurred because what comes after *agamiko* in the text is in Japanese. Later scholars did not know this; therefore, as in the passages above, they created the term "*kaminagara naru michi*," which seemed as though it was an ancient word. (I will explain in detail in a later chapter how Norinaga and Atsutane thought and the changes in the meaning of terms like "*kaminagara naru michi*" or "*kaminagara no michi*.")

However, even in Chinese, there are some examples of using the two characters 惟神 as one term. It is found in a passage from the preface of *Private Transmission of the History of the Chin Dynasty*[38] that I discussed in the book noted above, "The only constant spiritual way is that living things ordinarily have a nature that is soft, and that they are harmed too much by this." This comes from Taoist thought, and when we consider it from that perspective, we can surmise that it takes its two characters 惟神 from *Chuang tzu*'s "Ingrained Thinking" chapter quoted above, "The simple way through purity, only the spirit 惟神 protects it, if you protect and do not lose it, you become one with the spirit." (The *Chuang tzu*'s 惟 also originates from 唯, but these two characters can be used interchangeably, and in terms of their meaning, there are many examples of it as 惟.) However, while in the *Chuang tzu* the two characters 惟神 do become used as one term, they are so in the *History of the Chin Dynasty*. That is because it is trying to express the entire meaning of the words quoted above from the "Ingrained Thinking" chapter by the two characters 惟神. As long as they were already being used this way, it must be accepted as a separate term in the sentence. However, we cannot consider that the compilers of the chronicle of Emperor Kōtoku took the two characters 惟神 from here because if so the annotation would be meaningless. While it can be inferred that the compilers of the *Nihonshoki* read the *History of the Chin Dynasty*, we must consider these two characters in the way mentioned above.

While thinking about the characters from the *History of the Chin Dynasty,* I would like to add that in the *Hsiao wuchi,* a text included within it, "The official in charge of public records said, '[But if] one's heavenly gift is nothing but excellent (惟神), and one succeeds the throne splendidly.'" The term 惟神 is used even here, but it is completely different from the *Private Transmission.* It is just expressing Emperor Kōtoku's superior nature by the term 惟神 with the use of *shen* as an adjective, and these two characters do not form one term. The *shen* of the *I ch'uan,* is both spirit (as opposed to form) and is also the state of tranquil non-action (*wu wei*) which in Taoist thought marks the dawning of the ability to be a True Person whose spirit has grasped the way. When used in this way, it is a noun. (The meaning of heavenly gift [天挺], *t'ien ting*) is clearly understandable because in the *Chronicle of Emperor Hsüan* "Emperor Hsüan said, 'Guide our fate in response to the times with the support 資 (*tzu*) of heavenly gifts.'"[39] In the popular edition the character 資 becomes 姿 (*tzu,* looks or appearance), and it is clear that this was a copying mistake.) Can we not go so far as to conjecture that, while the *History of the Chin Dynasty*'s "The only constant spiritual way" (惟神之常道) has a completely different meaning, it invited Atsutane's Chinese-inspired term "*kaminagara naru michi*"? We must bear in mind that Atsutane read many Chinese books and also had some knowledge of Taoist thought. However, in Atsutane's time it was believed that 惟神 signified the Japanese term *kaminagara,* so it is right to see "*kaminagara naru michi*" as something that was created and originated from the Japanese term, *kaminagara.* Since it is even written with different Chinese characters "神隨なる道," such a conjecture is therefore implausible.

I think I have made clear in the above disquisition that there are various meanings for the word Shinto, that it originally was adopted as a Chinese compound word, further, how it came to be, and what meanings it carried. With this in mind, let us proceed to my main argument.

Notes

1 John S. Brownlee, *Japanese Historians and the Nationalist Myths, 1600–1945; The Age of the Gods and Emperor Jinmu* (Tokyo: The University of Tokyo Press, 1997), 186–89.
2 Joel Joos, "'Love Thy Emperor': Tsuda Sōkichi's views on 'Tennō' and 'Minzoku,'" *Japan Forum* 20 (November, 2008): 388.
3 Ibid., 195.
4 See Brownlee, Chapter 11, "Eminent Historians in the 1930s: The Betrayal of Scientific History," in *Japanese Historians,* 130–79..
5 Ibid., 192–93. This official view was basic to the school curriculum as seen in the *Kokutai no hongi* (1937), an approved text by the Ministry of Education that involved scholars that included Kōno Seizō and Watsuji Tetsurō.
6 Emperor Yōmei (518–87) reigned from 585 to 587.
7 Emperor Kōtoku (596–654) reigned from 645 to 654.
8 According to the *Nihonshoki,* a highly Buddhist document purportedly authored by Shōtoku Taishi in 604, offering a code of virtuous conduct so that the state would be prosperous and harmonious.
9 Emperor Tenmu (631–86), reigned from 672 to 686.
10 A Heian period chronicle created by imperial command and completed by Sugano Masamichi in 797. As the second of six national histories, it covers ninety-five years from 607 to 791.
11 This is a collection of legal codes compiled between 1002 and 1089.
12 This is a historical text commissioned by Emperor Uda and edited by Sugawara Michizane in 892. It categorizes and chronicles the events listed in the *Rikkokushi* (the six national histories).
13 He was a mid-Heian period literati and Confucian scholar (933–1002).

14 A Chinese-style poetry anthology dating from the mid-Heian period compiled by Fujiwara Akihira (989?–1066).

15 The late Heian period court diary of Fujiwara Munetada.

16 Scholar, official, and poet (1041–1111) of the late Heian period, who served as a tutor of Emperors Shirakawa, Hirokawa, and Toba and author of the famous *Gōke Shidai,* which documented court ceremonial and public functions.

17 A Heian-period text compiled by Miyoshi Tameyasu in thirty volumes containing poems, government documents, letters, official documents, imperial decrees, and so on.

18 The *Shoku Nihon kōki* is an historical work created in the Heian period from 869, the fourth of the six national histories.

19 Heian-period Chinese poetry collection in sixteen volumes.

20 An interpretative commentary on the *Nihonshoki* presumed to have been composed at the end of the Kamakura period between 1274 and 1301, in twenty-eight volumes.

21 This term generally refers to early modern nativist Shinto thought (or *kodō,* "teachings of the ancient way"). Nativist thinkers like Norinaga conceived an idealized "Shintō" ostensibly existing before the arrival of influences from Buddhism and Confucianism.

22 This is an encyclopedia-style set of essays written by the late Edo-period national learning scholar, Oyamada Tomokiyo (1783–1847), whose work, beginning in 1815 extended over a forty-six year period and 120 volumes.

23 Or *Keijiden,* "Commentary on the Images," a key part of the "Ten Wings" (*Jūyoku*) or commentarial works attributed to Confucius that are included in the classic Chinese book of divination, the *I ching* or *Book of Changes* (*Ekikyō*).

24 This passage is from Chapter 39 of the *Tao te ching.*

25 Two chapters (one and seven) of this famous Taoist classic from the second century BCE.

26 Types of souls in Chinese traditional religion. *Hun* is a spiritual *yang* soul that departs the body post-mortem, and the *po* is the *yin* corporeally linked soul that remains.

27 The earliest surviving Buddhist sutra said to have been translated into Chinese by two Yüeh-chih monks, Kasyapa-Matanga (迦葉摩騰) and Dharmaratna (竺法蘭) in CE 67 with no extant Pali or Sanskrit version.

28 The Jung and the Hu are names the Han Chinese gave to barbarian peoples of the West. So, the terms here refer to the Buddha as a barbarian or non-Chinese divinity.

29 Period of political instability and warfare in Chinese history beginning after the fall of the Han dynasty in CE 220 and extending to the conquest of south China by the Sui in CE 589, marked religiously by the growing power of Taoism and Buddhism, which became a popular religion during this period.

30 The first two of the "Ten Wings" or commentaries on the *I ching* purported written by Confucius. It is divided into two chapters and interprets King Wen's judgements on the sixty-four hexagrams based on their structure and other elements.

31 A Tendai Buddhist priest of the Kamakura period, fourteenth century, learned in the Ise, Ryōbu, and Sannō schools of Shinto of his time, who was a major influence on Yoshida Shinto and espoused the idea of Imperial Rule.

32 Kamo no Mabuchi (1697–1769), one of the four great National Learning scholars of the Tokugawa period. See Peter Nosco, *Remembering Paradise: Nativism and Nostalgia in Eighteenth-Century Japan.* Cambridge, MA, Harvard University Press, 1990.

33 This text, dating from 1811–19, is one of Hirata's major studies of ancient Japanese traditions, in which he argued that an ancient Japanese script from the "Age of the Gods" (*Kamiyo no moji*) existed prior to the introduction of Chinese characters from the continent. Hirata argued that Chinese characters increasingly were used for their sound value until they replaced the original written Japanese script. See Christopher Seeley, *A History of Writing in Japan* (Hawaii, The University of Hawaii Press, 2000), 3.

34 The Shirakawa Hakuo house was a powerful family in charge of the Jingikan from the twelfth century who also served in Shinto rites performed at the imperial palace. They were also major competitors with the Yoshida family for control and influence over Shinto shrines through the Tokugawa period. The *Jingihakke gakusoku,* a text composed in 1816, contains a compendium of their doctrines. See *Encyclopedia of Shinto,* http://eos.kokugakuin.ac.jp/modules/xwords/entry.php?entryID=367.

35 He lived from 1791 to 1844.

36 The passage from the *Nihonshoki* is: "Summer fourth month, twenty-ninth day. An edict was issued as follows: 'The Empire was entrusted (by the Sun-Goddess to her descendants, with the words) "My children in their capacity as Deities, shall rule it."'" The phrase of the commentary comes after this. See Aston, *Nihongi,* Vol. 2, 226.

37 History of the Sui Dynasty, thirteenth of the twenty-four dynastic histories compiled under Wei Zheng in 636 during Tang dynasty, eighty-five scrolls. This section of the text is the *Annals of Music.*

38 The Chin dynasty was from 265 to 420 and is divided into two parts, the Western Chin period ([西晉], 265–316) and the Eastern Chin period ([東晉], 317–420). This history is the fifth of twenty-four dynastic histories, compiled by Fang Hsüanling in 648 during the T'ang dynasty.

39 Emperor Hsüan, who reigned (569–82) during the Ch'en (or Southern Ch'en) Dynasty, the fourth and last of the Southern Dynasties in China, eventually superseded by the Sui Dynasty.

SUGGESTED READINGS
(PARTS 1 AND 2)

Bernstein, Gail Lee. *Japanese Marxist: A Portrait of Kawakami Hajime 1879–1946.* Cambridge, MA: Harvard University Press, 1976.

Brownlee, John S. *Japanese Historians and the Nationalist Myths, 1600–1945; The Age of the Gods and Emperor Jinmu.* Tokyo: The University of Tokyo Press, 1997.

Chamberlain, Basil Hall. "The Invention of a New Religion". London: Watts & Co., 1912.

Irokawa Daikichi. *The Culture of the Meiji Period.* New Haven: Princeton University Press, 1985.

Freidel, Wilbur M. *Japanese Shrine Mergers 1906–1912.* Sophia University, Tokyo: Monumenta Nipponica Monograph. 1973.

———. "The Establishment of Shrine Shinto in Meiji Japan." *Japanese Journal of Religious Studies* 2 (1975):137–68.

———. "A Fresh Look at State Shinto." *Journal of the American Academy of Religion* 44 (1975):547–61.

Fukase-Indergaard, Fumiko and Michael Indergaard. "Religious Nationalism and the Making of the Modern Japanese State." *Theory and Society* 37 (2008):343–74.

Garon, Sheldon M. "State and Religion in Imperial Japan, 1912–1945. *Journal of Japanese Studies* 12 (Summer, 1986):273–302.

Hardacre, Helen. *Shintō and the State 1868–1988.* Princeton, NJ: Princeton University Press, 1989.

Harootunian, Harry. *Overcome by Modernity: History, Culture, and Community in Interwar Japan.* Princeton, NJ: Princeton University Press, 2000.

Holtom, Daniel C. *The Political Philosophy of Modern Shinto, A Study of the State Religion of Japan.* Tokyo, Asiatic Society of Japan, 1922.

———. *The Japanese Enthronement Ceremonies: With an Account of the Imperial Regalia* (New York: Kegan Paul International, 1996).

———. *Modern Japan and Shinto Nationalism: A Study of Present-Day Trends in Japanese Religions.* Chicago, IL: The University of Chicago Press, 1943.

Huffman, James. *Japan and Imperialism, 1853–1945.* Ann Arbor, MI: Association of Asian Studies, 2010.

Hylkema-Vos, Naoimi. "Katō Genchi—A Neglected Pioneer in Comparative Religion." *Japanese Journal of Religious Studies* 19 (1990):375–95.

Inoue Nobutaka. "The Formation of Sect Shinto in Modernizing Japan." *Japanese Journal of Religious Studies* 29 (2002):406–27.

Isomae Jun'ichi. "The Conceptual Formation of the Category 'Religion' in Modern Japan: Religion, State, and Shintō." *Journal of Religion in Japan* (2002):226–45.

———. "The Formative Process of State Shinto in Relation to the Westernization of Japan: The Concept of 'Religion' and 'Shinto.'" In *Religion and the Secular: Historical and Colonial Formations,* edited by Timothy Fitzgerald, 93–101. London: Routledge, 2016.

Itō Yūshi. "Kawakami Hajime and Inoue Tetsujirō's Conflicting Views of Religion and State." In *Japan in Crisis: Essays on Taishō Democracy,* edited by Bernard Silberman and H.D. Harootunian, 172–83. New York: Routledge, 1974.

Kawada Minoru. *The Origin of Ethnography in Japan: Yanagita Kunio and His Times.* Translated by Toshiko Kishida-Ellis. New York: Kegan Paul, 1993.

Mehl, Margaret. "Scholarship and Ideology in Conflict: The Kume Affair, 1892." *Monumenta Nipponica* 48 (Autumn, 1993):337–39.

Mori Kōichi. "Yanagita Kunio: An Interpretative Study." *Japanese Journal of Religious Studies* 7 (June–September, 1980):83–115.

Morse, Ronald. *Yanagita Kunio and the Folklore Movement: The Search for Japan's National Character and Distinctiveness.* New York: Routledge, 1990.

Murakami, Shigeyoshi, *Japanese Religion in the Modern Century.* Translated by. H Byron Earhart. Tokyo: University of Tokyo Press, 1980.

Nakai, Kate Waldman, "State Shinto." In *Routledge Handbook of Modern Japanese History,* edited by Sven Saaler and Christopher W.A. Szpilman, 147–59. London: Routledge, 2018.

Ohnuki-Tierney, Emiko. "The Emperor of Japan as Deity (*Kami*)." *Ethnology* 30 (July, 1991):199–215.

Okuyama Michiaki. "Religious Nationalism in the Modernization Process: State Shintō and Nichirenism in Meiji Japan." *Nanzan Bulletin* 26 (2002):19–31.

———. "'State Shinto' in Recent Japanese Scholarship." *Monumenta Nipponica* 66 no. 1 (2011):123–45.

———. "Recent Research on 'State Shinto.'" *Nanzan Institute for Religion and Culture Bulletin* 42 (2018):8–22.

Rimer, J. Thomas, Editor. *Culture and Identity: Japanese Intellectuals During the Interwar Years.* Princeton, NJ: Princeton University Press, 1990.

Sakamoto Koremaru. "The Structure of State Shinto: Its Creation, Development, and Demise." In *Shinto in History: Ways of the Kami,* edited by John Breen and Mark Teeuwen, 272–94. Honolulu: University of Hawai'i Press 2000.

Scheid, Bernard, Editor. *Kami Ways in Nationalist Territory: Shinto Studies in Prewar Japan and the West.* Vienna: Österreichischen Akademie der Wissenschaften, 2013.

Shillony, Ben-Ami, Editor. *The Emperors of Modern Japan.* Leiden: Brill, 2008.

Shimazono Susumu. "State Shinto and the Religious Structure of Modern Japan." *Journal of the American Academy of Religion* 73 (December, 2005):1077–98.

———. "State Shinto and Emperor Veneration." In *The Emperors of Modern Japan,* edited by Ben-Ami Shillony, 53–78. Leiden: Brill, 2008.

———. "State Shinto in the Lives of the People: The Establishment of Emperor Worship, Modern Nationalism, and Shrine Shinto in Late Meiji." *Japanese Journal of Religious Studies* 36 (2009):93–124.

Stalker, Nancy K. *Prophet Motive: Deguchi Onisaburō, Oomoto, and the Rise of New Religions in Imperial Japan.* Honolulu: The University of Hawai'i Press, 2008.

Tipton, Elise. *Modern Japan: A Social and Political History.* New York: Routledge, 2002.

Thal, Sarah. "A Religion that was Not a Religion: The Creation of Modern Shintō in 19th Century Japan." In *Inventing Religion: Rethinking Belief in Politics and History,* edited by Derek R. Peterson and Darren R. Walhof, 100–14. New Brunswick, NJ: Rutgers University Press, 2002.

Ueda Shinji, "Japanese Imperialism: Political Philosophy based on the Shinto Emperor Ideology." *Journal of Asia-Pacific Affairs* 5 (February, 2004):89–113.

Part 3

SHINTO AND ULTRA-
NATIONALISM IN THE
1930S AND 1940S

INTRODUCTION

This section contains works by propagandists, government ministries, and agencies published during the 1930s and early 1940s. "The way of *kannagara*," is an essay by Kōno Seizō, a major propagandist for the state orthodoxy in the 1930s and 1940s. The *Kokutai no hongi* (Cardinal Principles of National Polity), published by the Ministry of Education (*Monbushō*), was designed to instruct students about the underlying spirit that runs through Japan's history, unifying the Japanese people. The third selection, dating from 1941, is the Ministry of Education's *Shinmin no michi* (The Way of Subjects), a short guide defining the basic duty of imperial subjects as being loyal and obedient to the will of the emperor. The fourth selection, the *Jinja hongi* (The Cardinal Principles of Shrines) published by the Board of Divinities in 1944, served as a means of fulfilling the Board's mission to promote reverence for the *kami*. These readings show how State Shinto played an important role in the government's increasingly authoritarian efforts at national indoctrination. These texts were tied institutionally to the ministries and agencies directly associated with the state-supported system of national shrines, imperial worship, and public education.

Historical overview

1930 to 1945 was a tumultuous time for Japan. Beginning with the Hara Takashi cabinet of 1918, the "Taishō Democracy" had promised a genuine parliamentary-based monarchical system. However, by 1930, the possibility of a stable civilian constitutional government was in trouble. Civilian officials' authority was increasingly being usurped by the military, whose generals and admirals increasingly wielded authority over domestic as well as foreign affairs. By 1937, the last vestiges of a civilian party-based system had all but disappeared as Japan went to war with China. By 1940, the new Prime Minister General Tōjō Hideki (1884–1948) commandeered an autocratic state on a war footing. By then, Japan was already caught in its quagmire in China, while unknowingly rushing headlong toward disaster as it planned its attack on Pearl Harbor.

Economically, Japan careened from boom to bust during this period. Throughout the 1920s, the banking system had been plagued by financial instability, exacerbated by the devastating Great Kanto Earthquake of 1923 that caused substantial damage to the country's infrastructure.

In 1927, despite special measures taken by the Bank of Japan, massive bank failures occurred, leading to a nationwide financial panic. Economic turmoil in turn produced political instability, with the opposition party, the Seiyūkai, coming to power after the resignation of the then ruling Kensei party's Wakatsuki Cabinet. While the new Tanaka Cabinet (1927–29) restored calm to the markets through financial relief bills and banking reforms, Japan's return to economic stability was short-lived. Following the New York Stock Exchange crash in 1929, Japan was badly hit by the global Great Depression, made worse by protectionist policies of the United States that levied high tariffs on Japanese imported goods. The rapid appreciation of the yen due to the government's ill-timed decision to return to the gold standard was yet another financial blow.[1]

The "Shōwa Depression" of 1930–32 that followed was the worst economic downturn in Japan's modern history. Over 20 percent of all urban workers became unemployed, and rural farmers faced starvation in the face of collapsing agricultural prices, coupled with the devastating crop failures in 1931 and 1934, particularly in north-eastern Japan.[2] A cacophony of ephemeral Marxist-leaning and left-wing parties, like the National Masses Party (Zenkoku Taishūtō), called for radical changes, such as immediate unemployment benefits, lowering tenant fees, the legalization of labor unions, and "doing away with the violent oppressive bureaucracy."[3] In response to Japan's economic woes, Prime Minister Inukai's new finance minister, the great statesman Takahashi Korekiyo, was able to put Japan on the road to fiscal recovery, although his austerity budget in 1934 had dire social and political consequences.[4] The fires of civil unrest arose with growing anger at government indifference to rural poverty, corruption and incompetence, and the rapacious *zaibatsu*, the family-controlled businesses with a vice-like grip on the Japanese economy; and at an international system seemingly hostile to Japan's national interests.[5] This anger ultimately weakened Japan's civilian parliamentary government.

Along with economic problems, Japan also faced domestic social and political turmoil with the rise of rightist extremism. The ultranationalism of the 1930s was partly the fruit of Meiji and Taishō officialdom's efforts to create a State Shinto centered on the emperor as the "august descendant" of the sun goddess Amaterasu. The Japanese emperor, worshipped along with other imperial *kami* at state sponsored shrines and whose benevolent reigns were "unbroken from ages eternal," was the focus of compulsory moral education courses (*shūshin*). His sacred image (*goshin'ei*) and his Imperial Rescript on Education were piously venerated in public schools, and he served as a symbol of the unique essence of the Japanese nation (*kokutai*).

Right-wing societies styled themselves as patriotic defenders of imperial Japan. Some saw their mission as defending Japan's unique national character against dangerous left-wing radical movements challenging imperial authority. The Anti-Red League (Sekka Bōshidan), for example, was dedicated to combating Communism and the labor union movement in Japan. Others, like the Society for the Foundation of the State (Kokuhonsha), founded by Baron Hiranuma in 1924, were jingoists calling for Japan's special mission in Asia, by which they meant Japan's unfettered imperialist expansionism. By the 1940s, these colonialist sentiments had evolved into official policy as Japan expanded its control of China, Korea, and other parts of Asia under the anodyne banner of the Greater East Asia Co-Prosperity Sphere (*Dai tōa kyōeiken*).

By 1936, these rightist groups significantly increased in numbers reaching over 600,000 members.[6] Many of them saw their mission to free Japan from its "national emergency" by calling for a "Shōwa Restoration." This idea had its source in the thought of radical nationalist Kita Ikki (1883–1937) whose book *A Plan for the Reorganization of Japan* (1923) pushed for revolutionary violent change. Domestically, Kita called for the forcible removal of the privileged cliques of corrupt counselors, military and party power brokers, and *zaibatsu* special interests who surrounded the emperor. Kita called for a *coup d'état* with "the people as the main force and the emperor their commander" to restore the pure union that originally existed between the emperor and the Japanese people.[7] Economically, he also wanted to eliminate the huge concentration of land and capital controlled by big business and landowners to benefit all of the people. Socially, he proposed a host of welfare measures that would remove inequality and improve conditions for the working class.[8] Internationally, he argued for Japan's military hegemony over all of East and South Asia, with the goal of freeing Asia from Western colonialism, a policy which became a cornerstone of Japan's foreign policy after 1940.[9]

Although his book was banned, Kita's ideas spread among the masses, particularly among young army and navy officers whose families at the farm and factory had endured great suffering during the Depression. Disillusioned by the status quo, they took action to save Japan from its "national emergency"—economic depression, the glaring wealth disparity between the elite and working classes, and worrisome external threats from abroad. What these rightist groups shared was a rejection of materialism and individualism in favor of a faith in the unique powers of the "Japanese spirit" and a faith that the emperor could directly unite with the people to save Japan. However, they vehemently opposed the existing Japanese imperial system with its officially sanctioned ideology of unswerving obedience and unquestioned loyalty to a state that legitimated and, in turn, was backed by a capitalist system that enriched special interests.[10]

Ultra-right groups engaged in many acts of terrorism and intimidation, causing enormous political chaos. The first of these occurred in November 1930 when Prime Minister Hamaguchi was assassinated by a fanatic outraged by the London Naval Treaty, signed April 22, 1930.[11] In 1932, a former finance minister, Inoue Junnosuke, and Dan Takuma, the managing director of Mitsui, were assassinated by an extremist group called the League of Blood (Ketsumeidan). Soon afterward came the "May 15 incident," when a group of young navy officers tried to destroy civilian government by killing the Seiyūkai party's Prime Minister Inukai. The result was that the party-run civilian government was replaced by a "national unity cabinet" of eminent civilian and ranking military leaders, appointed by the elder statesman Prince Saionji.

Academic freedom also came under assault. Right-wing extremists attacked leftist and liberal academics whose work they viewed as an affront to the imperial dignity. An important example is the 1935 "Minobe Incident" where the former Tokyo Imperial University constitutional scholar and then member of the House of Peers, Minobe Tatsukichi (1873–1948), was forced to resign for his "emperor organ theory" (*tennō kikansetsu*), a theory that envisaged true sovereignty lying in the state rather than the emperor. This liberal reading of the Meiji Constitution, uncontroversial in the Taishō period, became vilified by ultranationalists who attacked Minobe for subverting the notion of the emperor's absolute sovereignty. It spawned a movement, ratified by a resolution passed in the Diet, to "Clarify the National Polity" (*kokutai meichō*).[12] Another case was the censorship of Waseda University historian Tsuda Sōkichi (1873–1961). His books, *Kojiki oyobi Nihonshoki no kenkyū* (Research into the *Kojiki* and *Nihonshoki*, 1924), *Jindaishi no kenkyū* (Study of the Divine Age, 1924), *Nihon jōdaishi kenkyū* (Research on the History of Ancient Japan, 1930), and *Jōdai Nihon no shakai oyobi shisō* (The Society and Thought of Ancient Japan, 1933), got him convicted

123

in 1940 of the crime of *lèse-majesté* (*fukeizai*) under the Publications Law (Shuppanhō Ihan). As is apparent from his work in this reader, he was a historian who cast doubt on key elements of State Shinto faith: the historicity of the first Emperor Jinmu, the precept that the imperial line of emperors existed "unbroken from ages eternal," and the historical veracity of the imperial chronicles. His academic research ran afoul of the official imperial way (*kōdō*) ideology underpinning state nationalism.

On February 26, 1936, young officers staged a second *coup d'état* to eliminate what they called traitors and evildoers surrounding the throne. They led fifteen hundred troops who took control of government installations in Tokyo while dispatching assassins to murder the top civilian and military leadership. The revolt collapsed in four days, when Emperor Shōwa summarily ordered troops to put down the rebellion by arresting and ultimately executing the rebel leaders.[13] Nonetheless, many senior military leaders remained sympathetic to the rebels' cause. A key reason was that the military's interests remained opposed to the civilian government's policies. For example, the austerity budget of Finance Minister Takahashi, one of the assassinated officials, included large cuts to military spending, which the army and navy vehemently opposed.[14]

The February 26 Incident points to a third major characteristic of this period—Japan's increasingly bellicose activities abroad. In the 1920s and 1930s, the Japanese empire found itself increasingly embattled internationally as it aggressively advanced its sphere of influence, especially in regard to its "special interest" in China. Foreign relations with the West had gradually deteriorated on several fronts. The Japanese felt the humiliating sting of racism with the U.S. Exclusion Act of 1924, which stopped Japanese immigration to curb "the yellow peril." The public, which broadly approved of Japan's imperialist ambitions abroad and a strong national defense, grew increasingly boisterous, chafing at the unfair treaties they believed directly opposed Japan's interests. In particular, they were deeply offended by the London Naval Treaty of 1930. The navy also viewed the treaty as a blatant attempt to weaken its defensive capabilities, ensuring its inferiority to the West, and was infuriated when Prime Minister Hamaguchi Osachi ratified it. He became the victim of an assassination attempt soon afterward.[15]

The Manchurian Incident clearly displayed the military's willingness to act independently of civilian control. Extremists in the Japanese imperial Kwantung army, stationed in Mukden, had become anxious that Japan was losing its opportunity to control northeast China's valuable resources. They staged a fake terrorist incident, blowing up a small section of the South Manchuria Railway, which the army used as a pretext for a massive military response. It resulted in Japan's *de facto* control over their new puppet state of Manchukuo. Such adventurism by the Japanese in China was rejected by the great Western powers at the League of Nations in 1933. The Japanese response was to reject Western political pressure. They left the League of Nations and continued their aggressive military territorial expansionism in China. The outbreak of fighting at Marco Polo Bridge in Beijing in 1937 marked the beginning of the Sino-Japanese war. On the home front, the public's response to the war was initially enthusiastic. Patriotism was the order of the day, now that Japan had to defend itself against those who would try to thwart its ambitions in the East and the Pacific. Most Japanese citizens fully supported the army, the emperor, and the nation's goals to guard the colonies, expand control of needed resources abroad, and secure the prosperity of the empire.[16]

From 1937 until 1945, the Japanese economy was fully mobilized for war. During this period, an official Planning Board (1937), a National Mobilization Law (1938), Prince Konoe's formation of the Imperial Rule Assistance Organization (Taisei Yokusankai), and a strong one-party unity cabinet—ultimately led by the ultranationalist army general Tōjō Hideki—destroyed the last vestiges of Japan's civilian party-based system along with the country's fragile free market economy. By 1943, after preparing for total war in the Pacific, the military created a national defense state (*kokubō kokka*) that ruled over a planned economy, controlled industrial production, and designed a system of forced factory labor and public food rationing.

Developments in Shinto

The state in this period grew ever more authoritarian institutionally, legally, and ideologically. Different chronologies have been given to define this moment in the formation of State Shinto. Murakami Shigeyoshi calls it the "period of fascist state religion," dating from the 1931 Manchurian Incident to the end of World War II in 1945.[17] The goal was to foster the patriotism and national unity needed to support the war effort by indoctrinating and compelling Japanese subjects to conform to the imperial way.

The challenge of new religious movements

New religions continued to be a vibrant and controversial feature of Japanese life at the beginning of this period. But some posed challenges by resisting direct governmental control and by promulgating ideas and activities that were perceived as dangerous to the state. This is particularly true of one of the most powerful of them, Ōmotokyō, led by its colorful leader Deguchi Onisaburō. Nancy Stalker, a specialist in Ōmotokyō, has noted that Western studies of pre-1945 Shinto often assume that all that existed at the time was a "monolithic" State Shinto. But the existence of popular religious movements like Ōmotokyō show much more religious diversity. Ōmotokyō "clearly embodied a strong Shinto identity, but refused to conform to the modern state's definition of Shinto or religion, and they repeatedly came into conflict with authorities."[18]

In the 1930s Onisaburō drew inspiration from the radical right who sought a "Shōwa Restoration." Like them, he wanted to free Japan from unjust wealth inequality, political corruption, and threats from abroad. To that end, he launched a patriotic association tied to Ōmotokyō, called the Shōwa Shinseikai. While the organization's ultimate goal was to save Japan in its national emergency, its well-publicized mass petition campaigns and support of popular agrarianism deeply threatened the ruling powers. In 1935, the government acted to suppress Ōmotokyō for *lèse-majesté* and breaching the Public Security Preservation Law (Chian Ijihō). This led to the wholesale destruction of the group's facilities and the imprisonment of Onisaburō himself.[19] The important point here is that religious movements like Ōmotokyō offered alternative paradigms to the state nationalism of the imperial system. The government worked hard to craft a convincing ideological response to what it considered subversive groups.

Legal developments—Public Security Preservation Law (1925) and the Religious Organizations Law (1939/40)

This period saw ever-expanding government control and suppression of religious groups institutionally, politically and ideologically. The 1925 Public Security Preservation Law was designed to curb dissent by anti-government groups like the Japanese Communist Party.

But the law was ambiguously worded with a broad mandate to stifle anyone who went against national polity (*kokutai*). This law had the chilling effect of greatly limiting freedom of speech and religion.[20] For example, Oomoto's activities were considered dangerous by the authorities; in 1921 the government persecuted it as a heretical religion (*jakyō*), and in 1935–36 Onisaburō was ruthlessly prosecuted and imprisoned for violating this law.[21] Ōmotokyō's fate was a cautionary tale for other new religious organizations, both Buddhist and Shinto-based, which were subject to the same persecution if they were perceived as dangerous to the state.

The Religious Organizations Law (*Shūkyō Dantaihō*), passed by the Diet on April 8, 1939, was a complex thirty-seven article piece of legislation giving the state expansive authority over religious groups. It rationalized preexisting edicts and laws and clarified the legal status between religious organizations (*shūkyō dantai*), by giving them special official status and tax exemption. It also gave official recognition to some "quasi-religious groups" (*ruiji shūkyō dantai*). These were often the subject of police harassment but were now classified legally as "religious associations" (*shūkyō kessha*) under government administration, though without tax exempt status.[22] Key provisions included formal applications for building permits; official registration and regular reports detailing areas such as employees, facilities, and budget; a rule that each group must have one leader; and detailed penalties for any disruptions of general peace and order.[23] Given that the law allowed the state to ban any religious group deemed contrary to state orthodoxy, it was the ultimate tool for exerting absolute control over religious freedom. That was the reason why it was one of the first laws that the Supreme Commander for the Allied Powers (SCAP) rescinded in 1945.[24]

Institutional developments: The Jingiin

The governmental bureaucracy that administered Shinto shrines changed during this period. The Board of Divinities (Jingiin), an extra-ministerial government administrative agency of shrine affairs attached to the Home Ministry, was created by Imperial Rescript 736 on November 9, 1940 to replace the Bureau of Shrines (Jinjakyoku). According to Shinto scholar Sakamoto Koremaru, its creation marked an important milestone in Japan's officially approved myth-history, the 2,600th anniversary of the founding of the country by Emperor Jinmu. The Board's mandate was to administer Ise and oversee the network of national, imperial, and lower-ranked shrines, shrine priests, and shrine mergers of unranked shrines.[25] An important function in the Board's portfolio was propagating the reverence to the *kami*, a mission inspired by the 1935 political movement to "Clarify the National Polity" (*kokutai meichō undō*). This was designed to create an official State Shinto ideology that served the interests of the Japanese militarists at the head of the state.[26] It comes as no surprise, then, that the Board of Divinities was quickly dissolved by the Allies in 1946 in accordance with the Shinto Directive.[27]

Developments in pre-war Shinto—*Kokutai* ideology

This section's readings are from the works of propagandists, government ministries, and agencies published during this period. The first selection, "Kannagara no michi" (The Way of Kannagara, Reading #20) is by Kōno Seizō, a professor who became president of Kokugakukin University in 1935 and was a major propagandist for the state orthodoxy in the 1930s and 1940s. He authored many popular tracts and radio broadcasts on what he called the "cult of *kannagara.*" Kōno was also a member of a board of specialists assisting the Ministry of Education (*Monbushō*) in its indoctrination activities. In 1937, that ministry produced the *Kokutai no hongi* (The Cardinal Principles of Shrines, Reading #21), the second selection in this unit. This text was designed to instruct students about the underlying spirit that runs through Japan's history, unifying the Japanese people. It treats the divine origin of Japan and the imperial line recounted as the "Age of the Gods" in the *Kojiki* as an historical fact, and it highlights the theme that "Our country is a divine country governed by an emperor who is a deity incarnate." The third and fourth selections date from World War II. In August 1941 the Ministry of Education issued *Shinmin no michi* (The Way of Subjects, Reading #22), a short guide defining the basic duty of imperial subjects as being loyal and obedient to the will of the emperor. The *Jinja hongi,* published by the Board of Divinities in 1944, served as a means of fulfilling the Board's mission to promote reverence for the *kami.* Sakamoto Koremaru argues that the Board's publications were "milder in ideological tone" than the texts issued by Ministry of Education or the Bureau of Indoctrination and Education (Kyōgakukyoku).[28]

These readings are perfect examples of Helen Hardacre's definition of State Shinto, a definition that emphasizes the changed character of Shinto in imperial Japan. She uses State Shinto "to identify Shinto mediation of state-sponsored ideological campaigns."[29] These readings show how State Shinto played an important role in the government's increasingly authoritarian efforts at national indoctrination. These texts were tied institutionally to the ministries and agencies directly associated with the state-supported system of national shrines, imperial worship, and public education. All were designed to instill reverence for the divine emperor and the imperial *kami,* as well as to instill an ethic of loyalty, self-sacrifice, and obedience to the state. As such, they promoted what Stalker calls an "orthodox state nationalism" that countered the calls of the radical right for the revolutionary overthrow of the existing government.[30]

In his book, *Japan's Holy War,* Walter Skya has argued that the 1930s were very different from the earlier Meiji and Taishō periods. It was now very dangerous for anyone to question the "rigid ideological and religious conformity" as outlined in these texts.[31] It was a time, as Daniel C. Holtom has aptly described it, when state orthodoxy was

> so successfully imbued through constant reiteration in the schools, in the newspapers, in magazines, in books, over the radio, in all manifold agencies of propaganda of an all-powerful state, and which are so inextricably merged with the sanctions of religion that rejection of the stereotype becomes an indignity offered to the deity and criticism a form of treason.[32]

The great scholar of State Shinto, Murakami Shigeyoshi, calls this state orthodoxy the discourse on national polity (*kokutairon*). Western authors, such as William P. Woodard and Wilbur M. Fridell, also see this discourse as vital to what they call the "kokutai cult" of 1930s and 1940s Japan.[33] To be sure, *kokutai* (national polity) is a key concept of the period. Kōno Seizō, for example, was a key pre-war exponent of *Kokutai* Shinto.[34] In his lengthy 1939 essay, "Waga kokutai to shintō" (Our National Polity and Shinto), he unequivocally states at the outset, "The *kokutai* is our national characteristic."[35] In the reading included here, "Kannagara no michi" (the way as it is with the gods), Kōno substitutes *kannagara* for *kokutai,* but his term retains much of the meaning of *kokutai.* It refers to an ancient mystical unity between Shinto, the emperor, and the Japanese state. Of course, the *Kokutai no hongi* also uses the word in its title. The *Shinmin no michi* begins with the sentence, "The way of the imperial subject is the source of our national polity (*kokutai*)." The *Jinja hongi* (Reading #23) quotes approvingly the famous words of the Imperial Rescript on Education, describing "the glory of the fundamental character (*kokutai*) of Our Empire."

But what is *kokutai*? The term has a long and complex history, originating from the Chinese classics where it refers to a "form of government" or national dignity.[36] Without going into detail, by the eighteenth century in Japan, it was used by both Confucian and national learning scholars to refer to Japan's unique "national polity."[37] As the foundation of the modern Japanese nation state, *kokutai* is basically defined in Article 1 of the 1889 Meiji Constitution: "The empire of Japan shall be reigned over and governed by a line of emperors unbroken for ages eternal."[38] *Kokutai* stands for an ideology that glorifies "Japan's traditional uniqueness and superiority based on the rule of an unbroken line of emperors."[39] But *kokutai*, as intellectual historian Carol Gluck has noted, remains a very ambiguous concept. Although it became a legal term in the 1925 Public Security Preservation Law, its meaning remained vague: Anyone who organized a group with the intent of "changing the *kokutai*" was guilty of a criminal offense. The meaning the phrase seems to have here, then, is obscure: Anything that goes against the Japanese way goes against the *kokutai*.[40]

The fact of the matter is that *kokutai* was subject to multiple interpretations and remained unclear when it was used in key documents like the Imperial Rescript on Education (1890) and the Public Security Preservation Law. This ambiguity remained even after the ultrana- tionalist movement to "Clarify the National Polity" in 1935. A major result of this effort to clarify *kokutai* was to transform it from a secular-political into a "lofty, mystical, and sometimes impenetrable" concept.[41] John S. Brownlee defines the meaning of *kokutai* of this time as "the essential truths of Japan, which might be termed religious, or even metaphysical, because they required a faith at the expense of logic and reason."[42]

This definition drew upon the past. By the eighteenth and nineteenth centuries, national learning scholars like Motoori Norinaga had already emphasized the non-rational spiritual dimension of Japan's unique national polity. Norinaga and others believed it originated as an "ancient way," as recounted in the early Japanese chronicles and literature. Japan's ancient way was a utopian society ruled over by a line of benevolent emperors whose great ancestor, the sun goddess Amaterasu, had bequeathed to them the three divine treasures symbolizing their divine mandate to eternally rule Japan.[43] Norinaga's famous treatise, *Naobi no mitama,* opens by emphasizing Japan's divine and special origin:

> Japan is where the awesome sun goddess, the ancestor of all the gods, appeared. This is why Japan is superior to all other countries, since all countries receive her plentiful benevolence. The goddess held the heavenly symbol in her hands. These are the three divine treasures that have been transmitted by the court for genera- tions. She decreed that Japan was to be the land where her descendants would reign forever. Thus, in the beginning the imperial throne was established here along with heaven and earth.[44]

The myths of the "Age of the Gods" in the chronicles, treated as historical fact by Norinaga and other national learning scholars, became the inspiration of patriotic education texts like the *Kokutai no hongi* of the thirties and forties.[45]

Indeed, any pretense that State Shinto was simply a form of national morality that was non-religious in character disappears in works from this period. Katō Genchi (Reading #18), for example, distinguishes Shinto from sect Shinto, calling it, after Lafcadio Hearn, a "religion of loyalty." It is "Japanese patriotism suffused with religious emotion; or, in other words, a peculiar enthusiastic patriotic sentiment, often soaring into the plane of adoration or religious worship, towards the emperor or mikado, a manifest deity." Kōno Seizō begins his essay "Kannagara no michi" (The Way of *Kannagara*, Reading #19) by baldly stating that "*kannagara* has been from ancient times a national faith essentially Japanese, as well as the most fundamental belief of the race." This faith can be traced back to the age of the gods as noted in the *Kojiki* and *Nihonshoki*. This way from that time onward has been "the essence and life blood of the nation." For Kōno, the Manchurian Incident of 1931 was the critical moment for the reawakening of the spirit of the way. Shinto was much more than a moral code, being based on a reverence toward Amaterasu and the emperor as the spiritual foundation of Japan.

Both Kōno and Katō show the important role Shinto elements play in *kokutai* ideology of the time. But seeing State Shinto as a "religion" means redefining terms. *Kokutai* ideology is based upon what Norman Haven has called an "air" strategy. Shinto is not a voluntary organized religion, nor a local cult of the *kami*, but is part of the air Japanese breathe. It pervades Japanese culture, nationhood, and one's very being as a Japanese subject.[46] "Things Shinto," Isomae Jun'ichi points out, were neither sacred nor secular, religious nor ethical, but were "seen as part of an all-encompassing concept in which the national body (*kokutai*), and its closely related system of emperor worship, came to be emphasized."[47] Ultimately, *kokutai* is something supra-religious in character.

All of the readings point to beliefs, doctrines, or great principles that are the foundation for this supra-religious national faith. Kōno, for example, claims that the "way of *kannagara* was the fundamental principle and guiding power of rising Japan." This is also clear in the key documents, like the Imperial Rescript on Education and the Great Teachings (*taikyō*) of the Meiji government's Great Teachings Dissemination Campaign (Taikyō Senpu Undō, 1870–75). The five principles Kōno outlines in his essay are the essence of this way. The *Kokutai no hongi, Shinmin no michi,* and *Jinja hongi* also suggest an eternal spirit runs through history which is the basis of an ethical way that distinguishes Japanese subjects from other peoples. As the *Jinja hongi* puts it,

> [Japanese subjects] put the emperors' divine commands into effect by wholeheartedly and unconditionally respecting the ancestral will, serving generations of emperors, and exhibiting the fine virtues of loyalty and filial piety. This brings about an incomparable unity of the sovereign and his people that form one great family state . . . This is the essence of our national polity, incomparable and dignified, stretching back to ancient times and unchanged for eternity.

What are the key ideas and principles that define this "supra-religious national faith" of the *kokutai* cult?[48] The propaganda and moral textbooks of the 1930s and 1940s are noteworthy because they attempt to systematize and unify early elements of *kokutai* thought into an ultranationalistic patriotic faith.[49]

The first element is reverence of the emperor as a living deity (*akitsumikami* or *arahito-gami*) and direct descendent of the sun goddess, Amaterasu, through her grandson Ninigi no Mikoto and Emperor Jinmu. Reverence towards the emperor, who in the Meiji Constitution is described in Article 3 as "sacred and inviolable, " and to the unbroken line of emperors, who, as living *kami*, have reigned eternally over Japan (Article 1) as absolute rulers, is the foundation of the nation.[50] The sacredness of the emperor was a key component of nationalist policies around 1930 designed to counter what was perceived as the growing threat of left-wing social and labor movements. The government, for example, spared no opportunity to praise the activities of Emperor Meiji and to designate sites connected to him as "sacred." By 1945 there were over 1,375 sites nationwide that were so designated, and in government publications, Emperor Meiji's pronouncements and poetry were prominently displayed. Government in the 1930s seemed comfortable using the word "sacred' in their nationalist orientation. Isomae Jun'ichi argues the emperor system (*tennōsei*) became the "unchange-able national essence," an unfathomable beyond and "transcendent entity" that "seemed suitable for replacing the Christian god as the founding principle of the nation state."[51]

Second, the emperor, given sacred authority as a living deity, combined both religious and political roles as a divine ruler. The unity of rites and governance (*saisei icchi*) is a basic tenet of *kokutai* faith. But *saisei icchi* does not indicate a theocracy but rather a polity where the emperor serves both as the chief priest over Shinto rites and as sovereign head of state. According to Daniel C. Holtom, the emperor's role was as a ritual intermediary to the nation's *kami*, while his political authority was legitimated by his divine power as the descendent of Amaterasu. His divine power was such that "all important affairs of state of whatever nature were guaranteed and protected by supernatural sanctions."[52] By the Meiji period, however, the emperor's political role had dramatically changed. The Constitution explicitly stated the emperor wielded political power directly, rather than indirectly and cer-emonially. For example, Article 11 of the Constitution stipulates him as commander in chief of the military. The emperor's clearly defined direct role in governance, including his author-ity to wage war as Grand Marshal (*daigensui*) of the army and navy forces was a departure from most of Japanese history.[53]

Third, Japan is a divine country (*shinkoku*), a land of the *kami* created by the gods and presided over by the sun goddess Amaterasu. The divine creation of the Japanese isles and their sacred history are faithfully recounted in the "Age of the Gods" section of the official chronicles. Walter Skya describes this belief as a kind of "Shinto biblical creationism."[54] "Land of the gods," however, generally does not refer to particular local shrines dedicated to tute-lary spirits but to the country as a whole. Texts like the *Kokutai no hongi* describe Japan as standing "high above the other nations of the world" because of its pristine, incomparably beautiful mountains and rivers and blessed temperate climate. As Julia Adeney Thomas has argued in her book, *Reconfiguring Modernity*, this concept of nature differs from that in Western Romanticism where the solitary individual's soul merges with nature through a deeply personal experience of the sublime. Instead, what we have here is a "political image of nature as national consciousness"—an expression of an ultranationalist ideology where natural harmony reflects collective harmony. As Amaterasu rules over the heavenly and sacred *kami* of the world, so too the emperor rules over the divine land bequeathed by his ancestors, where the people live harmoniously in accord with the imperial will. According to the *Kokutai no hongi*,

> [s]uch a homeland as this and the national life which centers round the family, and which is expressive of the concord between the sovereign and the people, have together brought forth our national character that is cloudless, pure, and honest.[55]

Fourth, all Japanese subjects are part of a family state. They are unified harmoniously into a mystical whole—what Holtom called a "*corpus mysticum*"—by one collective purpose: to serve the imperial will.[56] The nation is nothing other than an extension of the traditional family unit (*ie*), with the emperor and empress ruling at its head as father and mother respectively. Imperial subjects are the emperor's children who must serve him like their own father. Loyalty is an extension of filial piety.[57] Ultimately, the state (*kokka*) replaces the family as the key collective whole. People find their true identity as imperial subjects of the emperor, to whom they owe their total allegiance.[58] The emperor therefore plays a unifying role as the divine embodiment of *kokutai* as the head of the family state.

The fifth element of *kokutai* faith is that the Japanese have "clear and bright minds" that reveal their unique spirit (*Yamatodamashii*).[59] That spirit is devoted to reverence of the emperor with the goal "to have our hearts become like the spirit of the *kami*." This is described by Katō Genchi (Reading #18) as a "unique spirit of national service of the people that comprehends not only their morality but their religion culminating in centripetal mikadoism or their own peculiar form of loyalty or patriotism towards the divine ruler." The core of this spirit defines "who they were—or should aspire to be—as a nation, people, and race."[60]

This "Yamato spirit" is at the heart of a fifth element of *kokutai*—Japan's unique national morality (*kokumin dōtoku*), which is detailed in officially approved texts like the *Kokutai no hongi* and the *Shinmin no michi*. But this spirit is not just a special emotional and reverential tie to the emperor as the divine ruler; it is also ethical in nature—defining the way of life for the Japanese people. Imperial subjects are enjoined to live a life of self-sacrifice, loyalty, obedience, and service to the emperor. This "imperial way" (*kōdō*) opposes the self-centered individualism and materialism of people from Western countries.[61] Such an ethic is based upon the traditional great Confucian principle of loyalty and filial piety (*chūkō no taigi*). But what was once a family-based ethic in Confucianism is now transformed into the imperial way, as we can see from documents like the Imperial Rescript on Education.[62] That way can be realized only by developing a spirit of self-sacrifice through ascetic mental and physical self-discipline. As the *Kokutai no hongi* describes it, imperial subjects should have "[a] pure, cloudless heart . . . which, dying to one's ego and one's own end, finds life in fundamentals and the true way." The kind of training advocated by this and other texts of the time is based on Bushidō, the way of the warrior.[63] Authentic mental and physical discipline, therefore, put "us in harmony with our moral natures as subjects of the imperial state and contribute to advancing the state's fortunes." By "dying to the self," these moral education texts assert, one can free oneself from the taint of self-interest and attain a "clean and cloudless heart" selflessly devoted to the emperor.[64]

Scholars like William P. Woodard and Wilbur M. Fridell take issue with identifying the *kokutai* cult with Shinto. For them it was an ideology that was invented by Meiji officials and later forced upon the Japanese public by ultranationalist extremists and militarists in the 1930s and 1940s; it is not a form of Shinto, but a distinct, separate, and independent phenomenon. In their view, the Shinto Directive mistakenly conflated the kokutai cult, an officially imposed system of teachings, doctrines, rites, and practices, with shrine Shinto, the organic beliefs and customs of the Japanese people at the folk, local, and regional levels.[65]

But others have noted that *kokutai* thought contains many Shinto elements. Early on, Daniel C. Holtom noted that while there is much truth in the view that modern State Shinto was "the artificial creation of sheer political utilitarianism, enforced by the authority of the gendarmerie," "*bona fide* historical aspects of Shinto" also lie at its heart. *Saisei icchi,* for example, has a long history; in ancient Japan, priestess rulers and later priest kings served dual roles as ritual intermediaries with the spirit world and government administration.[66] Generally, the view that prevails today is that the notion of *kokutai* was largely Shintoist in orientation.[67]

A second point of contention is over the extent to which *kokutai* thought really had influence over Japanese citizenry. Murakami Shigeyoshi's classic model of State Shinto describes four stages of development, the last, from 1931 to 1945 being when State Shinto becomes what he calls a "fascist state religion." State Shinto, according to Murakami, was a religion because it had a set of fixed beliefs and doctrines with *kokutai* ideology at their core, which, through governmental efforts, were forced on the Japanese people through compulsory attendance at shrines, official calendrical rites reverencing the emperor, and mandatory moral education classes in the schools.

However, others have criticized Murakami's model as exaggerated and overly simplistic. Historian of Japanese religions, Shimazono Susumu, for example, notes that few scholars would dispute that *kokutai* ideology was essential to the spiritual life of the nation from 1869 to 1945. However, he questions whether Murakami's top-down model of state coercion and manipulation of the people works to understand this. He raises several important questions: Were *kokutai* ideas and practices simply imposed from above on the Japanese people? To what extent did the ideology really influence people in their daily lives? In what ways can it also be considered a religion and a part of Shinto? In what ways was it different from other movements within Shinto? Shimazono is in favor of looking at State Shinto from a bottom-up perspective, one that examines how ordinary people were vital for the spread of *kokutai* ideology, especially through their everyday actions of emperor veneration.[68]

Others dispute the extent to which *kokutai* ideology was spiritually important, even in the 1930s and 1940s. Shinto scholar Sakamoto Koremaru, for example, notes that the state, even after 1931, "did not have the capacity, the 'fascist capacity' if you will, to force on the entire religious world shrine worship and, through it, reverence for the deities."[69] What they had built instead in the Meiji era was a jury-rigged system that defined shrine Shinto, by bureaucratic legerdemain, as non-religious in character. Shrines were officially prescribed as "objects of reverence." This designation, at least on paper, was supposed to avoid religious friction because compulsory attendance at Shinto shrines and moral education was solely to foster patriotism, loyalty, and good citizens rather than stirring religious fervor among the masses. But Sakamoto notes caustically that such coercive practices coupled with a bland *kokutai* ideology, much like the "Great Teachings" (*taikyō*) of the early Meiji period, "could never lead to more than a superficial concern for the nation's shrines."[70] He also notes that the Board of Divinities (Jingiin), which was established in 1940, marks the first time when State Shinto, in the strictest sense of the term as defined in the Shinto Directive, really comes into being. So, only late in this period, just before the onset of the Pacific War, does the government create an organization to disseminate its official political ideology.[71] Despite the government's compulsory shrine attendance policies and propaganda efforts, in the end there was nothing they could do to artificially spark people's fervor if they were not already interested in reverencing the deities, the emperor, and the imperial ancestors. For Sakamoto, the bureaucratic efforts to mass-induce reverence expose "the fragility of a faithless State Shinto."[72] This is a topic that the folklorist Orikuchi Shinobu discusses in his post-war essay, "A new direction for Shinto" (Reading #25).

The questions that Shimazono and others have raised about State Shinto in this period are still open to debate: To what extent were *kokutai* ideology and emperor veneration an essential part of State Shinto? To what extent were they simply imposed upon a docile public or embraced and actively spread from below? What exactly was State Shinto to the Japanese people? To what extent was the *kokutai* cult a modern invention of the Meiji state? To what extent does it share religious/political elements and structures from the past? Is the *kokutai* cult best understood as a part of Shinto, or it is different?[73] What was the relation between *kokutai* ideology or emperor veneration and local shrines? How is State Shinto related to other forms of nationalism? How do we make sense of official claims that State Shinto of the 1930s and 1940s was "non-religious in character," when it is sometimes described even by its proponents in religious terms.

Notes

1 Shizume Masato, "The Japanese Economy during the Interwar Period: Instability in the Financial System and the Impact of Worldwide Depression," *Bank of Japan Review* (2009):5.
2 James Huffman, *Japan and Imperialism, 1853–1945* (Ann Arbor, MI: Association of Asian Studies, 2010), 42–43
3 Christopher Gertais, "Political Protest in Interwar Japan—1 Posters and Handbills from the Ohara Collection (1920s–1930s)," https://ocw.mit.edu/ans7870/21f/21f.027/protest_interwar_japan/pij1_essay.pdf.
4 Shizume, "The Japanese Economy," 6–8.
5 Huffman, *Japan and Imperialism*, 42.
6 Peter Duus, *Modern Japan* 2nd ed, (Boston: Houghton Mifflin, 1998), 216.
7 Quoted in George Wilson, *Radical Nationalist in Japan: Kita Ikki 1883–1937* (Cambridge, MA: Harvard University Press, 1969), 68.
8 Ibid., 70–74.
9 Ibid., 67.
10 Nancy K. Stalker, *Prophet Motive: Deguchi Onisaburō, and the Rise of New Religions in Imperial Japan* (Honolulu: University of Hawai'i Press, 2008), 172.
11 Peter Duus, *The Rise of Modern Japan* (Boston: Houghton Mifflin, 1976), 210.
12 John S. Brownlee, *Japanese Historians and the National Myths, 1600–1945: The Age of the Gods and Emperor Jinmu* (Tokyo: University of Tokyo Press, 1997), 133–35; James Heisig and John C. Maraldo, eds., *Rude Awakenings: Zen, the Kyoto School, & the Question of Nationalism* (Honolulu: University of Hawai'i Press, 1995), 113.
13 Ibid., 212–13.
14 Shizume, "The Japanese Economy," 6–8.
15 James L. Huffman, *Japan and Imperialism*, 44.
16 Ibid., 44–46.
17 See Shimazono Susumu, "State Shinto in the Lives of the People, The Establishment of Emperor Worship, Modern Nationalism, and Shrine Shinto in Late Meiji," *Japanese Journal of Religious Studies* 36 (2009):101. Shimazono has problems with Murakami's chronology. Others, such as Isomae Jun'ichi have developed alternative timelines for the development of State Shinto. Isomae would see the 1930s as part of a larger third and final stage of development dating from 1906. It was a period when the state "actively pursued national indoctrination policies (*kokumin kyōka seisaku*) through the use of shrines and a rigid institutional form of State Shinto came to be spread" (97). See Isomae Jun'ichi, "The Formative Process of State Shinto in Relation to the Westernization of Japan: The Concept of 'Religion' and 'Shinto,'" in *Religion and the Secular: Historical and Cultural Formations,* ed. Timothy Fitzgerald (New York: Routledge, 2007).
18 Stalker, *Prophet Motive*, 3.
19 Ibid., 170–90.
20 Ueda Shinji, "Japanese Imperialism: Political Philosophy based on Shinto Emperor Ideology," *Journal of Asia Pacific Affairs* 5 (February, 2004):101.
21 Ibid., 98–99, 170–90.
22 Hans Martin Krämer, "Beyond the Dark Valley: Reinterpreting Christian Reactions to the 1939 Religious Organizations Law," *Japanese Journal of Religious Studies* 38 (2011):184; Sakamoto Koremaru, "Religious Organizations Law," *Encyclopedia of Shinto*, http://eos.kokugakuin.ac.jp/modules/xwords/entry.php?entryID=1098.
23 Ibid., 184–87.

24 Ibid., 182–83; Mark Mullins, "Religion in Contemporary Japanese Lives," in *Routledge Companion of Japanese Culture and Society,* edited by Victoria Lyon Bestor and Theodore C. Bestor (New York: Routledge, 2013), 64. Hans Krämer (see note 22 above) paints a different picture, arguing that its effects were less repressive in some cases than integrative.

25 Sakamoto Koremaru, "The Structure of State Shinto: Its Creation, Development and Demise," in *Shinto in History: Ways of the Kami,* edited by John Breen and Mark Teeuwen (Honolulu: University of Hawai'i Press 2000), 288–89. See also his "Jingiin," *Encyclopedia of Shinto,* http://eos.kokugakuin.ac.jp/modules/xwords/entry.php?entryID=1102.

26 Sakamoto notes, however, that neither the Jinjakyoku nor the Jingiin, which was established late in the war, really had much an effect on fostering reverence beyond its powers of exhortation to convince students or, for that matter, the general populace as a whole. See Sakamoto, "The Structure of State Shinto," 290–2.

27 Shimazono, "State Shinto in the Lives of the People," 97.

28 Sakamoto, "Jingiin."

29 Helen Hardacre, *Shinto: A History* (New York: Oxford University Press, 2017), 440.

30 Stalker, *Prophet Motive,* 172.

31 Walter A Skya, *Japan's Holy War: The Ideology of Radical Shintō Nationalism* (Durham, NC: Duke University Press, 2009), 285.

32 Daniel C. Holtom, *Modern Japan and Shinto Nationalism* (Chicago: The University of Chicago Press, 1943), 24. Also quoted in Walter A. Skya, *Japan's Holy War,* 284.

33 William P. Woodard, *The Allied Occupation of Japan 1945–1952 and Japanese Religions* (Leiden: Brill, 1972), 7–14; Wilbur M. Fridell, "A Fresh Look at State Shinto," *Journal of the American Academy of Religion* 44 (1976):547–61; Murakami Shigeyoshi, *Kokka Shinto* (Tokyo: Iwanami Shoten, 1970), 140–1.

34 Norman Havens, "Shinto," in *Nanzan Guide to Japanese Religions,* edited by Paul L. Swanson and Clark Chilson (Honolulu: University of Hawai'i Press, 2006), 16–17.

35 Walter A. Skya, *Japan's Holy War,* 282–84. This essay is his commentary on the *Kokutai no hongi.*

36 Shimazono Susumu, "State Shinto and Emperor Veneration," in *The Emperors of Modern Japan,* edited by Ben-Ami Shollony (Leiden: Brill, 2008), 59. Many scholars have surveyed this history including Daniel Holtom, Maruyama Masao, Muraoka Tsunetsugu, and others. See Mark Teeuwen, "State Shinto: An 'Independent Religion,'" *Monumenta Nipponica* 54 (Spring 1999):111–21.

37 For an incisive study of its development, see John S. Brownlee, "Four Stages of the Japanese Kokutai (National Essence), http://www.adilegian.com/PDF/brownlee.pdf. Of course, other lengthy studies also exist by Daniel C. Holtom, Muraoka Tsunetsugu, Carol Gluck, Klaus Antoni, Helen Hardacre, and others. However, Mark Teeuwen has pointed out important lacunae in some of these studies, particularly the absence of any discussion of the influence of Confucian *kogaku* (ancient learning). See his "State Shinto: An "Independent Religion?" *Monumenta Nipponica* 54:111–21.

38 Kawamura Satofumi, "The National Polity and the Formation of the Modern National Subject in Japan," *Japan Forum* 26 (2014):25.

39 Shimazono, "State Shinto and Emperor Veneration," 59. Shimazono is quoting Tsujimoto Masashi's general definition from his essay on "Kokutai shisō."

40 Carol Gluck, *Japan's Modern Myths: Ideology in the Late Meiji Period* (Princeton, NJ: Princeton University Press, 1985), 282. In effect, the law was directed against anyone from Communists to new religious movements like Ōmotokyō who challenged the status quo. Gluck observes that *kokutai* here has much the same meaning as being un-American during the "Red Scare" in America after World War II.

41 Ibid., 282–83.

42 John S. Brownlee, "Four Stages of the Japanese *Kokutai.*"

43 Kawamura, "The National Polity," 29.

44 Sey Nishimura, trans. "The Way of the Gods: Motoori Norinaga's *Naobi no Mitama,*" *Monumenta Nipponica* 46 (Spring, 1991):27.

45 For a more nuanced analysis, see Nelly Naumann, "Japanese Myth Ancient and Modern," *Bulletin of the European Association for Japanese Studies* 36 (December, 1991):5–12.

46 Norman Havens, "Shinto," in *Nanzan Guide to Japanese Religions,* edited by Paul Swanson and Clark Chilson (Honolulu: University of Hawai'i Press, 2006), 15.

47 Isomae, "The Formative Process," 98.

48 Many authors have summarized the key elements. See, for example, Woodard, *The Allied Occupation of Japan,* 10–13.

49 It is important to note that Isomae Jun'ichi and many other scholars have shown that *kokutai* teachings and doctrines have a long history. The totalitarian "kokutai cult" of the 1930s and 1940s is not as much a radical break as the outcome of long process of development throughout the Meiji/Taishō periods. Isomae, for example, traces three phases of development in State Shinto. His third is initiated in 1906 with the establishment of the government supervised system of official and national shrines (*kankokuheisha*). He thus abandons Murakami's model, which posits a third period of the "completion of the system, which he dates from 1931 to 1945. See Isomae, "The Formative Process," 97.

50 On the connection between the emperor and militarism in the pre-war period, see Daniel C. Holtom, "Shinto in the Postwar World," *Far Eastern Survey* 14 (February 14, 1945): 29–30; Skyra, *Japan's Holy War,* 214, 265.

51 Isomae Jun'ichi, "Religion, Secularity, and the Articulation of the 'Indigenous' in Modernizing Japan," in *Kami Ways in Nationalist Territory: Shinto Studies in Prewar Japan and the West,* edited by Bernhard Scheid and Kate Wildman Nakai (Vienna: Österreichische Akademie der Wissenschaften Wien, 2013), 43.

52 Daniel C. Holtom, "New Status of Shinto," *Far Eastern Survey* 15 (January 30, 1946):18–19.

53 Yanagawa Keiichi and David Reid, "Between Unity and Separation: Religion and Politics on Japan, 1965–1977," *Japanese Journal of Religious Studies* 6 (December, 1979):501–2. For more information on this see Murakami Shigeyoshi (Reading #28).

54 Ibid., 266.

55 Julia Adeney Thomas, *Reconfiguring Modernity: Concepts of Nature in Japanese Political Ideology* (Berkeley: University of California Press, 2001), 201.

56 Holtom, "Shinto in the Postwar World," 33.

57 Ueda, "Japanese Imperialism," 108–11.

58 This idea is also reflected in the thought of Watsuji Tetsurō. See Bernard Bernier, "National Communion: Watsuji Tetsuro's Conception of Ethics, Power, and the Japanese Imperial State," *Philosophy East and West* 56 (January, 2006):93.

59 As described in Nagao Ryūichi's theory of *kokutai.* See Shimazono, "State Shinto and Emperor Veneration," 56.

60 John W. Dower, *War Without Mercy: Race & Power in the Pacific War* (New York: Pantheon Books, 1986), 24.

61 Shimazono, "State Shinto and Emperor Veneration," 66–68.

62 Ueda, "Japanese Imperialism," 97; Walter Skya, *Japan's Holy War,* 267–70.

63 Christopher Goto-Jones, "The Way of Revering the Emperor: Imperial Philosophy and *Bushidō* in Modern Japan," in *The Emperors of Modern Japan,* edited by Ben-Ami Shollony (Leiden: Brill, 2008), 40–43.

64 Walter Skya, *Japan's Holy War,* 272–73.

65 William Woodard, *The Allied Occupation,* 11; Fridell, "A Fresh Look," 556.

66 Holtom, "New Status of Shinto," 18.

67 See Shimazono, "State Shinto and Emperor Veneration," 65.

68 Ibid., 54–55.

69 Sakamoto, "The Structure of State Shinto," 286.

70 Ibid., 287.

71 This effort was too little too late since the Jingiin's key work of political propaganda, the *Jinja hongi* was published only in 1944, near the end of the war.

72 Sakamoto, "The Structure of State Shinto," 290–91.

73 Shimazono, "State Shinto and Emperor Veneration," 55.

20

KŌNO SEIZŌ[1]

Kannagara no michi (The way of *kannagara*, 1940)

Kōno Seizō (1882–1963) was born in Kisai (present Kazo City), Saitama Prefecture. After entering Kokugakuin in 1902, he was deeply influenced by Shinto scholar Tanaka Yoshitō and the philosopher Inoue Testujirō, graduating in 1905. He also graduated from the Research Institute for the Imperial Classics (Kōten Kōkyūjo). While serving as a priest at the family shrine, from 1915 he taught at Kokugakuin University as a lecturer, and from 1918 he served as the superintendent of academic affairs and the director of the Research Institute for the Imperial Classics. He was appointed professor of Kokugakuin University in 1920 and submitted his Ph.D. dissertation on *Kokugaku no kenkyū* (Research on National Learning) in 1931. He was later named president of the university in 1935. Retiring from that post in 1942, he continued his professorship until 1946, when he was forced to resign because of his wartime activities. He became an advisor for the Association of Shinto Shrines in 1947. After being pardoned, he was reinstated as an emeritus professor at Kokugakuin in 1952, becoming the head of the Saitama Shrine Organization (until 1960).

Daniel C. Holtom referred to him as "one of the most influential of the contemporary teachers of the Shinto priesthood."[2] Kōno himself claimed to take his inspiration from Yoshida Kanetomo (1435–1511), the founder of a famous school of Shinto known as Yuiitsu Shinto ("The One and Only Shinto"), whom he admired for his marvelous abilities to spread Shinto teachings and deepen the national spirit.

Among his many works are: *Shintō no kenkyū* (Shinto Research, 1930), *Nihon seishin hattatsushi* (History of the Development of Japanese Spirit, 1932), and *Kokugaku no kenkyū* (Research on National Learning, 1932). Notably, he was also a member of the board of specialists assisting in the Ministry of Education's publication of the *Kokutai no hongi* (The Cardinal Principles of the National Polity, 1937) that was used to train students to give complete loyalty to the emperor and the imperial state.

The following essay appeared in July 1940 in the journal *Monumenta Nipponica*, published by Sophia University in Tokyo. In this essay, Kōno explains that Shinto or the "cult of *kannagara*" (the way as it is with the gods) is "the spirit of Japan" and "a national faith" devoted to Amaterasu, the sun goddess whose essence is embodied in the emperor himself.

Two points need to be briefly noted here. First, Kōno sees Shinto in explicitly spiritually patriotic terms. It is a national faith in the imperial way (*kōdō*) that has existed from the very beginning of Japanese history and has been revived anew since the Russo-Japanese War of 1904–5. Second, the exact meaning of the phrase, *kannagara no michi,* which originally appears in the *Nihonshoki* and other early texts, is open to dispute. Daniel C. Holtom, in editorial notes appended to the translation (not included here), raises several objections to

Kōno's uncritical use of the term. However, it was the great Japanese historian, Tsuda Sōkichi, who definitively showed that the term is deeply ambiguous and that in the early *Nihonshoki* could hardly have referred to the imperially based Shinto religion that Kōno espouses.[3]

KANNAGARA NO MICHI (THE WAY OF *KANNAGARA*)
(1940)

Translator unknown

The meaning of *kannagara*

Kannagara has been from ancient times a national faith essentially Japanese, as well as the most fundamental belief of the race. It has, however, from about the Meiji Restoration been formalized and defined as *kannagara no michi* or "the way as it is with the gods."[4] Although the origin of this faith can be found in "the Age of the Gods," the tense situation, the spiritual revival, the realization of the foundation of the empire, and the ideal of a progressing and expanding nation at the time of the Meiji Restoration were the causes which led to the conviction that this faith, defined as *kannagara no michi,* was the fundamental principle and guiding power of rising Japan.

The religion of *kami,* designated as the religion of the deities of heaven and earth (*amatsukami, kunitsukami*), has existed since the mythical ages. With regard to its substance we can refer to the *Kojiki* (Records of Ancient Matters), *Nihonshoki* (Written Chronicles of Japan), *Kujiki* (Ancient Records), and *Engishiki* (Institutes of the Engi Period, 901–23). Of the many deities, Amaterasu Ōmikami (Heaven Shining Great Deity) is the highest and most august, and her sublime soul is enshrined at Ise. The *kami* of heaven and the *kami* of earth included in the "eight hundred myriad" *kami* (*yao yorozu no kami*) are all enshrined in national and other smaller shrines, but the *kami* of *kannagara* signifies the deity of heaven (*amatsukami*) or Amaterasu Ōmikami, who is the centre of this religion.

That *kami* of *kannagara* signifies the divine imperial ancestor, Amaterasu Ōmikami, will become clear in further examples, but the fact is taken for granted, because *kannagara* was an ancient expression implying the sanctity of the reign of the emperor, thence signifying that the emperor is the reincarnation of Amaterasu Ōmikami and that he rules the empire of Japan according to the divine message of this ancestral deity.

In the application of Chinese characters to write *kannagara* we find the words "*yuishin*" (惟神, just as it is with the gods) and "*zuishin*" (随神、in accordance with the gods) and "*zuizai tenjin*" (随在天神、in accordance with the existence of the heavenly gods) used. The character *yui* or *i* (惟) is read in Japanese *kore* (such) or *tada* (just), which indicates absoluteness or pureness. In the case of *zuishin*, the character *zui* (随) indicates "in accordance with," hence "in accordance with the gods" signifies the existence and reign of the emperor being "in accordance with the gods", or "according to the will of Amaterasu Ōmikami." We find practically the same meaning in *zuizai tenjin*, this being the combined expression of *yuishin* and *zuishin*. The characters *yuishin*, which indicate the profound and fundamental meaning of *kannagara*, have mainly been used. In the ancient classics, however, such as the *Kojiki, Nihonshoki,* and *Manyōshū* (Collection of a Myriad Leaves), it is generally written *ka-mu-na-ga-ra* (加武奈賀良) according to the sound of the syllables.

A point worth considering in the explanation of *kannagara* is the use of *kami-gara* in the place of *kannagara* which is found in the *Manyōshū*. The interpretation also of the classic word *kuni-gara* (national character) as well as that of *ie-gara* in popular use (family standing, birth, descent, lineage, etc.) and *hitogara* (personal character, personality, etc.) is of considerable help. As has already been mentioned in relation to the Chinese characters applied to *kannagara*, the word signifies "just as the gods (or god)", "like the gods (or god)" or "being in accordance with the gods (or god)," but later on, the word is used in a lighter sense as a figurative expression denoting sacred articles or a metaphor for the unresisting and submissive form of nature. The fundamental meaning of the word, however, can be determined from the separate bearings of the three parts which constitute the word. Firstly, *kami*, which is an individual word itself and pronounced *kan* when forming the first part of the word, signifies Amaterasu Ōmikami. *Na* is a possessive particle equivalent to *no* (of), and *gara* is the same as in *hitogara* (personal character), *iegara* (family custom or tradition), and *kuni-gara* (nation), and can be interpreted as expressing the essence or fundamental nature of a certain object. Hence the literal translation of *kannagara* becomes the expression of the essence or nature of Amaterasu Ōmikami.

Then, what is the essence or nature of Amaterasu Ōmikami? It signifies the sublime and mightiest power of the nation, namely the throne, and the great-august-heart or the soul of the ruler, which is embodied in the throne. In other words, it represents the divine soul of the ruler of the empire, the emperor. The emperor is the divine manifestation of Amaterasu Ōmikami and rules the empire in accordance with her will. Thus the emperor and the imperial throne, transmitted in an unbroken line, are sacred and inviolable. The will of Amaterasu Ōmikami is expressed as follows in the *Kojiki*:

> This Reed Plain 1500 Autumn Fair Ears Land is the region of which my descendants shall be lords. Do thou, my august grandchild, proceed thither and govern it. Go! and may prosperity attend thy dynasty, and may it, like heaven and earth, endure forever!

This august message of the imperial ancestor has been looked upon by later generations as an expression of the divine will co-existent with heaven and earth. It also is considered as the fundamental faith of the nation and the motivating force of all activities. Furthermore, it is the source and foundation of Article I of the Japanese Constitution, which reads: "The Empire of Japan shall be reigned over and governed by a line of emperors unbroken for ages eternal."

Thus the cult of *kannagara* is to have faith in the emperor who is the divine descendant of Amaterasu Ōmikami, and to revere and serve the emperor who rules according to the divine message of the Imperial Ancestor.

It is made known to us by the *Kojiki* and *Nihonshoki* that the word *kannagara* first originated at the time of the Taika Reform, about 1,250 years ago. The words *yuishin* and *zuizai tenjin* were first used in the imperial edict promulgated by Emperor Kōtoku in the third year of Taika (CE 647). In the *Manyōshū*, a collection of poems written from about this time to the Nara period, the word *kannagara* is used exactly nineteen times. About nineteen examples also can be found in the imperial edict of the *Shoku Nihongi* (Supplementary Chronicles of Japan), which is one of the most valuable historical documents succeeding the *Nihonshoki*. Generally the word was used as a term modifying the sanctity of any event or august conduct of the emperor, such as, for example, *kannagara omohoshimesu*

(just as it is with the gods [the emperor] realized . . .) or *kannagara funade sesu* (just as
it is with the gods [the emperor] went by boat . . .). The following example is from the
Manyōshū and is used to praise the sanctity of the empire ruled by a manifest deity who is
the descendant and reincarnation of the founder-goddess of the country. *Kannagara kotoage senu kuni*, which means, "just as it is with the gods, the nation [Japan] is a nation which
has no words of dissertation or argumentation." This comes from the long-dwelt-upon faith
that Japan is a sacred nation. Another example is one which points out and praises the loyal
and self-sacrificing spirit with which the people toil and strive to construct the Imperial
Palace buildings, and through this spirit of national service the sanctity of the emperor is
emphasized. *Itawaku mireba kannagara narashi*, which means, "if [you] watch [the people]
most carefully, [they] are just as it is with the gods."

From these examples it is quite plain that the frequency with which the word *kannagara*
was used in ancient days and the occasions on which it was used originated the term *kannagara no michi*, "the way as it is with the gods," a term signifying faith in the sanctity of the
emperor, and the spirit of moral and national life through service to the emperor. In this way,
the relationship or connection between *kannagara no michi* and the emperor, and *kannagara
no michi* and the people is exactly the same as in the case of Shinto, or "the way of the gods,"
which holds *kannagara* as its fundamental principle; it is the way of the emperor as well as
the way of the people. This principle is made clear in the Imperial Rescript on Education
promulgated by the Emperor Meiji, in the words which signify the unity of the instructions
handed down by the imperial ancestors and the traditional customs of the people.

Motoori Norinaga, one of the greatest scholars of Japanese classics, speaks of *kannagara*
in his *Rekichō shōshikai* (Vol. I), which are interpretations of the imperial edicts of the *Shoku
Nihongi*, as follows:

> All sentences relating to things concerning the emperor shall begin with *kannagara*,
> and this example is most frequent in the *Manyōshū*. The emperor is actually called
> *kami* or god, and is in reality a god, so acts and works as a god.

So far, we have found the word used in denoting the sanctity of the emperor, or indicating
the sacredness of the emperor, or at times showing the sanctity of some sacred object. But
various social changes and the consequent change in thought brought about another understanding of the word—namely one of supernatural and mystic significance which had the
tendency of pointing directly at *kami*, or god, itself. Examples to this effect can be found as
early as the *Manyōshū*, when *kannagara* was used in praising a sacred mountain or in relating the history of a religious stone.

This tendency came to be most prominent during the Heian period succeeding the Nara,
when the Fujiwara family extended their political as well as their social power throughout the
country. It was also the time when the Chinese classics were being studied and Buddhism was
being propagated, and therefore almost no documents of this age can be found in which the word
is used. The very rare occasions are when the word designates some particular *kami* or god.

This fact indicates that during the Heian period the worshipping of the gods of heaven and
earth (*tenjin chigi*) in the various shrines (*jinja*) was quite popular, whereas the power and
authority of the emperor was weak and did not prosper.

The sacred or mystic usage of the word *kannagara* indicating *kami* or god itself, can be
considered quite natural from an historical and social point of view, but, as has already been
mentioned, *gara* represents the essence or substance of the noun it follows.

In the *Manyōshū* exactly seven examples can be cited where the word *kami-gara* is used in the place of *kannagara*. The following example is one which praises the beauty of the province of Sanuki.

> *Kuni-gara ka miredomo akanu.*
>
> *Kami-gara ka koko da tōtoki.*

> ([The province of Sanuki]. Is it its provincial character which makes one never weary of gazing? Is it its godliness which makes it seem so holy?)

In the above example, *kunigara* represents the essential character of the province, and *kami-gara* represents the essential character of *kami*, or gods.

From these examples, it is clear that *kannagara* and *kami-gara* have the same meaning. *Kannagara*, however, has been used only in relation with the emperor, and, as the centre of *kami* lies in Amaterasu Ōmikami, so does the centre of the faith of *kannagara* lie in the emperor.

In the Heian period, the term *kannagara-mo* was frequently used, but the additional *mo* was only to give a lighter and milder effect to the word and had no result upon the meaning. The term is frequently found in the *Shoku Nihongi*.

About seven centuries ago the word *jinnō* (神皇) was first used. This word originated from the faith that the emperor and Amaterasu Ōmikami were identical and were of one august body. The noted *Jinnō shōtōki*, or the "Emperor's Genealogy," a work on divine right by Kitabatake Chikafusa (1293–1354), is based upon this faith of *jinnō*. This faith was further expressed, politically and morally, as *jinnō no michi* (the way of jinnō), and this was later abbreviated as *kōdō* (皇道, the imperial way). This spirit or faith was the guiding light in every respect of the Meiji Restoration. The spirit and faith of *kannagara*, expressed in various different terms was what united Japan, making her realize both her divine lineage and her divine nationality, and awakening a racial self-determination.

Lastly, it must be mentioned that the faith of *kannagara* expresses within it a feeling of assimilation and harmony, a tendency towards avoiding argumentation and willful adherence to one's personal opinions, the result of submitting to one's superiors and respecting them. These characteristics come from the fact that the faith of *kannagara* expresses one's small self or ego through society or the nation and acts and works in accordance with a great family and the will of the ancestors of that family, and not through the small will of an individual. Hence the meaning of *kannagara* has come to be recognized as "natural" or "not unnatural." The significance of the use and meaning of the word *kannagara* lies in the fact that the nature or character of the historical development of our country can be found identical with the nature or character of *kannagara*.

The classics in relation to the word *kannagara*

One of the first uses of the word *kannagara* in the ancient Japanese classics can be accounted for by the characters 神長柄 in Volume I of the *Manyōshū*, and the characters 可無奈我良 in Volume XVII of the same book, which are distinctly read *kannagara*, according to the sound of each character. However, in Volume I of the *Shoku Nihongi* the characters 随神 are found used in exactly the same manner and with the same meaning as 神随 in the *Manyōshū*. This brings us to the conclusion that the characters 随神 in the *Shoku Nihongi* are to be read *kannagara*, which takes the origin of the word further back in date. But through a more careful study we are able to trace a still older origin of the word. This origin, mentioned in the foregoing chapter, is found in the use of the words *yuishin* (惟神) and *zuizai tenjin* (随在天神) in the imperial edicts promulgated in the third year of Taika (CE 647) by Kōtoku Tennō. As is made clear by the explanatory notes in some old copied manuscripts, thought to be of the latter Heian period, the above-mentioned words cannot be read otherwise than *kannagara*. Consequently, the oldest document or classic in which the word is found is the imperial edict promulgated by Kōtoku Tennō. It cannot be doubted, however, that the spoken origin of the word goes back much further.

The explanatory notes in the *Nihonshoki* concerning the characters *yuishin*[5] also confirm the theory that they should be read *kannagara*. Furthermore, this fact can be deducted from the ideas and religious feelings expressed in the various edicts and Shinto prayers of that period. The explanatory notes of *yuishin*, written with Chinese ideographs, have caused a discussion among scholars concerning the most appropriate reading. But in whatever way they may be read, the fundamental meaning, which indicates the sanctity of the ruler of the empire and the way that is the way of the gods, verifies the fact that the characters *yuishin* should be read *kannagara*.

In the study of *kannagara*, one of the most important sources of material to be consulted is the *Shoku Nihongi*. In this classical document there are sixty-two imperial edicts promulgated by eight emperors, from Monmu Tennō to Kōnin Tennō, and the word *kannagara* is used exactly twenty times, including an additional explanatory sentence written by Motoori Norinaga. The edicts in which the word is most characteristically used are noted below. If these edicts are carefully studied, the way in which the word was used as well as its deep meaning will become clear to the student.

First Edict:

This was promulgated by Monmu Tennō upon his accession to the throne. In this edict we find the words, besides *kannagara*, which read "according as it is with the august child of the heavenly god" and "rule together with the Heavenly-Founder-August-God," which express the fundamental idea of *kannagara*.

Third Edict:

Promulgated by Genmyō Tennō upon her ascension to the throne.

Fourth Edict:

Promulgated by Genmyō Tennō in January of the first year of Wadō (CE 708).

Fifth Edict:

Promulgated by Shōmu Tennō upon his ascension to the throne.

Sixth Edict:

Promulgated by Shōmu Tennō in August of the sixth year of Jinki (CE 729) on the occasion of changing the name of the era to Tenpyō.

In this edict we find the additional sentence written by Motoori Norinaga.

Ninth Edict:

> Promulgated by Shōmu Tennō in May of the fifteenth year of Tenpyō (CE 743) on the occasion of the Crown Prince learning the sacred dance of the Boys' Festival (*gosechi no mai*).

Thirteenth Edict:

> Promulgated by Shōmu Tennō in April of the first year of Tenpyō-Shōhō (CE 749) on the occasion of the construction of the Daibutsu (Great Buddha) at Tōdaiji in Nara.

Fourteenth Edict:

> Promulgated by Kōken Tennō in July of the first year of Tenpyō-Shōhō upon her ascension to the throne.

Nineteenth Edict:

> Promulgated in July of the first year of Tenpyō-Hōji (CE 754).

Twenty-third Edict:

> Promulgated in August of the second year of Tenpyō-Hōji.

Fifty-fourth Edict:

> Promulgated by Kōnin Tennō in May of the third year of Hōki (CE 772).

The edicts between the twenty-fourth and the fifty-third, which are not mentioned, cover an exceedingly long period of time, which includes the three reigns of Kōken Tennō, Junnin Tennō, and Shōtoku Tennō. It is during that long period that Buddhism was at its height of popularity and monopolized the realm of thought. The reflection of the age upon the imperial edicts is what accounts for the omission of *kannagara*. Attention should be called, however, to the fact that in the forty-eighth edict promulgated by Kōnin Tennō, although the word *kannagara* is not actually found, its spirit is most significantly expressed.

Fifty-ninth Edict:

> Promulgated by Kōnin Tennō in April of the first year of Ten'ō (CE 781).

With this all the imperial edicts in the *Shoku Nihongi* which include the word *kannagara* have been mentioned.

Reference will now be made to its use in the poems of the *Manyōshū*. Most of the poems in the *Manyōshū* that have any relation with *kannagara* are those composed after the Taika Restoration and during the Nara period. The names of the composers and the dates of composition, as well as a detailed explanation of the poems, will not be given here. Only the volume and number of the poem will be given, and for a more careful and comprehensive study the reader is asked to consult a commentary of the *Manyōshū*.

Vol. I   No. 38, No. 39, No. 45, No. 50.

Vol. II   No. 167, No. 199, No. 204.

Vol. V   No. 813.

Vol. VI   No. 935.

Vol. XIII   No. 3253.

In this last poem, the characters read *kannagara* are written 神在随, which is an unusual example. It may be assumed that they are closely connected with 随在天神 of the imperial edict of the third year of Taika.

Vol. XVII   No. 4003, No. 4004.

In poem No. 4001 of the same volume, we find the characters (*ka-mu-ga-ra-na-ra-n*). Kamochi Masazumi, the writer of *Manyōshū kogi* (万葉集古義), says that the character 奈(*na*) has been omitted here by mistake (between *Ka-mu* and *ga-ra*), but in various other documents 加武賀良 (*ka-mu-ga-ra*) is often found. Consequently, it has commonly been accepted that *kamu-gara* is used with exactly the same meaning as *kannagara*.

Vol. XVIII   No. 4094.

Vol. XIX   No. 4254, No. 4266.

The two examples in Vol. XIX are used exactly in the same manner as in the imperial edicts and express most significantly the philosophical background of the meaning of *kannagara*.

Vol. XX   No. 4360.

If we make a list of the different ways in which *kannagara* was written in the *Shoku Nihongi* and the *Manyōshū*, we find in the imperial edicts of the *Shoku Nihongi* the characters 随神 twelve times, 神随 once, 神奈我良母 five times, 神奈賀良 once; and in the *Manyōshū* 神随 six times, 神在随 once, 神良柄 four times, 神奈我良 three times, 可武奈何良 twice, 可無奈我良 twice, and 可牟奈我良 once.

It is exceedingly important for us to remember that the fundamental spirit and meaning underlying the use of *kannagara* and *kamu-gara* is absolutely the same. Also, the fact that *kannagara* is mainly used in expressing the deification of the Japanese dominion, as well as of mountains and rivers, is a significant point to be noted. Another point deserving mention is that in the Heian period the characters 神柄 (*kamu-gara*), which are found in Vol. II No. 126, Vol. VI No. 907, Vol. XIII No. 3250, are mainly used to indicate the divine activity or function of the gods.

In the Heian period, with the extreme popularity of the Chinese classics and Buddhism, and the decline of the imperial power, the word *kannagara* is scarcely ever found. This age, overshadowed by the political power of the Fujiwara family, was one in which the Japanese classics were practically forgotten. We are able, however, to find three examples, given below, in which the word *kannagara* is used. But it is only in connection with the ritual of the Shinto gods.

First, in the imperial edict issued as a message to Hirota Ōkami (The Great God of Hirota), by Seiwa Tennō in December of the tenth year of Jōgan (CE 868). Secondly, in the imperial edict issued as a prayer to Matsuo-no-Daimyōjin (The Great God of Matsuo) to stop the rain, by Kōkō Tennō in August of the second year of Ninna (CE 886). And lastly, in the imperial edict issued as a prayer to all the gods, asking for prosperity during the year, by Konoe Tennō in April of the second year of Kyūan (CE 1146).

From the Heian through the Kamakura and well into the Muromachi period we are unable to find any classical documents relating to *kannagara*. The spirit, however, which was expressed by the words *shinkoku* (divine nation), *jinkō* (divine emperor), *Shintō* (divine way or the way of the gods), *kōdō* (imperial way), etc., remained throughout the ages, and in the Edo period the enthusiastic study of the ancient classics was the cause of a vigorous revival in all things relating to *kannagara*.

We have thus made a brief study of the classics in relation to *kannagara*. In the next chapter we shall make a historical survey of the development of the spirit and doctrine expressed by the word.

Japanese history and the faith of *kannagara*

It has already been made clear to us in the previous chapters that the faith of *kannagara* signifies the divine character of the emperor and indicates that, being the son of the heavenly gods, he rules according to the will of his ancestors. This fact is manifested in the historical evidences of Jinmu Tennō, the first emperor of Japan who established the nation according to the faith of *kannagara*. Receiving the divine message of the ancestral gods he undertook the great mission of establishing the empire of Japan. This fact is evidence enough to recognize in him the spirit and faith of *kannagara*.

In the historical records and achievements of Sūjin Tennō, the tenth emperor in line, and Ōjin Tennō, the sixteenth emperor in line, we also find marked evidence of the promotion of this faith. Later, at the time of the Taika Restoration in the era of the Emperor Kōtoku, the thirty-sixth emperor in line, this faith was manifested most conspicuously and, as has previously been mentioned, it was in this age that the characters *yuishin* and *zuizai tenjin* were first used to express the faith. It was also in this age that such words as the following, which express the divine character and supremacy of the emperor, came to be written in historical documents

明神御神御宇日本天皇詔旨

Akitsumikami to ame no shita shiroshimesu

Yamato no sumera mikoto no ohomikoto:

The heavenly-shining goddess and the heavenly-

august emperor of Yamato speak.

明神御宇日本根子天皇

Akitsumikami to ame no shita shiroshimesu

yamato neko sumera mikoto:

The heavenly-shining goddess and the heavenly-

august emperor of the Yamato country.

現為明神御八嶋国天皇

Akitsumikami to ohoyashima guni shiroshimesu

sumera mikoto:

The heavenly-shining goddess and the heavenly-

emperor of the august eight island country.

The following sentences also, praising the divine character of the emperor, later developed into the written forms of the imperial edicts proclaimed during and after the reign of Tenchi Tennō:

> First of all, the gods should be revered and comforted, and then after that political matters should be discussed.
>
> As two suns do not exist in the heavens, so it is that two sovereigns do not exist in the nation. It is for this reason that in heaven and on earth the emperor is the only being who should rule the people.

The spirit of *kannagara* thus developed a racial faith based upon the "spirit of the establishment of the empire" (健国精神), which later in the Nara period produced a culture indigenous to the nation. During this same period the nationalistic idea that Japan is "a nation which, as it is with the gods, makes no unnecessary argumentations" (*kannagara kotoage senu kuni*) was born. This idea is that Japan, being a divine nation, finds it unnecessary to argue or discuss over superfluous matters. In other words, it is a nation of deeds, not words. The pride also in the national language was expressed in terms that indicate a mystic element in the language. This was an outcome of a nationalistic tendency of the times, which stood in opposition to the Chinese culture and language which was then pouring in.

This nationalistic spirit was expressed in the Heian period by the word *Yamatogokoro* (Yamato spirit) and *Yamatodamashii* (the spirit of Japan), and in the Kamakura period it was expressed by the words *kami tsu kuni* or the country of the gods. From about the Kenmu Restoration it was expressed in the idea of *jinnō* (神皇), namely the idea or faith that the emperor is the divine descendant of Amaterasu Ōmikami and that he is identical with the ancestral gods. This idea was expressed theoretically and most emphatically in the *Jinnō shōtōki* (神皇正統記—The Emperor's Genealogy: Work on Divine Right by Kitabatake Chikafusa). This idea of *jinnō no michi* (神皇ノ道) or the way of the divine emperor is another expression of the faith of *kannagara*.

In the middle of the Muromachi period, with the advancement in the study of the various classics such as the *Nihonshoki* (Chronicles of Japan) and *Kojiki* (Ancient Chronicles), a demand for a national faith arose. The cause of this also can be found in the social uneasiness of that period. It was during this period, to fulfill the demand of the times, that Urabe Kanetomo of the Yoshida family established a systematic doctrine of Shinto called Yuiitsu-Shinto, or the

One and Only Shinto. This doctrine held, indeed, a prominent position in the realm of thought and in the religious circles of the time. It was a profound theory, based upon the principles of Shinto and at the same time harmonizing with the teachings of Confucianism and Buddhism. Later, in the Edo period, however, the doctrine was criticized in regard to the historical facts it contained, and rejected because of its impurity in respect to the Confucian and Buddhist elements that it included.

Nevertheless, Yuiitsu Shinto can be considered as the foundation of the systematic analysis of *kannagara*, and its social significance during that period plays a most important part in the historical development of *kannagara*.

In the Edo period, during the three hundred years of the Tokugawa shogunate, this Shinto doctrine, established by Yoshida Kanetomo, served as a stimulus for the development of various other branches in the Shinto faith and doctrine. For example, among the Confucians a doctrine advocating the unity of Confucianism and Shinto was promoted; the Buddhists supported a doctrine which claimed the unity of Buddhism and Shinto; and among the common people an instructive moral code upon Shinto was encouraged.

From about the middle of the Edo period with the advance of studies in the national classics, a Shinto theory or doctrine based upon the racial faith of worshipping the ancestral gods was established and promoted by the national learning (国学) scholars. This was Pure Shinto (純正神道) or Revival [Restoration] Shinto (復古神道), which awakened in the nation the racial and nationalistic faith of *kannagara*. It was a spiritual impetus to the nation at that time and acted as a motivating force which led to the Meiji Restoration.

The great way of *kannagara* was the fundamental principle of the national policy at the time of the Restoration, and Western civilization was introduced according to the ideals of ancestor-worship and nationalism. Owing, however, to the terrific speed with which new thoughts, customs, and principles were introduced after the Restoration, a marked decline in nationalistic ideas and in the spirit of *kannagara* was experienced. The introduction of democracy and Marxism particularly harassed the national faith during the Taishō era.

Later, however, after the Manchurian Incident in 1931, nationalistic ideas began to be promoted once again, and the realization of the national faith was vigorously promulgated. This spirit or faith was at the time recognized as *Nihon seishin* (日本精神), or the spirit of Japan; later with the development of the China Affair, *kōdō* (皇道) or the imperial way was recognized as the basis of *Nihon seishin*; and the fundamental principle of *kōdō* is no other than the spirit of *kannagara*. Thus the spirit of the nation, in its essential form, is known as the "great way of *kannagara*."

In the historical development of religious and spiritual ideas in Japan, the fact that Confucianism and Buddhism, as well as Christianity, were greatly influenced by the spirit of *kannagara*, is indeed worthy of notice.

The spirit of the foundation of the empire, which is based upon the spirit of *kannagara*, should be made clear to make us realize the practical merits of *kannagara* and also the activities of the nation. What, then, is the substance of the spirit of the foundation of the empire? Various definitions have been attempted, but the following five principles can be given as the essence of this spirit.

1   To have faith in the prosperity of the imperial throne, co-existent with heaven and earth.
2   And upon that faith to base a spiritual confidence in the activities of the nation, which consists in the unity of the one sovereign and his subjects.

3   To hold firm confidence in the nation, based upon the family system, with the emperor at the head, who guides the national activities and rules his subjects according to the spirit of "reverence to the gods and love of the people," and the people who revere the gods and respect the emperor.

4   Sincerely to desire the realization of a practical life based upon the above-mentioned nationalistic spirit.

5   To hold the ideal of perfecting the high and superior nation of Japan by ever endeavoring to keep in mind the faith and realize the desires which have been mentioned above.

The spirit of the foundation of the empire consists in the spirit and ideals which have hitherto been mentioned and have permeated the history, culture, racial characteristics, and life of the people. When imported cultures are judged by this spirit or when it acts as a motivating force in the activities of the nation, it emanates among the people as a practical and systematic racial spirit or moral code; and this racial spirit or moral code is the way of *kannagara*.

Shinto and *kannagara*

Kannagara is the quintessence of Shinto (神道). As to the first use of the Chinese characters relating to it in the *Nihonshoki* (Chronicles of Japan) reference has already been made in the previous chapters. It is clear, from the explanatory notes in the *Nihonshoki*, that *kannagara*, signified by the characters *yuishin* (惟神), was in compliance with Shinto and, at the same time, included in itself the doctrine and ideas of Shinto. Furthermore, from the Kamakura period, in which classic words were, on the whole, seldom used, through the Muromachi on to the first part of the Edo period, the doctrine of *kannagara* was expressed by such words as *jinnō* (神皇), *kōdō* (皇道), Shinto (神道), etc. In the latter part of the Edo period, *kōdō*, *Shinto*, and *sumegami no michi* (皇神の道) or the way of the emperor-god, were most prominent. Later, following the Meiji Restoration, it was expressed by *kannagara no daidō* (惟神 の大道) or the great way of *kannagara*. Nevertheless, throughout these various periods, the term Shinto was most popularly used, and its fundamental doctrine or principle was in accordance with *kannagara*. As to this point, Motoori Norinaga has given a comprehensive illustration in his famous book, *Naobi no mitama* (直毘霊).

In the writings concerning Yōmei Tennō found in the *Nihonshoki*, the word Shinto is used about fifty years earlier than *kannagara*. In the same book, about thirty years later, in relation to Jōmei Tennō, the following words are found: "From the point of view of the ancient way (*kodō*, 古道) . . ." Likewise, in the *Kojiki*, in the reign of Ōjin Tennō about a hundred and fifty years before this, the following sentence is found: "In this reign of mine all things should be well done according to the gods." These references are of great importance in the study of the doctrine of *kannagara*.

Later in the reign of Kōtoku Tennō, the word Shinto was again used, and its usage in this period was to distinguish the traditional doctrine, characteristic of the Japanese, from the various doctrines and religions, such as Buddhism and Confucianism, which were being enthusiastically introduced at that time. It was particularly used in referring to rites and ceremonies for the gods, and this was the reason which led to its broader use, as a term for the doctrine of "reverence to the gods."

In the Heian period, which was more or less one of literary prosperity, the doctrine of *kannagara*, or "Shintoistic" ideas, was expressed in religious ceremonies and public rites.

The influence also of Chinese studies, so popular during that period, led to the tendency to explain Shinto as a mystic doctrine which can be referred to in the Chinese classics. This was the main reason for which during this period the doctrine or faith of *kannagara* had no systematic development in any particular racial characteristic.

During this time, however, gradual adjustment and attunement between Confucianism and the indigenous faith of the nation took place. Particularly in regard to Buddhism, adjustment and assimilation with Shinto was necessary for its propagation, and a marked tendency developed both in theory and in practice. This led to the spread of the theory implying the "unity of the gods and Buddhism" or the "oneness of *kami* (神) and *hotoke* (仏)."

In the field of religion, during the Kamakura period, there was a strong demand, on the one hand, for a religion and faith characteristically Japanese and, on the other, for a religion most befitting the times. The Buddhist doctrines and Chinese ideas, which were being imported most enthusiastically, filled the demand of the latter, while the various theories of the Tendai and Shingon sects, which had been going through a gradual process of adaptation and assimilation since the Heian period, contributed a great deal to the establishment of a systematic theory or doctrine of the former. Moreover, the classical documents kept in the shrine and the traditional customs and ceremonies held a prominent position in forming a theoretical basis for the Shinto faith. It should also be noted that this age was one that welcomed philosophical speculation and mystical illustrations in various lines of religious thought; this can be considered as another reason for the comparatively rapid diffusion of the philosophical and intellectual aspects of Shinto during this period.

At the time of the "Restoration" in the Kenmu era (1334–36), which can be called the transitional period from the Kamakura to the Muromachi, Kitabatake Chikafusa, a loyal subject of the emperor, and a profound thinker, established a grand theory which united and harmonized the three doctrines of Shintoism, Confucianism, and Buddhism.

In the middle of the Muromachi period, however, Yoshida Kanetomo established a doctrine of Yuiitsu Shinto (唯一神道) or "the One and Only Shinto." This doctrine placed Shinto in a much higher position, emphasizing its authority and value, and incorporating into it the various ideas and theories of Confucianism and Buddhism. Particular emphasis was placed upon the principle: "The nation is a nation of the gods. The way is the way of the gods. And the ruler is the divine emperor."

Though there still remained various Buddhist elements whose presence prevented Yuiitsu Shinto from claiming a pure doctrine of its own, the application of traditional rites and the creation of complicated observances, together with various new theories, later led to a pure, fundamental, and more systematic doctrine. Thus, towards the latter part of the Kamakura period, with the gradual progress in the study of the *Nihonshoki* and various other classics, a strong national spirit began to arise.

Influenced by Yoshida Kanetomo's Yuiitsu Shinto, and owing to the marked development in education on various lines of study, the Edo period saw the development of numerous Shinto doctrines. It was through the efforts of the Confucian scholars, which included the Mito School and the *kokugakusha* (国学者) as well as many other Shinto scholars, that the Shinto faith, with its various doctrines, came to be intelligently appreciated under a more systematic order. Among the Confucian scholars there were Hayashi Razan, Yamaga Sokō, Yamazaki Ansai, Kaibara Ekken, and Yoshida Shōin. Among the national learning scholars there were Kamo Mabuchi, Motoori Norinaga, and Hirata Atsutane. Among the many Shinto scholars, Yoshikawa Koretari, Watarai Nobuyoshi, and Yoshimi Yoshikazu deserve mention. It should be remembered that, although diversities could be found among the various doctrines, the fundamental faith of Shinto, namely reverence to the gods and the emperor, and ancestor worship, was awakened, and a strong racial and national spirit began to be highly esteemed.

It was this spirit, during the Meiji Restoration, that promoted the idea of the imperial way and became the fundamental basis of Motoori's and Hirata's doctrine of *kannagara*. It was also the essence or the fundamental principle of Pure Shinto (*junsei Shintō*, 純正神道) or Revival Shinto (*fukko Shintō*, 復古神道) which can be considered as the motivating power of the Meiji Restoration. Directly following the Restoration, great emphasis was placed upon the idea or spirit of the imperial way, and from the first year of Meiji for six or seven years, a nationwide moral or spiritual campaign was carried on by the government for the diffusion of the "great way" of *kannagara*. The doctrine of *kannagara* at this time was a leading moral code representing the faith and spirit of Shinto.

To illustrate how greatly the "way of *kannagara*" was a leading factor in the polity of the nation, and to show how strongly it was emphasized in order to unite the nation, morally and spiritually, a brief reference may here be made to two or three Imperial Edicts promulgated during the first three years of the Meiji era.

> Reverence to the gods and regard to the ritual constitute the proprieties of the empire and are the fundamental principles of the national polity and education . . . On this occasion of reestablishment, Tokyo shall be the new capital, and we shall, in person, rule the nation. First of all, the rites shall be initiated and rules and regulations to govern the country shall be firmly established, thus reviving the way of *saisei icchi* (the unity of religion and state, 祭政一致). (An imperial edict promulgated on the seventeenth of the tenth month in the first year of Meiji [November 30, 1868] upon the emperor's visit to the Hikawa Shrine.)

> From the very day our great ancestor undertook the establishment of the empire, she paid homage to the gods, and treated her subjects with tender affection. The origin of 'the unity of religion and state' lies far back. (At the commemoration ceremony of the foundation of the empire held on the third of the first month in the third year of Meiji [February 3, 1870]).

> The heavenly gods and our heavenly ancestor have constituted the highest principle, and upon it they founded the first undertakings of a great achievement. Ever since, the emperors in line have acknowledged, inherited and proclaimed it. The ideal of 'the unity of religion and state' is held by the whole nation; the right ways in polity and education are clear to those on high, and the customs and manners of those below are in perfect order . . . At this time, the heavenly course of the nation has turned, and thus all things are become new. By all means, polity and education should be made clear to the nation, and thus the great way of *kannagara* should be promulgated. Therefore, preachers shall be ordered to propagate the way far and wide. (The imperial edict on the great teaching of *kannagara* promulgated on the same day.)

In the fifth year of Meiji, with the extension of religious propagation, professional instructors took the place of the preachers mentioned in the imperial edict. These professional instructors, consisting of Shinto priests, Buddhist priests, and various other people connected with social education, preached the doctrine of *kannagara* throughout the nation. Their activities and sermons were determined by the following three articles of the educational decree.

No. 1. Particular stress should be laid upon reverence to the gods and the love of the nation.

No. 2. The way of the gods and the way of man should be made clear.

No. 3. The emperor shall rule over us, and his subjects shall obey his will.

This exceedingly active movement influenced the people greatly until about the eighth year of Meiji, when a disagreement occurred between the Shinto priests and Buddhist priests concerning their religious propagation.[6]

After this, the necessity of laying more stress upon principles other than those of the popular Shinto religion was recognized. Furthermore, from about the eighth and ninth years of Meiji, with the successive establishment of religious organizations relating to Shinto, religious propagation terminated, and in its place there arose a marked tendency towards manifesting the national significance of the Shinto shrine. Following this, from about the twelfth to the thirty-sixth year of Meiji, a general decline in the idea of "reverence to the gods" and in the doctrine of "the way of *kannagara*" took place. Such words also as *kōdō* (皇道) or imperial way, and Shinto became rare terms among the people.

However, towards the end of the Meiji era, after the Russo-Japanese War, a great self-awakening of the nation took place, and this led to a strong revival of Shinto. In the beginning of the Taishō era, various decrees relating to the Shinto shrines were enforced, while court ritual and court ceremonies were gradually reestablished. This led to the rise and progress of the Shinto doctrines. The great achievements also of the Meiji emperor, sinking into the hearts of the people, steadily revived in them a racial spirit which motivated the awakening of the national faith of *kannagara*. In the Taishō era, for about ten years from the middle of the World War, with the introduction of democracy and Marxism, Japan came to a most critical stage in her national spirit, or in her spiritual, religious, and social trends of nationalistic thought. However, from the beginning of the Shōwa era, particularly from the time of the Manchurian Incident, in 1931, the national spirit, or the spirit of the foundation of the empire, once more came to be recognized and valued with ardent enthusiasm. Thus it was recognized that "the way of *kannagara*" was the essence and lifeblood of the nation and, also, that its doctrine was the moral and practical code of the people.

Despite the fact-that the nation was greatly harassed by utilitarian and materialistic ideas introduced from the West, the China Incident served as an impetus in arousing demand for a sincere self-realization of things purely Japanese. Naturally, this led to the emphasis upon the spirit of Shinto and the imperial way and, in the re-establishment of the culture of Japan, the way of *kannagara* is expected in the future to hold a most significant position.

In the beginning of the Meiji era, when the way of *kannagara* was systematically preached, the following six principles of Shinto were laid down by one of the head professional instructors.

Revere the heavenly gods,

Love the country,

Live according to the way of man,

Worship the ancestors,

Strive, each man in his appointed post,

And do not do things evil.

Simple as these principles seem, they constitute the basis of the national cause, piety to the gods, and reverence to the emperor, and they are the practical manifestation of the way of *kannagara*. This proves that Shinto is and has been the practical code of the nation throughout our history, and it is here that we find the close relationship between Shinto and the "way of *kannagara*."

Notes

1 The original translation of this essay in the journal, *Monumenta Nipponica*, transliterates the author's name incorrectly as Shōzō Kōnō.
2 Daniel C. Holtom, *The National Faith of Japan* (London: Kegan Paul, Trench, Trubner and Co., 1938), 123.
3 For more information, see *Encyclopedia of Shinto*, "Kōno Seizō," http://eos.kokugakuin.ac.jp/modules/xwords/entry.php?entryID=493, and Walter A. Skya, *Japan's Holy War: The Ideology of Radical Shintō Ultranationalism* (Durham: Duke University Press, 2009), 280–83.
4 The term used here by Kōno is preferred by ultranationalist writers of the time, given that the word "Shinto" is the *onyomi*, or Chinese pronunciation for the two characters, hardly suitable to refer to an indigenous Japanese religion. In the original essay, the Sophia University editors of the essay appended a commentary by the great Western Shinto scholar D.C. Holtom. Holtom was critical of Kōno's philological analysis of the term and its original meaning. In his original "Note on *kannagara*," Holtom cautions that much "private interpretation" has been made of the original reference to this term in the *Nihonshoki*. He takes issue with Kōno's conclusion that the term means a "dogma and the institution of divine imperial sovereignty" or any "specific system of thought and action, that is, of an ancient term for Shinto itself" (28). See "Some notes of Dr. D.C. Holtom." *Monumenta Nipponica* 3, No. 2 (July, 1940), 387–91.
5 Found in the imperial edict promulgated in April of the third year of Taika by Emperor Kōtoku in Volume XXV of the *Nihonshoki*.
6 Kono is alluding here to the dissolution of Daikyōin by the separation of the Shin Buddhist group.

21

MINISTRY OF EDUCATION (MONBUSHŌ)

The inherent character of the people and ceremonial rites and morality, from *Kokutai no hongi* (The Cardinal Principles of the National Polity) (1937)

Published on May 31, 1937 by the Ministry of Education (Monbushō), the *Kokutai no hongi* was designed as an ethics textbook (*shūshinsho*) and also moral guide to teach state orthodoxy on the sacredness and centrality of the emperor. It was widely distributed to teachers from elementary schools on up to the university level. By March 1943, during the height of the war, over 1.9 million copies, along with numerous additional commentaries unpacking the formal and difficult prose of the original, had been disseminated.[1]

Among its teachings is that the emperor was the center of national polity (*kokutai*). Japan is distinct among sovereign nations because of the divine origins of the imperial line, which makes Japan unlike Western nations by not depending upon the will, choice, or consent of the people. *Kokutai* is based upon the will of the imperial *kami* and an unbroken line of emperors as manifest deities (*arahitogami*) to whom the Japanese nation owes its existence. The imperial throne's divine origin, its fundamental role in national polity, and the notion that its citizens, as imperial subjects, should deeply express their loyalty to the emperor from their spontaneous heart are unique to Japan; it reflects an eternal spirit running through Japanese history. Students must learn that at the ethical core of being a Japanese imperial subject is an unswerving and self-sacrificing devotion to the emperor.[2]

While a Hegelian idealism underlies its philosophy of Japanese history, the *Kokutai no hongi*'s core faith has Confucian-Shinto origins. It was a conservative reaction to Western ideas of individualism, individual liberty, and people's rights, which were perceived as stirring up social turmoil endangering the state. More specifically, the text was the government's response to the Minobe incident of 1935. Minobe Tatsukichi (1873–1948), a constitutional scholar and the professor emeritus of Tokyo Imperial University, was forced to resign his post at the House of Peers for proposing his "emperor organ theory," a theory of polity that envisaged true sovereignty in the state rather than the emperor, who was simply an organ of government as the head of a constitutional monarchy. This view of polity was popular in the 1920s but became increasingly controversial with the rise of right-wing extremism in the 1930s. After the government issued a formal condemnation of Minobe's theory, the Ministry of Education created a Committee for the Renewal of Education and Scholarship in order to clarify national polity.[3] This theory is definitively rejected in the *Kokutai no hongi*, which emphasizes the emperor as an absolute sovereign ruling through his own centralized imperial bureaucracy.

While the original draft was composed by a committee of fourteen scholars, the text was extensively revised, particularly by Itō Enkichi, the chief of the Ministry's Bureau of Thought (Shisōkyoku).[4] What follows is Book II Chapter 3 "The inherent character of the people" and Chapter 4 "Ceremonial rites and morality." Chapter 3 discusses the following topics: "Natural features and inherent character of the people," "A clean and cloudless heart," "Self-effacement and assimilation," "The national language," and "Manners and customs." Chapter 4 discusses the following topics: "Ceremonial rites," "Morality," "Bushidō," and "Buddhism." The other contents of this text are Book I "The national entity of Japan" (Part 1 "The founding of the nation," Part 2 "The sacred virtues," Part 3 "The way of subjects," and Part 4 "Harmony and truth.") Book II "The manifestation of our national entity in history" (Part 1 "The spirit that runs through history," Part 2 "The homeland and the life of the people," Part 5 "National culture," and Part 6 "Political, economic, and military affairs.")

THE INHERENT CHARACTER OF THE PEOPLE AND CEREMONIAL RITES AND MORALITY, FROM *KOKUTAI NO HONGI* (THE CARDINAL PRINCIPLES OF THE NATIONAL POLITY) (1937)

Translated by John Owen Gauntlett

Natural features and inherent character of the people

Yamaga Soko[5] [CE 1622–85] states in the *Chūchō jijitsu*: "The land of Japan stands high above the other nations of the world, and her people excel the peoples of the world." And indeed her natural features are blessed with a temperate climate and beautiful mountains and rivers, and rich in vernal flowers and autumn tints and scenic changes that accompany the seasons, Japan (*Ōyashima no kuni*) has been referred to since her birth as a region adapted to the lives of the people and as a "land of peace." However, natural catastrophes that from time to time visit the nation in their utmost fury occasionally menace the lives of the people, but the people do not on this account fear nature, nor are they cowed before it. Disasters go rather toward tempering the people's spirits so as to make them indomitable and, by awakening in them a power to start afresh and by increasing their attachment for the homeland, strengthen more than ever their desire to become one with the land. Clashes with nature such as are found in Western mythologies do not appear in our legends, and this homeland is to the Japanese a very paradise in which to live. It is not by mere chance that Yamato[6] has been rendered as "Great Harmony" using Chinese characters."

The now classic poem by Rai San-yō [CE 1780–1832], which has earned popular fame, reads:

A gaze across Yoshino's mount
Where the awakening glow of the cherry flowers ushers in the dawn—
And the hearts of Chinese and Koreans that see
Must surely turn to Yamato.

And this poem shows how our beautiful natural features have nurtured this heart of Yamato. Again, when we note, too, the words of a poem on the "Yamato Spirit of Japan" by Motoori Norinaga [CE 1730–1801], we see how deeply Japanese sentiment is bound up with Japan's natural features:

> What cherry blossoms are those
> That send forth their aroma in the morning sun!

Furthermore, one reads in *Seiki no uta* by Fujita Tōko [CE 1806–55]:[7]

> The sublime "spirit" of the universe
>   Gathers pure over this land of the gods—
> Rising high, it forms the peak of Fuji;
>   Towering aloft, it kisses the skies to a thousand autumns—
> Pouring itself forth out of rivers, it flows as waters of the great deep;
>   And boundless it courses around our land—
> It blossoms forth as countless clusters of cherry flowers,
>   And nought there is compares to their clustered beauty and scent.

And this speaks of the manner in which our homeland, her trees, and verdure vie to clothe our spirit and its beauty.

A clean and cloudless heart

Such a homeland as this and the national life which centers round the family, and which is expressive of the concord between the sovereign and the people, have together brought forth our national character that is cloudless, pure, and honest. In effect, the following, which forms a part of an imperial rescript by the Emperor Monmu [CE 697–707], on the occasion of his enthronement, is found repeated in this and other passages:

> A genuine heart that is cloudless, pure, and candid;
>
> A candid heart that is pure, cloudless, and righteous.

This character also appears in our legends as the Shindō[8] spirit that accompanies the purification rites, and in the name of an official rank instituted by the Emperor Tenmu [CE 673–86]; in the fourteenth year of his reign, the characters, "cloudless," "pure," and "honest," are placed above the rank name, "pursuance of one's duties," showing how deeply this inherent national character was esteemed. This translucence, purity, and honesty bespeak a spirit of sterling quality, clothed in strength and candor, and this quality is, in short, the utmost sincerity and truth. It is the actions and attitudes that stand for outward manifestations of this truth that are pursuance of one's duties. That is to say, the name of this official rank was a manifestation of an open and fresh national character and bespoke the people's attitude toward their way of life. Thus, a cloudless, pure, and candid heart, whose intrinsic nature is truth, does not confine itself merely to the world of sentiment, but as the Emperor Meiji says in one of his poems:

The valor of a Yamato heart
　When faced with a crisis
　　Its mettle proves.

And this heart reveals itself as patriotism. It has been written in the *Manyōshū*:

Out to the deep,
　A watery course—
Across the hills,
　A grass-grown course—
Oh, I would die beside my Lord,
　Come what may!

And, after the Mongolian Invasion, the conception that this is the land of the gods developed notably and was realized as the Yamato spirit. Indeed, the Yamato spirit has "prayed for the perpetuity and peace of the imperial throne," and in more recent times has been aroused forcibly and manifested concretely in the Sino-Japanese and Russo-Japanese Wars.

A pure, cloudless heart is a heart which, dying to one's ego and one's own ends, finds life in fundamentals and the true way. That means it is a heart that lives in the way of unity between the sovereign and his subjects, a way that has come down to us ever since the founding of the empire. It is herein that there springs up a frame of mind, unclouded and right, that bids farewell to unwholesome self-interest. The spirit that sacrifices self and seeks life at the very fountainhead of things manifests itself eventually as patriotism and as a heart that casts self aside in order to serve the state. On the contrary, a heart that is taken up with self and lays plans solely for self has been looked upon, from of old, as filthy and impure, so that efforts have been made to exorcise and to get rid of it. The purification ceremony as it exists in our country is a function in which one exorcises this adulterated heart and returns to the mainspring where the heart is pure, unclouded, and contrite. It is a function that has been practiced widely among our people ever since prehistoric times, and a passage in the Shinto purification rites reads:

Since thus informed—beginning with the imperial court of his augustness the imperial grandchild and going on to all lands under heaven—that there might be nothing left that could be termed sin, exorcise and sanctify until no sin remains, we pray; as the God of Wind scattereth abroad the multifold clouds of heaven; as the morning and evening winds do sweep aside the morning and evening mist; as the winds set free the bow of a large ship that lieth in a haven, and, setting free her stern, chaseth her free out to the great deep; as with a sharp, well-tempered sickle yonder shrubs are cut down to the roots. Then perhaps the Goddess Seoritsu-hime will bear our sins out to the great deep, a goddess whose abode is on the moving surface of the swift streams that tumble headlong from the heights of mountains lofty and low. If our sins are thus borne along, the Goddess Haya-akitsu-hime, whose dwelling is on the briny concourse of multitudinous sea streams of wild, briny tides, will surely swallow them up. If our sins are thus swallowed up, the God Ibukido-nushi that dwelleth at the door of spray spumes will surely spue them out into the nether land of the nether world. If our sins are thus spued out, the Goddess Hayasasura-hime, whose abode is in the nether land of the nether world, will surely carry them hence and bring them to nought. If our sins are thus brought to nought, from this day on and throughout the length and breadth of our realm, there can be nothing left in the way of sin, beginning with the officials that serve at the court of the emperor.

This passage indeed is an expression of the bright and sublime spirit of our purification ceremony. And our people have always preserved and exalted this pure, unclouded, and contrite heart by means of the purification rites.

When man makes self the center of his interests, the spirit of self-effacement and self-sacrifice suffers loss. In the world of individualism there naturally arises a mind that makes self the master and others servants, and that puts gain first and gives service a secondary place. Such things as individualism and liberalism, which are fundamental concepts of the nations of the West on which their national characteristics and lives are built, find their real differences when compared with our national concepts. Our nation has, since its founding, developed on the basis of a pure, unclouded, and contrite heart; and our language, customs, and habits all emanate from this source.

Self-effacement and assimilation

In the inherent character of our people there is strongly manifested, alongside this spirit of self-effacement and disinterestedness, a spirit of broadmindedness and its activities. In the importation of culture from the Asiatic continent, too, in the process of "dying to self" and adopting the ideographs used in Chinese classics, this spirit of ours has coordinated and assimilated these same ideographs. To have brought forth a culture uniquely our own, in spite of the fact that a culture essentially different was imported, is due entirely to a mighty influence peculiar to our nation. This is a matter that must be taken into serious consideration in the adaptation of modern Occidental culture.

The spirit of self-effacement is not a mere denial of oneself but means living according to the great, true self by denying one's small self. Individuals are essentially not beings isolated from the state, but each has his allotted share as forming part of the state. And because they form part of it, they constantly and intrinsically unite themselves with the state, and it is this that gives birth to the spirit of self-effacement. And at the same time, because they form part of it, they lay importance on their own characteristics and through these characteristics render service to the state. These characteristics, in union with the spirit of self-effacement, give rise to a power to assimilate things alien to oneself. In speaking of self-effacement or self-sacrifice, one does not mean the denial of oneself toward the state, such as exists in foreign countries, where the state and individuals are viewed correlatively. Again, broadmindedness and assimilation mean not being alienated by losing one's unique personal qualities and thereby losing one's individuality. Rather, broadmindedness and assimilation mean the casting aside of one's personal defects to make the best use of one's good qualities, so that by searching widely one may enrich oneself. Herein do we find the great strength of our nation and the depth and breadth of our ideologies and civilization.

The national language

The spirit of self-effacement and unity clearly appears also in the national language. The Japanese language is characterized by the fact that the subject does not often appear on the surface, and also by its highly developed honorifics. This is due to the fact that things are not viewed from mutually opposite angles but are weighed disinterestedly and in their entirety. Thus in foreign countries, whether in China or the West, honorifics are few, but in our country they have developed systematically since of old and are an eloquent manifestation of the spirit of respect so that with the development of honorifics the use of the subject grew rare. This spirit of reverence, needless to say, means death to oneself with one's mind centered on the imperial household and for the sake of the throne. This is seen in such examples as the use of *watakushi* ["private"] for the first person as against *ōyake* ["public"], and the turning of such verbs as *tamō, haberu,* or *saburō,* which have been in use from of old, into auxiliary verbs expressing respect or deference. Thus, from the term *saburō* or *samurō* [written *samarafu*] is derived the word *samurai,* which means a "knight", and this accounts for the development of the epistolary style, *sōrōbun. Gozaimasu*[9] for instance, which is in use today, is composed of *goza-aru,* which stands for "honorable seat," and *masu,* which comes from *imasu,* meaning "is" or "is present."

Manners and customs

Next, in our manners and customs, too, we find a spirit of reverence for the deities and the emperor, of self-effacement, and of concord. In referring to our daily meals, too, we speak of receiving our august meals,[10] and the practice of a whole household celebrating a meal after first placing the first fruits before the spirits of our ancestors by offering them to the deities reveals the sentiment that food is received from the deities and that it is this same food of which we are partaking. In the New Year's functions, too, we see the traditional life that has come down to us from our distant ancestors in the planting of pine trees in the front of our gates, in the use of water drawn for the first time in the year, and in the feast of the rice-cake soup. There is a connection between celebrating the New Year with the exchange of expressions of felicitation and the ancient spirit seen in the words of clan chiefs celebrating the emperor's age. The term *banzai,* too, is a felicitous term having the same meaning.

Guardian deities, needless to say, and clan deities may be considered on the whole as deities of one's place of birth, and these have come down to us as forming the nuclei of the local life of communities. The Buddhist services performed during the equinoctial week and the Bon Festival of the Dead, which are in practice today, are looked upon as a merging of Buddhist functions and the people's faith. Then again, in the Bon Festival dance seen in the precincts of tutelary shrines and temples, one witnesses a merging and uniting of two streams of faith in the entertainments of those living in farming villages. In the world of agriculture, one witnesses such manifestations as the spirit of celebrating a good year for crops, of harmony and co-prosperity, and of ancestor worship; and again, in our type of dance in which people form circles, one sees a characteristic of self-effacement in uniting in a dance facing inward. And this is in contradiction to the types of dance in which men and women dance in couples, a feature common to Western community dances. There is a widely practiced custom of paying a visit to the local shrine when a child is born, and this is a manifestation of a sentiment toward the tutelary deity, which has come down to us from olden times.

Among the annual functions are such things as the annual festivals, and in these are seen alliances to nature and the fusing and harmonizing of imported culture; and further, when we come to ancient court and military practices and usages, the traditional spirit that lies deep behind the outward forms of these activities cannot be overlooked. As already cited, among the annual functions, there are those which carry traces of clan life, those which find their origin in court life, and those which in the days of chivalry [CE 1192–1868] became established as ceremonial functions. At the root of all these functions, one sees our glorious traditional spirit. In the Dolls' Festival, the functions at first centered on exorcism, but, with the ushering in of the life of the nobility in the Heian period [CE 794–858], the thing turned into an amusement with dolls, and became a ceremonial function which combined within itself both pleasure and proper upbringing. Later on, with the arrival of the Edo period [CE 1603–1868], the doll emperor and empress were placed in view, to foster the spirit of reverence for the imperial household.

Ceremonial rites and morality

Ceremonial rites

The Emperor Meiji was referring to the rites that ushered in our administrative activities at the beginning of the year when he wrote in one of his poems:

> This year again
> I would hear of the Ise Shrine
> Before all things.

In these rites, the prime minister reports to the throne the perfect manner in which ceremonial rites were conducted at the shrine during the previous year. In this we see the great august will to preside over ceremonial rites, which are looked upon as being of the greatest importance in the administrative activities of our nation. We read in the *Jingishi* in the *Dai Nihonshi,*

> Ceremonial rites are the basis of religion and politics. If the entire realm vibrates with reverence for the deities, respect for one's ancestors, and devotion and honor toward one's parents, all systems and institutions will be established thereby.

And this brings out our national characteristics in which ceremonial rites, government, and education are united fundamentally. Our country is a divine country governed by an emperor who is a deity incarnate. The emperor becomes one in essence with the heavenly deities by offering them worship, and thereby makes all the clearer his virtue as a deity incarnate. Hence, the emperor lays particular importance on ceremonial rites; and, in the ceremonial rites held in the three shrines in the Imperial Palace, namely, the Imperial Sanctuary, the Imperial Ancestors' Shrine, and the Imperial Tabernacle, the emperor conducts the services himself. In the second year of Meiji [CE 1869], his majesty sanctified and enshrined the deities of heaven and earth and the spirits of the successive emperors by building a shrine within the Jingikan [in the grounds of the Bureau of Shinto Shrines], and in the third year [CE 1870], promulgated a rescript consoling the spirits of the deities, saying:

> We reverently call to mind how that our imperial ancestor, at the time of the founding of the empire, held the deities in high esteem, and loved and cared for the people. The genesis, therefore, of the unity of ceremonial rites and administration [*saisei icchi*] is seen to be in the very distant past. We, conscious of our weakness, accede to the throne; and day and night we are fearful lest we fall short in our sacred mission. Wherefore, we now repose the spirits of the deities of heaven and earth, the spirits of the eight deities,[11] and the sacred spirits of the successive emperors in the

159

Jingikan [in the grounds of the Bureau of Shinto Shrines], and so give expression to our devotion and reverence. We pray that our subjects throughout the realm may follow this example.

It is the nature of subjects to make this great august will their own, to receive the spirit of the founding of the empire as their own by means of ceremonial rites, to pray for the emperor's peace by sacrificing themselves, and to enhance the spirit of service to the state. Thus, the emperor's service to the deities and the subjects' reverence for the deities both spring from the same source; and the emperor's virtues are heightened all the more by means of the ceremonial rites, and the subjects' determination to fulfill their duties is made all the firmer through their reverence for the deities.

Our shrines have served, from of old, as the center of the spirit of ceremonial rites and functions. Shrines are expressions of the great way of the deities and places where one serves the deities and repays the source of all things and returns to their genesis. The oracle on the sacred mirror is the object of the rites at the Shinto shrines and the Imperial Sanctuary;[12] and the fundamental significance of the existence of Shinto shrines is found in the oracle on the Amatsu Himorogi [Heavenly Sanctuary] and the Amatsu Iwasaka [Sanctuary Precincts] in the passage on the descent to earth of the imperial grandchild, which appears in the *Nihonshoki*. That is, this answers to the august will expressed in the words of the deity Takamimusubi no Kami[13] addressed to their Augustnesses Ame no Koyane no Mikoto and Futotama no Mikoto:

We shall build the Amatsu Himorogi [Heavenly Sanctuary] and the Amatsu Iwasaka [Sanctuary Precincts] and offer services to the deities for the sake of our imperial grandchild. Ye augustnesses, Ame no Koyane no Mikoto and Futotama no Mikoto, descend ye to Ashihara no Nakatsu Kuni,[14] bearing with you the Amatsu Himorogi, and offer ye services also for the sake of our imperial grandchild.

The deities enshrined in the Shinto shrines are the imperial ancestors, the ancestors of the clans descended from the heavenly deities or the imperial family,[15] and the divine spirits who served to guard and maintain the prosperity of the imperial throne. These ceremonial rites of Shinto shrines serve to foster the life of our people and form the basis of this spirit. In the festivals of the clan deities, one sees expressions of the spirit of repaying the source of all things and of returning to their genesis, and of the consequent concourse of clansmen. Then again, in the festival rites of the guardian deities, in which portable shrines are borne along, there is the friendly gathering of parishioners and the peaceful scenes of the villages. Hence, Shinto shrines are also the center of the people's life in their home towns. Further, on national holidays, the people put up the rising sun flag and unite in their national spirit of devotion to the state. Thus, all functions of the Shinto shrines ultimately unite in the services rendered by the emperor to the imperial ancestors; and it is in this that we find the basis of our national reverence for the deities.

At festivals we serve the deities by purifying ourselves, with sincerity revere the dignity of the deities, return thanks for their benefits, and offer earnest prayers. The sentiment in coming before the deities springs in our country from the most fundamental element seen in the relationship between parents and children. In effect, it is found in drawing near to our ancestors by purifying ourselves of our sins and stains, in leaving self behind to unite with the public, and in "dying to self" to become one with the state.

And as a natural expression of a devout heart which has been purified we find an example in a poem by Saigyō Hōshi [CE 1118–90][16] which reads:

> What is enshrined I do not know,
> But the awe of a sense of gratitude
> Brings tears to my eyes.

As Shinto shrines have their basic significance in being national entities, they have, since the establishment of the Bureau of Shinto Shrines in the Code of Laws,[17] come down to us as national organs and institutions; so that they are differently treated from all the Shinto sects[18] and other religions of a general nature.

A poem by the Emperor Meiji runs:

> Great Goddess of Ise,
>   Preserve our world,
> For which we pray,
>   "May this people
> Rest well for aye."

Hafuribe Yukiuji also says in a poem:

> True is the heart
>   That serves my lord
> When at the shrine it prays
>   For a peaceful reign

Thus, the Grand Shrine of Ise is the focal point of our Shinto shrines, and all shrines, as belonging to the state, form the pivot of the spiritual life of the people.

The true purport of our nation's ceremonial rites has been expounded in the foregoing passages, and when this is compared with faith toward god as it exists in the Occident, the result is a great gap. In the mythologies and legends of the West, too, mention is made of many deities, but these are not national deities that have been linked with the nation since the days of their origin, nor are they deities that have given birth to the people or the land or have brought them up. Reverence toward deities in our country is a national faith based on the spirit of the founding of the empire and is not a faith toward a transcendental god in the world of heaven, paradise, paramita [Sanskrit], or the ideal, but it is a spirit of service that flows out naturally from the historical life of the people. Hence, our ceremonial rites have a deep and broad significance, and at the same time are truly national and allied to actual life.

Morality

It is this spirit of reverence for the deities and one's ancestors that forms the basis of our national morality, and it is also this that has embraced and assimilated Confucianism, Buddhism, and other things imported from abroad into every field of our culture and created things truly Japanese. Our national morality is founded on reverence for the deities and our ancestors, and has brought forth the fruits of the great principle of loyalty and filial piety.

By making the nation our home, loyalty becomes filial piety, and by making our homes our nation, filial piety becomes loyalty. Herein do loyalty and filial piety join in one and become the source of all good.

Loyalty means engaging ourselves zealously in our duties by making it our fundamental principle to be candid, clean, and honest, and it means fulfilling our duties, and thus to serve the emperor; and by making loyalty our basic principle is filial piety established. This is the great way of the deities which our people have faithfully followed since the days of their ancestors and throughout the past and the present.

In the Imperial Rescript on Education, his majesty declared by way of teaching the fundamental principles of national morality:

> Know ye, our subjects: our imperial ancestors have founded our empire on a basis broad and everlasting and have deeply and firmly implanted virtue; our subjects, ever united in loyalty and filial piety, have from generation to generation illustrated the beauty thereof. This is the glory of the fundamental character of our empire, and therein also lies the source of our education.

And he also says:

> The way here set forth is indeed the teaching bequeathed by our imperial ancestors, to be observed alike by their descendants and the subjects, infallible for all ages and true in all places. It is our wish to lay it to heart in all reverence, in common with you, our subjects, that we may all thus attain to the same virtue.

That candor, purity, and honesty have been highly esteemed in our country is made evident by the fact that these appear in our legends, are seen in the imperial edicts, and in the names of crowns according to rank. There is a passage in the *Hōkihongi*[19] which reads: "Honesty is the basis of divine protection." Again, in *Yamatohime no Mikoto seiki*[20] it says:

> Behave with discretion and with utmost purity, with hearts made sincere, cleansed of sins. Move not to the right that which is on the left, nor move to the left that which is on the right, but serve the great goddess, keeping what is on the left on the left and what is on the right on the right, so that in returning to the left or taking a turn to the right ye may have nothing go amiss. This is because the genesis must be made the genesis and the source made the source.

This, in short, brings to light the spirit of candor, purity, and honesty, and it shows a heart which does not confuse the proper order of things, which speaks of things on the right as being on the right and of those on the left as being on the left, and which gives to all their proper place, making their respective duties clear and not going amiss in the least. And it is a heart that has no patience for anything crooked and has no room for wickednesses and injustices. And it is only through this honesty that will not waver in the least and through its practice that we can make fundamentals our fundamentals. Kitabatake Chikafusa's [CE 1293–1354] *Jinnō shōtōki* reflects this spirit and lays emphasis on honesty, and the name of the works attributed to him, namely, *Gengenshū*, seems to have been taken directly from the foregoing passage; but what should be particularly borne in mind as national morality is to treat things on the left as being on the left and things on the right as being on the right, to have things abide in their true state and be as they should be, thereby making the genesis of things their genesis and the sources their sources.

Bushidō

Bushidō[21] may be cited as showing an outstanding characteristic of our national morality. In the world of warriors, one sees inherited the totalitarian structure and spirit of the ancient clans peculiar to our nation. Hence, although the teachings of Confucianism and Buddhism have been followed, these have been transcended. That is to say, though a sense of indebtedness binds master and servant, this has developed into a spirit of self-effacement and of meeting death with a perfect calmness. In this, it was not that death was made light of so much as that man reconciled himself to death and in a true sense regarded it with esteem. In effect, man tried to fulfill true life by way of death. This means that rather than lose the whole by being taken up with and setting up oneself, one puts self to death in order to give full play to the whole by fulfilling the whole. Life and death are basically one, and the monistic truth is found where life and death are transcended. Through this is life, and through this is death. However, to treat life and death as two opposites and to hate death and to seek life is to be taken up with one's own interests and is a thing of which warriors are ashamed. To fulfill the way of loyalty, counting life and death as one, is *Bushidō*.

In the Sengoku (age of civil wars) period [CE 1490–1600], too, the feudal lords gave ample expression to their patriarchal spirit and took good care of the serfs. This expression should also be true of Bushidō. The warrior's aim should be, in ordinary times, to foster a spirit of reverence for the deities and his own ancestors in keeping with his family tradition; to train himself to be ready to cope with emergencies at all times; to clothe himself with wisdom, benevolence, and valor; to understand the meaning of mercy; and to strive to be sensitive to the frailty of nature. Yamaga Sokō [CE 1622–85], Matsumiya Kanzan [CE 1686–1780], and Yoshida Shōin [CE 1831–60] were all men of the devoutest character, who exercised much influence in bringing Bushidō to perfection. It is this same Bushidō that shed itself of the outdated feudalism at the time of the Meiji Restoration, increased in splendor, became the way of loyalty and patriotism, and has evolved before us as the spirit of the imperial forces.

Buddhism

Buddhism was cradled in India and was introduced into our country by way of China and Korea. It is a faith as well as a rule of morals, and at the same time a system of knowledge. Hence, its introduction into our country saw its fusion into and sublimation in our national spirit, and it developed in a way befitting the people. Far back in history, in the "vernal" February in the reign of the Empress Suiko [CE 593–628], it pleased her majesty to issue an imperial edict to devote more attention toward the elevation of the *Sampō*,[22] and, through this edict, temples and pagodas were built to answer to imperial benevolences and parental attentions. This traditional spirit of the early days of Buddhism, to build temples in answer to imperial and parental benevolences, manifested itself later as the spirit of national deference in Nanto Buddhism,[23] and this was made the dictum by the Tendai[24] and Shingon[25] sects. This spirit later on took shape in the advocacy for protecting the nation by reviving the teachings of Zen in the case of the Rinzai sect, and in the advocacy for assuring the peace of the state by the rule of righteousness in the case of the Nichiren sect. Besides, the founders of new Buddhist sects similarly esteemed the laws established by the throne. Hence, their doctrinal developments, too, were truly noteworthy. The spirit of reverence for the deities of heaven and earth and of unity and self-effacement that centers on Amaterasu Ōmikami is found in the teaching of the Shingon sect, which holds that everything in the universe is a manifestation of *Mahāvairocana Tathāgata* and that each mind is a living Buddha, and in the teaching of the Tendai sect, which declares that there is Buddhahood in plants and trees as well as the homeland, saying that even an ordinary person is a Buddha when enlightened and that the whole creation has access to *moksha* or spiritual salvation. And one also finds in these things the spirit of universal benevolence and something that accords with a mind that embraces all. Some of the sects of Nanto Buddhism preach discrimination in *moksha*, but, after the days of Heian Buddhism, equality of all came to be preached, with clarification of the original purport of Buddhism which, based on self-annihilation, stood in particular for the idea of equality in spite of individual differences and of differences in spite of the fact that all are equal. This is due to the fact that their doctrines were likewise adapted and sublimated through our clan and family spirit and our self-effacing and totalitarian spirit, which our nation possesses as believing in equality in spite of individual differences. For instance, we see Shinran [CE 1173–1262][26] speaking of his fellow men as comrades and as companions on the way. The Jōdo and Shin sects held the tenets of salvation by faith by means of Buddhist invocations as against the tenets of salvation by works, and so preached the instability of life, while the Ji sect went on pilgrimages in order to indoctrinate and transform others; in this manner these sects made Buddhism a religion of the masses. In Shinran's search after natural law by preaching absolute belief in salvation by faith in Amida Buddha, fullest play is given to the spirit of self-effacement and unity, while the manner in which teachings carried out by Hōnen [CE 1133–1212][27] —by chanting prayers irrespective of time or place to the effect that one should fulfill the "mission" of death in one's natural state—portrays the kinetic and practical view of life taken by the Japanese. Again, there is a similarity in the disinterested and practical stand taken by Dōgen [CE 1200–53], who looked on industries and measures to control natural havoc as works done in return for benefits received, believing that deeds done by those who have emptied themselves of self indeed comprised the way. This spirit gradually took form in a view, for instance, that the three religions, Shintoism, Confucianism, and Buddhism, harmonized with each other. One sees a spirit of esteem for history and tradition in the rise of the movement for return to Shōtoku Taishi [CE 572–621][28] in the Tendai and other sects, which made as their basis the teachings of masters historically transmitted from generation to generation from Shakya[29] down. In this manner, our nation, which has been looked upon as adapted to Mahāyāna Buddhism, has made Buddhism what it is today, and in this we see naturally manifested a true picture and character of the people befitting the nation. It is Buddhism assimilated in this manner that has enriched our culture, deepened our way of looking at things, schooled us in meditation, and permeated our national life, at the same time inciting our national spirit and giving rise to functions in which reverence for one's ancestors is seen, as in the case of Paramita and Ullambana [Sanskrit].

Notes

1 Robert King Hall, ed. and John Owen Gauntlett, trans. *Kokutai no Hongi* (Cardinal Principles of the National Entity of Japan) (Cambridge, MA: Harvard University Press, 1949), 9.
2 Christopher Goto Jones, "Revering the Emperor: Imperial Philosophy and Bushidō," in *The Emperor in Modern Japan,* ed. Ben-Ami Shillony (Leiden: Brill, 2008), 39–40.
3 Ibid., 36–37.

4 For a full list of the scholars on the committee and its history, see Walter A. Skya, *Japan's Holy War: The Ideology of Radical Shintō Ultranationalism* (Durham, NC: Duke University Press, 2009), 280ff.

5 Samurai of the Aizu clan, a leading scholar of the official Neo-Confucian philosophy of the Tokugawa regime, and a noted military strategist.

6 One of the very many names of Japan.

7 A patriot whose love of country was stamped with a hatred of foreigners.

8 The way of the gods, and another name for Shinto.

9 A polite affirmative ending.

10 This is the literal meaning of a common expression, in which the verb "to receive" is an expression conveying an idea of receiving something from someone above you.

11 Namely: Kamimusubi no Kami, Takamimusubi no Kami, Tamatsumemusubi no Kami, Ikumusubi no Kami, Tarumusubi no Kami, Ōmiyanome no Kami, Miketsuno Kami, and Kotoshironushi no Kami.

12 Until CE 93, the mirror was kept at the imperial palace, but the Emperor Sujin, awakening to the fact that it was too sacred a thing to be kept beside him, since it reflected the very image of the sun goddess, Amaterasu Ōmikami, had a temple built for the three sacred treasures.

13 Spoken of in mythology as one of the three creators of the world.

14 Literally, "Central Land of the Reed Plain," which is one of the many ancient names for Japan.

15 Literally, "the Princes of the Ancestors of the clans."

16 He became a monk at the age of twenty-three, abandoning his wife and children, and traveling through the provinces preaching and reciting poetry. This particular poem expresses his reaction as he came under the awe-inspiring influence of the Ise Jingū.

17 Promulgated in the first year of the Taihō era (CE 701).

18 Of these there were thirteen.

19 One of the sacred Shinto books (CE 725) which is reputed to be a forgery.

20 A biography of Yamatohime, the fourth Imperial Princess of the Emperor Suinin, traditionally the eleventh emperor of Japan.

21 The code of warriors; chivalry. Literally, "the way of warriors."

22 Literally, "the Three Treasures" (*Ratnatraya*): namely, the Buddha (The Awakened One), Dharma (Truth), and Sangha (Community). But it has come to connote Buddhism.

23 The older schools of Buddhism of the Nara period, Nanto meaning southern capital or Nara.

24 A sect of Buddhism introduced from China by Saichō, later known as Dengyō Daishi, who introduced it to Japan in 805 with its headquarters at Mt. Hiei.

25 A sect of Buddhism introduced from China by Kūkai, later known as Kōbō Daishi, in 807.

26 A famous monk and founder of the Shin sect.

27 Monk who founded the Jōdo or Pure Land sect of Buddhism.

28 Famous political figure in early Japanese history and proponent of Buddhism.

29 Another word for Gautama Buddha.

22

MINISTRY OF EDUCATION (MONBUSHŌ)

Practicing the way of imperial subjects, from
Shinmin no michi (The Way of Subjects, 1941)

Shinmin no michi is an official government tract ordered published and disseminated to schools on March 31, 1941, by the Ministry of Education in the months before the bombing of Pearl Harbor. Commissioned by Prime Minister Konoe Fumimaro (1891–1945), the short three-chapter work was designed to be a simple primer for indoctrination. Like the *Kokutai no hongi*, it was designed for spiritually mobilizing the public while the Sino-Japanese War continued to rage and before the Great Pacific War began with the attack on Pearl Harbor. It makes the case that contemporary Japan has become polluted by the alien Western ways of individualism, materialism, liberalism, and utilitarianism.

By contrast, the *shinmin* or "subjects," a term used in the Meiji Constitution for all Japanese citizens not members of the imperial family, should follow a *michi* or moral "way" of absolute self-sacrifice and obedience to the imperial state. This way is based on filial piety and an unquestioned loyalty to the emperor as the direct sacred descendant of the sun goddess Amaterasu of an imperial line "unbroken for ages eternal," as stated in Article 1 of the Meiji Constitution. *Shinmin no michi* outlines a theocracy in which the emperors are sacred; they are described as "manifest *kami*" who lovingly care and rule while their subjects' ideal is to manifest hearts that are as pure as the *kami,* born to naturally obey the emperor and advance the fortunes of the imperial state. Faith here means "faithful service to the state." Like the *Kokutai no hongi,* the earlier Meiji and Taishō constitutional niceties are abandoned for an explicitly spiritual ideology where the emperor is a divine source whose political, moral, and heavenly authority are rooted in his descent from Amaterasu.

Chapters of this text include Chapter 1 "The building of the new world order" and Chapter 2 "National polity and the way of subjects." What follows is a translation of Chapter 3 "Practicing the way of imperial subjects," the first two thirds of Part 1, "The discipline of imperial subjects."

PRACTICING THE WAY OF IMPERIAL SUBJECTS FROM
SHINMIN NO MICHI (THE WAY OF SUBJECTS)
(1941)

The discipline of imperial subjects

The way of the imperial subject is the source of our national polity (*kokutai*). Each is united as one heart, each sincerely renders service to the country and humbly assists in advancing the fortunes of the emperor. At this time, we have chanced upon a great turning point in world history, and our country's historical calling becomes more urgent day by day. The great work of establishing a new order in the Far East has been placed on every person's shoulders and is waiting for them to earnestly rouse themselves in this effort. Without questioning where their duty lies, all the people are equally charged to bear the burden of this heavy but great duty, and should work earnestly together to advance the cause and fully offer their assistance in this great imperial undertaking (*tengyō*).

Those who are subjects of the empire in this new age must discipline themselves, body and soul, as imperial citizens. By living as subjects of the imperial state, firm in faith and steadfast to our true national principles, honoring our resolute spirit, strengthening our powers of discernment, refining our resoluteness of will and our complete physical energies, and actualizing them fully through practice, we can push toward achieving the historical mission of the imperial state. This is the discipline that subjects of the imperial state should deepen further. The noble character of our great people will flourish and should lead to the Greater East Asia Co-Prosperity Sphere (*Dai tōa kyōeiken*). If we are neglectful, not paying enough attention to the mission of this new age like a hermit crab vainly trying to hide inside his old shell, we will undermine the work our ancestors have bequeathed to us, neglect our duty to our descendants, and be guilty of transgressing the way of subjects.

In the imperial rescript graciously bestowed upon young people and students, it states,

> The duty is exceedingly heavy, and the way is extremely long that tries to cultivate our fundamental national principles and nurture our country's strength in order to eternally preserve our course toward national prosperity. You should fully make this your great responsibility, and you should carry it on your young shoulders with the earnest wish to be faithful and with high regard for your nobility of character and sense of honor. You should also carry out this responsibility by developing your powers of discernment of past and present history, considering the course of events domestically and internationally, and carefully appraising them without losing sight of what is the right direction to go.
>
> Each of you honor your duty, master your literary (*bun*) and military (*bu*) arts, and strive for a simple and solid character.

This is a teaching that young people should take to heart and endeavor to follow day and night. Everyone must also put this great spirit of the emperor fully into practice, overcome the troubles of the times, and dedicate more and more of their energy to contributing to a prosperous state.

It is a matter of the first importance that imperial subjects devote themselves fully to the fundamental principles of our national polity. If people are not isolated individuals, then neither are they universal citizens of the world. Surely, they are a specific people with a history, and people who belong to a particular nation. Therefore, for us, morality—that is, the way that people should behave—is not some abstract way of humanity or conceptual norm. Rather, it is the imperial way that has developed based upon a concrete history. To be human is to be Japanese, and to be Japanese is to practice the way of subjects in accordance with the imperial way. That is to say, in our unwavering faith based upon our national polity, we can be imperial subjects.

National polity is the great unchanging and eternal foundation of our country. Along with heaven and earth, it has no limit. The imperial ancestress, Amaterasu Ōmikami, had her grandson, Ninigi no Mikoto, descend (*kōrin*) to the islands of Japan (*Ōyashima*), bestowing her divine message, establishing the great principle between sovereign and subjects, and revealing the way subjects should live. Thus was established the foundation of our country's rites, politics, education, and industry. Our country is founded on this eternal and profound beginning and will never cease to develop and grow. Truly, what is taking place before our eyes is an undertaking of great consequence unparalleled in other countries.

The line of emperors down through history make Amaterasu Ōmikami's divine will their own, become united with her, and, as manifest *kami* (*akitsumikami*), rule all the subjects under them. That is to say, by relying on the will of the imperial ancestress, emperors broaden the scope of their heavenly work and lovingly care for their subjects as though they were infants. With the help of their subjects, emperors have tried to extend their imperial projects. In an imperial rescript that Emperor Taishō gave on the day of his Enthronement Ceremony at the Shishinden in the palace, he declares, "By having a duty, namely, between sovereign and subjects, like the bond between a father and his child, we have a national polity which is without peer in contrast to all other countries." In addition, in an official imperial decree on inspiring the people's spirit, he states, "By relying on the assistance of the people, I ardently desire to extend my great work and establish a firmer foundation for the country."

It is self-evident that our way as imperial subjects is to pay our respects to such a broad and limitless divine will. Our way is to have our hearts become like the spirit of the *kami*. As they offered their service to the imperial descendant Ninigi no Mikoto when he descended from heaven, we should give our obedience to the emperor. We are born *to receive the commands* of the emperor, to assist in advancing the fortunes of the imperial state, and to follow this way. The most fundamental thing in that way is evident both in the loyalty (*chū*) in the relations between a sovereign and his subjects, and also in the filial piety (*kō*) between a parent and a child.

All emperors in history are the divine descendants of the imperial ancestress, and the relationship between them is like a parent and child. So, too, the relationship between the emperor and his subjects is one of loyalty between sovereign and subjects while it is also like the bond that exists between a father and his child. Divinity and sovereign, sovereign and subject are truly one. In this lies the basis for honoring the *kami* and venerating the ancestors, the way that unifies loyalty and filial piety. With this kind of national polity, the nation eternally exists and develops equal to heaven and earth. In this respect, national polity becomes the model or norm for the people. Development is realized in deeds that lend support for the great divine undertaking. Indeed, this eternal and limitless undertaking is the very foundation of our lives and the real form of truth.

Thus, the way of subjects is for each person to fully master the spirit of building the country and offering sincere and absolute obedience to the emperor. Through this actual practice, a self-centered utilitarian thinking disappears and service to the state becomes of primary importance. No matter how hard you try to eliminate self-centered utilitarian thinking and advocate service to the state, it is a fundamental error to forget the national polity by trying to practice the way of subjects without true sincerity. If individualism and libertarianism, materialism and utilitarianism lead you away from your duty as an imperial subject, then even the most earnest effort will be of no avail. On the contrary, it will prove an obstacle in improving the country's fortunes. The life of imperial subjects comes from the fundamental belief that each person lives to fulfill his or her own duty; by performing that duty, each person sincerely offers service to the state and advances the imperial state's fortunes. It is through this spirit and with the help of constant and diligent discipline that the way of subjects is actualized.

Even the law establishing a national school system emphasizes this point for it stipulates that "offering elementary general education is in accordance with the way of our imperial country and achieves the fundamental training of the people."

After the Meiji restoration, our country's education at times was burdened with Western ideas. The unfortunate result was that the principles of educating imperial subjects were not fully implemented. The effect was that our country's traditional heritage was forgotten, and the discipline for the way of being subjects was neglected. Those who are imperial subjects must rectify this neglect, hold fast to the fundamental principles of national polity and our steadfast convictions, and strive hard through constant discipline to incorporate the way of subjects into their everyday lives.

We, as imperial subjects in this new age, need to constantly discipline ourselves. This is because training people to value a resolute spirit heightens their nobility of character, an essential condition for the people of a great country. If people lapse into vulgarity and laziness, indulge in greed for personal gain, and escape responsibility without shame, this will not only prevent the country's fortunes from improving but will bring ridicule. In order for our country to act resolutely and proceed calmly in our national emergency, a strong and steadfast spirit is essential. Discipline cultivates this magnificent spirit and sublime noble character of our great people, and this in turn should lead to a new order and a sphere of mutual prosperity.

Naturally ours is a maritime country, and formerly many went abroad full of ambition. But since Japan was closed to the outside world for three hundred years during the Edo period, the people's indomitable spirit became somewhat constricted. With the onset of the Meiji period and the bold, forward-looking policy of opening up the country, the country's fortunes improved remarkably. However, the general populace lacked awareness of our country's historical mission and also that indomitable resolve of a great people. At home, their hearts had no room for unity and harmony; abroad, they unintentionally humbled themselves and occasionally followed others. In assuming responsibility for this new age, our people should embody the fundamental spirit of our country through their magnificent energy and morality, which other countries respect and look up to.

If our country's fortunes are to be developed and our great work for Asia is to be realized, then we must ennoble the people's sense of good judgment and understanding. The way to cultivate good judgment and understanding is not simply by copiously assimilating knowledge without any reflection. It is accomplished by broadly observing and deeply thinking from various standpoints as imperial subjects; we must also acquire concrete knowledge and learning to truly offer assistance in advancing the empire's fortunes. Learning that cannot unify itself with the imperial way cannot be true learning and surely is no more than abstract theories irrelevant to our lives. The way, when it is traveled, becomes the way of teaching and learning. Learning causes us to grasp and be aware of the way in every aspect of our lives. Teaching, which contains learning within it, embodies the way. For that reason, teaching and learning, knowledge and virtue are one and the same in the way. Thus, in order to obtain that lofty sense of good judgment and understanding that is rooted in our calling as imperial subjects, we must gain a broad perspective, meticulously reflecting on things, such that it solely accords with the way of the imperial state.

As imperial subjects, our discipline has the potential for bold and vigorous practice. The true power of true practice—doing what should be done without hesitation, and absolutely never doing what should not be done—is founded upon a deep conviction in our national polity (*kokutai*). The wellspring of action is faith, and faith is power. This idea can also be seen in the rules and regulations for our national schools, where it is also stipulated that "You should put the way of the imperial state into practice in every aspect of your education, and especially you should deepen your faith in the national polity." We must honor a resolute spirit and develop an unbreakable will, good judgment, and understanding; we must also hone our physical strength and cultivate true practical abilities embodying a faith based on national polity. Here is why we must emphasize a discipline where heart and body are one and knowledge and virtue coincide.

In recent times, we have experienced progress in the material side of our civilization. Our daily lives have improved to a remarkable degree. However, all sorts of institutions stimulating vulgar and base desires have also spread, and a tendency to pursue a hedonistic lifestyle has gradually become more common. We as a people must do some deep soul searching about this.

Under these circumstances, the inclination is to make light of such virtues as self-control and self-restraint. These along with other impediments make it more difficult to discipline the will. In addition, increasing our physical strength is one of the most important tasks our country is facing. In order to endure the long period we need in order to strengthen our country, all citizens must not only refine their spirit but increase their physical strength. However, it should always be remembered that the reason for keeping our bodies physically fit through training is to discipline ourselves as citizens of the state. If you are simply interested in exercise and competition, or if you get carried away over the results of winning or losing, you will lose sight of why you are becoming physically fit and will end up confusing what is trivial and what is important. Mental and physical discipline become an authentic form of practice only when they put us in harmony with our moral natures as subjects of the imperial state and contribute to advancing the state's fortunes.

Our country has always held discipline in high esteem as the ancient way of our country, and this is a special feature of our education and learning. We call this opportunity for teaching and learning merging with the way through discipline or, put differently, ascetic practice (*gyō*). In Bushidō, if at a young age you drill and drill night and day, you can uncover Bushidō's divine essence (*shinzui*). It does not matter whether you practice *kendō*, *judō*, the way of archery, the tea ceremony, or the ways of flower arranging and the arts (*geidō*); all of these can reveal to the practitioner their innermost meaning through ascetic practice. Even Buddhism was adopted as a teaching to defend the state (*chingo kokka*) in our country; it was assimilated into the lives of our people as an ascetic practice for fostering loyalty and filial piety. The same spirit is also present even in Confucianism. Even when adopting Western science and technology, we should continue to foster this spirit. In this new age, we subjects of the imperial state must fully make this important duty our own. We should reflect deeply on our ancestors' example, uplift ourselves with the ascetic discipline of the way of subjects, constantly practice in our daily lives, and achieve success by faithful service to the state.

23

THE BOARD OF DIVINITIES (JINGIIN)

National polity and the great way of the gods, national history and shrines, and the state and shrines from Chapter 1, National Polity and Shrines of the *Jinja hongi* (The Cardinal Principles of Shrines, 1944)

Jinja hongi is a propaganda tract produced by the Japanese government in 1944. Like other governmental tracts, such as the *Kokutai no hongi* (1937), it gave the official line, in this case regarding the status and role of shrines in imperial Japan. Texts like the *Jinja hongi* were often used for educational purposes, in this case, as a way of clarifying the role shrines played in moral education, particularly as a means of expressing love of country and loyalty to the emperor. These texts delineated the official view but were open to interpretation, and they spawned several commentaries as a consequence.[1]

The source of the text, the Board of Divinities (Jingiin), was the administrative agency in charge of shrine affairs, attached to the Home Ministry. Originally founded by imperial rescript number 736, on November 9, 1940, the Board replaced the Bureau of Shrines (Jinjakyoku) at the time of the celebration of the 2,600th year of the imperial reign beginning with Emperor Jinmu. This text fulfilled one of the official mandates of the board to increase reverence for the *kami,* an ideological purpose that was inspired by the movement to clarify national polity (kokutai meichō undō) of 1935. Shinto scholar Sakamoto Koremaru notes that, ideologically speaking, this text and others like it published by the Jingiin were not as extreme as the *Kokutai no hongi* that was published under the auspices of the Ministry of Education (Monbushō).[2] The following selection is a translation of Chapter 1 in three sections: "National polity and the great way of the gods," "National history and shrines," "The state and shrines." Other contents include: Chapter 2 "The enshrined deities at shrines," Chapter 3 "Shrine pavilions and grounds," Chapter 4 "Shrine officials, priests and shrine parishioners (*ujiko*) and worshippers," Chapter 5 "Shrine rites," and Chapter 6 "Shrines and the life of the people,"

NATIONAL POLITY AND THE GREAT WAY OF THE GODS,
NATIONAL HISTORY AND SHRINES, AND THE STATE
AND SHRINES FROM CHAPTER 1, NATIONAL POLITY AND
SHRINES OF THE *JINJA HONGI* (THE CARDINAL PRINCIPLES
OF SHRINES)
(1944)

The great Japanese empire is a country that the imperial ancestor Amaterasu Ōmikami graciously began. The emperors, of one line unbroken for ages eternal, and who are her descendants, have reigned over Japan from eons past, as directed by her divine commands.

This is our national polity unrivaled in all other countries. What Kitabatake Chikafusa states at the beginning of his *Jinnō shōtōki* (The Chronicle of Gods and Sovereigns) is truly apt:

> Great Japan is a divine land (*shinkoku*). The heavenly ancestor initially founded it, and the sun goddess transmitted the line of rule for it for the ages. This is something that only our country has. There is nothing comparable to it in other dynasties. That is the reason why we call our country the land of the gods.[3]

The emperor who descends from this reigning line of the imperial ancestor Amaterasu Ōmikami inherits this divine blessing and the goddess's divine will and strives to expand the great undertaking that began with the foundation of the country. Our divine land of Japan is the only country that has at its core such a glittering national polity and has the great spirit of its founding pervading throughout its history.

When you look at other countries, you see that they do not always have firm spiritual foundations and that their histories are riven and marred by revolutions and internal unrest. These countries and their peoples repeatedly unite and break apart, fuse and fragment. Often the state as an entity ceases to exist, and then a new history arises, making an abrupt change. We can see that many countries, both in the past and in modern times, have not existed perpetually and have a history of revolutions. These histories also show that the people's lives, with no constant faith, lack ideals and are weakened at their roots.

In our country, a succession of emperors has always been united as one with the imperial ancestors, and has ruled as manifest *kami* (*akitsumikami*), just as in the age of the gods. They have broad, unlimited, and unsurpassed virtues. The people bask in their compassionate imperial kindness, and they put the emperors' divine commands into effect by wholeheartedly and unconditionally respecting the ancestral will, serving generations of emperors, and exhibiting the fine virtues of loyalty and filial piety. This brings about an incomparable unity of the sovereign and his people that form one great family state. The life of this eternally undying state continues to develop vigorously. This is the essence of our national polity, incomparable and dignified, stretching back to ancient times and unchanged for eternity. This way of being, practiced ceaselessly at home and abroad, is the great way of the gods (*kannagara no taidō* [also *kamunagara*]).

It is in the shrines, however, where we see the great way of the gods in its most sublime and venerable form. These shrines, which begin with Ise Jingū, enshrine divinities in each area, manifest our august national polity, and eternally guard our imperial country.

National polity and shrines

The meaning of the great way of the gods

The word *kannagara* appears many times in the *Nihonshoki* as well as in the *Shoku Nihongi* and the *Manyōshū*, but it appears with different Chinese characters such as 惟神, 随在天神, 随神, 神随. Regardless of how it is written, this word means the way the *kami* such as it is, the way the gods are as they are. Norinaga interpreted the great way of the gods to mean the way emperors rule this realm, and it means the way of the emperor as a manifest *kami* (*akitsumikami*), ruling this country by following the will of the *kami* as it is. Because it is the way of imperial rule inherited from the heavenly *kami,* it is also referred to as the way of the divine emperor (*shinnō no michi*) or the imperial way (*kōdō*), and people also broadly refer to it as Shinto.

This way is founded upon the divine command, which is eternal with the heaven and earth, and which Amaterasu Ōmikami graciously bestowed on her divine grandson Ninigi no Mikoto at the time of his descent from heaven. In this divine command, she states,

> The land of the bountiful reed plain with its fifteen hundred autumns of auspicious rice ears is the place where my descendants shall be rulers. With my blessing now, my grandson, go rule it! Go and may there be prosperity for those succeeding the imperial throne, and may that reign, like heaven and earth, last forever.[4]

Just as there are no limits to heaven and earth, there should be no limits to the flourishing of Amaterasu's royal descendants or to the good fortune of our country. For generations after, Amaterasu's descendants carry out the work of their predecessors according to the divine command. They make their hearts one with Amaterasu Ōmikami, and their great reigns show the cardinal principle of the great way of the gods.

Emperor Kōtoku in August of the first year of Taika (1305),[5] in a decree handed down to the governors of the Eastern provinces, stated, "In accordance with the charge given to me by the heavenly deities, we shall try now for the first time to rule the various provinces."[6] Moreover, in a decree of the third year of Taika (1307), there appears, "It was entrusted by the sun goddess that our children shall rule just as the gods did (*kannagara mo*). Because of this, since the beginning of heaven and earth, this has been a country ruled by monarchs."[7]

After this, Emperor Monmu in a decree at his Enthronement Ceremony, stated,

> I now announce my thoughts that, in accord with the will of the gods (*kannagara*), I humbly accept this noble, lofty, expansive, and profound imperial command that Empress Yamatoneko (Jitō), who rules over the great country of eight islands, has bestowed on me to bear. Beginning in Takamanohara, throughout the reign of our distant imperial ancestors and up to the present, there has been an unceasing succession of emperors ruling over the great country of eight islands, that continues next to my ceremonial act of sitting on the throne of Amaterasu Ōmikami, which the heavenly deity and even her children have entrusted to me as a manifest *kami*. I will arrange to rule the country as her successor, subdue it, and offer kindness and tender loving care to its people.[8]

Recently, Emperor Meiji, on January 3 in the third year of Meiji (1870), announced in his Imperial Rescript for the Proclamation of the Great Teachings (*taikyō*),

> I deferentially consider that the heavenly deities and the heavenly ancestors established the foundations and left directions, which each of later emperors in succession have proclaimed. As for the unification between rituals and governance and billions and trillions of people, whose hearts are one, governance and teachings clarify it on a higher level, while folk customs ornament it on a lower one. After the middle ages, however, through occasional ups and downs, lightness and darkness have in turn prevailed. Now the heavenly destiny returns full circle, bringing about the restoration of the hundred institutions. Now we should clarify the governance and teachings, thus upholding the great divine way. We order anew missionaries to go forth to propagate [the Great Teachings (*taikyō*)] under the heaven. You, my subjects and commoners, be convinced of their significance.

Further, in a rescript that the present Emperor [Shōwa] gave at the Hall for State Ceremonies (Shishinden) on the day of his enthronement, he declared,

What I have considered is that my imperial ancestors have followed the great way of *kannagara*, have prepared themselves for heavenly rule, laid the unshakable foundations of our great undertaking, and passed down the eternal throne through a line unbroken for ages eternal, thus extending to my own person.

In another rescript given at the ceremony celebrating the 2,600th year since Emperor Jinmu's reign,[9] he stated,

You my subjects, have taken to heart the purport of my decrees that were previously issued long ago. Make it known both at home and abroad as the great way of the *kami*. So, I hope you will definitely contribute to the welfare of humankind and harmonious relations of all countries.

As we have discussed, generations of emperors have considered the great way of *kannagara* an important point of politics. This goes back to the time of Emperor Jinmu who stated, "I shall respond affectionately to the values when the heavenly *kami* granted the country to me and shall extend the moral correctness cultivated by Ninigi no Mikoto." This is common to all ages.

Successive generations of emperors offered up immutable divine decrees like these, together with an eternal line of rulers for this country. History teaches us that our eternal imperial country has always exhibited, and continues to exhibit, the noble essence of the great way of *kannagara*. The great way of *kannagara*, fundamental to our empire's rule, is based on the rescripts of past emperors. Since the emperors rule by humbly receiving the divine will, generations of emperors ardently worship the gods of heaven and earth and revere the rites. This is where their plans for ruling the country and their plans to enlarge upon imperial rule and the spirit of the unity of ritual and governance begin.

The descent of the imperial ancestor and the expansion of imperial rule

Humbly reflecting upon the history of the age of the gods shows us that the names of the seven generations of deities reveal a process of the development from chaos. Then the two deities, Izanagi no Mikoto and Izanami no Mikoto, received a command from the heavenly gods to solidify the drifting land, descend from heaven, and accomplish this sacred work.[10] After this, the oversight of the earth depended upon the two deities Ōnamuchi[11] and Sukunahikona.[12] When the earth was pacified, the imperial grandchild Ninigi no Mikoto descended to the earth for the first time. In other words, once the gods had given birth to and formed the lands, Amaterasu Ōmikami instructed the imperial grandchild, in a profound divine command, to delegate the rule of the Central Land of the Reed Plains to his descendants for eternity. Ninigi no Mikoto descended from heaven to manifest the divine will from the Plain of High Heaven on earth, and in reign after reign succeeding emperors followed that divine will and advanced its sacred work.

The following generations of imperial rulers after Ninigi no Mikoto resided in the area of Kyūshū, cultivated uprightness and enlightened the simple folk. Ninigi's great-grand child, Emperor Jinmu, led his army eastward. Here we see a remarkable advance in the history of the imperial state. The noble task of the imperial line is typified by the story of expansion of the heavenly undertaking, recorded in the *Nihonshoki*'s chapter on Emperor Jinmu. The emperor had heard from the Old Man of the Sea (*Shiotsuchi no oji*) that there was a beautiful land surrounded on all sides by green mountains to the east. As he departed for that place,[13] he declared, "Because this land shall definitely be suitable for the expansion of the heavenly undertaking, I think that it will make the entire world full of glory."[14] He led his ships through Kyūshū and Chūgoku to the land of Yamato in the east. After long months and years of travails, he finished the great work of pacifying central Japan. The emperor cleared the mountains and the forests, oversaw the construction of his palace, and held a great Enthronement Ceremony at the Kashihara palace. In the third month of the second year before the Japanese era began, after he had settled on a place for the capital, the emperor noted in a decree, "Should I not build the capital in such a way that it embraces the heavens, the earth, and the four directions and puts a roof over the eight corners of the world by making my house?"[15]

After his enthronement, he erected a sanctuary in the mountains of Tomi in the land of Yamato and worshipped his imperial ancestor, the heavenly goddess. It is presumed that, along with expressing his gratitude to the ancestral spirits for their protection, he reported to them about the fruition of his great undertaking. We can infer, then, that there is an intimate and inseparable connection between the expansion of the imperial work and the veneration of the deities of heaven and earth.[16]

The reverence of deities in the imperial house

The source of reverence for deities in the imperial house is exceedingly profound. When the imperial grandchild Ninigi no Mikoto descended from heaven, Amaterasu Ōmikami issued her immutable divine command. At the same time, with her own hands, she gave her precious glorious mirror to her grandchild, and said, "This mirror—have [it with you] as my spirit, and worship it just as you would worship my very presence."[17] This is honored in the world as the divine command to humbly worship the sacred mirror, and it is the origin of the reverence at [Ise] Jingū and the Kashikodokoro.

This precious mirror was worshipped for a long time in the Imperial Palace. Emperor Sujin, however, due to his awe of the mirror's divine power, had the imperial princess Toyosukiirihime no Mikoto enshrine it in the village of Kasanui in Yamato. In the next reign of Emperor Suinin, he put the imperial princess Yamatohime no Mikoto in charge of worshipping Amaterasu Ōmikami instead and moved the sanctuary upstream of the Isuzu river of Watarai in Ise province. The princess became the priestess charged with performing rites by the side of the great goddess, and thus began the custom of having an imperial princess or another female imperial member serve as the Saigū.[18] Emperor Sujin also enshrined Ōkunitama no kami[19] and other deities in places where they had a historical connection. Subsequent reigns followed the emperor's example, working tirelessly to show piety towards the deities and care for the people. On the eighth day of the second month of the twenty-fifth year of his reign (656), Emperor Suinin gathered together five senior officials like Takenunakawawake and said,

> My predecessor Emperor Mimakiirihikoinie (Sujin) acted wisely here. He was reverential with a deep understanding of things, acted with humility and aspired to be unassuming. He united the system of government and worshipped the gods of heaven and earth. Calling himself to account, he endeavored to improve himself and lived by moderation day by day. Because of this, the people were sufficiently prosperous, and the realm was at peace. Now, while I reign, can there be, contrary to expectations, any neglect in worshipping the gods of heaven and earth?[20]

During Empress Suiko's reign, she invited monks to the palace to read the Buddhist sutras. But still she profoundly honored the great way which was the foundation of the country, declaring on the ninth day of the second month of the fifteenth year of her reign (1267),

> I hear that in the past our imperial forbearers governed the world bending their backs low to heaven, tiptoeing lightly on the earth, showing devout respect to the gods of heaven and earth, dedicating shrines at mountains and rivers everywhere, and traveling far and wide in heaven and earth. Because of this, *yin* and *yang* improve, are set at ease, and arranged together with heaven and earth. Now, in my reign, how can I neglect the worship of heavenly and earthly gods? Thus, because of this, it is essential that I, along with my subjects, devote ourselves to reverencing the gods of heaven and earth.[21]

It became part of the successive emperors' daily duty to offer deep and heartfelt piety. The imperial records written by Emperor Uda[22] show that he humbly worshipped the major, minor, and middling heavenly and earthly gods every day of his reign. He was especially reverent toward Ise Jingū. The *Kinpishō*,[23] in which Emperor Juntoku attentively recorded his daily customs and rituals, shows that he started every morning by washing his hands and face and then going to the *Ishibai no dan* prayer altar, facing the south-east corner, and bowing toward Ise Jingū and the Hall of the Sacred Mirror. We can infer his intentions from his own words:

> As a rule, etiquette at the imperial residence gives priority to divine rituals first and relegates other things until later. From dawn to dusk one does not neglect pious thoughts. One never regards Ise Jingū and the Hall of the Sacred Mirror as relics of the past. No matter what one cooks, it is put first on the table in the Daibandokoro and the court ladies are called so that they can offer it to deities.

It is therefore quite apparent that successive emperors have sought to rule by passing down the divine will of the imperial ancestress Amaterasu Ōmikami and deeply revering the heavenly and earthly gods. This shows clearly that rites and governance were the foundation of their reigns.

The spirit of the unity of ritual and governance (saisei icchi)

The unity of ritual and governance is the essence of our imperial country's rule. At the time of Emperor Kōtoku's Taika governmental reforms, the great minister Sogano Ishikawa Maro[24] replied, "And so, first celebrate and appease the gods of heaven and earth, and then after that it is suitable to deliberate over governmental matters." This exemplifies the traditional concept of the unity of rites and governance.

As for the unity of rites and governance the emperor humbly worships the *kami* and hears the divine will, to realize it in the affairs of state. "Worship" refers to serving the imperial ancestress Amaterasu Ōmikami and internalizing that spirit. "Governance" refers to actualizing the great spirit that has been internalized in imperial rule. And so, in our country, rituals and governance are one, united together in complete harmony.

This has been the case since the distant past. Emperor Jinmu built a sanctuary in the mountains of Tomi and fostered great filial piety by worshipping his ancestor Amaterasu

Ōmikami. We can see from this historical fact—and from the fact that he envisaged sovereign power according to his ideal of expanding the realm under his control (*hakkō iu*)—that the unity of rites and governance existed more than 2,600 years ago.

It is apparent from Emperor Meiji's great desire for the restoration of imperial rule that he took his cue from the foundational work of Emperor Jinmu. The term *saisei icchi* can frequently be found even in the imperial decrees of early Meiji. Among these is a rescript for a ceremony he performed himself in October of the first year of Meiji at Hikawa Shrine, the principal shrine of Musashi province,[25] in which the emperor stated,

> Praying to the gods of heaven and earth and holding their rites in high esteem are the major ceremonies of our imperial nation and have become the foundation of religion and politics. Nevertheless, it gradually came to be the case for some time after the middle ages that, as the way of politics weakened, ceremonial rites were no longer performed, and, finally, the moral fiber of the nation decayed. I deeply regret this. Now, at the autumn of the reformation, I set forth to the new capital of Tokyo and intend to restore the unity of rites and governance anew by attending to governance, reinstating ceremonies again, and firming the moral fiber of the nation.

Furthermore, on January 3 of the third year of Meiji in a decree for a *chinsai* ceremony that was widely disseminated to the public, the emperor stated,

> With the greatest respect, I think deeply about worshipping the gods and spirits and tenderly caring for the people, something that began with the acts of my great ancestors. The origin of the unity of rites and governance is in the distant past. Because of my weaknesses, I have worried night and day, especially after receiving this sacred bond, and fret over my deficiencies occasionally in the heavenly work. Therefore, I extend my filial piety by worshipping the heavenly and earthly *kami,* the eight guardian deities, and the spirits of my imperial ancestors, something performed by the Council of Divinities. My wish is that the people follow the same way.

The fundamental spirit of the restoration of imperial rule, which was the great ideal of the Meiji Restoration, can clearly be seen in this noble proclamation. Moreover, the imperial decree on the unity of rites and governance is apparent again in the promulgation of Japan's Imperial Constitution, the fundamental code for the rule of the empire. Before granting and promulgating it, Emperor Meiji first reported to the spirits of his imperial ancestors with the prayer in which he intoned,

> I now reverently make my prayers for divine help from them and from my father, and also make a solemn oath to them that neither now nor in the future will I fail to be an example to our subjects in the observance of the laws hereby established. May the divine spirits witness this solemn oath.

Later he decreed, "By the supreme power granted by my ancestors, I proclaim this Imperial Constitution granted for eternity for the people both now and in the future."

In the Imperial Rescript on Education, he stated:

> Know ye, our subjects: Our imperial ancestors have founded our empire on a basis broad and everlasting and have deeply and firmly implanted virtue; our subjects

ever united in loyalty and filial piety have from generation to generation illustrated the beauty thereof. This is the glory of the fundamental character of our empire [*kokutai*], and herein also lies the source of our education.[26]

And further, he states, "The way here set forth is indeed the teaching bequeathed by our imperial ancestors, to be observed alike by their descendants and the subjects, infallible for all ages and true in all places."[27]

In these statements, the emperor explains clearly that education should come from the essence of our national polity because education and learning in the empire should follow the great principles of the founding of the nation, in accordance with the great way of *kannagara*. Education must therefore be fundamentally in harmony with rites and governance.

The Taihō codes, the *Rikkokushi*, and other sources all provided that the emperor should be considered a manifest *kami* (*akitsukami, akitsumikami*) or else a *kami* who is a human being (*arahitogami*); they also provided that the emperor himself issued imperial orders as manifest *kami*. This noble belief about the emperor's rule shows the unity of rites and governance. Here we respectfully see the noble divine will of the great goddess Amaterasu, passed down through eternity and developed into the sovereign governance of the emperor as a manifest *kami*.

A particularly awe-inspiring part of the annual ceremony which marks the year's first court work (*matsurigoto hajime*) is the initial report to the emperor from the prime minister and the cabinet. This tells the emperor that the previous year's special and everyday ceremonies at Ise Jingū were all performed without any hindrances.

In Emperor Meiji's poem he also wrote, "This year too, at the ceremony of the first court work, I hear about the sanctuary for the *kami* at Ise of the divine winds." This shows the emperor's profound thoughts on the unity of rites and governance and his deep piety toward the gods.

Reverence for the deities and the way of subjects

Successive generations of emperors have inherited the divine will of the imperial ancestor and have embodied the great way of *kannagara* in the actual forms of the great governance. Likewise, the imperial subjects, respectfully mindful of divine and imperial blessings, follow the great way of *kannagara*, and serve the imperial house with sincerity, as they have from time immemorial. This is the accepted duty of Japanese subjects, and it also conforms to the great way of *kannagara*. The fundamentals of the great way of *kannagara* lie in the reign by the generations of emperors as manifest *kami* in one continuous hereditary line, whereas the subjects' part in the great way of *kannagara* has, for generations, manifested itself in the Japanese people's sincere obedience and loyalty to their emperor.

Because of their pure loyalty, the two deities Amenokoyane no Mikoto and Futotama no Mikoto,[28] graciously received the divine command to serve closely and protect the divine grandson, Ninigi no Mikoto. They accompanied him when he descended from heaven, and it is apparent that their descendants have served loyally ever since. In addition, the ancient ancestral *kami* Amenooshihi no Mikoto of the Ōtomo clan and Amekushitsuōkume of the Kumebe clan took the vanguard during the divine grandson's descent from heaven. Their descendants have followed suit, continuing to serve as protectors of the imperial house. The poet of the Nara period Ōtomo no Sukune Yakamochi[29] gave his blessing to the great reign and, among the poems he composed, tells about the unstinting loyalty of his family since the time of his ancestors.

To the Ōtomo clan belongs a great office.
In which served our far-off divine ancestor
Who bore the title of Okume-nushi.
We are the sons of the fathers who said,
"At sea be my body water-soaked,
On land be it with grass overgrown,
Let me die by the side of my sovereign!
Never will I look back";
And who to this day from olden times
Have kept their warrior's name forever clean.
Verily Ōtomo and Saheki are the clans
Pledged to the maxim, as pronounced
By their ancestors: "Extinguish not, sons, The name of your fathers!
Serve your sovereign!"[30]

The spirit behind this poem is the fundamental spirit of Japanese subjects that can be seen throughout the country's history. The subjects of the divine country Japan venerate each and every ancestor of the clans as a *kami*. They have been part of the country's history since the beginning; they regard the souls of these ancestral *kami* as their own souls and work hard to be loyal to and supportive of the imperial house and the state.

The great ancestral goddess Amaterasu is worshipped at shrines, and most of the other *kami* piously worshipped at shrines are clan ancestral spirits who serve the imperial state helping to secure the emperor's good fortune. Since these *kami* have been the objects of piety for generations of our ancestors, venerating the shrines means filial piety towards one's ancestors as well as loyal service to the imperial house; being devout, venerating the emperor, and worshipping the ancestors harmonize together.

Since the emperor's great heart is filled with respect toward the *kami* and love towards his people, and since he rules with great virtue according to the divine will of the great ancestral goddess, the way of *kannagara* has progressed resolutely and correctly. It also progresses because the hearts of the emperor's subjects overflow with pious and reverent thoughts and people of high and low stations are united by their deep sense of sincerity.

Since the country was founded, Japanese subjects have tirelessly exerted themselves for the imperial house without thinking about their own or their families' interests. Even through the national crises we have faced, these loyal and patriotic acts have clearly come from genuine feelings of piety and belief in public service. For example, Fujiwara Kamatari[31] was the loyal courtier who, assisting Prince Naka no Ōe,[32] chastised the Soga clan and helped initiate the beginning of the Taika reforms. If we look further into his background, we will see that he is a descendant of Ame no Koyane no Mikoto who served Amaterasu Ōmikami, always giving his unalloyed loyalty. He carried along sacred enclosures for the gods (*himorogi*), accompanied the divine grandson on his descent from heaven, and performed important duties as a palace guard and protector, and his family line originated in mythical events. Also, Wake no Kiyomaro[33] was sent to Usa Shrine and humbly received a divine oracle; he risked his life to deliver it and destroy the ambitions of the monk Dōkyō in order to protect the eternal imperial throne bestowed by the gods of heaven and earth. And both loyal courtiers, Kamatari and Kiyomaro, became *kami*, supporting the foundations of imperial rule and transmitting their influence down to today.

179

Even the loyal retainers of the Yoshino period, Kusunoki Masashige[34] and Nitta Yoshisada,[35] are all pious men. It has been said that Masashige deeply revered Takemikumari,[36] the deity of his birthplace, while Yoshisada, before heading into battle, would worship at shrines to pray for the deity's protection.

Therefore, unity came through the combination of venerating the gods of heaven and earth, obeying the divine will, and revering the emperor with unstinting loyalty. It is a remarkable historical fact that Oda Nobunaga,[37] who feared the weakening of the imperial house and offered his loyalty to it, also lamented shrines falling into ruin and worked to assure their reconstruction and repair. There were few feudal lords or military commanders whose fervent spirit of devotion was not directed toward the shrines in the fief. The Meiji Restoration itself came from the movement to overthrow the shogunate and revere the emperor; this came about based on Suika Shinto, which Yamazaki Ansai advocated, as well as Restoration Shinto, which Motoori Norinaga advocated. That is, needless to say, especially noteworthy and glorious. At every opportunity, Motoori Norinaga emphasized how important shrines are for the state. He also noted that the great way of *kannagara* is an essential way of piety for deities, for imperial governance as a manifest *kami* ruling by following the divine will of the imperial ancestor, and also even for subjects who earnestly follow that great imperial rule. Even after the Meiji period, loyal subjects, pillars of the state, and illustrious generals have shown great piety toward deities and reverence toward the emperor. Today, senior statesmen and military commanders who bow to the royal commands regarding state affairs are among the first to worship at Ise Jingū offering their devotion. There is no need at present to tell subjects that they should never forget even for a second their great duty to venerate the gods and shrine rites. That is because Japan's subjects serve the emperor who regards his piety and his love of the people as important parts of his imperial rule.

National history and shrines

The origin and development of shrines

The country's history shows the perpetual development of the imperial state. Japan's development is on a firm trajectory because it is based on an eternally unchanging national polity. While some aspects of that development change in response to particular times and circumstances, the great way which has the state as its basis simply makes no missteps no matter what the vicissitudes. The emperor, coming from a line unbroken for ages eternal, is above; below are his subjects, who hold to their duties while treading the path of fidelity and offering their utmost loyalty. This will never change.

This foundation of the country is also clearly visible in the history of shrine development. That is, shrines have an eternal life, but even as they preserve their ancient form they continue to develop with the times.

What do we mean by shrines? To put it most simply, they are a place for humbly worshipping the gods and their spirits who reside there peacefully. Although it is unclear exactly when shrines took on their present form, with buildings to worship *kami,* people in the past worshipped the gods at *himorogi* and *iwasaka.* A *himorogi* is a tree that gives an abode for the deity. Sakaki trees—evergreen trees which grew in sacred places—were preferred in ancient times. And, *iwasaka* means a sacred area divided off by rocks.

The first reference to *himorogi* and *iwasaka* in national history occurs when Takamimusubi no Mikoto gave the divine command to the two deities, Amenokoyane no

Mikoto and Futodama no Mikoto, who accompanied the divine grandson's descent from heaven. According to an entry from the section of the "Age of the Gods" in the *Nihonshoki*, Takamimusubi no Mikoto gave the following command to the chief accompanying deities:

> I shall immediately set up a heavenly *himorogi* and *iwasaka* and will surely prac-
> tice religious abstinence for my descendant. You, Amenokoyane no Mikoto and
> Futodama no Mikoto, take a heavenly *himorogi* with you when you descend to the
> Central Land of the Reed Plains and practice religious abstinence for my descendant.

This is commonly known as the divine command to set up tree altars and rock sanctuaries. The national significance of shrine rites comes from this divine decree.

Today, we distinguish between *himorogi* and shrines. *Himorogi* are set up to invite the temporary presence of divine spirits, but in ancient times there was no distinction. Although the standard Chinese characters for *himorogi* are not specifically used, there is an entry in the *Nihonshoki* when Emperor Jinmu prayed at the headwaters of the Niu river in Yamato for victory in battle. He commanded that a five-hundred-branch *sakaki* tree be selected and then prayed to all the gods; this is an example of an ancient rite which relied on a tree altar.

The architecture of today's shrines generally dates from later on. We can surmise that there is no strict distinction between an age of tree altars and shrine buildings, and that both coexisted together in certain periods.

We can therefore see that even though institutions for the worship of the gods in our country do change more or less with the times, they have not changed drastically because of the power of tradition born from the cardinal principles of shrines. We can see this in a work composed by Emperor Meiji where he graciously states, "What was precious is that shrines of the *kami* have not changed; they have the same form as in the distant past."

Shrines and the progress in the fortunes of the nation

The prosperity of shrines appears to parallel the rise in the country's fortunes. Although it is not clear how many shrines there were in ancient times, the *Jinmyōchō*, or *Shinmeichō* (Register of Deities) of the Heian period's *Engishiki*,[38] recorded 2,861 public shrines throughout the country, with 3,132 enshrined divinities. There were also a considerable number of shrines venerated by provincial governors and ordinary people, so the total number is probably over 30,000 shrines. Shrine numbers have also continued to increase annually. This trend partly comes from the very ardent devotion of generations of emperors, and deep reverence of lords and generals. We could also explain this by saying that this increase followed population increases, the opening up of land for cultivation, and the development of villages, which involved dividing and moving clan deities and inviting certain deities from another shrine. An additional reason for this increasing piety, particularly after the Meiji Restoration, was the deepening sense of national polity and the strengthened sense of national self-consciousness which sprang from the progress of the age. According to a recent survey, the number of shrines in the country has reached approximately 110,000 overall.

We can make the same connection between the expanding national destiny and the increased number of shrines in Japan's foreign territories. There is a famous story about Yamada Nagamasa,[39] who voyaged from his hometown of Suruga to what is now Thailand (then known as Siam) and built a Japanese colony there, which reveals our growing national prestige. Yamada was so devoted to venerating his home country's local deity that it is said that he had a big painting of his ship offered to Asama (or Sengen) shrine, located in his far away home of Shizuoka. This is a commonplace for people separated from their country while pursuing their activities abroad. Because they are Japanese, they find that they must purify their new location by building shrines, which indeed manifests their pious devotion.

It is striking that when our country's power expanded after the Meiji period, shrines were built one after another—not only in such places as Taiwan, Sakhalin, and Korea, but even in many foreign countries. Taiwan contains the official major Taiwan Shrine (*kanpeitaisha*), the government-supported middle-ranked Tainan Shrine (*kanpeichūsha*), the lower national Hsinchu Shrine (*kokuheishōsha*), Taiching Shrine (*kokuheishōsha*), Chiayi Shrine (*kokuheishōsha*), and more than sixty other shrines. In Sakhalin, besides the imperial Karafuto (Sakhalin) Major Shrine (*kanpeitaisha*), we see over 120 shrines enshrining a *kami*. In Korea, people worship the *kami* at the imperial major shrine, Chōsen (Korea) Jingū (*kanpeitaisha*), and at Puyō Jingū (*kanpeitaisha*), the national lower-ranked Seoul Shrine (*kokuheishōsha*), Yongdusan Shrine (*kokuheishōsha*), Taegu Shrine (*kokuheishōsha*), Pyongyang Shrine (*kokuheishōsha*), Gwangju Shrine (*kokuheishōsha*), Gangwon Shrine (*kokuheishōsha*), Jeonju Shrine (*kokuheishōsha*), Hamhung Shrine (*kokuheishōsha*), and many others. The enshrined *kami* vary based on the origins of each shrine, but many of them are dedicated to the reverent worship of Amaterasu Ōmikami. There are also more than a few instances of shrines taking as their enshrined *kami* deities like Emperor Meiji or such deities associated with cultivating undeveloped lands as Ōnamuchi, Sukunahikona, and Kunitama.[40] The major official Nanyō Shrine (*kanpeitaisha*) was constructed in Koror Island of Palau to celebrate the 2,600th year of the founding of the empire,[41] and enshrines Amaterasu Ōmikami as the deity for worship; there are many other shrines dedicated to the deity in places like the Marshall, Mariana, and Caroline islands.

In the province of Canton as well as Manchukuo there are close to 200 shrines in various places, including the major official shrine Canton Jingū (*kanpeitaisha*) as well as Dalian (Port Arthur), Yingkou, Shenyang (Mukden), Changchun, and Harbin. In Mongolia as well as the Republic of China, in areas of critical importance such as Zhangjiakou, Ta Fong, Hohhot, Peking, Tianjin, Shanghai, Hankow, Nanking, Tsing Tao, and Canton, people enshrine the deities of the imperial state. After the Greater East Asia War suddenly broke out, as imperial power became increasingly stronger, shrines were constructed one after the other in important places in the south, beginning with Singapore and Hong Kong. This is because the divine power shining over the four seas reveals the ideal that all the world should be under Japan's imperial roof.

The state and shrines

Core rituals of the state (sōshi)

Shrines which are based on a unique national polity are naturally closely tied to the state. Shrines have been institutions of the state since the ancient period, so every aspect of their management—priests, construction, rites—was overseen by the state. As mentioned before, shrine rites grew to national significance due to the divine decrees of the heavenly *kami*. This is evident even in a prayer (*norito*) of the Toshigoi Festival recorded in the *Engishiki*:

I humbly speak before you,

Sovereign deities whom we offer praises

With heavenly and earthly shrines

By the command of sovereign ancestral gods and goddesses

Who divinely reside in the High Heavenly Plain.[42]

Emperor Sujin specifically decided which were to be heavenly and earthly shrines, and he devised a plan to support and manage them with offerings of land, men, and housing. However, over time, an administrative system developed that involved appointing full-time officials to take charge of the shrines.

According to the *Nihonshoki,* the official title of head of the Council of Divinities (*jingi-haku*) already appears in the first year of Emperor Keitai's reign (1167).[43] The most detailed knowledge of this system, however, comes from the Taihō codes. With respect to shrine administration, we can cite the code for divinities, in twenty articles. These articles laid out the fundamental principles governing such areas as the customary annual rites, government offerings, and the supervision of shrine finances. It also made the Council of Divinities the central bureau in regard to the administrative structure. Although local governors were in charge of shrine administration in the provinces, the Council of Divinities was placed at the top of the hundred bureaus, separate and independent of the other major bureau, the Council of State (Dajōkan). In any case, provincial governors' administration of the shrines takes priority among all their tasks because of their spirit of reverence for the heavenly and earthly gods.

With the enactment of the *Engishiki*, shrine administration became increasingly well organized. Shrines were classified throughout the entire country as those administered by the central government or those admistered by the provincial governor. In particular, the provincial governors were given responsibilities for carrying out repairs and ensuring the strict performance of the rites in the shrines of their provinces or districts.

The system was later altered somewhat in response to the changing world. But the fundamental spirit of reverence for the heavenly and earthly gods in the affairs of state remained the same. Especially after Meiji period, as shrines grew more and more prosperous, the institutions of those shrines were orderly, formulated in ways that far surpassed ancient times. The government established the ordinance of Jingū rituals and the ordinance of shrine rituals for official and national shrines. For these, they instituted specific provisions regarding offerings for the gods, proper ceremonial forms and etiquette. These were put into effect at shrines throughout the country, and, accordingly, the ceremonial protocol for rites was carried out in what was considered to be a more proper and reverential manner. Additionally, the basis of shrine finances was strengthened due to a system for monetary support from the national treasury as well as local public entities. Even the status of shrine priests was fixed, either being recognized as formal government officials or being treated as if they had official rank. The administrative structure also gradually became established. At present, the Board of Divinities, under the jurisdiction of the Home Ministry, publicly administers all matters related to Jingū, official and national shrines, and all shrines below them.

As we can see, the past and present shrine administrative systems differ, but managing shrine-related matters had always been an important affair of state. It is clear that all shrines are venerated as sites for the state's core rituals. "Core state rituals" is a phrase that best expresses the essential character of shrines. It appears in a proclamation of the Council of State in May of Meiji 4 (1871), "It is clear that rituals at shrines are fundamental rites of the state that should not be privatized by anyone nor any family." This makes it clear that shrines are not the focus of private faith but are for the state to revere and worship. This is fundamentally different from the thirteen sects of sect Shinto, which are based on a religious faith and are treated as religions.

Jingū

Ise Jingū is a large shrine in our country that enshrines and worships with absolute reverence the imperial ancestress Amaterasu Ōmikami. There are two shrine buildings housing deities; these are known as Amaterasu's great shrine and the goddess Toyouke's great shrine. The ancestress's great shrine dates from the twenty-sixth year of the reign of Emperor Suinin (657), and it enshrines the deity at the headwaters of the Isuzu river at the base of Mount Kamiji, Uji Yamada city. This is where people humbly worship the imperial ancestress Amaterasu Ōmikami, who beautifully shines her light over the whole universe. Toyouke's great shrine was founded 481 years later, in the twenty-second year of Emperor Yūryaku (1138), and is devoted to Toyouke no Ōkami, who is the deity in charge of foodstuffs for Amaterasu. Amaterasu's great shrine is referred first to as the Inner Shrine (Naikū), while Toyouke's great shrine is secondly referred to as the Outer Shrine (Gekū).

Since Jingū is a large shrine and absolutely revered in our country, people of all ranks since ancient times have considered it essential and worshipped the deity as the great ancestor of Japan. For that reason, the Jingū did not have any specific shrine ranking; it transcended them all by being outside the general shrine system.

In accord with the ancient regulations, the shrine buildings of Jingū were to be rebuilt every twenty years by the national treasury. This is called the *shikinen* reconstruction, and the Agency for the Construction of Jingū was especially established for the shrine rebuilding. The reconstruction is synchronized with various rituals that continue for several years. *Shikinen sengū*, the ceremony which transfers the deity to the new *kami* hall, is the most important ceremony at the shrine, and, as an important state ceremony, it is extremely splendid. In the Jingū's ceremonial transfer of the *kami* to the new hall, the emperor personally is to bow from afar from the Imperial Palace, and all the official and national shrines perform the ceremony of bowing from afar.

Besides the main shrines of the Naikū and Gekū in the Jingū, there are detached shrines (*betsugū*), subsidiary shrines (*sessha, massha*), and shrines under management (*shokansha*).[44] The detached shrines have the highest rank and receive sacred offerings from the imperial house, which are proportionate to the offerings to the main shrine. These are rebuilt in the ceremonial year along with the main shrine.

At present, fourteen detached shrines are linked to the two shrines. The ten for the Inner Shrine are Aramatsuri Shrine, Tsukiyomi Shrine, Tsukiyomi Aramitama Shrine, Izanagi Shrine, Izanami Shine, Takihara Shrine, Takiharanarabi Shrine, Izawa Shrine, Kazahinomi Shrine, Yamatohime Shrine. The four in the Outer Shrine are Taka Shrine, Tsuchi Shrine, Tsukiyomi Shrine, and Kaze Shrine.

The rank of jinja

Since ancient times there have been various classifications for shrines. The oldest of these is the distinction between heavenly shrines (*amatsuyashiro*) and earthly shrines (*kunitsuyashiro*). This classification appears as early as the Emperor Jinmu chapter of the *Nihonshoki*, and it is interpreted to mean that heavenly shrines are those for worshipping heavenly deities and earthly shrines are those for worshipping earthly deities. Later, during the time of Emperor Sujin, the records of instructions for providing court donations of land (*kamudokoro*) and households (*kamube*) supporting the shrines seem to show that a regular system for shrines was established for the first time. Here *kamudokoro* means land where a *kami* is enshrined as well as a shrine estate, and *kamube* refers to the people who are attached to the shrine.

In the third year of Hōki (1432) in the Nara period, the word *kansha* (public shrine) already existed, appearing in the *Shoku Nihongi*. It referred to shrines that were noted in the records of the Council of Divinities and given offerings for prayers for the new crops (*kinen*). In the *Jinmyōchō* or *Shinmeichō* (Register of Deities) section of the *Engishiki*, which Emperor Daigo ordered compiled in the eighth month of the fifth year of Engi (905), the 2,861 shrines (with 3,132 deities) recorded there were all public shrines at the time. These shrines were further classified as receiving offerings from the Council of Divinities[45] or receiving offerings from the provincial governors. The former are shrines where worship was administered by the Council of Divinities, and the latter are shrines where worship was administered by the provincial governors. Five hundred and seventy-three shrines (737 enshrined deities) received offerings from the Council of Divinities, and 2,288 (2,395 enshrined deities) received support from the provincial governors. Both shrine types were sub-divided into major and minor shrines. Major shrines of both types totaled 353 (492 enshrined deities), and minor shrines of both types totaled 2,508 (2,640 enshrined deities). These were also called the "shrines in the *Engishiki*," abbreviated simply in Japanese to the *shikinai* shrines. By contrast, other shrines not mentioned in the register were referred to as *shikige,* meaning shrines not included in the *Engishiki.*

Among the *shikige* shrines, those whose names appear in Japan's six national histories (*rikkokushi*) are referred to as "shrines noted in the national histories" (*kokushi shosaisha*) and also "shrines present in the national histories" (*kokushi genzaisha*). They have a noble origin comparable to the shrines listed in the *Engishiki.*

There are additional groups from the Heian period that are comparable to this shrine ranking system: one is the twenty-two shrines, and the other is the *ichinomiya* shrines (principal or first shrines). The twenty-two shrines are shrines that (irrespective of whether they were *shikinai* or *shikige*) received special treatment from the imperial court, such as at the Toshigoi Festival for a good harvest. Other than Ise Jingū and Hie Shrine in Ōmi, all of these shrines are found in the Kinai region and include Iwashimizu, Kamo, Matsuo, Hirano, Inari, Ōharano, Umenomiya, Yoshida, Gion, Kitano, Kifune of Yamashiro; Kasuga, Ōmiwa, Isonokami, Ōyamato, Hirose, Tatsuta, Niukawakami of Yamato; and Sumiyoshi and Hirota of Settsu. Ise Jingū is the exception, but the other twenty-one shrines are presently all ranked on or above the middle rank of official shrines. Next, *ichinomiya* are shrines of the first rank among those shrines held in high esteem in the provinces. They are in that first rank on the occasions when the provincial governor comes to worship there and give offerings to the *kami*. Most are *shikinai* shrines, but among these were also notable *shikige* shrines. The majority of them are presently ranked as official and national shrines.

In time, the number of shrines gradually increased with the rise of piety among the people, and, as explained previously, reached their present state today. The following is an overview of the rank system.

Official shrines and national shrines

These are called public shrines (*kansha*) or *kankokuheisha*, generally referring to both *kanpeisha* (official shrines) and *kokuheisha* (national shrines). *Kanpeisha* are *kanpei no yashiro* in the *Engishiki* that received official offerings for the *kami*. Similarly, *kokuheisha*, based upon the term *kokuhei no yashiro*, are shrines that receive offerings for the *kami* from the province. However, in contrast to the official and national shrines in the *Engishiki*—all of which were classified into the two ranks of major and minor shrines—the present shrine ranking divides *kanpeisha* and *kokuheisha* into three ranks: major, intermediate, and minor. Besides these three ranks for *kanpeisha* there are also shrines classified as special category (*bekkaku kanpeisha*).

This shrine-ranking system is generally based on the old *Engi* system. It is now formulated after repeated debates that considered such factors as the origin of the enshrined deity; who actually worships there, beginning with the imperial household, samurai generals, and feudal lords; the facilities such as the shrine halls and grounds; and the level of people's piety. Thus, compared to all the nation's shrines, official and national shrines were those with unequaled distinguished histories. In the *Engishiki*, one of the differences between *kanpei* shrines and *kokuhei* shrines is that, while the former received offerings from the Council of Divinities, the latter received offerings from the provincial governors. At present, however, *kanpei* shrines receive donations for the *kami* from the imperial house for the Toshigoi and Niiname great festivals, annual festivals, and shrine-transfer ceremonies. By contrast, *kokuhei* shrines only receive donations from the imperial household for the Toshigoi and Niiname festivals. For annual festivals and shrine-transfer ceremonies, the donations come from the national treasury. The donations themselves depend on whether the shrine is ranked as a major, intermediate, or minor official and national shrine. The special category *bekkaku kanpeisha* is treated the same way as minor shrines.

Special category *bekkaku kanpeisha,* exceptional official shrines, was established under the Meiji shrine system. The first of these is Minatogawa Shrine, which was established as such in the fifth year of Meiji (1872). Subjects who offered their pure loyalty to the imperial house and the state are enshrined and worshipped as the deities in these shrines. These include such loyal retainers of the Yoshino period as Kusunoki Masashige, Kikuchi Taketoki, Nawa Nagatoshi, Kitabatake Chikafusa, and Nitta Yoshisada, and they stretch back to Fujiwara no Kamatari, Wake no Kiyomaro, and samurai generals like Oda Nobunaga, Toyotomi Hideyoshi, and Tokugawa Ieyasu. They also enshrine some feudal lords from early modern times who gave their complete loyalty to those meritorious retainers of the Meiji Restoration. However, there are also both the middle-ranked official Kitano and Dazaifu shrines where Sugawara no Michizane is worshipped, and the middle-ranked national shrine Ube Shrine where Takeuchi no Sukune is worshipped. These three were already given the official or national statues. In addition to these three, Emperor Meiji implemented the separate way of ranking for the shrines treating an emperor's faithful retainers as *kami* in *bekkaku kanpeisha*. Yasukuni Shrine is one of exceptional official shrines; needless to say, it worships spirits of the war dead (*eirei*) who protect the nation as *kami*. Thus, after Tokyo was designated as the new capital, the government constructed the Tokyo Shōkonsha at the top of Kudan Hill in June of the second year of Meiji (1869), worshipping first the warriors who had died in battle since the Boshin War.[46] Later it was combined with the worship of the war dead after the sixth year of Kaei (1853) and was granted the new name of Yasukuni Shrine in 1879, as well as being ranked as an exceptional official shrine.

Subsequently, every time a war or an incident occurred, an order was issued to include the war dead as enshrined at the shrine. At present, in May of Shōwa nineteen (1944), more than 313,800 enshrined *kami* are there. Every year at the annual spring and autumn festivals, his majesty always graciously sees that an imperial envoy is dispatched, and on certain occasions we most humbly observe an imperial visit of the emperor and the empress.

Some official shrines, known as the *chokusaisha,* receive special treatment. *Chokusaisha* refers to shrines where an imperial envoy visits during its annual festivals. Even at the average official and national shrines, an imperial envoy is dispatched on the day of the Great Enthronement Ceremony as well as at special offerings ceremonies, but at annual festivals only the local head of government visits as the messenger bearing offerings for the *kami.*

After the Meiji Restoration, the list of *chokusai* shrines where imperial envoys visit these annual festivals and give offerings grew to more than ten. They are the shrines on the following list:

Official major shrine	Kamowakeikazuchi Shrine
"	Kamomioya Shrine
"	Iwashimizu Hachimangū
"	Kasuga Shrine
"	Hikawa Shrine
"	Atsuta Jingū
"	Izumo Taisha
"	Kashihara Jingū
"	Meiji Jingū
"	Chōsen Jingū
"	Katori Jingū
"	Kashima Jingū
Exceptional official shrine	Yasukuni Shrine

In addition, both major official shrines, Usa Jingū and Kashiigū, are examples of shrines where every ten years an imperial envoy is dispatched to make offerings.

Regional shrines (fusha)*, prefectural shrines* (kensha)*, local district shrines* (gōsha)*, and village shrines* (sonsha)

Regional and prefectural shrines are venerated in each prefecture, or Tokyo, Hokkaido, Osaka, or Kyoto. Each of Japan's administrative divisions gives the donation for the *kami* of its own regional or prefectural shrine for the three great festivals—the Toshigoi, the Niiname, and the shrine's annual festival. Generally, the official leader of each division acts as the messenger with the donation. Local district shrines are those originally venerated in the district; they are positioned between regional or prefectural shrines and village shrines. For the three great festivals, donations are furnished by the Japanese prefectural administrative divisions. In the early Meiji period, village shrines were affiliated with the local district shrines by regulation; later, however, they became independent from the district shrines.

Generally, village shrines are tutelary shrines of each village. They have a deep historic relationship with the inhabitants and are the hereditary ancestral deity (*ujigami*) and tutelary *kami* (*ubusunagami*) for families who have inhabited the same locality for generations. For the three great festivals of the village, shrine offerings were provided for the *kami* from the city, town, or village, and those in charge of these would visit as their bearer of the offerings. Besides these divisions, there are what are called unranked (*mukakusha*). These have not been designated with a rank although they are officially recognized; they will deserve being ranked with a proper status after some future preparations.

As stated above, shrines of the imperial country are classified, from official and national shrines to regional, prefectural, and then to local district, village, and unranked shrines. Official and national shrines are categorized as public shrines, while regional, and prefectural shrines as well as the other lower shrines are called various shrines or, more colloquially, private shrines. However, they are the same in that they are all shrines for core rituals for the state.

Shrines for the protection of the state

In the second year of Meiji (1869) a shrine memorializing the war dead (*shōkonsha*) was built at the top of Tokyo's Kudan Hill by special favor of the emperor, which later became Yasukuni Shrine. *Shōkonsha*, which were built in various prefectures, had features that were a little different from ordinary shrines. Among the *kami* enshrined at Yasukuni Shrine, some were worshipped at a local *shōkonsha* as divine spirits connected to their localities. *Shōkonsha* were divided into officially administered *shōkonsha* and privately administered *shōkonsha*. These were renamed shrines for the protection of the nation (*gokoku jinja*) in the fourteenth year of Shōwa (1939), and it was stipulated that the general system governing shrines below regional and prefectural shrines was also to be applied to the shrines with this new name. More and more these shrines' rites were considered important so that they would expect a boost of divine authority. Therefore, the Home Ministry designated an important shrine for the protection of the nation in each prefecture, equivalent to a regional and prefectural shrine, and the other *gokoku* shrines as equivalent to village shrines. They accordingly made decisions that local government heads or city and village leaders should visit the shrines at annual ceremonies, the enshrinement of the *kami* as well as ceremonies to apotheosize groups of souls of those who died in battle. But it is customary that they do not attach ranks to these shrines for the protection of the nation from the onset.

Shrine nomenclature

There are various designations for shrines. *Shagō* are terms for designating shrines, and the names of shrines are different. For example, Meiji Jingū and Yasukuni Shrine (*jinja*) are shrine names, and *jingū* and *jinja* are terms for designating shrines. Generally, there are four different classifications for shrines—*jingū*, *gū*, *jinja*, and *sha*.

Shrines that have the *jingū* designation tend to have an especially noble origin such as Atsuta Jingū, Isonokami Jingū, Katori Jingū, Kashima Jingū, Hinokuma Jingū, Kunikakasu Jingū, Usa Jingū, and Kehi Jingū. Kirishima Jingū, Kagoshima Jingū, as well as Udo Jingū venerate the ancestral *kami* of the imperial line. Others, such as Kashihara Jingū, Miyazaki Jingū, Ōmi Jingū, Shiramine Jingū, Heian Jingū, Akama Jingū, Minase Jingū, Yoshino Jingū, and Meiji Jingū, have an emperor as their enshrined *kami*. All of these are major official shrines.

The *gū* designation is for a shrine that either has a highly respected enshrined *kami* or that has a special origin. Examples of these are shrines that have a deep connection to the great *kami* Hachiman, such as the official shrines of major rank, Iwashimizu Hachimangū, Kashiigū, Hakozakigū, and the national shrine of middle rank, Tsurugaoka Hachimangū. A national shrine of middle rank, Kotohiragū, is also one example. The official shrines of middle rank, Kamakuragū, Iinoyagū, Kanegasakigū, and Yatsushirogū, are shrines where some of the historical figures of the imperial line were enshrined anew in the Meiji years, and they all have the *gū* designation. The recent rules forbid the indiscriminate use of the *jingū* and *gū* designations.

Those shrines with *jinja* as their shrine designation are the most common. Reading these characters as *jinja* dates from later generations. In the records from ancient ages and the *Jinmyōchō* or *Shinmeichō* (Register of Deities) of the *Engishiki*, they all are read as the shrine (*yashiro*) of a certain *kami*. There is not one example among the official and national shrines where they are simply named only as shrines (*sha*), and the Great Shrine of Izumo is a special example of a shrine that is designated as a great shrine (*taisha*). Not a few shrines below regional and prefectural shrines have passed down the *sha* designation.

However, even if they are referred to as *jinja* or *sha*, there really is no difference between them because that is based on history and origin.

Notes

1 Isomae, Jun'ichi, *Religious Discourse in Modern Japan* (Leiden: Brill, 2014), 278.
2 Sakamoto Koremaru, "Jingiin," *Encyclopedia of Shinto*, http://eos.kokugakuin.ac.jp/modules/xwords/entry.php?entryID=1102.
3 Kitabatake (1293–1354) came from an aristocratic house that served Emperor Godaigo during the chaos of the Northern and Southern dynasties. After the failure of the Kenmu Restoration, he retreated from the capital and ended up in Ise, where he studied Watarai Shinto, which led to his writing of this history by 1339. Taking his cue from Ise Shinto, Kitabatake emphasizes the uniqueness of Japan as a land protected by the *kami* and ruled by an unbroken line of emperors descended from the sun goddess. See H. Paul Varley, trans., *A Chronicle of Gods and Sovereigns: Jinnō shōtōki of Kitabatake Chikafusa* (New York: Columbia University Press, 1980), 49.
4 See W.G. Aston, *Nihongi: Chronicles of Japan from the Earliest Times to A.D. 697*, 2 vols (Rutland, VT: Charles E. Tuttle Co., 1972), 2:77.
5 This Emperor's (?–654) rule began in the first year of Taika 645. The date 1305 is according to the government-inspired dating system popularized in 1872, which dated the first year of the first Emperor Jinmu's reign as February 11, 660 BCE. As Jinmu is only a legendary figure, this date was fictional.
6 Aston *Nihongi*, 2:200.
7 Aston translates *kannagara* as "in their capacity as deities." He then glosses that as meaning "to follow the way of the gods or again to possess in oneself the way of the gods." See Aston *Nihongi*, 2:226.
8 A passage from the *Shoku Nihongi*, Vol. 1, Monmu no. 42.
9 This annual ceremony was called Kigensetsu, a national holiday that was celebrated from 1872 to 1948.
10 The stories of their creation of solid land is found in chapter three of the "Age of the Gods" in the *Kojiki* and *Nihonshoki*. See Donald Philippi, trans., *Kojiki* (Tokyo: The University of Tokyo Press, 1968), 49 and Aston, *Nihongi* 1:7ff.
11 This is an alternate name for the god Ōkuninushi although this deity is described in the chronicle literature as a land-forming deity. See Philippi, *Kojiki*, 92ff.; Aston, *Nihongi*, 1:54. This deity represents the lord of the Central Land of Reed Plains who transfers the land to Takemikazuchi, the deity commanded to descend from heaven to pacify the land in the *Kojiki*. See Philippi, *Kojiki*, 134–36).

12 A deity who worked with Ōnamuchi to form and administer the land. See Philippi, *Kojiki,* 115–17; Aston, *Nihongi,* 1:59.

13 Aston translates his name as the Ancient of the Sea. This deity is an offspring of Izanagi and is an enshrined deity of Shiogama Jinja in Miyagi prefecture; he is worshipped as the god who taught people how to make salt. In the *Nihonshoki,* he tells Emperor Jinmu about the fair land to the East (the main island of Honshu in Japan) that should be his new capital. See Aston, *Nihongi,* 2:110–11.

14 Ibid., 2:110–11.

15 Aston, *Nihongi,* 2:131. The pre-war slogan, *hakkō ichiu,* "the eight corners (of the world) under one [imperial] roof," has its source in this passage. The Buddhist Nichiren nationalist Tanaka Chigaku invented this modernist term to sloganize Japan's militaristic policy of expansionism

16 Ibid., 2:134.

17 Phillipi, *Kojiki,* 140.

18 The term used here is *mitsueshiro* for imperial priestess (Saigū or Saiō) who served in the abstinence palace (*Saigū*) at Ise. The account of this is found in the *Nihonshoki.* See Aston, *Nihongi,* 1:176. This post probably existed from the early Heian period until the fourteenth century.

19 Another name for Ōkuninushi no Kami.

20 See Aston, *Nihongi,* 1:175–76.

21 See Aston, *Nihongi,* 2:135.

22 Lived from 867–931 and ruled from 887 to 897.

23 The book, "A Selection of Palace Secrets," composed between 1219 and 1221, was a compilation of court practices intended as a reference for future emperors.

24 He was a prominent figure in court politics who died in 649.

25 A shrine in Ōmiya, in what is now Saitama prefecture, particularly favored by the emperor and designated as a first-ranked official shrine until 1946.

26 Translation from William Theodore de Bary, Carol Gluck, and Arthur E. Tiedemann, eds. *Sources of Japanese Tradition, Part 2 1868–2000* (New York: Columbia University Press, 2006), 108–9. The rescript was issued on October 30, 1890 (Meiji 23).

27 Ibid., 109.

28 Deities found in the *Kojiki* and *Nihonshoki.* Ame no Koyane no Mikoto was the ancestor of the Nakatomi (Fujiwara) clan, and Futotama no Mikoto was the ancestral *kami* of the Inbe clan, who were court ritualists.

29 He lived from 718 to 785 as a Nara period official of the Yamato court and famous *waka* poet. See Paula Doe, *A Warbler's Song in the Dusk: The Life and Work of Ōtomo Yakamochi (718–785)* (Berkeley: The University of California Press, 1982).

30 Nihon Gakujutsu Shinkōkai trans., *The Manyōshū* (New York: Columbia University Press, 1965), 151.

31 A famous courtier and statesman of the Nakatomi (and later founder of the Fujiwara clan), who lived from 614–69. He was a major figure involved in the affair of the assassination of Soga Umako's grandson, Iruka, which led to the Taika era and T'ang Chinese influenced political reforms.

32 Later he becomes Emperor Tenji (626–71), who ruled 668–71.

33 A Nara court official (733–99) who was sent to Usa shrine to receive an oracle from the *kami.* The oracle he delivered, saying that only those directly descended from Amaterasu could become emperors, thwarted the plans of the Buddhist monk Dōkyō, whose affair with Empress Kōken had spurred his own ambitions to rule.

34 Kusunoki Masashige (?–1336) was a military commander during the Northern and Southern dynasties period particularly revered as an exemplar of imperial loyalty to his emperor, Godaigo (1288–1339).

35 Nitta Yoshisada (1301–38) was a military commander who also supported Emperor Godaigo's quest for imperial restoration. With his defeat, Godaigo's hopes were dashed, and the Ashikaga samurai became the head of a new military shogunate.

36 This deity is enshrined at Mikumari Shrine, which was moved to its present location near Osaka in 1334 by Kusunoki under the command of Emperor Godaigo.

37 A famous warlord (1534–82) of the Sengoku (or Warring States) period who attempted to unify Japan under his control.

38 A list of deities with their shrines found in this famous collection of administrative codes (*ritsu*) and procedures (*ryō*).

39 Yamada (?–1630) was a former Japanese privateer who was the chief of a colony built by Japanese traders located in the city Ayutthaya in what is now Southern Thailand.

40 These deities are perfect objects of worship, given that these overseas lands had been developed, in effect, as colonial territories under Japanese jurisdiction since their victory in 1895 at the end of the Sino-Japanese War.

41 This occurred in 1940, the date commemorating the founding of the empire of Japan by the first Emperor Jinmu in 660 BCE.

42 Translation from Donald Philippi, trans., *Norito: A Translation of the Ancient Japanese Ritual Prayers* (Princeton, NJ: Princeton University Press, 1990), 15. See also Robert S. Ellwood, Jr., "The Spring Prayer (*Toshigoi*) Ceremony of the Heian Court," *Asian Folklore Studies* 1 (1971):1–30.

43 He ruled from 507 until 531. So, this would be the year 507.

44 All of these terms refer to different types of shrine ranking, but generally mean small-scale auxiliary shrines that are under the management of main shrines.

45 They were offerings given for the Spring Harvest Festival, the shrine monthly festival, and the New Tasting Festival.

46 The war against the Tokugawa shogunate by imperial loyalist forces of 1868–69 that led to the Meiji Restoration.

SUGGESTED READINGS

Antoni, Klaus, Hiroshi Kubota, Johann Nawrocki, and Michael Wachutka, Editors. *Religion and National Identity in the Japanese Context*. London: Lit Verlag, 2002.

Bernier, Bernard. "National Communion: Watsuji Tetsuro's Conception of Ethics, Power, and the Japanese Imperial State." *Philosophy East and West* 56 (January, 2006):84–105.

Brownlee, John S. *Japanese Historians and the National Myths, 1600–1945: The Age of the Gods and Emperor Jinmu.* Tokyo: University of Tokyo Press, 1997.

———. "Four Stages of the Japanese Kokutai (National Essence)," http://www.adilegian.com/PDF/brownlee.pdf.

Dower, John. *War Without Mercy: Race & Power in the Pacific War.* New York: Pantheon Books, 1986.

Duus, Peter. *Modern Japan*, 2nd edition. Boston: Houghton Mifflin, 1998.

Fridell, William. "A Fresh Look at State Shinto." *JAAR* 44 (1976):547–61.

Goto-Jones, Christopher. "The Way of Revering the Emperor: Imperial Philosophy and *Bushidō* in Modern Japan." In *The Emperors of Modern Japan,* edited by Ben-Ami Shollony, 23–52. Leiden: Brill, 2008.

Gluck, Carol. *Japan's Modern Myths: Ideology in the Late Meiji Period.* Princeton, NJ: Princeton University Press, 1985.

Havens, Norman. "Shinto." In *Nanzan Guide to Japanese Religions*, edited by Paul Swanson and Clark Chilson, 14–37. Honolulu: University of Hawai'i Press, 2006.

Holtom, Daniel C. *Modern Japan and Shinto Nationalism.* Chicago: The University of Chicago Press, 1943.

Huffman, James. *Japan and Imperialism, 1853–1945.* Ann Arbor, MI: Association of Asian Studies, 2010.

Isomae Jun'ichi. "The Formative Process of State Shinto in Relation to the Westernization of Japan: The Concept of 'Religion' and 'Shinto.'" In *Religion and the Secular: Historical and Cultural Formations*, edited by Timothy Fitzgerald, 93–102. New York: Routledge, 2007.

Kawamura Satofumi. "The National Polity and the Formation of the Modern National Subject in Japan." *Japan Forum* 26 (2014):25–45.

Krämer, Hans Martin. "Beyond the Dark Valley: Reinterpreting Christian Reactions to the 1939 Religious Organizations Law." *Japanese Journal of Religious Studies* 38 (2011):181–211.

Naumann, Nelly. "Japanese Myth Ancient and Modern." *Bulletin of the European Association for Japanese Studies* 36 (December, 1991):5–12.

Nishimura, Sey, Trans. "The Way of the Gods Motoori Norinaga's *Naobi no Mitama.*" *Monumenta Nipponica* 46 (Spring, 1991):21–42.

Sakamoto Koremaru. "Religious Organizations Law." *Encyclopedia of Shinto*, http://eos.kokugakuin.ac.jp/modules/xwords/entry.php?entryID=1098.

———. "Jingiin." *Encyclopedia of Shinto*, http://eos.kokugakuin.ac.jp/modules/xwords/entry.php?entryID=1102.

————. "The Structure of State Shinto: Its Creation, Development and Demise." In *Shinto in History Ways of the Kami*, edited by John Breen and Mark Teeuwen, 272–94. Honolulu: University of Hawai'i Press, 2000.

Shimazono Susumu. "State Shinto and Emperor Veneration." In *The Emperors of Modern Japan*, edited by Ben-Ami Shollony, 163–84. Leiden: Brill, 2008.

————. "State Shinto in the Lives of the People, The Establishment of Emperor Worship, Modern Nationalism, and Shrine Shinto in Late Meiji." *Japanese Journal of Religious Studies* 36 (2009):93–124.

Shizume Masato. "The Japanese Economy during the Interwar Period: Instability in the Financial System and the Impact of Worldwide Depression." *Bank of Japan Review* (2009):1–10.

Skya, Walter A. *Japan's Holy War: The Ideology of Radical Shintō Nationalism.* Durham, NC: Duke University Press, 2009.

Stalker, Nancy K. *Prophet Motive: Deguchi Onisaburô, and the Rise of New Religions in Imperial Japan.* Honolulu: University of Hawai'i Press, 2008.

Teeuwen, Mark. "State Shinto: An 'Independent Religion'?" *Monumenta Nipponica* 54:111–21.

Thomas, Julia Adeney. *Reconfiguring Modernity: Concepts of Nature in Japanese Political Ideology.* Berkeley: University of California Press, 2001.

Ueda Shinji. "Japanese Imperialism: Political Philosophy based on Shinto Emperor Ideology." *Journal of Asia Pacific Affairs* 5 (February, 2004):89–113.

Wilson, George. *Radical Nationalist in Japan: Kita Ikki 1883–1937.* Cambridge, MA: Harvard University Press, 1969.

Woodard, William. *The Allied Occupation of Japan 1945–1952 and Japanese Religions.* Leiden: Brill, 1972.

Yanagawa Keiichi and David Reid. "Between Unity and Separation: Religion and Politics on Japan, 1965–1977." *Japanese Journal of Religious Studies* 6 (December, 1979): 500–21.

Part 4

RECASTING SHINTO—POST-WAR
REFORMS AND REFORMULATIONS

INTRODUCTION

The readings in this section are reactions to the post-war Occupation's Shinto Directive, the key document that led to the disestablishment of State Shinto. The Directive forced Shinto to be treated as a privatized religion like Buddhism, Christianity, and the Japanese new religions.

The authors in this section, however, respond in fundamentally different ways to the Occupation's new policy. In his "A new direction for Shinto" (1949), Orikuchi Shinobu writes about possibilities for Shinto in post-war Japan; a new Shinto religion might rise from the ashes of Japan's wartime defeat. Watsuji Tetsurō, in his "Feudal thought and Shinto doctrine" and "Representative of the whole people" (1948), re-visions the emperor to fit his new post-war status as a symbol of a democratic Japan. Ashizu Uzuhiko's "The various issues related to contemporary shrines" (1956) offers a critical retrospective of the harm the Shinto Directive wrought upon Japan. Murakami Shigeyoshi's selections, "The emperor as a deity in human form," and "The development of imperial house rites" (1977), show how the emperor's political, military, and religious authority as a living god (*arahitogami*) of the pre-war Japanese imperial state was a meticulously wrought construct by the Meiji government. The final reading, Kuroda Toshio's "Shinto in the history of Japanese religion" (1981) is a seminal critique of the idea that Shinto as a religious system is archaic.

Historical overview

On August 6, 1945 the United States dropped an atomic bomb on Hiroshima. Shortly thereafter, on August 9, the United States dropped a second bomb on Nagasaki, the results of which were devastating. Over 200,000 people, mainly civilians, were killed. The stage was set for Emperor Hirohito's unprecedented *Gyokuon-hōsō* "Jewel voice" radio broadcast on August 15, 1945, announcing the termination of the war. Speaking directly to his subjects on the radio for the first time, Hirohito (posthumously known as Emperor Shōwa) averred that despite the "best that has been done" by the gallantry of its fighting forces and the "devoted service" of his subjects, Japan had not prevailed. Given the awful reality of the "cruel bombs," the only choice other than total annihilation was "enduring the unendurable and suffering what is insufferable." After accepting the Potsdam Declaration for unconditional surrender to the Allied Powers, the emperor ended his broadcast with a tired moral bromide:

Let the entire nation continue as one family from generation to generation, ever firm in its faith of the imperishableness of its divine land, and mindful of its heavy responsibilities, and the long road before it.

Unite your total strength to be devoted to the construction for the future. Cultivate the ways of rectitude, foster nobility of spirit, and work with resolution so that you may enhance the innate glory of the imperial state and keep pace with the progress of the world.[1]

It was the last gasp of the pre-war *kokutai* rhetoric calling for continued noble sacrifices on behalf of the divine land (*shinkoku*) and the imperial-centered family state (*kazoku kokka*). How were his Japanese subjects to endure the unendurable? How would they be able to rebuild Japan from the ashes of destruction? What was the "way ahead" when the imperial way (*kōdō*) had so obviously failed? On that, Hirohito remained silent.

The war had devastated Japan, leaving the country largely destroyed and its survivors exhausted. Over 2.7 million had died in the war. One quarter of Japan's national wealth was lost; 80% of its ships, 34.2% of its industrial machinery, and 24.6% of its structures had been demolished, ruining the Japanese economy. Immediately after the war, economic output cratered to only 30% of its pre-war peak with real GNP in 1946 slightly below its 1918 level.[2] U.S. aerial bombing had wreaked havoc on almost every major city in Japan. For example, the March 10, 1945 firebombing of Tokyo had caused over 100,000 deaths. William P. Woodard, who ran the Religions Research Unit of SCAP (Supreme Commander of the Allied Powers) described the scale of the destruction as unbelievable: "Charred brick, stone and concrete storehouses, gutted factories, steel skeletons of former machine shops, and towering chimneys rising from the ashes were gaunt reminders of what were once thriving factory communities, industrial centers, and residential districts."[3] In fact, 40% of urban areas in Japan had been destroyed, leaving a third of the population homeless. Food shortages were endemic, and inflation, particularly in the black markets, made life difficult from 1946 to 1949. Living standards dropped precipitously to 35% in rural and 65% in urban areas compared to pre-war levels.[4] Given the great physical devastation and massive loss of life, the early days after the defeat were ones of desperation and despair for Japanese, as they tried to eke out their survival in their shattered country.

A daunting task of reconstruction, reform, and reinvention lay ahead. Initially, this work was overseen by the Supreme Commander, General Douglas MacArthur, during the Occupation of Japan (1945–52). It was an operation largely run by the Americans. However, it could not have succeeded without the Japanese "embracing defeat," to borrow the title of John Dower's classic history of the early post-war era. Led by Liberal Party prime ministers beginning with Yoshida Shigeru, who was in power for most of the period between 1946 and 1954, the Japanese welcomed rather than resisted the Occupation, and largely cooperated with American authorities. The "Yoshida Doctrine" became a guiding principle for post-war Japan, which relied on the United States for military protection and guidance in foreign affairs while prioritizing domestic policies for rebuilding Japan's industrial and economic strength.

The most urgent policy of the Occupation initially was demilitarization. This included resolving the immediate crisis of repatriating over six million Japanese soldiers and civilians from overseas. But SCAP also embarked on a broader mission to transform Japan into a peaceful country. Steps toward this goal included abolishing the armed forces (Article 9 in the new Constitution), purges and war crimes trials of culpable militarists and ultranationalists, and eliminating the patriotic moral education curriculum from the schools.

The Occupation was also involved in a host of initiatives aimed at democratizing politics and liberalizing Japan's economic system. They forced major reforms in government, the economy, education, and religion. These included a host of initiatives such as anti-monopoly laws designed to break up Japan's powerful pre-war business conglomerates (*zaibatsu*), encouraging the spread of labor unions, curtailing the rural absentee landlord system, promoting land redistribution and women's suffrage (legalized in 1945 and enforced in the 1946 general election), instituting reforms to family law to end the old (i.e. patriarchal) *ie* system, and introducing new educational ideas like the 6-3-3-4 model, textbook reform, local school boards, co-education, and a democracy-centered civics curriculum in the school.

The so called MacArthur Constitution of 1947, while retaining some key elements of Japan's pre-war polity, helped form a stable democracy with sovereignty directly vested in the people, not the emperor's person. Prime Minister Kishi Nobusuke (who held power from 1957 to 1960) spearheaded the Security Treaty between the United States and Japan of 1952, which was renewed as the Treaty of Mutual Cooperation and Security between the United States and Japan, in 1960. This made Japan America's most valuable ally in East Asia by permitting military bases on Japanese soil. From the Korean War to the escalating Cold War, Japan became indispensable for American strategic interests in the East.

Japan's recovery after World War II was fueled by its own "economic miracle" of the 1950s to the 1970s. Historian Peter Duus has described this post-war social and economic transformation as moving "from Imperial Japan to Japan Inc."[5] In 1945, economic conditions were dire—industrial production declining precipitously, and mining and manufacturing production falling to between 20% and 30% of pre-war levels.[6] In addition to the political reform measures and American economic aid, other important factors helped dramatically transform Japan's economy from ruin to resurgence. The Dodge plan of 1949 stabilized the Japanese economy through tough austerity measures for balancing the budget, controlling inflation, and repaying government debts. These policies ultimately restored Japan's financial independence. The Korean War in 1950–53 was also a huge economic stimulus, boosting Japan's national production by almost 70%. By 1952, Japan's GDP had already returned to its pre-war high.

On the domestic front, the "Yoshida Doctrine" also spurred Japan's growth rate of roughly 9.7% between 1960 and 1973. This doctrine was intended to foster growth at any cost, and it included policies that stimulated technological innovation in Japan's industries and oversight of private industrial development through government agencies like MITI (Ministry of International Trade and Industry). Other factors contributing to growth were the rise of powerful business conglomerates (*keiretsu*) like Mitsubishi and Toyota, and a meritocratic educational system producing highly skilled technicians and white-collar professionals. During this period, Japan developed a hugely successful export economy, with Japanese brands becoming household names globally. For example, the electronics company Sony, which was founded in 1946 as Tokyo Telecommunications Engineering Corporation, became famous for its high-quality products such as transistor radios and TV sets. As early as 1964, Japan's reemergence as a respected member of the international community was symbolized when it hosted the Summer Olympic Games. By 1968, Japan's GNP had surpassed that of West Germany as it became the second largest economy in the world. By the 1970s and 1980s, electronics, automobile, toy, watch, and camera companies, like Casio, Canon, Honda, Toshiba, Bandai, and Nintendo, had become the international corporate face of Japan Inc.

Japan's rapid industrialization and wholehearted embrace of corporate capitalism spurred important social and cultural changes. Japan developed a large middle class and a new culture of mass consumerism. Ezra Vogel, in his 1963 book *Japan's New Middle Class*, saw Japan's rising affluence as symbolized in the "bright new life" (*akarui seikatsu*) of the successful salaryman working in a large corporation. By 1964, the white-collar Japanese dream had expanded to include a broad swathe of the population; over 90% of Japanese households now possessed their own "three divine treasures"—a TV, a fridge, and a washing machine.[7] To Vogel, rising income levels for white- and blue-collar workers alike indicated that "all these aspirations for security, material possessions, and regular hours have been realized not only by the salary man, but by most of the population of Japan."[8]

This led to a broadening of the middle class from the mid-1960s onward; 85–90% of Japanese considered themselves part of the middle class. They wanted to live the "good life" that was epitomized by the American dream as graphically displayed in Hollywood films, TV, and newspapers. This middle-class consciousness sparked an explosion in consumer demand for all sorts of luxury goods to fill the middle-class Japanese home.[9] A cultural symbol of this was the popular comic strip *Sazaesan*, which has been a fixture of post-war Japanese life since its debut in a Kyushu newspaper in 1946 and its serialization in the *Asahi shinbun* in 1949 and then turning into a weekly TV show that started in 1969. The main character, Isono Sazae (after her marriage, Fuguta), was a middle-class suburban wife whose house was filled with the latest appliances—courtesy of Toshiba, the TV show's sponsor.

And yet, the "Japan Inc" that was symbolized by the gleaming skyscrapers built in Shinjuku in Tokyo in the 1970s and 1980s was not as stable as it looked. The "oil shock" of 1973 proved that Japan's economic miracle was extremely vulnerable to external threats. The terrible price of its post-war success was also clear with the blight of urban sprawl, vast overdevelopment, rampant political corruption, and horrific environmental pollution.

It is clear that the pre-war ethic of self-sacrifice for the good of the state had become irrelevant. Duus has argued that it was replaced by a new individualism which legitimized private prosperity and affluence.[10] This very "unwholesome self-interest," which had been scorned in old pre-war government screeds like the *Kokutai no hongi* and *Shinmin no michi,* had become the new ethos of Japan Inc. At the same time, the very individualism which underlay the post-war salaryman's hard work began to raise questions. As Vogel put it,

> Why should one sacrifice for the good of the company? Why should one labor so assiduously for so many years at the same place? Are there not other, more interesting things to do? Why should the youth study so hard to be admitted to the good colleges and the good firms? Are there not other values of greater importance?[11]

These questions gained urgency in the 1970s and 1980s.

Post-war developments in Shinto

According to prominent Shinto scholars Inoue Nobutaka and Sakamoto Koremaru, Shinto has undergone two major transformations in the modern period. The first, as we have seen, occurred during the Meiji Restoration when, under government auspices, Shinto was refashioned into a state-supported shrine system and imperial-centered cult. The second occurred after World War II, when the religious reforms spearheaded by the Occupation's GHQ dissolved that same system.[12] The time was ripe for major changes.

Japan's defeat in World War II ended the state's authoritarian control over religious matters while revealing the spiritual bankruptcy of its *kokutai* ideology. Its ultimate expression, the way of the warrior (*bushidō*) described in the *Kokutai no hongi* as the "outstanding characteristic of our national morality," was a spirit of self-effacement. The ideal was meeting death with a "perfect calmness" through offering one's loyalty and reverence to the emperor.

However, the great work of advancing the emperor's fortunes and establishing a new imperial order in the East under his benevolent rule was a chimera. Japanese subjects' loyalty and reverence had tragically led them into the darkness of wartime defeat and destruction. This was personified by Hirohito's own wartime prime minister, General Tōjō Hideki, who was executed as a class-A war criminal in 1948. Even those Japanese who had paid only lip service to the imperial cult often found themselves, as Japan specialist Ian Buruma has described it, "lost without a faith."[13]

According to Woodard, the Allied Powers saw "State Shinto," named as such in the Directive, as a major impediment to achieving their twin objectives of occupying Japan: first, eliminating ultranationalistic militarism, and, second, establishing a peaceful democratic government.[14] The danger, as they saw it, was not in the ties between the emperor and Shinto, but in Japan's pre-war authoritarian polity of *saisei icchi,* the unification of rites and governance in an emperor who was, according to the Meiji Constitution, "sacred and inviolable." As a "priest king," the emperor was not only an object of reverence but was granted full civil and military authority.[15] SCAP therefore became involved with religious reform because religious freedom was seen as the foundation for democracy.[16] It is with this in mind that we briefly survey the post-war developments related to Shinto.

The Shinto Directive (*Shintō shirei*)

According to Tokyo university religious studies professor Kishimoto Hideo (1903–64), the Shinto Directive (Reading #24) was one of the most important documents issued by the GHQ during the Allied Occupation.[17] It was the first step in the dramatic post-war transformation of Shinto from a public national faith into a private religion.[18] Public comments by a State Department official on the need to abolish Shinto were reported in Japanese newspapers in early October 1945, and subsequently SCAP ordered Lieutenant William K. Bunce, the head of the Religions branch of the Civil Information and Education Section (CIE), to draft a formal directive to that effect. Bunce, with the assistance of scholar of Japanese religions Kishimoto Hideo and others, composed multiple drafts over the next seven weeks. He issued a staff study of the problem on December 3 and the actual Directive on December 15, 1945. Daniel C. Holtom has noted that, "If it were true that the content of a national culture could be determined chiefly by injunction," the Directive "might well mark the end an age."[19]

Kishimoto notes two major objectives of the Shinto Directive. The first objective was to disestablish Shinto, so the government could no longer use it as a vehicle to promote ultranationalism and militarism.[20] Bunce had initially blamed Shinto for Japanese warlike aggressiveness. However, under Kishimoto's tutelage and drawing on the work of Western specialists like Holtom, Bunce gained a more nuanced understanding. He learned that Shinto was much more than the neologism he coined in the Directive, "State Shinto" (*kokka Shintō*). The real problem was not Shinto but the Japanese government's state-sponsored cult of *kokutai*, an ideology that placed faith in Japan's distinctive spiritual essence as a nation or national polity.[21] Its cardinal principles were the divine origin of the land, emperor, and Japanese people, which fostered a sense of racial superiority and legitimated a jingoistic belief in Japan's imperial destiny to rule all nations—especially Asia.[22] But the Directive goes on to show that State Shinto was more than just an ideology. It was enshrined within a bureaucratic state system, from the imperial household to the Shinto shrines, which forced people to comply with state-sanctioned ceremonial, educational, and institutional beliefs and practices. As such, SCAP thought State Shinto needed to be dealt with.[23]

A key goal, therefore, as the full title of the Directive indicates, was the "Abolition of the Governmental Sponsorship, Support, Perpetuation, Control, and Dissemination of State Shinto (*Kokka Shinto, Jinja Shinto*)." This meant, in effect, the termination of all shrine religious laws issued since 1871.[24] The Directive severed shrine Shinto's special state sponsorship and financial support. Some of the particular effects of the Directive included the abolition of the Board of Divinities (Jingiin), thus eliminating government oversight, forcing the Japanese government to cease and desist teaching Shinto in public schools, in particular, prohibiting propaganda tracts like the *Kokutai no hongi* and ending compulsory official and school visits to Shinto shrines.[25] According to the Directive, in abolishing "State Shinto," SCAP had eradicated a militarist and politicized "perversion" that did not represent Shinto as a whole.[26] By contrast, Bunce considered shrine and sectarian Shinto *bona fide* religions with their own particular beliefs and practices. So long as they were privately held faiths of the Japanese people, they were entitled to the same rights and protections as any other religious organizations.[27] This included the imperial household rites, which were allowed to continue as a "private" religious practice of the emperor and the imperial family.[28]

The second objective, according to Kishimoto, was to provide a general religious policy. The purpose of the Directive was to separate religion from the Japanese state. Abolishing State Shinto ensured religious freedom and equality in thought and belief. It permitted the private religious practice, including worship at Shinto shrines. Bunce hoped the Directive would lead to the enshrinement of religious freedom in a new Japanese Constitution.[29]

Religious reforms in the 1947 Constitution

In the so-called "MacArthur Constitution" of 1947, which was largely drafted by SCAP, several provisions deal directly with religion: Article 19 ensures freedom of thought and conscience. Article 20 strictly separates religion from the state, guaranteeing a larger degree of religious freedom than even the American Constitution does. The key part of Article 20 states that "[n]o religious organization shall receive any privileges from the State, nor exercise any political authority," and adds that the state cannot engage in religious education or religious activities.[30] Article 89 strictly prohibits the use of public funds for religious purposes. These constitutional provisions sought to legally disentangle Shinto from its former public role.[31] Shrine Shinto now had to compete alongside other religions in the vibrant "free market religious economy" which filled the spiritual vacuum left by the demise of the prewar state-sponsored shrine system.[32]

As a result, Shinto emerged as one religion among many in a context of contemporary religious pluralism, and writings on religion more openly considered Shinto as a religion. The Religious Corporations Ordinance (Shūkyō Hōjinrei), promulgated and enforced on December 28, 1945 (which developed into the Religious Corporations Act [Shūkyō Hōjinhō] of 1951) codified constitutional principles by ensuring that all religious organizations including Shinto shrines, sectarian and Shinto-styled new religious movements received private legal status.

The precise interpretation of these constitutional provisions with respect to Shinto is a fascinating story. Neither the Constitution nor the "Religious Corporations Ordinance" explicitly defines religion. So the interpretation of Shinto has largely been defined by the courts. The judiciary has defined religion very broadly, including shrine Shinto within the regulatory purview of Article 20.[33] That being said, the 1977 Tsu City Supreme Court case which dealt with the legality of the city's 1965 fund appropriation for a Shinto opening ceremony (*jichinsai*) for a new gymnasium, showed how nuanced such a definition was. In that decision, the court ruled that such a ceremony was not religious but secular and customary in nature. Therefore, Tsu City did not violate the Constitution by financially subsidizing a religious act.[34] The court found that "religious," within the meaning of the Constitution, involved "a feeling and a behavior which places its faith in the existence of a supernatural, superhuman entity (i.e. the absolute, the creator, the highest being, especially God, Buddha spirits, etc.) and worships it."[35]

The Humanity Declaration (Ningen Sengen)

Another aspect of the disestablishment of State Shinto was the status of the emperor. While some wanted to force his abdication or eliminate the imperial system altogether, the Occupation saw the utility of retaining the emperor as the new face of Japan's democracy. But before taking on his new role, it was essential that the emperor renounce his divinity. The popular view, as stated in a *Time* magazine article of May 21, 1945, was that Americans were "waging war against a god" in the great Pacific war. The emperor's status as a living *kami* was seen as the origin of Japan's malignant jingoism of racial and national superiority.

The imperial rescript of Emperor Hirohito, in which he formally denied his divinity was issued on January 1, 1946.[36] In it he stated:

> We stand by the people and we wish always to share with them in their moment of joys and sorrows. The ties between us and our people have always stood upon mutual trust and affection. They do not depend upon mere legends and myths. They are not predicted on the false conception that the emperor is divine and that the Japanese people are superior to other races and fated to rule the world.[37]

This declaration had its impact. An elderly woman of our acquaintance, for example, who came of age during the war, refuses to visit Meiji Shrine to this day because, she says, "why would you go to a shrine to worship merely a human being?" The new Constitution of Japan transformed the emperor into a "symbolic" figurehead. Unlike the 1889 Meiji Constitution, Article 1 of the new Constitution no longer treats emperors as "sacred and inviolable."[38] Rather, they become "the symbol of the state and of the unity of the people, deriving his position from the will of the people with whom resides sovereign power."

To sum up, the post-war religious system constructed during the Occupation has three essential components: (1) A formalized separation between religion and state with the declaration of freedom of belief; (2) the removal of Shinto as a national ritual institution, disestablishing its special status so that it was now just another part of a rich Japanese religious pluralism; and (3) the emperor system survived, although the emperor was now a symbol of the new national polity—a state whose sovereignty lay in the Japanese people.

The rise of the Association of Shinto Shrines (Jinja Honchō)

As part of its reforms, in February 1946, GHQ abolished the Board of Divinities (Jingiin), leaving Shinto shrines without direct government oversight. In its place arose a national Association of Shinto Shrines (Jinja Honchō), which merged some 86,000 of the country's approximately 106,000 Shinto shrines. Its responsibilities include shrine administration, training priests, fund-raising for the rebuilding of Ise Jingū (*shikinen sengū*, which was originally planned for 1949 but successfully accomplished in 1953), the distribution of Ise amulets (*jingū taima*), and political lobbying.[39]

Although the Association supports local shrine beliefs and practices, it also strongly supports a pre-war imperial-centric Shinto. Its important statement of faith, "General Principles for a Life of Reverence toward Deities" (*Keishin seikatsu no kōryō,* 1956) underscores this. While this document prescribes reverence for the *kami* and ancestors, duly observing Shinto rites, and selfless public service in accord with the will of the *kami*, it also requires respecting "the emperor as a mediator of the wishes of the sun goddess," praying not only for Japan's good fortune but for the peace and prosperity of all nations.[40] Mark Teeuwen has argued that "pre-war Meiji ideas and rituals are very much at the core" of its policies.[41] Even the Association's campaign to have all Japanese enshrine the Ise *taima* in their home altars underscores this: "the worship of this *taima* serves to unify the nation in worship of the imperial deity Amaterasu Ōmikami, irrespective of people's religious beliefs."[42] Historian of religions Shimazono Susumu notes that this idea of national unity under Ise Shrine and the emperor "leans toward State Shinto in its broad meaning,"[43] The Association's political campaigns likewise reveal its ultimate goal of restoring Shinto to the pre-war public role which focused on reverence toward the emperor. For example, the Association was able to restore national Foundation Day (Kigensetsu), which had been abolished in 1948. It was restored in 1966, renamed as Kenkoku Kinen no Hi, and is now celebrated annually on February 11.[44]

To conclude, Shinto has become integrated within contemporary Japan's new religious pluralism, and writings on religion now consider Shinto more explicitly as a religion. To survive economically, shrines pursue a variety of entrepreneurial religious activities such as Shinto funerals and weddings, the sale of talismans (*omamori*) and amulets (*ofuda*), and various efficacious rites and prayers that attracted parishioners and visitors. Shrine Shinto competes within the dynamic spiritual marketplace that characterizes Japanese religions today.

Yasukuni Shrine's sacred persistence

Yasukuni ("peaceful country") is a shrine in Tokyo which honors the souls (*eirei*) of soldiers who had loyally sacrificed their lives for the emperor and nation, and which is considered an important nation protecting (*gokoku*) shrine. After 1945, it faced an uncertain future. The army and navy had directly controlled it since 1879, so it seemed a key symbol of the direct link between militarism, emperor worship, and Shinto that the Occupation wanted to sever. It was famous as the shrine where Kamikaze "special attack" pilots (*tokkōtai*) pledged to meet after their deaths. Yasukuni's cherry blossoms became the symbol of their heroic sacrifice.[45]

The United States government had initially decided as early as March 1944 that Yasukuni was a "nationalist shrine" rather than a place of religious worship.[46] However, the policy changed during the Occupation. Kishimoto Hideo, who served as the Japanese consultant on religious matters for CIE, helped to disabuse Bunce and other staff members of the notion that Shinto itself was tied to military aggression. He took them to the special grand festival at Yasukuni Shrine in the fall of 1945, an event that deeply moved General Kenneth R. Dyke, the chief of the CIE section. Kishimoto related that he later heard that, "whenever Shinto was discussed, [Dyke] would refer to that festival and say that he could not think that Shinto itself was inflammatory."[47] By 1947, the Religious Division had decided Yasukuni was permitted to continue, albeit without its state patronage.[48] A February 2, 1946 amendment to the Religious Corporations Ordinance made it clear that Ise Jingū and Yasukuni were to be regarded as religious institutions. Yasukuni had incorporated as a private religious organization in accordance with this amendment by September 1946, opting to remain independent rather than affiliating with the Association of Shinto Shrines. It was finally granted approval for the transfer of its state-controlled shrine property in 1951.

In the post-war years, Yasukuni's militaristic calling increasingly made it the subject of great controversy. Emperor Hirohito renewed his visits, attending rites eight times until 1975, and Prime Minister Yoshida Shigeru made the first governmental official visit in 1951. In 1952 the Japan League for the Welfare of the Bereaved (Nippon Izoku Kōsei Renmei), which had approximately one million members—later renamed the Bereaved Society of Japan (Nippon Izokukai)—lobbied for the shrine to be completely state supported and renationalized as a public institution. Legislation to that effect came before the Diet in 1969 and was debated on and off until 1974. In 1975, Prime Minister Miki Takeo was the first to visit the shrine on August 15, the day marking the end of World War II. This custom, which was followed by several succeeding prime ministers, sparked protests from both China and South Korea. In 1978, Yasukuni enshrined fourteen Class-A war criminals, including the executed wartime militarist Prime Minister Tōjō Hideki. Later documents suggest that Emperor Shōwa stopped visiting Yasukuni because of this enshrinement. Yasukuni's history thus raises important questions over religious freedom and religion and state issues.

Redefining Shinto

All the readings in this section share one common trait: They are all reactions to the Shinto Directive (Reading #24), which led to Shinto becoming a privatized religion. The authors' reactions to the Occupation's new policies, however, differ in fundamental ways.

Orikuchi Shinobu's "A new direction for Shinto" (1949) (Reading #25) takes an opportunistic stance. By that, we mean simply that the brilliant Kokugakuin literary scholar and folklorist saw the opportunity for new religious forms of Shinto, arising from the ashes of the wartime defeat. Shinto was grounded in Japan's ancient folklore traditions that had become obscured by the heavy hand of the state. The mysterious and creatively potent *kami* of the natural world (*musubi no kami*) transcended imperial ancestor cults and the state's ethical interpretation of Shinto as a way of loyalty to the state. Orikuchi argues that Shinto is essentially religious and looks forward to the emergence of a new "Shinto religion" (*Shintōkyō*) that would mark a spiritual rebirth for the Japanese people.

Watsuji Tetsurō's essays, "Feudal thought and Shinto doctrine" and "Representative of the whole people" (1948, Reading #26) take an accommodationist stance. Watsuji, aware of the momentous changes of the new Constitution, sought to re-vision the emperor's role to fit his new status as a symbol of the nation. Watsuji aims to prove that Japan's aggressive militarism was never essentially a part of the imperial institution and that, even in ancient times, the emperor served as a peaceful collective symbol of the will of the Japanese people. The imperial institution, in his view, is crucial for Japan's unity and its spiritual-ethical core.

Reverence to the emperor, as Watsuji noted in his pre-war writings, is Japan's unique way of intuiting the "absolute" and forms the ethical foundation binding its citizens into a holistic community (*gemeinschaft*). It is the key characteristic which distinguishes Shinto from other world religions like Christianity and Islam, which posit the absolute in a transcendent God.[49]

Ashizu Uzuhiko's "Various issues related to contemporary shrines" (1956, Reading #27) is a critical retrospective of the harm the Occupation's Shinto Directive wrought upon Japan. Ashizu, a founding father of the Association of Shinto Shrines, is blunt in his criticisms, rejecting the Occupation policies as trying to spark "a spiritual revolution that would reform Japan by 'turning it into a model American colony.'" He criticizes the new constitution because it destructively severs the link between the state and Shinto. The Occupation's goal was to undermine Shinto's special public status in Japanese society, which Ashizu found intolerable due to Shinto's positive moral and spiritual role.

Murakami Shigeyoshi's selections, "The emperor as a deity in human form," and "The development of imperial house rites," from his important work, *Imperial Rituals, 1977* (Reading #28), are significant examples of the critical work historians have done in the post-war period. Murakami spent his career analyzing the ideology, ritual structure, and political impact of State Shinto, which he defines as a national religion, unique in the history of religions. In this selection, Murakami meticulously details the particulars of the Meiji era Imperial House Law. He shows how the Meiji government constructed the emperor's political, military, and religious authority as a living god (*arahitogami*) and the head of the new imperial Japanese state. His analysis reveals that the imperial absolutism in the Meiji was in fact an invented tradition, a system that "caused untold havoc and corruption, both intellectually and morally."

We have already discussed the final reading, Kuroda Toshio's "Shinto in the history of Japanese religion" (1981, Reading #29) in detail in the introduction. Needless to say, it is a seminal critique of the idea that Shinto as a religious system is archaic. Kuroda shows that the major premise of pre-war Shinto—that it was the true and original way of the Japanese people—is false.

Notes

1 "The Text of Hirohito's Radio Rescript," *The New York Times* August 15, 1945, 3

2 Kenichi Ohno, *The Path Traveled by Japan as a Developing Country:Economic Growth from Edo to Heisei* (Tokyo: GRIPS Development Forum,2006), 144–60; W.J. Macpherson, *The Economic Development of Japan 1868–1941* (Cambridge: Cambridge University Press, 1995), 3.

3 William P. Woodard, *The Allied Occupation of Japan 1945–52 and Japanese Religions* (Leiden: E.J. Brill, 1972), 7.

4 John Dower, *Embracing Defeat Japan in the Wake of World War II* (London: W.W. Norton and Co., 1999), 45.

5 Peter Duus, "Shōwa-era Japan and Beyond: From Imperial Japan to Japan Inc.," in *The Routledge Handbook of Japanese Culture and Society,* eds. Victoria Lyon Bestor and Theodore C. Bestor (New York: Routledge, 2011), 13.

6 Tetsuji Okazaki, "Industrial Policy in Japan: 70-Year History since World War II," *Japan Spotlight* (March–April, 2017), 57.

7 Ezra Vogel, *Japan's New Middle Class: The Salary Man and His Family in a Tokyo Suburb* (Berkeley, CA: The University of California Press, 1971), 73.

8 Ibid., 272

9 Duus, "Shōwa-era Japan," 20–23.

10 Ibid., 15.

11 Vogel, *Japan's New Middle Class,* 273.

12 Inoue Nobutaka and Sakamoto Koremaru, "Modern and Contemporary Shinto," *Encyclopedia of Shinto*, http://k-amc.kokugakuin.ac.jp/DM/detail.do?class_name=col_eos&data_id=22950.
13 Ian Buruma, "Lost without a Faith," *Time* (June 24, 2001), 34.
14 Woodard, *The Allied Occupation of Japan,* 14.
15 Ibid., 66.
16 Ibid., 9.
17 Ibid., 70.
18 Mark R. Mullins "Secularization, Deprivatization, and the Reappearance of 'Public Religion' in Japanese Society," *Journal of Japanese Religion* 1 (2012):63.
19 D.C. Holtom, "New Status of Shinto," *Far Eastern Survey* 20 (January 30, 1946):17.
20 Kishimoto Hideo, "The Constitution and Religion: Meeting on March 9, 1960," *Contemporary Religions in Japan* 4 (March, 1963):107.
21 Woodard makes this same argument, seeing the equation of Shinto with militarism as a "mistaken belief" of the Allied Powers. See Woodard, *The Allied Occupation of Japan,* 9.
22 Urs Matthias Zachmann, "The Postwar Constitution and Religion," in *Handbook of Contemporary Japanese Religions,* eds. Inken Prohl and John Nelson (Leiden: Brill, 2012), 216.
23 Woodard, *The Allied Occupation of Japan,* 9.
24 Inoue and Sakamoto, "Modern and Contemporary Shinto." http://eos.kokugakuin.ac.jp/modules/xwords/entry.php?entryID=738
25 Woodard, *The Allied Occupation of Japan,* 66.
26 For his part, Kishimoto thought that the premise of the Directive was mistaken; State Shinto was more secular custom than national religion for the country. He likened its practices to non-religious state ceremonies, such as the prayers held before the opening of the American Congress. He hoped it would be allowed to continue if its compulsory components were prohibited. See Kishimoto Hideo, "The Constitution and Religion," 114.
27 Mullins, "Secularization," 66
28 Shimazono argues SCAP purposely minimized its mention of imperial household Shinto in the Directive because it wanted to use the emperor's authority for the Occupation's political ends. In any case, imperial household rites were observances with a national import. His worship of the sun goddess and the people's reverence of the emperor were a powerful source of Japan's identity. The persistence of these rites means that State Shinto in the broadest sense of the term is not extinct, even under the Directive. See Shimazono Susumu, "State Shinto and Religion in Post-War Japan," in *The Sage Handbook of Sociology of Religion,* eds James A. Beckford and N.J. Demerath III (London: Sage Publications, 2005), 697–709.
29 See also Woodard, *The Allied Occupation of Japan,* 62–65.
30 Article 20 reads: "Freedom of religion is guaranteed to all. No religious organization shall receive any privileges from the State, nor exercise any political authority. 2) No person shall be compelled to take part in any religious acts, celebration, rite or practice. 3) The State and its organs shall refrain from religious education or any other religious activity." See Zachmann, "The Postwar Constitution," 216–22.
31 Article 89 reads: "No public money or other property shall be expended or appropriated for the use, benefit, or maintenance of any religious institution or association, or for any charitable, educational or benevolent enterprises not under the control of public authority."See Michiaki Okuyama, "Religion and Japanese Constitutional Law," *Academia Humanities and Social Sciences* 83 (June, 2006):133–46.
32 Mullins, "Secularization," 67.
33 Zachmann, "The Postwar Constitution," 217–18.
34 Okuyama, "Religion," 137–40.
35 Zachmann, "The Postwar Constitution," 218.
36 For the story behind the drafting of this imperial rescript, see John Dower *Embracing Defeat,* 310–18.
37 Wikelmus H.M. Creemers, *Shrine Shinto After World War II* (Leiden: E.J. Brill, 1968), 226–27.
38 The exact wording of the rescript generated some controversy. The word for "divine" used in the text in is *akitsumikami* ("manifest deity"), an archaism appearing in early Japanese documents but with little meaning for modern Japanese. A more concrete term used in the original draft, "descendants of the gods," was replaced by the more literary and ambiguous term *akitsumikami* (literally,

"manifest *kami*"). John Dower has argued, based on the evidence, that the emperor was willing to renounce that he was a god in the Western sense of the term but was resolute in maintaining that he was a descendant of Amaterasu. Daniel C. Holtom, writing soon after the rescript was issued, noted that this term had been used by the Ministry of Education in pre-war tracts. True reform, he advised, meant discontinuing the use of *kami* (translated variously as god, sacred, deity, or divine) for the emperor under any circumstances. But just as importantly, legal changes needed to take place as well, especially the abolishment of Imperial House Law. See his, "The 'New Emperor,'" *Far Eastern Survey* 15 (March 13, 1946):69–71.

39 Inoue Nobutaka, et al., *Shinto—A Short History,* 170; Woodard, *The Allied Occupation,* 57ff.
40 Ibid., 170–71.
41 Mark Teeuwen, "Jinja Honchō and Shrine Shintō Policy." *Japan Forum* 8, No. 2 (1996):185.
42 Ibid., 184.
43 Shimazono, "State Shinto and Religion," 705.
44 Ibid., 185. See also Ueda Kenji, "Contemporary Social Change and Shinto Tradition," *Japanese Journal of Religious Studies* 6 (March–June, 1979):304f.
45 See Emiko Ohnuki-Tierney, *Kamikaze, Cherry Blossoms, and Nationalisms: The Militarization of Aesthetics in Japanese History* (Chicago: The University of Chicago Press, 2010).
46 John Breen, "'The Nation's Shrine' Conflict and Commemoration at Yasukuni, Modern Japan's Shrine to the War Dead," in *The Cultural Politics of Nationalism and Nation-Building: Ritual and Performance in the Forging of Nations,* eds. Rachel Tsang and Eric Taylor Woods (London: Routledge, 2013), 145.
47 Kishimoto, "The Constitution and Religion," 107.
48 For a full account, see Mark R. Mullins, "How Yasukuni Shrine Survived the Occupation: A Critical Examination of Popular Claims," *Monumenta Nipponica* 65 (Spring 2010):89–136.
49 See Robert Bellah, "Japan's Cultural Identity: Some Reflections on the Work of Watsuji Tetsuro," *The Journal of Asian Studies* 24 (August, 1965):573–94.

24

GENERAL HEADQUARTERS, SUPREME COMMANDER FOR THE ALLIED POWERS

THE SHINTO DIRECTIVE
(DECEMBER 15, 1945)[1]

MEMORANDUM FOR: IMPERIAL JAPANESE GOVERNMENT

THROUGH: Central Liaison Office, Tokyo

SUBJECT: Abolition of Governmental Sponsorship, Support, Perpetuation, Control, and Dissemination of State Shinto (*Kokka Shinto, Jinja Shinto*)

1   In order to free the Japanese people from direct or indirect compulsion to believe or profess to believe in a religion or cult officially designated by the state, and

In order to lift from the Japanese people the burden of compulsory financial support of an ideology which has contributed to their war guilt, defeat, suffering, privation, and present deplorable condition, and

In order to prevent a recurrence of the perversion of Shinto theory and beliefs into militaristic and ultra-nationalistic propaganda designed to delude the Japanese people and lead them into wars of aggression and

In order to assist the Japanese people in a rededication of their national life to building a new Japan based upon ideals of perpetual peace and democracy,

It is hereby directed that:

a   The sponsorship, support, perpetuation, control and dissemination of Shinto by the Japanese national, prefectural, and local governments, or by public officials, subordinates, and employees acting in their official capacity are prohibited and will cease immediately.

b   All financial support from public funds and all official affiliation with Shinto and Shinto shrines are prohibited and will cease immediately.

    (1) While no financial support from public funds will be extended to shrines located on public reservations or parks, this prohibition will not be construed to preclude the Japanese Government from continuing to support the areas on which such shrines are located.

    (2) Private financial support of all Shinto shrines which have been previously supported in whole or in part by public funds will be permitted, provided such private support is entirely voluntary and is in no way derived from forced or involuntary contributions.

c   All propagation and dissemination of militaristic and ultranationalistic ideology in Shinto doctrines, practices, rites, ceremonies, or observances, as well as in the doctrines, practices, rites, ceremonies, and observances of any other religion, faith, sect, creed, or philosophy, are prohibited and will cease immediately.

d   The Religious Functions Order relating to the Grand Shrine of Ise and the Religious Functions Order relating to State and other Shrines will be annulled.

e   The Shrine Board [Board of Divinities] (Jingiin) of the Ministry of Home Affairs will be abolished, and its present functions, duties, and administrative obligations will not be assumed by any other governmental or tax-supported agency.

f   All public educational institutions whose primary function is either the investigation and dissemination of Shinto or the training of a Shinto priesthood will be abolished and their physical properties diverted to other uses. Their present functions, duties, and administrative obligations will not be assumed by any other governmental or tax-supported agency.

g   Private educational institutions for the investigation and dissemination of Shinto and for the training of priesthood for Shinto will be permitted and will operate with the same privileges and be subject to the same controls and restrictions as any other private educational institution having no affiliation with the government; in no case, however, will they receive support from public funds, and in no case will they propagate and disseminate militaristic and ultra-nationalistic ideology.

h   The dissemination of Shinto doctrines in any form and by any means in any educational institution supported wholly or in part by public funds is prohibited and will cease immediately.

   (1)   All teachers' manuals and textbooks now in use in any educational institution supported wholly or in part by public funds will be censored, and all Shinto doctrine will be deleted. No teachers' manual or textbook which is published in the future for use in such institutions will contain any Shinto doctrine.

   (2)   No visits to Shinto shrines and no rites, practices or ceremonies associated with Shinto will be conducted or sponsored by any educational institution supported wholly or in part by public funds.

i   Circulation by the government of "The Fundamental Principles of the National Structure" (*Kokutai no hongi*), "The Way of the Subject" (*Shinmin no michi*), and all similar official volumes, commentaries, interpretations, or instructions on Shinto is prohibited.

j   The use in official writings of the terms "Greater East Asia War" (*daitōa sensō*), "The Whole World under One Roof" (*hakkō ichiu*), and all other terms whose connotation in Japanese is inextricably connected with State Shinto, militarism, and ultra-nationalism is prohibited and will cease immediately.

k   God-shelves (*kamidana*) and all other physical symbols of State Shinto in any office, school, institution, organization, or structure supported wholly or in part by public funds are prohibited and will be removed immediately.

l   No official, subordinate, employee, student, citizen, or resident of Japan will be discriminated against because of his failure to profess and believe in or participate in any practice, rite, ceremony, or observance of State Shinto or of any religion.

m   No official of the national, prefectural, or local government, acting in his public capacity, will visit any shrine to report his assumption of office, to report on conditions of government, or to participate as a representative of government in any ceremony or observance.

2   a   The purpose of this directive is to separate religion from the state, to prevent misuse of religion for political ends, and to put all religions, faiths, and creeds upon exactly the same basis, entitled to precisely the same opportunities and protection. It forbids affiliation with the government and the propagation and dissemination of militaristic and ultra-nationalistic ideology not only to Shinto but to the followers of all religions, faiths, sects, creeds, or philosophies.

b   The provisions of this directive will apply with equal force to all rites, practices, ceremonies, observances, beliefs, teachings, mythology, legends, philosophy, shrines, and physical symbols associated with Shinto.

c   The term State Shinto within the meaning of this directive will refer to that branch of Shinto (*kokka Shintō* or *jinja Shintō*) which by official acts of the Japanese Government has been differentiated from the religion of sect Shinto (*shūha Shintō* or *kyōha Shintō*) and has been classified a non-religious cult commonly known as State Shinto, National Shinto, or Shrine Shinto.

d   The term Sect Shinto (*shūha Shintō* or *kyōha Shintō*) will refer to that branch of Shinto (composed of 13 recognized sects) which by popular belief, legal commentary, and the official acts of the Japanese Government has been recognized to be a religion.

e   Pursuant to the terms of Article I of the Basic Directive on "Removal of Restrictions on Political, Civil, and Religious Liberties" issued on 4 October 1945 by the Supreme Commander for the Allied Powers in which the Japanese people were assured complete religious freedom,

(1)   Sect Shinto will enjoy the same protection as any other religion.

(2)   Shrine Shinto, after having been divorced from the state and divested of its militaristic and ultra-nationalistic elements, will be recognized as a religion if its adherents so desire and will be granted the same protection as any other religion in so far as it may in fact be the philosophy or religion of Japanese individuals.

f   Militaristic and ultra-nationalistic ideology, as used in this directive, embraces those teachings, beliefs, and theories which advocate or justify a mission on the part of Japan to extend its rule over other nations and peoples by reason of:

(1)   The doctrine that the emperor of Japan is superior to the heads of other states because of ancestry, descent, or special origin.

(2)   The doctrine that the people of Japan are superior to the people of other lands because of ancestry, descent, or special origin.

(3)   The doctrine that the islands of Japan are superior to other lands because of divine or special origin.

(4)   Any other doctrine which tends to delude the Japanese people into embarking upon wars of aggression or to glorify the use of force as an instrument for the settlement of disputes with other peoples.

3 The imperial Japanese government will submit a comprehensive report to this Headquarters not later than 15 March 1946 describing in detail all action taken to comply with all provisions of this directive.

4 All officials, subordinates, and employees of the Japanese national, prefectural, and local governments, all teachers and education officials, and all citizens and residents of Japan will be held personally accountable for compliance with the spirit as well as the letter of all provisions of this directive.

FOR THE SUPREME COMMANDER:

/s/ H. W. Allen H. W. ALLEN,

Colonel, A.G.D.,

Asst Adjutant General

Note

1 *Contemporary Religions in Japan* 1, No. 2 (June, 1960):85–89, http://www.jstor.org/stable/30232810.

25

ORIKUCHI SHINOBU
A new direction for Shinto
(1949)

Orikuchi Shinobu (1887–1953) was a brilliant scholar of classical literature and folklore and an accomplished tanka poet (under the *nom de plume* of Shaku Chōkū). Born in Kizumura village in the Nishinari district of Osaka, Orikuchi attended Kokugakuin University where he graduated in 1910 with a degree in Japanese literature. After a brief stint of teaching at a middle school in Osaka, he returned to Tokyo where his interest in folklore and culture studies was sparked by meeting Yanagita Kunio.

In 1916–17, he published his first major work on ancient Japanese literature, the *Kōyaku Manyōshū* (The Translation of the *Manyōshū*, in three volumes). He was subsequently appointed to temporary lecturer status at Kokugakuin in 1919. In 1922, he became a full professor at Kokugakuin University; in 1923, lecturer at Keio University in Tokyo; and, from 1928 onwards, also an adjunct professor. In 1921 and 1923, he traveled to Okinawa, which deeply stimulated his thinking on the interconnections between ancient Japanese literature and the folklore. From 1929 to 1930, he published his important study, *Kodai kenkyū* (Studies of Antiquity) in three volumes, a curious mishmash of memoir, poetic fancies, and folklore studies. It contained some of Orikuchi's tantalizing insights into ancient Japanese literature and folklore—for example, his notions of the divine guest (*marebito*), the everlasting realm (*tokoyo*) and the literary trope of the nobleman in exile (*kishu ryūritan*).

After the war, Orikuchi turned his attention to theological concerns related to Shinto. He began a series of introductory lectures on Shinto at Kokugakuin. Shinto's transformation during the Meiji period into the systematized state-supported shrine Shinto had eroded Shinto's original framework, and this distortion had contributed to the war disaster. However, while the defeat caused a spiritual crisis for Japanese people, it also allowed for a rebirth of Shinto for the new age. In particular, what he called "popular Shinto" (*minkan Shintō*, a term that was also used by the GHQ during the Occupation) transcended more narrow pre-war categorizations of Shinto as a religion, a moral way, or a political ideology or institution. Orikuchi refers to a broader phenomenon—the unobstrusive folk manners and customs that have been passed down from ancient times. "Shinto," as he defined it, "was Japan's ancient folk customs," something he explored through the study of classic texts like the *Manyōshū*. In his view, popular Shinto had a religious sensibility to it that shared comparable elements with the great universal religions like Christianity. While sect Shinto as "new religions" showed an ongoing religious vitality at work beyond State Shinto, Orikuchi believed that post-war Japan needed new religious visionaries to begin a new form of Shinto, transforming the myths and ritual practices of the past into a new universal religious faith for the present. He calls this new faith variously "Shinto religion" or "Shinto Teachings." (*Shintō shūkyō, Shintōkyō*)

The following essay summarizes Orikuchi's thinking on these matters. "A new direction for Shinto" was included in *A Talk in Folklore Studies*, published in June 1949.

A NEW DIRECTION FOR SHINTO
(1949)

It was the summer of 1945. I had not yet realized the miserable fact that the end of the war was getting closer day by day, hour by hour. Then one day I was shocked by a revelation I felt rising in my chest. It happened when I overheard the following conversation: "Perhaps American youth have the same fervor as their crusader ancestors, who strove so zealously to retake Jerusalem. Aren't they working just as zealously in this war too?" If that were so, was there any chance of winning this war? I began to do some quiet soul searching.

Yet, our own zeal was certainly boiling fiercely at that time. But we could hardly stop feeling anxious, worrying over whether there were young people in our own country of Japan who had the same degree of religious fervor. Perhaps young Japanese have lived lives excelling in moral virtue, but in terms of religious zeal their lives were, by comparison, quite inferior. I have to say this without mincing words and worrying about my own safety. More than anything else, our country lacked what we might call a social sense of civility and humility (*reijō*). The situation after the end of the war reveals that the lack of proper respect caused a loss of discipline, which, in turn, has caused great suffering. This comes from a lack of religious devotion. While it is due to the lack of a spiritually grounded life, it is more than simply a disposition we share. In fact, it is the cause for why we continue to live our lives without any sense of civility and humility. There is no way we can save ourselves from this without religion. Those of us who live in Buddhist households still go to temples to worship regularly, but our religious zeal has completely vanished from that too. And such devotions become empty of whatever sense of civility and humility we once had.

However, one good outcome is that now is an extremely opportune time for our salvation. It goes without saying that the situation at present is not at all a happy one. But one benefit coming out of this is the knowledge that we can indeed rectify things by beginning a new life based on a true religious humility. This suggests that we can live a good life in our society by becoming righteous people.

And yet, from time to time, I have my doubts. For example, does Japan really have a basis for living a religious life? Do the Japanese themselves have any religious devotion? Do the proper circumstances really exist for creating a Japanese religion from this point on? When one looks at how Buddhists act, they seem to observe religious customs. But while they act religiously and are seemingly spiritually devoted, it is mostly no more than just rote behavior. Similarly, those who follow a more "enlightened" philosophy seem to do no more than think about Buddhist ideas and act accordingly. And when it comes to Shinto, something is fundamentally lacking religiously speaking.

Up until now, the general view has been that transforming Shinto into a religion would be totally wrong. In other words, by treating it as a religion we would lose the moral component of Shinto. However, this thinking has turned Shinto into too much of a moral code, so that taking even one step away from this paradigm would apparently detach it from morality. The original vision of Shinto depends on a strange distinction which did not define it as a religion; this led to the thinking that identified religion with Shinto sects (*kyōha Shintō*). Any association of Shinto with religion was rejected.

Before we were born—around the Meiji Restoration—sect Shinto suddenly appeared on the scene. It flourished at that time because the sharply defined moral vision of Shinto, which I mentioned earlier, could not oppose it. In essence, this sharply defined but mistaken view of Shinto as a moral code created an open space where the buds of a free [sect] Shinto suddenly appeared and sprouted.

If someone—whether a true leader or someone truly enlightened or an intellectual heir with the right standpoint—had appeared then and founded Shinto as a religion, then perhaps several offshoots of it would be available to us today. But unfortunately, this did not happen, and the work of the Restoration fell quickly into place. And, at least temporarily, things settled down and stabilized felicitously. It became generally believed that making Shinto religious was morally wrong and interfered with its moral clarity. Therefore, what we call Japanese Shinto tried to materialize outside religion.

Yet, even now, a number of people think that the source of Shinto is in shrines. I think some think that Shinto does not exist outside of shrines. This idea deserves further reflection. If we continue as we have, we will continue living a life with little religious devotion, one that does not match the level found among young people in the West. But come to think of it, there was once a time when Buddhists incorporated the Japanese *kami* into Buddhism adding to their character. And the result was that Japanese *kami* were revitalized through Buddhist doctrines.

In this case, you have traditional Japanese *kami* but also the Japanese Buddhist *kami* who appeared later. And yet people believed in both types of the *kami*. Moreover, those Japanese *kami* who had been redescribed through Buddhist doctrines were not worshipped as religious divinities. For example, through the prism of the *Lotus Sutra,* some viewed our country's *kami* as Buddhist guardian deities, and they were worshipped as nothing more than that. It was simply not true that they were worshipped independently as Japanese *kami*. Therefore, I think it is safe to say that up until now Japanese *kami* were not religiously autonomous [from Buddhism], nor were they objects of deep religious devotion.

When we speak about the nature of Japanese *kami* as a whole, they are often thought of polytheistically. However, in truth, people think about Japanese *kami* monotheistically. For example, even though there are many *kami*, when people think about them, they tend to think of either Amaterasu Ōmikami or Takamimusubi no Kami or Amenominakanushi no Kami.[1] They feel like there is only one divinity. At the other end of the spectrum, the conventional view is that there are "myriads of *kami*" (*yao yorozu no kami*); but given the fact that we tend to think about just one divinity at a time, the notion of myriads of *kami* does not carry much weight. Our commonplace view that there are an almost infinite variety of *kami* is quite limited. This is really the way it is in our religious traditions. And yet this is how our country's faith appears to be. So, although Buddhism has polytheistic tendencies, it tends to adopt very few or even one Buddha or bodhisattva as an object of devotion. Be it Shakyamuni, Kannon, Yakushi, or Jizō, such objects of faith become central to worship. Similarly, I think that [more generally] this applies to the faith of the Japanese people.

Although the Japanese seem to worship a large number of *kami*, I think that in practice they typically focus on one or just a few divinities. In retrospect, the practice of enshrining Amaterasu Ōmikami in Japan's colonies caused many problems, due to the mistaken ideas of those who adopted this colonial policy or the Shinto leaders who guided them badly. However, such mistakes all originate from the same proclivity to the focus on one deity.

Thus, we need to think whether the religious pattern of worshipping the *kami* at shrines has continued as a deep devotion. For over a thousand years, our faith in shrines has waned. To borrow a turn of phrase, we can think of that period in Greece and Rome that lasted for over a thousand years, known as "the death of the gods." During this time, Japanese *kami* existed as guardian deities in order to support the Buddhist faith, just as the ancient European gods continued to exist syncretistically [in Christianity] in the guise of saints.

We must free the Japanese *kami* from the yoke of the last thousand years in order to revitalize them religiously. We must wake them up for the first time with a new set of believers. If we do not, Japan will remain in its current fallen state, a nation where we have lost all civility, humility, and beautiful customs. And that is not all. If the people who advocated ideas like Japan's spirit (*Nihon seishin*) made a fundamental mistake, it was in their failure to have and think about religion. The idea that overlaying Shinto with religion was a mistake that would lead to the defiling of the *kami* was a grave error. Thus, no matter what, we should seek out and intensify our passion for a Shinto made manifest as a newly revitalized religion.

However, enthusiasm is not enough to give birth to a religion. Instead, it requires a founder who has awakened religiously. Unless there is someone who can sense the *kami*, no amount of scriptures and systematic theologies will bring meaning to any such a doctrine. No matter how much we anxiously and eagerly wait, it is by no means certain that such a person will appear. However, if enough people yearn and long for this as we do—whether it is a hundred, a thousand, or ten thousand, or more—then I believe someone will appear who can actually experience the *kami* spiritually, and, because of that, a religion will emerge. Furthermore, I believe it likely that we will soon see an individual who is not only highly sophisticated but also deeply spiritually aware of the Shinto religion (*Shintō shūkyō*). But we must encourage these persons to come forward with their revelations. Through deep soul searching, we must urge them strongly to come forward, with that request rising from our heart and soul deeply within. Put more boldly, what is important is whether from among the tens of thousands of Shinto faithful a prophet appears who has fulfilled the principles of the highest god.

We must wait patiently for that time. Perhaps, I might become awakened and grasp the deep will of the *kami*: Will I be able to be prepared for when that time comes? What kind of *kami* are we trying to get? What kind of *kami* did we have before? We must keep asking these questions in order to resolve these issues.

However, with the end of the war approaching, something strange happened. On the surface it appeared quite silly, but in fact it is important to consider. There was a dispute that occurred between Shinto leaders and government officials over which was the most important deity—Amaterasu Ōmikami or Amenominakanushi no Kami. Some of those involved tried to settle this dispute as if it were a secular or almost secular problem. At that time, I really felt angry about it. What do you do to settle things intellectually over the *kami*? What reason is there for trying to resolve something that way? I thought it was regrettable—it was a blasphemous thing that sullied the *kami*, and I felt almost like sobbing with indignation. Thus we were defeated by the *kami*. But if we now soberly reflect on what happened, the dispute was over the religious *kami* that should emerge in Japan from now on. Doesn't something divine, a mixture of certain religious qualities that wafts up and lingers among these deities—Amaterasu Ōmikami or Amenominakanushi no Kami—point to a divine being that will be the focus of worship in the coming new religion?

It is safe to say that the Japanese faith contains something beyond all religion and something that is unique to Japan, even though it borrows some elements from other countries. That is the faith in those *musubi no kami* –known as Takamimusubi no Kami and

Kamimusubi no Kami.² The characters are literally *musu* (産) for birth, *hi* (霊) for soul (*tamashii, rei*), but faith in the *kami* itself does not mean that. *Musubi* means the planting of a soul in a living body or the insertion of the soul in lifeless matter. In this way, as the matter grows larger, the soul grows with it, and so they both grow up together.³ Ancient people thought that the most perfect of these entities became the *kami* as well as human beings. Those that were physically imperfect, or else remarkable things that were very powerful, became land and the islands. This appears in ancient Japanese myths such as the story of the creation of Japan—Ōyashima—or in the stories about the birth of the *kami.*

In other words, the soul unified with the body by the *kami* gradually develops, and this allows matter and the body to grow together simultaneously. *Kami* who perform this sacred act, that is to say, Takamimusubi no Kami and Kamimusubi no Kami, are thus *musubi no kami.* The belief in *kami* who can provide life and a soul, through the soul and the body, is a basic tenet of Shinto teaching. From ancient times in Japan there were also families that considered these *musubi no kami* as their ancestors, which is an easy error to make.

This same way of thinking led some ancient texts to describe *musubi no kami* as the ancestors of those at the imperial court. There are many examples of *kami*, in particular, Takamimusubi no Kami and Kamimusubi no Kami, being described as imperial founders or ancestors of the nobility. However, the *musubi no kami* who implant souls are not personal *kami* for these people. It was easy to feel that such *kami* were one's ancestors, so the rationale is understandable.

Up to now, the Japanese have considered those *kami* with which they have a deep faith relationship to be their ancestors. Therefore, in the past it has been common that *kami* who were not ancestors were nonetheless treated as such. It is true that neither Takamimusubi no Kami and Kamimusubi no Kami are human ancestors of the Japanese people. They are *kami* who are thought to implant human souls; in other words, they offered the essence of life, which grew and developed in human bodies. We must first stop thinking of *musubi no kami* as our ancestors. Thinking of religious *kami* this way, as our human ancestors, leads Shinto teachings into error. It ends up inserting into Shinto a peculiar ethical view weakly connected to religion. Therefore, I think that one of the initial difficulties is these great *kami.* We must start by separating these great *kami* from our own human pedigree and regard them as religious *kami* that are independent from human lineages. I think we have to start from this standpoint and then rethink what we believe in, remembering that our minds and bodies develop as they do due to these divinities. In our myths, these *kami* bestow a suitable soul in everything—the land, the mountains, the rivers, the grasses the trees—so that they grow and live as the land, trees and grasses, mountains and rivers, perfecting the life of humans, animals, and the landscape. In other words, we must start by reconsidering and revitalizing the way we understand things.

We must move toward reconsidering Shinto teachings (*Shintōkyō*) based on the line of religious *kami* that focuses on Takamimusubi no Kami and Kamimusubi no Kami. Preparations for that have generally already been laid, through the long discipline of Shinto studies. But we lack the spiritual passion to make Shinto into a religion; we are waiting for the right person to appear.

In order for us to really restore order in this world by making it a good and beautiful place of civility and humility, we must beg once more to gods who are completely forgotten. For our revitalization, we must recover a heart that believes in these *kami*. So long as that does not occur, I think that we will not be able to realize in Japan a beautiful social life that has order.

Until that day, we will work hard to systematize the theory of Shinto (*shingaku*), and we will wait quietly for a sacred revelation that will reveal Shinto religion.

Notes

1 Amenominakanushi was made a central deity at the Daikyōin in the early Meiji period. This reflected a long history where this deity was favored by a variety of National Learning scholars. See Sasaki Kiyoshi, "Amenominakanushi no kami in Late Tokugawa Period Kokugaku," *Kami— Contemporary Papers on Japanese Religion* 4 http://www2.kokugakuin.ac.jp/ijcc/wp/cpjr/kami/index.html. However, in the emperor system (*tennō seido*) eventually constructed by the Japanese state, Amaterasu became the primary deity of the state supported Shinto pantheon. See Carol Gluck, *Japan's Modern Myths: Ideology in the Late Meiji Period* (Princeton, NJ: Princeton University Press, 1985), 139.

2 Both *kami* are included in the Kojiki's "three *kami* of creation" (*zōka sanshin*) along with Amenominakanushi.

3 *Musubi* (産霊)is an important term that dates from at least the Nara period and is found in the "Age of the Gods" section of the *Kojiki* and *Nihonshoki*. For a more detailed discussion of this term, see Jacques H. Kamstra, *Encounter or Syncretism: The Initial Growth of Japanese Buddhism* (Leiden, Netherlands: E.J. Brill, 1967), 105ff.

26

WATSUJI TETSURŌ

Feudal thought and Shinto doctrine (1945) and
Representative of the whole people (1948)

Watsuji Tetsurō (1889–1960) is a towering figure—a man of letters, philosopher, and cultural historian. Born in Hyogo Prefecture as the second son of a local physician, his academic talent and literary passion, particularly for Western literature, allowed him to enter the elite First Higher School in Tokyo in 1906. In 1909, Watsuji entered the Faculty of Literature of Tokyo Imperial University and graduated in 1912, after submitting a graduate thesis on Schopenhauer. As a student, he was influenced by Okakura Kakuzō (1863–1913), noted author of the *Book of Tea*, which explores Japanese spiritual aesthetics; Raphael von Koeber (1848–1923), the Russian born philosopher who introduced Watsuji to Western existentialism; and the famous novelist Natsume Sōseki (1867–1916), whose critique of Western individualism resonated with Watsuji's desire to free the lonely and isolated individual of modernity through an identity and purpose that identifies with a larger communal whole.[1]

Watsuji taught at a number of universities until he landed a lectureship at Kyoto Imperial University in 1925. After an important interlude during which he studied in Germany (1927–28), he was finally appointed professor of ethics at Tokyo Imperial University in 1934, where he taught until his retirement in 1949.

Watsuji was an enormously productive scholar, whose complete works stretch over twenty volumes, revealing his deepening academic interests in Japanese and Asian art, religion and ethics, and culture. Among Watsuji's most important works are his 1919 *Koji junrei* (translated as *Pilgrimages to the Ancient Temples in Nara,* 2012), an account of his own pilgrimage to the art treasures of Nara, where he rediscovered the rich spiritual aesthetic of ancient Japan that pointed to a Japanese spirit. In 1935, he published *Fūdo* (translated as *Climate and Culture: A Philosophical Study,* 1988), a response to Heidegger's famous work on *Being and Time* (1927). Watsuji argues that space—particularly natural surroundings, society, and culture—is just as important as time for defining human identity. His work on ethics is seminal. Of particular note are his *Rinrigaku* (Ethics, a three-volume work published in 1937,1942, 1949, translated as *Watsuji Tetsurō's Rinrigaku,* 1996), and *Nihon rinri shisōshi* (The History of Ethical Thought in Japan, 1952).

It should also be noted that Watsuji also served on the committee of scholars who revised the draft version of the *Kokutai no hongi* (Cardinal Principles of the National Polity, 1937), the ultranationalist work that was designed for Japanese students' civic education and that clarified the basic nature of the Japanese state by defining the emperor as the holder of supreme sovereign power over his subjects rather than as simply serving as one organ of the state.

The following are two of five short essays Watsuji wrote during the Occupation (in 1945 and 1948 respectively).[2] All of them focus on the emperor and the meaning of the imperial institution in post-war Japan. The overarching title of Watsuji's 1948 book, which includes these essays, borrows the language used for the emperor in Chapter 1, Article 1 of the post-war so-called MacArthur Constitution: "The emperor shall be the symbol of the State and the unity of the people, deriving his position from the will of the people with whom resides sovereign power."[3]

Watsuji's view comes from his belief that human beings are essentially formed through their interconnections between social, environmental, cultural, and historical actualities; individuals are not solitary egos but exist linked to a greater collective whole that defines their humanity and ethics. Watsuji believed that Shinto gave mythic and ritual expression to a distinctive Japanese spirit (*Nihon no seishin*) revealed in an ethic of willing sacrifice of the individual for the greater good of the Japanese state (*kokka*).

Watsuji was in favor of preserving the emperor system in the post-war period. He believed that from ancient times the emperor had served as the human expression of the collective will of the Japanese people; ever since, the community was unified by the emperor and Amaterasu, who embodied the quiet love and spirit of unselfishness that was characteristic of the Japanese spirit. His view dovetails nicely with the democratic reforms under the Occupation, where sovereignty lay in the people not the emperor. The emperor remained, however, as a vital cultural and spiritual symbol that served to preserve Japan's unity as a people. Shinto and reverence to the emperor offered a distinctive Japanese religious way; this differed from religions like Islam and Christianity, which centered around a transcendent god known primarily through dogmas and theological speculation.

"FEUDAL THOUGHT AND SHINTO DOCTRINE" (1945) AND "REPRESENTATIVE OF THE WHOLE PEOPLE" (1948)

Feudal thought and Shinto doctrine (1945)

The institution of imperial rule in Japan is not intrinsically linked to the feudal system and doctrinal Shinto, which dates from the middle ages. Since this link is merely contingent, springing from specific historical circumstances, even casting it aside will not affect imperial rule. Indeed, by doing so, the essential meaning of imperial rule becomes clear.

As a starting point I want to consider the relationship between the institution of imperial rule and the feudal system. The feudal system in Japan formed after the appearance of the samurai or warrior families (*buke*). Indeed, the samurai's appearance was what caused the system of constitutional government, which had been in place since the Taika reforms, to succumb to a gradual paralysis from within.[4] In an age when emperors took the throne, proclaiming "the rule by law," there was no such thing as ruling by military force. However, the samurai used their military might to gradually amass political power and establish a feudal system based upon force of arms. This period is perhaps most concisely and accurately described as a system of military rule legitimated by the "Imperial Rescript to Soldiers and Sailors" (Gunjin Chokuyu).[5]

The rise of the samurai coincided with the fall of the publicly run government land system established through the Taika reforms.[6] Since public land ownership had resulted in stagnating productivity, the policy had been garnished with a dash of private ownership in order to encourage land cultivation. However, the policy was revised a number of times and, in its final form, became private control of paddy cultivation. Thus, the *shōen*, that is, land not under the purview of provincial imperially appointed governors, came into being.

Since this land was outside of government jurisdiction, it was not under state control, nor did it receive any state protection. Military power thus began to be wielded for the purpose of self-defense. From the very beginning, then, the samurai were intertwined with the possession of land.

The contemporary politicians of the court bear the most blame for failing to prevent this shift of power. Beginning with the Fujiwara clan, the nobility who played important roles politically were also preoccupied with managing their own *shōen* estates. However, the nobility were able to use the sovereign authority of the law to manage their private holdings and did not need to rely on military power. At the time, Japan was peaceful because of a civil administration that, for over two centuries, had prevented civil war as well as external threats. Yet, when the Tengyō disturbance broke out in 939, it was clear that the samurai's military power could quell the rebellion where the state's armed forces could not. This situation became, if anything, even clearer in the subsequent civil disturbances, such as the nine-year (1056–64) and, later, three-year (1085–87) wars.

From the outset, the samurai, who proved that their power could support civil order, were organized as lords and vassals rather than as groups of comrades in arms. These groups originated from the rise of the aristocratic families which led them, like the Genji and Heike, but they also depended on the close personal ties that developed between their members. The most visible and typical example of this was the ties of mutual affection acquired when people became foster children (*menotogo*). The parents experienced a lord–vassal relationship while, in the next generation, the foster child and his new siblings forged deep emotional ties to one another. Thus, the saying, "serving a lord to whom one is indebted for three generations," was more than just words; it reflects these deep personal bonds freighted with considerable personal experience.[7] Yet, in the final analysis, groups built upon these close personal ties were private warrior bands rather than a public army responsible for the state's protection. This is clearly revealed in the series of civil wars in which samurai grasped political power and ended up establishing military rule (*buke seiji*). They used their military power to prosecute their internal factional conflicts, and the victors who eventually emerged began to follow the same course. Needless to say, such a warrior government was contrary to a national polity (*kokutai*) that based itself on traditional notions of the rule of law. Thus, the lord–vassal relationship, "loyalty toward one's lord" (*chūkun*) and so on, was part of a phenomenon generally at odds with Japanese national polity.

But then, military rule was not fully achieved overnight. The Kamakura shogunate, as it were, ruled those within the Minamoto clan's house, and not Japan as a whole. The rule of the aristocratic houses paralleled that of the military houses. Samurai authority was clearly limited, since they did not directly control much land. Nevertheless, by the Muromachi period, samurai land holdings had increased, and political power generally shifted into the hands of the samurai until the shogun became the unifying figure who governed the entire country. Finally, through such factors as these territories' political autonomy, daimyō rivalries, wars, and the rise and fall of new samurai houses, it developed into an elaborate feudal system in the Edo period. As a consequence, much thought was also given to military rule, and efforts were made to understand the way of the warrior (*bushidō*) based upon Confucian principles as *shidō* (that is, the Confucian way of the gentleman [*shitaifu*]).[8] According to this way of thinking, the lord–vassal relationship was not only a simple, direct bond of love and affection; it was also the most important of the five Confucian relations (*gorin*). This basic doctrine permeated Japanese society for over three centuries.

According to this doctrine, the ruler is, in the last analysis, a feudal lord. The designation "lord" usually refers to those in charge of individual feudal domains (*han*), but the shogun, as the unifying ruler, was similarly called a "lord" (*kun*). In both instances, what mattered was the particular relationship between a lord and his vassals. In each feudal domain there was the "lord's house" (*shuka*) with anywhere from three hundred to a thousand samurai "retainers" (*kachū*); they formed a close family-like union. The lord and vassal were bound not only by ties of loyalty but by sentiments approximating those of father and son. The staunch loyalty of the samurai therefore came not only from a moral imperative but also from their feelings of heartfelt respect. Conversely, since the large number of ordinary people who belonged to the *han* were not vassals, they did not treat their ruler as their lord and thus were not obligated to give him their utmost loyalty as the samurai class did. Because they were not vassals but people living in the domain, they were not in a lord–vassal relationship.

In addition to the lord–vassal relationship, samurai also had their own "households" (*ie*). To some degree, these households were based on master–servant and lord–vassal relationships between the samurai and their attendants; however, the samurai were also obliged to put into practice the moral principle of humanity in their relationships with their fathers, wives, children, and siblings. The most significant of these was the parent–child relationship, which was characterized by the way of filial piety (*kō no michi*). That is why "loyalty" (*chū*) toward one's master and filial piety (*kō*) toward one's parents became central to the life of samurai. If one lacked filial piety even while loyal to one's master, one could not claim to be walking on the path of humanity. Therefore, if these two were at odds, it was impossible to achieve the way of the warrior. Samurai could only realize the custom of serving a lord for three generations through their family's relationship of love and affection, and this in turn could only be realized by the harmony of loyalty and filial piety. Indeed, some explained that since both could also be harmonious, loyalty and filial piety were in effect the same thing (*chūkō ippon*).

When the feudal system was abolished with the Meiji Restoration and the legacy of imperial rule was alive and strong once more, people enjoyed again a spirit "of rule by law" both institutionally and legally. But their effort to correctly comprehend anew the relationship between the emperor and his people (*kokumin*) was glaringly deficient. They tried, quite imprudently, to apply wholesale a feudalistic lord–vassal relationship here. Some historians have concluded that its effect was to distort loyalty and devotion through seven hundred years of military rule, denigrating true loyalty as nothing other than a subject's (*shinmin*) service to the emperor.[9] However, this is not a historical fact. Emphasizing loyalty (*chūkun*) and devotion (*chūgi*) to one's master as the fundamental way of life is ultimately *a peculiarity of the age of the samurai*, and is no older than that. Of course, sincerity (*makoto*) was valued in human relationships from antiquity and was always seen as key in one's relationship with sovereigns. And yet, a specific sense of loyalty evolved to meet the needs of the feudal lord–vassal relationship. In the period where intense devotion to the emperor was a main force in forming national unity, the words to express "*makoto*" toward the emperor were not "loyalty" or "devotion" but a "pure heart" (*seimei shin*), an honest heart (*shōjiki shin*), sincerity of pure devotion (*chūmei no makoto*), and so on. The relationship between the emperor and the people is different in kind, not just in degree, from the lord–vassal relationship of the samurai.

This is even more apparent because this relationship developed under the conditions of the "Restoration" after Meiji. It entails complex organizations and relationships, beginning with the Constitution and expressed in various laws and institutions that are beyond easy comprehension. They are not so simple as the relationship between a feudal lord and hundreds of his retainers. As the unifier of this complex organization, the emperor represents the whole of his people; Therefore, individual members of society simply cannot have a relationship with this "whole" that is as rudimentary as the lord–vassal bond. Individuals' service to this "whole" must be mediated through the web of human relationships to which they belong. For instance, service to the whole could involve performing one's duty as a family member, as a city resident, as a church member, as a research analyst, as a friend, or in any number of other relationships. This matter is most clearly revealed in none other than in the Imperial Rescript on Education. While it indicates a way of acting for many forms of human association, such as filial piety towards parents, devotion to friends, bearing oneself with modesty and moderation, extending benevolence to others, learning and cultivating the arts, advancing the common good, obeying the laws, and courageously offering oneself to serve the state, loyalty (*chūkun*) and devotion (*chūgi*) are conspicuously absent. Devotion to the emperor (*chūsetsu*) is not mentioned in the text of the rescript, because it goes beyond filial piety and other ways of action, while including them all. In order to be "deeply loyal and good subjects" (*chūryō no shinmin*), you do not have to perform any specific personal service for the emperor; instead, you have to serve the emperor through scrupulously honoring other forms of human association. Those who do not perfect themselves by deepening their intellectual faculties and honing their moral virtues are not devotedly loyal and good subjects; neither are those who fail to honor the national Constitution and follow the law. This devotion is essentially carrying out the duties of citizenship, and it is different from the loyalty that bound the samurai lord to his retainers.

The confusion between these two modes of loyalty came about because of a faction of people who were "without loyalty" (*fuchū*), choosing the line of least resistance rather than developing their intellectual and contemplative faculties. The structure and organization of the constitutional state can be comprehended only through one's power of inference, which grasps these intangible and invisible associations much more easily than the visible ones. To try to replace that nuanced structure with the simplistic lord–vassal relationship is to abandon wholesale any effort at thought. In particular, it is extremely unfortunate that this approach insinuated itself even among academics and gave birth to concepts like the family state (*kazoku kokka*).

The concept of the family state was taken from a current of feudalistic thought, most particularly from the notion that there is a unity between filial piety and loyalty to one's superior (*chūkō icchi*). It was intended to give expression to the fact that our state is a community based on strong interpersonal ties, which developed on its own from a time before there were historical records. Certainly, our state strongly bears the character of a community based on strong interpersonal ties. However, in order to express this by calling our state familial is, in the final analysis, an analogy. It is impossible for it to be anything more than that. The family is the simplest form of human association, and therefore it is direct and intimate. It does not depend on internal rules or contracts. However, the state is the highest level of human association, and no matter how strong its interpersonal communal character, it probably has to have an impersonal character—that is, it must organize social relations in a calculated manner. In any event, a state that starts with a constitution and regulates itself according to numerous laws cannot have the same character as a simply structured family. No matter how much you expand the family, a state limited to familial relations is still out of reach. Thus, all attempts to try to understand the state in familial terms fundamentally misunderstand the state. The way to revitalize the *gemeinschaft* character of our state is not by explaining that the state is like a family but by deepening the ethical sense of the state and by using the powerful force of that ethic to underpin the nation's laws.[10]

While the notions of loyalty and the unity of loyalty toward one's superior and filial piety, as they were realized in the samurai lord–vassal relationship, should not be tied to the institution of imperial rule, these notions are not in themselves without meaning or value. We should recognize that these concepts were extremely important insofar as they adapted to the needs of *society and the times.* In particular, it is quite significant that in pre-modern times, warriors understood the way of the gentleman (*shidō*) in terms of the way of the warrior (*bushidō*), which has considerable historical significance. *A situation where politics is carried out through brute military coercion* is contrary to national polity. And yet, samurai, who stood in positions of power, endeavored to cultivate themselves as statesmen rather than as experts in the military arts. Thus, warriors thoroughly and appropriately mastered the Confucian ethic of the gentleman-bureaucrat (*kunshi*).[11] The result was that as statesmen they did not make blunders severe enough to wrong the Japanese nation. After the Meiji period, the duty of soldiers was not politics but the "protection of the state." The army was not supposed to flex its coercive military powers in order to influence internal national politics. Thus, servicemen were specialists in the military arts and did not have to learn how to be statesmen. The harm caused by this was much greater than was caused by a military government, since these soldiers ran the government through the coercive use of their military power. The Imperial Rescript to Soldiers and Sailors (Gunjin Chokuyu) was originally issued as a warning against any such harmful meddling in politics. If servicemen had mastered this rescript and understood it, the Japanese nation would not have fallen into its present difficult situation.[12]

Next, I will consider the connection between the institution of imperial rule and Shinto doctrines. When the institution of imperial rule was first depicted in the "Age of the Gods," a supreme god was not mentioned. Moreover, the concept is not even framed doctrinally as a divine teaching. What is clearly indicated here is simply governance (*matsurigoto*, 政治), which began as rites (*matsurigoto*, 祭事), together with the sacredness of the imperial line of succession to the throne.[13] Thus, if we think of faith as an approved fixed set of doctrines, shrine festivals do not express such a faith. This is probably why shrine rituals did not cause any serious conflicts when world religions like Buddhism gained acceptance in Japan. Over a long period of time, the imperial household adopted the Buddhist faith, and the Japanese people also began to satisfy their spiritual needs by practicing Buddhism while continuing to worship at their local shrines.

Shinto began to create its own creed much later, after this had been the situation for over several centuries. The first impetus for this was the Buddhist effort to understand the *kami* theoretically, which was in essence an attempt to incorporate the *kami* into a Buddhist framework. This made the shrines see the need for a theoretical underpinning to their own *kami* cult and led to *Ise Shinto,* which centered on the Watarai clan priests of the Outer Shrine at Ise and arose during the Kamakura period, after the samurai had established a feudal system. A main goal of this movement was to heighten the status of the Outer Shrine. At the same time, however, it endeavored to establish *a fundamental principle of Shinto in and of itself,* making it as independent as possible from Buddhist thought and trying to explain it in terms of faith in *a supreme being.* Since there is no foundation for this in the "Age of the Gods" section in the *Kojiki* and *Nihonshoki*, this family of Shinto priests forged documents, added fanciful interpretations, and dealt with these materials by drawing on Taoism, the *I ching,* and other aspects of Chinese thought, and, indeed, some aspects of Buddhist thought.

The supreme being Daigenshin ("divine origin of the universe") was none other than the main deity (*saijin*) of the Outer Shrine, the great imperial deity Toyouke, and the goddess was considered identical to the creator deities Amenominakanushi[14] and Kunitokotachi. The teaching of the *kami* is made clear in a prayer in an oracle from the great imperial goddess to Yamatohime no Mikoto.[15] From this vantage point, it goes on to argue that the emperor and the *kami* are a unity, by locating the imperial essence at the beginning of heaven and earth. We can discern Shinto's character as a faith movement through these particular points. On the one hand, we should think of Shinto as opposing Buddhism while trying to become a religion in the same way that Buddhism is; on the other hand, we should think of it as a religion which lays the foundation for the institution of imperial rule. The success of this movement would lead naturally to the establishment of Shinto as a state religion (*kokkyō*).

In subsequent years, these characteristics generally remained the same while Shinto went through its various doctrinal developments with the rise of Yoshida Shinto and Confucian Shinto. This signals a consistent trend in several respects, because Shinto priests continued to advance heavy-handed and self-serving doctrines based on the *I ching* and Confucianism; people became more interested in worshipping a supreme deity like Taigen Sonshin[16]; and given that the ultimate origin of the imperial line became more strongly linked to and promoted by this religious standpoint. Restoration Shinto (*fukko Shintō*) alone differs, insofar as it is based on a close literary study of the *Kojiki* and a repudiation of Chinese thought and the need for a supreme deity. However, even serious scholars like Norinaga, given his position as a Shintoist, had to adopt a stance of *credo quia absurdum* ("I believe because it is absurd"). This was because he was unacquainted with scholarly approaches that treated the stories [in the *Kojiki*] as myths. Like other intepreters before him, he continues the trend of seeing Shinto as a religion that undergirds imperial rule. It is clear, therefore, that Hirata Shinto, which inherits this side of Norinaga's thought and expands on it, develops the most extreme version of this literalist approach and, indeed, argues baldly for Shinto as the state religion.

However, this spiritual movement was not intrinsically necessary for the institution of imperial rule. The interest in establishing Shinto as a state religion, which flared up after the Meiji Restoration, soon died down, and the principle of freedom of religion was promulgated. Even during the six hundred years when Shinto was being continually developed, the majority of the population as well as the imperial household practiced Buddhism. Shinto was recognized as one of many faiths, and it was not the only one which supported the institution of imperial rule. The Meiji Restoration was largely motivated by the desire to *unify the people,* rather than the rabid desire to promote faith.

This matter was already fully understood by our forebears when freedom of religion was declared in the Imperial Constitution; it was important, too, to let the world know that Christianity could operate freely and fully in our country. Nonetheless, during the past decade or so, the movement to establish Shinto as the state religion has developed new forms and intensified. Even though we saw this unfold before our very eyes, we do not know precisely where this movement came from. What we do know is that it did not come out of the imperial household and that, furthermore, it was not needed for the institution of imperial rule. The imperial household treated both Buddhism and Christianity very well; in the spirit of tolerance, all religions were accepted, and, in our country, it is particularly striking that they were allowed to develop fully. A narrow-minded, closed nature is something contrary to our national polity. Thus, we can only say that it is clearly wrong to blame the institution of imperial rule for the unfortunate mistake of these ten years or so.

The movement toward making Shinto into a state religion does not just hinder the domestic principle of religious freedom. It also leads to the mistaken notation that imperial rule invariably manifests itself as an aggressive imperialism directed against the rest of the world. This is probably the greatest sin of this movement. The sacredness of the emperor sprang directly from the larger community of the Japanese people, and it is not something that should be forced on other peoples. Despite this, Hirata Shinto made the *kami* Amenominakanushi into an absolute deity who presided over the cosmos; from there, it explained the phenomenon of the entire cosmos by reference to divine action, which in turn came from two gods who manifested creative powers (*musubi*). It was only natural, then, that the emperor who was a direct descendent of this god should rule all the nations in the world. Teasing this interpretation out of the "Age of the Gods" section of the chronicle literature is already an act of madness, but applying it to the modern world in order to explicate the providence of a "Greater East Asia" is absolutely shameful. I wholeheartedly pray that the narrow-minded gang which popularized this theory has not harmed the institution of imperial rule.

(November, 1945)

Representative of the whole people[17]

At the close of 1945, following a request from Amano Kimiyoshi[18] of the Federated News Agency,[19] I wrote the following short piece in a minute. Amano intended to offer it to newspapers as something to read for the New Year.

"To say people have sovereignty does not mean that people are sovereigns individually. The unanimous will of the people, that is to say, the common will (*sōi*) of the people is what has the greatest authority in the land. What becomes an important problem in this case is how this will of the people is formed and given expression. Formerly, on their way to grabbing power, the military clique had forced their unreasonable ideas on the country by imposing "the consensus of the army." However, there was no way for the Japanese armed forces to mold a "common will." Thus, they usurped the word "will," so that it meant nothing more than the resolve of a few military men. Similarly, if a few political activists impose their own convictions under the guise of the "will of the people," and force unreasonable ideas on the country, we will be forced to repeat our miserable failure over and over again. We must honestly and precisely mold a true common will. And further, we must express it through the most suitable form for the will of the people. For us, no one but the emperor embodies this form and most suitably represents "an expression of the will of the people." In other words, the sovereignty of the people and the sovereignty of the emperor are one and the same thing. It is unnecessary to overthrow the imperial system in order to acknowledge the people's sovereignty.

Although I think that this will finally be made clear when "what history reveals is that already in the past the Japanese people pointed this out by freely expressing their own will." Relying only on myths to grasp the significance of imperial rule is narrow-minded and leads to misinterpretations. Myth must be understood as arising from a specific cultural stage; Seeing it this way allows us to recognize clearly how early Japanese society manifested their will in the person of the emperor. Primitive societies commonly projected their common will on to something which was then accepted as sacred; this is not confined to Japan. However, our country is different because this tradition, although it has changed its form at different cultural stages, has continued through the ages. After the Taika period,[20] in an age where "rule by law" was advocated and efforts were made to provide a legal system, the will of the people was projected onto the newly organized state's sovereignty. Such projects as public

224

ownership of the land and the well-field system[21] could be carried out without military force and repression because they reflected the will of the people. In this period the sacredness of the imperial throne was fused with myth. That said, it is important to note that myth is not the source of the people's reverence to the emperor and, indeed, that some of the most reverent art and literature from the age of the Fujiwara discarded myths. In the next period of military government, the imperial house lost both its military and political power. And yet, as ever, the people recognized the emperor as an expression of their will. No matter how much shoguns tried to grasp absolute power, the people simply viewed them as oppressors because of it. During the Muromachi period, when people wanted to symbolize Japan as a country, they used the name of the emperor instead of focusing on the shogun or the daimyō. The same phenomenon appears at the moment at the end of the Edo period when the people, with foreign countries as the catalyst, realized that they existed as *one nation*. The unity of the nation, the common will of the people was always represented by the emperor. This was not manufactured or coerced through military force. Although military power had worked for over seven hundred years to separate the people from the imperial family, that effort was not successful. Even though our recent unfortunate situation tried to bind the emperor by the force of arms, he wielded his authority for a long time before that without ever resorting to it whatsoever. This was only possible because that authority was, in essence, the expression of the people's will.

Passing through the crucible of history over the long centuries carries with it a great significance. "The classics" acquire their value by enduring the crucible of history. Even if many people do not recognize the value of a classic work in a particular period, it never perishes. By contrast, a work that enjoys praise and respect from lots of people in one period ends up completely forgotten and disappears in the next. In like manner, the means by which the people express their will has survived the trials of history and is thus a constant. We hope for the people's calm and objective recognition of this."

These lines were all written in haste, and the argument is inadequate in many ways, but what I have stated so far are views I have held for many years and not something I have made up in the last four months after the defeat. Incidentally, it was around that time that arguments for the overthrow of the imperial system dramatically increased. I think it is for that reason that none of the Tokyo newspapers *en masse* carried this short piece, contrary to Amano's expectations. Only the radio stations broadcast it in the morning hours, I hear. Amano was sorry, but I felt fine about it happening that way. I have lived a quiet life and have been thinking deeply about the troubles over the past five thousand years of humanity.

However, a reaction came from unexpected quarters. It seems that local newspapers across the country carried my short piece. Letters, both critical and approving, made their way to me in the course of time. The newspaper from Akita had a big headline, "The Emperor System and Watsuji-like Philosophy—Serious Distortions of Japanese history, Rehashing Fanatical Logic," and the reporter ran my short piece with a rather lengthy introduction to it. The text had terrible typos, and there were quite a number of passages where the meaning was hard to follow. The headline suggests that the reporter believed that my piece was a restating of distortions of Japanese history and fanatical logic, but whether that is the case is not at all clear from his preface. The reporter first introduces the current theories that reject the emperor system; he then lists

> those dismissing its mythological quality viewed from reexamining Japanese history . . . those dismissing the view of the emperor's divinity, a position built solely upon exposing *its distortion of Japanese history*—such as the imperial clan, who

professed that their remote ancestors were the same as the average citizen's distant ancestors, were the conquerors of most indigenous groups and had no ancestral ties to most citizens, and including the false claim of [there being an extra] six hundred years to ancient [Japanese] history. The reporter states that,

> While established political parties, conservative scholars and so on are developing counter arguments unanimously opposed to those who reject the emperor system, we can hear it espoused by Tokyo University professor Watsuji Tetsurō, who seems to have fashioned its key argument.

Above all, the article suggests two or three apparent weak points in my original argument. The most important of these is the lack of clarity about the following: "Which social strata is he referring to when I say, 'the people in the past'?" [Another question concerns] "Whether or not ordinary people were granted a political culture or the freedom to express their convictions." [Third is] "Is there a difference essentially between the will of the people voiced in various ways and one that will be voiced through the democratic process from now on?" The points he raises are justifiable. In a short essay I could not cover these points in sufficient detail. That said, I do not understand the reason for writing such a headline as "The Emperor System and Watsuji-like Philosophy—Serious Distortions of Japanese history, Rehashing Fantical Logic." Where are the distortions and where is the fanatical logic? He offers no justification whatsoever.

Did he judge that because my argument was *conservative*, I supported the distortions of Japanese history that those opposed to the emperor system had exposed and I was someone who defends the view of the emperor's divinity. If I supported the distortions, he could say "serious distortions," and if I defended the view of the divine emperor, he could say, "rehashing fanatical logic." However, I have never defended making the imperial clan, who were conquerors, into our nation's forefathers, nor the *so-called distortions of Japanese history* such as the insertion of the imperial line's false chronology, beginning with emperor Jinmu, into ancient history. Quite to the contrary, I have never treated the ancient part of the chronology offered in the *Nihonshoki* as a real chronology. That can be gleaned by looking at my book, *Japanese Ancient Culture,* first published thirty years ago. Any real scholar among national historians does not attempt to definitively date Japan's ancient period before CE 400. The *Nihonshoki* adds about six hundred years to its chronology. No one these days takes these numbers seriously, given that scholars of old from the mid-Meiji period decided that eliminating this made the chronology accurate. If anyone asserted that this fictitious six hundred years distorted Japanese history, it would be truly unprofound and unworthy given Dr. Tsuda Sōkichi's brave struggles in the courts, for his textual criticism of imperial chronicles. It is the same regarding the imperial clan as our ancestors. I have never supported such an idea. First, I cannot find in any document that a "clan' (*uji*) known as "the imperial clan" ever existed. On the contrary, I have already given a detailed argument in *Japanese Ancient Culture* that the *uji* is an extremely recent concept and system in Japan. The idea that the descendents of the heavenly gods were conquerors is also a relic of the mid-Meiji period; it is no more than a theory based upon a historical interpretation of a myth, and it has no academic value. What kind of evidence is there to make a distinction such as indigenous people or conquered people anyway? However, just because I deny that the Japanese were a subjugated people does not mean that I believe that the imperial household are the ancestors of the entire Japanese nation. Do not the legends in the imperial chronicles themselves reveal that such a theory does not hold water? Indeed, ancestor worship in ancient times in our country was not so striking as it was in Greece and Rome; rather, it became more and more intently practiced through the influence of Chinese thought. If this kind of argument could deny the divinity of the emperor, the issue of the divine emperor should have been explained away thirty years ago.

Similarly, I do not recall defending the emperor's divine status in the way that the lunatics did. In our time, astronomy and biology have advanced to the point that no one can seriously believe that the emperor is a descendent of the sun goddess and, therefore, is a manifest kami (*akitsukami*). Some of those who advocated this type of thing were the zealous devotees of the Hirata School of Shinto. I have already clearly pointed out in my book *Revering the Emperor, Its Thought and Tradition* that Hirata Atsutane could only be thought of as psychologically abnormal and deranged. Having said that, I have no wish to deny *the historical fact* that twelve to thirteen hundred years ago the emperor upheld the myth and through it supported his divinity. This fact is clearly revealed in the established legal codes and myths that were compiled in that age. No matter how many times it is reexamined, it can never be obscured. To our eyes, there is a rational explanation for this historical fact. It is common for a people at certain cultural stages to produce a myth which shows their larger group is be sacred. The imperial chronicles are simply the final culmination of such a stage. The imperial throne has now lost its sacred mythological basis, but it has continued to exist as an institution while adapting to each successive cultural stage. This is also a historical fact and cannot be denied. I have worked to prove these historical facts by analyzing them objectively as cultural products; this, however, is a rational approach and not a crackpot argument that attempts to press an ancient mythological way of thinking on modern people.

When we consider it this way, it is not only reckless but logically inconsistent to say that I have made "serious distortions of Japanese history," and am "rehashing fanatical logic." These are essentially the same irrational criticisms that the lunatics have previously inflicted on my argument. Indeed, "rehashing fanatical logic" fits to a tee the act of a reporter who writes headlines such as this. What could I do but disappointedly stay silent?

About one week later, the *Hokkoku Mainichi* newspaper from Kanazawa arrived. Andō Takatsura,[22] over a four-day period, wrote a critique of my piece. This analysis was quite reasonable and was not off-base like the previous case. However, what initially caught my eye were big headlines like "In Japan there were no citizens. What existed were people who were nothing more than subjects," or "The perpetuation of the imperial rule is nothing more than the blessing of powerlessness and a fig leaf for the ruling classes," or "The imperial household is surely the authoritative family? This sense of emotional affinity is nothing more than a myth." I felt it was happening all over again. I had never said that the imperial household was the authoritative family. Neither did I say that the continuation of imperial rule was the blessing of military power and authority. These headlines did not actually reflect the content. What's more—with respect to what it means to be a Japanese citizen—we have to start from scratch, beginning with an inquiry into the very concept of citizenship. I got disgusted and threw the paper away without reading the article.

But, when I calmed down later and read it, Andō's first critical attack involved three points: (1) Has our country ever had something called the will of the people? (2) If there were a will of the people, what form would it take? (3) If there is a will of the people and it has always supported the emperor in the past, why should that mean that the emperor system should also continue into the future? Coincidentally, this was very similar to what the reporter of the Akita newspaper had suggested were the points in my article *that lacked clarity*. I have to think that this coincidence comes from some deficiency in my writing. Thus, to answer these critiques and redress these inadequacies, it is my duty to write a rough response.

However, even as I thought about writing a retort, I was pressed by lectures I had to do for the first academic year since the war and had no time to embark on something so bothersome.

In the meantime, the first government draft of the new Constitution[23] was finally released. When I looked at it, I saw inscribed at the beginning, "The Emperor is in accord with the sovereign will of the Japanese people and should be a symbol of the Japanese state and the unity of the people" (天皇は日本国民至高の総意に基づき、日本国及び其の国民統治の象徴たるべきこと).[24] That seemed to largely agree with what I tried to say in my earlier article. I had used the phrase "An expression (hyōgen) of the will of the people," and not the word "symbol" (shōchō). And yet, if you treat the subjective desires of the people by giving it a visible form, then what you have is a symbol. Thus, making the emperor the symbol of the unity of the people is correct. Provided that the Constitution in fact came from the freely expressed common will of the people, it ultimately accomplishes what I had tried to articulate in my short article. So, I decided to watch the deliberations over the Constitution without making any comments at all.

Finally, the Constitution was resolved. The phrase Nihon kokumin shikō no sōi (the sovereign will of the Japanese people) was revised into "shuken no sonsuru Nihon kokumin no sōi" (the will of the Japanese people with whom resides sovereign power). Either shikō or shūken no sonsuru carries the same sense of sovereign.[25] I think that for the time being this issue has been settled.

* * *

In my earlier article I used the common phrase "the will of the people" without giving any explanation at all. I think that this was certainly a flaw. I used the word, kokumin, originally in the same sense as the German word, Nation. In this case, kokumin is a cultural unit that has the same language, customs, and beliefs; it does not necessarily overlap with the state (kokka). However, one meaning kokumin can have is everyone in a state or the state's individual members. Therefore, if I am discussing people as a community with a common culture, I use the word minzoku or the folk. I have also used the word kokumin, but only in cases when I particularly view this folk as members of the state and want to distinguish them from a group related by blood. Thus, I can use the concept of kokumin to express both a people of a state and a community sharing a common culture of language and customs. The Japanese people are both a group linked by custom and a part of the Japanese state. When Korea and Taiwan were part of Japan's territory, there was criticism because Taiwanese and Korean people could not be included as Japanese nationals. However, the official term at the time for designating people who were part of the Japanese state was subjects (shinmin) and not the people (kokumin). And the word kokumin includes the connotation of a community who share a common culture. For example, you do not take Indian character into account when you think about the English. Vietnamese culture is not at issue when you think about the achievements of the French. Even in the enthusiastic debates that took place around the time over Japanese nationality, no one at all considered the Koreans or the Taiwanese. If that is the case, the right thing conceptually is not including Koreans or Taiwanese among the Japanese people.

If we regard kokumin, on the one hand, as the people of one state, and, on the other, along with it, as a single cultural community, they are not individuals, but a single group of people. Therefore, the common will of the people is their collective will and not the specific desires of individuals. Originally, the word kokumin (people) could also mean the individual members who belong to a group. However, such an individual is shaped collectively; no individuals are independent of society. This sense of collectivity, which exists in the word *kokumin* should be taken very seriously. Japanese have no problem referring to young people or soldiers as though they were one youth or soldier, and they likewise denote separate individuals with words like *kokumin* and *jinmin*. However, an individual soldier can only be labeled as such because he is defined by a group of soldiers; by analogy, then, a particular person (*jinmin, kokumin*) can also be spoken of this way only as a member of a group. When it is said that the people have sovereignty, it is important not to lose sight of *kokumin*'s sense as a collectivity. The authority comes from *the collective will of the people* and not the inclinations of particular individuals. Further, the collective will of the people is not simply the sum of individual desires. Rather, it originates from conditions different from that of individual wills—in the unity of its whole nature. I think that phrase, "the common will of the people," can indicate a supra-individual will, a collective will such as this, and I have used it in short order. That is perhaps nothing more than one small nod of approval.

I have stated that if the common will of the people has sovereignty in the above sense, the important question then becomes *how it is formed, and given expression.* I have repeated that word, formation (*keisei*) in that sense, many times since. I must say that this too is very inadequate. If the will of the people is the collective will of a group, then it already exists within that group with *no need for it to be actualized anew.* What I am trying to raise is how one determines that collective will. You elect a representative by voting, and then that elected representative votes for something in the Diet. This is not the first time that a *collective will has been formed.* That collective will is decided at this time over some issue. To put it a differently, *the collective will, which is inclined to go in a certain direction regarding a specific matter,* is made manifest at this time. I have somewhat obscurely described it as a common will that is formed. Therefore, the common will in this case is the collective will that has made a concrete choice about something.

In our time, the most advanced way of determining this kind of collective will is by such mechanisms as legislative resolutions, elections, and voting. However, needless to say, this is not a *perfect method.* How can one sufficiently give voice to the collective will by voting once in several years? Determining the collective will in an assembly by debate, *like authentic citizens* of an ancient Greek polis, comes much closer to perfection. However, that only works in a state which is small enough to allow its individual citizens to discuss things together, and it is not a suitable approach for a state consisting of millions or tens of millions of people. Therefore, a method was devised for large states for selecting a small number of members of the Diet from among the citizenry. By representing the convictions of many people, they work to determine the collective will. Provided that such legislators as these abandon all selfish motives and only act with sincerity as public servants, the collective will of the people will be decided exactly as the majority wants.

However, the reality is far from this ideal. It is still fresh in our memories that in our country, where we expected our citizens to choose their representatives freely, thoughtfully, and eagerly, the Diet lost its efficacy in the face of the tyranny and threats of a small number of militarists, and the collective will was finally decided in a manner that most found undesirable. It was in actuality a military government—a dictatorship by a minority through force of arms. But the danger of such a dictatorship today remains completely undiminished. There is a movement already afoot among those who burn with desire for leaders like the former militarists. In order to prevent such a dictatorship, individuals must stiffen their resolve and defend freedom of thought and volition. Completely sacrificing oneself for the emperor (*yokusan seiji*) was simply acting like slaves who have cast away their freedom; this new movement, however, which blithely flows with the currents of the times, is also a way of acting slavishly. Our task for the future is to shake off this servile attitude and determine the true collective will of the people as a whole.

* * *

The crux of the matter is determining how to express a "vibrant collectivity" *invisible and unavailable as an object in a form visible to an objective eye.* In our country it has been represented by the emperor. But now, in late 1945 and early 1946, the time has come where *we must decide* according to "the freely expressed will of the Japanese people" whether this representation will persist as ever, or whether it will be replaced with an elected president as in other countries. I have argued in this regard that if it is clear that "the person who represents our nation's collective will is none other than the emperor," then the sovereignty which resides in the collective will of the people and the sovereign emperor who represents that collective will are one and the same. This refutes the argument that the sovereignty residing in the people and the existence of the emperor are completely incompatible.

After this, the draft of the Constitution was announced, making the emperor the symbol of the Japanese state and of the unity of the Japanese people. The members of the Diet, who were elected to debate the Constitution, decided to recognize the emperor as the representative of the collective will of the people according to "the freely expressed will of the Japanese people." My predictions, then, were on the mark. On this point, there is no longer any need for further debate. Before the decision was made, however, the part of that prediction that engendered the most severe doubts was my comment that "What history reveals is that already in the past the Japanese people pointed this out by freely expressing their own will." Is it a fact that somewhere in the past the Japanese people, "by their own freely expressed will," recognized the emperor as the representative of their collective will?

I have given a rather over-simplistic rendering of that history from primitive times through the age of the samurai. What is initially problematic, however, is whether we can accept that people in primitive Japanese society did indeed freely express their convictions. One opinion is that the common will of primitive societies is not an expression of any personal conviction by an autonomous individual self-consciousness; rather, it is an *unmediated and innately collective consciousness.* Furthermore, it is largely driven by its religious, magical, and mystical worldview. In primitive societies, there is no tyrannical monarch, but likewise no member of that society is free. Indeed, some argue that, conceptually speaking, chiefs as well as the clan members are slaves. Indeed, one has to acknowledge that there is no individual self-conscious in primitive societies as there is in modern democratic society. However, even so, it is an overstatement to say that primitives lack almost any individual consciousness, in the same way as it is to say that they are free and independent. According to recent field surveys of primitive societies, among societies strongly knit together by totems and taboos, individual opposition is directly proportional to the strength of those ritual bonds. Malinowski,[26] who stresses this point, even argues that the relationship between the individual and society in primitive societies is scarcely different from what is found in civilized society. Obeying the collective will in primitive society is not innate. It is achieved through much self-denial—that is, the conscious subordination of the self to those things it could willfully oppose. The fact that the worldview holding sway is magical does not, in and of itself, usurp an individual's freedom. The individuals are shaped by a collective consciousness to which they always belong, but it is simply untrue that the only truly free people are those rare geniuses whose intellect can transcend that consciousness. Even if individuals adopt that collective consciousness, so long as they do so without coercion, they remain free. In primitive societies, for example, people who subscribed to a magical worldview venerated those in charge of their religious festivals—who ultimately came to represent the collective will—and, *for the first time*, created a national polity which was rooted in that sacred authority. We must acknowledge that this sprang from *those people's* freedom of expression, and therein lies the creative significance of that age. When something is created for the first time in any system, it carries a positive significance as a step forward. While its originality will harden over time and may even turn into its opposite, that does not lessen the creativity of that first moment.

Given these considerations, it is quite appropriate to attach great importance to the fact that when our national polity first came into being, it was united *by religious authority* and not by coercive military force. This was probably the usual way of primitive states. State authority began as religious authority and then shifted to military power. Those who had the authority were strong, and the powerful did not obtain authority. That ended up being reversed because the tradition of the sacred ruler eventually turned into its opposite. After such a development occurred in Mesopotamia, it also started in China. And after this process finally came to an end in China, it began anew in Japan. When the Japanese wrote down this developmental sequence in their myths and legends, they were influenced by Chinese culture, so they were apt to use its fossilized version to portray this initial creative phase. As this is a mixture of simple mythical content and concepts associated with dynasties who took control through force, we can definitely offer a critique of it if we are careful. That is because works like the *Jinmu tennōki* (Record of Emperor Jinmu) are considered products of a time not too distant from when the *Kojiki* and *Nihonshoki* were compiled.[27] If we consider these criticisms in light of the archeological record, those within the group *preferred and encouraged* the use of the emperor as a *living representation of the collectivity* and not something *forced upon them* by a few oppressors. It is not precisely clear how this collective decision was made, but if we assume that it is reflected in the myths, then surely it appears in the "assembly at Kawara."[28] Here everyone in the group assembled and made the *kami* that embodied the *power of thought* express his opinion.[29] It signifies that what rules over the assembly is the power of thought so that the collective will is determined both by the assembly and the *logos*. Is it so odd to see free will being expressed here?

* * *

Some argue that what I say in my above short essay is that myth should be understood according to the age in which it was created and that, therefore, the authority of the emperor, while it originates in myth, also changes its content as the culture goes through different stages of development. However, what originates in myth stays around forever. Regarding the emperor as a manifest deity (*akitsukami*), *this is a tradition that continues in all periods throughout Japanese history*. We have now reached the moment when this tradition should be destroyed. That *would be the greatest revolutionary act since the founding of the country*. Make no mistake: In order to achieve this revolution, conservative sophistries, such as those that see value in reviving the country under the emperor, must be smashed.

Recognition of the inevitable historical relationship between the emperor system and Shinto was generally prevalent both before and after the defeat. Nonetheless, I have to see historical understanding as being wrong here. The emperor gained his sacred authority during the age when vast high-mounded tumuli were being built; this antedated the compilation of the myths by three to four hundred years.[30] And at the time when the myths were compiled and the idea of the manifest deity had clearly appeared in the legal system, the country's religion had already shifted to Buddhism, beginning with the emperor and the intellectual classes generally. Even though shrine rites had not yet ceased to exist, most of these shrines were local and communal *with no relationship to a manifest deity*. And whether in legislation or in literature, while a manifest deity indicates a high degree of respect, *it was never an object of religious belief*. There is no room for dispute about this, which is clearly indicated in the huge monuments of the Hakuhō and Tempyō periods.[31]. The idea of a manifest deity had already been severed from religious belief even in the period it was most conspicuously in use. In an age when Buddhist beliefs had spread more and more among the people, the term "manifest deity" itself became defunct. And therefore, it simply cannot be argued that a myth-based faith, which treated the emperor as a manifest deity, continued.

A Shinto that revived myth and endeavored to restore its religious vitality came much later with the sudden rise of Kamakura Buddhism. A Shinto that worked to connect itself to the imperial family came still later, after the mid-Edo period. These efforts on the part of Shinto were due to the continuing veneration of the emperor among the people; it is wrong to say that Shinto by nature supported the imperial family. Explaining how the emperor system and Shinto flourished and fell together requires an argument which relies solely on the views of Hirata Shinto in and after the *bakumatsu* period and the recent militarists who advanced this point of view. It is apparent from the writings of the Confucian scholars of the Edo period, as well as the earlier war tales, that the emperor is not a manifest deity in the sense of a superhuman person. This understanding is the greatest revolution since the founding of the country only from the viewpoint of the Hirata school.

Still another rebuttal is that the whole purpose of revising the Constitution is to oppose considering the emperor as the representative of the collective will of the people. According to this argument, the main idea behind revising the Constitution is to prevent such dangers as usurpers monopolizing the imperial prerogative. Nevertheless, over the long period of time the emperor system was preserved, one usurper after the other continued to monopolize political power. Thus, the continued existence of the emperor system is not useful for preventing this danger. If the emperor were the representative of the collective will of the people, what would be preferable for the people would be an increase in the emperor's real power and not its restrictions. Therefore, that would entail an expansion of royal prerogative and an all-out drive to make the emperor's direct rule a reality. That clearly is moving in the opposite direction from the aim for revising the Constitution.

This argument was made in January 1946 prior to the revision of the Constitution. It seems no longer necessary to debate this since the Japanese Constitution, which considers the emperor as a symbol of the unity of the nation, has been enacted based upon the freely expressed views of the people. However, I want to make an additional comment because the thinking here reveals a remarkable misunderstanding of the role of the emperor. In this view, if the people as a whole decide to take one position on an issue, the emperor simply reflects that decision as his imperial will. This will not be "the emperor's direct rule," meaning that the emperor orders his people according to his own individual views. Making the emperor a sacred figure from the beginning, rather than having a particular individual conquer the group and impose that sacredness, means that the collective will of the people becomes the imperial will. Even under the Imperial Constitution, the emperor did not rule based on his own individual views. What was decided in the Diet and the other government agencies established by constitutional law was promulgated in the name of the emperor. Probably the exception was when the emperor actively expressed his opinion over the decision to surrender. Therefore, appointing the prime minister based on the nomination of the

Diet or promulgating laws based on the consent on the counsel of the cabinet does not alter the essential significance of the emperor in any way. What matters is that the collective will is carried out as precisely and justly as possible. Grabbing the people's hearts through false propaganda, no matter what the ideology, must be avoided. And, yet, making decisions directly through the collective will is a different issue from whether the emperor system should continue. Hitler's dictatorial politics made their appearance even under a republic.

If we regard the emperor as the representative of the collective will of the people in the sense discussed above, then the argument that we are already repudiating the emperor system by entrusting this decision to the people collapses. From the outset, the will of the people created the emperor as their own representative. And afterward, even at different cultural stages of development, they did not try to abandon it. This reaffirmation of it is, in principle, not a denial of the emperor system. As has been argued several times, it will need to be reaffirmed again. However, until that time, individual members of our nation should actively participate even more by making decisions according to the collective will and by clearly protecting the independence of their judgments and opinions. In this way, even the politicians who burn with ambition to rule and who devote all their energy to spreading false propaganda will become extinct. An attitude of service toward all the people is even more important under a democratic system. Even in advanced countries, that is achieved only after a prolonged period of hard national labor. In our country as well, it will take much work to achieve this. Yet, it seems that when this attitude and individual self-awareness have prevailed among our citizens, reaffirmation will happen again in an even more definitive form. There is an insuperable power latent in the classics.

July 1948 (partially abridged)

Notes

1 Robert Bellah, "Japan's Cultural Identity: Some Reflections on the Work of Watsuji Tetsurō," *The Journal of Asian Studies* 24 (August, 1965):578. "Watsuji Tetsurō," *Stanford Encyclopedia of Philosophy*, http://plato.stanford.edu/entries/watsuji-tetsuro/.
2 Both essays were republished in book form as *A Symbol of the Unity of the People* (*Kokumin tōgō no shōchō*, Tokyo: Keisō Shobō, 1948).
3 In his preface to his essays, Watsuji notes that up to this point, he used in his writing the term, *tōitsu*, instead of *tōgō*, the term found in the Constitution itself. He notes that the term was used in the field of education referring to one's *Konzentration* (in the sense of a deliberate focusing of attention on a particular activity). See "Hōken shisō to Shintō no kyōgi," *Watsuji Tetsurō zenshū*, 20 vols. (Tokyo: Iwanami, 1962), 14:315.
4 A set of government reforms dating from 645 during the reign of Emperor Kōtoku and modeled after the Chinese system and Confucian principles that centralized power on the imperial throne.
5 Watsuji here is referring to the practice, beginning with the shogun Yoritomo in the Kamakura period, of the emperor legitimizing military government. This was done through a formal appointment as the emperor's designated *seii taishōgun*. A key modern example of such a rescript is the Imperial Rescript to Soldiers and Sailors (Gunjin Chokuyu), issued by Emperor Meiji to the new imperial army on January 4, 1882. Among its Confucian principles were loyalty to the emperor, valor, faithfulness, righteousness, and simplicity. It admonishes them to "with single heart fulfill your essential duty of loyalty, and bear in mind that duty is weightier than a mountain, while death is lighter than a feather." See Tsunoda, et al., *Sources of Japanese Tradition*, 2 vols. (New York: Columbia University Press, 1958), 2:198–200.
6 Key to the Chinese-inspired Taika Reforms was a policy of land redistribution that wrested private control from the great clans to the direct control of the central imperial government. See Kozo Yamamura, "The Decline of the Ritsuryō-System: Hypotheses on Economic and Institutional Change," *Journal of Japanese Studies* 1, No. 1 (Autumn, 1974):3–37.

7 Heian aristocrats were typically raised by wet nurses and socially were much more intimately familiar with their foster siblings than with their actual ones, who remained distant and, indeed, often were considered rivals. See Haruo Shirane, *The Bridge of Dreams: A Poetics of the Tale of Genji* (Stanford, CA: Stanford University Press, 1987), 145.

8 The *shitaifu* is a scholar official in Confucianism while the *bushi* in Edo are warrior officials. The character, *shi*, in the two compounds, while meaning "officials," has very different references. Originally, for Confucians, government officials were scholars who had mastered the literary arts and, through them, the Confucian virtues, whereas the *bushi* were masters of the military arts as conceived in Confucian terms. For Confucians, the military *shi* originally served the scholar official and had no place in Confucius's moral ideal of the gentleman.

9 Based upon the Meiji Constitution, "subjects" (*shinmin*) refers to the Japanese people other than the emperor, the imperial family, and, after the annexation of Korea after 1910, Korean nobility (*ōkōzoku*).

10 Watsuji is drawing upon the distinction the German sociologist Ferdinand Tönnies (1855–1936) makes between two social groups—*gemeinschaft* types and *gesellschaft* types.

11 Literally, "noble or exemplary person," the *kunshi* is the Confucian idea of the scholar gentleman who embodies the moral ideal of human-heartedness (*jin*) and ritual propriety (*rei*) that instills harmony in the five relationships. It is particularly made manifest in filial piety in the family but can be extended to ensure virtuous, prosperous, and harmonious rule.

12 In particular, its first precept warns as follows: "Remember that, as the protection of the state and the maintenance of its power depend upon the strength of its arms, the growth or decline of this strength must affect the nation's destiny for good or for evil; therefore, neither be led astray by current opinions nor meddle in politics, but with single heart fulfill your essential duty of loyalty, and bear in mind that duty is weightier than a mountain, while death is lighter than a feather. Never by failing in moral principle fall into disgrace and bring dishonor upon your name."

13 Here, for *matsurigoto*, Watsuji is using different *kanji* compounds to distinguish two meanings of this ancient word. This idea is also expressed in the Meiji era term, *saisei icchi*, the "unity of rites and governance."

14 On the identity of Toyouke with Amenominakanushi see Richard Bowring, *The Religious Traditions of Japan 500–1600* (Cambridge: Cambridge University Press, 2005), 353–54. On intellectual developments of this deity in eighteenth- and nineteenth-century National Learning, see Sasaki Kiyoshi, "Amenominakanushi no Kami in Late Tokugawa Period Kokugaku," http://www2.kokugakuin.ac.jp/ijcc/wp/cpjr/kami/sasaki.html.

15 This is found in the *Yamatohime no mikoto seiki* (Chronicles of Princess Yamatohime), one of the five key texts (*Gobusho*) of Watarai Shinto. These texts, attributed to the Watarai priestly family, were created during the early to mid Kakamura period. See Mark Teeuwen, *Watarai Shintō: An Intellectual History of the Outer Shrine in Ise* (Leiden: CNWS, 1996).

16 Taigenkyū, originally known as Kunitokotachi, was the major deity enshrined at Yoshida Shinto's main ritual site in the fifteenth century. Yoshida Kanetomo regarded Taigen as the original source of the cosmos.

17 The word Watsuji uses here for people is *kokumin*, which can be translated as people, citizens, or nation, rather than the term *jinmin*, a Japanese equivalent for what was used in documents like the Declaration of Independence and the United States Constitution. As historian John Dower has explained, *kokumin* is "an inherently conservative term used for pre-war propaganda purposes—with its nationalistic connotation, signifying the Japanese people or race. Composed of the ideographs for country (*koku*) and people (*min*), it connotes citizens who are 'harmoniously merged with the nation.'" It reinforced the view that the people and the emperor were one. The conservative Kijūro Shidehara cabinet's Special Committee to Investigate Constitutional Matters insisted on including *kokumin* in its negotiations with GHQ for the new post-war Constitution. See John W. Dower, *Embracing Defeat: Japan in the Wake of World War II* (New York: W.W. Norton and company, 1999), 381–82.

18 Amano Kimiyoshi (1921–90) was a graduate of Tokyo Imperial University's faculty of letters, where he studied with Watsuji. He became a reporter at the Federated News Agency and, in 1949, won the general election to serve in the Lower House of the Diet as a representative of the Minshu Jiyū Party for several terms. He also served as Home Minister.

19 The Federated News Agency (Dōmei Tsūshinsha) was the official news organ for the Japanese government from 1936 to 1945, after which it was replaced by the National non-profit Kyōdō News service.
20 The Taika period was noted for its reforms (645) instituted by Emperor Kōtoku along T'ang dynasty Chinese lines. It created a centralized system of imperial government with a *tennō*, or "emperor" at its head and organized through civil (*ritsu*) and administrative (*ryō*) legal codes.
21 Two of the legislative innovations of the Taika reform based along Chinese lines. The *handen* system (*akachida*) distributed land to peasant families from which the state would receive approximately one twentieth of the harvest as tax revenue.
22 Andō Takatsura was a Kanazawa University philosopher (1911–84) who specialized in Aristotle.
23 This draft was the Japanese cabinet's response to the GHQ Government Sections draft presented on February 13, 1946. The "first government draft" for the revised Constitution was written in response and presented to the GHQ on March 4.
24 The final wording for Article 1 in the Constitution enacted on May 3, 1947 is as follows: "The Emperor shall be the symbol of the State and of the unity of the people, deriving his position from the will of the people with whom resides sovereign power" (天皇は、日本国の象徴であり日本国民統合の象徴であつて、この地位は、主権の存する日本国民の総意に基く).
25 Another change in the language used in the revised draft was the substitution of *shikō* for *shuken* (sovereignty). As John Dower has noted, *shikō* is an archaicism meaning literally "supreme height," whose meaning was obscure, and, as such, was an attempt to water down GHQ's efforts to base Japanese national polity on popular sovereignty rather than the imperial will. Dower and others would disagree with Watsuji here, finding in "supreme" a nuance that is not identical with what the GHQ wanted to clearly identify—that sovereignty was vested in the people rather than the emperor.
26 Bronislaw Malinowski (1884–1942) was a famous social anthropologist and pioneering ethnographer of Trobriand Islanders in Melanesia whose works, *Argonauts of the Western Pacific* (1922) and *Magic, Science, and Religion* (1948) were highly influential, particularly with respect to his theories on magic and religion.
27 The *Kojiki*, compiled in 712 by the imperial court to give an authoritative historical statement about its own origins, was based on a variety of source documents dating from the sixth century. The *Nihonshoki* contains a record of such works in an entry dating from 620, which includes, among other works, the *Tennōki* (Record of Emperors). See Donald L. Philippi, trans. *Kojiki* (Tokyo: The University of Tokyo Press, 1968), 4–5.
28 In the *Kojiki* and *Nihonshoki*, the meeting of the gods is at *Ama no yasu no kawara*, where they consulted on ways to get the sun goddess Amaterasu out of the heavenly rock cave, where she had retreated leaving the land in darkness after the depredations of her brother Susanoo. See Philippi, *Kojiki*, 82.
29 This is the child of Takamimusubi no Kami, Omoikane no Kami, who possesses the ability to "think over" (*omoikane*).
30 This is a period extending from the third or fourth to the end of the seventh century.
31 These periods were from 650 to 710 and 710 to 794 respectively.

27

ASHIZU UZUHIKO

The various issues related to contemporary shrines (1951)

Ashizu Uzuhiko (1909–92) was born in Hakozaki, Fukuoka prefecture. Until the end of the war, he worked as a representative for a company involved in shrine construction. In 1945, after Japan's defeat, he worked with Miyagawa Munenori and Yoshida Shigeru (who had the same name as the prime minister but was a different person) to form the Association of Shinto Shrines (Jinja Honchō), a key religious administrative organization representing over 80,000 Shinto shrines. This association was organized after the Occupation's Shinto Directive, which ordered that Shinto be disestablished from the Japanese state.

Along with defending and maintaining shrine activities under the Occupation, Ashizu also served as the chief of the *Jinja shinpōsha* publishing house and wrote several important books and articles on Shinto, including: *Tennō shintō kenpō* (The Emperor, Shinto, and the Constitution, 1954), *Nihon no kunshusei* (Research into Japan's Monarchy, 1966), *Kokka shintō to wa nan datta no ka?* (What was State Shinto? 1987), and *Tennō: Shōwa kara Heisei e* (The Emperor from Shōwa to Heisei, 1989).

Ashizu has been described as an "imperial loyalist and activist" who worked tirelessly to protect the Japanese monarchy and to preserve the emperor as an object of loyalty and unifying spiritual force for the Japanese people.[1]

In the following essay, written around 1956 as a brochure, Ashizu gives his critique of the Occupation's Shinto Directive, and the American government's view of Shinto. Ashizu argues that the American policy of treating Shinto like any other religion, ending its connection with the state and severing its ties to the emperor, ignores Shinto's own unique history. He is also critical of folkloric approaches to Shinto, like those of Orikuchi and Yanagita, which deemphasize the deep imperial connections to shrine Shinto. Religious studies scholar Shimazono Susumu has recently described Ashizu as representative of a group of scholars who define Shinto—and particularly State Shinto—narrowly. In this view, Shinto is nothing more than shrine worship connected to the Japanese state; however, this ignores the broader reality of Shinto-inspired ideas and practices, often promoted by the government and right-wing political groups, which continue to have influence throughout Japanese society today.[2]

THE VARIOUS ISSUES RELATED
TO CONTEMPORARY SHRINES
(1951)

The Allied Forces' occupation of Japan

After Japan's defeat on August 15, 1945, shrine Shinto ended up facing a crisis it had never experienced before. There are several issues facing contemporary shrine Shinto, all of which are directly or indirectly connected to Japan's defeat in World War II.

The Supreme Commander during the time the United States occupied Japan was Douglas MacArthur. MacArthur's military occupation of Japan appeared remarkably different from what was contemplated by existing international law.

The Hague treaty on the laws and customs of war on land[3] anticipated that the occupying army would respect the common religious practices and laws of the occupied country. However, the Americans who occupied Japan reformed its entire legal system, starting with the Constitution. Their ultimate goal was to reform the very mentality and thought of the Japanese people. Therefore, they did not stop with demands for reforming the shrine Shinto system, the center of Japanese folk beliefs, but unhesitatingly interfered with such matters as shrine rituals and prayer texts.

John Gunther, discussing MacArthur, says that, "the fact of the matter is what America tried to do through its Occupation policy, to put it bluntly, was, in effect, to remake the entire culture and civilization exactly according to the American model." It might be more exact to say their goal was a spiritual revolution that would reform Japan by "turning it into a model American colony." The most effective and potent weapon the United States used for promoting this serious and thoroughgoing Occupation policy was the "war tribunal." The war tribunal was not a criminal court based on constituted criminal laws and codes; indeed, the conduct and persons which fell within the court's jurisdiction were completely unpredictable. The anxiety that this uncertainty naturally caused was used most effectively by General Headquarters (GHQ).

From the fall through the winter of 1945, accused war criminals from General Tōjō on down were arrested one after the other. At that time, some identified as war-crimes suspects were tied to shrine Shinto, such as, on December 2, 1945, his imperial highness, the ritual head of Ise, Nashimotonomiya Morimasa;[4] the vice president of the Research Institute for the Imperial Classics (Kōten Kōkyūjo), Hiranuma Kiichirō;[5] and Mizuno Rentarō,[6] the President of the Greater Japan Board of Deities (Dai-Nippon Jingikai). Under such conditions, the press of the Allied Powers fiercely criticized Shinto as a pillar of Japan's militarism and insisted that militaristic Shinto thought therefore needed to be excised from the hearts of the Japanese. Many in the Shinto community clearly felt spiritually panicked by this attitude.

The American army, occupying the entirety of Japan, searched shrines throughout the country and confiscated shrine treasures such as swords. Although the conduct of the American army depended on the local military commanders and thus was not uniform, there were certainly more than a few cases where armed soldiers raided shrines. There was very little resistance to this desecration.

Even the imprisonment of the ritual head of Ise caused no protest movement among the Shinto community. Since the ritual head was also the president of the Research Institute for the Imperial Classics, which managed Kokugakuin University, some Kokugakuin students attempted a drive to lodge petitions with GHQ. The university authorities put a stop to this, however, which gives some idea of the tenor of the times. The Shinto Directive was issued in the midst of this panic-ridden situation.

The issuance of the Shinto Directive

The aim of the Shinto Directive can be generally summarized as follows:

1   The guarantee, support, preservation, and promulgation of Shinto by the Japanese government and public institutions was strictly prohibited.

Further, the Directive prohibited the use of public resources to support shrines; it also abolished the Board of Divinities and also the Jingū Kōgakkan University as a Shinto-based institution of public education.

2   The propaganda and promulgation of a militaristic ideology in Shinto doctrines, customs, ceremonies, and rites were prohibited. This portion of the Directive aimed to stamp out Shinto doctrines from public education, and it ordered the removal of all things connected to Shinto doctrine from textbooks and reference works for teachers.

The Directive was explained as an attempt to guarantee freedom of belief based on the principle of the separation of religion and state, thus building a new Japanese edifice of eternal peace and democracy. The Directive was officially announced on December 15, 1945 by "Army Colonel H.W. Allen, adjutant staff officer acting on behalf of the Supreme Commander." (Note: *Shintō shirei no kaisetsu,* ed. Jinja shinpōsha.)

By means of the Shinto Directive, the Board of Divinities was abolished, and fundamentally reforming the shrine system became unavoidable. Shrines had to cope with this new situation amidst the social panic, confusion, and uncertainty.

Therefore, the Association of Shinto Shrines was established on February 4, 1946 as a national organization to cope with this new situation, and it became the central mechanism through which shrines coped with postwar problems. Needless to say, the Shinto Directive was fundamental for legally adjudicating all problems related to shrine Shinto under the Occupation. The key points of the Shinto Directive were transferred into the draft document of the new Japanese Constitution almost completely verbatim (especially Articles 20 and 89). Even after the Occupation had ended, American policy continued to exert a strong pressure on Shinto.

That is to say, once Shinto's connection with the state and its institutions was severed, the state not only became unable to offer Shinto financial support but was also foreclosed from turning to the religion educationally and ceremonially. Accordingly, the following big changes occurred:

1   Coinciding with the alterations in the Constitution, the old imperial household rules and law became invalid, and new laws arose to take their place. In the new Imperial House Law, the Ceremony of Transferring the three divine treasures (*sanshu no jingi*) and the performance of the Great Harvest Festival, part of the Imperial Enthronement Ceremony were deleted. The traditional rites of the imperial household came to be considered "private matters of the imperial court," and thus the state could not participate. Even after the new Constitution,[7] although the imperial court continued, as in the past, to give offerings (*hōhei*) to the old *kanpeisha* shrines, this shortly was discontinued even as a private ceremony. Imperial offerings were continued only at the shrines formerly devoted to imperial worship, and even so, the participation of the emperor was curtailed.

2   Not only was all Shinto influence removed from public and state rituals, celebrations, and so on, but Shinto elements within the moral training of public education, history, Japanese language instruction, and so on were also completely eliminated. Indeed, education came to include active criticism of and attacks on Shinto.

The Shinto Directive uses an expression calling for the elimination of "extreme" nationalism. Its actual meaning is to expel all nationalism and militarism that existed in the Japan of the past. This also resulted in the destruction of bronze statues of soldiers from the Russo-Japanese War and the Sino-Japanese War and the annulment of Emperor Meiji's Imperial Rescript on Education. Intense propaganda abetting this was spread through the radio and newspapers, and "old Japan" was censured beyond all reason. Angry throngs raising the communist red flag marched on the Imperial Palace on several occasions.

Along with directing the government to fully implement the Shinto Directive, GHQ even instructed "revisions of ceremonies, events and etiquette," and "the drawing up of new collections of model prayers" (*norito*). This policy of interference even influenced the religious observances within the shrines. (Note: D.C. Holtom is a good source that reveals an American's view on Japanese Shinto.[8])

The establishment of the Association of Shinto Shrines and its character

The trend of the Allied Occupation's policies was predictable before the Shinto Directive was issued. To cope with these policies, the need was keenly felt for a national organization that would consolidate the power of the entire nation's shrines, both to protect them from the chaos and to preserve shrine Shinto's power in society. It was natural that the organizers turned first to other religious groups as models. To give one example, one set of bylaws that was drafted was called, "The Shrine Organization of the Fundamental Teachings" (Jinja Honkyō), adopted a "head administrator system," and stipulated that "the head administrator would rule on whether religious doctrines were right or wrong."[9]

The Occupation authorities denied the prior legal system that publicly acknowledged shrines as state institutions, and they gave orders that shrine Shinto should become more like other religions. However, shrines have their own unique history and character. People had some strong opinions, such as,

This kind of head administrative system is really essentially far removed in character from shrines. To establish a head administrative system, decide on doctrines and scriptures, and have a central religious association giving orders and controlling each shrine throughout the country both organizationally and spiritually is neither possible nor even desirable.

The specific nature of the Association of Shinto Shrines as we see it today developed as a consequence. The Association was established without having any definitive doctrines and scriptures. At the time, this was a particularly wise approach to take. If the Association had established doctrines and scriptures and had installed a head administrator with authority to issue rulings about doctrine, the Association's head administrator would have had to establish a MacArthur style Shinto which the Allied Forces wanted to institute.

When the Association was founded, Shintoists balked at giving it central authority not only over doctrine but also over the management of shrines as individual corporate entities; each shrine forcibly asserted its own sovereignty. As a consequence, the Association has very little actual regulatory and governing authority. By contrast, from then until today, although there are various points at issue, it is undeniable that the Association, newly established under the pressing conditions of the times, has no legal or historical basis whatsoever for even exerting authority over individual shrines throughout the country. (Three groups formed the womb that created the Association: The Research Institute for the Study of Imperial Classics, the Greater Japan Board of Deities (Dai-Nippon Jingikai), and the Association of Devotees of the Ise Jingū (Jingū Hōsaikai). Even though all these earlier groups supported shrine people, they did not have commanding status over them. Ruling authority belonged solely to the state's Board of Divinities.)

There is a natural, straightforward reason why the Association did not assume any powerful regulatory or governing authority. It is quite possible that if such a system with centralized power had been established forcibly, the Association would have fallen apart by itself.

However, without powerful national supervision from either a religious organization or the state, an unfortunate phenomenon has risen in the shrine Shinto—what we might call the negative effects of "laissez-faire, non-interventionism." Priestly misconduct and errors that would have been punished under government supervision are now overlooked. And fiscal mismanagement, which also would deserve punishment, is allowed to continue until they finally collapse as institutions. Appointing new people is inhibited, personnel matters needing attention pile up, and a spirit for religious education and learning slackens. I should note that this will be an important topic in the future for shrine administration.

The history of the Association of Shinto Shrines

The "draft of the new Constitution" was announced soon after the Association of Shinto Shrines was founded. It paralleled the Shinto Directive and raised a number of important issues, but one of the most urgent problems that shrines needed to solve at that time was the issue of shrine property. When the government administered shrines, the property within shrine precincts was generally regarded as state-owned land. But, in order to comply with Article 89 in the Constitution, it was necessary to transfer state-owned land to the shrines. In order to do this, regulations were rushed. At the time right after the Association was founded, this was the most important matter to resolve. And that was what the first secretary general of the organization, Miyagawa Munenori, accomplished on his own. (Note: "Miyagawa Munenori's Reminiscences, Informal Talk," *Jinja shinpō senshū* 1 (February 4, 1951)).

Along with the issue of shrine property, the GHQ also had a serious interest in changing the ritual character of the Ise Jingū. In particular, serious negotiations continued over whether Yasukuni Shrine and the shrines for the protection of the nation should continue to exist. Although the Association completely acquiesced to the Shinto Directive, it considered the preservation of the traditions of the Ise Jingū and shrines, in line with the strictures of the Directive, as its fundamental policy.

In 1948 General Secretary Miyagawa resigned, and the next person to be appointed to the post was Hase Toyoo. Shrines had already been separated from state administration, and some felt a danger that shrine rites and prayers might fall into disorder. General Secretary Hase sought to point a way toward a new model for rites as well as prayers. However, there was intense pressure from the Occupation authorities concerning this issue, and these revisions had to be carried out through negotiations under the authority of the Occupation. (Note: Compare and contrast the prayers (*norito*) in the pre-war period when shrines were under government control, such as those found in "Rites for Shrines" at the levels of and under the official and national shrines (*kankokuheisha*), the sample prayer texts of the Association of Shinto Shrine, and, again, these when they were revised again in 1955 after Japan emerged from the Occupation. For many who do so, the traces of the Occupation's policy of interference are clear.)

Throughout these times, shrines were dealt with as if they were individual religious corporations as defined by the Religious Corporations Ordinance. Another law, the

Religious Corporations Act, was enacted during the time of Takashina Ken'ichi, the third General Secretary. The legislation this time followed a proposal drawn up by the Ministry of Education and was carried forward under the direction of the GHQ. The Association, under Mr. Takashina's leadership, was dissatisfied that shrines were treated like new religious corporations, despite the fact their circumstances were completely different. Nonetheless, given the political exigencies of the time, the Association decided to agree in principle to the legislation, but went no further than issuing a statement expressing some qualifications and reservations. (Note: In the Diet's public hearing over enactment of the Religious Corporations Act, the Association's director Tomioka Morihiko, while agreeing in principle with the legislation, publicly declared that shrines should perhaps in the future request their own independent law over their legal status.)

When discussing the history of the Association of Shinto Shrines under the Occupation, it is important to make special mention of the regular construction of a new shrine and transfer of the enshrined object from the old to the new location (*shikinen sengū*) at the Ise Jingū, which is the main ritual center of the Association.

The Grand Shrine's *shikinen sengū* was scheduled for 1949. However, it had to be canceled after the Shinto Directive was issued and the new Constitution came into effect. This was one of the few times in Japanese history that the regular removal and replacement of the shrine buildings of Ise had not been done on the appointed date. It had previously occurred once because of the rebellions during the Yoshino Dynasty and a second time as a result of the chaos of the Warring States Period, making this only the third time such a change had taken place.[10] The Grand Shrine's worshippers organized the fifty-ninth Ise Jingū Shikinen Sengū Support Organization (the chair was Satō Naotake and the director was Miyagawa Munenori) and carried out a campaign for soliciting funds throughout the country. It was a unique *shikinen sengū*, for it was the first time since the founding of the Ise Jingū that it was accomplished through private donations from ordinary citizens. The Association, as well as Shintoists from shrines throughout the country, was quite active in the movement to support the shrine rebuilding. The result of this was that the Sengū Festival was held in the fall of 1953, and it should also be noted that this movement to support Ise clearly revealed that Ise Jingū enjoyed nationwide (non-sectarian) support.

The issue of post-war Shinto doctrine

The aim of the Shinto Directive of the Occupation army was to sever the connection between the emperor and the Japanese state, on one hand, and Shinto on the other. The discourse of pre-war Shinto meant national learning (*kokugaku*), which taught about the excellent qualities of our national polity (*kokutai*), and imperial learning (*kōgaku*), an effort that tries to make clear the reasons why we should venerate the imperial family. However, the Shinto Directive has exactly as its key goal the termination of national and imperial learning.

Although the tendency of *kokugaku* and *kōgaku* in the early modern period had as its aim the restoration of ancient Shinto, these terms clearly mean *the modern growth and development of Shinto*. Moreover, it is no exaggeration to say that Emperor Meiji perfected Shinto's modern growth and development. Shinto as a faith for Japanese who live in modern times was revealed by Emperor Meiji.

Emperor Meiji completely changed the character of the rituals both within the Imperial Palace and at the Ise Jingū and other shrines. Through Emperor Meiji, Shinto was established as a living faith for a new age. Even non-Japanese confirm Emperor Meiji's important status in terms of Shinto's history, and therefore, the points they especially wanted to denigrate were the ritual observances, the system, and the spiritual quality (*seishin*) that Emperor Meiji originated (Note: See Holtom, *Modern Japan and Shinto Nationalism*).

However, it must be said that among the Japanese people, some cannot presume to fathom the depths of Emperor Meiji's thinking. It is really foolish that they find seemingly little value in what Emperor Meiji created just because it was accomplished not all that long ago historically speaking. Matters of faith should not be valued just because they are old. Even if they are new, it does not mean that they are less valuable. Shinto is by no means an ancient cultural asset. (The only ritual observances in the Imperial Palace said to be traditional are the Niinamesai (New Tasting Festival), the Toshigoi Festival, and kagura performances before the Imperial Sanctuary (Kashikodokoro). Almost all of the rest of the large and small festivals were creations of Emperor Meiji.)

Many books on national learning and the imperial learning were prohibited by the authorities during the Occupation. Scholars and thinkers connected to Shinto were treated as "nationalists" and banished from public office and teaching positions. Under such pressure against Shinto doctrine, it was natural for Shinto scholarship to tend to concentrate in the areas of folklore and religious studies. Shrine Shintoists who gathered around the Association of Shinto Shrines tended to be deeply rooted both in national learning and the imperial learning. This is expressed in the way they regard "Ise Jingū as their main ritual center." And therefore, their scholarship seems to have been completely eclipsed for the time being. On the other hand, the folkloristic research into Shinto of Yanagita Kunio and Orikuchi Shinobu, was given the freedom and opportunity to develop substantially, even under the Occupation.

Religious studies and the folklore of Orikuchi and others were considered ancillary fields in Shinto doctrine up to that time. While this scholarship was given the opportunity to disseminate widely among Shintoists, we should by no means overlook the fact that it also enriched their scholarship and broadened their field of vision. "Shinto," which had put down deep roots within the Japanese ethnic mentality, was discovered anew through this new meaning. And, in addition, through comparative research between Shinto and foreign religions, Shinto came to be studied in a broader perspective. These are the points of progress in Shintoist scholarship.

However, the disinterested research and scholarship into Shinto, coming from such areas as religious and folklore studies, should not be the mainstream of Shinto doctrine. Even when this research is favorable towards Shinto, it essentially amounts only to research done by outsiders; they can just as easily be negative as positive in their outlook. (Note: Correctly balancing this relationship between the outsider's scientific and the insider's approach in Shinto studies and education is quite a difficult problem. See "Editorial," *Jinja shinpō*.)

What is obviously called for is the construction of a Shinto theology that would be at the mainstream of Shinto scholarship. However, not much of consequence has happened up to now. It is safe to say that future efforts in this direction are eagerly anticipated.

The new phenomenon of post-war shrines

At the time when the Association of Shinto Shrines was founded, members of the Shinto community, who were now separated from the emperor and the state, established a basic administrative provision that "the Association and each shrine have as their main ritual center (*honshū*) the Grand Shrine." Although the meaning of *honshū* is not exactly clear, it can be interpreted as meaning "a place of ritual observances which should receive the highest respect." There are a number of problems with this, however, since the shrines, which were once united under the emperor and the state, were prohibited from having any direct connection with the emperor. Nonetheless, the desire to keep that unification through pious faith in the Grand Shrine which enshrines the imperial ancestor probably gave rise to this principle. Yet, a connection between Ise Jingū and individual shrines remains theoretically unclear. Further, a folklore-based understanding of Shinto also ends up taking the critical stance that this kind of connection between the Grand Shrines and shrines is forced and unnatural. They would have administrative provisions reformed to read, "The Ise Jingū is the main ritual center of the Association," and scratch out the sentence, "each shrine has the Ise Jingū as the main ritual center."

On the one hand, the idea that "Ise Jingū is central" has very strong roots. There is also a way of thinking that considers Ise Jingū the main headquarters of shrines throughout the country and treats each shrine like a branch of and subordinate to the Grand Shrine. This way of thinking is difficult to support given both the history and the essence of the Grand Shine as well as other shrines. However, even if you are able to mount a rational argument, following religious and folklore studies, that separates ordinary shrines from the emperor, the state, or the Grand Shrine, what becomes "Shinto religion" in this sense is limited to the earliest primitive faith. It simply cannot retain a vitality that will make it continue to live on as a Shinto faith for contemporary Japanese people.

The one characteristic phenomenon of the present day that should not be overlooked is that each shrine's faith retains a national and ethnic consciousness. This is due to their tendency to maintain close ties to the Grand Shrine, which is ensured through the cooperation of shrines nationwide in the regular construction of a new shrine and transfer of the enshrined object from the old to the new location (*shikinen sengū*) at the Ise Jingū and also by the annual distribution of the shrine amulets (*jingū taima*).[11] (Note: The emperor, the citizenry and Shinto in the period of the Tokugawa shogunate.)

* * *

Besides the above, another remarkable phenomenon of post-war shrines that should be noted is what could be called their tendency toward (high) culture (*bunka shugi*). This is a popular trend that spread throughout the country in the difficult times immediately after the end of the war, when Shinto's significance as a faith was not widely recognized. It was enabled when Shintoists as well as their supporters made a strong case that their shrines hold properties that are culturally important in both tangible and intangible ways; they realized a certain measure of success in this effort. This tendency toward culturalism, together with shrines' connections with the tourist industry, is a phenomenon of the times, exerting a great influence over the financial operation of contemporary shrines. We must not overlook the critical influence of this trend on authentic shrine faith.

In addition to the tourism industry, the large number of weddings at each shrine should be seen as a new phenomenon in the way shrines operate. Weddings in Japan used to be part of family celebrations and were not performed at public shrines. But, in the Meiji period, after the Crown Prince was married in the Imperial Sanctuary in the palace and common people's ceremonies began to be performed before the *kami* at Hibiya's Great Shrine,[12] this type of wedding spread throughout the country.[13] After the war, such occasions as marriage ceremonies and funeral rites came under renewed scrutiny in relation to shrine management; it was in any case difficult for ordinary Japanese to associate funerals with shrine Shinto, and shrine-based funerals did not see any great development. Yet the connection between a happy event like a marriage and shrines was considered extremely natural, and wedding ceremonies were performed at shrines in each area.

This contains serious issues that, together with the development and changing views of the family and marriage since Meiji, should be a matter for considerable reflection. However, despite the fact that weddings before the gods became popular, it is regrettable that there has been no significant research into the Shinto view of marriage. It is one of the open questions assigned to future Shintoists to investigate. (Note: The problem of Shinto and funerals, and shrines and graveyards.)

In light of a history where funeral rites and graveyards were monopolized by Buddhism, even members of the Shinto community since the Edo period discussed whether Shinto had any role to play, and, in early Meiji, there was a noteworthy controversy over Shinto's view of purity.

However, in 1882, the government prohibited "the participation of shrine priests in funeral rites," and grave sites remained almost totally a monopoly of Buddhist temples. After the end of the war, these laws were abolished, but, other than the occasional involvement of shrines in this area, nothing all that remarkable is apparent.

Contemporary Shintoists' views (Part 1)

Given the pressures Shinto was under in the post-war period, the religion had little energy left to attempt to make its views known publicly. To a large extent, Shintoists responded to this heavy pressure passively. Immediately after the Association of Shinto Shrines was founded, it published its weekly newspaper, the *Jinja shinpō*. It was a notice board for publicly expressing the views of the shrine community, and one could describe it as offering a window to the outside world. Thus, let us reflect here on the views of Shintoists as expressed mainly through the *Jinja shinpō*.

The editorial stance of the *Jinja shinpō* at the time of its founding was extremely understated. Yet, given the tenor of journalism right after the occupation, it offered a distinctive perspective. In particular, the publication publicly stated the case for protecting and maintaining Yasukuni Shrine; it also noted the flaws of the new Constitution and requested future amendments.

In the midst of the journalistic turmoil after the time of the Occupation, *Jinja shinpō* was unique among periodicals in that it consistently and strictly observed the use of honorifics for the imperial family and always admired the sacred virtue of Emperor Meiji; this shows the spirit which remained among Shintoists.

In 1948, under the direction of the GHQ, the government started to reorganize national holidays. At this juncture, members of the Shinto community insisted on preserving Foundation Day (Kigensetsu) and other national holidays, actively resisting the currents of the times. The views of Shintoists were not only expressed in the *shinpō* but also in radio debates, where many students were mobilized and, in line with their view, large numbers of petitions were sent to the Diet.

Although public opinion was against the reorganization of national holidays, the government and the Diet, following the implicit instructions of the GHQ, carried out the reorganization. However, this movement of Shintoists did not just remain a temporary opposition movement, but afterwards has been doggedly continuing as a movement for the "restoration of the Kigensetsu."

* * *

In 1949, the Japanese Communist Party rapidly expanded its power as a political party. Following the overt principle of the separation of religion and state, Shintoists also strongly believed that the policy should be one of non-interference. The *Jinja shinpō* worked intensively, however, on anti-communist education and the Shinto Youth Association (Shintō Seinen Kai) entered the foray by organizing anti-communist speeches in the streets.

In 1950, a bill for the abolition of era names was being discussed in the Upper House of Councilors. At a public hearing by the Councilors, the Association's Head Administrator, Takatsukasa Nobusuke, insisted on the continuation of era names, and the *Jinja shinpō* appealed to Shintoists throughout the country for support. Public opinion against the measure grew and finally stopped the proposal all together.

The next year, a bill was introduced to reform the existing Religious Corporations Ordinance. Although voices of discontent grew among Shintoists concerning this matter, they did not actively oppose the bill but simply expressed their reservations. Because I have already discussed this matter, I will omit it here.

Contemporary Shintoists' views (Part 2)

In June 1950, the Korean War began, and MacArthur's American army was dispatched to the Korean peninsula. The American Occupation, having deprived Japan of any military power for self-defense, smugly and for their own advantage incited arguments among the Japanese with respect to rearmament. There were some who argued in favor of a Japanese volunteer militia participating in the war. Public opinion in Japan wavered over this. The opinions of Shintoists concerning the situation were not uniform.

At this time the *Jinja shinpō* as well as the Shinto Youth Association were absolute in their opposition to "the establishment of an enslaved colonial army." There were not a few who were opposed to this position, viewing it as lending support to the left wing's anti-war movement. However, both Shinpōsha and the Youth Association considered this movement critically important in freeing the Japanese from their spiritual subordination to the United States and helping them realize true independence and peace (*bansei taihei*).[14]

* * *

In 1951, the Religious Corporations Act was put in effect and a deliberative council was established. Its composition, however, reflected the bureaucratic smugness of the Ministry of Education, pointedly ignoring the authority of the Association of Shinto Shrines. The Association vehemently objected to this, and the *Shinpō* issued a series of denunciations of the Ministry. When the authorities at the Ministry finally proposed a compromise, they ended up completely following the views of the Association.

In 1952, in the national election for the Upper House of Councilors, Miyagawa Munenori was nominated by people connected to shrines and stood for the election. Although he lost, Miyagawa argued for "reform of the Imperial House Law" (Kōshitsu Tenpan).[15] It should be noted that this was an open expression of Shintoists' opposition to the consequences of the Shinto Directive.

* * *

Around the same time as Miyagawa Munenori's argument for the reform of the Imperial House Law, some Shintoists made their views known regarding public education and public national ceremonies after the war.

Article 20 of the Japanese Constitution inherits the aims of the Shinto Directive in every respect. It prohibits religious education and religious activities related to the state and its agencies.[16] For this reason, the state suppressed not only Shinto-inspired moral education but also education which offered knowledge related to Shinto.

For this reason, history, social studies education, and so on have become seriously deficient. Since around the end of the Occupation, Shintoists have frequently noted this and eventually insist on addressing this problem in public education.

Article 20 is also interpreted as banishing all religious ceremonies from the national public square. The commonly accepted understanding of the law is that public funerals for those with distinguished national service or for consoling the spirits of the war dead must all be ceremonies that are non-religious in character. In the shrine community, many are opposed to such a legal interpretation and assert that rituals such as funerals, which are recognized social customs, may naturally be performed in a religious style.

Actually, the state funeral for the chair of the Upper House of Councilors, Mr. Matsudaira Tsuneo, was performed in the Shinto style at the Upper House. The funeral of the chair of the Lower House of Representatives, Mr. Shidehara Kijūrō, and of Mr. Ozaki Yukio[17] were performed under the responsibility of the Diet in Buddhist style. Indeed, Shinto, Buddhist, Christian, and other religious representatives were to accompany the delegates on the boat dispatched abroad to retrieve the remains of those who died in battle.

However, soon after we were freed at the end of the Occupation, the government's National Memorial Service for the War Dead had any religious hue thoroughly eliminated from it. The two interpretations of Article 20—the one which completely separates religion from the state and that favored by Shintoists—remain at odds with each another.

Along with Article 20, Article 89 of the Constitution is also a source of recurring controversy.[18] One example that is especially noteworthy is the incident over a military unit of the Self-Defense Force at Shibata, Niigata. A number of soldiers had erected a small shrine to worship the gods of Ise as well as Yasukuni, and the authorities forced them to dismantle it. When this incident happened, the *Shinpō* protested to the government, and the matter was concluded when Secretary of the Japan Defense Agency Sunada Shigemasa acknowledged that "the authorities had gone too far."[19]

The Shinto Directive ordered the removal of god shelves (*kamidana*) from public buildings. Thus, *kamidana* and small shrines were removed from public buildings all over the country, although there are a few national sanitariums and some railway offices and police stations where they still remain. The Shinto Directive became invalid at the same time as the Occupation's administration ended. We can add that there is one other problem that should also be noted. That is the view, which arose among jurists and politicians throughout these controversies, that "shrines are not religious."

Reflecting upon these arguments, what is most evident is that the "Constitutional issue" occupies a very important central place for solving all these societal issues related to the shrine community.

For this reason, in 1953, Yoshida Shigeru, then secretary general of the Association of Shinto Shrines, requested that the *Jinja shinpōsha* "do research on the Constitution."[20] The next secretary general, Hirata Kan'ichi, was bequeathed all aspects of this policy concerning the Constitution. *Shinpōsha*'s views on this were published, expressing a sentiment shared by many Shintoists. In 1955, both the board conference of the Association of Shinto Shrines and the National General Representative Assembly of Shrine Parishioners (Zenkoku Ujiko Sōdaikai) expressed considerable interest in the constitutional problem.

Thus, it is not too much to say that in the near future many issues regarding shrine Shinto will be focused, directly or indirectly, on constitutional issues.

Notes

1 John Breen and Mark Teeuwen, *A New History of Shinto* (Chichester, UK: Wiley- Blackwell, 2010), 6.
2 Susumu Shimazono, "State Shinto and Religion in Post-War Japan," in *The SAGE Handbook of the Sociology of Religion,* eds. James A Beckford and N.J. Demerath III, (London: Sage Publications, 2007), 699–701.
3 The Hague Conventions of 1899 and 1907, the latter being signed on October 18, 1907, were the first treaties that, along with the Geneva Conventions, created a set of international laws on war and war crimes. The provisions Ashizu notes in his essay are found in the 1907 treaty, section number 4.
4 Nashimotonomiya Morimasa (1874–1951) was a member of the imperial family and decorated soldier, who was army field marshal, chief councilor on military affairs, and a recipient of the Grand Cordon of the Supreme Order of the Chrysanthemum. He was appointed chief priest at Ise in 1943.
5 Hiranuma Kiichirō (1867–1952) was a pre-war right-wing politician and government official who briefly served as prime minister of Japan in 1939 and an unofficial senior advisor to Hirohito in World War II. He was sentenced to life imprisonment as a Class-A war criminal.
6 Mizuno Rentarō (1868–1949) was a politician, and government official from the Meiji through Shōwa periods who served several important capacities in government as Home Minister and Minister of Education. After the war he was initially listed (but later exonerated) as a Class-A war criminal due to his association with a wartime nationalist society, the League for a Prosperous Asia (Dai Nippon Kōa Dōmei).
7 See also Ashizu Yoshihiko, "The 'Shinto Directive' and the Constitution: From the Standpoint of a Shintoist," *Contemporary Religions of Japan* 1 (1960):16–64.
8 Ashizu is referring to Daniel Clarence Holton's *Modern Japan and Shinto Nationalism: A Study of Present-Day Trends in Japanese Religions* (Chicago: The University of Chicago Press, 1943), published in Japanese as *Nihon to tennō to shintō* (Tokyo: Shōyō Shoin, 1950).
9 The organization under the same name exists as an independent inclusive shrine organization and as a religious judicial person (*shūkyō hōjin*), that is, an independent religious organization not supported by public funds. It calls itself a *kyō*, like many other religious organizations; in particular, it follows the precedent of thirteen *kyōha* or sect Shinto religious organizations that were made separate entities from State Shinto in the Meiji period, such as Tenrikyō, Konkōkyō, and so on.
10 These eras were 1334–93 and 1467–1573 respectively.
11 These are amulets from the Ise Jingū that are blessed at New Year and distributed through associated shrines throughout the country. In the pre-war period, they were spread to each household and ward under the auspices of the Ise Jingū Agency of Shrine Corporations (Kanbesho) that was established in 1900, and the National Association of Shinto Priests (Zenkoku Shinshokukai) in 1898. In 1946, this duty was carried out by the Association of Shinto Shrines, whose goal is to install an amulet in every household throughout the country. The amulets are generally understood to be symbolic emblems of the imperial ancestor, signifying the sun goddess Amaterasu Ōmikami's divine virtue (*shintoku*) and one's gratitude for her divine blessings (*shin'on*). See "Jingū taima," *Encyclopedia of Shinto*, http://eos.kokugakuin.ac.jp/modules/xwords/entry.php?entryID=283.
12 Founded in 1880 by the decision of Emperor Meiji, Tokyo Daijingū (as it is known now) enshrines many deities related to the imperial house and particularly Ise Shrine, including Amaterasu, Toyouke, and Yamatohime no Mikoto. After Emperor Taishō (the then Crown Prince) and his consort were married in 1900, this shrine invented the wedding in Shinto style.
13 Known as "marriage rites before the gods" (*shinzen kekkon*).

14 This phrase is based on a line from the Shōwa emperor's imperial decree formally accepting the Potsdam Declaration, in effect, surrendering and ending the war, which was given in a radio broadcast on August 15, 1945. The line reads, "However, it is according to the dictates of time and fate that we have resolved to pave the way for a grand peace for all the generations to come (*bansei no tame ni taihei o hirakan to hossuru*) by enduring the unendurable and suffering what is insufferable."

15 The law regulating the imperial family, such as Imperial House Council, imperial succession, and so on that was first established in 1889 and reorganized in 1947.

16 See note 5 above.

17 Ozaki Yukio (1858–1954), was a well-known politician known as the "*kamisama* of Constitutional government" who participated in the founding of the Constitutional Reform Party (1882) and was a member of the Japanese parliament for sixty-three years.

18 See note 5 above.

19 Ashizu is referring here to Sunada Shigemasa (1884–1957), a well-known politician who was appointed as Defense Secretary in 1955.

20 Yoshida Shigeru (1885–1954), with the same name as the Prime Minister, was a pre-war bureaucrat in the Home Ministry and Tokyo city, and later became the Minister of Health and Welfare, and the Minister of Munitions. After the war, he worked with other Shintoists for the survival and reorganization of shrine Shinto.

28

MURAKAMI SHIGEYOSHI

The emperor as a deity in human form and the development of imperial house rites
(1977)

Murakami Shigeyoshi (1928–1991) was a scholar of religion. Born and raised in Tokyo, he graduated from the Faculty of Letters at the University of Tokyo, finishing in 1952 with a specialization in religious studies, and continued on to graduate studies. He became a lecturer at various colleges, such as the University of Tokyo and Keiō University, while pursuing an active scholarly life, in particular, research into modern new religious movements. In 1959, he won the prestigious Japanese Association for Religious Studies Anesaki Memorial Award for outstanding scholarship with his book *Kindai minshū shūkyōshi no kenkyū* (Research into the History of the Modern Folk Religions, 1958). Influenced by Marxist historiography, Murakami's approach was "to consistently view religion and religious developments in terms of prevailing economic, political, and social conditions."[1]

However, Murakami is best known for his groundbreaking work about the emperor system and what he termed "State Shinto," the phrase used in the Supreme Commander of the Allied Powers' (SCAP) Shintō Directive, which abolished the pre-war state-supported, emperor-centered shrine system and the educational curriculum with its militaristic brand of ultra-nationalism. His book, *Kokka shintō* (State Shinto, published in an inexpensive Iwanami paperback edition in 1970), was the first comprehensive study of the topic, and was widely influential, elevating Murakami to the status of an opinion leader for the political left, whose writings reached a general reading public. Murakami welcomed the post-war democracy and called attention to the dangers posed by continuing the emperor system and by the movement to reestablish Yasukuni as an officially supported state shrine.

Murakami's argument is simple but powerful. In his preface to *Kokka shintō*, he argues that during the eighty years from the Meiji Restoration to the end of the Great Pacific War, State Shinto was a religious political system which exerted a profound influence over every corner of the Japanese people's lives and consciousness.[2] As Hayashi Makoto has argued, Murakami's model of State Shinto as a religious phenomenon was both structural and historical.

Structurally, he defined it as an ethnic "religious political system" that combined shrine Shinto and imperial household Shinto with a set of national rites and an ideology of national polity (*kokutai*) at its core. It was supra-religious in character, privileged over and above the other organized religions that were officially allowed by the Meiji Constitution. While the terms ethnic and national religion were used by some pre-war scholars, Murakami argues (unlike Katō Genchi) that this national religion is unique in the history of world religions. Historically, Murakami developed a four-part periodization of State Shinto's history: (1) The formative period (1868–87), (2) the doctrinal completion period (1889–1905), (3) the systematic completion period (1900s to the late 1920s), and (4) the fascist national religion period (1931–45).[3]

Needless to say, many critics have attacked Murakami's work for oversimplification, historical inaccuracies, errors in his periodization schema, and exaggerated claims about the coercive force and range of State Shinto's influence. These include prominent critics such as Yasumaru Yoshio, Nakajima Michio, Sakamoto Koremaru, Nitta Hitoshi, Shimazono Susumu, and Isomae Jun'ichi, among others.

The following selections are excerpts from a later work *Tennō no saishi* (Imperial Rituals, 1977) taken from Chapter 3 "The emperor as a deity in human form" and Chapter 4 "The development of imperial house rites."

THE EMPEROR AS A DEITY IN HUMAN FORM AND THE DEVELOPMENT OF IMPERIAL HOUSE RITES (1977)

Chapter 3: The emperor as a deity in human form

Part 4: The establishment of imperial authority—the Imperial House Law, the Imperial Constitution, and the Imperial Rescript on Education

The promulgation of the new Constitution

The Imperial House Law[4] and the Constitution of the Empire of Japan were promulgated in the twenty-second year of the Meiji era, on the Foundation Day, February 11, 1889. A formal announcement to the imperial ancestors took place at the Imperial Ancestor's Altar (Kōreiden) in the Imperial Palace and formal announcements were also made at shrines throughout the country.

The enactment of the Imperial House Law and the Constitution of the Empire of Japan signified the establishment of imperial authority in the modern state; this also created the legal foundation of the Japanese empire as a religious state. Coinciding with these enactments, Emperor Meiji offered the following announcement to the divine spirits of his imperial ancestors:

> I do humbly and solemnly swear to the divine spirits of the imperial founder and the other imperial ancestors that, following their eternal and great plans, I have succeeded to and secured the divine throne of the emperor, and I will be true to their ancient intentions and preserve them from corruption.
>
> In consideration of human progress in the course of its affairs and with the advance of civilization, I deem it expedient to give clarity and distinctness to the instructions that have been bequeathed by the imperial founder and the other imperial ancestors. I shall establish the Imperial House Law and the Constitution, with the formulation of specific provisions, so that, on the one hand, we may possess an explicit guide for the course we are to follow for posterity, and that, on the other, our subjects shall thereby enjoy a broader means of giving us their support, and that these means shall continue to the end of time.

We will thereby ensure greater stability of the country and promote the welfare of the people's life within the boundaries of the Japanese islands.

We now establish the Imperial House Law and the Constitution. These laws amount to only a model for the rule of government, bequeathed by the imperial founder and by the other imperial ancestors. That I have been so fortunate, in keeping with the tendency of the times, as to accomplish this work, I owe to the glorious spirits of the imperial founder and of the other imperial ancestors.

I now reverently make my prayers for divine help from them and from my father, and also make a solemn oath to them that neither now nor in the future will I fail to be an example to our subjects in the observance of the laws hereby established.

May the divine spirits witness this solemn oath.[5]

The Imperial Constitution was granted by the emperor, who also decided upon its provisions. As this proclamation indicates, the Constitution was founded and became supreme because of the religious authority of the emperor, who was united in spirit with his imperial ancestors. The proclamation is permeated by religious concepts such as imperial ancestors, divine spirits, and divine assistance, and it shows the intense religious character of the state. The emperor ruled the empire of Japan, and the imperial throne and its succession were governed by the Imperial House Law. The first "Tennō" chapter in the Imperial Constitution established his royal prerogatives.

The Imperial House Law

Imperial House Law is comprised of twelve chapters and sixty-two articles in the following order: Chapter 1 "Succession to the imperial throne," Chapter 2 "Succession and enthronement," Chapter 3 "Majority, institution of the empress and the heir apparent," Chapter 4 "Style of address," Chapter 5 "Regency," Chapter 6 "The imperial guardian," Chapter 7 "The imperial family," Chapter 8 "Imperial hereditary estates," Chapter 9 "Expenditures of the Imperial House," Chapter 10 "Imperial family litigation and disciplinary matters," Chapter 11 "Imperial family council," and Chapter 12 "Supplementary provisions," which contains several provisions related to the emperor, the imperial house, and the imperial family.

Article 1 stipulates, "The imperial throne of Japan shall be succeeded to by male descendents in the male line of imperial ancestors." Article 2 establishes that the succession to the imperial throne is based on the succession of the male line through the oldest son. Cases where there is not an eldest son in the male line are considered in detail later in Chapter 1, so that there is no confusion about the order of succession.

Article 10 of Chapter 2 on the rules for succession and enthronement specifies that "Upon the demise of the emperor, the imperial heir shall ascend to the throne and shall acquire the divine treasures of the imperial ancestors." It is stipulated that the emperor has the throne until the end of his life but that the new emperor must ascend to the throne on the day of his death and will receive the three divine treasures (*sanshu no jingi*). This provision publicly bestows an official national status on the three divine treasures, although the real character of the treasures is not fully clear. Article 11 stipulates that "The ceremonies of enthronement shall be performed and a Great Harvest Festival (Daijōsai) shall be held at Kyoto," and Article 12 stipulates one era name per reign.

The edict associated with Imperial House Law states that "Our imperial throne of the Japanese empire is gifted with heavenly blessings, and successive generations have been bequeathed it, and so it has come to me" and thus emphasizes the everlasting successive generations of imperial rule. The enactment of Imperial House Law legally completed the imperial house system over the course of more than twenty years following the Meiji Restoration. Later, on February 11, 1907 (Meiji 40) Imperial House Law was further expanded with eight supplementary articles enacted.

The emperor in terms of the Imperial Constitution

The Imperial Constitution was the legal foundation of the state; it was in that sense a pair to the Imperial House Law, and it was comprised of seventy-six articles in seven chapters. The chapters listed consecutively are: "The emperor," "Rights and duties of subjects," "The Imperial Diet," "The ministers of state and the Privy Council," "The judiciary," "Finance," and "Supplementary rules." It thus proposed the articles undergirding the state system of government.

The main purpose of the Imperial Constitution was to legally establish imperial authority. Chapter 1, "The emperor," totaled seventeen articles, all of which dealt with the emperor's status, character, and royal prerogatives. Article 1 establishes that "The empire of Japan shall be reigned over and governed by a line of emperors unbroken for ages eternal." Article 3 establishes his sacred inviolability, stating that "The emperor is sacred and inviolable."

Articles 4 through 16 lay out the imperial power both politically and militarily, and Article 17 provides for a regency. According to these provisions, the emperor is the head of state and controls the right of sovereignty (Article 4), possesses legislative power, and orders the promulgation and execution of laws (Articles 5 and 6). The emperor orders the convening, opening, closing, and proroguing of the Imperial Diet and the dissolving of the House of Representatives (Article 7). In extreme situations the emperor can issue imperial ordinances when the Imperial Diet is not in session, and moreover he can issue necessary orders within the existing legal framework (Articles 8 and 9). The emperor has the authority to appoint and dismiss officers in the civil and military administrations (Article 10).

Article 11 stipulates that, "The emperor has the supreme command of the army and navy." It thus establishes that the emperor is the supreme military commander of the imperial army and navy. He has the power to organize the army and the navy, decide how many soldiers are in the standing army, declare war and peace, and conclude treaties (Articles 12 and 13). In addition, the emperor declares martial law (Article 14), confers honors (Article 15), and grants amnesty (Article 16).

These provisions gave the emperor complete authority over the government's political and military operations and made him a sacred being. The second chapter of the Imperial Constitution lays out the various rights of subjects and their duties of military service and paying taxes. The rights of "subjects," however, did not include freedom of thought, and freedom of religious belief was only recognized "within limits not prejudicial to peace and order, and not antagonistic to their duties as subjects." Furthermore, Article 31 stipulates that "The provisions contained in the present chapter shall not affect the exercise of the powers appertaining to the emperor, in times of war or in cases of a national emergency," which clearly indicates that the extreme power of the emperor prevails over human rights.

The enactment of the Imperial Constitution signified the judicial fulfillment of the doctrine of national polity (*kokutai*). This is perhaps most apparent from the imperial rescript which was issued when the Constitution was promulgated:

Whereas we make it the joy and glory of our heart to behold the prosperity of our country, and the welfare of our subjects, we do hereby, in virtue of the supreme power we inherit from our imperial ancestors, promulgate the present immutable fundamental law, for the sake of our present subjects and their descendants.

The imperial founder of our house and our other imperial ancestors, by the help and support of the forefathers of our subjects, laid the foundation of our empire upon a basis, which is to last forever. That this brilliant achievement embellishes the annals of our country, is due to the glorious virtues of our sacred imperial ancestors, and to the loyalty and bravery of our subjects, their love of their country and their public spirit. Considering that our subjects are the descendants of the loyal and good subjects of our imperial ancestors, we doubt not but that our subjects will be guided by our views, and will sympathize with all our endeavors, and that, harmoniously cooperating together, they will share with us our hope of making manifest the glory of our country, both at home and abroad, and of securing forever the stability of the work bequeathed to us by our imperial ancestors.[6]

As the supreme commander of the military

As we have seen, the emperor's authority that came from Imperial House Law and the Imperial Constitution, combined in the secular sphere his power as the military commander with his political power as the sovereign and head of state. The idea of giving the emperor direct control over the army and the navy, keeping any political interference away from the military, initially came from the Takebashi disturbance in August, 1878 (Meiji 11), the first insurrection that occurred within the Japanese army.[7] After its suppression, Field Marshal Yamagata Aritomo throroughly indoctrinated all officers and men in the military with the ideology of imperial supremacy and made it his urgent business to prevent the infiltration of ideas of personal freedom and people's rights.[8] That same year in October, he issued "The Admonition to the Military." This discusses the inviolability of the emperor and the strict observance of military order and prohibits soldiers from participating in politics.

When the movements for freedom and human rights gained ground, the government permitted the adoption of a legislative political body based on the Constitution granted by the emperor. The promise was to prepare for the extension of the people's rights in the future, putting the military under the direct command of the emperor. At the same time, the government stiffened its policies of isolating the army from politics including the Imperial Diet and using military power to suppress human rights. On January 4, 1882 (Meiji 15) the Imperial Rescript to Soldiers and Sailors (Rikukaigun Gunjin no tamawaritaru Chokuyu, abbreviated Gunjin chokuyu) was issued.[9]

The Imperial Rescript to Soldiers and Sailors states:

Since I have control over the great power of leading the army, although I delegate various duties to the people in my service, at its foundation I alone command and this is not something that I should entrust at all to our subordinates . . . Soldiers and sailors I am your Supreme Commander-in-Chief!

This clearly suggests that the emperor had supreme command of the armed forces. In addition, the Imperial Rescript to Soldiers and Sailors posited five articles that military personnel were ordered to uphold as imperial commands: (1) "Soldiers and sailors should regard loyalty as their essential duty," (2) "They should manifest the proper respect," (3) "They should esteem bravery," (4) "They should honor faithfulness and righteousness," (5) "They should make simplicity their aim." The essence of this edict was in Article 1, which ordered unconditional allegiance to the emperor and prohibited military personnel's participation in politics. Despite the preface to the rescript, which states, "Emperors have for generations commanded our country's armies," there are few historic examples (other than the legendary time when the Japanese state was founded) of an emperor directly commanding an army. The emperors only appointed military commanders, although even this task has become nominal after the middle ages. Considering the traditional character of the emperor, it was extremely rare to see a soldier emperor; rather, the supreme command is the basis of the militaristic character of the imperial Japanese state.

The emperor was regarded as the Grand Marshal (*daigensui*) of the army and navy forces. *Gensui* means marshal. The Board of Marshals and Fleet Admirals (Gensuifu) were set up as the supreme advisory council for the Japanese armed forces in 1898 (Meiji 31). Those army and navy chiefs who had particularly distinguished themselves were bestowed the title of *gensui* and promoted to the Board. The emperor as the Grand Marshal occupies the highest military rank above even the chiefs of the army and navy who were marshals and fleet admirals. His lapel and shoulder pins indicating his rank were a paulownia leaf and flower crest added to the chief's three stars on a gold backing (for the army) or three cherry blossoms (for the navy). After the emperor became the Grand Marshal, his formal photographs were largely taken in military uniform, and it was *de rigueur* for all male members of the imperial family, starting with the crown prince, to become servicemen in the army or navy. Ordinary citizens thought of the emperor as a military leader above all else, and he became nothing other than "His Majesty the Supreme Commander" (*daigensui heika*) who led the imperial armed forces.

The prerogative of the emperor depended on his religious authority along with his supreme political and military power. In religious terms the emperor's ritual prerogative came from his official status as the highest priest (*daikannushi*) of State Shinto (*kokka Shintō*). This conception of the imperial ritual prerogative derives from the tradition of the emperor as an officiating priest-king and can be regarded as the enhancement of this tradition.

The emperor as an absolute god

The emperor, with his political, military, and ritual prerogatives, was regarded as a *kami* while he was alive. He was described as a manifest deity (*arahitogami*) or manifest *kami*, a deity of the spirit world who takes a distinctive form in this world (*akitsumikami*). In the modern imperial system, the emperor is conceived as a living god, in contrast to the times before the Meiji restoration when he was considered to be a priest-king. The new fundamental conception of the emperor as a living god is a sharp departure from the imperial tradition, and it was newly created after the Meiji Restoration. Previously, throughout the history, the emperor had primarily been charged with officiating rituals, but he or she never was a *kami*; while it was believed that he united himself with a deity on ritual occasions and held magical and spiritual powers that no one else could possess, there was no doubt that the emperor remained human.

At the time when the ancient imperial system was flourishing, the emperor was compared to a deity. We see words like *arahitogami* (in the "Records of Emperor Keikō," *Nihonshoki*) and *akitsumikami* (*Manyōshū* #1264), which means *kami* originally supposed to be invisible who manifests a visible form in this world. Additionally, in book 18 of the *Manyōshū* there is also a poetic verse by Ōtomo no Miyuki that intones, "Because his majesty is a *kami . . .*" In ancient times, honorific expressions such as *arahitogami, akitsukami, akitsumikami* were widely used, along with "*sumera,*" *sumeraki, sumeroki,* and *sumeramikoto,* and so on, which honored the reigns of dynamic sovereigns. These were honorific titles based on the natural assumption that the emperor was human, and they did not mean that he was a deity in and of himself.

Since ancient times we have amassed a tremendous number of documents which hold records of emperors. Including the *Kojiki* and *Nihonshoki,* which are official histories, there are plenty of stories of emperors who committed atrocities or acted according to human greed. In the middle ages, there are also examples of those who argued that even an emperor would receive divine punishment and die an untimely death if he opposed Buddhism. We find this in the writings of Nichiren, who described the emperor as a political figure and never recognized his religious authority (See his *Shijō kingo dono gohenji, Sushun Tennō gosho*). In the Edo period, Empress Kōken's special affection for the monk Dōkyō offered good fodder for *senryū* poems,[10] and while the masses knew that the emperors were of noble blood, they did not consider them sacred and inviolable.

The imperial absolutism since the Meiji Restoration finally established an emperor in the Imperial Constitution as a sacred and inviolable *kami.* But this new attribute of the emperor, the concept of divinity, is a monotheistic concept that is quite different from the concepts of *hitogami* and living *kami* (*ikigami*). While these latter arose from a thoroughly shamanistic Japanese folk religion, the former is really close to the concept of God in Christianity.

The idea among the ruling classes in the modern imperial Japan of making the emperor an absolute god was heavily influenced by Christianity. Considering the emperor as a deity appearing in human form transformed him into an embodiment of supreme virtue and absolute truth separate from humanity. This was the natural result of the State Shinto system where the emperor's religious authority dominated religions such as Buddhism, Christianity, and sect Shinto, all of which had their own universal values. The modern imperial system in Japan was decidedly different from other monarchical systems precisely because of the way the emperor was regarded. He was in his person both unified with the imperial clan *kami* (*kōsoshin*) and his ancestral spirits (*kōrei*), and a god who embodied universal values.

The complex nature of the emperor

The emperor who was manufactured by the modern imperial system thus offered a complex structure. He was a deity appearing in human form, while retaining supreme power in the secular areas of politics and the military and in the religious area of ritual. Even though this concept was filled with contradictions, the emperor's individual person unified his fundamental nature as well as his supreme powers in the sacred and the secular. For example, as the supreme military commander, the emperor's main duty was to find the most effective way to slaughter the enemy in war. It is virtually impossible to reconcile this duty with the idea that the emperor was an *arahitogami* who supposedly embodied supreme virtues. Furthermore, although he had complete military and political power, as a *kami* the emperor had played no part in taking responsibility, while those who were supposed to advise him had to take responsibility.[11]

This kind of fundamental contradiction, coupled with the thorough indoctrination by the imperial system, caused untold havoc and corruption, both intellectually and morally.

However, we can say that its root really lay in the contradiction between the attributes ascribed to the emperor and the functions he performed.

The Imperial Rescript on Education

The Emperor, who had become a deity appearing in human form, issued his Rescript on Education (Kyōiku ni kansuru Chokugo) on October 30 of the following year, 1890 (Meiji 23), after the Constitution was issued. This laid the emperor's religious authority squarely at the foundation of education. In its opening, the Imperial Rescript on Education states, "Our imperial ancestors have founded our empire on a basis broad and everlasting, and have deeply and firmly implanted virtue." Virtue is clearly considered to come from imperial forbears. Next, it states, "Our subjects ever united in loyalty and filial piety have from generation to generation illustrated the beauty thereof. This is the glory of the fundamental character of our empire, and herein also lies the source of our education." Thus, the edict emphasizes loyalty and filial piety, and considers the source of education to be rooted in Japan's national polity (kokutai). Continuing, it ordered,

> Ye, our subjects, be filial to your parents, affectionate to your brothers and sisters; as husbands and wives be harmonious, as friends true; bear yourselves in modesty and moderation; extend your benevolence to all; pursue learning and cultivate arts, and thereby develop intellectual faculties and perfect moral powers; furthermore, advance public good and promote common interests; always respect the Constitution and observe the laws; should emergency arise, offer yourselves courageously to the state; and thus guard and maintain the prosperity of our imperial throne coeval with heaven and earth.

This is a list of the Confucian virtues, and they are to be respected and defended ultimately by offering everything to the emperor and the state in times of war and other emergencies. It goes on to state, "So shall ye not only be our good and faithful subjects, but render illustrious the best traditions of your forefathers," and adroitly combines the concepts of allegiance to the emperor and ancestor worship. In the final paragraph, it states,

> The way here set forth is indeed the teaching bequeathed by our imperial ancestors, to be observed alike by their descendants and the subjects, infallible for all ages and true in all places [domestic and foreign]. It is our wish to lay it to heart in all reverence, in common with you, our subjects, that we may thus attain to the same virtue.

These virtues are enshrined as a teaching of the imperial ancestors; this in turn transformed into universal virtues of humanity that transcended the state and the times. Regarding these virtues that come from the emperor as universal underscores that he, a deity in human form, embodies universal values.

The Imperial Rescript on Education was distributed to each school as the virtual doctrinal canon of State Shinto, and special repositories in its honor were constructed on the school grounds (hōanden). Preceding the promulgation of the Imperial Rescript on Education, imperial picture portraits of the emperor and empress (goshin'ei) were granted, initially to a Shiba District Elementary School in Tokyo, on February 11, 1890 (Meiji 23). The next year, in 1891 (Meiji 24), on June 17, the "Regulations for Elementary School of National Holidays and Festival Rites" were established. In this way the *goshin'ei,* the virtual sacred icons of State Shinto, and The Imperial Rescript on Education, its doctrinal text, and the *Kimigayo,* the sacred song of State Shinto, were incorporated into school education. Education under the emperor system was intensified in short order through State Shinto events and rites performed at schools.

The notion of the emperor as an *arahitogami* was disseminated so that it regulated every corner of Japanese people's consciousness, and it eventually manifested an intensely political-religious function without peer in modern nation states. War in the name of the emperor was regarded as a "holy war," which would shine the bright imperial power throughout the world and ultimately bring "all the corners of the world under one roof" (*hakkō ichiu*) [of the Japanese empire]. Foreign invasion was justified in order to spread the god-emperor's universal values throughout the world. Whether in times of war or peace, everyone was expected to show unlimited allegiance by "sacrificing their own self-interest" (*messhi hōkō*) for the emperor and the state.

Chapter 4: The development of imperial house rites

Part 1: Regulations for imperial house rites and the emperor's enthronement

The emperor has held the authority to preside over imperial house rites as long as there has been an emperor, and this was referred to as his royal ritual prerogative (*saishi taiken*) during the period of the modern emperor system. However, neither in the Imperial Constitution nor in the Imperial House Law there were any clear provisions about that prerogative, and its legal standing was unclear. The Imperial Household Ritual Ordinance, which generally established imperial house rites, was issued as Imperial House Rule #1 on September 18, 1908 (Meiji 41); this was nearly twenty years after the Imperial House Law had been enacted. This was issued together with an imperial rescript countersigned by Count Tanaka Mitsuaki, Imperial House Minister, which stated, "I have officially approved the regulations concerning imperial house rites and promulgate them here."

The Imperial Household Ritual Ordinance amounted to twenty-six articles in three chapters. These were legal regulations which systematized the emperor's rites and the ceremonial order, which was outlined in detail in the supplementary rules. In the first chapter, "General Rules," a distinction is drawn between the "major ceremonies" of the imperial house rites, which the emperor performs himself, and the "minor ceremonies" carried out by the chief ritualist, who served as the emperor's proxy over such matters, and handling mourning and preparatory purification is prescribed. The emperor, while in mourning, did not perform Mikagura[12] or Azuma Asobi,[13] and further, those in mourning were unable to serve or attend any rites. It was further ordained that ritual officiates undergo purification on the day of and two days preceding the great ceremonies, and on the day of the small ceremonies.

The second chapter, "Major ceremonies" (*taisai*), stipulates that, "In the major ceremonies, the emperor celebrates the festival himself, leading the imperial family and officials. At times when the emperor is in mourning or there is some other misfortune, the festival noted in the previous clause shall be performed by a member of the imperial family or the chief ritualist" (Article 8). Next, it set up ten regularly scheduled rites and three special rites as major ceremonies, and indicated the locations and the specific times for performing them:

Festival of Origins (Genshisai), January 3, at the Kashikodokoro, Kōreiden, and Shinden

Foundation Day (Kigensetsu), February 11, at the Kōreiden (afterward at the three shrines at the Imperial Palace)[14]

Spring Festival for Imperial Spirits (Shunki Kōreisai), celebrated on the vernal equinox, at the Kōreiden[15]

Spring Shinden Festival (Shunki Shindensai), celebrated on the vernal equinox, at the Shinden

Emperor Jinmu Festival (Jinmu Tennōsai) April 3, at the Kōreiden (with offerings made at the Jinmu mausoleum)[16]

Autumn Festival for Imperial Spirits (Shūki Kōreisai), celebrated on the autumnal equinox, at the Kōreiden

Autumn Shinden Festival (Shūki Shindensai), celebrated on the autumnal equinox, at the Shinden

The First Fruits Festival (Kan'namesai), October 17, at the Kashikodokoro (making offerings and worshipping Ise Shrine from afar)

The New Tasting Festival (Niinamesai), November 23–24, at the Shinkaden (presenting food offerings to the *kami* (*shinsen*) and offerings made at Ise Jingū and official and national shrines)

Memorial Service for the Previous Emperor (Senteisai), on the anniversary of the passing away of the previous emperor, at the Kōreiden (offerings made at his mausoleum)

Memorial Service for the Spirits of the Three Imperial Ancestors Preceding the Last Emperor (Shikinensai), on each anniversary of their passing away, at the Kōreiden (offerings made at his or her mausoleum)

Memorial Service for the Preceding Empress (Shikinensai), on the anniversary of her passing away, at the Kōreiden (offerings made at her mausoleum)

Memorial Service for the Deceased Empress (Shikinensai), on the anniversary of her passing away, at the Kōreiden (offerings made at her mausoleum)

Furthermore, with respect to the New Tasting Festival, the law stipulated that the emperor should perform a ceremony for spirit pacification (*chinkon*) at the Ryōkiden[17] on the previous day; on years when the Daijōsai is performed, the New Tasting Festival is not celebrated. In addition, the memorial services (*shikinen*) were designated to take place on the third, fifth, tenth, twentieth, thirtieth, fortieth, fiftieth, one hundredth, and every hundredth year thereafter. When the Emperor Jinmu Festival (Jinmu Tennōsai) and the Memorial Service for the Previous Emperor (Senteisai) coincided with the *shikinen*, they were performed at the Kōreiden and the imperial mausoleums. But festivals at the Kōreiden were to be performed by the chief ritualist.

The other four rites were established as festivals next to the great ceremonies: (1) rites offering formal notice about great events of state or the imperial house given at Ise Jingū, the three Imperial Palace shrines, Emperor Jinmu's mausoleum, and the mausoleum of the previous emperor; (2) the rite dedicating the new shrine (*sengū*) constructed at Ise Jingū; (3) the rite for moving between the main shrine (*honden*) and the temporary shrine at the occasion of the reconstruction of the three shrines of the Imperial Palace; (4) the rite for moving the spirit token or tablet of the emperor, the previous empress dowager, and the empress dowager into the Kōreiden. The dates of these ceremonies were determined by the emperor and announced by the Imperial House Minister.

For the "Minor Ceremonies" (*shōsai*), Chapter 2 required that

> in the minor ceremonies the emperor offers worship himself, leading the imperial family and the officials, and the chief ritualist performs the ceremony. When the emperor is in mourning or when there is some other misfortune the worship noted in the previous clause will be offered by a member of the imperial family or the chamberlain. (Article 20)

The next provision defines the four regular and four special minor ceremonies, the specific dates, and the places where they are to be performed.

New Year Rite (Saitansai), January 1, at the three shrines in the Imperial Palace

The Festival for a Bountiful Year (Kinensai), February 17, at the three shrines in the Imperial Palace (offerings made at Ise Jingū and official and national shrines)

Classical Theatrical Dance in Honor of the Deities (Kashikodokoro Mikagura), mid-December, at the Kashikodokoro

Celebration of the Emperor's Birthday (Tenchō Setsusai), every year on the Emperor's birthday, at the three shrines in the Imperial Palace

Annual Rites for the Three Previous Emperors Preceding the Last Emperor (Sentei izen Sandai no Reisai), every year on the respective anniversaries of the emperors' passing, at the Kōreiden

Annual Rite for the Preceding Empress (Sengō no Reisai), every year on the anniversary of the preceding empress's passing, at the Kōreiden

Annual Rite for the Deceased Empress (Kōhi taru Kōgō no Reisai), every year on the anniversary of the current empress's passing, at the Kōreiden

Annual Rite for the Emperors from Emperor Suizei up to the Emperor Fourth Generations Past (Suizei Tennō[18] ika Sentei izen Yondai ni itaru Rekidai Tennō no Shikinensai), every year on the anniversaries of the emperors' passing, at the Kōreiden

In addition, preceding the New Year rite, the emperor should perform a prayer to the four directions (*shihōhai*) unless he was in mourning or there was some other calamity. The ceremonies of moving spirit tablets of the empress, crown prince and princess, the first son of the crown prince and his spouse, the sons and the brothers of the emperor and their spouses, the daughters and the sisters of the emperor, the other imperial princes and their spouses, and the other imperial princesses to the Kōreiden were classified as the rites next to minor ceremonies. On these occasions, the emperor did not offer the worship unless there were some special circumstances.

Supplementary rules in the regulations for Imperial Household Ritual Ordinance consisted of volume one "Major Rites" (*daisaishiki*) and volume two "Minor Rites" (*shōsaiskiki*). "Major Rites" set the ritual arrangement in the order of ceremonies at the Kashikodokoro, the Kōreiden, and the Shinden, and at the altar for imperial offerings to the *kami* (Shinkaden) of the New Tasting Festival (Niinamesai).[19] This also covered the ceremonies for spirit pacification (*chinkon*) occurring the day before the New Tasting Festival, ceremonies for dispatching imperial envoys to Ise Jingū, ceremonies for making offerings at Ise Jingū, ceremonies at imperial mausoleums, and ceremonies for dispatching imperial envoys to mausoleums. Additionally, this volume explained ceremonies making offerings at imperial mausoleums, ceremonies for moving the spirit tablets of emperors (ceremonies reporting to the imperial ancestors at the Kōreiden, ceremonies at the Temporary Hall for Enshrining the *Kami* (Karidono), and ceremonies performed by the emperor himself at the Kōreiden).

The "Minor Rites," were arranged as follows: ceremonies at Kashikodokoro, ceremonies at the Kōreiden, ceremonies at the Shinden, the prayer to the four directions, *mikagura* at the Kashikodokoro, the ceremony of sending an imperial envoy to Ise Jingū, and making offerings at Ise Jingū. They also included ceremonies for moving spirit tablets of the empress, crown prince and princess, the first son of the crown prince and his spouse, the sons and the brothers of the emperor and their spouses, the daughters and the sisters of the emperor, the other imperial princes and their spouses, and the other imperial princesses to the Kōreiden (ceremonies reporting to imperial ancestors at the Kōreiden, ceremonies at the Temporary Hall for Enshrining the *Kami* (Karidono), ceremonies at the Kōreiden).

Major rites in supplementary rules were performed on a large scale and governed by exceedingly detailed regulations, down to the manner of dress. The text adds a warning to prepare for times when the emperor is an infant, "When the emperor is dressed in diapers, a shrine priestess will carry these." In addition, it considers the possibility of extreme situations. It adds an annotation that even for major and minor rites, "Depending on the circumstances, one should perform these by simplifying what is in the explanatory notes of these rituals."

Regulations for the enthronement and supplementary rites

Foundation Day (Kigensetsu) of the year following the Imperial Household Ritual Ordinance, February 11, 1909 (Meiji 42), commemorated the twentieth year since the issuance of the Imperial Constitution. On this commemorative day, the Enthronement Ordinance and Supplementary Rules were issued as imperial house regulations. The rule of Emperor Meiji had already lasted over forty years. Since his health was uncertain, the government might have prepared for the next successor's coronation and Enthronement Ceremony and the Great Harvest Festival (Daijōsai) and formulated the regulations that generally stipulated these. The same day, provisions for a regency, for investiture of the crown prince, and for the imperial family's coming-of-age ceremony were issued as imperial house regulations, with the supplementary rules. Thus, important legal rules were provided concerning the imperial house.

The Enthronement Ordinance consisted of eighteen articles. Imperial House Minister Count Tanaka Mitsuaki, Cabinet Prime Minister and Finance Minister Marquis Katsura Tarō, and all the Cabinet Ministers all signed the public imperial edict. Each of its articles stipulated the fundamental matters on the succession, era names, order of the Enthronement Ceremony, and the Great Harvest Festival. As for supplementary rules, the first volume consisted of "Rites for the succession" and volume two, "Rites for the accession to the throne and the Great Harvest Festival."

The Enthronement Ordinance prescribed in the first article, "At the time of the imperial succession, the chief ritualist shall immediately perform the ceremony at the Kashikodokoro and shall report the details of succession at the Kōreiden and Shinden." It was determined that the era name change immediately after the succession. The new era name would be set by the emperor after consultation with advisors of the Privy Council, and it would be issued publicly by official proclamation (Articles 2 and 3).

Articles 4 through 18 prescribe the Enthronement Ceremony and the Great Harvest Festival. They are performed continuously in the fall and winter, and an official for major rites is appointed in the court who oversees their management. The Imperial House Minister and the ministers in the cabinet sign and issue a public proclamation of the dates of ceremonies. If the dates have been decided, that will be announced before the three shrines at the palace, and the imperial envoys sent to and offerings made at Ise Jingū, at the mausoleum of Emperor Jinmu, and at the mausoleums of the previous four emperors (Articles 4 to 7).

The announcement at Emperor Jinmu's mausoleum was an innovation at the time of Emperor Meiji's Great Harvest Festival. Article 7 prescribes that "At the time when the Enthronement and Great Harvest Festival are set to be performed, it shall be announced at the Kashikodokoro and Kōreiden, and an imperial envoy shall make announcements at Ise Jingū, the mausoleum of Emperor Jinmu, as well as at the mausoleums of the four former emperors." This effectively abolished the announcement at Emperor Tenji's tomb, which had been considered to represent ancient imperial tombs in Kyoto, and Emperor Jinmu's mausoleum came to serve that function for all imperial tombs.

An imperial edict was issued concerning the rice fields for the Great Harvest Festival, selecting the direction of the *yuki* to the south and east, and the *suki* to the west and north of Kyoto. The rice fields for offerings to the *kami* (*saiden*) were decided by the Imperial Household Minister or the local head of government, and the owner was responsible for the procedures which preceded the offerings of the newly harvested rice.[20] When the time of the ripening of the rice had arrived, an imperial envoy was dispatched who performed the rite for picking out the rice ears (*nuibo no shiki* or *nukiho no shiki*) (Articles 8 to 10).

Article 11 specifies that, "In advance of the time of performing the Enthronement Ceremony, the emperor carries the divine treasures and moves together with the empress to the palace in Kyoto." On the day of the Enthronement Ceremony, the imperial envoy makes an announcement at the Kōreiden and the Shinden, while others are dispatched to make offerings at Ise Jingū, the Kōreiden, the Shinden and official and national shrines (Articles 11 and 12).

The Great Harvest Festival requires a spirit pacification ceremony (*chinkon*) the day before and a great banquet after the Enthronement Ceremony at the Daijōsai's end. After these rites are performed, the emperor and empress go to worship at Ise Jingū, the mausoleum of Emperor Jinmu and the mausoleums of the four previous emperors. After returning to Tokyo, the emperor and empress worship at the Kōreiden and the Shinden (Articles 13 to 17). In the Enthronement Ordinance, the word *essu* ("to meet a member of the nobility") is particularly apropos for this worship (*sanpai*) and veneration (*hairei*). This word was used because the Great Harvest Festival made the emperor one with the sacred mirror (*yata no kagami*) of the three divine treasures; he was thus equivalent to the imperial ancestral *kami*, imperial spirits, the *kami* of heaven and earth, and the myriads of deities existing in this world. Even regarding the empress and the crown prince, who were connected to the emperor, this word came to be used. The Enthronement Ceremony and Great Harvest Festival could not be performed during the mourning period for his parents (Article 18).

In volume one of the supplementary rules, "Rites of succession," the ritual order is set out in detail as follows: the rites of the Kashikodokoro (three days), announcement rites at the Kōreiden and the Shinden, the rite of transfer of the sword and seal, and the rite of imperial audience after the succession.

The second volume "Enthronement and Great Harvest Festival rites," details the rules for the rites of announcing to the deities the day of enthronement at the Kashikodokoro, the Kōreiden and the Shinden; the rite of making offerings at Ise Jingū; and the rite of making offerings at the mausoleum of Emperor Jinmu and the mausoleums of the previous four emperors. This volume also explains the rite for determining the rice fields for offerings to the gods (*saiden*), the rite for picking out the rice ears (*nuibo* or *nukiho*), the rite for the imperial procession to Kyoto, the rite of departing for the Kashikodokoro Spring Palace (at the Kyoto Palace), the rite of making announcements on the day of the Enthronement Ceremony at the Kashikodokoro and the Shinden, and the rite on the day of the Enthronement Ceremony before the Kashikodokoro. Also discussed are the rite at the Shinden on the day of the Enthronement Ceremony; the Kagura rite at the Kashikodokoro the day after the Enthronement Ceremony; the spirit pacification rite one day before the Daijōsai; the rite of dispatching an imperial envoy to Ise Jingū, the Kōreiden, the Shinden, and official and national shrines; and the rite of making offerings at Ise Jingū on the day of the Great Harvest Festival. Additionally, the volume covers the rite of making offerings at the Kōreiden, the Shinden on the day of the Daijōsai, the rite of offering consecrated rice to the Kashikodokoro on the day of the Daijōsai, the rite of the Daijō Shrine, the rite of offering rice at the Yukiden,[21] and the rite of offering rice at the Sukiden.[22] It also explains the rites of the grand banquet one day after the Enthronement Ceremony and the Great Harvest Festival and of the grand banquet on the second day after, the rite of imperial worship at Ise Jingū after the Enthronement Ceremony and the Great Harvest Festival, and the rite of imperial worship at the mausoleum of Emperor Jinmu and the mausoleums of the four previous emperors after the Enthronement Ceremony and the Great Harvest Festival. These regulations, like the supplementary rules for the Imperial Household Ritual Ordinance, were extremely detailed. In the case that the emperor was a minor or an infant, it offered detailed prescriptions of when a court lady and when a previous empress, an imperial princess, or a prince's spouse should hold the emperor. Since the enthronement rules were for a great ritual event occurring once in a reign, these supplementary rules were not permitted to be abbreviated or shortened in any way and were instituted wholesale just as they had been stipulated.

* * *

Wedding ceremonies before the kami

In 1899 (Meiji 32), with the marriage of the crown prince close at hand the following year, the Imperial House Marriages Ordinance was formulated in haste as a forerunner of the Imperial Household and Family Ordinance. The next year, in 1900 (Meiji 33) on May 10, the crown prince held his wedding ceremony before the Kashikodokoro with Sadako, the daughter of Duke Kujō Michitaka[23] (later Empress Teimei). The rite was in Shinto style. In March of that year, it had been announced at Hibiya Shrine that the wedding ceremony before the *kami* would follow the imperial court's ceremony, and a mock wedding ceremony was publicly performed by the students at the girls' peerage school. Weddings before the *kami* did not increase all that much even after this event; the norm continued to be home weddings without a religious component. But, from 1940, wedding ceremonial halls increased. As they became more widely used, weddings before the *kami* were accepted as an ancient Japanese tradition, and they became widespread and commonplace in daily life.

The Great Wedding Ceremony, which had become standardized as a supplementary ritual in the Imperial Household and Family Ordinance, included a gift-exchange rite at the three sacred halls of the palace; a rite for notifying the deities of the marriage contract at the three sacred halls of the palace; ritual offerings at the mausoleums of former emperor and empress, at the mausoleum of Emperor Jinmu, and at Ise Jingū; a ceremonial presentation of decorations of honor and swords; a formal announcement of the day of the wedding; and a ritual offering letters (customarily *waka* poems were offered to the empress and she would give a reply). The day of the wedding ceremony required an announcement ceremony for the crown princess, a rite of the empress entering the palace, a rite before the Kashikodokoro and a ceremonial audience at the Kōreiden and Shinden, a ritual offered meal at the great dining table (*daishōji*), a rite of the *mikayo* rice cake (a rice cake served on the first to the third night of the wedding), ceremonial audiences with the empress dowager and the grand empress dowager (*tai kō taigō*), receiving the morning greeting from the emperor and empress, and palace banquets (an evening feast on the first and second day). Additionally, after the wedding, the procedure was for the emperor and empress to present themselves at Ise Jingū, the mausoleum of Emperor Jinmu, and the mausoleums of former emperor and empress.

* * *

The imperial family's rights and duties

Through the workings of its ceremonial system, the imperial house established its foothold as the linchpin of the modern imperial state. Various rules and regulations related to the imperial house and the Imperial House Law determined the registry of honorary titles, as well as the rights and duties of the imperial family below the emperor. Under Articles 17 and 18 of the Imperial House Law, the emperor, grand dowager empress, dowager empress, and crown princess held the title of "his [her] majesty" (*heika*), and others in the imperial family had the title of "his [her] royal highness" (*denka*). The *hei* of *heika* means the stairs used to enter the palace and is an honorific title signifying someone of nobility who can only be reached through the efforts of his attendants who are at the bottom of the stairs. The registry of the imperial family below the emperor is different from the family registry of ordinary citizens and was recorded in the imperial family registry (*kōtōfu*), which included the birth registry and life history of the empress, emperor, etc. (*daitōfu*) and the imperial family birth registry and life history (*kōzokufu*). Following tradition from ancient times, the emperor does not have a family name, but the members of the imperial family have surnames (*miya*), and new surnames are bestowed by the emperor. There were fourteen collateral imperial family houses (the *miya* houses). Formally, each house was ranked in the following order: Chichibu no Miya, Takamatsu no Miya, Mikasa no Miya, Kan'in no Miya, Higashi Fushimi no Miya, Fushimi no Miya, Yamashina no Miya, Kaya no Miya, Kuni no Miya, Nashimoto no Miya, Asaka no Miya, Higashikuni no Miya, Kitashirakawa no Miya, Takeda no Miya.[24] Further, accompanying the "annexation" (*heigō*) of Korea in 1910 (Meiji 43), the old Korean royal house, the Yi, was treated as a royal family on par with the imperial family. The honorific title for Korean royalty and aristocracy was royal highness (*denka*), and they were treated formally in the order of the Yi royal family, the Ikon, and the Iu aristocratic houses.

The imperial family had special privileges, which included the right to succeed to the throne, the right to hold public office, the right not to have ordinary laws and ordinances be applicable to them, honorary entitlements, and special prerogatives in terms of property and estates. Where public offices were concerned, an adult male member of the imperial family was allowed to be appointed as regent, to become a member of the imperial family council, to participate in the privy council, and to become a member of the House of Peers. Additionally, they had special rights to be appointed to offices; the crown prince and his children when they reached ten years of age were appointed as military officers in the army and navy. This commission did not depend on recommendations from the cabinet. It was based on the minister of the imperial house's recommendation to the emperor and was promoted outside of the mandatory minimum term regulation. Also, in the absence of special circumstances, a prince or monarch would be appointed an army or navy officer upon reaching the age of eighteen. They did not have to wait for a vacancy, and when they fulfilled the minimum term, they would be promoted immediately.

Along with special privileges, the imperial family had special obligations. In order to preserve the dignity of and obedience toward the imperial house, the imperial family members were limited in areas such as duties, travel, and residence, and their relations and property ownership. The imperial family could not join public organizations or become members of the Diet. The boys of the family entered the Gakushūin school, which was under the direct control of the Imperial House Ministry, and girls enrolled in Gakushūin's girls' school.

* * *

Myth education in the emperor system

The taboos, together with the completed ceremonial system, kept the imperial house strictly isolated from the eyes of the general public. Strange taboos that a modern society today can barely imagine were repeatedly devised. A special palace vocabulary, started in the Heian period and remote from modern Japanese, was commonly used at the palace; in effect, it formed a completely different world. The people were not permitted to know anything about the daily life of the emperor and the imperial family and looked up to the emperor and the imperial house earnestly as beings who were "above the clouds." Soldiers and sailors, as a part of their military education, were forced to memorize the five articles of the Imperial Rescript for Soldiers and Sailors. Students were forced to memorize the names of successive emperors from "Jinmu, Suizei, Annei, Itoku[25] . . ." to the current emperor, and, in addition, memorizing the Imperial Rescript on Education was strongly encouraged.

The emperor system's mythology also developed in tandem with the creation of its festival and ceremonies. Even concerning the origin of the three divine treasures, they created a consistent narrative by picking and choosing what they felt suitable from documents and many different explanations, inculcating it in young people by inserting it in compulsory national textbooks. In May 1937 (Shōwa 12), on the eve of the Sino-Japanese war, the Ministry of Education published the *Kokutai no hongi* (Cardinal Principles of the National Polity), distributing it to groups for indoctrination and schools throughout the country as a commentary on the fascist dogmas of the emperor system.

In this period, "the divine edict on the eternal sovereignty" (*tenjō mukyū no shinchoku*), which was bestowed to the divine grandson Ninigi no Mikoto by Amaterasu Ōmikami when he descended from the High Plain of Heaven, was treated as an imperial edict by elementary school textbooks on "national history" and "ethics" (*shūshin*):

> Then she commanded her august grandchild, saying: "This Reed Plain 1,500 Autumns Fair Rice Ear Land is the region which my descendants shall be lords of. Do thou, my august grandchild, proceed thither and govern it. Go! And may prosperity attend thy dynasty, and may it, like heaven and earth, endure forever."[26]

This divine edict was the sacred phrase that consolidated the religious foundation of the national polity (*kokutai*) of the empire of Japan. However, this sentence is nothing more than from a document that represents one line of transmission, which was recorded in book 1 in the opening paragraphs of part 2 of the "Age of the Gods" section of the *Nihonshoki*. Furthermore, what is "Ashigahara" (Reed Plains) in the original, changes into "Toyoashihara" by the Eikyō text, which is one of the textual variants. A sentence whose sources are as unclear as this was made absolute by the machinations of the state as the divinely inviolable words of the *kami*, and it forced all the people to believe it as a divine edict.

In this way, the development and expansion of the imperial house's ceremonial system stimulated the development of the emperor system's myths and systematized the fictional doctrine of the national polity (*kokutai*), which was far removed from historical fact. The modern state under the emperor system did nothing other than deepen its own self-contradictions as time went on by enlarging its rituals and myths until it ran out of room to maneuver.

Notes

1 H. Byron Earhart, "Translator's Introduction," in Murakami Shigeyoshi, *Japanese Religion in the Modern Century*, trans. H Byron Earhart (Tokyo: University of Tokyo Press, 1980), xiii.
2 Murakami Shigeyoshi, *Kokka shintō* (Tokyo: Iwanami Shinsho, 1970), 1.
3 Hayashi Makoto, "Religion in the Modern Period," in *The Nanzan Guide to Japanese Religions*, eds. Paul Swanson and Clark Chilson (Honolulu: University of Hawai'i Press, 2006), 208–12.
4 The law comprised rules regarding succession to the imperial throne, ascension to the throne, styles of address, the imperial family, and so on in minute detail. It was considered coequal in status to the new Constitution in terms of its importance and authority.
5 Ito Miyoji, trans. The Constitution of the Empire of Japan (1889), https://history.hanover.edu/texts/1889con.html.
6 Ibid.
7 This was a mutiny among 260 members of the imperial guard at Takebashi near the Akasaka Palace in Tokyo. The revolt, which was over grievances regarding remuneration for their part in putting down the Satsuma rebellion, was suppressed , and fifty-five of the insurgents were ultimately executed.
8 Yamagata Aritomo (1838–1922), originally from Chōshū, was an early leader in the Meiji Restoration, and later a key member of the Meiji oligarchy who dominated the government behind the scenes. As war minister, chief of the army general staff, and field marshal, he was an important military and political figure. He also encouraged Emperor Meiji to issue the Imperial Rescript to Soldiers and Sailors (Rikukaigun Gunjin ni tamawaritaru Chokuyu).
9 The Imperial Rescript to Soldiers and Sailors is a document that outlined the key moral tenets for the imperial army until its dissolution at the end of World War II.
10 A type of short poetry with three lines of seventeen or fewer syllables popularized by the Edo period *haikai* poet Karai Senryū (1718–90). These poems focus on human peccadilloes, foibles, and light humor.

11 This was specified in the Meiji Constitution, for example, in Article 55, "The respective ministers of state shall give their advice to the emperor, and be responsible for it."
12 Literally, "god entertainment," a Shinto theatrical dance performed before the *kami.*
13 Literally, "entertainment from the east" (Azuma); these were ancient Shinto song-dances that, by the Meiji period, had been revived and incorporated within official court rituals and were performed three times annually before the Kōreiden.
14 This commemorated the accession of Emperor Jinmu, the first mythical emperor of the imperial dynasty.
15 This collectively commemorated all imperial ancestors.
16 This commemorated the death of Emperor Jinmu.
17 A small hall located close to the three shrines of the Imperial Palace.
18 The second emperor of Japan after Jinmu.
19 A building to the west of the Kōreiden.
20 Part of the preparations involved in this festival was the selection of two districts for the growing of rice used in the ritual. The central rites for the festival were performed in two small buildings—the Yuki and Suki Halls—each with their separate rice fields. See Daniel C. Holtom, *The Japanese Enthronement Ceremonies with an Account of the Imperial Regalia* (London: Kegan Paul International, 1996), 97ff.
21 The ceremonial hall located to the east in the Daijō Shrine.
22 The ceremonial hall located to the west in the Daijō Shrine.
23 He lived from 1839 to 1906, and was a court noble, Meiji period politician, and patriarch of one of the five regent families (*gosekke*).
24 Imperial surnames were associated with the *shinnōke* and *ōke* branches of the imperial household and were considered part of the imperial family until 1947. The Seshū Shinnōke were four royal branches of the imperial family that until 1947 had the privilege to provide a successor to the throne if the main line failed to produce an heir. The other ten were called "princely houses" (*ōke*).
25 Emperor Jinmu, the legendary first emperor of Japan as related in the chronicle literature, followed by other emperors in the lineage.
26 W.G. Aston, *Nihongi: Chronicles of Japan from the Earliest Times to A.D. 697* (Rutland, VT: Charles Tuttle Co, 1972) 1:77.

29

KURODA TOSHIO

Shinto in the history of Japanese religion
(1981)

Kuroda Toshio (1926–93) is a famed historian of the Japanese medieval period. Kuroda grew up in the countryside in Toyama prefecture, in a family affiliated with the Jōdo Shin sect of Buddhism. He entered Kyoto University in 1945, and, after graduating in 1948, he continued to study as a graduate student until 1955; during his studies, he became deeply interested in the Japanese medieval period. He began teaching history, first, at Kobe University in 1955 and, later, at Osaka University in 1961. In 1989 he moved to Otani University, teaching there until his death.

Kuroda is best remembered as a revolutionary scholar who challenged not only conventional Japanese historiography but also prevailing modes of thought within Buddhist and Shinto studies. Beginning with his key 1963 essay, "Chūsei no kokka to tennō" (The Medieval State and the Emperor), followed by a succession of major works, he refuted the commonplace view that the Japanese middle ages was the time of the samurai. He proposed, instead, a more complex model of medieval polity that he called the "ruling elites system" (*kenmon taisei*). The warrior was not the sole proprietor of political sovereignty in this period but ruled alongside the older aristocracy and the powerful Buddhist schools of Nara and Kyoto.

In his later works, Kuroda increasingly focused on the important role of religion in undergirding this medieval political structure. Here he challenged another widespread academic view—that Zen, Pure Land, and Nichiren, the new schools of Buddhism that emerged during this period had supplanted the older schools of Buddhism. Kuroda argued instead that the eight old schools, which he collectively called the *kenmitsu* (exoteric-esoteric) Buddhism system, remained the most powerful intellectual, economic and political force of the time. Kuroda's seminal essay on Shinto, presented below, appeared in English in 1981 (the Japanese version appeared later, in 1983). This essay challenges the belief, which continues to be widely espoused today, that Shinto has existed from time immemorial as the indigenous religion of Japan. While Shinto in this sense was invented during the Meiji period with the forced separation of shrines from Buddhism, it cannot be found in earlier or later periods. As Kuroda has shown, the worship of the *kami* during the medieval period was intimately connected with *kenmitsu* Buddhist temple-shrine complexes, systems of esoteric Buddhist thought, and ritual practices. Kuroda finds claims to the contrary to be historically erroneous and based in the totally discredited ultranationalistic Shinto ideology that was anathema to him. It is ironic that even William Kenneth Bunce, the head of CIE's Religions Branch (later, Religious and Cultural Resources Division of the Civil Information and Education Section), in his report to the Occupation authorities, accepts uncritically the ideologically tinged notion of Shinto as the ancient indigenous religion of Japan.[1]

KURODA TOSHIO

SHINTO IN THE HISTORY OF JAPANESE RELIGION
(1981)

Translated by James C. Dobbins and Suzanne Gay

Shinto has long been regarded as a crucial element in Japanese religion that gives it distinctiveness and individuality. The common man's view of Shinto usually includes the following assumptions: Shinto bears the unmistakable characteristics of a primitive religion, including nature worship and taboos against *kegare* (impurities), but it has no system of doctrine; it exists in diverse forms as folk belief but at the same time possesses certain features of organized religion—for example, rituals and institutions such as shrines; it also plays an important role in Japan's ancient mythology and provides a basis for ancestor and emperor worship. In short, Shinto is viewed as the indigenous religion of Japan, continuing in an unbroken line from prehistoric times down to the present.

Many people have discussed the role of Shinto in Japanese history and culture, but depending on the person, there are slight differences in interpretation. These can be divided into two general categories. The first includes those who believe that, despite the dissemination of Buddhism and Confucianism, the religion called Shinto has existed without interruption throughout Japanese history. This has become the common man's view, and it is the conviction of Shinto scholars and priests particularly. The second includes those who think that, aside from whether it existed under the name Shinto, throughout history there have always been Shinto-like beliefs and customs (*shinkō*). This kind of interpretation is frequently found in studies of Japanese culture or intellectual history. This view can be traced back to the national learning (*kokugaku*) scholar Motoori Norinaga in the eighteenth century, and it is reflected more recently in Yanagita Kunio's work on Japanese folklore. The same trend is discernible in the writings of Hori Ichirō, who claims an opinion similar to Robert Bellah's and Sir Charles Eliot's.[2] Hori defines Shinto and "Shinto-ness" as "the underlying will of Japanese culture." He argues that Shinto has been the crucial element bringing the "great mix" of religions and rituals absorbed by the Japanese people into coexistence. Moreover, it has forced them to become Japanese in character. Maruyama Masao, speaking as an intellectual historian on the historical consciousness of the Japanese people, is also of this school. He maintains that the thought processes found in the myths of the *Kojiki* and the *Nihonshoki* continue to exist as an "ancient stratum," even though other layers of thought have been superimposed in subsequent ages.[3] Maruyama is somewhat sympathetic to "Shinto thinkers of the Edo period"—including of course Motoori Norinaga—"down to the nationalistic moralists of the 1930s," and he even construes their assertions to be "a truth born of a certain kind of intuition."

Of these two groups, the views of the second demand special attention, but they should not be looked upon separately from those of the first. The two represent in a sense the external and the internal aspects of the same phenomenon. The views of the second group can be summarized as follows:

1) Shinto, with the Japanese people, is enduring. It is "the underlying will of Japanese culture," to borrow Hori Ichirō's phrase, an underlying autonomy which transforms and assimilates diverse cultural elements imported from outside. In the words of Motoori, any cultural element of any period (even Buddhism and Confucianism) is, "broadly speaking, the Shinto of that period."[4]

2) Even though one can speak of Shinto as a religion along with Buddhism and Taoism, "Shinto-ness" is something deeper. It is the cultural will or energy of the Japanese people, embodied in conventions which precede or transcend religion. Here, the "secularity of Shinto" is stressed. Whether people who maintain this position like it or not, what they advocate is akin to the Meiji Constitution, which did not regard State Shinto as a religion and on that basis placed restraints upon the thought and beliefs of Japanese citizens. It is also similar to the rationale adopted by certain movements today which seek to revive State Shinto.

3) Based on this line of thought, "the miscellaneous nature of Japanese religion," whereby a person may be Buddhist and Shinto at the same time, is taken as an unchanging characteristic of Japanese culture. When such a formula is applied to all cultural phenomena in history, then a miscellaneous, expedient, irrational, and non-intellectual frame of mind, more than any effort at a logical, unified, and integrated world view, is extolled as that which is most Japanese.

The views of the second group when compared to those of the first differ in conception and central argument, but insofar as they both regard Shinto as a unique religion existing independently throughout history, the two share a common premise and reinforce one another. This view, however, is not only an incorrect perception of the facts but also a one-sided interpretation of Japanese history and culture. It is hoped that this article will demonstrate that before modern times Shinto did not exist as an independent religion. The main points of my argument will be as follows:

1) It is generally held that an indigenous self-consciousness is embodied in the word Shinto. I would argue that the original meaning of the word differs from how it is understood today.

2) The ceremonies of lse Shrine, as well as those of the imperial court and the early provincial government, are said to have been forms of "pure Shinto." I would like to show that they actually became one component of a unique system of Buddhism which emerged in Japan and were perceived as an extension of Buddhism.

3) It is said that Shinto played a secular role in society and existed in a completely different sphere from Buddhism. I would maintain that this very secularity was permeated with Buddhist concepts and was itself religious in nature. The greater part of this paper will examine this question and the preceding two in their ancient and medieval contexts.

4) Finally, I would like to trace the historical stages and the rationale whereby the term Shinto came to mean the indigenous religion or national faith of Japan and to clarify how and when Shinto came to be viewed as an independent religion.

Shinto in the *Nihonshoki*

The word Shinto is commonly taken to mean Japan's indigenous religion and to have had that meaning from fairly early times. It is difficult, however, to find a clear-cut example of the word Shinto used in such a way in early writings. The intellectual historian Tsuda Sōkichi has studied the occurrences of the word Shinto in early Japanese literature and has divided its meaning into the following six categories: (1) "religious beliefs found in indigenous customs passed down in Japan, including superstitious beliefs"; (2) "the authority, power, activity, or deeds of a *kami*, the status of *kami*, being a *kami*, or the *kami* itself"; (3) concepts and teachings concerning *kami*; (4) the teachings propagated by a particular shrine; (5) "the way of the *kami*" as a political or moral norm; and (6) sectarian Shinto as found in new religions.[5] From these it is clear that the word Shinto has been used in a great variety of ways. Tsuda maintains that in the *Nihonshoki* Shinto means "the religious beliefs found in indigenous customs in Japan," the first definition, and that it was used from that time to distinguish "Japan's indigenous religion from Buddhism." He also claims that this basic definition underlies the meaning of Shinto in the other five categories.

It is far from conclusive, however, that the word Shinto was used in early times to denote Japan's indigenous religion,[6] and for that reason Tsuda's analysis of examples in the Nihonshoki should be re-examined. The following three sentences are the only instances of the word Shinto in the *Nihonshoki:*

1) The emperor believed in the teachings of the Buddha (*Buppō* or *hotoke no minori*)[7] and revered Shinto (or *kami no michi*). (Prologue on Emperor Yōmei)
2) The emperor revered the teachings of the Buddha but scorned Shinto. He cut down the trees at Ikukunitama Shrine. (Prologue on Emperor Kōtoku)
3) The expression "as a *kami* would" (*kamunagara*) means to conform to Shinto. It also means in essence to possess one's self of Shinto. (Entry for Taika 3/4/26)

In examples (1) and (2) it is possible to interpret Shinto as distinguishing "Japan's indigenous religion from Buddhism," but that need not be the only interpretation. Tsuda himself indicates that in China the word Shinto originally meant various folk religions, or Taoism, or sometimes Buddhism, or even religion in general.[8] Therefore, the word Shinto is actually a generic term for popular beliefs, whether of China, Korea, or Japan, even though in examples (1) and (2) it refers specifically to Japan's ancient customs, rituals, and beliefs, regardless of whether they were Japanese in origin. Since the *Nihonshoki* was compiled with knowledge of China in mind, it is hard to imagine that its author used the Chinese word Shinto solely to mean Japan's indigenous religion. Though there may be some validity in what Tsuda says, the word Shinto by itself probably means popular beliefs in general.

In examples (1) and (2) Shinto is used in contrast to the word *Buppō,* the teachings of the Buddha. Tsuda takes this to mean "Japan's indigenous religion," but there are other possible interpretations of this without construing it to be the name of a religion. For example, it could mean "the authority, power, activity, or deeds of a *kami*, the status of *kami*, being a *kami*, or the *kami* itself," Tsuda's second definition of Shinto. In fact, during this period the character *dō* or *tō,* which is found in the word Shinto meant not so much a road or path but rather conduct or right action.[9] Hence, Shinto could easily refer to the conduct or action of the *kami*.

In example (3) there are two instances of the word Shinto. While it is not unthinkable to interpret them as "popular beliefs in general," Tsuda's second definition, "the authority, power, activity, or deeds of a *kami* . . ." is perhaps more appropriate, since the word *kamunagara* in the quotation means "in the nature of a *kami*" or "in the state of being a *kami*." The sentences in example (3) were originally a note explaining the word *kamunagara* as it appeared in the emperor's decree issued on the day of this entry, and according to Edo period scholars it was added sometime after the ninth century when the work was transcribed.[10] Therefore, it is not reliable as evidence for what Shinto meant at the time the *Nihonshoki* was compiled. Even if it were, it is more likely that the compiler did not use the same word in two different ways but rather applied the same definition, "the authority, power, activity, or deeds of a *kami* . . ." in all three examples.

Another possible interpretation of Shinto in the *Nihonshoki* is Taoism. Based on recent studies, it is clear that Shinto was another term for Taoism in China during the same period.[11] Moreover, as Taoist concepts and practices steadily passed into Japan between the first century AD and the period when the *Nihonshoki* was compiled, they no doubt exerted a considerable influence on the ceremonies and the beliefs of communal groups bound by blood ties or geographical proximity and on those which emerged around imperial authority. Among the many elements of Taoist origin transmitted to Japan are the following: veneration of swords and mirrors as religious symbols; titles such as *mahito* or *shinjin* (Taoist meaning-perfected man, Japanese meaning the highest of eight court ranks in ancient times which the emperor bestowed on his descendants), *hijiri* or *sen*[12] (Taoist—immortal, Japanese—saint, emperor, or recluse), and *tennō* (Taoist—lord of the universe, Japanese—emperor); the cults of Polaris and the Big Dipper; terms associated with Ise Shrine such as *jingū* (Taoist—a hall enshrining a deity, Japanese—Ise Shrine), *naikū* (Chinese—inner palace, Japanese—Inner Shrine at Ise), *gekū* (Chinese—detached palace, Japanese—Outer Shrine at Ise), and *taiichi* (Taoist—the undifferentiated origin of all things, Japanese—no longer in general use, except at Ise Shrine where it has been used since ancient times on flags signifying Amaterasu Ōmikami); the concept of *daiwa* (meaning a state of ideal peace, but in Japan used to refer to Yamato, the center of the country); and the Taoist concept of immortality. Early Japanese perhaps regarded their ceremonies and beliefs as Taoist, even though they may have differed from those in China. Hence, it is possible to view these teachings, rituals, and even the concepts of imperial authority and of nation as remnants of an attempt to establish a Taoist tradition in Japan. If that is so, Japan's ancient popular beliefs were not so much an indigenous religion but merely a local brand of Taoism, and the word Shinto simply meant Taoism. The accepted theory today is that a systematic form of Taoism did not enter Japan in ancient times,[13] but it is not unreasonable to think that over a long period of time Taoism gradually pervaded Japan's religious milieu until medieval times when Buddhism dominated it completely.

Three possible interpretations of the word Shinto in the *Nihonshoki* have been presented above. It is not yet possible to say which of these is correct, but that should not preclude certain conclusions about Shinto. What is common to all three is that none view Japan's ancient popular beliefs as an independent religion and none use the word Shinto as a specific term for such a religion. Also, there is no evidence that any other specific term existed. Moreover, when Buddhism was introduced into Japan there was a controversy over whether or not to accept it, but there is no indication that these popular beliefs were extolled as an indigenous tradition. Hence, Shinto need not imply a formal religion per se, and it need not indicate something which is uniquely Japanese.

The significance of Shinto deities in the ancient period

In the previous section the word Shinto was analyzed to show how it was used and what it meant in ancient times. Now it is necessary to consider the institutional significance and place of *kami* in Japan during that period, especially as evidenced in the *jingiryō* codes and in Shinto-Buddhist syncreticism.

The *jingiryō* is a set of code of ancient Japan which instituted ceremonies to the *kami.* Needless to say, they include only those rites which had state sponsorship, but nonetheless represent a fair sampling of the ceremonies current at that time. In brief the *jingiryō* codes cover the following topics: (1) the season, title, and content of official annual ceremonies; (2) imperial succession ceremonies and *imi* (seclusion to avoid things tabooed); (3) the supervision and administration of ceremonies; (4) *ōharai* (an official ceremony to exorcise evils and offenses from people); and (5) the administration of government shrines.

It is well known that the *ritsuryō* law code of ancient Japan was modeled on the codes of Sui and T'ang China. Many scholars have already pointed out that the *jingiryō*, one section of the *ritsuryō*, was based on the Chinese *shiryō* or *tz'u-ling* code, which has been reconstructed in forty-six articles.[14] When compared to the T'ang *shiryō*, the *jingiryō* is seen to occupy an identical position in the overall order of the law code and to correspond to the *shiryō* in topic and sentence structure. The official ceremonies described in the *shiryō* include: (1) *shi* or, in Chinese, *ssu* (veneration *of kami* of heaven); (2) *sai* or *chi* (veneration of *kami* of earth); (3) *kō* or *heng* (deification of the spirits of the dead); and (4) *sekiten* or *shih-tien* (deification of ancient sages and masters). From these the *jingiryō* of Japan incorporated only the first two and then added imperial succession ceremonies and *ōharai* ceremonies, not found in the *shiryō*. These changes probably reflect differences in the use of ceremonies in Japan and China which the compilers of the *ritsuryō* code took into account. Notwithstanding these differences, both codes are alike in that they record popular ceremonies of society at that time, even though they include only those ceremonies which had official or political significance. The importance which Japan's *ritsuryō* code placed on *kami* derived ultimately from such ceremonies. Originally, *kami* were popular local deities connected to communal groups bound by blood ties or geographical proximity, and later to the imperial concept of state as well. The *kami* associated with ancestor worship are one example of such local deities. As the section following the *jingiryō* in the *ritsuryō*, the government drew up the *sōniryō*, laws for Buddhist institutions, to regulate priests and nuns. By compiling the *sōniryō* separately from the *jingiryō*, the government placed ceremonies for *kami* in a different dimension from religions such as Buddhism which exerted a special influence on society through its high doctrines.

In subsequent centuries the significance of *kami* changed somewhat from what it had been under the original *ritsuryō* system. During the eighth century the state enthusiastically embraced Buddhism, and the Empress Shōtoku [also known as Kōken], in collusion with the priest Dōkyō, established a policy that was pro-Buddhist in the extreme. Recent scholars have shown how this policy met with opposition in aristocratic and court circles, and they claim that in conjunction with political reforms at the beginning of the ninth century there emerged the concept of Shinto as an independent indigenous religion.[15] Certainly, it was during these ninth-century reforms that court Shinto ceremonies and Ise Shrine's organization were formalized. Nonetheless, it is highly unlikely that Shinto was perceived as an independent religion in opposition to Buddhism at this time.

As is already well known, between the late eighth century and the eleventh century, Shinto and Buddhism gradually coalesced with one another (*shinbutsu shūgō*) or, more precisely, veneration of the *kami* was absorbed into Buddhism through a variety of doctrinal innovations and new religious forms. Among the doctrinal explanations of the *kami* were the following: (1) the *kami* realize that they themselves are trapped in this world of samsara and transmigration, and they also seek liberation through the Buddhist teachings; (2) the *kami* are benevolent deities who protect Buddhism; (3) the *kami* are transformations of the Buddhas manifested in Japan to save all sentient beings (*honji suijaku*); and (4) the *kami* are the pure spirits of the Buddhas (*hongaku*). Among new religious forms were the *jingūji* (a combination shrine and temple) and Sōgyō Hachiman (the *kami* Hachiman in the guise of a Buddhist monk). Such religious forms are exemplary of ceremonies and objects of worship which could not be distinguished specifically as Shinto or as Buddhist. The first stage in this process of Shinto-Buddhist syncretization covered the late eighth and early ninth century. During that period the first two doctrinal explanations of *kami*, mentioned above, became current.

It is only natural that at this stage people became more cognizant of the *kami,* especially in relation to the Buddhas. Examples of this are found in the *Shoku Nihongi.* The entry there for 782/7/29 states that Shinto cannot be deceived and that numerous recent calamities are retribution meted out by the great *kami* of Ise and all the other *kami* in return for the negligent use of mourning garb widespread among men. Such disrespect for decorum, and by extension for the *kami*, indicates implicitly the popularity of the Buddhas over the *kami.* Another example from the *Shoku Nihongi* is an imperial edict of 836/11, which states that there is nothing superior to Mahāyāna Buddhism in defending Shinto and that one should rely on the efficacy of Buddhist practices to transform calamity into good. This passage indicates that it is the Buddhas who guarantee the authority of the *kami.*

These examples reflect a heightened awareness of *kami* during this period, but they by no means imply that Shinto was looked upon as an independent and inviolable entity. On the contrary, there was more of a sense that Shinto occupied a subordinate position and role within the broader scheme of Buddhism.

The meaning of the word Shinto in medieval times

The *Konjaku monogatarishū*, composed around the eleventh century, contains the following two references. First, an old woman in China was possessed with heretical views: she served Shinto and did not believe in Buddhism. Second, there was an outlying province in India which was a land of *kami*, and to this day the words of Buddhism have not been transmitted there.[16] Here "Shinto" and "land of *kami*" have nothing to do with Japan but clearly indicate "local deities" and "a land devoted to its local deities." Although these references are from a collection of Buddhist tales, they show that even in this period the word Shinto was used in its classical sense, as it was in China and in the *Nihonshoki.*

In medieval times the word Shinto generally meant the authority, power, or activity of a *kami*, being a *kami*, or, in short, the state or attributes of a *kami.* For example, the *Nakatomi no harai kunge,* a work on Ryōbu Shinto of Shingon Buddhism, discusses the relationship of *kami* and Buddha in the following way: "The Buddha assumes a state in which *kami* and Buddha are not two different things but are absolutely identical. The Buddha constantly confers his mark (*suijaku*) on Shinto."[17] Here Shinto must mean *kami* or the state of being a *kami.* The word Shinto is used in the same way in the *Shintōshū,* a collection of tales from the Sannō Shinto tradition of Tendai Buddhism:

> Question: For what reason do the Buddhas and the Bodhisattvas manifest themselves in the form of Shinto?

> Answer: The Buddhas and the Bodhisattvas manifest themselves in various forms out of compassion for and to save all living beings.[18]

Besides these there are numerous other examples of Shinto used to mean *kami.*

A saying in common parlance in medieval times was, "Shinto is a difficult thing to speculate about." This example, if any, is representative of what Shinto ordinarily indicated in that period. It does not mean that one cannot conjecture about the religion or doctrines of the *kami* but rather that it is difficult to fathom the conduct, the intentions, and the existence of the *kami* by human intellect. Such a definition of Shinto was current throughout the medieval period, and even the *Japanese Portuguese Dictionary* of 1603 contains the following entry: "Xinto *(camino michi). Kami* [*camis* in the original] or matters pertaining to *kami.*"[19] The *camino michi* recorded here is the Japanese reading of the Chinese characters for Shinto. It is clear that this word *michi* likewise does not mean doctrine. *Michi* in the medieval period, just as in ancient times, indicated conduct or ideal state like the *michi* in *mononofu no michi* or *yumiya no michi* (the way of the warrior). Hence *kami no michi* means the state of being a *kami* or the conduct of a *kami.* Even when *michi* is compounded with another character and read *tō* or *dō* as in Shinto, the compound can have the meaning of the other character alone. An example of this is found in the *Gishi wajinden* which states in reference to Himiko that "she served the *kidō* (demons)." The same can be said of the *dō* and *tō* of *myōdō* (deities of the world of the dead) and *tentō* (deities such as Bonten and Taishakuten), words which appear in *kishōmon,* medieval documents containing oaths sworn before *kami* and Buddhas.

The next question that must be dealt with is what religious content this word Shinto was said to have contained. As pointed out earlier, during medieval times Shinto was generally interpreted as one part of Buddhism. This was possible because the concepts contained in Mahāyāna Buddhism provided a rationale for absorbing folk beliefs. Just as a unique form of Buddhism evolved in Tibet, so in medieval Japan Buddhism developed a distinctive logic and system of its own.

Nominally, medieval Buddhism comprised eight sects, but it was not unusual for individuals to study the teachings and rituals of all the sects. The reason is that the eight held a single doctrinal system in common, that of *mikkyō* or esoteric Buddhism (Skt. Vajrayāna). The Buddhist teachings that were recognized as orthodox during the medieval period had *mikkyō* as their base, combined with the exoteric teachings or *kengyō* (Buddhist and other teachings outside of *mikkyō*) of each of the eight schools—Tendai, Kegon, Yuishiki (Hossō), Ritsu, etc. These eight sects, sometimes called *kenmitsu* or exoteric-esoteric Buddhism, acknowledged their interdependence with state authority, and together they dominated the religious sector. This entire order constituted the fundamental religious system of medieval Japan. Shinto was drawn into this Buddhist system as one segment of it, and its religious content was replaced with Buddhist doctrine, particularly *mikkyō* and Tendai philosophy. The term *kenmitsu* used here refers to this kind of system.[20] At the end of the twelfth century, various reform movements arose in opposition to this system, and there even appeared heretical sects which stressed exclusive religious practices—the chanting of the *nenbutsu, zen* meditation, etc. Nonetheless, the *kenmitsu* system maintained its status as the orthodox religion until the beginning of the sixteenth century.

In *kenmitsu* Buddhism, the most widespread interpretation of the religious content of Shinto was the *honji suijaku* theory, based on Tendai doctrine. According to this theory, the *kami* are simply another form of the Buddha, and their form, condition, authority, and activity are nothing but the form and the acts by which the Buddha teaches, guides, and saves human beings. Shinto, therefore, was independent neither in existence nor in system of thought. It was merely one means among many by which the Buddha guides (*kedō*) and converts (*kegi*) sentient beings. The *Shintōshū* cited earlier contains about fifty tales in which the Buddha takes on the form of a *kami* and saves human beings. The word Shinto in its title presupposes this meaning—i.e., conversion by the Buddha. With Shinto interpreted in this way and with people's beliefs based on this kind of interpretation, individual Shinto shrines sought to emphasize the distinctive capacities and lineage of their own *kami* as a manifestation (*suijaku*) of the Buddha, as well as the unique teachings and practices passed down in their shrine or school. These claims were expanded through complicated doctrines and tortuous theories into a class of teachings how called sectarian or *shake* Shinto (Tsuda's fourth definition of the word Shinto, "the teachings propagated by a particular shrine"). Ryōbu Shinto of the Shingon tradition and Sannō Shinto of the Tendai tradition are typical examples of such teachings. Individual shrines in different areas adapted these teachings in such a way that during the medieval period countless theories of Shinto arose.

The theory of Shinto propounded by the Ise Shrine tradition, sometimes called Ise or Watarai Shinto, is of decisive importance in a consideration of medieval Shinto. Modern intellectual and Shinto historians have generally regarded Ise Shinto, which became active in the thirteenth century, as evidence of Shinto's tenacious, though hidden, existence as "Japan's indigenous religion" throughout medieval times. Moreover, they see it as the starting point for subsequent medieval theories of Shinto as they began to break away from Buddhism.[21]

It is well known that, even during Buddhism's apex in the medieval period, Ise Shrine maintained ancient rites—whether uniquely Japanese or Taoist in origin—and upheld proscriptions against Buddhist terminology, practices, and garb. But it is equally important to realize that Ise Shrine did not completely reject Buddhism, for Buddhist priests would visit the shrine and Ise priests themselves possessed considerable knowledge of Buddhism. In this light, the proscription against anything Buddhist was probably regarded as a peculiar and mysterious practice, incomprehensible to society in general and even to the Shinto priests at Ise. This proscription, for example, is treated as strange in Mujū's *Shasekishō* and Tsūkai's *Daijingū sankeiki,* works closely associated with Ise Shrine, and in treatises by outstanding priests of Ise, such as the *Daijingū ryōgū no onkoto* by Watarai Tsunemasa. For the medieval mind this was only a natural response. The problem that arises here is how to explain in Buddhist terms what was a truly peculiar practice for the times, or even more so, how to advocate it in all good conscience as a praiseworthy feature of the shrine. The works mentioned above actually begin with this kind of question and end up expounding the immeasurable virtues of the *kami* at Ise. Also in Ise Shinto there is the expression "not to breathe a word about Buddhism." This in fact does not imply a rejection of Buddhism but rather indicates a special attitude or etiquette assumed in the presence of the *kami.* As stated previously in another article, this view draws on the philosophy of innate Buddhahood (*hongaku shisō*) found in esoteric Buddhism which was popular at that time, the thirteenth century.[22] In the final analysis, Ise Shinto was nothing more than one form of sectarian Shinto, which took for granted the existence of the Buddhas.[23]

In the *Hieisha eizan gyōkōki* of the early fourteenth century, it states:

> There are identical as well as differing aspects in the method of conversion used by the *shinmei* (*kami*) in other lands and that used by Shinto in our own land. Our land, which is a land of the *kami*, is superior in that human beings are benefitted by "the light of the Buddha melded to become one with our world of dust" (*wakō dōjin,* i.e., the power of the Buddha harmonized with our mundane world and manifested as *kami*).[24]

This passage is indicative of how the word Shinto was interpreted in medieval times. It was not used to distinguish popular beliefs from Buddhism but rather to signify the form in which the Buddha converts and saves human beings.

Shinto's secular role

If Shinto is a manifestation of the Buddha and one form in which he converts and saves human beings, there arises the question of whether *kami* play precisely the same role as the Buddha. Here it is important to note the secular character of Shinto in medieval times. Many of the representations of *kami* familiar to people in the medieval period were secular in form. Admittedly, there were also numerous examples of syncretism with Buddhism, for instance, Sanskrit letters used to symbolize invisible *kami* or a Buddhist image enshrined in the inner sanctuary (*shinden*) of a shrine, or again Hachimanshin portrayed as a Buddhist monk, or Zaō Gongen as the Buddhist deity Myōō (Skt. Vidyārāja). Nevertheless, in many of the Shinto statues, portraits, and narrative drawings that survive today, *kami* were depicted in such secular guises as noblemen, ladies, old men, young boys, Chinese gentlemen, travelers, and hunters. A number of these became formalized iconographically during the thirteenth century.[25]

The same can also be said of how the word *suijaku* (manifestation) was comprehended. *Suijaku,* as understood by the common people in medieval times, was not the abstract or philosophical idea found in the doctrines of Mahāyāna Buddhism but was mythological in nature or perhaps associated with concrete places or events. The term *suijaku* literally meant to descend from heaven to a given spot and to become the local or guardian *kami* of that spot.[26] Hence, at that spot there would arise a legend of the mysterious relationship between men and *kami,* and the very area enshrining the *kami* would be looked upon as sacred ground where profound doctrinal principles lay concealed. The history of this manifestation—that is, its development over time—was related in the form of an *engi* (a historical narrative), and the positioning of its enshrinement—that is, its location in space—was depicted in the form of a mandala (a rational layout). This indicates that the legends, the architectural form of early shrines, and the rituals of worship were interpreted as mysterious principles expressing Buddhist philosophy. In short, secular representations in Shinto actually expressed an essence which was strongly Buddhist. The link between Buddhism and Shinto in medieval times is exemplified by the Kike school at Enryakuji. This school, which specialized in chronicles, concentrated on mysterious legends, especially Shinto legends, as a means of plumbing the depths of Buddhism.[27]

Also in the medieval period Shinto was associated with numerous secular functions and duties. Shinto observances at court, such as the *Daijōe* (a rite performed by the emperor upon his succession) and the Jinkonjiki (a biannual offering to the *kami* by the emperor) had no other purpose than to enshroud in mystery secular authority. Nonetheless, they derived their meaning from the fact that secular mystery lay within a world encompassed by Buddhist law. Eventually, the worship of *kami* became inseparable from secular authority, but at the same time it was incorporated into the multi-leveled *kenmitsu* system with its unique logic and structure resulting from Buddhism's development in Japan. Secular though it was, Shinto did not coexist aloof from Buddhism, nor did it constitute a non-Buddhist stronghold within the Buddhist sphere. Rather, its secularity functioned, in the final analysis, within a Buddhist world.

Because shrines were Buddhism's secular face, their upkeep was the responsibility of the secular authority, even though they themselves were integrated into Buddhism's system of control. For that reason, the imperial court made regular offerings to twenty-two specially designated shrines, and the provincial government bore the responsibility for ceremonies and maintenance at major shrines (*sōsha, ichinomiya,* and *ninomiya*) in the provinces. In the

Kamakura period the bakufu stipulated in Article 1 of the *Goseibai shikimoku,* the Jōei law code, that "efforts must be made to keep shrines in repair and not to neglect their ceremonies," thereby stressing the importance of maintaining shrines in the provinces and on *shōen* under bakufu supervision. In Article 2 it dealt with Buddhist temples and their functions. These indicate not only the responsibilities that the bakufu inherited from the provincial government of the previous period but also the obligations which secular administrative authority had to fulfill to religion.

As stated earlier, Shinto was looked upon as a skillful means by which the Buddha, in his compassion, might lead people to enlightenment or deliver them to his Pure Land. Nonetheless, it is important to note that in actuality Shinto played an important role in the administrative power upholding the secular order. As pointed out in the previous section, the ability of "the light of the Buddha to meld and to become one with our world of dust" (*wakō dōjin*) was constantly stressed in medieval times, but that expression reflects an understanding of Shinto's ultimate significance or its final objective. On an everyday level, people felt a strong sense of fear toward the *kami.* For example, in many medieval oaths (*kishōmon*), it is recorded, "If I violate this pledge, may the punishments of Bonten and Taishakuten, of the *kami* of the provinces, and especially of the guardian *kami* of this *shōen* be visited upon this body of mine." It goes without saying that what was sworn in such oaths was, without exception, actions of worldly significance or things relating to the preservation of the secular order, rather than anything to do with religious affairs. It is true that in Buddhism also people would petition the Buddha for "peace in this world and good fortune in the next" (*gense annon gosei zenshō*), but as a general rule matters of this world were addressed to the *kami* and those of the coming world to the Buddha. In times of worldly difficulty, one might pray for the protection of the *kami* and the Buddha, but first and foremost for that of the *kami.* Or, when heading into battle, one would beseech the *kami* for good fortune in war. Concerning the *kami* and their power, it was generally said that they were strict in both reward and punishment. Such views simply highlight the influence and control which religion exerted over secular life.

Though there is not enough space to deal with it adequately here, the belief that "Japan is the land of the *kami*," with both its political and religious implications, was based on the secular role of Shinto described above. The secularity of Shinto and the political applicability of the concept of "the land of the *kami*" does not indicate that Shinto was without any religious character but rather shows that the Buddhist system which lay behind it pervaded all aspects of everyday life. The present-day illusion that Shinto is not a religion derives historically from a misunderstanding of this point.

The emergence of the concept of Shinto as an indigenous religion

The following two sentences are found in the *Shintōshū*:

1) Question: On what basis do we know that Shinto reveres the Buddha's teachings?
2) Question: How are we to understand the statement that the Buddha's realm and Shinto differ in their respective forms but are one and the same in essence?[28]

Both of these questions pose *kami* and Buddha against one another. In the first, Shinto clearly indicates the *kami* themselves, whereas, in the second, Shinto may be interpreted as the deeds, state, or authority of the *kami*, but it also conveys the idea of a realm of the *kami* by contrasting it to the Buddha's realm. A similar passage is found in the *Daijingū sankeiki* by Tsūkai: "Amaterasu Ōmikami is paramount in Shinto and the Tathāgata Dainichi is paramount in Buddhist teachings. Hence in both *suijaku* (manifestation) and *honji* (origin or source) there is the supreme and the incomparable."[29] In this case Shinto may be understood as the ideal state of being a *kami,* but it is also important that, as a concept juxtaposed to "Buddhist teachings," it assumes a sphere of its own, meaning "the realm of *suijaku,*" teaching and converting in the form of a *kami.* This is especially true of the Ise School's theory of Shinto. For example, in the *Hōki hongi* Shinto is contrasted to the "three jewels" (the three basic components of Buddhism—the Buddha, the Buddhist teachings, and the Buddhist order), or in the *Ruishū jingi hongen* it is juxtaposed to *bukke* (Buddhist schools).[30] These imply that Shinto and Buddhism belong to separate spheres in the phenomenal world even though they are identical in essence. Examples which transfer emphasis to the word Shinto in this way are quite conspicuous in Ise Shinto. This was a natural tendency, since the Ise School's theory of Shinto had to stress the efficacy of Shinto above all, even more than other schools of sectarian Shinto.

The word Shinto, when set up as an object of contrast in this way, emerged with a sectarian meaning or with a special sphere of its own, even though fundamentally it meant the authority of the *kami* or the condition of being a *kami.* This is not to say that it immediately assumed the meaning of a separate teaching or religion liberated from the framework of Buddhism. Rather, what Ise Shinto tried to do was to cast the realm of Shinto in a resplendent light. This was attempted by reducing the terms contrasted with Shinto to purely Buddhist phenomenon and forms—i.e. Buddhist teachings, "three jewels," Buddhist schools, etc.— and by defining Shinto relative to them. All the while, Buddhism, the overarching principle which embraced and unified both, was left intact as the ultimate basis. The Ise School also attempted to aggrandize Shinto by diverse embellishments and additions to Shinto that were non-Buddhist and by cloaking it in a dignity similar to that of the Buddhist scriptures. Nonetheless, in this case also the principles which Shinto held in common with Buddhism were likewise stressed.

In this way the word Shinto came to refer to a Japanese phenomenon, school, or sphere of Buddhism qua religious truth. This meaning of the word paved the way for later stages in which Shinto became a term for Japan's indigenous religion. The writings of the priests at Ise as well as the theories of fourteenth-century Shinto thinkers such as Kitabatake Chikafusa, Jihen, and Ichijō Kanera (corresponding to Tsuda's third definition of Shinto, "concepts and teachings concerning *kami*") played a particularly important role in this process. Nevertheless, it was not because these thinkers were critical of *kenmitsu* Buddhism, which was the orthodox religion of the medieval period. Rather, they were all adherents of the orthodox teachings, so that any statements they made, which might at first seem to oppose those teachings, were nothing more than an attempt, extreme though it may have been, to enshroud in mystery the authority of the governing system at a time when it was isolated and in decline. With the rise of the Shinto-only school (Yuiitsu or Yoshida Shinto) at the end of the fifteenth century, the word Shinto became increasingly identified as an indigenous form of religion. It was even interpreted as the highest religion, though identical in essence with Buddhism and Confucianism. At this point the meaning of the word began to depart from the orthodox teachings of *kenmitsu* Buddhism. It just so happened that during this period the power of the orthodox religious order was in a state of decline because of the strength of various heretical movements of so-called "new Buddhism," particularly of Shinshū uprisings (*ikkō ikki*). The Shinto-only school, which was one branch of sectarian Shinto, simply took advantage of this situation for its own unfettered development.

Beginning in the seventeenth century, a Confucian theory of Shinto, with much the same structure as medieval theories, was formulated by Hayashi Razan and other Edo period scholars. Based on this interpretation of Shinto, the definition of Shinto as the indigenous religion of Japan, as opposed to Taoism, Buddhism, or Confucianism, became firmly fixed. Moreover, the Confucian concept of *dō*, the way, also influenced the word Shinto, imbuing it with the meaning of "the way, as a political or moral norm" (Tsuda's fifth definition of Shinto). Of course, Confucian Shinto amounted to nothing more than theories of the educated class subordinating Shinto's true nature to Confucianism. Actual belief in the *kami*, however, as found among the common people at that time, remained subsumed under Buddhism.

The notion of Shinto as Japan's indigenous religion finally emerged complete both in name and in fact with the rise of modern nationalism, which evolved from the National Learning School of Motoori Norinaga and the Restoration Shinto movement of the Edo period down to the establishment of State Shinto in the Meiji period. The Meiji separation of Shinto and Buddhism (*shinbutsu bunri*) and its concomitant suppression of Buddhism (*haibutsu kishaku*) were coercive and destructive "correctives" pressed forward by the hand of government. With them Shinto achieved for the first time the status of an independent religion, distorted though it was. During this period the "historical consciousness" of an indigenous religion called Shinto, existing in Japan since ancient times, clearly took shape for the first time. This has remained the basis for defining the word Shinto down to the present. Scholars have yielded to this use of the word, and the population at large has been educated in this vein.

There is one further thing which should be pointed out. That is that separating Shinto from Buddhism cut Shinto off from the highest level of religious philosophy achieved by the Japanese up to that time and inevitably, moreover artificially, gave it the features of a primitive religion. Hence, while acquiring independence, Shinto declined to the state of a religion that disavowed being a religion.

Conclusion

This article is an attempt to trace Shinto throughout Japan's entire religious history by extracting samples dealing only with Shinto from each period. The reader may be left with the impression, contrary to the assertion at the beginning of this essay, that Shinto has indeed existed without interruption throughout Japanese history. This is only natural considering the sampling method used. Moreover, it is undeniable that there is certain continuity to it all. Therein lies the problem. Up to now all studies of Shinto history have emphasized this continuity by means of such a sampling process. In doing so they have applied to all periods of history a sort of surgical separation of Shinto from Buddhism and thus from Japanese religion as a whole. By such reasoning, anything other than Shinto becomes simply a superficial overlay, a passing thing.

The meanings of the word Shinto, as well as changes over time in customs and beliefs, would indicate that Shinto emerged as an independent religion only in modern times, and then only as a result of political policy. If that is so, can this continuity be regarded as a true picture of history? Or could it be that what is perceived as indigenous, or as existing continuously from earliest times, is nothing more than a ghost image produced by a word linking together unrelated phenomenon? Up to just one hundred years ago, what constituted the religion and thought of the Japanese people in most periods of history was something historical—that is, something assimilated or formulated or fabricated by the people, whether it was native or foreign in origin. This thing was something truly indigenous. In concrete terms, this was the *kenmitsu* Buddhist system including its components, such as Shinto and the Yin-yang tradition, and its various branches, both reformist and heretical. It, rather than Shinto, was the comprehensive, unified, and self-defined system of religious thought produced by Japan in pre-modern times. Even today it is perpetuated latently in everyday conventions as the subconscious of the Japanese people.

Throughout East Asia, Mahāyāna Buddhism generally embraced native beliefs in a loose manner, without harsh repression and without absorbing them to the point of obliteration. The question here is how Japan should be interpreted. While acknowledging Japan as an example of this East Asian pattern, should one consider the separation of Shinto and Buddhism to be an inevitable development and, in line with Meiji nationalism, perceive Shinto as the basis of Japan's cultural history? Or, should one view *kenmitsu* Buddhism's unique system of thought, which evolved historically from diverse elements, including foreign ones, as the distinguishing feature of Japanese culture?

Considering the magnitude of the problem, this article leaves much to be desired. It is hoped, however, that it has served to dispel fictitious notions about Japan's religious history and religious consciousness, and about Japanese culture in general.

Notes

1 For further reading, see James C. Dobbins, "Editor's Introduction: Kuroda Toshio and His Scholarship," *Japanese Journal of Religious Studies* 23, Nos. 3–4 (1996):217–32.
2 Hori Ichirō, *Sei to zoku no kattō* (Heibonsha, 1975).
3 Maruyama Masao, "Rekishi ishiki no kosō," *Rekishi shisōshū,* ed. Maruyama Masao (Chikuma Shobō, 1972).
4 Taken from the *Tōmonroku* by Motoori Norinaga, thought to have been written between 1777 and 1779. This work is a compilation of answers to questions asked by his students. *Motoori Norinaga zenshū,* Vol. 1 (Chikuma Shobō, 1968), 527.
5 Tsuda Sōkichi, *Nihon no shintō* (Iwanami Shoten, 1949), Chapter 1. Kami is the Japanese word for a deity or spirit. The word Shintō, which is of Chinese origin, is made up of two characters: *shin* meaning *kami* and *tō* meaning way or upright conduct.
6 *Nihonshoki,* II, Vol. 68 of *Nihon koten bungaku taikei* ed. Sakamoto Tarō (Iwanami Shoten, 1965), note on "Shintō," p. 556
7 In an early manuscript, the Japanese gloss *hotoke no minori* is added to the Chinese characters *Buppō.* Of course, this was written after the ninth century, but it may have been read that way from the time of the manuscript.
8 Tsuda, Chapter 1.
9 *Jidaibetsu kokugo daijiten* (Sanseidō, 1967); *Iwanami kogo jiten* (Iwanami Shoten, 1967). Both works give examples of *michi* used to refer to Buddhist doctrines, but this is not to say that the meaning doctrine is included in the word *michi.*
10 *Nihonshoki,* II:574.
11 Fukunaga Mitsuji, "Dōkyō ni okeru kagami to tsurugi—sono shisō to genryū," *Tōhō gakuhō* 45 (1973):59–120; Fukunaga Mitsuji, "Tennō to shikyū to shinjin—Chūgoku kodai no Shintō," *Shisō* 637 (1977):955–73.
12 Here both *hijiri* and *sen* are written with the character *ninben* with *yama.*
13 Shimode Sekiyo, *Nihon kodai no jingi to Dōkyō* (Tokyo: Yoshikawa Kōbunkan, 1972).
14 *Ritsuryō,* Vol. 3 of *Nihon shisō taikei* (Tokyo: Iwanami Shoten, 1976), 529.
15 Takatori Masao, *Shintō no seiritsu* (Heibonsha, 1979).
16 *Konjaku monogatarishū,* fasc. 7, story 3; fasc. 3, story 26.

17 *Kōbō Daishi zenshū* (Tokyo: Yoshikawa Kōbunkan, 1909), 5:160.

18 *Akagi bunkobon Shintōshū*, Vol. 1 of *Kichō kotensekisōkan* (Tokyo: Kadokawa Shoten, 1968), 12.

19 *Vocabvlario da Lingoa de Iapam* (Nagasaki, 1603); *Nippo jisho* (Tokyo: Iwanami Shoten, 1960).

20 Kuroda Toshio, *Nihon chūsei no kokka to shūkyō* (Tokyo: Iwanami Shoten, 1975), Chapter 3.

21 Ōsumi Kazuo, "Chūsei shintōron no shisōteki Ichi," *Chūsei shintōron,* Vol. 19 of *Nihon shisō taikei* (Tokyo: Iwanami Shoten, 1977).

22 Kuroda, 521.

23 Kuroda Toshio, "Chūsei shūkyōshi ni okeru shintō no ichi," in *Kodai Chūsei no shakai to shisō: Ienaga Saburō kyōju taikan kinen* (Tokyo: Sanseidō, 1979), 151ff.

24 Okami Masao hakase kanreki kinen kankōkai, ed. *Muromachi gokoro—chūsei bungaku shiryōshū* (Tokyo: Kadokawa Shoten, 1978), 366.

25 For Hie Shichisha, see *Enryakuji gokoku engi* in *Dai Nihon Bukkyō zensho,* Chapter 1; for Kasugasha, see Kageyama Haruki, *Shintō bijutsu* (Tokyo: Yūzankaku, 1973), 170.

26 Kuroda, *Nihon Chūsei,* 451.

27 Hazama Jikō, *Nihon Bukkyō no kaiten to sono kichō,* 2:245ff.

28 *Akagi bunkobon Shintōshū*, 226–27.

29 *Jingū sankeiki taisei,* in *Daijingū sōsho,* 70.

30 *Watarai Shintō taisei,* I, in *Daijingū sōsho,* 54, 695.

SUGGESTED READINGS

Bellah, Robert. "Japan's Cultural Identity: Some Reflections on the Work of Watsuji Tetsuro." *The Journal of Asian Studies* 24 (August, 1965):573–94.

Bernier, Bernard. "National Communion: Watsuji Tetsuro's Conception of Ethics, Power, and the Japanese Imperial State." *Philosophy East and West* 56 (January, 2006):84–105.

Bix, Herbert P. "Inventing the 'Symbol Monarchy' in Japan." *Journal of Japanese Studies* 21 (Summer, 1995):319–63.

Creemers, Wilhelmus H.M. *Shrine Shinto after World War II.* Leiden: E.J. Brill, 1968.

Dower, John. *Embracing Defeat: Japan in the Wake of World War II.* London: W.W. Norton and Co., 1999.

Holtom, Daniel. "The 'New Emperor.'" *Far Eastern Survey* 15 (March 13, 1946):69–71.

———. "Shinto in Postwar Japan." *Far Eastern Survey* 14 (February 14, 1945):29–33.

———. "New Status of Shinto." *Far Eastern Survey* 15 (January 30, 1946):17–20.

Kamata Tōji. "The Disfiguring of Nativism: Hirata Atsutane and Orikuchi Shinobu." In *Shinto in History—Ways of the Kami,* edited by John Been and Mark Teeuwen, 272–94. Honolulu: The University of Hawai'i Press, 2000.

Mullins, Mark. "How Yasukuni Shrine Survived the Occupation: A Critical Examination of Popular Claims." *Monumenta Nipponica* 65 (Spring, 2010):89–136.

Okuyama Michiaki. "Religion and Japanese Constitutional Law." *Academia Humanities and Social Sciences* 83 (June, 2006):133–46.

Shimazono Susumu. "State Shinto and the Religious Structure of Modern Japan." *Journal of the American Academy of Religion* 73 (December, 2005):1077–98.

Ueda Kenji. "Contemporary Social Change and Shinto Tradition." *Japanese Journal of Religious Studies* 6 (March–June, 1979):303–27.

Woodard, William P. *The Allied Occupation of Japan 1945–52 and Japanese Religions.* Leiden: E.J. Brill, 1972.

———. *The Religious Juridical Persons Law.* Tokyo: The Foreign Affairs Association of Japan, 1965.

Yanagawa Keiichi and David Reid. "Between Unity and Sepration: Religion and Politics on Japan, 1965–1977," *Japanese Journal of Religious Studies* 6 (December, 1979):500–21.

Part 5

CONTEMPORARY WAYS OF
DEFINING SHINTO

INTRODUCTION

The essays in this section argue that Shinto should be classified as a religion but define Shinto religiosity differently. Ueda Kenji finds underlying theological principles, arguing for a "basic Shinto," that is an essentially clear conceptual framework underlying Shinto in all its manifestations—at shrines, in sects, folk Shinto, etc. Kamata Tōji defines Shinto spirituality in terms of a distinctive non-rational experience of the *kami* in the natural world. This divine sensibility is a basic feature of Shinto as a "forest religion" with its "guardian forests" (*chinju no mori*). The other readings in this section move from interior psychological or doctrinal definitions to exterior institutional, ritual, and social factors. Miyata Noboru's essay shows that what is central to Shinto in its long history is ordinary people's deep personal piety toward the enshrined *kami* at the village level obscured beneath the state-supported facade of the imperial way. Sonoda Minoru argues that Shinto is not an individual private faith or a personal quest for salvation in the standard Western sense of the term. Shinto is defined much more broadly as a cultural religion (*bunkateki shūkyō*) tied to the local community. Inoue Hiroshi defines Shinto shrines and faith in the *kami* not, as some would have it, as an unchanging ancient tradition from ages eternal but as distinctive religious institutions showing how Shinto has undergone significant changes over time.

Historical overview

Japan's post-war "economic miracle" produced a high-tech industrialized society with stable employment, a strong middle class, and a vibrant consumer culture. By the 1980s, Japan seemed on the verge of catapulting into the world's greatest superpower, as optimistically predicted by Ezra Vogel in his best-selling book, *Japan as Number One: Lessons for America* (1979). Yet, despite Japan's rising affluence in these boom years, rapid industrial growth ultimately fizzled. The economic fundamentals proved hollow, fueled by an unsustainable overinvestment in hyper-inflated stocks and skyrocketing property prices. When the bubble finally burst, Japan plunged into its worst recession since World War II. The financial collapse ushered in the "lost decade" of the 1990s. Credit tightened, banks failed, the GDP declined, and unemployment rose as companies downsized, merged, and entered into bankruptcy (a process referred to as "restructuring" or *risutora*).[1] Japan was further buffeted by the "Great Recession" in 2008, which weakened export growth and caused steep cuts in corporate spending.[2] Today, Japan remains an East Asian success story with a GDP outranked only by the US and China, but it continues to struggle against the twin banes of deflationary pressures and tepid economic growth. The need for systemic fiscal reforms remains paramount despite a massive government stimulus program, known as "Abenomics," promoted by the current prime minister, Abe Shinzō.[3]

Japan also faces political uncertainty. A succession of weak prime ministers (seventeen since 1989) and ingrained political corruption has not been good for Japanese democracy.[4] Moreover, the official ineptitude seen in the responses to the Hanshin earthquake in 1995 and the Great Tōhoku tsunami and Fukushima nuclear disaster in 2011 has caused a loss of confidence. In a poll taken five months after the latter catastrophe, 82% responded that they had deep doubts about the government.[5] Consumer confidence has recovered somewhat from its all-time low in 2009, but it still remains lower than in the 1980s.[6] Finally, Japan faces social and demographic uncertainties. Divorce rates continue to increase, and as of 2016 the marriage rate had dropped to half of what it was in 1970. By 2060, it is projected that 40% of the population will be 65 or over, and the population will fall from 128 million to 87 million.[7]

These factors combine to create what anthropologist Anne Allison has called Japan's "precarious sociality." The traditional post-war "family-corporate system," typified by the middle-class ideal of owning "my home," the work ethic of the salaryman operating within Japan's corporate capitalism, and the goal of increasing children's standard of living through a meritocratic educational system, is under increasing strain.[8] In the post-bubble years, Japan's economy has become increasingly privatized. In effect, Japan is turning into a "temp nation" where in 2016 over 40% of workers were "frītā" (freelance and part time workers) who lack a satisfactory social safety net, whether due to underemployment, part-time work, or irregular employment.[9] New subcultures of the disenfranchised are also evident, including social recluses (hikikomori) and NEETs (young people "not in education, employment or training").[10]

This has harmed the young in particular. Many find themselves adrift, alone, alienated, with a sense of hopelessness about their future and their prospects a far cry from the old dream of lifetime employment at a big Japanese firm. Bereft of an *ibasho*—a stable center at home, work, and in the nation on which to base their personal identity—many look for a new source of meaning, belonging, and hope for a better future.[11] What the future holds after the "demise of Japan Inc.," as Peter Duus has aptly called the old post-war corporate-political-social order, remains an open question.

Trends

If the key question for these times, as Susan Tipton has asked, is "whither Japan?," it is also key to ask, whither Shinto?[12] There are four trends in Shinto that must be considered: (1) the secularization of Japanese society and Shinto; (2) Shinto's religious role, with Shinto shrines as local centers for private personal piety and collective identity; (3) restorationist attempts to recover Shinto's pre-war public and civil character; and (4) econationalist portrayals of Shinto as a green religion—an ecologically based nature religion that directly addresses the environmental crisis.

The secularization of Japanese society and Shinto

Some would argue that one key trend is Japan's increasing secularization. The so-called "classical model" of secularization posits that, according to sociologist of religion Rodney Stark, modernization is "the causal engine dragging the gods into retirement."[13] Secularization is generally defined as: (1) an increase in industrialization, urbanization, and rationalization leading to a decrease in religiousness; (2) the decline of the social power of religion as it loses its hold over public political and educational institutions (deinstitutionalization); (3) a marked drop of personal individual piety in the private sphere; (4) corrosive effects of science on religious belief and morality eroding their plausibility and causing disenchantment.

Ian Reader, a specialist in contemporary Japanese religions, is a leading proponent of the view that Japan is becoming increasingly secularized. He argues that secularization is not an outmoded social theory, as Stark and other sociologists of religion have claimed. Rather, he believes that it is an accurate assessment of the current situation: Japan is experiencing a "rush hour away from the Gods," he argues. He points, for example, to the steady decline of belief in religion, from 64.7% in 1952 to 22.9% in 2005, and to the similar decline in those who find religion important, from 46.2% in 1979 to 27% in 1998. Moreover, in 2000–03 only 9.3% claimed an individual religious affiliation.[14]

In the case of Shinto, evidence exists suggesting an "estrangement from religion" (shūkyō banare). We can see this in the progressive loss of private Shinto altars (kamidana); according to the Association of Shinto Shrines, this fell from 51% of households in 1996 to 43.8% in 2006. The data also show low percentages of actual worship in Japanese households.[15] Moreover, well-educated young people believe and participate in religion at a markedly lower rate. For example, a study between 1999 and 2001 showed that the number of college-age students who believed in the existence of Shinto kami declined from 19.7% to just 13%.[16] Adding to this picture is a long-term trend of closing Shinto shrines, especially in rural areas.[17] As we have seen, this began in the pre-war period with official efforts at consolidation (jinja gōshi); Between 1902 and 1938, shrine numbers declined from a high of 196,000 to 110,000 shrines; after the war this number dropped again and remained steady at roughly 80,000.[18] It is therefore unclear what the future holds, particularly in rural Japan with its declining population. Some have argued that up to 41% of local rural shrines are in danger of disappearing in the near future.[19]

Other adverse effects of modernization include loss of parishioners (ujiko) due to rural depopulation, especially since 1965, and difficulties staffing shrines with new priests. Between 1980 and 2006, the number of Shinto priests decreased by almost 20%.[20] New bed towns and housing developments (danchi) in and around cities often have no nearby shrines. folk Shinto festivals, originally annual rites tied to rice agriculture, have not always survived in an increasingly urbanized society where less than 4% of the working population engages in agriculture. Where they have survived, they have become increasingly commercialized "civic pageants" and tourist attractions, losing their religious character.[21]

Shinto scholar Ueda Kenji also points to the deleterious effects of modern society's rationalization (which he conflates with Westernization). Some of the examples he cites include scheduling festivals on Sundays to fit the Western calendar and replacing the traditional New Year's pine decoration or kadomatsu with commercially produced cheap, paper substitutes. All are instances of modern efficiencies that erode rituals' religious meaning.[22] The post-war separation of religion from public education has also contributed to low levels of religious literacy and thus to increasing secularization. Many are ignorant of basic facts about Shinto and would be hard-pressed to distinguish a Shinto shrine from a Buddhist temple.

Yet, other trends seem to belie the notion that Shinto has lost its modern relevance. Many social commentators note that visits to shrines at New Year (known as hatsumōde) have become increasingly popular in the post-war period, particularly at large urban shrines like Meiji Jingū in Tokyo. Even during the economic downturn, these numbers skyrocketed from

45.1 million in 1970 to 98.19 million in 2008, about 70% of the population.[23] However, the question is over what these mass visits really mean. Is it a key example of Shinto's secularization, or does it mark Shinto's resurgence as a vital part of contemporary private and public life? Certainly, festivals and shrine annual events have become increasingly commercialized and commodified; they are often treated as non-religious, simply as part of Japan's unique traditional and cultural heritage.[24]

Shinto's privatization—shrines as local centers for personal piety and collective identity

Many argue against the secularization thesis. That is, they argue that "the idea of secularization in Japan, if taken to refer beyond institutions to the attenuation of all forms of faith, spirituality, beliefs and practices, is clearly mistaken."[25] Even in the case of shrine Shinto, some do not see an institutional decline but rather a continued relevance despite secularizing forces at work.

Japanese engineer and industrialist Honda Sōichirō, for example, claims that Shinto has adapted as Japan transitioned from an agricultural society to an industrial one—from "land of vigorous rice plants" to the "land of the integrated circuit."[26] The *kami* and festivals are not living fossils; they are alive today in urban high-tech Japan because they are compatible with modernity. New shrines are found in seemingly secular settings such as electronics factories, department stores, and automobile plants. In the Ginza district in Tokyo, for example, shrines have moved from their original location on the ground to the top of high-rise buildings; Kakugo Inari Shrine, which dates from the early nineteenth century is now on the roof of the Matsuzakaya store at Ginza 6-chome. Shrines are not incompatible with urbanization; they adapt to the new urban realities, and people come to pray there for the prosperity of family and company.[27]

Shinto ceremonies are performed when satellites are launched at the Tanegashima Space Center, with Shinto priests performing rituals for the safety and success of the mission. Honda argues that Shinto has not succumbed to the corrosive and disenchanting effects of modern society but has, rather, found its niche. No matter how much technological know-how scientists have, they remain humble before the unknown, relying on the *kami* to protect them.[28]

Mark Mullins argues that the post-war disestablishment of State Shinto with the new constitutional guarantees of freedom of religion has meant that "[i]n stark contrast to earlier periods, contemporary religious lives unfold in the context of a free-market religious economy."[29] Shinto shrines, independently registered separately as religious juridical persons (*shūkyō hōjin*), no longer depend on state support, but on the support of their "customers," the parishioners who visit them. According to some scholars, despite the momentous changes in the post-war period, this marks a continuity with the past: The core of Shinto faith is the worship of the *kami* at local shrines. As we have previously seen, Yanagita Kunio made this point in critiquing the Taishō state policy that Shinto was non-religious in character. Who is it, asks Yanagita, that "distributes charms and talismans, receives offerings, and hears the prayers of the priests and parishioners?" Local *kami* are a central spiritual presence for shrine worship. No matter how the government may try to refashion Shinto into a secular institution, the *kami* remain at the heart of Shinto practice. Shrines are more than a means of enforcing a bureaucratically devised national patriotism centering around the divine figure of the emperor.

Yet, damaging misconceptions of Shinto continue to this day. In an essay written in 1993, entitled, "Is a Shinto Renewal Possible?," University of Tokyo professor Saeki Shōichi argues that the great tragedy of post-war Japan was the wholesale spiritual dismantling of Shinto. The Occupation, as expressed in the Shinto Directive, completely misconstrued Shinto. The nuances and complexities were reduced to the simplistic stereotype of a state cult, based upon jingoistic ultra-nationalist beliefs and spurring on Japan's aggressive militarism.[30] This characterization overlooked Shinto's vibrant roots in the local customs of mountain religious traditions which were historically combined with Buddhism (*shinbutsu shūgō*). Local *kami* worship makes a Shinto renewal possible.

Local shrines continue to offer an animistic world, within which individuals and communities can freely commune with the *kami*. They can create a special space where people experience a "radical personalization of the universe," and "the boundaries between human/ natural/divine are extremely permeable."[31] Shinto scholar Bernard Scheid sums up the powerful role shrines can play by noting that,

> [T]he common people's approach to the *kami* seems to provide a stabilizing factor in shrine Shinto. For most Japanese, shrines are symbols of local identity. By extension, this localism may include patriotic pride but nationalism does not seem to be the primary motivation to pay a visit to a Shinto shrine. Rather the shrines are places to pray for this worldly benefits and protection from immediate risks and dangers.[32]

This points to two important functions that shrines continue to serve in contemporary Japan. First, the shrines continue to provide a place for private individual piety. Shinto scholar John Nelson has observed that shrines remain relevant in an industrialized society by providing a space for people to freely choose when, how, where, and why they want to worship. For example, although Kamigamo Shrine in Kyoto has a long history allied to state interests as a "nation preserving shrine," very few visitors today are aware of its past status.[33] Nelson cautions against using "binary models" to determine whether people visit for either sacred or secular reasons. Signs advertising religious services for a variety of prayers, purification ceremonies, and similar rituals present shrines as a spiritual gateway to their enshrined *kami*. But visitors are just as likely to be tourists, attracted to the shrine for its rich historical heritage and natural beauty. The shrine allows them the freedom to do what they want—they can sightsee, purchase fortunes (*omikuji*) and charms (*omamori*), and exhibit "deference" whether to a presence of the deity, ritual propriety, or something else. Contemporary Shinto tolerates freedom of choice—informal, "innovative and highly personal forms of worship"— that allows highly subjective practices that suit personal spiritual needs.[34]

Second, Nelson reaffirms the centrality of shrines to their villages, neighborhoods, cities, and regions. In his study of Suwa Jinja in Nagasaki, Nelson demonstrates how the annual round of ritual and festival events (*nenchū gyōji*) at the shrine make it central to the community. Drawing on anthropologist Clifford Geertz's work, Nelson shows how Suwa Shrine supplies a system of cultural, traditional, and religious symbols through which people build meaning in their lives. This allows them in turn to build a collective sense of communal pride and self-esteem. While shrines in rural areas are struggling, urban ones show increasing participation in their larger festivals, such as Suwa Shrine's famous Okunchi *matsuri*.[35] Suwa Shrine exemplifies the trend, begun in the 1970s, of reviving shrine practices and festivals for people "to recover their traditional value orientation."[36] Of course, this often bumps up against the realities of modern urbanization. As a classic example, Ueda Kenji notes difficulties of reviving the Kanda Festival in downtown Tokyo due to police concerns over traffic control.[37] Some traditional shrine activities also challenge the lines drawn between secular and sacred. Ueda cites the case of Ikuta Shrine in Kobe in 1970, which ran afoul of municipal tax laws in constructing a new parking lot to perform traffic safety rituals. A parking lot, which seems like a secular space, is in reality a sacred locale for religious purification and prayers for safety. Shrine Shinto is accommodating itself to contemporary social changes.[38]

Restorationist trends

Another critique of the secularization thesis notes that the model does not fit Japanese realities. Shimazono Susumu has noted that "State Shinto," defined broadly as Shinto-inspired ideas and practices propagated in the governmental and political sphere to unify the nation, is still socially powerful in postwar Japan.[39] There is a concerted effort today by conservative right-wing groups, whose discourse is similar to the religious right in the U.S., to restore Shinto to its civil role in the public sphere.[40] Mark Mullins sees these "restorationist initiatives" as a counter-reaction against the secularizing effect of Occupation policies privatizing religion.[41]

It is a movement that has gained steam during and after Japan's troubles in the 1990s. The effort to restore the public pre-war role of Shinto continues to be spearheaded by the Association of Shinto Shrines, which, as we have seen, was inspired by Ashizu Uzuhiko's opposition to a shrine religion exclusively focused on local *kami* cults. According to Shinto scholar Mark Teeuwen, the Association's key principle is that a faith based on private rituals (*minkan saishi*) is insufficient; shrines should serve a public role by unifying people's national consciousness. As the Association's own Hase Haruo stated in 1993, this is to be accomplished through "national rituals (*kokkateki saishi*) which pray for the peace (*goantai*) of the imperial house and the prosperity of the state and the people."[42] A major policy of the Association then, is distributing Ise Jingū amulets (*taima*) to local shrines so that parishioners (*ujiko*) can install them in their homes on their god shelf (*kamidana*). They see this practice as central, not only for the financial support of Ise Jingū but "to unify the nation in worship of the imperial deity Amaterasu Ōmikami."[43] Understanding the "why" of distributing these Ise amulets, notes another Shinto scholar, John Breen, is key for understanding twenty-first-century Shinto. The *taima* serve as a vital link between Ise, the emperor, and the Japanese people; they are a means of "returning to the origins," by restoring a sense of awe for the transcendent as embodied in the emperor and his ancestral *kami* enshrined at Ise.[44] The goal here is restorationist—resurrecting the Meiji era's civil form of Shinto centering on reverence to the emperor in order to foster a unified patriotic nationalism.[45]

The Jinja Honchō's agenda has advanced in both the political and judicial spheres. Politically, the Association expanded its influence by establishing its own political wing, the Shinto Seiji Renmei (the Shinto Association of Spiritual Leadership), in 1969. This organization, which seeks to renew "Japanese spiritual values," now boasts the current prime minister, Abe Shinzō, as its secretary-general, and, in the fourth Abe administration starting in November 2017, sixteen out of the twenty members belong. As of March 2018, over 205 among 465 members of the House of Representatives and 82 among 242 members of the House of Councilors are also affiliated, the majority of whom belong to the LDP party.[46]

Shinto Seiji Renmei has scored several political victories. These include the government restoration of the use of era names in 1979 and, in 1999, the national flag and anthem, *Kimigayo*. In 2007, it lobbied successfully to establish a new holiday on April 29 in honor of Emperor Shōwa to reflect "in awe" at his "sacred virtues."[47] Most recently, Abe's initiatives to restore Shinto's "rightful place" in the public sphere have included his hosting the 2016 summit of the Group of Seven at Shima, a resort area near Ise Jingū, to highlight Japan's Shinto-based imperial heritage.[48] Abe has also continued earlier LDP prime ministers' support of the special character of Yasukuni Shrine, the controversial shrine based on the earlier state-supported "shrine to beckon the souls" (*shōkonsha*) for commemoration of the "glorious war dead" (*eirei*). Although Yasukuni is now a private shrine, it remains an object of conservatives' patriotic fervor for Japan's militarist past.[49] Abe, like prime ministers Nakasone Yasuhiro and Koizumi Jun'ichirō before him, last visited the shrine and has supported it repeatedly with his private offerings.

A key goal of the Shinto Seiji Renmei is educational reforms to combat young people's moral and spiritual decay. This relies on restoring the ideals of the 1890 Imperial Rescript on Education.[50] For example, Abe's former education minister, Shimomura Hakubun, said in a 2015 interview that he wanted schools to inspire patriotism by increasing students' respect for Japan's national symbols and removing "self-deprecating" views of history and "disputed war crimes." Citing a survey that over 84% of Japanese high school students feel worthless at times, double the figures in the United States, Shimomura argues that "without changing that, Japan has no future."[51] The government is also attempting to enforce the singing of the national anthem in school and to install revised textbooks that promote a more positive image of Japan and love of country. Such initiatives are reminiscent of the pre-war morals and patriotic (*shūshin*) education found in works like the *Kokutai no hongi*.[52]

Key to this restorationist trend is the Meiji era tactic of defining *jinja* as non-religious in character. Here Shinto is defined as fundamental for understanding a uniquely Japanese traditional and cultural identity.[53] The Supreme Court has also defined Shinto as a secular practice. The landmark case is the ruling which allowed Tsu City to disburse tax funds for Shinto ground-purification ceremonies (*jichinsai*). Despite Article 20 of the Constitution, these practices can be supported by the state so long as they are secular "customary practices" that people no longer see as having a religious character.[54] The proposal of the Liberal Democratic Party in 2012 to revise the Constitution adds an exception to Article 20 following this legal precedent, allowing state support for activities originally deemed religious but now regarded as customs or matters of social etiquette.[55]

Econationalist Shinto as an ecological religion

The fourth trend is to revision Shinto as an ecological religion. Kamata Tōji, Saeki Shōichi (discussed above), and others argue that a renewal is possible by recovering what they perceive is Shinto's fundamental nature as an "ancient nature religion."[56] This characterization of Shinto as an "ancient nature religion" or "green Shinto" began in the 1970s with priests like Sonoda Minoru and Ueda Masaaki,[57] who sought to protect shrines' "guardian forests" (*chinju no mori*).[58] Shinto for them was synonymous with natural beauty, tied especially to local forest groves. It emphasized human intimacy with a mysterious natural world and accented the power of purification rituals for reestablishing a harmonious spiritual balance between the human, divine, and natural world.[59]

It is increasingly popular to think of Shinto as an ancient cult of nature worship that is alive and well in modern, industrialized Japan. While this was certainly not the Association of Shinto Shrines' original view, times have changed.[60] The Association's weekly newspaper, the *Jinja shinpō*, regularly discusses Shinto environmentalism in highly nationalistic terms. Shrines are the national guardians of the environment, and the Shinto "natural way" is a noble way to exercise "responsibility to future generations and the national good."[61] On the Association's home page under "Spiritual Beliefs," a section entitled "Nature Worship" notes that

> Shinto has always made one of its highest priorities coexistence with nature. It could even be said that Shinto could not exist apart from nature. In Shinto, we believe that both humans and nature are children of *kami*, and live together as members of the same family.[62]

The major new role of this paradigm was symbolized by the international conference the Association organized at Ise Jingū on June 24, 2014, entitled, "Tradition for the Future: Culture, Faith and Values for a Sustainable Planet." As an ancient nature religion, Shinto offers spiritual resources for solving the environmental crisis.[63]

Redefining Shinto

The essays in this section reflect the above contemporary trends. All of them accept the postwar assumption that Shinto should be classified as a religion. However, the way each goes about defining Shinto religiosity is creatively different.

Ueda Kenji finds underlying theological principles that define Shinto as a unique form of religiosity. He challenges the basic stereotype of Shinto as predominantly based on practice rather than doctrines like Western religions. He argues for a "basic Shinto," which is essentially a clear conceptual framework underlying Shinto in all its manifestations—at shrines, in sects, folk Shinto, etc. Defining that conceptual framework is key for identifying Shinto's unique value orientation, while avoiding essentialist arguments identifying it with Japaneseness (*Nihonjinron*). Ueda also believes this conceptual framework transcends narrow restorationist models of Shinto as a nationalist, imperial-centered way.

Kamata Tōji defines Shinto spirituality in terms of a distinctive non-rational experience. There is ever-available potential to experience the *kami* in the natural world. This is the distinctive experiential core of the religion that is intimately associated with local environments and geographies. Kamata relies on Lafcadio Hearn's Romantic definition of Shinto. By visiting a shrine, Hearn argued, one can intuit an essential "sense of Shinto," a deeply numinous feeling of the divine intuited within the natural world. This is a "feeling of awe and gratitude toward the eternal in life and creative power active within nature." This divine sensibility is a basic feature of Shinto as a "forest religion" with its "guardian forests (*chinju no mori*).[64] Nonetheless, for Kamata, this eco-religious vision is not a form of Shinto nationalism, as epitomized by the Jinja Honchō's neo-conservative formulation. Kamata believes this "spiritual ecology," while key for understanding religiosity in the Japanese archipelago, forms a wider common heritage shared throughout Asia and the Pacific Rim. Elsewhere, Kamata, like Ueda, also talks about Shinto having a "latent doctrine," with its seven key characteristics as a religion of place, way, beauty, festival, technique, poetry, and ecological wisdom.[65] But Shinto ultimately is distinctive because rather than fixed doctrines like Buddhism and Christianity, it relies on spiritual intuition of the *kami* made manifest (*miare*) in the natural world and on the indigenous traditions associated with these experiences.

The three other readings in this section take a different approach to define Shinto as a religion. All three move from interior psychological or doctrinal definitions to exterior institutional, ritual, and social factors. All three look to the dynamic local folkways, tales, and rituals, and festivals centered on at local shrines. These local traditions tied to shrines have been a communal faith that, while temporarily obscured beneath the facade of State Shinto, continues to exist.

Miyata Noboru's essay analyzes Yanagita's post-war writings on folk Shinto as a way of offering an extended critique of State Shinto. For Miyata, the official version of State Shinto is superficial—merely a modern bureaucratically invented tradition. What is central to Shinto in its long history, however, is ordinary people's deep personal piety toward the enshrined *kami* at the village level, which continued in the modern period, only temporarily obscured beneath the state-supported facade of the imperial way.

Sonoda Minoru, like Kamata, defines Shinto as essentially a nature religion, and, like Miyata, argues that its "religious roots have always rested in Japanese folk culture." It cannot be classified as a world religion founded upon the teachings of a master with a clearly marked path for personal salvation. It belongs to the anonymous folk who "superimpose an invisible spiritual world on their natural environs and make piety and reverence worshipping the gods and ancestors their main principle." Sonoda calls this folk Shinto "climatic" (*fūdo*) cults.

These *kami*-centered cults based in local shrines are anti-secular in character. Local shrines are sanctified places where local worshippers can commune with manifestations (*miare*) of the invisible *kami*. Shrine-related festivals (*matsuri*) for the *kami* are different from secularized community "events." Sonoda here is very much responding to his historical moment—when commercial events from rock concerts to the upcoming Tokyo Olympic Games have become a fixture of the Japanese world. Such modern spectacles are produced by a culture industry and designed to attract mass audiences of consumers for entertainment, as the Western cultural critic Theodor Adorno has described them.[66] Shrine festivals, according to Sonoda, are anything but commodities. Shrines and their festivals are "a source of order, and, above all, inspire a collective sense of belonging to one's native home (*kokoro no furusato*) for local people." Shinto is not an individual private faith or quest for salvation in the standard Western sense of the term. Sonoda defines Shinto in a much broader sense as a cultural religion (*bunkateki shūkyō*) that reflects and supports the interests of the local community.

Inoue Hiroshi's essay also highlights Shinto's ancient polytheistic heritage based on animism, something that is not distinctively Japanese but is "humanity's common religious foundation." What is distinctive about Shinto as one form of Japanese animism is the way it has been handed down and changed in Japan. In particular, Inoue notes that the religious institution of the shrine (*jinja*) for the worship of the *kami* is unique to Japan. What does Inoue mean by the title of his book, "Shinto's false and true image"? Unlike pre-war texts like the *Jinja hongi*, Inoue is arguing that Shinto shrines and faith in the *kami* are not, as some would have it, an unchanging ancient tradition from ages eternal. That image is false. Shrines are distinctive religious institutions that have developed in Japan. Looked at historically, they reveal that Shinto has undergone significant changes over time. Even the word Shinto, as we pronounce it today, is a relatively recent term. Inoue's historical genealogy of Shinto shrines is a critique of the "restorationist" model revealing Shinto's constantly changing and evolving character; particularly important are the creation of *ichinomiya* shrines during the middle ages.

Notes

1 Peter Duss, "Shōwa-era Japan and Beyond: From Imperial Japan to Japan Inc.," in *The Routledge Handbook of Japanese Culture and Society*, eds. Victoria Lyon Bestor and Theodore C. Bestor (New York, Routledge, 2011), 25–26.

2 Only after 2006 did Japan again attain 1991 levels of industrial production. "Japan as Number One Land of the Setting Sun," *The Economist*, November 12, 2009, http://www.economist.com/node/14861545.

3 James McBride and Beina Xu, "Abenomics and the Japanese Economy," Council on Foreign Relations, http://www.cfr.org/japan/abenomics-japanese-economy/p30383.

4 See Roger Bowen, *Japan's Dysfunctional Democracy: The Liberal Democratic Party and Structural Corruption* (New York: Routledge, 2003); Yoichi Funabashi and Barak Kushner eds., *Examining Japan's Lost Decades* (New York: Routledge, 2015).

5 "Majority of Japanese People Lack Confidence in Government," *The Telegraph*, September 2, 2016. The results are based on Associated Press-GfK poll, http://www.telegraph.co.uk/news/world news/asia/japan/8735801/Majority-of-Japanese-people-lack-confidence-in-government.html.

6 Cabinet Office, "Consumer Confidence Survey," http://www.esri.cao.go.jp/en/stat/shouhi/shouhi-e.html.

7 Statistics Bureau of Japan, Statistical Handbook of Japan 2018, http://www.stat.go.jp/english/data/handbook/c0117.htm.

8 Anne Allison, *Precarious Japan* (Durham, NC: Duke University Press, 2013), 8–9.

9 "Plight of Irregular Workers," *The Japan Times*, January 5, 2016, http://www.japantimes.co.jp/opinion/2016/01/05/editorials/plight-of-irregular-workers/#.WQQRSLGZPwc. Others become *johatsu,* "the evaporated people," simply vanishing off the grid due to shame, hopelessness and debt.

10 The *hikikomori* who have withdrawn from society—over half a million in 2016—is suggestive of the difficulties Japanese youth are having living in contemporary Japan. "Japan home to 541,000 young recluses, survey finds," *The Japan Times*, September 7, 2016, http://www.japantimes.co.jp/news/2016/09/07/national/japan-home-541000-young-recluses-survey-finds/#.WQQTlLGZPwd.

11 Allison, "Precarious," 174–76. The key early manifestation of youth anomy occurred in 1995 with the shocking sarin gas attack on the Tokyo subway by members of the fringe new religious movement, Aum Shinrikyō.

12 Susan Tipton, *Modern Japan: A Social and Political History*, 2nd edition (New York: Routledge, 2008), 239–60.

13 Rodney Stark, "Secularization, RIP," *Sociology of Religion* 60, No. 3 (Autumn, 1999):251.

14 Ian Reader, "Secularization, R.I.P.? Nonsense! The 'Rush Hour Away from the Gods' and the Decline of Religion in Contemporary Japan," *Journal of Religion in Japan* 1 (2012):12–13. These numbers dropped steeply after the Aum subway sarin gas attack in 1995.

15 Ibid., 22. The 2003 COE "Social Survey Regarding Japanese People's Religious Consciousness and Conceptions of *Kami*" found only 44.1% of households using a *kamidana*. See Kokugakuin University, *Newsletter* No. 3 (March 2007), 15.

16 Ibid., 14. Other surveys of adults in general show higher percentages: The 2003 COE study notes higher percentage of 35.6% (ibid., 15). The NHK Hōsō Bunka Kenkyūjō longitudinal survey, "Nihonjin no ishiki," shows that belief in the *kami* remains remarkably stable between 1973 and 2013 over 30%. See Bunkachō, *Shūkyō kanren tōkei ni kansuru shiryōshū* (2015), http://www.bunka.go.jp/tokei_hakusho_shuppan/tokeichosa/shumu_kanrentokei/pdf/h26_chosa.pdf.

17 Reader, "Secularization," 19.

18 Bunkachō, *Shūkyō kanren tōkei*, 22. See Ishii Kenji, *Databook gendai Nihonjin no shūkyō* (Tokyo: Shin'yōsha, 2008), 76. Bunkachō ed. *Shūkyō nenkan* 2016, http://www.bunka.go.jp/tokei_hakusho_shuppan/hakusho_nenjihokokusho/shukyo_nenkan/pdf/h28.

19 Isabel Reynolds, "Abe Treads Fine Line in Ise Shrine Tour as Shinto Religion Faces Challenges," *The Japan Times*, May 25, 2016, http://www.japantimes.co.jp/news/2016/05/25/national/politics-diplomacy/abe-must-tread-fine-line-g-7-ise-shrine-tour-shinto-overall-fears-slipping-shadows/#.WTB4JbGZPwc.

20 Bernard Scheid, "Shintō Shrines: Traditions and Transformations," in *Handbook of Contemporary Japanese Religions,* eds. Inken Prohl and John Nelson (Leiden: Brill, 2012), 81. See also Ueda Kenji, "Contemporary Social Change and Shinto Tradition," *Japanese Journal of Religious Studies* 6 (March–June, 1979):322–25. According to Ueda, even in 1976, approximately one chief priest served seven shrines.

21 Inoue Nobutaka and Sakamoto Koremaru, "Modern and Contemporary Shinto." *Encyclopedia of Shinto*, http://eos.kokugakuin.ac.jp/modules/xwords/entry.php?entryID=738.

22 Ueda Kenji, "Contemporary Social Change," 20–21.

23 Mark R. Mullins, "Religion in Contemporary Japanese Lives," in *Routledge Companion of Japanese Culture and Society,* eds. Victoria Lyon Bestor and Theodore C. Bestor (New York: Routledge, 2013), 68–69. This is in contrast to a very low percentage visiting shrines as a daily routine, 1.9%. See COE's "Social Survey Regarding Japanese Participation in, Recognition of, and Evaluations of Religious Organizations," in *Kokugakuin University Newsletter* No. 3 (March 2007), 20.

24 Ueda, "Contemporary Social Change," 321–22.

25 James Beckford, *Social Theory and Religion* (Cambridge: Cambridge University Press, 2003), 52.

26 Honda Sōichirō, "Shinto in Japanese Culture," *Nanzan Bulletin* 8 (1984):24.

27 Ishii Kenji, "The Secularization of Religion in the City," *Japanese Journal of Religious Studies* 13 (February–March 1986):202–06.

28 Ibid., 25–6. Honda also makes an argument for the "spirit of Shinto" underlying modern capitalism: The communal effort of the village in cooperation with the *kami* (*shinjin kyōdō*) to produce a good harvest translates into the common cooperative work ethic at the heart of the means of production of the corporation. Here the pre-war ideology found in texts like *Shinmin no michi* is abandoned. Its moral ideal that "imperial subjects devote themselves fully to the fundamental principles of our national polity" (*kokutai*) is replaced with the salaryman who is devoted fully to the modern corporation.

29 Mullins, "Religion in Contemporary Japanese Lives," 64.

30 Saeki Shōichi, "Is a Shinto Renewal Possible?," *Nanzan Bulletin* 17 (1993):34–35. They also misconceived it given their own Western "faith in progress," that saw Christian monotheism as the most advanced religion that "has swept through the world like a bulldozer toppling and tramping the ancient gods and native deities," dismissing them as a primitive "ancient and outmoded mentality," 35.

31 John Clammer, "The Politics of Animism," *Interculture* 137 (April, 2000):228–29.

32 Bernard Scheid, "Shintō Shrines," 103. Scheid's point seems underscored by data that numbers of people who carry with them talismans (*omamori*) or charms (*ofuda*) from shrines and temples, who offer prayers for well-being, business success, and passing school entrance exams have remained the same or increased slightly from 1973 to 2013, roughly in the 30% range of those surveyed. See Bunkachō, *Shūkyō kanren tōkei*, 65.

33 John Nelson, "Freedom of Expression: The Very Modern Practice of Visiting a Shinto Shrine," *Japanese Journal of Religious Studies* 23 (Spring, 1996):129.

34 Ibid., 135–36.

35 John Nelson, *A Year in the Life of a Shinto Shrine* (Seattle, WA: The University of Washington Press, 1996), 10–12, 159. See also Michael K. Roemer, "Shinto Festival Involvement and a Sense of Self in Contemporary Japan," *Japan Forum* 22 (3–4) 2010:491–512 and Sonoda Minoru, "The Traditional Festival in Urban Society," *Japanese Journal of Religious Studies* (June–September, 1975):103–36.

36 Ueda Kenji, "Contemporary Social Change," 320.

37 Ibid., 319–20.

38 Ibid., 319.

39 Susumu Shimazono, "State Shinto and Religion in Post-War Japan," in *The SAGE Handbook of the Sociology of Religion*, eds. James Beckford and N.J. Demerath III (Thousand Oaks, CA: Sage Publications, 2005), 707.

40 Ibid., 707.

41 Mark Mullins, "Secularization, Deprivatization, and the Reappearance of 'Public Religion' in Japanese Society," *Journal of Japanese Religion* 1 (2012):71–73. See also Elisabetta Porcu, "Religion and State in Contemporary Japan," in *Religion and Politics*, eds. Johann P. Arnason and Ireneusz Karoleewski (Edinburgh: Edinburgh University Press, 2014), 168–82. This may also reflect a traditional response of "turning to the gods in times of trouble" (*kurushii toki no kamidanomi*).

42 Mark Teeuwen, "Jinja Honchō and Shrine Shintō Policy," *Japan Forum* 8, No. 2 (1996):185; Mullins, "Secularization," 72.

43 Ibid., 184.

44 John Been, "Resurrecting the Sacred Land of Japan: The State of Shinto in the 21st Century," *Japanese Journal of Religious Studies* 37, No. 2 (2010):297–98.

45 Teeuwen, "Jinja Honchō," 185; Mullins, "Secularization," 72. Teeuwen notes that the Association of Shinto Shrines sees it as a restored rather than an invented tradition of Meiji bureaucrats.

46 Mullins, "Secularization," 72–73. For a list of LDP restoration initiatives, 1998–2009, see 77–78. For a general overview, see also Michael Holtz, "Japanese Prime Minister, Party Leaders Seek Policies that Revive Shinto Religion," *Christian Century* 133, No. 2 (January 20, 2016):16, https://www.questia.com/magazine/1G1-441765734/japanese-prime-minister-party-leaders-seek-policies.

47 David MacNeill, "Back to the Future: Shinto's Growing Influence in Politics," *Japan Times*, November 23, 2013, http://www.japantimes.co.jp/news/2013/11/23/national/politics-diplomacy/back-to-the-future-shintos-growing-influence-in-politics/#.WSMirbGZPaY.

48 It should be noted that in the post-war era, Ise Jingū has also served as a ritual center attracting politicians and government officials. The first prime minister who annually visited Ise was Hatoyama Ichiro in 1955. Abe also attended Ise's *shikinen sengū* ceremonies held every twenty years marking the construction of its new shrine. On October 2, 2013 he attended the *sengyo no gi* evening rites when the physical transfer of the divine object and divine treasures occurred. Although he attended the ceremony as a private citizen (with eight cabinet ministers), this was the first time since 1929 that a prime minister had attended this ceremony. These activities, among others, have garnered scholarly debate over whether some form of State Shinto continues today. This idea was first advanced by Murakami Shigeyoshi in his book, *Kokka shintō*, in 1970, and is advanced today by historian of Japanese religions, Shimazono Susumu, Koyasu Nobukuni and others. See, for example, Shimazono, "State Shinto and Religion in Post War Japan," in *The SAGE Handbook of the Sociology of Religion*, eds. James A Beckford and N.J. Demerath III (London: Sage Publications, 2007), 697–709.

49 John Breen, *Yasukuni, the War Dead, and the Struggle for Japan's Past* (Oxford: Oxford University Press, 2008).

50 Mullins, "Secularization," 74.

51 Ibid.

52 Yet these efforts to turn back the clock face significant hurdles. In a 2009 poll, for example, 82% of respondents are satisfied with Emperor Heisei's post-war constitutional role as a symbol of state and the Japanese people; only 6% would want him to have any real political authority. Any return to the emperor's pre-war sovereignty does not seem to have much support. See Katō Motonobu, *Heisei kōshitsukan—sokui 20 nen kōshitsu ni kansuru ishiki chōsha kara* (NHK Chōshabu, February 2010), 24.

53 The recent Ministry of Education Center of Excellence (COE) Program-funded "National Learning Institute for Shintō and Japanese Culture" at Kokugakuin University seems to have this as the heart of its mission. Their goal is to do research into "the original Japanese culture that arose out of Shintō" that is "a symbol of Japanese culture and the Japanese worldview." See Sakamoto Koremaru, "Thoughts on Shintō Research," 21st Century Center of Excellence Program Establishment of a National Learning Center Institute on Shinto and Japanese Culture, http://21coe.kokugakuin.ac.jp/articlesintranslation/pdf/07Sakamoto_en_ver11.pdf.

54 The Kakunaga v. Sekiguchi case in 1977 marks the first major Supreme Court decision on the separation of religion and state. See Michiaki Okuyama, "Religion and Japanese Constitutional Law," *Academia* 83 (June, 2006):147–48.

55 Mullins argues that the secularism at work here still "masks a religious spirit." See Mullins, "Secularization," 80. See also Michiaki Okuyama, "The Yasukuni Shrine Problem in the East Asian Context: Religion and Politics in Modern Japan," *Politics and Religion Journal* 3 (January, 2017):235–38 and Helen Hardacre, "Japan," in Robert Wuthnow, ed. *Encyclopedia of Politics and Religion*, 2nd edition (Washington DC: CQ Press, 2007), 492–98.

56 Ibid., 46; Saeki, "Shinto Renewal," 35.
57 1927–2016, Shinto priest, historian in ancient Japanese history, professor and later professor emeritus of Kyoto University.
58 Aike P. Rots, "Sacred Forests, Sacred Nation," *Japanese Journal of Religious Studies* 42 (2015):212–13; Kamata Tōji, "Shinto Research and the Humanities in Japan," *Zygon* 51 (March 2016):46–47. For some case studies, see also Ueda, "Contemporary Social Change," 316–18.
59 Rosemarie Bernard, "Shinto and Ecology: Practice and Orientations to Nature," Forum on Religion and Ecology at Yale, http://fore.yale.edu/religion/shinto/.
60 See Teeuwen, "Jinja Honchō," 185.
61 John K. Nelsen, *Enduring Identities: The Guise of Shinto in Contemporary Japan* (Honolulu: University of Hawai'i Press, 2000), 246–47.
62 Jinja Honchō Association of Shinto Shrines, "Spiritual Beliefs," http://www.jinjahoncho.or.jp/en/spiritual/index.html.
63 Rots, "Sacred Forests," 206.
64 Ibid., 47.
65 Kamata, "Shinto Research," 48–50.
66 Theodor Adorno, *The Culture Industry: Selected Essays on Mass Culture*, ed. J.M. Bernstein (London: Routledge, 1991), 11, 67.

30

MIYATA NOBORU

State Shinto
(1999)

Miyata Noboru (1936–2000) is a well-known folklorist and prolific writer on Japanese folklore. Born in Yokohama, Kanagawa Prefecture, Miyata grew up to be an academic, graduating from Tokyo University of Education (later Tsukuba University) in 1960 and earning his Ph.D. in 1976 on folk beliefs related to Miroku (Maitreya Bodhisattva). In 1982, he became a professor of history and anthropological studies at Tsukuba, and, after his retirement, Miyata joined the faculty at Kanagawa University, working with the famous medieval historian Amino Yoshihiko.

His numerous publications reveal his wide-ranging intellectual curiosity in Japanese and comparative folklore. Key publications include: *Miroku shinkō no kenkyū: Nihon ni okeru dentōteki meshiakan* (A Study of Miroku Belief: A Traditional View on Messiah in Japan, 1970), *Ikigami shinkō: hito o kami ni matsuru shūzoku* (Belief in Living Deities: Customs to Venerate Persons as Deities, 1970), *Toshi minzokuron no kadai* (Challenges in the Studies of Urban Folklore, 1982), and *Nihonjin to Shūkyō* (The Japanese and Religion, 1999).

The following essay, published near the end of Miyata's life, discusses his views of "folk Shinto" (*minzoku Shintō*). While this term is close to Orikuchi's "popular Shinto," (*minkan Shintō*) it clearly reflects Miyata's indebtedness to Yanagita Kunio. Miyata is interested in looking at actual contemporary everyday folkways and rituals, with their accompanying spiritual consciousness. This folk Shinto is difficult to systematize, but it may be described as a dynamic religious force existing beyond particular shrines, religious groups, and, of course, the pre-war system of "State Shinto" (*kokka Shintō*). Miyata builds upon Yanagita's post-war critique of the Occupational authorities' Shinto Directive, arguing that the Directive misses the complexities of shrine Shinto before, during, and after the government's attempts to institutionalize it. The dynamism of a folk and village-based religion has several elements—rites of passage, annual calendrical festivals and rites, notions of the other world, ancestral spirits and *kami*, and so on. It is also particularly associated with local *ujigami* shrines, which were closely tied to the local society and environs and which persisted despite the overarching authority of the pre-war state cult. Folk Shinto was impervious to any governmental controls and reforms. Indeed, State Shinto ultimately failed because it could not replace this local, dynamic folk piety. This localized folk Shinto continues in post-war Japan.

STATE SHINTO
(1999)

Yanagita Kunio's perspective in his *Ujigami to ujiko*

In the diary of Hori Ichirō, the son-in-law of Yanagita Kunio, there is a passage from August 12, 1945 about Yanagita Kunio visiting the Hori household bearing the news of Japan's defeat in the war. Hori wrote movingly about Yanagita's demeanor at this time.

> Yanagita picked up a text, *Jinja to saishi* (Shrines and Religious Observances), and told me, "Now that things have come to such a pass, I think that the problem is how to deal with what comes afterward. How can scholarship be useful from now on?"

Heading the list of Yanagita's works completed immediately before and after the war is his *Senzo no hanashi* [A Discussion about Ancestors][1] followed by *Yamamiya kō* [Thoughts on Mountain Shrines], *Saijitsu kō* [Thoughts on National Holidays], and *Ujigami to ujiko* [Local Divinities and Their Parishioners]. Of these, the latter three works are well known, collected under the title, *Shin kokugaku dan* [Discourses on a New National Learning].[2] The zeal of this seventy-year-old scholar in his quest to make folklore studies meaningful to the spiritually devastated people of post-war Japan is deeply touching. It is particularly important that he came to grips with "Shinto" from the perspective of a folklore scholar. The concept of *Shin kokugaku dan* was influenced by such works as Yano Harumichi's *Yasono kumade*, Kodera Kiyoyuki's *Kōkoku shinshoku kō*, Muraoka Tsunetsugu's *Nihon shisōshi kenkyū*, Maeda Natsukage's *Inari jinja kō*, Inoue Enryō's *Tengu ron*, and *Mikanagi Kiyonao shū, Jingū nenchū gyōji taisei, Shihei kōben, Kujiki setsugi*, and Arakida Tsunetada's *Gishikichōge*. Yanagita read them not from a research, historical, or theoretical perspective for professional Shinto priests but rather because they were useful for investigating the future of Shinto and the problems related to Japanese faith. Rather than investigating so called State Shinto (*kokka Shintō*) shrines which occupied mainstream Shinto until just before the end of the war, he was interested in popular Shinto (*minshū no Shintō*) based upon ordinary citizens' lives, and his overarching goal was to discover the intrinsic value in that.

Yanagita does not use the term "State Shinto" in his work. It is common knowledge that on December 15, 1945 the Shinto Directive (understood to mean the Directive to Abolish State Shinto (Kokka Shintō Haishirei) or the Directive to Separate State and Religion (Kokkyō Bunri Shirei) was issued from the Supreme Commander of the Allied Powers (SCAP) to the Japanese government. The Shinto Directive defines State Shinto in institutional terms. Namely, it regards State Shinto as

> [t]hat branch of Shinto (*Kokka Shintō* or *Jinja Shintō*) which by official acts of the Japanese Government has been differentiated from the religion of sect Shinto (*Shūha Shintō* or *Kyōha Shintō*) and has been classified a non-religious cult commonly known as State Shinto, national Shinto, or shrine Shinto.[3]

This provision singles out Ise Jingū, Yasukuni Shrine, and several others from among those generally understood as shrine Shinto, and yet simultaneously classifies them as "a non-religious national cult."

Yanagita was very critical of the Shinto Directive. He presented a number of valid and important points about Japan's Shinto that SCAP had not grasped in its definition.

Specifically, he argued for the importance of restoring the essence of shrine Shinto at the village level, rather than viewing it as a national cult, and tried to ascertain the conditions that should be a starting point for that. He believed this would be particularly critical after the war:

> It is fine to criticize the example of Occupation authority's Directive concerning Shinto shrines issued in December of last year as ridiculously rough and reckless. Because of this Directive, people who worship the *kami* at small country shrines have almost no clue of how to keep their faith in the future. But, from my perspective, I think that even this may present yet another golden opportunity for us to wise up.

This statement comes from Yanagita's *Ujigami to ujiko,* in which he also describes the concrete details of Shinto at the village level and criticizes the Shinto Directive's definition of State Shinto. He states as follows:

> Japan's so-called shrine Shinto (such a term did not exist until now) is an extremely imprecise and also misleading concept that foreigners all seem to share. Its origin is clear, and, moreover, is a matter of quite some embarrassment, but basically, the people who ought to explain it have done nothing at all until now. Or, if they are forced to try, their attempts are crude and inappropriate. So even if others err and, for the time being, make silly judgments, you cannot wring your hands over it.

Here, Yanagita is emphasizing that there is an original Shinto, deep in the Japanese people's hearts, that they have known from ancient times. It should be considered the people's own indigenous faith, but this is thoroughly denied by the Shinto Directive. Yanagita goes on to state:

> Japan, from the time it was founded to the present day, has not officially recognized its own people's native faith. There is hardly any evidence of any constraints on its development and, especially after the middle ages, the country selected bits and pieces from this faith and gave it special treatment beyond the bounds of simple piety. Even if their faith did not really benefit them, the Shinto Directive's sudden elimination of its special protected status really interfered with people's spirituality. People would become shaken, and their souls would wither, and it might be decades before they could regain any measure of spiritual equanimity. As a coping mechanism, I think that it is good to look forward, accepting whatever comes without holding on to what vanishes away. It is also good to be careful not to trample on things or push them aside so that we do not crush that which lies within people's hearts. I hear that even some of my fellow countrymen insist that we will become thoroughly Christianized, but I wonder if they are really dreaming under the present circumstances? I'd say, "Let them just try it." Even I am a bit curious.

The key to this passage is that Yanagita does not accept the Shinto that had been officially recognized as so called "State Shinto." It is particularly important that, in order to understand national rituals, Yanagita explained them by distinguishing between prayer (*kigan*) and reverence (*keishin*). The gist of *Ujigami to ujiko* concerned this point. In other words, being reverent is being moral, and it is a way that all the people should follow. The officially recognized shrines throughout the country have various differences. If we provisionally accept morality as reverence, then that is something that is encouraged through the public instruction. For example, each house establishes its own god shelf (*kamidana*) and gets an Ise talisman (*Ise taima*) every year; this originates from people's devotion to Ise Jingū. In other words, it is out of reverence. And yet, even followers of Shin Buddhism, which has a strongly sectarian character, were forced to show their reverence toward Ise. Yanagita explains that "regardless of whether it is a good or evil thing, there are occasions when the state can force people to accept an Ise talisman. That is, if necessary, it can even require it through legislation." In other words, even though the state has forced Shinto on people as a form of morality, the officials don't recognize it as "State Shinto."

Prayer is something that cannot be expressed in form; it comes from people's hidden wishes and faith, and thus has a passive side to it. And so, Yanagita says the following:

> No matter how much they force the issue, it is hard to make people without faith to pray to the *kami*. You cannot force such people whatsoever to depend on the *kami* for spiritual blessings by saying they will definitely get some help from the *kami*. It is impossible to sometimes force people to pray, or at other times to let them just remain reverential depending on the nation's needs. Faith is something that should completely depend upon the natural tendencies of the people's hearts.

Yanagita clearly mentions that the state cannot force people to pray to uniformly meet the nation's needs. He regards the idea of reverence as "something that completely depends upon the natural tendencies of the people's hearts."

However, given its importance for the state, it was necessary to unify people's hearts. Shrines did not just remain objects of reverence; they also gave people a place to perform acts of prayer. Yanagita says that this could not have been anticipated, and, at the same time, argues that the reality is that it should itself be criticized. Minakata Kumagusu[4] had criticized local leaders who led people to visit a shrine within their district to hold prayer rites there at the time of the Russo-Japanese War. Yanagita Kunio did not agree with Minakata. He believed that there was a difference between prayer and reverence, and that prayer was something that should be in each citizen's heart. You can never force people to pray by applying external pressure. Yanagita not only opposed such policies but insisted that one should further emphasize the impossibility of forced prayer. This, in Yanagita's view, was why priests were so important. Administrative officials saw the shrine cult as part of their political duties; they did not understand the spirit of prayer and, thus, could not be trusted to manage the shrines' religious observances.

Ujigami to ujiko was published in 1947. At the proofreading stage, this book was censored by the Occupation. Etō Jun, in his "The Original *Ujigami to ujiko*—the Occupation's Censorship and Yanagita Kunio" (*Shinchō* 78, No. 1, January, 1981) notes that the original content is apparent from the galley proofs of the copy at the University of Maryland's Prange Archive. After his book was censored, Yanagita made some stylistic changes and then published it. It has long been unclear to readers which parts were deleted; however, since Etō has now published these censored parts, it is possible to judge Yanagita's response to the Shinto Directive.

The Shinto Directive is comprised of four parts and nineteen paragraphs, and its intent is to ban all public financial support for Shinto and shrines. In addition, it conditions the shrines' freedom to practice their religion on the removal of militaristic and nationalistic elements from the Shinto faith. While the Directive seems clear-cut, it was horribly unclear and unspecific. For example, it seems that the reality of "State Shinto" in and of itself from early on was anything but clear for priests of small local shrines.

Yanagita's *Ujigami to ujiko* are lectures he delivered in July of 1946 as part of his course on culture at Yasukuni Shrine. At first, it was advertised as "discussions on folklore studies," and because of that few professional priests were among the participants although Yanagita had wanted priests to attend and listen. Afterward, the lectures in their censored form were published by Koyama Booksellers. On the other hand, on October 15, 1944, Yanagita appeared in response to a request by the Board of Divinities (Jingiin) to discuss the subject of "Reverence and Prayer." In the wartime, he seems to have tried to explain the essence of prayer to the priests. Actually, it is also clear that Yanagita did not himself feel there was any inherent connection between the life of village shrine festivals (*matsuri*) and their official priests and "State Shinto."

There were about 110, 000 state-sanctioned shrines recorded in the official shrine register. These included more than 200 official and national endowed shrines (*kankokuheisha*) and approximately 1,200 prefectural shrines. The important issue is the existence of the more than 100,000 small "clan shrines" (*ujigami sha*) as Yanagita had noted. The deep connections between these small shrines, their devotees, and the land on which they live and grow is still not clearly understood, insofar as no surveys exist that sufficiently examine the local conditions. However, of the more than 200 officially and nationally endowed shrines, the vast majority are said to have been founded for local parishioners to worship their "clan" *kami*. One exception is Yasaka Shrine in Kyoto, a large shrine that has no clan associated with it. Famous large shrines are easy to understand because their documents are still extant. But, the middle to small shrines become "actual examples revealing before our eyes every stage that the local 'clan' *kami* has transformed into for the last thousand years."

The move toward making Shinto into a state religion

The shrine parishioner (*ujiko*) organization is a system that is intimately related to Japanese society. It spread the same way as the *danka* parishioner system did for temples in early-modern Japan. As Japan entered the modern age, the Meiji era *ujiko fuda* [a registration card designating a person as a shrine parishioner] became widely used for registering the family officially with the government.[5] The shrines took some steps toward participating in this administrative work, but, in the end, shrine registration never fully took root. A person entered the ranks of the *ujiko* by being brought as a new-born baby to the shrine to worship. So long as they lived their lives there and were accepted by the *kami,* they would enjoy the divinity's protection. Although the custom today dates from the middle ages, if people move repeatedly as happens nowadays, they had to become the *ujiko* of several different *ujigami* respectively in the places where they lived. A woman's household's *ujigami* and her prospective husband's *ujigami* could be different, and it was quite normal to be *ujiko* of two or three different *ujigami* over time. At the time, this new phenomenon was a response to increasing urbanization. But it also ended up being a problem during the war years, and particularly by the end of the war, because of the criticisms made by the Imperial Rule Assistance Association (Taisei Yokusankai).[6] Specifically, it caused disputes over who was financially responsible for a shrine's festivals. Because these disputes could not be officially resolved, given the circumstances, the shrine-parishioner system could not become a unified focus of faith. As to the future direction, Yanagita insisted that academics needed to keep a tight focus on the relationship between the *ujigami* and the *ujiko*.

From the vantage point of Yanagita's folklore studies, there is no reason for the historical emergence of "State Shinto." The history after the middle ages revealed that each region of Japan had developed a society which centered upon the relationship between *ujigami* and *ujiko*. The typical style of a village *ujigami* is that each village has a shrine known as the village shrine. These number over 45,000. Under them were close to 60,000 officially unranked shrines, but their history displayed regional differences. Although some officially unranked shrines should have been given village-level status, unavoidable circumstances prevented it from happening. Since these unranked shrines were important to local parishioners, Yanagita noted that we should be "attentive to the *ujigami* who are not officially recognized as village deities."

In the original villages, furthermore, there are estate *ujigami* (*yashiki ujigami*) which are worshipped. These are neither ranked or unranked shrines; rather, they are enshrined in a corner of the estate in a small shrine (*hokora*). They are maintained as sites for rituals. They are called "*ubusuna*," to which the Chinese characters "birthplace" (産土) are applied. Like the village *ujigami,* estate *ujigami* were also a product of the middle ages. And when the number of village *ujigami* grew substantially with parishioners affiliated to each, the ties of faith villagers had with them weakened, so it became quite natural to amalgamate them. The basis for this kind of amalgamation, Yanagita suggests, was fomented by the interaction between the *ujigami* and the *ujiko*. He summarizes this process in the following seven points:

1   Festival days and seasons are a common part of Japanese culture throughout the archipelago. Japanese folk have a sense of the seasonal festivals; two times every year they have festivals to worship the *kami* both before and after the rice is cultivated.
2   The ceremonial sites of households are located close to each other, without any permanent building. The households agree on the ceremonial sites where they can welcome the *kami* who descends from the mountain.
3   Festivals in large households offer the opportunity to be deeply moved by feelings of gratitude and respect. People tend to prefer to consolidate festivals with fewer participants into a bigger one.
4   Full time priests become increasingly important, ultimately serving in place of the *ujiko*. Amalgamation of festivals therefore becomes easy with the mediation of priests.
5   Formerly, when people died, they become worshipped as *kami* after a certain amount of time. But at present, under the influence of Buddhism, it is now customary to have a Buddhist altar for performing rites for the dead (*kuyō*) inside the household. This makes the gap between *ujigami* and *ujiko* more distant, and while the divinity's individual connections with the household have weakened, a common faith in the *kami* has strengthened. Since it changed the faith that treated ancestral spirits as *ujigami,* this shift also made it possible to enshrine *kami* together to be worshipped as a great *kami*.
6   A tendency develops to use festivals (*matsuri*) as social events. As these enterprises gained notoriety, people contributed money to support them; it also became deeply enjoyable to perform them collectively.
7   For the unity of the village and the harmony of the population, it is essential to have festivals on the same day at the same place. That need became stronger.

Yanagita mentions the above seven points as factors that increase the need for divinities to be enshrined together. He considers the shift in the village's small *ujigami* festival divinities, from ancestral spirits to a part of the nationally prominent great *kami*, as an outcome of this unification of Shinto faith. Thus, I can speculate about the reasons why this period's national policy made it possible to stress Shinto's transformation into a state religion. I can speculate that Yanagita himself recognized that it reflects a transition of the village *ujigami* and that it was smoothly tied to the villagers' intrinsic values. Points five, six, and seven of his summary are particularly important elements of the historical mindset underlying *matsuri*. And examining Yanagita's points also leads us to look at the village level of Shinto to explain the original meaning of "State Shinto."

It is understood that the transformation of Shinto into a state religion occurred along with Japan's modernization. The term *kokka Shintō* that I have used is a translation of the term "State Shinto" that the Occupation employed in its Shinto Directive and other documents. Although there were many conceptual elements of the emperor system making up State Shinto, it is clear that State Shinto is based on the concept of national polity (*kokutai*) of Restoration Shinto (*fukko Shintō*) and the Mito School that existed prior to the Meiji period.[7]

In January of the first year of the Meiji period (1868), the new government established seven departments within the Council of State (Dajōkan), which included among them the Departments of Divinities, Domestic, and Foreign. In September of the same year, they set up seven councils including the Legislative (Giseikan), Administrative (Gyōseikan), and the Council of Divinities (Jingikan). In the *Meiji jibutsu kigen* (The Origin of Meiji Things), the great Meiji chronicler Ishii Kendō notes the current conditions of the times: "This marks the first step for the restoration of the imperial way and the unification of rituals and governance (*saisei icchi*). This marks a period of glory for priests throughout the country and the Hirata school's national learning scholars." In 1869, the government underwent restructuring again, this time emerging with six ministries below the Council of State and Council of Deities. In August of 1871, the Council of Divinities was changed to the Ministry of Divinities (Jingishō), and, in March of 1872, this became the Ministry of Public Instruction (Kyōbushō).[8] These facts make clear that the government had prepared gradually to make Shinto a national religion. Most consider that the keys to making Shinto a state religion were the forced separation of buddhas and *kami* (*shinbutsu bunri*) and compulsory shrine parishioner registration (*ujiko shirabe*).[9] In March of 1868, the Bureau of Deities (Jingi Jimukyoku) [The Department of Deities was reorganized into the Bureau of Deities in February] prohibited Buddhist words in the names of Shinto deities, like *gongen* (Buddhist incarnations) and Gozu Tennō,[10] and enshrining Buddhist statues as *shintai* [or sacred objects of worship]. Before the *kami*, temple gongs, bells, and other types of Buddhist implements were forcibly removed. Further, supervising Buddhist priests (*bettō*) and attendants known as "shrine monks" (*shasō*) were ordered to be removed from the Buddhist priesthood. In particular, gods of heaven and earth, starting with the imperial gods of Ise, were among the thirty-three gods that were installed in some Nichiren temples. While these had quite a popular following, this practice was now prohibited because of its connection to shrines.[11] It is well known that the separation of buddhas from kami was thoroughly carried out via the people's drive for "abolishing Buddhism and destroying Shākyamuni" (*haibutsu kishaku*). This was conducted under the policy that Shinto should be established as a state religion, but, since Buddhist elements had permeated people's lives in the Edo period, they were virtually impossible to remove, however. Historical research has shown that in some localities, the new government policy provoked violence and outrage. Although this cannot be explained simply as the transfer of authority from the temples to the shrines, it did indeed strip temples of much of their institutional power. Socially, the policy targeted catalpa-bow diviners (*ichiko azusa miko*),[12] mountain ascetics (*yamabushi*), *rokujū rokubu* itinerants,[13] and Inari ascetics. While these popular religious practitioners' activities effectively stagnated, it was not so easy to destroy them, particularly given their traditions' long and intimate connection with the lives of ordinary people. They continued to survive by changing their form to meet the new challenges.

The Ministry of Public Instruction (Kyōbushō), which was established in 1872, proclaimed as the three articles for teaching that people should (1) Learn the meaning of reverence to the deities and of love of country. (2) Clarify the natural principles of heaven and the human way of morality. (3) Guide people to respectfully uphold the emperor and to follow the imperial way. Not only the priests but also the remaining Buddhist monks who had not actually been killed were made public instructors (*kyōdōshoku*) and assigned to proselytize.[14] It is obvious that extreme religious policies inevitably invite a backlash. Despite the efforts at abolishing Buddhism and destroying Shākyamuni, it became clear after nearly ten years that the policy had failed. For example, the shrine parishioner registration (*ujiko shirabe*), which was intended to regulate people's lives under the shrine, ended up being applied superficially. Additionally, in November of 1872, the practice of monks' begging was banned by the Ministry of Public Instruction, although by August 1881 this ban was rescinded.

On May 14, 1871, at the same time that it reformed the system of heredity priesthood at shrines, the Council of State declared jurisdiction over many shrines under the charge of the Council of Divinities which established a clearly ranked shrine hierarchy with ninety-seven shrines classified as either large, medium, or small *kanpeisha* (official (endowed) shrine) or *kokuheisha* (national (endowed) shrine). The result was a framework which forced provincial, domain, and district (*gōsha*) shrines, as well as village tutelary deities, placed under regional administration. Further, in July of the same year, the Council gave district shrines the highest ranking in the smallest administrative district and ranked all others as village shrines (*sonsha*) attached to them. So, at least on the surface, shrine organization had become consolidated into a system.

But if we look at how worship actually occurred within (for example) family households (*ie*), nothing changed. Families allowed god shelves (*kamidana*) and Buddhist altars (*butsudan*) to coexist in their homes. Ancestral spirits visited each house at New Year just as they had done during the festival of the dead, Obon, in the summer. No one thought that the ancestral spirits came from the cemeteries of the Buddhist temples. However, no matter where they were from, the spirits came to people's houses and feasted together with their descendants, during the New Year festivities. The ancestral spirits would enter the household via the New Year pine decoration attached to the gate or door (*kadomatsu*), come further inside, and stay, taking the shelf for the yearly god (*toshigamidana*) in the living room. They received exactly the same treatment that they had during Obon, when they had settled in the Buddhist or spirit altars (*shōryōdana*). Since these were established customs, they would always be a part of people's daily life, and it was barely possible for either of them to be removed by force.

At the village level, the local temples and shrines had the same arrangement as the household *butsudan* and *kamidana*. Since the intent of abolishing Buddhism was to destroy a long-standing custom, the situation was really impossible from the outset. In July of 1881, the government ordered all the shrines and temples to establish parishioner representatives, except for the state sponsored *kankokuheisha* (official and national shrines). The purpose was that these parishioner members (*ujiko* or *danka*) should participate in the management of the shrine or temple with an eye to establishing its regional associations.

The nullification of State Shinto

In September of 1872, a deity festival of the Ise Jingū ended up under governmental regulation. First, the First Fruit Festival at Ise (Kan'namesai) became the focus for the imperial household's offering (*hōhei*) in Tokyo. That is to say, a palace ritual observance was directly connected to a specific divine ritual at Ise. Before this, the New Tasting Festival (Niinamesai) had also been an important ritual event for the imperial house, so every year, on the second day of Rabbit in the eleventh month according to the lunar calendar, that year's new grain was offered to the great goddess Amaterasu. Unlike some other divine rituals, this one was typical among ancient religious services, and therefore a prohibition against Buddhist bell ringing and sutra recitation had been enforced in the Yamashiro province of Kyoto from the day of the festival until the next morning.

Moreover, the government constructed new shrines that venerated special people who had devoted their lives to serving the emperor and the state. Among these, Yasukuni Shrine is important due to the state's apotheosis of humans into divinities. On May 10, 1868, they created the prototype of the "shrine to beckon souls" (*shōkonsha*) in the Higashiyama district in Kyoto to venerate those patriots who had died in the battle of Fushimi. On June 29, 1869, after Tokyo became the capital, a spirit-appeasing shrine was founded at Banchō Kudanzaka. Three thousand five hundred and eighty-eight spirits from the battles of Toba-Fushimi to Hakodate during the Boshin War (1868–69) were consolidated for worship. This shrine at Kudanzaka was originally known as the Tokyo Shōkonsha. However, this shrine was neither prosperous nor well attended until the first several years of the Meiji period. It was renamed Yasukuni Shrine and was given a new status as an imperially endowed shrine with a special grade (*bekkaku kanpeisha*) in 1879.

The first volume of the *The Origin of Meiji Things* [written by Ishii Kendō] includes an extremely interesting article about this, which reports that in 1869 the first female divinity was enshrined at Yasukuni Shrine. This was a woman from Akita Prefecture, Yamashiro Miyo, who died in a battle. Twenty-four additional female divinities, all said to have been loyalists before and after the Restoration, were enshrined in November of 1891. The shrine also included three foreigners who had served on the Hitachimaru and lost their lives after it was sunk by a Russian warship near Okinoshima on June 15, 1904—Captain John Campbell, Steersman First Class Samuel Bishop, and the Engineer James Hugh Grass, were enshrined together on April 19, 1907. It did not seem at all odd, given people's understanding of the spirits of the dead, that English foreign nationals were enshrined at Yasukuni. By this point in time, the significance of appeasing spirits was even stronger than later for this shrine.

Spirits who had devoted themselves to the state were invited to reside in one place, regardless of their gender or nationality. The move toward making the invited spirits into divinities gave birth to a new custom of divinizing human beings. The founding of Toyokuni Shrine (or Hōkoku Shrine), enshrining Toyotomi Hideyoshi;[15] Toyosaka Shrine for Mōri Motonari;[16] and Takeisao Shrine (Kenkun Shrine) for Oda Nobunaga[17] indicates that a special characteristic of Meiji Shinto was its focus on the deification of human beings (*hitogami*). Other such shrines include Kusunoki Masahige's Minatogawa Shrine,[18] dating from the Shōwa era; Tōgō Heihachirō's Tōgō Shrine;[19] and, at the pinnacle of all of these, Meiji Jingū, which was determined to be founded on May 1, 1915 in order to enshrine Emperor Meiji and Empress Shōken. In any case, these new shrines were incorporated under the state's bureaucratic control. After the Japanese Imperial Constitution of 1889 had provided for freedom of religion, these shrines for state ritual observances, particularly, were not considered religious. It is also noteworthy that these were not administered by the Ministry of Education's Bureau of Religion (Shūkyōkyoku) but rather by the Bureau of Shrines (Jinjakyoku) in the Home Ministry.

The question of whether Shinto can objectively be considered a religious system surely depends on whether it contains any doctrinal tenets unique to Shinto. The Great Teaching Institute (Daikyōin), which can be called the great head temple of Shinto, found itself especially weakened in the late 1870s, and this trend continued when those on the Buddhist side withdrew their cooperation. In 1879, when the Administrative Office of Shinto was set up in Tokyo's Hibiya, disputes erupted over which *kami* should be enshrined for the Office.[20] In short, the lesson emerging from these disputes is that you cannot easily formulate a common doctrine for Shinto. On the one hand, the thirteen Shinto sects (*kyōha Shintō*) including such groups as the Shintō Shūsei sect, Shinshūkyō, and Tenrikyō had diverged from the main branch of Shinto.[21] The attempt to unify the country effectively through Shinto could not overcome the regionalism which drove the festival forms of each particular shrine, which became one characteristic of State Shinto that was based on the notion that Shinto was not a religion. In his *Kamigami no Meiji ishin* (Iwanami Shinsho, 1979), Yasumaru Yoshio argues out this is because advocates of State Shinto tried to escape the onus of any doctrinalization that had any religious meaning, inheriting a state religious framework that was no more than shrine religious observance. Similarly, people were also disgusted by the self-righteous nature of *kokutai* theology and its policy failure to make Shinto a state religion.

Yanagita's folklore studies recognize that the attempt to make Shinto into a state religion did not extend to the level of the village *ujigami*. General shrines (*sōja*),[22] which can be seen as reflecting a national policy for unification, and the transfer of tutelary *kami* to shrines allowed deities to be enshrined together at ceremonial sites. As a result, there emerged a customary practice that had minor *kami* grouped together and enshrined in a confined area. However, these divinities are independent of each other, and it is not appropriate to present them with the same offerings. Generally speaking, religious services should be performed separately for *kami* or buddhas individually. An *ujigami* is an ancestral spirit, and the basic principle is that each one is enshrined separately. But the *kami* are eventually merged together; which bears resemblance to the folk tradition where, for example, thirty-three years after someone dies, the departed is incorporated into an ancestral spirit after gradually losing its individuality. However, some ancestral spirits have such individual and independent characters that they continue to enjoy separate religious services. Some of these who have kept their individuality become "spirits who have not been enshrined." Given such historical processes, however, there seems a natural tendency to syncretize *kami* who are originally worshipped separately and individually, above and beyond the cases where the government encouraged their unification as part of its national policy.

At he local and regional level, there are two types of shrines for the *ujigami* and for the *sōja*. At the national level, the government selected a small number of publicly recognized *sōja* shrines that represented regional *kami* and established policies focusing on them. Yanagita emphasizes in *Ujigami to ujiko* that we must recognize that there are two structurally different types of regional shrines; this is because, over and above "the village and my home's *ujigami*," powerful divinities with special powers may be ceremonially transferred from elsewhere.

"Faith originally occurs spontaneously, and no experiment of any theory or policy has been able to control it." However, after it became apparent that the government could no longer seek to turn Shinto into a state religion, shrine Shinto was able to find a new way forward by "noticing the realities which most people were not conscious of in their daily lives."

Some shrines, particularly those village *ujigami* of specific localities, continue to pass down festivals as solemn and dignified as they have been since early modern times. This can only mean that these festivals are sustained by a faith that is unconnected to so-called State Shinto.

When people were thinking in terms of State Shinto, it was fashionable to use particular words like "heavenly grace" (*ten'yū*) or "divine wind" (*kamikaze*). For example, people also used *tenyū* when a critically ill person fully recovered, or, even worse, lots of people would say *tenyū* when they won a game of *go* they thought they would lose. I detest such frivolity, and although it is better to live without using these words, nonetheless some people still try somehow or other to popularize expressions like "the divine wind still will blow."

Yanagita here expresses his disapproval of superficial prayers at shrines, which was often the practice at particular shrines and became quite conspicuous after the Sino-Japanese and Russo-Japanese Wars in Meiji. Yanagita was critical of "those who thought simply that because Japan was a divine country (*shinkoku*), the divine wind would probably come and such. They were people who had forgotten their most precious history of pious reverence."

The local administrative arm of the Council of Divinities publicized the official notices and directives that came down unilaterally from on high. But the effects of these proclamations were only superficial, for they could not influence people's personal piety. This was difficult for local government officials to understand, as they only regarded shrine festivals as part of their official work. But the actual life of small village *uji* shrines, however, depends on the piety of local parishioners, and it is a welcome discovery that it perseveres there.

As we have seen, Yanagita's writings explain why State Shinto could lie only on the surface of shrine Shinto. The reasons why the attempt to make Shinto into a state religion failed may also lie in the traditions of religious observances at the local *uji* shrines; this, at least, would appear logical.

Notes

1 See Fanny Hagin Mayer and Ishiwara Yasuyo, trans., *About Our Ancestors: The Japanese Family System* (Westport, CT: Greenwood Press, 1970).
2 See *Yanagita Kunio zenshū*, 32 vols (Tokyo: Chikuma Shobō, 1989–91), Volume 16.
3 "The Shinto Directive," *Contemporary Religions in Japan* 1, No. 2 (June, 1960):88.
4 Minakata Kumagusu (1867–1941) was a famous biologist, folklorist, and scholar who was a life-long resident of Wakayama prefecture. He was actively involved in the anti-shrine consolidation movement as well as nature conservation. Minakata became an ardent opponent of shrine consolidation in Wakayama prefecture, worried about the environmental, cultural and spiritual harm it might cause. He fought to have the government policy halted and was arrested for his protests in 1910. In his efforts, he found an ally in Yanagita, then a government official, and, by 1920, in large part due to his efforts, the shrine consolidation law of 1906 was abolished by the Diet.
5 This was a responsibility that was originally associated with the parishioner system (*danka seido*) of Buddhist temples. It was a way to register citizens through their temple affiliation that was used by the Tokugawa *bakufu* and known as the *terauke* system.
6 This organization tried to create a single party totalitarian state. This caused friction for those people who had associations with different neighborhoods with different *ujigami.*

7 The Mito School was an influential school of thought of the Tokugawa era that advocated defense against foreign incursion, nativism, and reverence to the emperor (*sonnō jōi*) founded by Tokugawa Mitsukuni (1628–1700), lord of the Mito domain, and led by Tokugawa Nariaki in the nineteenth century.

8 These changes in the bureaucracy coincide with efforts to promulgate a government-approved national doctrine (*kokkyō*) in 1870 to instill ethical conduct among the masses through a program known as the "Great Teaching" (*taikyō*).

9 Like the temple registration that was a key bureaucratic function of Buddhist temples during the Edo period, with the new Meiji state, this function shifted to state-supported local Shinto shrines. The practice of registering parishioners was instituted as a governmental policy in 1871 and was abandoned by May 1873.

10 Literally "ox-head-heaven-king," Gozu Tennō is a product of *kami*-buddha combinatory religion, and is worshipped at the Gion Shrine (Yasaka Jinja) in Kyoto, famous for its summer Gion festival where this deity occupies a central ritual role.

11 This assembly of Shinto gods, again showing the combinatory paradigm of *kami*-buddha worship, had the duty of protecting the Buddhist sutras, particularly the *Lotus Sutra*. In the Tokugawa period, *banshin* shrines were found mainly in the precincts of Nichiren temples. In Nichiren Buddhism the central sacred Buddhist text was the *Lotus Sutra*.

12 Wandering female shamans, unaffiliated with particular shrines, who act as spirit mediums and are known for characteristic ritual use of a catalpa-bow. They were found primarily throughout Eastern Japan.

13 These were wandering ascetics or holy men (*hijiri*) who had made sixty-six copies (*rokujūrokubu*) of the *Lotus Sutra*, which they offered at the sixty-six sacred temple-shrines on their sacred circuits. Originally, they were wandering Buddhist mendicants in the Kamakura, but by the Edo period ordinary lay pilgrims engaged in this religious practice called *rokujūrokubu kaikoku kuyō*.

14 On this educational effort, see James Ketelaar. *Of Heretics and Martyrs in Meiji Japan: Buddhism and Its Persecution* (Princeton, NJ: Princeton University Press, 1990), 87–135.

15 The first such shrine dedicated to Hideyoshi's spirit was founded in 1599 in the Higashiyama district in Kyoto. There are many others which were founded in the Meiji Period, such as the one in Nagoya city, founded in 1885, and in Osaka in 1879. Toyotomi Hideyoshi (1536–98) was the famous *daimyō* of the Warring States period who tried to unify Japan.

16 This shrine, now located in Yamaguchi city in Yamaguchi prefecture, was founded in 1762 and enshrines Mōri Motonari (1497–1571), a famous Warring States period general who became one of the most powerful lords of the Western Provinces during this period. In response to Mōri's support and reverence for the imperial house, the Meiji emperor honored his memory by giving him the divine name "Toyosaka" in 1869 and renaming the shrine Toyosaka Shrine in 1871. In 1882 it was given a new ranking as a shrine in a special grade financed by the state (*bekkaku kanpeisha*).

17 Located in the northern district in the city of Kyoto, the shrine is dedicated to the famous general of the Warring States period, Oda Nobunaga (1534–82), who made efforts to unify Japan. The shrine was founded in 1870 to honor his spirit and due to his support for the revival of court rituals. In 1875 it was given the shrine ranking as shrine in a special grade financed by the state.

18 This shrine located in the Central district of Kobe city enshrines Kusonoki Masashige (1294–1336), the loyal general who famously fought and died for Emperor Godaigo during the Kenmu Restoration.

19 Tōgō Heihachiro (1848–1934) was the famous Japanese admiral who heroically defeated the Baltic fleet at the Battle of Tsushima in 1904 during the Russo-Japanese War. His shrine, located in Shibuya district in Tokyo, was founded in 1940 after receiving an outpouring of contributions from all over the country. The shrine was listed as a shrine in a special grade financed by the state (*bekkaku kanpeisha*) in 1945.

20 The agency was privately created to replace the Daikyōin and presided over by Ise Jingū.

21 These three are examples of sect Shinto, the specifically religious organization created separately from State Shinto in the Meiji period.

22 These are shrines that for the convenience of worship have relocated several *kami* so that they can be worshipped together in the same sacred area.

31

UEDA KENJI

The structure of Shinto faith
(1995)

Ueda Kenji (1927–2003) is a well-known Shinto theologian and scholar. Born in Ōita Prefecture, he studied at Kokugakuin University where he completed his Master's in Shinto studies in 1954. From 1958 to 1960 he continued his graduate studies at Harvard University, specializing in religious psychology under the guidance of Gordon Allport, and Shinto theology under the influence of Paul Tillich. In 1966, he became an assistant professor at Kokugakuin, and in 1975 he became a full professor. He received his doctorate in literature in 1982 and became the director of the university's Institute for Japanese Culture and Classics in 1984 and president of Kokugakuin University in 1995. Ueda retired in 1999.

His publications include *Kokugaku no kenkyū: sōsōki no hito to gyōseki* (Research into National Learning: The People and their Achievements in the Beginning, 1981), *Shintō shingaku* (Shinto Theology, 1990), *Shintō shingaku ronkō* (An Inquiry into Shinto Theology, 1991), *Kiki shinwa no shingaku* (The Theology of Japanese Mythology in *Kojiki* and *Nihonshoki,* 2002).

The following selection comes from Chapter 3 "The Structure of Shinto Faith" of his book *Shintō shingaku: soshiki shingaku e no jōshō* (Shinto Theology: A Preface to a Systematic Theology, 1986). In this essay, Ueda challenges the common stereotype that Shinto is not a religion because unlike Buddhism, Christianity, and other world religions it has no commonly accepted beliefs and doctrines. Typically, Shinto is defended as a religion by the argument that its defining characteristic is ritual; however, Ueda argues that Shinto does in fact have a coherent theology, identifiable in terms of certain principles, which he outlines below.

THE STRUCTURE OF SHINTO FAITH
(1995)

Shinto—an attempt at its ontological understanding

Introduction

Even these days in the world of shrine Shinto, one can often hear people claim, "Shinto is not a religion." What they mean by this is that Shinto is not a religion that proclaims teachings as its center like Buddhism and Christianity. Certainly, after the Outer Shrine Shinto at Ise was established in the medieval period, attempts at the formal study and doctrinal elaboration of Shinto occurred, taking various forms. However, none of these has ever been widely accepted or become settled canon in the world of Shinto. This is not only because of the variety of different deities enshrined at the over 80,000 officially recognized individual shrines, or because of the difficulty of singling out any doctrinal unity. Rather more fundamentally, it is because people involved with Shinto commonly view it as something that cannot be essentially fixed in doctrine. This way of thinking about Shinto considers ritual its defining characteristic as a religion. This is apparently an attempt to identify Shinto's own special quality by making a distinction between doctrinal and practical types of religions. The fact is that Shinto is a religion without a founder, which exists within an indigenous ethnic culture oriented around myths and ritual traditions. Even so-called "sect Shinto," which developed in the unique political and social conditions at the end of the Edo and Meiji period as a religious organization centered on a founder, is remarkably weak in its systematization of doctrine. This is particularly notable when it is compared to other religions and sects. Moreover, from the middle ages until the appearance of the National Learning School, Shinto's scholastic development consisted of borrowing a few Confucian, Buddhism, or Taoist concepts, or extracting syncretic elements of Shinto faith based on these other faith perspectives. Thus, the noted national learning scholar Motoori Norinaga could even claim, "There is no way (*michi*) to the way of Shinto." It is interesting that many of those identified as national learning scholars tended to be poets or classicists; there were thus very few of them who left behind any lasting intellectual achievements. Even the claims presented by those few who have made lasting intellectual contributions have been harshly criticized by those poets or classicists. It is also well known that shrine Shinto lost its state support after World War II, finding itself in the position of having to promulgate its own teachings independently of the state. Given this course of events, many within the Shinto priesthood clearly demanded doctrine. Yet all that the Association of Shinto Shrines (Jinja Honchō), the parent organization for shrines all over the country, could do in response was issue a document entitled, "General Principles for a Life of Reverence toward Deities,"[1] which delineated some of the practical goals. Of course, I am not taking a theoretical position that doctrine is necessary or even possible in shrine Shinto. Rather, my focus here is on the almost complete absence of doctrinal disputes over the faith that forms the basis of the general principles of Shinto, the seeming deficiency of doctrinal disputes in the world of Shinto today. I would argue that this very absence reveals the special character of Shinto.

As difficult as this is, I would like to identify the basic conceptual framework underlying Shinto faith or at least to identify its special characteristics logically. Doubtless, it is problematic if I do anything more here than just offer a few provisional observations. And yet, this challenge has also inspired me. Perhaps, I am like the *Manyōshū* poet Kakinomoto Hitomaro (CE 662–710) who wrote, "The Land of Reed Plains that is Abundant with Rice, sacred as it is, requires nothing more to be said," and then fervently added, "I will make a proclamation" (poem #3253). He said that because it was basic to his faith that "The land of Yamato, of many islands, is a country rich in the spirit of words (*kotodama*)" (poem #3254).

The following assumptions underlie my work. First, I have found my standard of comparison in the way "existence" or "being" (*sonzai*) is understood in Shinto. It is well known that Buddhism is a religion that developed from an ontology and that Western philosophy also has ontology as one of its central themes historically, which explains why Christian theology shows conspicuous development along these lines. However, we must also not forget that taking an ontological perspective in studying religion will not exhaustively reveal everything significant about its thought. For this reason, I feel compelled to emphasize that this essay can be no more than a prolegomenon.

My second assumption concerns what we call "Shinto." What, specifically, does this term refer to? It is often said that Shinto is Japan's indigenous religion. We have already noted that it is also rooted in an ethnic faith that has no founder or scriptures. Because of this, Shinto first became historically conscious of itself only after it was influenced by so-called continental culture, including Buddhism, Confucianism, and Taoism. Indeed, the word "Shinto" first appears in Japanese chronicle literature in an entry on Emperor Yōmei in 585. The same word also appears in the entry of Emperor Kōtoku in 645, but there is some doubt whether this has the same meaning as the word "Shinto" that we use today. While I cannot go into detail here, I should note that "Shinto" is used both times in contrast to Buddhism. So, it seems reasonable to conclude that Shinto refers to the country's indigenous faith. Therefore, it seems that before the introduction of Confucianism and Buddhism and, certainly before the age when the chronicles were compiled, we can assume that a Japanese faith existed that can be regarded as "Shinto." Linguistically, the word probably means something like the "ancient way" (*kodō*), a word appearing in a chronicle entry under Empress Kōgyoku in 642, and becomes widely accepted as a term during and after the Kamakura period. Thus, my own view is that phenomena such as shrine Shinto, sect Shinto, scholastic Shinto, and folk Shinto all reflect formulations of a basic Shinto; this basic Shinto is itself Japan's unique value orientation, formed in reaction to the stimulus of foreign cultures.

And yet, this does not receive much support even among Shinto scholars, whose reasoning highlights the danger in identifying Shinto and Japaneseness as one and the same. It is generally accepted that Shinto, like Japanese Buddhism and Confucianism, developed around a core value orientation of Japanese culture, and that a special Japanese character is therefore a key element of all these religions. Clearly, however, Buddhism and Confucianism were both founded on values and concepts that were very different from Japan's. It is commonly accepted that Buddhism and Confucianism in Japan have undergone a high degree of Japanization. Shinto, then, occupies a very different position from Buddhism and Confucianism. Why? Because Shinto originally developed as a religion that was founded on a basic Japanese value orientation; it is based upon a quality which is also at the core of Japanese culture. Any gap between these two would have to come from the influence of the continental culture. Thus, national learning scholars of the early modern period worked very hard to eliminate foreign influences in order to discover the pure ancient way. The effect of these scholars' efforts and the Shinto characteristics of their approach are beyond the scope of this essay. I would concur, however, that when trying to grasp the vagaries of Shinto thought, reflecting on its original form is both necessary and meaningful.

The lack of an absolute perspective

One of the most basic challenges for understanding Shinto as a religion is to analyze its concept of the *kami*. This task is in line with my essential goal, which is to grasp Shinto's characteristics ontologically. Probably the first scholarly task should be sorting out and classifying all those *kami* that have historically been the focus of belief and reverence; next, those *kami* should be defined and their essential natures clarified. However, in this essay, I plan to closely analyze the first characteristic that I have identified, comparing Shinto conceptually to other religions.

In Shinto, people believe in myriads of gods. This is an obvious and key difference between it and monotheistic religions. In perhaps more abstract philosophical terms, Shinto "lacks an absolute perspective." Of course, absolutism and relativism are conceptually inseparable insofar as a self-conscious relativist must assume an absolute perspective. In point of fact, documentary evidence, particularly from the period that gave rise to the classics, reveals that Japan had already been influenced by continental Confucianism and Buddhism. So, the Japanese of that era were clearly familiar with the concept of the "absolute." And yet, despite this, it seems that most people then lived in a relativistic world where the absolute was never absolutized. In order to understand this point, I shall analyze the cosmogonic myth in the *Kojiki*, which contains two different types of *kami*. The first are "the gods who "come into being" (*naru kami*) and the second are the "gods who are born" (*umareru kami*). The latter, as is well known, appear in the myth at the point when the land is born (*kuni umi*), after the two *kami,* Izanagi and Izanami, have sexual intercourse (*mito no maguwai*), giving birth to the islands of Japan, in the forms of many deities from Torinoiwakusubune to Hinokagutsuchi. And, what is interesting is that all the *kami* who traditionally perform important roles, from the three deities of the creation and the *kami* of the five grains[2] to the three august deities (*sankishin*) centered around Amaterasu,[3] belonged to the *naru kami*. This suggests that the *kami* of Shinto were all deities generated from the basic stuff given at the beginning. They do not precede the world as existing beings *a priori*, nor are they transcendental absolute beings that create the world *ex nihilo*. However, beyond this generalization, we have to accept that there are different interpretative approaches to the classics. These are particularly concerned with understanding the divine character of the first three deities of creation. In order to discuss this particular point, let us look at the original text from the *Kojiki*:

> At the time of the beginning of heaven and earth, there came into existence (*naru kami*) in Takamagahara a deity named Amenominakanushi no Kami, next, Takamimusubi no Kami, and, next, Kamimusubi no Kami. The three deities all came into being as individual deities and then hid themselves.[4]

Motoori Norinaga, after completing his commentary on the particulars of the original text, summed it up as follows:

> It is difficult to know for what reasons and through what creative life process (*musubi*) the three *kami* mentioned above came into being since no traditions have been passed down. One imagines that they came into being through some extraordinary and miraculous means, and, since this event is also beyond thought or words, one has to accept that there are no solid traditions that have been passed down . . . Furthermore, since these *kami* appeared before there was a heaven and earth . . . they came into being *ex nihilo* . . . The phrase, "came into being in Takamagahara," indicates, however, that after the creation of heaven and earth, the place in which they appeared became Takamagahara. And it was only afterward that the gods resided in Takamagahara," etc.

Clearly, there are conceptual confusions here. Norinaga, on the one hand, understands that the three gods of creation existed before the creation of the world, and honors and respects them for that. In this respect, he seems to treat these three gods as pre-existing beings with a transcendental character. On the other hand, Norinaga also thinks that, although such gods do exist, they rely on the power of the creative life process (*musubi*). His interpretation sows confusion because he conflates the place where the three *kami* come into being with Takamagahara, which appears after the creation of heaven and earth. What causes this confusion is the inherently contradictory attempt by Norinaga, who does not seem to have a concept of transcendence, to attribute a transcendental nature to the finite world.

As for the Yamato word *naru*, "coming into being," Norinaga commits almost the same predictable mistake, thus inviting the same confusion and contradiction. He defines *naru* this way:

> For the word, *naru*, there are three distinct meanings. First, it refers to things that appear from nothing (this also refers to human birth), and the appearance of the *kami* also has this sense. Second, it refers to things that change to become other things, for example, [in the *Kojiki*] the time when the sea goddess Toyotamahime gave birth and turned into a large serpent (*yahirowani*). Third, it refers to finishing or completing an action; an example is [the phrase] "it became a national disaster" (*kokunan nari*).

For Norinaga, "nothing" (*mu*) is simply nothing more than something that does not actually exist. Therefore, his understanding is that both human birth and the *kami* coming into being is a "creation" from "nothing." This logic, when applied to the genesis of the three gods of creation, identifies them in this way. Deities who are "generated" from "nothing" are considered to be gods who already exist transcendentally and who retain that same character even after the creation of Takamagahara. Because I can see this logical contradiction, my reaction is simple as well as impartial: For Shinto, there is no logical or theoretical concept about the origin of things. Shinto considers the three gods of creation as nothing other than *kami* within whom the power inherent in the world becomes manifest through their own self-development. That world is the land Takamagahara that existed from the beginning as one world; even if it is the land of the gods, it is the given world. In Shinto, there is no conception of an absolute god as a transcendental reality.

Nevertheless, there are those who would argue critically against this standpoint. That is because Shinto has historically been quite capable of misunderstanding its own traditions, conceiving Amenominakanushi (also known as Kunitokotachi no Mikoto) as having a monotheistic absolute divine character. This doctrinal view is first seen in the middle ages, starting with the development of Ise Shinto of the Watarai priestly family from the Outer Shrine at Ise, and reaching its zenith at Yoshida Shinto faith in Daigenshin. Subsequently, Hirata Atsutane took this position too, although not one of the disciples who belonged to his school wrote anything about this god. A detailed debate about these issues, however, is best left for another time. Limiting my focus here, I would like to make the following points.

First, this belief about Amenominakanushi during the period when the classics were formed neither existed widely nor had deep significance for most people. To be sure, Inbe no Hironari's compilation, the *Kogoshūi* (807) contains a discussion of the genealogical relationship between this *kami* and the *musubi no kami*. However, this text, like the other classics, reveals nothing about the activities of this deity. Furthermore, in the entry on clans descended from the gods in the land of Yamato in the second book of the *Shinsen shōjiroku* (815), this *kami* is identified as an ancestral god of Hattori Muraji and Miteshiro Obito. However, when we compare this with the large number of clans that had *musubi no kami* as their ancestral deities and also consider their clan's high ranking, we will be naturally able to know more about the actual historical conditions behind the faith in this *kami*. Perhaps this *kami* is a Japanese adaptation of a faith in a heavenly deity that was introduced by foreign immigrants from China who held this belief, or perhaps the Chinese faith had an impact on the formation of the Japanese mythological traditions and thus gave rise to this *kami* conceptually.

My second point is to underscore that it is not hard to understand why later doctrinal history emphasizes this *kami*. Why? It is because there always lurks in the background an intense anti-Buddhist and anti-Confucian sensibility. Of course, this does not obviate the historically documented faith in Amenominakanushi. However, faith in this *kami* never develops in a way that negates the divine nature of the other myriads of *kami*. Further, it is important to remember that, from the onset, the three deities—including Amenominakanushi—and the *musubi no kami* are understood as manifesting themselves at the same time. Therefore, it is hard to regard Amenominakanushi as a transcendental or monotheistic absolute God.

So what conceptual and practical characteristics define Shinto, a polytheistic religion lacking an absolute? In terms of basic principles, Shinto is focused on the particular rather than the universal. This tendency has been integrated even into such representations as emperor worship and faith in *ujigami* and *ubusunagami*. At the anthropological and sociological level, we can find concrete examples in Japanese ways of living which emphasize such attributes as "loyalty" (*chū*), duty or obligation (*giri*), and human wholehearted feeling (*ninjō*). The proverb, "When in Rome, do as the Romans do," is a teaching also rooted in this same ethical vision. That is, it means adapting your life to changing social customs, *die Sitte*, and also respecting one's family-based customs and moral codes. If we substitute the word truth (*shinri*) for the *kami*, Shinto takes the view that holds there is not a monistic truth, but pluralistic truths. Therefore, even when there are conflicts, your truth is only relative to your opponent's truth. The idea that I am correct and that my opponent is therefore wrong, at fault, and completely to blame for everything is not found in Shinto. Indeed, the framework of Shinto is ideal for encouraging spiritual growth based on harmony, especially through compromise.

This is consistently seen in the classical myths. For example, even the creators of the land, Izanagi and Izanami, commit a ritual error and give birth to the leech child, Hiruko.[5] Another example is Amaterasu, revered as the supreme divinity and ancestress to the emperor, who finds that she cannot control the violent behavior of her brother Susanoo. After her repeated attempts to understand his explanations for his inauspicious activities (pollution, *tsumi*) fails, she had to perform acts of religious purification (*harai*). This act of purification was not just imposed on Susanoo but applies to Amaterasu as well. The myth of Amaterasu hiding herself in the rock cave can be interpreted as symbolizing a rite of death and rebirth.[6]

The rite of death and rebirth was enabled by the festival of millions of *kami*. Amaterasu is certainly the *kami* who receives this festival in her honor, but she is also a *kami* who spiritually participates in this festival of the heavenly *kami*. At the root of this view of the *kami*, you can find a sense of awe and a simple awareness of the conditions that make life possible. This harmony, which is permitted by the synthesis of relative truths, could not itself be absolute, let alone eternal. Thus, even the *kami* of the land are not described in ideal terms in Shinto myths. This also explains why Shinto festivals have the cycle of life and death as their key principle and why they follow the mythological model of return to chaos and rebirth of order.

Accepting actual existence

The second characteristic of ontological thinking in Shinto is the acceptance of actual existence—understood as its simple and positive affirmation. That is to say, the foundation of ontological understanding in Shinto is present within the givenness of existence in and of itself. You could say that Shinto's first basic principle, the lack of a transcendental being, leads naturally to this second characteristic. A more appropriate way of putting it might be that these two ideas are like a theorem and a corollary, or even like two sides of the same coin. An idea like this accepts the existence of all that is given and cannot be expected to contain anything that would fundamentally deny that existence. It follows, then, that it is extremely natural for Shinto to be spiritually optimistic and think in a way that affirms this world as its center. I shall discuss this point more concretely below.

First, what view of human nature is found in Shinto? According to the creation myth in the classics, the various *kami*, as well as the country itself, are offspring of Izanagi and Izanami. But there is no part that directly explains the birth of human beings. However, each clan transmitted its own myths, including the *kami* who were their own ancestral deities. Also, terms like *aohitogusa*, meaning populace, appear in these stories. The word literally compares people's flourishing to luxuriantly growing grass, which suggests humanity is conceived as one and the same with the land. Based on this, it is fair to conclude that human beings were originally understood as offspring of the *kami* and that human beings and *kami* are essentially equal. Indeed, from the dawn of recorded history there have been humans who were enshrined as gods, even when still alive. This certainly does not contradict this belief. If we recognize a divine nature to our humanity, then we could never see humanity's original nature, what we might call our common instinctual desires, as inherently evil or sinful. In discussing this, Motoori Norinaga explains that the "sincere heart given at birth is what we have on the road of life, and the heart has been with us from the beginning, whether good or evil." Or, as he also states elsewhere,

> Delicious things people want to eat, silk clothes they want to wear, nice houses they want to live in, riches they want to have, they want to be respected by others, and they want to live for a long time—all these are sincere manifestations of the human heart . . . Someone who does not stop to gaze at a woman's charms lacks the sentiments people usually have.

This kind of thinking, for ethical religions, suggests crude and unprincipled attitudes toward life. However, Shinto tradition conceives the creator *kami* as creating the land, the ancestral *kami*, and our own realm through sexual relations. Human sexuality is, therefore, undeniably sacred, and it is perfectly understandable that at festivals for praying for an abundant harvest there are Sarume Kagura dances[7] as well as other rites provocatively reenacting the sexual acts of the *kami*.

What becomes problematic for understanding human nature is sin (*tsumi*) in Shinto. According to the "Great Purifying Words" (*Ōharai no kotoba*) mentioned in the *Engi norito shiki* (927), there are two types of *tsumi*—heavenly and earthly. Among the latter are not just personal infractions but things like pollution and natural calamities. The specific interpretation of this is a task best left to Shinto dogmatics, but the key point is that sin, in this sense of committing a moral wrong, is no different from pollution and natural disasters, and all are understood as something that can be expiated. Certainly, during the middle ages, in the time of the kami-buddha syncretism (*shinbutsu shūgō*), an idea that explained the suffering of *kami* was present, as illustrated in the *Kumano engi,* had its basis in the Buddhist belief that bodhisattvas could serve as substitutes by taking on the suffering of others. There are even scholars who connect this idea of sin to Susanoo's tale traditions to establish that there is a belief in original sin in Shinto. However, we not only need to question whether this is correct but also whether the idea was originally part of Shinto. If we believe that *tsumi*, taken as the word for original sin, is something that one originally possesses—in other words, that it is an immanent and essential thing—a notion like "Great Purification" (*ōharai*) does not make any sense. The "Great Purification" lumps pollution and natural disasters together with personal sin and regards them all as things that can be expiated through ritual. Original sin would also seem to require a transcendent or absolute being to explain it as well as such other faith components as repentance, moral precepts, atonement, absolution, and salvation. However, these faith elements are essentially incompatible with Shinto's framework for understanding existence. Here, rather than entering into a detailed analysis of medieval Shinto, taking an orthodox approach seems more natural historically. The notion of purity of heart is seen for the first time in the chronicle literature under the imperial edicts of Emperor Tenmu; that literature considers that purity of heart to be the sincerity of the human heart, which we all originally have. The result is that we cannot avoid potential criticisms that Shinto lacks a deep awareness of sin or that its view of purity is merely sensory and superficial. Such criticisms are simply uncompromisingly self-righteousness arguments and clearly ignore the differences in cognitive systems and analytical classifications. How is that so? It is because criticisms like these come from a perspective that originally favors the ideas including the absolute.

Even within its worldview and historical perspective, Shinto consistently accepts and affirms actual existence. As we know, Shinto has no eschatology, as Christianity does, or Decline of the Law (*mappō*), as Buddhism does. The national learning scholars of the early modern period recognized something comparable, which they called "the end of the world" (*sue no yo*). This idea, however, was never about historical decline, nor did it view inevitable degradation of all existence; in actuality, it was a lament over the spiritual loss that resulted from a dependency on intellect and logic. Out of this comes national learning's yearning for ancient times and its insistence on their restoration. This way of thinking about restoration and renewal, however, was possible precisely because Shinto has always focused on new life. The classics tell us that the ancient Japanese believed that this world, along with heaven and earth, was boundless and infinite, and that its development was guaranteed and blessed by the imperial ancestral goddess, Amaterasu. The divine declaration that this universe be boundless can actualize the meaning of the faith traditions only when it is considered to be a development of the episode of Izanagi and Izanami, who in the birth of the land myth received a divine command from the heavenly *kami* to redo their rite of union. Shinto believes that the primary reason for being and meaning of existence is to receive the will (or "august command" (*kotoyozashi*)) of the heavenly *kami* (the creative energy or *musubi*) and to zealously carry that out as an emissary commissioned by these superior beings (*mikotomochi*). Thus, the secular tendencies in contemporary Christian societies can never be a major problem for Shinto. This is because even though Shinto distinguishes between extraordinariness (*hare*) and ordinariness (*ke*), it makes no conceptual distinction between the sacred (*sei*) and profane (*zoku*).

One can easily discover a similar line of thought in its traditional beliefs concerning the other world. Neither in the classics nor in its later history does Shinto describe in detail the land of the *kami* or the land of the dead where ancestral spirits are pacified. Moreover, these are not separate from this world but are understood as being nearly on the same plane of existence. The other world is not some idealized and perfected paradise but quite the opposite—a world that is closely connected with our own and is oriented in relation to the actual world. It is true that Hirata Atsutane, as well as some of his disciples, searched for a central conception of the other world; there is, however, hardly any doubt that this was again a response to the demands of the age and the influence of another religion. If we think of this as fundamentally at odds with the meaning of rituals for ancestors, then we are on to the central current of Shinto thought at work here.

Existence as function

The third principle of Shinto thought is that all existence can be grasped and understood through its operation or function. That is to say, for Shinto there is no distinction between substance or essence and function. Existing is activity, and activity is what existing is in itself; in other words, it is conceived as the essential nature of existence. Perhaps we can say that the Japanese proclivity to dislike abstract thought and indifference to logical rationalism is rooted in this same fundamental principle. Some examples of this among the *kami*, whose traditions are handed down in the classics, include the *musubi no kami* of the cosmogonic myth, Umashiashikabihikoji,[8] or Kunitokotachi,[9] Toyokumonu,[10] Uhijini and Suhijini,[11] and Tsunogui and Ootonoji[12] (although in the strictest sense, ambiguities remain as to the exact meaning of their names). All of these convey the belief that things coming into being and the course of their development are divine. Amenominakanushi is the sole exception in that his divine nature is an abstraction. Of course, the original nature of the *kami* is logically impossible to grasp in all respects, and therefore our limited grasp of their functions stands to reason. Nonetheless, over and above any understanding of a *kami*'s character common to other religions, what really stands out for Shinto is a functional understanding of its divine character. In what follows, we shall consider a number of examples where we can interpret the meaning of these gods' functional roles.

In Shinto, many *kami* have naturally divine characteristics. Ōyamatsumi,[13] Ōtokonushi,[14] and Ōwatatsumi[15] are representative examples in this regard. If we had to select one characteristic common to them all, it would be that Shinto is a religion of nature worship. However, I am very doubtful here about whether Japanese have an abstract conception of nature. One would assume that a precondition of nature worship would be a general awareness of nature that evokes a feeling of awe or fear. However, the contemporary Japanese word for nature (*shizen*) in this sense did not exist in ancient Japanese (*Yamato kotoba*). Rather, it is a translation of a word that was introduced from the West in the modern period. Before that the word pronounced, *jinen,* was a Buddhist term, which means "self so," "naturally," and "spontaneously."

One can verify this even in the classic myths. For example, the story of creation is not about creating the simple natural world but is rather about the birth (*umi*) of the "country" (*kuni*), that is, the islands making up the Japanese archipelago. At a stage preceding their creation, the two *kami,* Izanagi and Izanami, descended from heaven to the island of Onogorojima.[16] While Onogorojima is natural, so to speak, there is no evidence that it ever became an object of any belief. Similarly, it is fair to say that Awajima, another island that appears at the beginning of the creation story, is the same since it is also not numbered among the deities' children in the myth. However, the other islands created by the gods afterward are treated differently. They are referred to as gods; for example, the island, Okinomitsugonoshima is referred to as Princess-Good-Boiled-Rice (Amenooshikorowake). Can we not say that this indicates that the land created by the *kami* is not just simply a plot of land, but something alive that functions through its close connection with living. Through its operation, this type of nature makes us aware of its connection with our lives, and thus it is conceived as having a divine character.

What we call mountain gods (*yama no kami*) are much the same. For example, Ōyamazumi no Kami, who is mentioned in the classics as the offspring of Izanagi and Izanami, is considered to have the spiritual qualifications to rule over mountain spirits. This much is easily understood from the deity's name, which means the venerable great god of the mountains. However, this *kami*, now enshrined at Mishima in Shizuoka prefecture, is also believed to be a protector of those who go to sea, keeping them from harm. This dimension of its faith is contained in its history. Since sailors going to sea use the mountain as a landmark, the mountain, acting as a beacon on their voyages, dominates their lives. This way of understanding how Ōyamazumi, a mountain *kami*, becomes a sea god is not deduced from the *kami*'s original nature but rather by the god's function, a way of understanding divinity that must take precedence.

Ōkuninushi,[17] as a god who has many different names, is typical of what we find even in the classics. He is referred to as Ōnamuchi, Ashiharashikoo, Yachihoko no Kami, and also as Umashikunitama and Ōmiki no Mikoto. I will refrain from a detailed analysis of each of the gods' names, but they indicate the various special qualities historically possessed by this *kami*. These names leave no doubt that people believed in Ōkuninushi and grasped his divine nature by his functions that these names designate. Is it not likely that this emphasis on function made polytheism in Shinto possible while also providing a foundation for Japanese syncretism? The Japanese unhesitatingly worship different objects. People have clan gods and tutelary gods, but they also enshrine gods with specific powers relevant to what they do—according to their different occupations. Moreover, they also worship a variety of popular divinities when they hear that one divinity or another has a specific kind of efficaciousness. We can conclude that this is not simply because Shinto lacks a monotheistic or absolute God, but because the *kami* are perceived distinctively according to their particular functions. Based on this reading, then, the Magatsuhi, considered problematical in Shinto's doctrinal history, are not unnatural at all. The Magatsuhi are evil *kami* who originate from the pollution of the netherworld of Yomi. As Motoori Norinaga explains it, these deities cause all the misfortune and disasters that happen to people in the world. Building on this, Hirata Atsutane's basic view was that it was impossible for people to worship evil deities and that these *kami* were gods that signify evils. After Norinaga and Atsutane, theological disputes concerning these deities continued. Without going beyond what is directly relevant to my point, this is another example of how divine nature gets its "power" from what it does. When pollution or misfortune (impurity and disasters) appear, it is regarded as a function of some divine "power." This functional grasp of their divinity reflects a fundamental attitude of Shinto. Evil is certainly a negative power in life. However, like good, it has "power" and, thus, there is no difference between the two in this respect. Even Susanoo's haughty behavior (*kachisabi*) in the classical myths, which is regarded as the origin of heavenly pollution, fits this basic model for understanding evil in Shinto. The great purification ritual only makes sense as a religious rite because of this functional understanding of existence.

We should not forget that this basic functional understanding of existence permeates the very structure of serving shrine Shinto. For example, while everyone can theoretically be enshrined in shrine services as a child of the *kami*, in practice, historically, it was limited to those who played a major role in communal life as a whole. People do not just enshrine *kami* in order to express gratitude for their blessings and to commemorate their virtues, a practice referred to as *mitama no fuyu*,[18] but expect to serve and pacify the god's spiritual power.

A good example in this regard is Kitano Tenjin, a well-known instance of the faith in vengeful spirits (*goryō*). Looking back in Shinto history, we already find that from the Nara period the imperial court recognized him as a *kami* and granted him several promotions in rank. This means that they felt the same way facing this *kami* as they would toward a living human being. The main problem lay not in just being attentive to the deity but in taking into account differences in the divine rank in accordance with the *kami*'s spiritual power. If they wanted to confirm how important the god was, they did so by raising the *kami*'s ranking. The case of Usa Hachiman, who is connected to the forging of the statue of the Great Buddha at Nara, is also representative in this respect.[19]

What Shinto has passed down is a faith deeply focused on the benefits of this world (*genze riyaku*). While it is also true that Buddhism and Confucianism strongly influenced shrine Shinto throughout its historical development, the worship of *kami* icons as embodiments of divinity was never widely practiced. Both of these, I would argue, originate from the tendency I have described above; that is, they reflect a way of existence that does not grasp the essence of things ontologically, but instead through the way things function.

Existence as relationality

"Existence exists in relationality" is the fourth principle basic to that existential awareness that characterizes Shinto thinking. But this principle is not in itself meaningful. Why not? This is because everything that exists in the actual world is inevitably connected in some way to other existing things within the world, and those connections condition and give individuals or objects their orientation in life. To fully understand this, we have to acknowledge that this fourth principle relies upon the three previous principles. First, Shinto does not conceive of absolutes. Shinto does not have a way of thinking that situates a transcendent. Therefore, Shinto does not have an episteme which posits an absolute transcendent. It does not conceive our present existence in connection with an absolute, nor does it define and evaluate our existence based on interconnections within this world with reference to an absolute. A good way to understand how "existence exists in a relational quality" is to view how those connections we have with other things in the actual world determine the true nature of our own existence. To reiterate, Shinto does not have a way of thinking that situates a transcendent. This thinking with the element of a transcendent first postulates an essence to existence, and based on this postulation it considers, judges, and situates its interconnectedness in the actual world. Again, as problematized by the third principle, existence is understood by what a thing does, its function within Shinto's conceptual framework. Therefore, the connections that individually existing things have with each other within the actual world end up being determined through the functions that those things can and do perform. On this basis, the concept underlying the fourth principle should be completely clear. However, the relation between "function" and "relationality" is by no means unidirectional. Function is perceived as the essence of existing things, and, for that reason, the actual connection of existing things is determined and given an orientation through their function. Yet, at the same time, conversely, the relational nature of things is also perceived as their essence, and, for that reason, determines and orients the actual way things function. This, then, is the reason why the fourth principle has to exist in its own right. I will try to state this argument more concretely in what follows.

The historian of religion Kishimoto Hideo (1903–64) expressed this special religious character of Shinto by using the word "connection" (*tsunagari*). It has the same meaning as relationality (*kankeisei*) that I am using. The most obvious example of this relationality is in the vertical child–parent relationship, which Shinto recognizes as the most fundamental basis for human life. Thus, this principle underlies the mythological traditions about the creation as well as social relationships formed within the nation state and regional collectivities, which are originally organized around horizontal rather than vertical relationships. Children are children of a parent, and how they exist as their own person in actuality is determined by the parent–child relationship. This same idea is found in the creation myth in terms of "the logic of succession." That is to say, in the myths, Amaterasu, in accordance with the will of the other heavenly *kami*, decreed (*kotoyoza*) her divine descendant, Ninigi no Mikoto, to have sovereignty over the newly created land. This myth also emphasizes that members of each clan, who were descendants of *kami* were supposed to join cooperatively in Ninigi's rule over the land, became imperial emissaries by decree and given rank as regional governors of their local territories (*mikotomochi*). Thus, the meaning of one's actual existence, is found in these relationships—in one's work as the *mikotomochi*, as an officially designated function fixed through a familial relationship, or, more concretely, in the succession of the tasks of making the country following the gods' decree.

It is also very natural that Shinto developed as a form of religion centered on rituals for ancestors. This understanding of existence in terms of the parent–child relationship and coordinating actual existence in terms of this relationship manifests itself in a variety of ways besides the rituals for clan ancestral deities. For example, one myth tied to the heavenly gods (*amatsukami*) is Amaterasu's divine decree to Ninigi to keep her sacred mirror enshrined at Ise Jingū, a key request upon which the rituals at Ise are founded.[20] Even in the lineages of the gods of the earth (*kunitsukami*), we can see this. There is the entry from the seventh year of Emperor Sujin that records the deity Ōmononushi appearing in the emperor's dream and giving an oracle demanding that he establish a service for him, with the *kami*'s grandson, Ōtataneko, as the priest in charge. Both of these examples indicate that ancestral rituals according to blood kinship ties were a generally accepted ethnic practice. Thus, one of Shinto's peculiarities is that ritual functionaries gain office not based on individual qualifications or talent but on "heredity."

There are a great many other examples of this as well: The imperial family, at the apex of the collective unity that is the state, is the chief household related to all others, and the emperor is referred to as the great parent of the people. At the level of village life, there are the main (*honke*) and branch (*bunke*) houses, and the master (*oyakata*) and disciple (*kokata*) systems. There are also *oyabun–kobun* relationships found in special social groups, the *iemoto* system, and many others. What is important here is that the parent–child relationship is not necessarily restricted to actual blood kin. This is clear in the fact that people even accept a parent–child relationship that is a legal fiction, such as the Japanese practice of adopting a male heir (*yōshi*). In other words, Shinto finds meaning not in people standing isolated in a row but in the inter-relationship of a parent and child. The basis for how an individual exists is based on this relationship. Although locating individuals on the basis of this relationality gives character and meaning to their activities, it is not at all limiting. Why? Just as the Shinto perspective of history identifies its oscillations between opposites of growth and decay as a form of transcendence, part of the pattern of eternal return, so children transcend their role in the parent–child relationship, changing status by becoming parents and positioning themselves within a new relationship with their own child. Needless to say, what makes this possible is the functional character of actual existence.

It has been noted that the Japanese tend to introduce vertical relationships into social groups that were originally horizontally related. This reveals a strong sense of group identity that rejects individuality. For instance, people refer to the business where they work as their "home" (*uchi*) company and call their boss "my old man" (*oyaji*). Does this tendency exist in Shinto, even theoretically? I have some doubts. A faith in eight million gods eloquently conveys a way of thinking that recognizes individuals' functionally independent nature and, for that reason, their essential equality. Of course, the way things actually work invites differences in terms of their actual power to influence the course of events; it all depends on such functions as the quality of their work, and the size and strength of their effects. So, it is clear that Shinto does not rely on any basic principle of equality in the simplest sense of the term.

Moreover, the fact that it has vertical relationships as its organizing principle creates a possibility of establishing hierarchical classes and ranks in society. This has occurred historically with the development of distinct social classes in Japanese society. Having said that, we must not overlook the very large amount of social mobility between social classes. For example, the Fujiwara clan, considered as a classical example of the court aristocracy, was originally nothing more than a house occupying one of the lower rungs in terms of social status. Even in the case of the rise and fall of the military houses, beginning with the Taira and the Minamoto clans, or in considering the Genkun, originally lower-level samurai from clans marginalized by the Tokugawa shogunate in the Edo period, who became elder statesmen after the Meiji Restoration, we see that function clearly triumphs over social rank or connections.

The best proof that the horizontal principle is as important as the vertical principle as a critically important element of Shinto thought is the characteristic belief in local tutelary *kami* (*ubusunagami*) along with ancestral clan *kami* (*ujigami*). Thus, Shinto's sense of group identification relies on both principles, since the two are closely interrelated. The individual is conceptually situated at this interrelation, and the significance of the individual functions are grasped in terms of both vertical and horizontal relations. To my mind, this way of understanding group identity in the Shinto style offers a good opportunity to reveal its true form for the first time.

Finally, something should be said about Shinto ethical thinking, given that it issues from this principle of relationality. In his *Shinto: The Way of Japan* (1965), the American educator and clergyman Floyd H. Ross suggested that one can grasp the ethical character of Shinto with the term, "situational ethics." Such an ethics does not have a standard of behavior that is prescribed by commandments from an absolute God through divine revelation. Shinto ethics is explained rather in this sense: Taking existing social conditions as its premise, it aims at contributing toward developing a better life for society as a whole. It is not at all surprising that such an ethic, based on such views, has been criticized as a type of crass opportunism or expediency. But it seems natural enough if one thinks about it matter of factly. What this really means is not opportunism but rather the desire to develop—fully and harmoniously—vitality in life without having an absolute, within the conditions of life in which individuals find themselves and within that matrix of relationships. "Sincerity" (*makoto*) is not just striving to remain loyal in one's relationships but also means that "*koto*," that is to say, an individual existence or individual thing, exists in its original functions, Based on this, a good way of understanding Shinto is that it conceives ethics in terms of a process of moral development, in much the same way as other principles of understanding existence. This understanding is what is really special in Shinto thinking.

Notes

1 Issued in 1956, the *Keishin seikatsu no kōryō* emphasized three basic principles summarized as follows: (1) Being grateful to the *kami* and the ancestors and sincerely devoting oneself to Shinto rituals; (2) Serving society and the people by having the wishes of the *kami* in mind; and (3) respecting the emperor as the mediator for the sun goddess and following his wishes, praying for the good fortune of Japan and the world for peace and prosperity.

2 The five grains: wheat, rice, beans, millet (*awa* and *kibi*).

3 The other two deities are Susanoo and Tsukuyomi.

4 See Donald Philippi, trans., *Kojiki* (Tokyo: The University of Tokyo Press, 1968), 47.

5 Ibid., 51.

6 Ibid., 81. In the myth, a boisterous ritual celebration of the gods brings Amaterasu out from her solitary confinement in the rock cave into the world where she again radiates her life-giving powers (*musubi*).

7 Sarume (猿女 or monkey women), mentioned along with the Nakatomi and Inbe clans as taking part in the festival of first fruits and other court ceremonies, who performed comic dances (*saru-gakui*, 猿楽, monkey dances).

8 Found in the *Kojiki* and *Nihonshoki*, Umashiashikabihikoji is one of the gods who appears after the emergence of the first three deities emerging "from a thing that sprouted up like a reed-shoot."

9 Kunitokotachi (Kuninotokotachi in the *Nihonshoki*) is born with Umashiashikabihikode no Kami.

10 One of the seven generations in the "Age of the Gods" (*kamiyo*) as recounted by *Kojiki*. According to the main text of *Nihonshoki*, one of the three "solitary *kami*" (*hitorigami*) that came into being at the first stage of creation.

11 The first deity pair in the seven generations of the gods in the classics.

12 *Kami* appearing in the second and third pairings in the creation myth,

13 In Japanese myth, an elder brother of Amaterasu and an important god who rules mountain, sea, and war.

14 Also read as Jinushigami (Land Master Deity), a local tutelary spirit.

15 A legendary sea deity considered to be a dragon or tutelary water deity.

16 This is the island the *kami* created by dipping their jeweled spear into the sea from the floating bridge of heaven. The drips of curdled brine that fell from the spirit became the island where the rest of the creation story takes place. See Philippi, *Kojiki*, 49.

17 Literally "Great-Land-Master," this deity is the lord of the Central Land of the Reed Plains in the *Kojiki*.

18 *Mitama* means a soul or spirit (*reikon*) and *fuyu* means to come in contact with (*sawaru*), calling upon (*furi*), or to increase (*fuyu*).

19 Enshrined in Usa Hachimangū in the Kyūshū area; faith in this deity spread across Japan in the succeeding centuries, supported by both the imperial house and the Genji (Minamoto) military clan. When the temple Tōdaiji's Great Buddha was constructed in the Nara period, the "shrine priestess" (*negini*) of Usa, Ōga no Ason Morime, traveled to the capital and received a "message" (*takusen*) from Hachiman saying that the *kami* would assist in the sculpture's construction, thus introducing the cult of Hachiman to the center of Japan.

20 The mirror is one of the three regalia mentioned in the *Kojiki* and *Nihonshoki* that Ninigi received before his descent from heaven, one of the so-called three divine treasures (*sanshu no jingi*).

32

SONODA MINORU

Our way of shrines and Shinto, asking about what shrine Shinto will look like in the future, the local shrine grove—a Shinto model of one's home, and shrines and Shinto (1998)

Sonoda Minoru (1936–) is a Japanese historian of religions who is also the chief priest of Chichibu shrine, in Saitama Prefecture. Born in the city of Chichibu, he attended the University of Tokyo, where he received his degree in religious studies from the Faculty of Letters in 1960 and completed his Ph.D. in 1965. Sonoda served as a lecturer and assistant professor at Kokugakuin University from 1972 to 1981, when he was promoted to professor. In 1991, he went to Kyoto University, serving as a professor in the Faculty of Integrated Human Studies and the Graduate School of Human and Environmental Studies. At present he is Professor Emeritus of Kyoto University. His focus is research on Shinto from the perspective of religious and folklore studies.

Sonoda Minoru is the author of several books, including *Matsuri no genshōgaku* (A Phenomenological Study of Festivals, 1990) and *Shintō no sekai* (The World of Shinto, 1997). The following essays are taken from his *Daredemo no shintō: shūkyō no Nihonteki kanōsei* (Shinto for Everyone: A Possibility for Religion in Japan, 1998).

Building on folklore studies, particularly the work of Yanagita Kunio, and his own experience as a Shinto priest in the Kanto region of Japan, Sonoda looks at Shinto from the inside. His primary concern is dispelling some of the key mistaken conceptions of Shinto; he believes that at the local level the shrines, and particularly their annual communal festivals, form the heart and soul of Shinto. These traditions both form the ancient ethnic religion and carry it forward into modern Japan.

OUR WAY OF SHINTO SHRINES AND SHINTO, ASKING ABOUT WHAT SHRINE SHINTO WILL LOOK LIKE IN THE FUTURE, THE LOCAL SHRINE GROVE—A SHINTO MODEL OF ONE'S HOME, AND SHRINES AND SHINTO (1998)

* * *

Our way of Shinto shrines and Shinto

The theme I have been asked to write about is "looking at shrines from the outside and Shinto from within." That is to say, this chapter is about the identity of shrines and Shinto, and it is nothing more than our definition of shrine Shinto from a priestly perspective. It is like being asked to give my own description that I, as a Shinto man, find desirable. So, my intention here is simply to discuss how I serve as a priest at a shrine and what I think of Shinto. As I am quite aware of my own personal views and biases, I will accordingly try to do this by stating what amounts to six seemingly paradoxical negative propositions.

Shinto is not history

Needless to say, Shinto has a long history. And yet, is Shinto something that is precious because it has a long history? If a religion is precious because it is old, then Christianity and Buddhism are more so because they have a much older history. Ours is an age that takes pleasure in novelty, on the one hand, while inclined toward a type of conservatism that thoughtlessly privileges history, on the other. I find it puzzling that so many men and women who come to the shrine to worship are happy if you simply emphasize the shrine's long history. But when all is said and done, a shrine is a place for festivals (*matsuri*). And, since festivals have continued down through the ages, born anew each time they are performed, they are surely precious indeed. Shinto is always new because its archaic form nullifies history eternally. Indeed, Ise Jingū's shrine rebuilding festival (*shikinen sengū*) celebrates the rebirth of its enshrined divinity by remaking all its divine treasures for its newly reconstructed main hall. Shrines and Shinto are not venerable because of their history but because they are always renewed at their festivals.

Festivals are not community events

Recently, many have confused Shinto festivals with community events. There are even priests who do not understand the difference. While it is true that both traditional festivals and events are something to be performed, they have the completely opposite essences. Events are successful through their pursuit of novelty, coming up with something new for variety's sake. Festivals, on the other hand, convey important meaning through their repetition of the same idea. Every year that the same ancient dignified festival is performed gives a sense of reassurance and peace of mind for those who participate in it. If a festival gets turned into an event, it is ruined, becoming something corny. And yet, if an event becomes part of a festival, it becomes a "refined tradition" (*fūryū*) included among the lively activities associated with the entertaining of the *kami*. In the final analysis, festivals are the reappearance of myths, the myths of eternal return.

Kami *do not exist*

Gods are not present in the sense that actual things are present. They have their presence in the way that I or we have our presence. *Kami* indeed also exist in the same way that we do by being ourselves (*aru*). Kami also exist as well in so far as we try to have existence ourselves. Existing, then, is not only something that is present. To exist is to have; in other words, it is a way of being that *has* (*motsu*) something. *Kami* have existence and I do too; I have existence and *kami* also do too. The spiritual world of the gods does not exist objectively as things exist (*aru*). But we subjectively perceive a spiritual nature of *kami* that should evoke a sense of awe toward some essential thing that makes us feel alive. Mystery is not part of the objective way in which most things exist. Our way of being objectifies a mystery which we subjectively experience; it does not depend on the empirical validation of the *kami* through science or pseudo-science.

Shrines are not churches

Shrines are first and foremost for the worship of the *kami.* In other words, they are a festival place for welcoming and rendering service in the presence of the *kami.* Shrines are neither training halls for spiritual austerities nor churches for giving sermons. The shrine (*yashiro*) of the *kami* is also the grove (*mori*) of the *kami.* The idea of the shrine is a solemnly dignified sacred area, richly endowed with pure forest groves and natural scenery. In the verdant natural world in which they found themselves and built their native home, Japanese long worshipped the local nature *kami* that they discovered there and that affected their lives. The so-called local tutelary shrines and sacred groves are a means of giving form and substance to the invisible spiritual nature of the *kami* that local inhabitants perceive around themselves. That is why the word "*kami*" etymologically refers to a spiritual nature from which life originates, which lies hidden in the wellsprings of rivers, the recesses of forested mountains, and so on. It is likely that the small rustic village sanctuary, which awaits, welcomes, and enshrines a manifestation (*miare*) of the invisible *kami* that appears at different times throughout the changing seasons, is the prototype of the Shinto shrine.

The shrine is not a place for the private practice of religion

In this respect, the shrine is the source for a local village's sense of order and, above all, inspires a collective sense of belonging to one's native home (*kokoro no furusato*) among local people. The way Japanese villages are arranged lacks any centrally situated open area. Instead, the village is ordered around the sacred grove of the *kami,* which is found out in the rear of the village (*oku*) and which forms an "invisible order" as it were. While local residents may visit the shrine on their own, even if they do not do so, the important thing is that the local divinity is alive and well there, ensuring their lives are peaceful and secure. During the year, however, there are several occasions when they greet the *kami* who is carried out from the shrine. On these occasions, the village becomes a town—the commotion of the festival with its bustling market re-energizes everyone into a lively collective whole. The words for town (*machi*), market (*ichi*), and festival (*matsuri*) all come from the same linguistic root. This linguistic connection makes sense when one realizes that the original value of *matsuri* lay in their attracting people, turning villages into towns with busy markets; festivals turned regional societies into authentic communities. Thus, we must conclude that shrines transcend individual personal piety and are essentially the common religion (*kyōdō no shūkyō*) of a community. Herein lies the reason why shrines are the most appropriate foundation for our present-day community awakening and community building efforts in villages and towns.

The priestly vocation is not an occupation

We often make fun of ourselves, saying, "A head priest is a hungry lord" (*kannushi wa kuwan-nushi*) or "The priestly life is a poor life" (*shinshoku wa hinshoku*). Certainly, right now there are only 20,000 people in the country engaged in this kind of work. Probably no more than 20 percent support themselves primarily through the priesthood. In terms of our present expectations for employment, the situation is perhaps deplorable; on further reflection, however, being a priest was not originally meant to be a means to earn one's livelihood. A priest's role is that of a master of ceremonies; the priestly vocation, in the past, generally signified membership of a family of priests who served a shrine on a hereditary basis. Moreover, before the early modern period, genuine hereditary priests served only at a limited number of large shrines. The great majority of the small and middle-sized shrines, which even now total about 80,000, sprang from a syncretism between *kami* and buddhas (*shinbutsu shūgō*). In former times, they were directly controlled by Buddhist temples or, at best, entrusted to the village leader in charge of *kami* rituals for his local parishioners or to mountain ascetics. In other words, since most shrines were originally led either by people who combined both religious duties, held both jobs concurrently, or were appointed to serve both institutions, being a priest was not a full-time occupation. So, while it may be true that with the separation between *kami* and buddhas during the Meiji period all the shrines became independent, most shrines could not possibly offer people full-time employment. Therefore, any assumption that it was ever possible to earn a living at a shrine is improbable; given that, is there really anything to worry about? Shrines from which one expects to make a living will lose their original way of being.

I view the shrine priest neither as someone who renounced the secular life nor as a saint. He or she should neither abandon the secular world nor look down on it. As a Shinto priest, I want to serve the *kami* and to worship them as representatives of people who try to live a straightforward and honest life. If the priesthood only amounts to a side business, the shrine priests should be proud that their service is not simply a means to earn their living. If a person can be compensated for devoted service, then that is a rewarding life, whether or not that compensation is enough to live on.

Asking about what shrine Shinto will look like in the future

Being aware of Shinto's state as a single "religion"

To begin with, what I would like to note first is awareness of shrine Shinto's character as a single religion. It is vital to resign oneself to the fact that it is one "religion" ranked with other various religions in our bewildering society of today. It is no longer possible for any religion or worldview to have a monopoly in any open society that has developed an internationalized market civilization like ours today under conditions where all values coexist pluralistically. Especially in a developed country like Japan, all values have become objects of choice no matter what their material or spiritual aspects are. Although Shinto and Buddhism can boast of a long tradition, this is not a time when every Japanese person can be regarded as a follower simply because of it. Rather, it is a time that welcomes people inquiring about their sense of these faiths spiritually speaking. However, what is especially key for comprehending shrine Shinto as a "religion" is the need to free ourselves from the concept of it as a "religion," a narrow view recognizing its basis only in an individualistic private faith, which is how "religion" is stipulated in its usage in the present Constitution and Religious Corporations Act. We need to understand the concept of religion more broadly signifying how it can give intrinsic meaning to a traditional culture and collectivity as a symbolic system. "Religion," as part of human culture, is not just those religions of the modern era that are equipped with founders and doctrines, consisting of individual faith and salvation. In human history one can find many more examples of cultural religions (*bunkateki shūkyō*) that, even without having any personal faith or salvation, support the cultural life of a community and effectuate spiritual peace and enlightenment for all its members. We should be clearly cognizant that shrine Shinto has such a character and foster our pride and spirit in it, advocating shrine Shinto's relevance for contemporary society while closely questioning the narrow view that holds sway in contemporary laws and common sense.

How do we foster awareness of Shinto as a "religion"?

Well then, how do we foster awareness of Shinto as a "religion"? What is plain is that its religious roots have always rested in Japanese ethnic culture. It serves faithfully still as the spiritual outlook of the indigenous peoples who settled in this mountainous archipelago and is openly practiced in their cultural life. What is necessary to especially note here is that Shinto is not a grandiose religion like those that originated from the meritorious needs and great teachings of some master, nor is it a world religion of prophets urging people to convert by loudly berating and encouraging them. Instead, it belongs to the ordinary anonymous folk who, while naturally sharing together their lives and livelihoods, superimpose an invisible spiritual world on their natural environs and make piety and reverence worshipping the gods and ancestors their main principle. That is to say, it must be remembered that Shinto is a religious culture in which very ordinary Japanese worship as part of their daily life, rather than being members of a religious organization, such as those especially seeking enlightenment or salvation in another world by renunciation and conversion. And yet, the problem here is that, given its character, how can shrine Shinto really continue to make itself relevant and meaningful in this confusingly modern world?

The dominant view of religion today tacitly assumes that something religious should extend some kind of means of salvation to people who are suffering and in pain mentally and physically. Moreover, religion should be devoted to salvation and welfare beyond what is offered by secular institutions, involving itself in overcoming social conflicts and evil. Initially, what's understood is that religion is a system of salvation to confront human suffering and social troubles.

Certainly, religion generally has the function to overcome and resolve the fundamental contradictions and limitations endemic in human beings and society through some transcendental standpoint. However, just because a faith does not practice special charitable work or offer a means of salvation for individuals and society at large it does not mean it isn't a religion. One cannot necessarily claim, even by using as one's standard the social contributions of religious practice as independent organizations apart from secular society, that there is one specific parameter that is definitive for making religion continue to be relevant. One persistent question, especially for a cultural religion like shrine Shinto, which, as it were, exists inherently within secular society and is directly connected to its social life, is how it validates itself through its contributions to that society's continuity and revitalization.

Wagering that shrines will continue to exist due to a desire for community renewal

However, as stated above, local communities—most of whose shrines formerly functioned as worship places for their guardian spirits and patron deities—have almost completely lost their original communal character. This began with the reorganization of local administration from the Meiji period and accelerated with the rapid urbanization and occupational fluidity from the late 1950s onwards.

Formerly, local communities essentially had the form of a village (*mura*) inter-mutual association. People with livelihoods rooted in the local environs in agriculture, forestry, and fishing could actually live as a communal whole. Having festivals in honor of the local tutelary deities was also indispensable for bustling towns (*machi*) that were originally *mura*. Cities in those days were also none other than an aggregation of towns stemming from *mura*, as evinced in the old saying, "the countryside lies there in the capital of Kyoto." However, local societies nowadays have almost completely been transformed by a thoroughgoing urbanization that makes them uniform and eliminates any distinction between town and country. Although called farming villages, their community life has become hollowed out by industrialization and mechanization and diversification through the division of labor.

And, while one might conclude that festivals and tutelary deities that are intrinsically a part of local communities throughout the country would have disappeared with urbanization, it never happened. Their survival has depended on the efforts of shrine priests and representatives. Not a few of these shrines, facing the unavoidability of making necessary changes, show examples of renewed revitalization rather than being simply preserved as they were. Here we can see a renewed desire to seek a community founded on spiritual bonds of the heart but that differs from the self-contained *mura* communities of the past.

Thus, one can think about this either negatively, seeing shrines' continued existence against the backdrop of the fluid social conditions that join cities and villages together and erode any sense of local community life, or positively, betting on people's renewed desire for community even as village-based society is becoming transformed fundamentally into an urban-based type of society. Yet, isn't the path that priests should choose the latter alternative, that resigns them to hardship? If, for the time being, they content themselves with the other choice, taking a business-management approach to what faces them, then the original lifeline of the shrines will soon be severed and lost.

Clearly reformulating how priests and shrines ought to be

So, how can we bet that shrines will continue to endure? It is important to clearly reformulate how shrines and priests ought to be, something that somehow has been left untouched. Based on this reformulation, boosting shrine instruction will be important as well.

Thus, what follows is a list of what has come to mind.

1   Repeatedly and ceaselessly questioning the basis for how shrines can exist religiously: While many studies of each shrine's mythical and historical origins have been done, we should give some thought to the particular condition of shrine grounds shared by shrines and especially emphasize the contrast between the solemnity of their shrine groves and sacred trees, even in the case of urban shrines, and what lies outside.
2   Re-designating shrine priests and its leadership more broadly as "shrine keepers" (*yashiromori*): Although it seems self-evidently true that shrines have never been an exclusive possession of the priests, in point of fact it actually remains unclear. It is naturally important for priests, whose families have served at a shrine for generations, to instill in their descendants a sense of pride and duty even if their work will not make for a comfortable life. Yet, nonetheless, now is the time where it is possible for shrine parishioners and worshippers to do their duty. Isn't it possible to ask for their humility and generosity in their efforts along with those who serve as its leaders, to protect the shrines? Such efforts will preserve self-discipline so as to escape the fate where priests

end up putting livelihood first by making the shrine their meal ticket. So, I think I can safely say without fear of being misunderstood that there is a way for shrines to persist. That is by revitalizing them as a nucleus for creating the community so sought after by people today—that way has its source in the distinctive character of shrine Shinto, as a religion that exists within the secular world (*sezoku nai shūkyō*).

3   It is vital that we should confront the many problems that have flowed nonstop from today's ever-changing society with the view of life and humanity that Shinto conveys. We should encourage people to think long and hard about it.

To add a final brief comment, the Shinto passed down through shrines is not a religion that aims to be novel or different. From the past it has been a way of revering the deities and respecting the ancestors, practiced both in the past and the future for this reason—so ordinary and sincere people living their lives attain a sense of spiritual peace for themselves.

*   *   *

The local shrine grove—a Shinto model of one's home

Images of one's old homeland

As the philosopher Martin Heidegger once said, one word that accurately describes people today is "homeless." Yet, for many Japanese people, the image of the local shrine grove still evokes fond recollections of home. There are still quite a few people, I am sure, who during their childhood sang a song called "The Village Festival," with the lyrics, "Today for the village's local deity is a happy festival day," or who raised their voices and sang the song "Spring Foliage," with the lyrics, "Brilliant green, bright green! Enveloping the *torii* gate to the shrine, hiding the straw thatched roofs. Fragrant, fragrant, the Spring foliage is fragrant."

In the time after World War II, when religion was the object of intense criticism, it seemed that the custom of worshipping the *kami* and the buddhas was dying out. And yet, even so, people's zeal for preserving their local shrines and groves never disappeared.

Shinto and shrines

The Japanese ethnic religion generally known as Shinto has its own special character. It has inherited, without historical interruption, an ancient religious culture of a people who were directly involved in the natural world. In other words, Shinto is unique in that it inherited a primal religious heritage from antiquity that has disappeared throughout the rest of the world. Originally, it was a religion of the woods and festivals that fit ancient times. To be sure, classical Shinto as a consciously elaborated religious system only came into existence after Yamato sovereignty was established, a time which spanned the clan-based state system of honorary ranks (*shisei kokka*)[1] to the emergence of the *ritsuryō* state system, organized around a new system of administrative and legal codes. But popular Shinto folkways, as the basis of the classical Shinto throughout the country, are to be found in the shrines and festivals which are scattered in every corner of the land and which stretch back to ancient times. Around the time of the Meiji Restoration the number of shrines in the country was estimated to be more than 180,000, corresponding roughly to the actual number of villages at that time. *The Shrine Inventory Register,* composed in 1879, counted over 176,000 shrines and, while a 1906 survey done immediately before the Ordinance for Merging Shinto Shrines (*jinja gōshirei*) had the number climbing approximately to 193,000, by the end of Meiji the number soon decreased to around 110,000, a result of the government-enforced shrine mergers.[2] At present those shrines officially classified as religious corporations or "juridical persons" (*shūkyō hōjin*) number around 80,000. They are mostly maintained as large and small regional shrines of local tutelary deities throughout the country. And yet, if we added non-official and privately run shrines, it is conceivable that the numbers of shrines could climb to as much as 200,000–300,000 shrines even today.

Shrines and groves

In ancient times, the word for shrine was both "*kamu tsu yashiro*" (shrine of the *kami* as seen in the *Engishiki*) and *mori* (grove). In the *Manyōshū,* we find several examples such as these two poems exchanged between a certain young woman and Saeki Akamaro: "If the shrine (*yashiro*) of the *kami* were not there, I would sprinkle my millet in the field at Kasuga." "If you sprinkled your millet in the field at Kasuga, without any thought, I would go following the millet there, even if the presence of the shrine (*yashiro*) prevents me" (Scroll #3, poem # 404).

Another example is "Much tormented by love, I felt as if I could jump over this sacred grove (*mori*) where the paper Mulberry strips hang for the festival" (Scroll #7, poem #1378).

In verses from a long poem (*chōka*) we also find: "I pray that the wind will not blow hard down from the mountains, and I will cross then cross them and offer a festive celebration for the wind god at that famous grove (*mori*)" (Scroll #9, poem #1951), and "I offer votive paper offerings to the *kami* who resides in the grove (*mori*) at Yamashina, and will cross over the mountain of Ausaka" (Scroll 13, poem #3236).

The word *yashiro* does not originally refer to a shrine building, but indicates a place where a house (*yashiro*, 屋代 or namely, an *okusha* 屋舍) should be built. Accordingly, the *yashiro* of a *kami* is a sacred vacant piece of land where one should enshrine the *kami*. Usually, it is considered taboo or off limits, marked off by a *shimenawa* rope indicating that it is consecrated ground. Since the field at Kasuga was sacred as a *yashiro* of the *kami*, one could not sprinkle millet there. Since the Japanese word *miya* (宮), probably refers to *miya* (御屋, literally, "respectable housing"), it was probably a designation used after shrine buildings were erected at the *yashiro*. In a different vein, the relationship between the Japanese sound *mori* and such Chinese characters as *jinja* (神社), *sha* (舍), or *to* (杜) reveal a distinctive Japanese usage of them. In Japanese, the word *mori* refers to a grove that a *kami* quietly inhabits—most particularly a densely wooded area of a shrine (*shasō*). This is a different usage, since the character 社 (or *sha*) in Chinese refers to an earth god, and the Chinese character 杜 (or *zu*) originally refers only to a wild pear tree. Shrines in Japan, *jinja*, were originally nothing more than a sacred grove that a *kami* inhabits quietly.

Shrines and festivals

In addition, we find many instances of ancient shrines not just in wooded areas but in the mountains (*oyama*). The original form of the shrine was mostly rituals performed at the foot of mountains. For example, Ōmiwa Shrine in the Nara basin bequeaths to us its ancient rites, and thus Mount Miwa, which lies behind it, is the *kami* shrine without a main hall. Other nearby mountains associated with *kami* (which are also objects of worship known as *shintai-san*) include Mount Furu for Isonokami Shrine and Mount Mikasa for Kasuga Taisha as well as others. The upper and lower shrines of Kyoto's general tutelary shrine, Kamo Shrine, pre-serve a form of worship that greets the *kami* from the *shintaizan* of Mount Kōya (Kōyama) and Mount Migake (Mikageyama) respectively. What are generally called *shintaizan* are sacred mountains that in classical texts were called "*kamunabi*" (mountains) (神奈備). These moun-tains were not themselves embodiments of the *kami* (*shintai*) but were inhabited quietly by gods. All over the country, one can find mountains whose names tell us that they are regarded as *shintaizan*—examples of these include Kōyama (or Miyama), Miyayama, Ontake (Mitake or Utaki), Ōyama (or Daisen), and Moriyama (or Muriyama). There are also examples of local sacred sites not directly connected to actual groves or mountains. These include Obotsuyama in Amami region (in the Ryūkyū Archipelago, now Kagoshima Prefecture), Garōyama in Tanegashima island (lying in southern Kyushu in Kagoshima Prefecture), Moidon in Satsuma and Ōkuma (also in southern Kyushu), Kōjinmori in Western Iwami (in the Chūgoku region of the main island of Honshū), and Tendōyama in Tsushima island (located in the Korean Strait).

Most of these sacred sites are nicely shaped hills covered with densely wooded forests or impressive mountains that can be seen from nearby villages. All of them are landmarks that serve as a scenic backdrop for the village. More importantly, they are the source of water, indispensable for local people's livelihoods and daily lives. In villages along the shores of the ocean and lakes, the rocky outcrops out in the open sea and small islands where the fishing is especially bountiful are called *tachigami* (literally, "standing *kami*") or *kamijima* (literally, *kami* islands). There are also capes on the coast called *yamadate* and mountains inland that become landmarks for seafarers indicating the sea lanes and good fishing places and, as such, their object of faith.

The results of recent Japanese philological research suggest that the Japanese word *kami* means a spiritual nature that lies hidden in the mountains and valleys that served as water sources for the local villages. The word's ancient etymological origin is the word *kuma* or *kumu* (隈,"a corner deep inside"or "to hide there"). Having settled into the natural local environs of Japan's mountainous archipelago and begun to labor in agriculture, forestry, and fishing, the local inhabitants had a peaceful and secure *lebenswelt* that has lasted for gener-ations. It constituted a vitalistic cosmos where they found and worshipped a spiritual nature hidden within those natural mountains and groves—the *kami*.

The cosmology of one's homeland

The ritual structure lies within the framework, ordering the life of the towns and villages, an order which the Japanese have depended on for a peaceful and secure existence tradition-ally. This structure has two classic forms: either the mountain shrine (*yamamiya*)—village shrine (*satomiya*)—shrine of the rice field (*tamiya*), or the offshore shrine (*okimiya*)—the village shrine (*satomiya*)—the shore shrine (*hamamiya*), both of which are centered around the local shrines of the ancestral *kami* (*ujigami*). Although the village shrine was originally a grove intended to welcome the divinity from the mountain to the village, it was eventu-ally supplanted by shrine buildings, which became ancestral tutelary shrines where the *kami* perpetually dwelt. However, the buildings, like the groves before them, physically reveal a sacred spatial order, one that signifies for the villagers the deep inside, or the other world, located in a grove. The shrines of the rice field and the shore shrines supposedly offer a provisional shrine at ceremonial times when the *kami* appear where villagers live and work; essentially, these shrines can be considered transient shrines that lodge the *kami* (*kamiyado*), abodes for traveling *kami* (*otabisho*), or makeshift palaces (*tongū*).

Traditionally, Japanese villages are not centered around open areas like plazas or common greens but form their communities along roadways. The festival for the tutelary divinity changes the entire village into a sacred space by bringing kami from the mountain shrine to the village shrine and to the transient shrine along the village roadways. Indeed, on these public occasions, the village becomes transformed into a bustling town and a festive market that revitalizes the human spirit. Such communal gatherings where local people share their joy is a world of peace and security, a home brought about by the silent grove of the *kami* and its invisible order.

* * *

Shrines and Shinto

Although it is an advanced society on par with Western European countries, Japan maintains a cultural tradition rich in truly spiritual symbolism. Modern Japanese are quite adept at skillfully designing mechanical robots, but they never forget to endow their machines with souls. They think that there is a spiritual life force, not only in human beings but also in the rich natural world in which they live, as well as in the agricultural tools like plows, spades, and other implements they use, when they function fully. They sense that a *kami* (or divine spirit, *shinrei*) dwells in the subtle workings of both nature and human activities. That is a Japanese spiritual feeling; since ancient times, Japanese people have discovered *kami* in such Japanese beauties as the flowers, birds, winds, and various phases of the moon.

And it was in the beauty of natural locales that people experienced *kami*, not only throughout their own lives but for generations. This is not a nature that has become something that people own, not someone's private property as it is in our day, nor is it a nature that is pristine, still untouched and undeveloped by human hands. One might say that it is a natural world where the *kami* touch people in their ordinary lives. Evidence for this is found everywhere throughout the country, wherever people erect *torii* gates close to villages where they live, whether on the coast or at the foot of mountains. Wherever people tie a *shimenawa* rope on rocks near the shore or on large trees in forests, nature is regarded as a spiritual dwelling place for the *kami*.

According to philologist Sakakura Atsuyoshi the word *kami* originates from the ancient word, *kumu* (to hide) and *kuma* (a corner deep within and hidden).[3] Furthermore, the term also shares the same linguistic root with the word *kami* "above" (上) expressing the origin (*moto*) as opposed to "below" (*shimo*, 下), that is, the end of something (*sue*, 末). Therefore, in this respect, it indicates an original source, something that is hidden beyond where people can see, somewhere in the mountains and fields. Of course, if things are called *kami*, they are spiritual beings (*mitama*) that are not visible to the naked eye. Rather, they are manifestations (*miara*, 御現) or spiritual silhouettes (*mikage*, 御蔭), especially in living things and in pristine natural settings. Originally, when people violated a taboo and trespassed on the fields and mountains of the *kami*, it was dangerous because a "rough" or violent spirit (*araburukami*) would appear, taking forms like a bear, a wolf, a serpent, or thunder (*narukami* or *ikazuchi*). If people cordially welcomed it to the village with devotion and a sincere invitation, the *kami* would appear as a "young" (*wakamitama*) or "gentle" spirit (*nigimitama*) that offers creative or vitalistic power (*musubi*) and bestows blessings on the village. This is what Shinto calls a festival.

Moreover, the *kami* who are present at appropriate ritual times in the village are regarded as *mikoto*. Why were they referred to in this way? Since they were originally hidden spiritual beings, *kami* take their form by appearing to the festival celebrants who become their *mikoto-mochi* (those serving the will of the *kami*) as their words and actions (*kami no mikoto*). The forms of *kami* are none other than the celebratory words and actions of *kamunagara* (the way exactly like *kami*) that the celebrants perform.

If *kami* were originally hidden spirits, then surely the aim of *matsuri* is that people initially seclude themselves for religious purification and then wholeheartedly gather together to welcome the *kami*'s manifestation or hierophany. Certainly, the underlying principle of *matsuri* is to work to soothe these spirits and to foster peace and harmony. Since *matsuri*, as it were, are when *kami* appear via *mikoto* (sacred words and actions) *kami* and *matsuri* have an indispensable relationship with each other. Because of their hidden spiritual nature, *kami* have festivals in which they appear. If they reveal themselves only in *matsuri*, then *kami* also therefore have a hidden nature.

And human life also has a spiritual nature as well. The dead become *kami no mikoto* only after they receive due rituals. Therefore, people who through some misfortune died unexpectedly and did not thereafter receive duly respectful rituals can become enraged and vengeful spirits (*onryō*) that can harm people through curses (*tatari*). There are several frightening examples of this down through history. In addition, when people settled an area in ancient times, if they did not take due notice of the region's nature *kami* and perform rituals for them, the divinities soon made them realize their presence by sending them misfortunes. Ōmononushi, the enshrined deity of the old Nara shrine, Ōmiwa Jinja, for example, made Emperor Sujin aware of his presence in this way when the sovereign attempted to rule the country of Yamato.[4]

In other words, the spirits have festivals because they are *kami*, but they cannot be *kami* if they don't have festivals. The places where *kami* are respected and enshrined are sacred sites that from time immemorial have been called shrines (*jinja*).

Shinto is rooted in the formation of this kind of ethnic culture. It became an ethnic religion (*minzoku shūkyō*), in tandem with the unification of the ancient Japanese state, cognizant of and standing for the unity of the Japanese state. However, needless to say, words were necessary to express that self-consciousness. And those words were taken from ancient China's advanced culture. The first appearance of the word "Shinto" is in the ancient imperial chronicle, the *Nihonshoki*, under the entry before Emperor Yōmei's enthronement,[5] This emperor lived during the latter half of the sixth century, and the text was compiled in 720. Therefore, it is apparent that Japanese became conscious of "Shinto" as a distinct form of spirituality sometime between the Asuka and Nara periods.

But what is more important is the connection with the continental culture of that time. The chronicles indicate that Emperor Yōmei converted to Buddhism and additionally paid respect to "Shinto." Buddhism had officially been introduced to the imperial court during the time of Emperor Kinmei, two reigns earlier. In other words, the introduction of Buddhism stimulated the formation of Shinto.

So then, what was the content of this form of Shinto? It was none other than the rituals of all the gods of heaven and earth (*tenjin chigi*) as indicated in the ordinances of the Yōrō codes regarding deities (*jingiryō*). That is, it was nothing more nor less than a public festival for worshipping national and regional *kami* throughout the four seasons. A *matsuri* is in and of itself a formal public ceremony rather than part of a private form of faith. In this case, "public" has the additional meaning of the jurisdiction of the palace as well as the Council of Divinities (Jingikan), which supervised festivals and rituals where the emperors and the courtiers participated. Therefore, "Shinto" must originally have referred to the system of *kami* festivals related to the ancient imperial state.

However, the *kami* who were enshrined throughout the country were not only those of the ancient state. Rather, most were mythical ancestral or regional spirits, who date back to the ancient times and who were served by powerful regional clans. These Shinto *kami* were initially called "*oyagami*" (ancestral divinities) but later became known as "*ujigami*," a name that continues to this day. While these *kami* did occasionally adopt elements of the superior Buddhist culture, they never lost their natural divine character that rooted them to different localities. This is evidenced even now by the more than 80,000 shrines and associated festivals throughout the country.

Notes

1 The *uji kabane* (*shisei*) ranking system was created in 648 by Emperor Tenmu as a system of eight surname titles. The upper four were assigned to 120 lineages and established a privileged aristocratic elite which had access to power at court for the following century. See Richard Miller, *Ancient Japanese Nobility—The Kabane Ranking System* (Berkeley: The University of California Press, 1974).
2 See Wilbur M. Freidel, *Japanese Shrine Mergers 1906–1912* (Sophia University, Tokyo: Monumenta Nipponica Monograph, 1973).
3 Sakakura Atsuyoshi, "Gogen—'*kami*' no gogen o chūshin ni," *Kōza—Nihongo no goi daiikkan* (Meiji Shoin, 1982).
4 See Robert S. Ellwood, "The Sujin Religious Revolution," *Japanese Journal of Religious Studies* 17 (1990):199–217.
5 Some have argued that the proper pronunciation here is *jindō*. The phrase Sonoda refers to here is "The emperor believed in Buddhism and respected Shinto." It is commonly accepted that this phrase comes from a commentary on a hexagram from the Chinese Confucian classic, the *Book of Changes* (*I ching*). How this phrase is interpreted, however, is a matter of considerable scholarly controversy. Some argue that the phrase reflects a Chinese understanding of the spiritual way (*shen tao*) of heaven. Others argue that the Japanese simply appropriated the phrase to express their own understanding of divinity as *kami*. It is clear that Sonoda takes the latter view.

33

KAMATA TŌJI

What is Shinto?
(1999)

Kamata Tōji (1951–) is a philosopher of religion and professor of Shinto studies. He was born in Anan city, Tokushima prefecture. In 1975, he graduated from Kokugakuin University with a degree in philosophy; he also finished his doctoral course work in Shinto studies there in 1980, and in 2001 he completed his doctorate in literature at Tsukuba University. In 2003 he became a professor at the Kyoto University of Art and Design, and in 2008, he was appointed professor at the Kokoro Research Center of Kyoto University. In 2016, after retiring from Kyoto University, he moved to the Institute of Grief Care at Sophia University.

His many publications include: *Shinkai no fiirudo waaku* (Fieldwork in the Divine World, 1985), *Kigō to kotodama* (Symbols and the Spiritual Power of Words, 1990), *Shūkyō to reisei* (Religion and Spirituality, 1995), *Shintō no supirichuaritī* (Shinto's Spirituality, 2003), and *Gendai shintōron: reisei to seitaichi no tankyū* (An Essay on Contemporary Shinto—Spirituality and Inquiry into Ecological Wisdom, 2011).

The essay that follows comes from his edited book, *Shintō yōgo no kiso chishiki* (Fundamental Knowledge of Shinto Terminology, 1999). Here Kamata argues that Shinto cannot be understood in terms of the conventional categories used to define world religions. Kamata draws on the ideas of Lafcadio Hearn (1850–1904), the celebrated Greek-Anglo-Irish American man of letters and interpreter of Japan (who later became a naturalized Japanese citizen using the name, Koizumi Yakumo), arguing in favor of what Hearn calls the "sense of Shinto." By this, Hearn meant that at the heart of Shinto is a numinous experience of the mysterious power of the *kami* within the natural world.

WHAT IS SHINTO?
(1999)

Lafcadio Hearn (Koizumi Yakumo), who had come to Japan in the twenty-third year of Meiji when he was forty (1890) was, in the following year, the first Westerner to ever be granted permission to worship at the Grand Shrine of Izumo. Hearn wrote the following about that experience in his travelogue, *Kitzuki*: "There seems to be a sense of divine magic in the very atmosphere, through all the luminous day, brooding over the vapory land, over the ghostly blue of the flood—a sense of Shinto."[1]

This "sense of Shinto," as Hearn calls it, is a sense that something divine exists within the air, light, water, earth, wind, and so on that make up this natural world, that is to say, a sense of feeling the *kami* within nature. How come Hearn as a modern Westerner learned this sense of Shinto?

One can conclude that it was probably because Greek polytheistic animism also had this spiritual sensibility, natural to Hearn given that he was Greek by birth. And, it seems Hearn had nurtured a sensitivity toward spirits, souls, and gods that grew or developed in him through the various stories and myths and fairy legends of Ireland where he spent his childhood.

When he came to Japan and lived on its land, this sensibility that Hearn had toward the gods and spirits probably became even more acutely honed and sharpened. Rather than an intuition, this "sense of Shinto" was more visceral, manifesting itself as a physical feeling for him. Hearn's sense very much touches upon the basis of Japanese people's own religious sensibilities. In this sense of Shinto, Hearn recognized an important mode of thought.

A religion is generally considered as something that has founders, doctrines, scriptures, and a religious organization. However, this modern way of thinking toward religions is modeled after Christianity, Islam, and Buddhism. If we view Shinto by taking these kinds of world religions and religious classification as our sole model, Shinto is lacking all of these features—it has no founder, doctrines, or scriptures and is not clearly organized as a religious order; no matter what the perspective, it ends up not fulfilling any of the conditions for constituting a religion.

Rather Hearn finds that in the shrines and Shinto, which lacks such founders and scriptures, there is a positive quality of eternity. Hearn says, "Buddhism has a voluminous theology, a profound philosophy, a literature vast as the sea. Shinto has no philosophy, no code of ethics, no metaphysics; and yet, by its very immateriality, it can resist the invasion of occidental religious thought as no other oriental faith can."[2]

In other words, there is no philosophy at all, no systematic ethics, nor any abstract doctrine nor thinking either; Shinto finds its life within this "nothing" (nai). That life of Shinto, that is, the life pulse of an ancient faith, is the feeling one has of discovering the kami within nature and the atmosphere itself, and this physical feeling cannot be expressed in thought. Ancient people had it, and today many Japanese still secretly have this sense of eternity or, rather, this sense of the cycle of life. Hearn pointed out the spiritual reality of this feeling. Isn't it important for we modern Japanese to try to once again deeply grasp what Hearn has put his finger on here?

> Indeed the best of our scholars have never been able to tell us what Shinto is. To some it appears to be merely ancestor-worship; to others, again, it seems to be no religion at all; to the missionary of the more ignorant class it is the worst form of heathenism. Doubtless the difficulty of explaining Shinto has been due simply to the fact that the sinologists have sought for the source of it in books: in the Kojiki and the Nihongi, which are its histories; in the norito, which are its prayers; in the commentaries of Motoori and Hirata, who were its greatest scholars.[3] But the reality of Shinto lives not in books, nor in rites, nor in commandments, but in the national heart, of which it is the highest emotional religious expression, immortal and ever young. Far underlying all the surface crop of quaint superstitions and artless myths and fantastic magic there thrills a mighty spiritual force, the whole soul of a race with all its impulses and powers and intuitions. He who would know what Shinto is must learn to know that mysterious soul in which the sense of beauty and the power of art and the fire of heroism and magnetism of loyalty and the emotion of faith have become inherent, immanent, unconscious, instinctive.[4]

What Hearn calls here the vital living pulse beating "deep within the soul of the folk," the root of the folk's soul deep beneath its surface manifestations, the folk's instinct, vitality, and intuition—don't we need to reconsider this as the creative core of Japanese culture?

Shinto and the creative wellspring of the Japanese

There are a variety of views about Shinto. As Hearn says, there are some scholars who see Shinto as the living culture of ancestor worship. Again, there are also some who see it as a primitive and simple system of faith and nature worship. And then again, some look at it as having a form that combines animism and shamanism. One cannot dismiss any of these views as mistaken. It is possible to accept these as the various elements or conditions that form Shinto.

However, that which is the life and basis of Shinto is not something that can be exhaustively expressed through such words. It is necessary to discern, as Hearn says, the instinctive nature, vitality, and intuition that exists within Japanese culture or, more specifically, Japanese people's ethnic culture, in other words, its creative wellspring. In short, one cannot understand Shinto without grasping from the inside the eternal in life that Japanese people have experienced in an embodied way. Surely, that can be referred to as "the sense of Shinto." It seems Shinto lives on in the present because such folk instincts exist within it or because of its sensibility toward the eternal or life's everlastingness. Thus, if we look at Shinto historically, what kind of picture do we come up with?

First, about 10,000 years ago, at the end of the last ice age, the eastern tip of the Eurasian continent was cut off due to rising sea levels. A short time passed after that, and the islands at the western end of Eurasia likewise became separated from the continent. That is the course of the natural geographical formation of the islands of Britain and Ireland.

For Japan, the warming and the melting ice raised ocean levels at the end of the last ice age almost 10,000 years ago, causing the peninsula connected to the eastern edge of Eurasia to become detached from the continent because of the Japanese sea. Because of that dividing sea, Japan became an archipelago. The Japanese archipelago's geographical location and conditions proved decisive for the formation of Japanese civilization afterward including Shinto.

The Japanese islands were formed in a transitional period from the old Stone Age to the New Stone Age, during what is called the Jōmon period. It was from that time that the special quality or individuality that is at the root of Japanese culture came into being. First, broad-leaved and deciduous trees of beech and oak forests spread throughout the entire northern eastern region of Japan, and, from the southwest broad-leaved evergreen forests gradually advanced northward and spread eastward. The pottery culture that used cord mark patterns (jōmon) formed both at the western and eastern ends of Japan's archipelago. Why was this form of pottery culture created? What reasons were behind this turning point from the Stone Age to the age of pottery?

When considering this problem, we must reflect on the geographical and natural environmental conditions. The Japanese archipelago is situated in the Pacific Rim volcanic zone. One can discover active or the remains of now dormant volcanoes on every island. There is no doubt that the ancient people on these islands held this violent power of fire in awe as a great natural force. And, they doubtless discovered a mystery of nature in the earth and stones that were transformed by fire.

The power of fire and the ancient people of the archipelago

In order to make pottery you need clay. That clay was fired producing the first pottery. How did the ancient people living in the archipelago make sense of this kind of power of fire? They had a profound realization of the great might of nature as a function of a number of *kami*.

At the beginning of the *Kojiki,* it is recorded that when heaven and earth were first divided, three divinities, Amenominakanushi, Takamimusuhi, and Kamimusuhi, came into being in the High Plain of Heaven (Takamagahara). A divinity first appears in the center of heaven, namely, Amenominakanushi, and then the two divinities with creative and vitalistic power (*musuhi*), Takamimusuhi, and Kamimusuhi, appear.

These first kami are called the three deities of creation (*zōka sanshin*). It seems that the *kami* were constructed from Chinese thought and a kind of political theology of the age in which the *Kojiki* was formed.[5] However, clearly at their root, there is a faith in *musubi*. *Musubi* is a productive and generative power that manifests and reveals itself from the depths of earth or from the sky. In other words, from nature and all the world, new life forms are created and generated, and people profoundly realize the power of *musubi*, feeling a sense of awe and gratitude.

After the three *kami* of creation, the *kami* Umashiashikabihikoji[6] and Amenotokotachi appeared, followed by Kuninotokotachi,[7] Toyokumono, Uijini and Suijini, Tsunogui and Ikugui, Ōtonoji and Ōtonobe, Omodaru and Ayakashikone, and Izanagi and Izanami.[8]

Specifically, Umashiashikabihikoji is a plant that grew up vigorously from the soil like a mold or a reed, and also Uijini and Suijini symbolize sand, soil, clay, and mud. In other words, the *Kojiki* describes the overwhelming power of nature and activity of life where the earth is generative, and plants grow luxuriantly up from the soil as a function of the *kami*. The divine lineage given in the beginning of the *Kojiki* illustrates that idea in the process by which the *kami* manifest themselves.

In this we can discover the feeling of awe and gratitude toward the eternal in life, and the creative power active within nature and *musubi*, of which the ancient Japanese were keenly aware, continues unabated. In the Shinto sensibility, continuing unabated is that feeling of awe ancient people felt toward the vital and generative natural powers, particularly evident in volcanoes, especially, the power of fire.

Even in Ainu and also in Okinawan belief, the fire deity plays a very intimate and important role. Petitions to the *kami* were delivered to the gods through the fire deity before anything else. At the same time as occupying a central place in everyday life, fire also served a role as a messenger to various *kami*. In other words, the fire *kami* is a mediator who connects the human world to the highest deities. Fire was revolutionary for human life, having a powerful role in assuring life and culture.

Jōmon pottery and the sense of life

The pottery of the Jōmon period could not be produced without clay and fire. When you knead the clay, you use water. And when you fire the vessels, wind affects the flames. The power of what are called the four elements—earth, wind, fire, and water—combine together to produce the pottery.

The evidence suggests that Jōmon pots were used for removing the harshness and bitterness of acorns found in the Japanese beech and oak forests [they were boiled in them].

Given this possibility, the Jōmon people doubtless had a profound insight into the power and mystery of nature when they fired these pots themselves. The various spiral, whirlpool, or zigzag—called *raimon*—patterns that look like lightening, added to the outer surface of the pottery, graphically portray this dynamism at work in life, revealing the natural world's mystery and creative energy.

Probably, this deep sense of life, which continued unabated from the Old Stone Age, came to be fully grasped within Japan's volcanic archipelago culture through a clearer embodiment in the tangible creativity of Jōmon pottery. This deep sense of life continues, finally finding expression in the story of Izanagi and Izanami's creation of the land.

Izanagi and Izanami give birth to the fire god Kagutsuchi, and Izanami's genitals get burned in the process. That is to say, in order to give birth to the fire *kami,* the mother's body, her uterus, and her genitals get burned, and, weakening, she falls ill, excreting vomit, feces, and urine from her body. But from that vomit two gods of metal, Kanayamabiko and Kanayamabime, emerge as a divine husband-and-wife pair, and from the effluvia, Haniyasubiko and Haniyasubime, husband-and-wife gods of clay also emerge, as well as, from the urine, a water *kami* called Mitsuhanome.

This can be interpreted as a narrative divinizing the acts of nature, as a story in which rocks, metals, and earth form from the first erupting volcanoes, and springs and hot springs gush out from underground chasms. In this respect, a sense of awe toward nature that the people who lived in Japan's archipelago felt lies hidden within the representation collected together here as a myth, a sense that extends for thousands, even tens of thousands of years.

The Jōmon period continued for more than roughly 10,000 years, but in this long span of time, the culture formed out of a variety of special regional and climatological conditions. Even though it is called the Jōmon period, over that time span and also regionally, one can find much diversity and great modifications. However, at its base, it always maintained that feeling of awe toward the creative might of nature.

Water and sun in rice farming

In the fifth and sixth century BCE, rice farming culture was brought to the Japanese isles from the continent. Of course, it is certainly an archeological fact that before this time there was Jōmon farming. The shift from Jōmon to Yayoi farming was a decisive change to rice paddy cultivation and brought with it a structural transformation to Japanese archipelago culture. In order to do rice paddy farming, first you need to ensure that there are canals to channel the water to the fields. Up to that point, the faith that probably occupied center stage in ancient Jōmon people's belief was focused on fire, with which they were most intimately familiar. Naturally, they also probably worshipped various other powers of nature other than fire, such as the sun, water, the earth, and plants, but at the center of their nature worship was fire.

However, with the Yayoi period, this faith substantially changed from a focus on fire to worshipping the water or the sun. Water is essential for growing rice as well as the blessings of the sunlight and the sun. Without an abundance of sunlight and water, it would be impossible to have a rich rice harvest. Thus, the devotional focus on water and the sun gradually grew stronger. Perhaps the spiritual transformation from Jōmon to Yayoi can be located in this shift from the worship of fire to that of the sun and water.

In the formation of this kind of faith, the sun, in particular, is alone in the sky, and becomes symbolically meaningful as its light shines everywhere. Water falls from the sky and is stored in the earth, becoming the rivers that pour into the sea. That water is used when doing ritual purification (*misogi harai*). Along with purifying pollutions and sins, it moistens the earth, transforming it into fresh verdure. In other words, water is something that symbolizes the purifying and vitalistic power of nature as a whole.

On the other hand, at the same time, it fosters the growth of all things; the sun as one in heaven comes to have a symbolic nuance as something that unifies all things together. That is the reason why the sun is tied to the emperor. It is clear that the title of "emperor" (*tennō*) has its origin in the Taoistic worship of the North or Pole Star, but this devotion to the North Star and the Big Dipper, which formed the center of the Chinese imperial astrological worship, was transformed into a focus on the sun in Japanese imperial worship. It was thought that the sun itself bound the natural world together as a whole, and unified it, making it into one. Thus, the emperor came to hold the position as the descendant of the great *kami* Amaterasu Ōmikami, who was dispatched from the High Plain of Heaven (Takamagahara).

In this way, the myth was formed that the sun *kami* had a unique family line who properly ruled and unified the Japanese isles, referred to as Ashihara no Nakatsukuni (the Central Land of the Reed Plains) in the *Kojiki* and *Nihonshoki*. The unified state system that had the emperor at its center was organized politically, mythologically, and culturally. At the root of the economic system that supported the emperor was rice cultivation, and the political system that supported it was the *ritsuryō* system introduced from China in the seventh century. And the cultural system that supported the emperor came to fruition in the Tanka poetic form, like those *waka* recorded in the *Manyōshū*, that further refined and formalized the older songs. This marks the birth in Japan of a unified state power and religious authority.

The culture of the descendants of the heavenly *kami* and foundational culture

In this way, a political system of rule based upon rice cultivation was born as the Yamato court, created through the efforts of the imperial family and the aristocrats who supported them. The myths that express this clearly are the myth of the descent of Ninigi from heaven, the story of Emperor Jinmu's eastern progress to Yamato as he subjugated his enemies, and the story of Yamato Takeru's asserting control over the Kumaso Takeru and Izumo Takeru. Ninigi was granted the three divine treasures of the imperial regalia (*sanshu no jinki* [or *jingi*]) from Amaterasu: the mirror (*yata no kagami*), the jewel (*yasakani no magatama*), and the sword (*ame no murakumo no tsurugi* or *kusanagi no tsurugi*),[9] and, entrusted with ears of rice, he descended to this land, the Central Land of the Reed Plains. This was probably a mythological system that immigrants from the continent transmitted to Japan along with rice cultivation and metallurgical technology.

Therefore, the speculation is that the origin of the imperial system lay in the continent and the Korean peninsula. In Japanese myth, heavenly deities (*amatsukami*) dispatched from the High Plain of Heaven conquer the indigenous deities (*kunitsukami*) who lived on the land before them, and the recorded tales tell of the battles forcing them into submission. If there were some among these indigenous deities who were obedient and cooperated with the heavenly deities, some also resisted and were destroyed. Those peoples who did not yield were called the Tsuchigumo, among others,[10] and were treated as inferior savages. From their name, we can surmise that the Tsuchigumo were a people who were more rooted to the earth and nature and closer to animals. The word reflects the viewpoint of those who enjoyed the benefits of the civilization that had been transmitted from the continent, scornfully singling out those who lived a more natural life and had a simple form of nature worship.

However, from the archeological remains of the Jōmon that we find today at sites like Uenohara in Kagoshima prefecture[11] and Sannaimaruyama in Aomori prefecture,[12] it is clear that the Tsuchigumo's way of life was far from the lowest cultural level. One can say that there is a structural difference between the Yayoi cultural system, which was based upon rice paddy cultivation, and Jōmon culture, which was based on hunting and gathering and primitive agriculture.

In this way, the culture of the Japanese isles underwent a great transformation. Namely, Jōmon as the indigenous culture formed the foundation of Japanese culture. But on top of it was the Yayoi, integrating its culture based on metal technology and rice cultivation systematically with it. In this respect, a unified state developed that was reliant on an ancient metallurgical culture of bronze and iron implements, and so a Japanese culture came into being that was centered on the ancient *ritsuryō* legal system and compiled the *Kojiki* and the *Nihonshoki*, which served to guarantee that state political system of authority theologically, and also the *Manyōshū*.

What we call Japanese culture formed out of the Old and New Stone Age before Jōmon and Jōmon pottery culture, in the process of establishing a single unified state system that was constructed with the addition of the Yayoi period rice farming and metal working culture, and after that of Taoism, Confucianism, and Buddhism transmitted from China. Shinto came to occupy a position as a traditional belief system that existed from ancient times, in contrast to the religions that had been transmitted from the continent, in other words, Confucianism and Buddhism, and so on.

Shinto and the transmission of Buddhism

The word "Shinto" first appears in the entry for Emperor Yōmei in the *Nihonshoki*. Emperor Yōmei is regarded as a sovereign who both had faith in Buddhism and respect for Shinto. This phrase "*shin buppō son shintō*" points to his achievement; while during his tenure he appointed the imperial princess Sukatehime as the Saiō high priestess at Ise Jingū, he fostered a faith in Buddhism by praying for his own recovery from illness. In other words, while respecting traditional Shinto rites, he had faith in Buddhism—newly transmitted from China—as something that would solve his own personal suffering.

It is recorded in the *Nihonshoki* that in the thirteenth year of the Emperor Kinmei (552), Buddhism together with scriptures and various temple ornaments was officially introduced from the Korean Kingdom of Kudara [Paekche] to Emperor Kinmei, who was Emperor Yōmei's father. Probably, Buddhism captivated people of that time with its voluminous writing (that is, the scriptures), its new technology for constructing huge buildings such as temples, and its dazzling and exotic system of rites. People reacted to the new religious civilization with amazement. Buddhism as a world religion entered ancient Japanese society with a marvelously deep system of thought, extensive writings, new highly developed technological prowess, and an enormous organizational framework. With the appearance of this new religious system, the Japanese grew increasingly self-conscious of their own earlier faith in various *kami*, in which they performed festivals tied to the four seasons for the various *kami* of the mountains, rivers, grasses, and trees.

In the fifteenth year of Suiko's reign,[13] the empress proclaimed that "Shinto are rites transmitted from the ancestors to worship the many *kami* of the mountains and streams in each of the four seasons,"[14] and an imperial decree was issued to the effect that the nation should not neglect these rituals ("Devotedly venerate the *kami*, worship at mountains and streams everywhere, and let your heart spread far and wide through the heavens and the earth. Then summer and winter will harmonize, and all the creation will be perfected"). She put to practical use the traditional festival life together with Buddhism as a new system of salvation, institutional order, and doctrines. After the conflict between the Mononobe and Soga clans over *kami* and buddhas during the reign of Empress Suiko, Prince Shōtoku constructed the foundations for the mutual cooperation between *kami* and buddhas in the Japanese religious world.

Prince Shōtoku was one of the earliest Japanese to carefully delineate the main differences between Buddhism and Shinto. However, at the same time, he tried to combine both systematically into a religious system that would ease Japanese minds and allow the peaceful rule of society. Confucianism, Buddhism, and the traditional Shinto together were used by Prince Shōtoku as a practical means of stabilizing Japanese life, culture, and political system. In this respect, Prince Shōtoku, it can be said, is the person who created the foundation for the Japanese people's deity-buddha system.

He was venerated by Shinran as a great teacher of Japanese Buddhism. As *The Great Teacher of Japan*, Shinran expressed his high regard and praise for him. Moreover, these feelings of intense admiration toward Prince Shōtoku in later ages gave rise to the devotion for the prince and formed a unique folk religious faith.[15] On the other hand, he was reassessed by the various Shinto lineages of the middle and early-modern periods, who ranked him as a pioneer of syncretic thought who had introduced Buddhism and Confucianism to the country by grafting them onto Shinto at the base.

The synthesis of *kami* and buddhas originating and rooted in Shinto

Yoshida Kanetomo, who belonged to a Shinto priest lineage in the middle ages, is the person who advanced "the theory of the origins, leaves and branches, flowers and fruit" (*konpon shiyō kajitsu setsu*).[16] Why had Buddhism gradually moved eastward toward Japan? Kanetomo explained why this happened in the following way: Shinto is like a tree that had rooted and grown in Japan, with its trunk spreading its branches and leaves to China, which then flowered and ripened into the fruit that was the Buddhism of Central Asia and India. In other words, he considered Shinto as the foundation, the leaves and branches as Chinese Confucianism, and their flowers and fruit as Indian Buddhism. In his theory, Kanetomo argues that this process of the fruit falling to earth and returning to its roots is a basic principle of the natural world. He thought that Buddhism's gradual spread eastward was the same case of natural law in which the fruit from a large tree growing from the earth, once again returns to its origins.

Kanetomo ends up elevating Shōtoku Taishi as the person who first formulated such a theory. Prince Shōtoku's status underwent further revision by early-modern Shinto priests who ranked him as the person who, besides authoring the Seventeen-Article Constitution,[17] founded various *kami* systems and a priest's code. It is recorded in the *Sendai kuji hongi taiseikyō*[18] that, besides the Seventeen-Article Constitution, Prince Shōtoku composed codes for *shakke*, that is, for Buddhists, and one for Shinto priests. The idea expressed here envisages Prince Shōtoku as a pioneer of Shinto-Buddhist syncretism or the coexistence of *kami* and buddhas.

In the history of Japanese faith, Shinto has adopted foreign religions and faiths, and time after time has formed doctrinal systems for each age. One of these was the *honji suijaku* (original ground and traces—or manifestation) theory of the middle ages.[19] Another was its early-modern version of Shinto, Buddhism and Confucian syncretism. What is consistent in these cases is that, as Shinto discovers *kami* in various people and natural powers, it discovers new divinities, *kami* that have power and can be relied upon even if they are from foreign religious systems and faiths. These have been able to be accepted and incorporated within Shinto as part of its myriads of deities (*yao yorozu no kami*). In other words, with its belief in many *kami*, Shinto is essentially accommodating toward Confucianism, Taoism, and Buddhism and creates a foundation for firmly establishing them in Japan. That is certainly the reason why Shinto can be thought of as forming the basis of Japanese religion.

The separation of *kami* and buddhas (*shinbutsu bunri*) and the weakening of Shinto

The great change that occurred in this *kami*-buddha syncretism and Shinto-Confucian-Buddhist syncretic thought was an ordinance formally separating buddhas from *kami* (*shinbutsu bunri rei*, or the Ordinance Differentiating Buddhas and *Kami* (*shinbutsu hanzen rei*)), issued in the first year of Meiji (1868). While this ordinance has its background in the theological ideas of national learning (*kokugaku*) thought, it also originated from the political policies that would import Western civilization into our country and create a modern Japanese nation state. First, the leaders of the early Meiji government located the basic principle of the Japanese state in the revival of the ancient *ritsuryō* system which was centered on the emperor. This was the ideal of the restoration of imperial rule.

The restoration of imperial rule was the reason for the revival of the Council of Divinities (Jingikan) and the Council of State (Dajōkan), and, conceptually speaking, this system ranked the Council of Divinities above the Council of State.[20] However, in actual fact, such a faith as advocated by this government council did not have enough power to unify the modern nation state, and, furthermore, the government came under pressure in the face of a host of modern principles, such as freedom of religion and the separation of politics and religion. The Jingikan gradually devolved into lower-ranking bureaucracies such as the Ministry of Divinities (Jingishō), the Ministry of Public Instruction (Kyōbushō), and the Bureau of Shrines (Jinjakyoku). Finally, Shinto ended up being cast as "not a religion, but as state rites and morality." Here is where Shinto became disconnected from the Japanese people's sensibility toward an eternal quality of life and became categorized as a separate form of traditional culture that was different from the modern conception of religion. In other words, Shinto came to be regarded as a type of folk custom and a moral system.

We can argue that this policy profoundly weakened, nullified, and vacated the feelings toward the *kami* of Japanese who believed in the myriads of deities. It made the emperor a *kami* appearing in human form (*arahitogami*), the supreme commander of the nation, and its unifying principle. However, this system ended up weakening the faith in the multitudes of other *kami* that had transmitted from ancient times. And the anti-Buddhist movement to "abolish Buddhism and destroy Shākyamuni" (*haibutsu kishaku*) was unleashed, triggered by the new ordinance for the separation of *kami* and buddhas. The Buddhist world, sensing a crisis, ended up responding to the situation by advocating particularly the separation of religion and politics and by developing new Buddhist religious movements in modern

343

society. By contrast, Shinto lost its religious hue, with its priests as officials working under government control and reduced to serving in the capacity of official administrators of rites and national morality.

This separation of *kami* and buddhas has both advantages and disadvantages. One feature that can be considered a plus is it carries on the spirit of Edo period national learning scholars by asking what exactly our country's traditional faith is—that is, our worship of the gods of heaven and earth, Shinto, and so on. The attempt is to reexamine and revive the form and essence of a purer traditional culture. To put it differently, this can be viewed as an impulse and a movement to try to clarify the essential features of Japanese culture.

But, on the other hand, it also ended up destroying the creative Japanese religious syncretism that had lived and breathed within ordinary cultural life. That is, while Shinto had combined and coexisted with a variety of other religions, the ordinance suppressed and shredded politically Shinto's own expression of the eternal in life found in its tolerant nature. We can doubtless argue that the separation policy suppressed and tore apart the traditional view of the *kami* that Japanese people used to have.

The separation of religion and politics and making Shinto a "non-religion"

Shinto became a system of nationally administered rites in the Meiji period. But after the World War II, there was a time when it was loathed as a tool of militarism and nationalism that served to encourage Japan's warmongering. However, it is fair to say that, if one examines its history closely, Shinto had always been used by the state's ruling ideologies and organizations. In the ancient *ritsuryō* system, it was treated as *ritsuryō* Shinto; in the middle ages, as Ise Shinto and Yoshida Shinto, and, again, as the Shinto of Buddhist priests, Sannō Ichijitsu Shinto and Shingon Shinto. In the Meiji period, it was used politically taking on a new guise courtesy of the Meiji government. After Japan's defeat in World War II, all the various ways that Shinto was used in that period's politics, institutions, and systems of thought ended up being repudiated. Indeed, the time had come when shrines became independent and had to survive on their own.

The religious policy of the Meiji period substantially changed the Japanese belief system. One change is its policy of separation of *kami* and buddhas, but another is the separation of religion and politics. The separation of religion and politics is a religious policy introduced from the West. More exactly, it is the "the separation of church and state." The cause precipitating this is attributed in some ways to the Catholic Church's sovereignty over Western nations and its control over and oppression of the political, economic, and cultural spheres including scholarship and thought. The modern nation state sought freedom, and independence from such religious authority. For that reason, along with ideas on human rights and democracy, the separation of church and state appeared as an important principle in the formation of modern civil society.

The Meiji government ended up adopting the separation of religion and politics, which seemed inevitable given its support of modern Westernization. Promoting Westernization means promoting modernization—industrialization—and urbanization. In line with the formation of such a modern nation state, even Japan adopted the same policy since it was a fundamental principle of Western society that separated the state from religion (church religion).

However, the separation of church and state is completely different from the separation of Shinto, its shrines, and the state. The Meiji government introduced something new in Japanese history, culture, and institutions by making a policy to separate religion from politics. The Japanese religious system includes elements that are completely different from religion as conventionally conceived in the modern separation of church and state. Shrines are completely different organizationally from churches.

As previously stated, this is not unrelated to Shinto's origin as a faith with no founders, scriptures, or organization that could be identified as a religious order. Shinto as well as shrines are a culture and a system rooted fundamentally in Japan's natural environment and locale. Although connected to the state, Shinto is rooted in its own unique regionalism, history, and local conditions. It was essentially impossible to adapt shrines, with their intimate natural and regional ties, to the separation of religion and politics in terms of a modern religious policy.

For that reason, the Meiji government saw shrines as different from church-like religions, that is, they had to classify shrines not as religions but as centers for the performance of state rites. And, Shinto became not a focus of faith for the people, but of rites and morals.

The appearance of sect Shinto

Religious Shinto in the Meiji period is later designated as the thirteen groups of sect Shinto. But Shinto as a religion in this sense occurs at the end of the Edo period, starting with the mystical experiences of Kurozumi Munetada, namely, during his religious experiences when he attained union with the goddess Amaterasu and gained healing powers. And sects like this [Kurozumikyō] appeared as Shinto religious systems, newly arisen, having founders, organizations with a religious order, and, additionally, scriptures and doctrines.

This formed upon the soil of shrine Shinto or of Shinto thought in the middle ages and the early modern period, and of folk religious belief. This new religious Shinto possesses qualities found in world religions. Their founders, based upon their individual religious experiences, formed new views of the *kami*, faith, and visions of salvation on top of a preexisting folk belief in deities. Moreover, based upon such views of the *kami*, they taught ordinary people by explaining in what directions the world was moving in this age and their *kami*'s process of salvation and healing. One can argue that newly arising religions with a Shinto pedigree, such as Kurozumikyō, Tenrikyō, Konkōkyō, and so on, were new forms of Shinto, based upon their own idiosyncratic views of the *kami*, and expressing the founders' own distinctive religious experiences and thinking.

After Meiji 15 (1882), new Shinto religions like these were lumped together along with the more traditional Shinto groups and reorganized as Izumo Ōyashirokyō, Misogikyō, and Shinto Shūseiha, and so on, to be regarded as the thirteen groups of sect Shinto. Another example of a new Shinto that eventually formed from out of this stream of sect Shinto is Ōmotokyō.[21] Especially in its mythological system, Ōmotokyō emphasizes a view of salvation in which the original deity (Ushitora no Konjin), hitherto unknown or hidden away, appears in a modern society filled with flaws and suffering, to rebuild, transform, and save the world. It emphasizes world salvation depending on the original *kami*, with the founder Deguchi Nao and her assistant, Deguchi Onisaburō, as leaders in this effort, who are given a mythologically sacred status as embodiments of the divinities Izunomitama and Mizunomitama respectively. The religion is also based upon the founder's prophecies, called the *Ofudesaki* [Tip of the Writing Brush], interpretations of Japanese classic texts, Ōmoto rituals for calming spirits to be returned to god (*chinkon kishin*), or spirit studies, and so on. One can argue that this was a restoration of a long-buried shamanistic impulse, that is to say, a shamanism renaissance.

However, in Taishō 10 (1921) and again Shōwa 10 (1935), Ōmotokyō ended up twice coming under pressure from the authorities due to crimes of *lèse-majesté* as well as the violation of the Newspaper Law and the Peace Preservation Act.[22] Ōmotokyō was viewed as a danger that caused a lack of respect, or, worse, destroyed internally the Meiji state's myths as well as its political system by undermining its mythological worldview. Thus, yet again, the inherent power of shamanism was suppressed.

Spirit studies and shamanism

A variety of world religions and mysticisms entered the religious world of the Meiji period. Christianity from the West, and spiritualism, the occult, psychic research, theosophy, and so on had a great influence on intellectuals and religious people of that time. Out of these influences, "spirit studies" (*reigaku*) emerges, and people like Tomokiyo Yoshizane—who ended up leaving Ōmotokyō—and Deguchi Onisaburō promulgate such studies.

In Taishō 10, Tomokiyo Yoshizane authored his *Reigaku sentei* (Useful Guide for Spirit Studies), and argued that not even half of human potential could be researched and developed by "human engineering," as understood only one-sidely from the modern sciences of psychology, physiology, and kinetics.[23] What was necessary was learning and the actual practice of "Shinto spirit studies," a form of "spiritual human engineering" that he thought of as true human engineering. According to Tomokiyo, the purpose of spiritual studies was to investigate our true human nature (spirit nature), to master and then put into practice firsthand the goals of cosmic human life. But in order to do so, one had to engage in a variety of ascetic practices, such as the method of purifying the heart and calming the spirit (*jōshin chinkon hō*), the great breathing method (*okinaga hō*), the Tamafune arts (*Tamafune jutsu*), and breathing methods (*ibuki hō*).

One can argue that the "method of purifying the heart and soothing the spirit" that Tomokiyo Yoshizane advocated was refashioned from the *chinkon kishin* method taught by Honda Chikaatsu and Deguchi Onisaburō. The "*chinkon kishin* method" in Ōmotokyō was a means of becoming possessed by a spirit in order to know one's own true spiritual nature and the source of spirituality. Such spirit studies have a goal and methodology similar to Western spiritualism and psychic research. It is arguable that it represents a modern revival of ancient shamanism.

Shamanic elements, on the one hand, became reconfigured as a new religion called sect Shinto and, on the other hand, as supra-scientific study called Shinto spirit studies. However, shamanic elements once again were hidden from view after the Ōmoto incidents and throughout the wartime chaos. In this way, Meiji period Shinto was suppressed by the government, which oppressed repeatedly these views of the *kami*, nature, and life that were so full of energy. The argument can be made that State Shinto was founded on the basis of nationally hiding away and repressing this kind of traditional worldview and view of life.

After the war, both sect Shinto and shrines had to be active as individual religious corporations. A variety of new religious organizations were founded from religions derived from the Shinto pedigree, such as Sekai Kyūseikyō, Shinji Shūmeikai, Sūkyō Mahikari, and Tenshō Kōtaijingūkyō. Most of these are religious groups based on the shamanistic religious experiences of their founders.

The global challenges and Shinto's view of nature, life, and death

A variety of problems brought about by the principles of modern life have violently erupted these days. As examples, there is the urge for consumption based on wage labor in a capitalistic society, physical oppression and the destruction of nature, and the collapse of communities and the family. But a trend has also developed within these conditions. This trend is to reconsider Shinto as animism, shamanism, totemism, and ecological—as a system of thought and cultural way of life that retains ancient wisdom.

Minakata Kumagusu, who opposed the shrine consolidation of Meiji, is the person who first used the word "ecology" in Japan. He emphasized the real importance of shrine forests as the basis of the Japanese people's fundamental view of life, view of nature, and world-view. The wisdom and lifestyle of Shinto is being revived once again as a key means for reexamining ecology and our views of life and nature, and for pondering a way of life in harmony with nature and the communities in which we live. Today when people are crying out about the numerous ways that ideas like symbiosis and natural cycles are important, reconfiguring Shinto as a type of wisdom about living in symbiosis and attuned to the cycles of nature is substantially relevant.

However, just revisioning Shinto simply this way, ends up providing a rather impoverished understanding of it. As related in the myth in which Izanagi pursues Izanami to the country of Yomi, the *kami* also die. In other words, life is filled with death. Being able to live life together with others is nothing other than to die in death together with others. Without this principle of "to die in death together," it would be impossible to simply talk about a symbiotic view of life. In the Shinto worldview, along with living life together is dying in death together. There is nothing living that does not die. The relation invisible things (spirits—human and otherwise) have in facing death, being reborn, and moving on to the next life is very important.

If this is so, then likewise, ecology is not just for the living but must be an ecology that encompasses the dead. To put it differently, it is important that there be a shamanistic ecology or a spiritual ecology. That is, Shinto's spiritual nature is something connecting the worship of nature and the ancestors. As Hearn put it, "the center of the folk soul," "the folk instincts, energy and intuition" that pulses with life must clearly be recognized.

Yanagita Kunio appraised Japanese folklore studies as the Japanese people's own "introspective science." That is to say, he even appraised it as the Japanese people's own "science of searching for and realizing happiness." Both Yanagita and Orikuchi thought of Shinto as something that occupied the axis of Japanese folklore studies.

Among the three examples of the word "Shinto" appearing in the *Nihonshoki*, there is the entry in which Emperor Kōtoku reveals his behavior toward it: "He venerated the Buddhist law and made light of Shinto." Then, if you ask more specifically what he did to slight Shinto, there is this annotation, "Things like cutting down the tree of Ikukunitama shrine."[24] He cut and felled the sacred tree of Ikukunitama shrine in Osaka and used it for his palace or as timber for something.

If that is the case, one might argue, as a matter of fact, that venerating Shinto would be treating each tree as if it were precious. A tree forms the living forest. It is the source of life and the symbol of the cycle of life. In the sentiment and behavior that regards each tree as something precious is "the sense of Shinto" and happiness. Thinking that *kami* reside in the mountains, rivers, grasses, and trees is "the feeling of Shinto," a heart that has reverence and experiences awe toward nature and life.

Thus, we can conclude that Shinto is the culture of questing for and realizing the happiness of a people who live within the natural environs and historical tradition of Japan's archipelago. This "way following the *kami*" (*kannagara no michi*), which is a Shinto that aims to convey its inheritance of the eternal in life from the ancestors to their descendants, continues to live on as the prayers, desires, and actions that will never change for the Japanese, even in the future.

Notes

1 Lafcadio Hearn, *Glimpses of an Unfamiliar Japan*, 2 vols. (New York: Houghton Mifflin, 1922, Rinsen Book, 1988), 1:202. On Hearn see Roy Starrs, "Lafcadio Hearn as a Japanese Nationalist," *Japan Review* 18 (2006):181–213.
2 Hearn, *Glimpses*, 1:242–43 [in 1894 Edition, 1:209]. The Japanese translator of the passage that Kamata cites translates "and yet, by its very immateriality" as "*shikashi, sono masashiku 'nai' koto ni yotte*."
3 This is cited from Hearn, *Glimpses* [1894 Edition], 1:209–10.
4 Lafcadio Hearn, "Kizuki: The Most Ancient Shrine of Japan," in *Complete Works of Lafcadio Hearn* (Hastings, East Sussex: Delphi Classics, 2017, Section 19). On Hearn and Izumo, see Klaus Antoni, "Izumo as the 'Other Japan': Construction vs. Reality," *Japanese Religions* 30 (2005):1–20; Cf, 12–14.
5 On this point, see Matsumae Takeshi, "Early Kami Worship," in *The Cambridge History of Japan, Ancient Japan* (Cambridge: Cambridge University Press, 1993), 1:317–58; Inoue Nobutaka ed., *Shinto—A Short History*, trans. Mark Teeuwen and John Breen (London: RoutledgeCurzon, 2003), esp. 29–62.
6 The versions in the *Nihonshoki* have this deity also appearing as the first and second *kami* produced.
7 The *Nihonshoki* has three alternative accounts that place this *kami* of the "foundation of the land" as the first deity to appear in the creation. These first five separate deities are abstract beings, that appear by themselves (*hitorigami*) (rather than in male–female pairs) and then vanish. They are referred to as a group in the *Kojiki* as the five separate heavenly deities (*kotoamatsukami*).
8 The last pair comprise the seventh generation of the age of the gods (*kami no yo*) and are the first whose activities are described in detail in the narratives.
9 See "Sanshu no Shinki," *Encyclopedia of Shinto*, http://eos.kokugakuin.ac.jp/modules/xwords/entry.php?entryID=1220.
10 The term means literally "ground spiders."
11 The site's stratification has several phases, the earliest (ninth strata) dating back more than 9,500 years, contains Maehira style pottery and marks the oldest fixed village settlement in Japan.
12 This is a large-scale village site dating from the early to late Middle Jōmon period (5500–4000 BCE).
13 She ruled during the Asuka period from 592 to 628; her nephew was the famous Prince Shōtoku.
14 The original quotation does not contain the word "Shinto." It reads, following Aston's translation, "We heard that our imperial ancestors, in their government of the world . . . paid deep reverence to the gods of heaven and earth." See W.G. Aston, *Nihongi*, (London: Kegan, Paul, Trench, Trübner, 1896), 2:135.
15 See Michael I. Cuomo, *Shōtoku: Ethnicity, Ritual, and Violence in the Japanese Buddhist Tradition* (New York: Oxford University Press, 2008).
16 A theory he set forth in his major work, *Yuiitsu shintō myōbō yōshū*. In this, Kanetomo was directly infuenced by the late Kamakura period Tendai priest Jihen, who argued in the first fascicle of his work, the *Kuji hongi gengi*, that Japan was initially a land of the *kami* with buddhas entering only later. In the fifth fascicle of the same work, Jihen develops the seed metaphor that Kanetomo makes his own later in his creation of Yoshida Shinto. See also Kamata Tōji, *Shintō to wa nani ka: shizen no reisei o kanjite ikiru*, 177ff.
17 According to the *Nihonshoki*, the Constitution was set forth in the twelfth year of Empress Suiko's reign, as noted in the entry dated April 3, 604, where the text is quoted. Modern scholars doubt the attribution of Prince Shōtoku's authorship, most notably Tsuda Sōkichi in his *Nihon jōdaishi kenkyū* (1930).

18 This significant twenty-seven volume work, discovered at an Edo bookstore in 1679, caused controversy because it supported the claims of priests from Izawanomiya that their shrine enshrined the sun goddess while the inner and outer shrines at Ise Jingū enshrined only a star and moon deity respectively. While the *bakufu* banned it as a forgery in 1681, it still influenced the development of Suika Shinto. See Nozawa Tadanao, *Kinsho Shōtoku Taishi gokenpō* (Tokyo: Shin Jinbutsu Ōraisha, 1990).

19 This is the idea the *kami* were in fact manifestations of Buddhist divinities. On this concept see, Susan Tyler, "*Honji Suijaku* Faith," *Japanese Journal of Religious Studies* 16 (June–September, 1989):227–50.

20 In reality, however, the Council of State was more powerful. Those who served at the Council of State had higher ranks in the imperial court, and the Council had considerably more officials.

21 For a recent detailed study of this group see Nancy K. Stalker, *Prophet Motive: Deguchi Onisaburō Oomoto and the Rise of New Religions in Imperial Japan* (Honolulu: University of Hawai'i Press, 2008).

22 Both incidents resulted in Onisaburō's arrest, with the latter resulting in his imprisonment along with many Ōmotokyō followers, the confiscation of the group's land, and the destruction of its spiritual centers, dealing a severe blow to the movement.

23 Tomokiyo Yoshizane (1888–1952) founded Shindō Tenkōkyo, a Shinto-derived new religion with its headquarters on Mount Iwaki in Yamaguchi prefecture.

24 Aston, *Nihongi* 2, 195.

34

INOUE HIROSHI

Introduction and a syncretism based upon differentiation—the formation of 'Shinto' (2011)

Inoue Hiroshi (1941–), a noted Japanese historian, was born in Kyoto. After entering Osaka University's doctoral program in its Graduate School of Letters, he became an assistant in the School of Letters in 1968. In 1975 he moved to the Faculty of Literature and Science at Shimane University, where he eventually was promoted to full professor. From 1997 to 2007, he was a professor at Osaka Institute of Technology. He is now a professor emeritus at both institutions.

Inoue's principal academic focus is the history of the middle ages. His major publications include: *Chūsei shokoku ichinomiyasei no kisoteki kenkyū,* (Fundamental Research into the Provincial Ichinomiya System in the Middle Ages, 2000), *Nihon no jinja to "shintō,"* (Japanese Shrines and "Shinto," 2006), *Nihon chūsei kokka to shokoku ichinomiyasei* (The Provincial Ichinomiya System and the Japanese Medieval State, 2009), and *Shintō no kyozō to jitsuzō* (Shinto's False and True Image, 2011).The following selection is taken from the last book, the Introduction and Chapter 2, "The formation of 'Shinto'—a syncretism based upon separation."

Inoue argues that Shinto's emphasis on acceptance of religious diversity and animistic orientation set it apart from other religious traditions. These characteristics alone, however, do not distinguish Japanese religious creativity. To understand what makes Shinto distinctive, we must focus on the institutional history of Shinto's development. Here Inoue differs from his predecessors, particularly the Shinto nationalists from the 1930s and 1940s and builds upon the work of Kuroda Toshio by placing Shinto's religious origins in the medieval period rather than in ancient Japan. These earlier views of Shinto are ahistorical and anachronistic. The medieval period did not corrupt an originally pristine archaic Shinto religion. Rather, the creation of the distinctive *ichinomiya* shrine system came out of a period of creative institutional development and formed the framework for what we know as Shinto today. Here Inoue is closer to Sonoda, who emphasizes the institutional foundation provided by shrines (*jinja*) as key to understanding Shinto's religious character. Inoue's focus on the medieval period allows for an interesting comparison with Kuroda's thesis that Shinto as an independent organized religion dates from the modern period. Inoue argues that the formation of the medieval shrine system marks the beginning of an organized form of Shinto that was distinctive—institutionally and ideologically—from the *kenmitsu* Buddhism system that Kuroda argues was hegemonic throughout this period.

INOUE HIROSHI

INTRODUCTION AND A SYNCRETISM BASED UPON DIFFERENTIATION—THE FORMATION OF 'SHINTO' (2011)

Introduction

"Not having a religion" and the social conventionalization of religious ceremonies

Religion in Japan today, including the way we are involved with religion and think about religion, occupies a unique status in the world. I will discuss the following four points, which are the most important.

First, an overwhelmingly large number of Japanese citizens refer to themselves as not religious. By this they mean that they do not belong to a specific religious group or believe in specific religious doctrines, so this is not the same as atheism. The statistical data show that this may include up to 70 percent of the population (Ama Toshimaro, 1996).

Despite this, there is a second point: The total number of adherents reported by all kinds of religious groups far exceeds Japan's population. This is in accordance with data from sources such as *The Japan Statistical Yearbook* edited by the Ministry of Internal Affairs and Communications Bureau of Statistics (2011), which shows that there was no substantial change in the total number of Japanese adherents between 1980 (Shōwa 55) and 2007 (Heisei 19); this number is over two hundred million. This is about double the total population of Japan including infants. This does not make sense unless you consider that it includes the members doubly or triply reported by organizations, shrines, temples, and so forth. It is clear that there exists a large gap between people's awareness and their actual circumstances.

This brings us to point three: What is really going on? In everyday life, people tend to have the same fundamental stance towards such formal ceremonies as weddings, funerals, and annual festivals and events (*nenchū gyōji*). They do not especially worry about differences between religions and between denominations, and deal with them unaware that they are religious ceremonies. What has clearly developed is the social and customary conventionalization and routinization of religious rituals.

If we take the yearly round of festivals and events as an example, so many Japanese people go to pray at a shrine or temple that the first visit to the shrine or temple in the new year (*hatsumōde*) is aptly called a national annual event. Visiting family graves (*hakamairi*) during the Ohigan and Obon season is also regarded by many Japanese as very natural. In the same vein, decorating a Christmas tree yearly and enjoying Christmas Eve has become an extremely commonplace sight.

It is the same for rites of passage too. Many people's lives begin with the 7-5-3 festival for young children to visit the shrine (*shichigosan*), progress through weddings before the *kami* or at a Christian church, and end with a Buddhist funeral ceremony. For the most part, these are common social practices and are scarcely recognized as religious ceremonies.

The fourth point is closely related to these things and might perhaps be called the "peaceful coexistence" of various religions and a diverse "museum of religions." For the period

1980–2007, the Ministry of Internal Affairs and Communications counted as many as 220,000 religious organizations. That number is large, but a rather important feature is their diversity, which divides them into the Shinto, Buddhist, Christian, and various other faiths. For example, the Buddhist line of faith is really rich in its doctrinal and ritual variation. It includes several schools that have already almost vanished in Korea and China that transmitted Buddhism to Japan, like the Hossō, Kegon, Tendai, and Shingon schools, and the Jōdo, Jōdo Shin, Ji, and Nichiren schools that originated in Japan. There are also the many faiths that can be classified as new religions, such as Tenrikyō and Konkōkyō, which arose in Japan as a reaction to the older Buddhist schools, as well as the many religions and schools that were created after World War II. They are very diverse in content, but peacefully coexist together and continue to be active even today.

Flexible and free-flowing polytheism—based in animism

Why does Japan's religion have these specific characteristics? In comparing Japan with (for instance) other Asian countries, it is best understood as a flexible and free-flowing polytheism. Rather than following the monotheistic tradition of Europe, North America, the Middle East, and western Asia, which includes Judaism, Christianity, and Islam, Japan belongs to the polytheistic tradition that is more prevalent in the rest of the world.

As is apparent in the phrase "myriads of *kami*" (*yao yorozu no kami*), there are many *kami*, buddhas, and bodhisattvas in Japan, and these are considered objects of worship. This also allows for adaptation to a particular time and place, which is a special feature that differs from many other Asian countries.

It is unnecessary to point out that Japan's religion is characterized by the so-called "synthesis of *kami* and buddhas" (*shinbutsu shūgō*), which was created through the opportunity for syncretism with different religions. However, the term *shinbutsu shūgō* was introduced from China (Yoshida Kazuhiko, 1996), and therefore cannot by itself account for the difference between Japan and China, or Japan and other Asian countries. Where, then, does that difference come from?

The people who lived on the Chinese continent, the Korean peninsula, and the Japanese archipelago all held animism (the worship of nature) as their object of faith. They recognized that all things in the universe and the natural world had a spiritual life. This belief system has been shared by all primitive societies, including those in the West and in many Islamic countries. Simply put, animism is humanity's common religious foundation.

The issue, then, becomes how this tradition has been handed down to the present day in the Japanese archipelago, and how it has been changed in the process. And also how does it differ from the traditions of other Asian countries, such as China and Korea?

Shrines and faith in the kami

It is noteworthy here that the religious institution of the shrine (*jinja*) and the worship of the *kami* (*jingi shinkō*) exist only in Japan. *Jingi* is an abbreviation for the gods of heaven (*tenjin* or *amatsukami*) and the gods of the earth (*chigi* or *kunitsukami*); it refers to deities who have descended from heaven and those who originally existed on earth. Worshipping all these *kami* is *Jingi shinkō*.

How and when did these institutions and faith become established in the Japanese archipelago? This question must be carefully considered in tandem with a second question: How do we understand the special characteristics of Japan's religion?

There is a widespread understanding both in Japan and in the world that Japanese shrines and faith in the *kami* originated in the ancient past and have been handed down uninterrupted without any changes up to the present.

This understanding, as will be discussed later, is clearly based on factual errors. However, another important point is that after these institutions were first formed, they went on to experience great changes and transformations. Therefore, while we still have shrines and faith in the *kami* today, they are not fundamentally the same as they were when they were first instituted.

This is extremely natural given that things change historically. Nonetheless, as soon as we begin to discuss Japan's culture and historical traditions, we tend to lapse into highly unscientific and ahistorical ways of thinking, such as "theories about the basic strata of culture" (*kisō bunkaron*).[1] Why is this? There are many reasons, but two points are particularly important.

Originality in dealing with extraordinary cultural shocks

First, we tend to overlook the unprecedented cultural shocks which Japan has experienced.

Japan is unusual in that it carved out its own comparatively independent history and developed its own culture. This was helped by the geography and natural environment, which situated it at the eastern end of Asia, surrounded on all four sides by oceans. Perhaps the best example of this is Jōmon culture, a special Neolithic culture unassociated with agriculture, which lasted approximately ten thousand years. This does not, however, mean that the history and culture of the Japanese archipelago were not influenced by other countries and regions. The truth was that the history of the Japanese islands was shaped by repeated close contact and exchanges with many nearby countries and regions. In particular, various influences arrived at various times from China and the Korean peninsula; these include iron tools, Chinese writing, and the introduction of Buddhism.

An overview of the history of the Japanese islands shows three particular times when foreign influences resulted in decisive breakthroughs and historical turning points.

(1) The introduction of rice cultivation from the Chinese continent.

This event ended the so called Jōmon and ushered in the Yayoi period. In the Jōmon period, agricultural projects were realized to some extent, such as the planned cultivation of acorns, chestnuts, and grain. The new technology and civilization transmitted from the Chinese continent brought about a fundamental transition from a society based on hunting, fishing, and gathering to one based on a foundation of rice cultivation.

(2) The introduction of the *ritsuryō* system.

The *ritsuryō* system as a means of centralizing state authority was introduced from China, and the first genuine state in the Japanese archipelago was born. It was during this period that both the name of the state, "Japan" (*Nihon/Nippon*), and the label of the country's ruler, "emperor" (*tennō*), both of which are used today, came into use.

(3) The rise of the modern nation state as well as the modern capitalist system after the end of the Tokugawa period and the Meiji Restoration.

Many momentous events have shaken the Japanese islands, from the Mongol invasion in the late Kamakura period to the introduction of the gun and Christianity in the sixteenth century. However, until the nineteenth century, none of these caused such a fundamental transformation of the nation and society as the nation state system and capitalism have caused.

"The extraordinary culture shocks" that we are discussing in this book refer to the second and third events. Although I will discuss this later in greater detail, it should be noted at this point that the special nature of Japan's religion is closely connected to these events.

Secondly, it appears that there is not sufficient understanding of the specific details of these cultural shocks or the way that Japan dealt with them. I shall discuss their specific content further a little later; however, it is clear that the geography that separates the archipelago by oceans from the Eurasian continent, and a history that cultivated Japan's original culture since the Jōmon period, bred a nationalistic response together with its unique geography and history. The significance of this has not been sufficiently understood.

These two points have had an enormous influence not only on Japanese shrines and faith in the *kami* but on the overall state of Japan's religion, whose uniqueness is closely related to Japan's unique history. Since that is so, it is only natural that we need to grasp both generally and concretely how the changes in shrines, faith in the *kami*, and the structure of Japan's religion itself have come to be the way they are today from that history.

It is crucial here to remember that history is made up of a complex mixture of various wavelengths—one part changing moment by moment and another persisting for a long period of time, continuing without easily changing. We need to generalize about the whole of it by taking a historical viewpoint. This is particularly so because events with a long wavelength carry a great weight in ordinary people's everyday lives, and it is vital to pay sufficient attention to the specific content and unique meaning it possesses.

Originally, it was the voiced consonant—Mark Teeuwen's observation

The word "Shintō" has itself become an issue. At this point, it is safe to say that the word "神道" read as "Shintō" has become the convention, both within and outside Japan. It has also become convention to compare this "Shintō" to religions such as Buddhism, Christianity, or to think of it as Japan's naturally developed indigenous national religion that can be compared to Chinese Daoism, and Indian Hinduism.

Based on this conventional wisdom, "theories of Japanese culture" (*Nihon bunkaron*) are offered up in various forms repeatedly in Japan. They also arise in connection to an indigenous emperor and the emperor system in Japan.

However, can we say that this kind of conventional view of Shinto is actually correct? In recent years Mark Teeuwen of Oslo University in Norway has clearly shown that this conventional view is clearly mistaken (Teeuwen, 2008). Teeuwen has clarified mainly the following three points:

(a) The word "Shintō" (神道) was originally used in China and was introduced as is to ancient Japan. Its reading also initially used the voiced consonant "Jindō."

(b) It has meaning as a Buddhist term that indicates the deities subordinate to Buddhism.

(c) During the Muromachi period around the fourteenth century in Japan, this Jindō changed into "Shintō," which is pronounced based on a voiceless consonant. It is thought that this accompanied the transformation of the word 神 (Chinese, *shen,* Japanese, *kami*) from a collective into an abstract noun.[2]

Teeuwen's findings can be accepted as basically correct given the corroborating historical materials, which have gained some scholarly notoriety. For instance, at the beginning of the *Nihonshoki kan daiichi kikigaki* (*Tendai shintō,* Vol. 1, *Shintō taikei ronsetsuhen*), written by the Tendai monk Ryōhen in Ōei 26 (1419) during the Muromachi period, "The word 神道 is not read *Jindō*, but the correct reading is plainly Shintō. It's correct in the sense that it means just what it says."

Although, at that time, "神道" was commonly read with the voiced consonant, "*Jindō*", Ryōhen emphasized that it should be changed to the voiceless consonant, "Shintō". By the beginning of the early modern era, that pronunciation had become broadly and firmly established, as we can see in the Japanese–Portugese dictionary published by the Society of Iezusu (the Jesuit order) in Keichō 8–9 (1603–4) *Nippo jisho* (Doi Tadao et al. eds., *Hōyaku Nippo jisho*): "Xinto (神道): *Camino michi* (神の道, the way of the *kami*). *Camis* and things related to the *Camis*."

The voiceless consonant "Shintō" arose not in Japan's ancient period or earlier but only in the middle ages. It became widely used as a form of expression later than that, from the end of the middle ages to the early modern era. It seems clear, therefore, that the conventional idea of the everlasting existence of Shinto without major changes cannot be justified any longer.

Looking at this from other different perspectives

However, what Teeuwen has taken as his problem is the question of the reading and meaning of "Shintō." That is itself important but in order to clarify what Japanese Shinto is, we must consider it more deeply taking other different standpoints. It is undeniable that Japanese "Shintō" has especially close connections with faith in the *kami* and shrines that are regarded as uniquely Japanese religious institutions. Therefore, it behooves us to base our study on the link between Japanese religions and their historical formation and special characteristics. Indeed, this is also where we find the biggest problem with the conventional view of present-day "Shintō."

So, while I want to take the word "Shintō" as one clue, I also want to take a historical approach considering the whole of Japan's religion, including shrines, temples, Buddhism, and other institutions. Like "Shintō," Japan's many other religions occupy a very special place in the religious world, and Shinto and Japan's religions are thought to be indivisible.

As a starting point, we need to consider Shinto in light of its connection with a general definition of religion, and the question of "What is religion?" "Shintō" has a unique and special character that create subtle differences distinguishing it from other religions. The confusion surrounding our understanding of Japanese "Shintō" has probably arisen because of this. The problem lies in ideas for political rule dressed in religious clothing, that is, a religious political ideology based on the political use of religion, appropriated by secular political authority with the intention to control the masses. We need to keep this point clearly in mind, too, if we are to advance our understanding.

Chapter 2: "A syncretism based upon separation—the formation of "Shintō"

The exoteric-esoteric system and the idea of the divine land (Shinkoku)[3]

[To summarize this section: Inoue traces the development of medieval society and its key Buddhist-based exoteric-esoteric *kenmitsu* religious system, which began during the Insei period,[4] from the end of the eleventh to the beginning of the twelfth century and continued until the early modern *baku-han* feudal system. Politically, it displayed continuities with emperor as king still at the apex of the old centralized state system. But it exhibited discontinuities with the rise of a new strata of ruling: powerful families (*kenmon*) and shrine-temple complexes whose power was based in their own manorial estates (*shōen*) that were organized along feudal lines. This arrangement with the emperor as the symbolic head of the state, the *kenmon* as the *de facto* arbiters of political authority, and shrine-temple complexes also performing religious functions is called the *kenmon* state system. This system was further stabilized by mid-level governing institutions and a regional system of rule enforced by provincial head officials (*zuryō*), their representatives (*mokudai*), and other local bureaucrats; or provincial head constables (*shugo*) and their representatives; or the first-ranked or principle shrines (*ichinomiya*) in each province that served as the tutelary guardians of the province.

By the Warring States period, in the fifteenth and sixteenth centuries, the civil power of regional governing authorities had evolved into many independent "states" ruled by war lords (*daimyō*), whose power was based upon feudal ties of authority, lord–vassal relationships.

Key to the legitimacy of the medieval political system was exoteric-esoteric Buddhism (*kenmitsu bukkyō*) with its theory of the "mutual dependence of imperial and Buddhist law" (*ōhō buppō sōi*). Under this theory, secular political authority, which was represented by the emperor, was supported and stable for the first time through the cooperation of religion (Buddhism). For its part, religion (Buddhism) also received protection from secular authorities and showed that it could function commensurably. Both were like "two wheels of a cart" and "two wings of a bird" that could not exist without the other, adding legitimacy and stability to the *kenmon* political order. The *kenmitsu* system effectively fused religion and state. Practically, shrine-temple complexes also fused with the civil authorities by having many monks from the imperial *kenmon* nobility and military houses serving in these institutions in an administrative capacity.

Kenmitsu thought essentially rested on the Buddhist theory of *honji suijaku*, the idea that things that exist are in actuality all buddhas that take a temporary form. The tutelary *kami* of each shrine came to have its own *honji* Buddha. *Kenmitsu* Buddhism really establishes the formation of an "indigenous religion in Japan" describable as a "flexible and free-flowing polytheism." Although the essence of buddhas and *kami* is the same according to *honji suijaku* theory, they were understood and interpreted according to the way that their manifestations differed. Such a unique Japanese form of religion with its theoretical basis in Buddhist thought and inclusive nature, nonetheless still distinguished between Buddhism, *kami* faith, *shugendō,* and *onmyōdō* practices. These different forms of faith centering on these exoteric-esoteric Buddhist ideas were a unified and mostly stable religious ideology until the demise of *kenmitsu* Buddhism by the end of the Sengoku period.]

The twenty-two shrine-ichinomiya system and medieval shrines

The principle of "distiguishing kami *from buddhas"*

Through the *kenmitsu* system and *honji suijaku* theory, buddhas and *kami,* temples and shrines came to be seen as one and the same. However, during this same period others followed a different view—that buddhas and *kami,* temples and shrines should be differentiated. What they supported is generally referred to as "the principle of differentiating *kami* from buddhas."

Such a view was natural to some degree, since shrines and *kami* worship were created to compete with temples and Buddhism. However, this principle of differentiating was also at work in the development of the second stage of kami-buddha synthesis (*shinbutsu shūgō*) (Fujii Masao, 1994).[5]

The formation of *honji suijaku* theory and the *kenmitsu* system, which is the third stage of the kami-buddha synthesis, is when *shinbutsu shūgō* had become fully systematized theoretically in terms of this principle of "differentiating *kami* from buddhas."

The question thus becomes how, within this system, did medieval shrines differ from what shrines were like in antiquity?

The first obvious difference is that shrines changed dramatically, both in their appearance and the way they operated institutionally. The shrine/temples (*jingū-ji*), each dedicated to its own *honji* buddha, were all built within or near the shrine grounds, according to how the *honji* buddha was identified based on *honji suijaku* theory. Similarly, such Buddhist facilities as sutra repositories and pagodas were built within the shrine precincts, and many clergy such as *jingū-ji* monks took on the important administration and ceremonial roles of the shrines as shrine monks (*shasō*). This accompanied a modified ceremonial structure which combined *kami*-related and Buddhist services.

The new hierarchy of medieval shrines

The second big change was the formation of the medieval shrine system that accompanied this new hierarchy of shrines.

Medieval shrines can be broadly divided into three types in a hierarchy:

(a) Powerful shrines that have an official, national character, such as the twenty-two shrines and the first-ranked shrines in provinces (*ichinomiya*) which held state authority. This authority included regional rule and functioned as an institutional control over ideology.
(b) Small and medium-sized shrines, such as those *chinju* at the village level, which ruled ordinary people through ties to the authority of individual feudal lords.
(c) Additional small sanctuaries and local shrines that became the object of simple ethnic worship.

The shrines in the first two categories can be traced back to ancient official shrines, while those in the third category can be ranked as descending from an ancient non-official shrine lineage. It is especially noteworthy that the first category of shrines was distinct from the second, and the former *ichinomiya*, which are particular to medieval society, became defined institutionally.

I will discuss this in more detail later, but here I want to lightly touch upon some other points.

The first concerns the meaning of hierarchy. The focus of Buddhism and of Buddhist temples is the spiritual salvation of individuals. By contrast, shrines were established for collective purposes, such as protecting the common benefits of a specific social group. This explains the essential difference between temples and shrines. If we consider it in this light, then the hierarchy of shrines comes directly from the character of the social groups or units whom they were intended to benefit. The first type of shrine was dedicated to the national tutelary *kami* representing the central and regional powers of the state; the second to the sovereign authority of the *shōen* estates and public land system; and the third type was dedicated to local tutelary *kami* that dealt with everyday village life.

We should also consider the connection this hierarchy has with the principle of differentiating *kami* and buddhas. Since temples and shrines fulfilled different functions, it was natural that they were distinguished from one another, as were buddhas and *kami*. The first two types of shrines were clearly and formally characterized by the way they distinguished buddhas from *kami*, although this was more apparent in the first shrine type than in the second. In the case of the third shrine type, which generally had neither a permanent shrine building (*shaden*) nor full-time priests, there was no need to make these distinctions. They retained the ability to shift "corresponding to the time and place."

The twenty-two shrines

The twenty-two-shrine system and the *ichinomiya* system were characteristic forms of shrine organization in medieval society. These forms of organization developed from around the end of the eleventh to the beginning of the twelfth century and were closely tied to the *ken-mitsu* Buddhist system of the middle ages (Inoue Hiroshi, 2009).

These twenty-two shrines are located in Kyoto and in its vicinity, such as is the case for Ise Jungū and Iwashimizu Hachimangū, and are also called "guardian shrines of the capital" (*ōjō chinju*). They functioned as guardian *kami* for the emperor and the capital where he resided, and, rather imaginatively, as the tutelary deities for the whole of Japan.[6] A sixteen-shrine system was created in the tenth century to accompany the ancient establishment of the emperor's direct control of the rites, and, to augment this older system, the twenty-two-shrine system was later established, almagamating with the *ichinomiya* system (discussed later) found in various provinces.

This system was institutionalized in the first year of Eihō (1081), when Hie Shrine in Ōmi Province was added to the ranking. The emperor made offerings at these twenty-two shrines regularly but also on the occasion of important national events. Official worship by the nobility, beginning with the emperor and the military houses, also occurred at shrines such as Iwashimizu Hachimangū and Kamo.

UPPER SEVEN SHRINES

Name of shrine	Name of shrine today	Location
Daijingū	Jingū (Ise Jingū)	Ise, Mie Prefecture
Iwashimizu	Iwashimizu Hachimangū	Yawata, Kyoto
Kamo	Kamowakeikazuchi Shrine (Kamigamo Shrine)	Kita-ku, Kyoto
	Kamomioya Shrine (Shimogamo Shrine)	Sakyō-ku, Kyoto
Matsunoo	Matsunoo Taisha	Nishikyō-ku, Kyoto
Hirano	Hirano Shrine	Kita-ku, Kyoto
Inari Shrine	Fushimi Inari Taisha	Fushimi-ku, Kyoto
Kasuga Shrine	Kasuga Taisha	Nara City, Nara Prefecture

MIDDLE SEVEN SHRINES

Name of shrine	Name of shrine today	Location
Ōharano	Ōharano Shrine	Nishikyō-ku, Kyoto
Ōmiwa Shrine	Ōmiwa Shrine	Sakurai, Nara Prefecture
Isonokami Shrine	Isonokami Jingū	Tenri, Nara Prefecture
Ōyamato Shrine	Ōyamato Shrine	Tenri, Nara Prefecture

Hirose Shrine	Hirose Taisha	Kawai, Kitakatsuragi-gun, Nara Prefecture
Tatsuta Shrine	Tatsuta Taisha	Sangō, Ikoma-gun, Nara Prefecture
Sumiyoshi Shrine	Sumiyoshi Taisha	Sumiyoshi-ku, Osaka

LOWER EIGHT SHRINES

Name of shrine	Name of shrine today	Location
Hie Shrine	Hie Taisha	Ōtsu, Shiga Prefecture
Umenomiya Shrine	Umenomiya Taisha	Ukyō-ku, Kyoto
Yoshida Shrine	Yoshida Shrine	Sakyō-ku, Kyoto
Hirota Shrine	Hirota Shrine	Nishinomiya, Hyōgo
Gion Shrine	Yasaka Shrine	Higashiyama-ku, Kyoto
Kitano Jinja	Kitano Tenmangū	Kamigyō-ku, Kyoto
Niu Shrine	Niu Kawakami Shrine Upper Shrine	Kawakami, Yoshino-gun, Nara Prefecture
	Niu Kawakami Shrine Middle Shrine	Higashiyoshino, Yoshino-gun, Nara Prefecture
	Niu Kawakami Shrine Lower Shrine	Shimoichi, Yoshino-gun, Nara Prefecture
Kibune	Kifune Shrine	Sakyō-ku, Kyoto

The provincial ichinomiya

By contrast, in many provinces there were shrines that were considered the tutelary guardian deities of each province (*kuni chinju*). The most powerful shrines were chosen to represent each province; they were described as having "the first-ranked miraculous deity of the entire province." Through the deity's divine grace, they were thought to protect not only the province but also the lives of those who resided there. Because of that, the provincial governor and other officials not only took responsibility for supporting these shrines financially (for example, in times of construction or festivals), but they also performed the ceremonies together with the priests and shrine monks (*shasō*).

This sort of provincial guardian shrine is called an *ichinomiya*. Some provinces had not only an *ichinomiya* but also a *ninomiya* (second shrine); these became dyads, sharing the function of provincial tutelary guardians. One example is found in Awaji Province, which contains Izanagi Jingū (an *ichinomiya*) with Izanagi as its enshrined deity and Yamato Ōkunitama shrine with Izanami as its enshrined deity (a *ninomiya*). Similarly, in Nagato Province [in today's Yamaguchi Prefecture] there are Sumiyoshi (an *ichinomiya*), with "Emperor Chūai" as its enshrined deity, and Iminomiya shrine, with "Empress Jingū" as its enshrined deity (a *ninomiya*), the latter in the middle ages being called Empress Jingū shrine (Jingū Kōgōgū). These two were united to take on the role of provincial guardian shrines.[7]

Additionally, powerful shrines within a province were given ranks such as *ichinomiya*, *ninomiya*, *sannomiya* as these terms came into usage. The case of Kōzuke Province [today's Gunma Prefecture], which organized its shrines from first to ninth in rank, was the largest of these. However, even in this case, the *ichinomiya* was still considered the most important protector of the province. Therefore, all these shrines are considered to belong to the *ichinomiya* system of various medieval provinces.

The Nihongi *of the middle ages*

The *ichinomiya* system followed by many provinces in the middle ages had several important characteristics.

First, these provincial tutelary shrines, by being established in all the sixty-six or sixty-eight provinces, not only protected the provinces but formed a collective system while also liaising with the central twenty-two shrines. This structure protected all of Japan, and thus they are also known as "guardian shrines of the capital (*ōjō chinju*) and of provinces" (*kuni chinju*). However, it is important to remember that, at the provincial level, the *ichinomiya* system was key to the medieval state's national shrine system by serving as provincial guardians (*kuni chinju*).

Secondly, these shrines were able to carry out their public and national functions, which distinguished them from the tutelary shrines of villages and small sanctuaries in hamlets, because of the medieval reorganization of the ancient imperial myths. Therefore, a third defining characteristic of the provincial *ichinomiya* was that they were the direct agents of medieval *shinkoku* thought. The *Ruiju kigenshō* (*Zoku gunsho ruijū*, Vol. 58) indicates this most concisely when it states, "The matter of the many provincial *ichinomiya*. 'They are provincial guardian spirits. Japan is a land of the gods' (*shinkoku*)" (the original *kanbun* marked by quotation marks is a two-line supplementary note).

To add to this point, the ancient imperial myths changed significantly during the shift from antiquity to the middle ages after the *kenmitsu* system was formed. One such change was the new and widespread interpretation of these myths in tandem with Buddhist thought; another was the creation of many new myths by excerpting and tying together certain sections of works like the *Kojiki* and *Nihonshoki*. This is commonly referred to as the medieval *Nihongi*.

Many of these new provincial *ichinomiya* created their own medieval myths particular to the tradition and history of these provinces and shrines. A typical example is the case of Izumo Province's *ichinomiya* Kizuki Taisha (Izumo Taisha). (In the case of the medieval Kizuki Taisha, unlike in antiquity or after the early modern period, it was not Ōnamuchi [Ōkuninushi] but Susanoo who was considered the enshrined *kami*.) [The shrine's origin story is as follows:]

Spirit Vulture Peak was regarded as a sacred place where the Buddha explained the *Lotus Sutra*. A piece of its peak broke off and drifted out to sea. Susanoo pulled it close, thus creating Izumo Province. He also decided to build a shrine there and enshrined himself in it. That shrine was Kizuki Taisha, and the newly made land was known as Furōsan (presently, Shimane peninsula).

This is a medieval myth that was fashioned based upon Buddhist thought. It derives from an ancient story in the *Izumo fudoki* that relates how the deity Yatsukamizu Omizunu created the province of Izumo by roping the land (*kunibiki*) and pulling it away from Oki, Hokuriku, and the Korean peninsula. The original story was refashioned to include Susanoo, who is regarded as the *kami* who was a manifestation of the principle Buddhist object of worship, Zaō Gongen, who was enshrined at Furōsan Gakuenji, a Tendai temple that was the main Buddhist temple tied to Shinto shrine, Kizuki Taisha.[8]

In this manner, the many medieval provincial *ichinomiya*, like the twenty-two shrines, created their own medieval myths based on their own unique interpretation. Additionally, by tying all their enshrined deities to the imperial myths, they established their status as official and national shrines. The provincial *ichinomiya* system was a truly appropriate organizational form for the medieval state, which some have called a "centrally authoritarian state" but which was, nonetheless, pluralistic and dispersed. If we consider this in relation to *kenmitsu* Buddhism as well as the theory of the mutual dependence of imperial and Buddhist law, Buddhism is, through *kenmitsu* temples, the bearer of its theoretical construct. In fact, the theory was realized through the shrines (the provincial *ichinomiya*), as there was a mutually complementary relationship and an allotment of functions between temples and shrines. This was the precise situation of what we call the medieval *kenmitsu* Buddhist system.

Village tutelary shrines and provincial shrines enshrining many gods (sōja)

In the middle ages, the village tutelary shrines (the second type discussed previously) were more numerous and widespread than the twenty-two shrines and the provincial *ichinomiya*. Their circumstances varied greatly, from those encompassing the entire area of public lands or *shōen* estates to those with their own small-scale sphere of belief that equates to village shrines.

Other conditions varied as well. Some traditional shrines were reconstituted as village tutelary shrines while others were newly sought out by the lords of the *shōen* or landowners. However, in all cases, the lords of the *shōen*, or similar officials, guaranteed a part of their construction and ceremonial expenses. Therefore, the festivals at all these shrines had official status for the *shōen* and public lands.

In the middle ages, permanent sanctuaries were constructed in these shrines as well, and they commonly employed full-time religious functionaries, such as priests and shrine monks, to oversee maintenance and administration. This highlights one major difference from antiquity. Also, one of the main characteristics of village tutelary shrines was that the villagers bore some of the expense for the festivals and held an important role as participants in the festivals. This is the primary difference between these shrines and provincial *ichinomiya*, which functioned as religious institutions chiefly for the landed ruling class; this kept villagers in the role of spectators and taxpayers.

In the middle ages, these shrines, together with the provincial tutelary shrines (*ichinomiya*), were placed under the control of *sōja* shrines (those enshrining several deities) at the headquarters of the provincial governor. They were listed in the provincial shrine register drawn up by the *sōja* and formed a large contingent of each province's tutelary deities.

The *sōja* were formed at the same time as the medieval *ichinomiya* system. Like the *ichinomiya*, they were established in all the provinces. They were responsible for religious functions at the provincial governor's headquarters, and their primary duty was the administration and management of shrines, including the *ichinomiya*, within the province.

The name *sōja* originated from the fact that they worshipped together all the enshrined *kami* of the shrines within the province and adjoined the provincial governor's headquarters in each province. They formed part of the power structure of the provincial governor's headquarters, and the *sōja* priests and shrine monks were bureaucrats of that office as well.

The metamorphosis of the "kami"

How did the medieval shrine system and the changing religious structure that we have discussed change "Shinto"?

In considering this, we must be careful to keep in mind that this does not include such definitions as "Japan's indigenous folk religion." The early modern *Nippo jisho*,[9] which interprets the word "神道" (today, Shinto) as "*kami* and things related to *kami*," does not include such definitions either. This means that even in the middle ages, just as in antiquity, the word "神道 (*shindō, jindō*)," was understood in extremely vague terms as "the function, power, and authority of the *kami* and the *kami* in and of itself."

Naturally, things did not remain the same from antiquity to the middle ages, especially in the following two regards.

The first great change was in the meaning of 神 *kami*. The 神 of antiquity was generally read as *kami*, with an extremely vague definition based on an animistic tradition. By contrast, in the middle ages, the *kami* metamorphosed into the *kami* of imperial myths. Let us provide a few examples:

1   "Now, this realm of ours is the land of the gods, where the paired shrines of the great imperial ancestors work many wonders . . . [W]ith the god's help and in conformity with this decree, chastise the Heike and disperse the enemies of the imperial line." (Tyler, *The Tale of the Heike*, 283–84)
2   "The Great Bodhisattva Hachiman in the past was an emperor of the imperial court and in the present is a spiritual being again worshipped at the altar of the imperial ancestors . . . Our deity whom we revere is the original ancestor of the current ruler . . . The purpose of the manifestation of deity (*Shintō*) is for the protection of the state, and the doubling of divine virtue is due to the high regard of the shrine-temple." (Kōan 9 (1286) January 23, in the Iwashimizu Hachimangū document, compiled in *Kamakura ibun*, #15787, Vol. 21 in the section of the historical documents, originally in Chinese).
3   "Great Japan is a divine land (*shinkoku*). The heavenly ancestor established its basis. The sun goddess bequeathed it to her descendants for eternity. Only in our country did this occur. There is nothing comparable to it in other dynasties. This is why our country is a divine land . . . Because this country is especially the land of the gods, not one day passes when it runs counter to the way of the *kami* (*Shintō*)." (*Jinnō shōtōki, Gunsho ruijū* Vol. 29).[10]

There are too many examples of this to enumerate all of them. In the second quotation above, however, the "manifestation of the deity (*Shintō*)" is "Emperor Ōjin" of the imperial myths, who manifested himself as the great bodhisattva Hachiman, the one enshrined at Iwashimizu Hachimangū shrine. The "Shinto" here clearly refers to "Emperor Ōjin." Thus, in the middle ages, "Shinto" is understood as the *kami* of imperial myths and their circumstances, which is different from ancient cases.

The formation of Japanese "Shinto"

Another great change occurred when various ideological and conceptual interpretations about the deities who appeared in the imperial myths and were enshrined at shrines ("Shinto" teachings) also began to be called "Shinto." We can see this from Urabe (Yoshida) Kanetomo's work, *Yuiitsu shintō myōbō yōshū*, which was composed at the beginning of the Warring States period:[11]

Question: What are the details about how many specific divisions there are in Shinto?

Answer: First, Honjaku Engi Shinto (Shinto Originating from the Buddhist Essence Manifesting Itself as *Kami* in this World), second, Ryōbu Shūgō Shinto (Two Mandala

Combinatory Shinto),[12] and third, Genpon Sōgen Shinto (Shinto as the Fundamental and Original Principle of the Universe).[13] That is why it is called the Shinto of the three lineages."

Question: What is Honjaku Engi Shinto?

Answer: Lineages of priests are so named based on orally transmitted secret teachings and established from the secret traditions of each shrine in the history of its origin since a deity's incarnation at such and such a shrine, its descent to earth, or its ritual invocation. Or, mastery of the subtle qualities of the essence of Buddhist law is likened to the laws and teachings of inner purity, and giving ritual offerings is qualified as a ritual of outer purity. They call this "the Shinto originating from the Buddhist essence manifesting itself as *kami* in this world" or also "the Shinto of shrine traditions and records."

Question: What is Ryōbu Shūgō Shinto?

Answer: It compares womb and diamond mandalas of the two realms to the Inner and Outer Shines of Ise and combines (合わす) the many Buddhist divinities with the many *kami*.[14] That is the reason it is called Ryōbu Shūgō (習合) Shinto. (*Nihon shisō taikei, chūsei shintōron*).[15]

Kanetomo criticizes the two "Shintos" that had existed up to that time by upholding "Genpon Sōgen Shinto," or, Yuiitsu Shinto. What is quoted here is Kanetomo's explanation about the two forms of Shinto that became the object of his criticism (Honjaku Engi Shinto and Ryōbu Shūgō Shinto).

Later on, we will reflect further on "Yuiitsu Shinto," as Kanetomo calls it. Here, however, I want to note that many doctrines about *kami* in myths are also understood as "Shinto." If we combine these two great changes, then it becomes apparent that in the middle ages, the *kami* of imperial myths, their circumstances, and in addition, the many interpretations (doctrines) concerning them were all understood as "Shinto." This is an obvious difference from antiquity.

This is particularly important because it was when a "Shinto" that was different from the Chinese tradition and conveyed a distinctively Japanese meaning first became established.

Thus, we can see that Japan's "Shinto" was established in the middle ages, not in a primitive society and in antiquity. Furthermore, it was not, as has previously been thought, "Japan's indigenous folk religion." It is especially important that it was rather, first, the *kami* in imperial myths regarded as the enshrined deities of a shrine and their circumstances and, second, ideological interpretations concerning them.

Respective theoretical arguments

What was the backdrop to the Japanese "Shinto" that was established in the middle ages? A hint for this is suggested in Kanetomo's explanation given above.

The former (Honjaku Engi Shinto) of the two traditions that Kanetomo explained originated when each shrine created its own respective history. These were based in Buddhist thought, as is implied by the description of this form as "the Shinto of shrine traditions and records." It had meaning in its way of interpreting the shrine's origin, the spiritual authority of the enshrined deity, and its blessings in relation to imperial myths. As stated above, it is regarded as one of medieval *Nihongi*, and, since the enshrined *kami* are deities within imperial myths, we can deduce that this was nothing other than a product of the twenty-two shrines and, even more so, of the *ichinomiya*.

As had happened in Izumo Province's *ichinomiya* Kizuki Taisha, a suitable imperial myth was rearranged to correspond to the conditions at each province and at each shrine. Each shrine also equipped itself with an appropriate ritual system, in addition to its own original medieval mythology. We can conclude that these were the concrete details of what Kanetomo calls Honjaku Engi Shinto, which coincides with the medieval national establishment of the twenty-two shrines and the *ichinomiya* network.

By contrast, the latter system, Ryōbu Shūgō Shinto, explained the enshrined deities of Ise Jingū (the Inner and Outer Shrines) by syncretizing them with the dual mandalas called in Esoteric Buddhism, the Womb and Diamond mandalas. These were illustrations that depicted the enlightened realm of many principal objects of worship, and they showed many buddhas, bodhisattvas, and *kami* together. This Shinto could be labeled "Shinto" teachings based upon esoteric Buddhist theory, and they were intended to explain Ise Shinto, which worships Japan's sovereign, Amaterasu, from the standpoint of exoteric-esoteric Buddhism. This coincided with the establishment of the *kenmitsu* Buddhist system.

This shows how these systems were established—Honjaku Engi Shinto mainly in the twenty-two shrines and the *ichinomiya* shrines and Ryōbu Shūgō Shinto at *kenmitsu* Buddhist temples. In that sense, we can call the former "shrine Shinto" and the latter "Buddhist Shinto." The recognizable special feature that both share is that imperial myths form their base. We can think of it this way: In the times of antiquity, the imperial myths adopted by the *ritsuryō* state remained political slogans, so to speak. The large majority of even state shrines (official and national shrines) had absolutely no connection with them. In the middle ages, however, as the *kenmitsu* system developed, there was a greater dependence on imperial myths with a theoretical underpinning of Buddhist thought. This came to occupy an exceedingly important position as a theoretical support for the state and society.

The real situation of "Ise Shinto"

Among the medieval Shinto tradition, Ise Shinto has been well known and indeed thought to lie at the core of Japan's "Shinto." This also explains why the *Shintō gobusho,* believed to date from the latter part of the Kamakura period, is regarded as a sacred book of Japan's "Shinto."

However, this belief should be reconsidered. Perhaps most importantly, the term "Ise Jingū" did not exist in the middle ages. All that existed at that time was one case of what Yoshida Kanetomo calls "the Shinto of shrine traditions and records." This is one of the many examples of "shrine Shinto" that were produced by the twenty-two shrines, including Ise Jingū, and the *ichinomiya*. That was the reality of what is now known as "Ise Shinto."

However, the important point is that even regarding "shrine Shinto," the *kenmitsu* monks affiliated with each shrine were the ones directly responsible. Ise Jingū was connected to the respective views of the Inner and Outer Shrines, and it was unique in that it was organized by the Watarai priestly family of the Outer Shrine. Similarly, Izumo Province, which contains the temple headquarters of *ichinomiya* Kizuki Taisha, namely, Gakuenji, and its monks produced medieval myths.

Still another "Shinto"

Some documents related to "medieval Shinto" distinguish between "Shintō" and "Butsudō" (the way of the Buddha). Here are two specific examples.

1   "In the beginning, the precinct of the temple (referring to Gakuenji) broke off from the north-east corner of Spirit Vulture Peak in the Western Pure Land and Susanoo caught and stopped it while it was drifting (*furō*), floating this way on the sea. That is why they call it Furōsan. At its base he identified a special place where many deities had descended to earth and built a great shrine for those with spiritual benefits (referring to Kizuki shrine). On the peak, he constructed an altar for the avatars appearing in this world as *kami*, and it reveals a sacred realm—the Buddhist heavens from which buddhas temporarily manifest themselves. Every night the reason the great *kami* Hirō would come before shrine was (for the purpose) of protecting the Buddhist law and making a vow to the state. Although there are two here, Kizuki and Gakuenji, they do not end up being two, and not for a moment is there any difference between the way of the Buddha and the way of the *kami* (*Shintō*)." (Date unknown, fragment from a letter, a document originally possessed by Gakuenji, *Taishachōshi* historical materials volume—ancient, medieval #1837, originally in Chinese).

2   "I do not know if the way of the Buddha and the way of the *kami* (*Shintō*) are at the bottom one and the same. On the surface they are exceedingly different, and the way they operate is like fire and water. However, how do people who are priests perform Buddhist rituals side by side (with Shinto ones)." (*Kokubun tōhō bukkyō sōsho, Kōgi zuiketsu shū*, originally in Chinese)

The first passage is from Gakuenji in Izumo Province, which we have already discussed. The second passage is related to Suwa Shrine in Shinano Province. While the way of the gods (*Shintō*) and the way of the Buddha (*Butsudō*) have a relationship that is neither too close nor too distant, it is emphasized that they should be distinguished, particularly in the second passage.

Can we consider these passages as referring to "Japan's indigenous folk religion," which is particularly contrasted to Buddhism? This simply is not correct.

The second passage, as indicated by the phrase "the way they operate is like fire and water," means only that we should distinguish between Shinto and Buddhist rites. This is because of differences in their practice and their ritual systems. Although both religions are based in Buddhist thought, their practices diverged during the middle ages. It is probably appropriate to consider the practice of *kami* worship within a "flexible and free-flowing polytheism," which is Japan's unique religion. We can think of this as "the way of the gods of heaven and earth (*jingidō*)," which ultimately became shortened to "Shintō" as a contrast with belief systems such as Butsudō, Shugendō, and Onmyōdō.

We can also glean this from the first passage, which discusses the unified relationship between Kizuki shrine and Gakuenji, based on the medieval Izumo mythology, and describes each as Shinto and Butsudō. It is important to remember, however, that this usage is highly circumscribed. In the middle ages, this nomenclature occupied a minor and secondary place. That should be considered as a metaphorical way of speaking, which is also true for the examples above.

* * *

The systematization based on Yoshida Kanetomo

Given what we know about the history of Japan's religion, particularly shrines and "Shinto," it is extremely important to know something about Yoshida Shinto.

Yoshida Shinto was a completely new religious system—Yoshida (Urabe) Kanetomo the priest of Kyoto's Yoshida Shrine created its new theories and rituals concerning the "Shinto" doctrines and, based on them, attempted to unify, control, and regulate the shrines and priests throughout the country (Inoue Horoshi 2006).

There are three main reasons why this was particularly significant. First, the "Shintō" theory raised by Kanetomo is different from the various "Buddhist Shinto" and "shrine Shinto" that had previously existed; it was characterized by a new theory and systematization.

As I have mentioned previously, Kanetomo classified the "Shinto" teachings after the formative period of the middle ages into two—Honjaku Engi Shintō (Shinto Originating from the Buddhist Essence Manifesting Itself as *Kami* in this World) and Ryōbu Shūgō Shintō (Two Mandala Combinatory Shintō). He insisted that both of these teachings contained errors and introduced Yuiitsu Shinto (Genpon Sōgen Shintō (Shinto as the Fundamental and Original Principle of the Universe)). This includes a unique and superior "Shinto" teaching that arose from the revered deity Daigensonshin, the source of heaven and earth, who manifests himself in the spiritual nature of all beings (the deity of the first generation of the seven generations of the heavenly gods Kuni no Tokotachi) and was conveyed directly to the present day through the Urabe family's ancestral spirit Ame no Koyane. This doctrine also contrasts with Indian Buddhism and Chinese Confucianism and is Japan's indigenous religion (Shinto).

Concrete ritual practices

This did not stop simply at "Shinto" doctrine; it contained a system of concrete rituals that provided a unique structure. Kanetomo thought of Yuiitsu Shinto as having two sides—an external surface teaching and a hidden spiritual teaching. The former is a "Shinto" doctrine that is based on works such as the *Kojiki* and the *Nihonshoki*.[16] The latter, by contrast, is an ultimate secret teaching founded upon the Wondrous Scripture of the Divine Metamorphoses of the Heavenly Foundation (*Tengen shinpen shinmyōkyō*), the Wondrous Scripture of the Wondrous Energies of the Earthly Foundation (*Chigen jintsū shinmyōkyō*), and the Wondrous Scripture of the Wondrous Powers of the Human Foundation (*Jingen shinriki shinmyōkyō*).[17] This spiritual teaching invented the method of prayers and incantations of eighteen-fold Shinto's[18] three foundations, three mysteries, and three practices, emphasizing the importance of realizing inner and outer purity through prayers and incantations.

The relationship between the external surface and hidden spiritual teachings here are comparable to the relationship between exoteric and esoteric teaching in Buddhism. The three books which form the canon of Kanetomo's hidden spiritual teaching were fabrications from Taoist and Esoteric Buddhist thought and actually did not exist. Further, Kanetomo designed a unique funeral ceremony "*shinsōsai*," which was a formal *kami* ceremony different from Buddhism; he tried to include teachings on the destinies of souls in the next world and worked on a unique systematization of religious ritual that could rival Buddhism.

Aiming for the construction of a religious organization in society

Yoshida Shinto's third goal was to build a religious organization in society that we could also call a single religious association.

In order to bring his teachings into practice, Kanetomo constructed the Daigengū, a shrine intended for religious services, at Yoshida shrine in Bunmei 16 (1484). He built a six-sided hall behind the eight-sided main hall, and he worshipped all the deities of heaven and earth at that shrine, as well as the enshrined deities of over three thousand shrines throughout the entire country. Kanetomo styled himself as "the director and head priest of heavenly and earthly deities" and "the head priest of Shintō." He issued documents, called written commands from the foundation of all things, as well as a Shinto Conditional Approval, and he bestowed rank on shrines and priests all over the country, recognized divine names, and gave approval for shrines, festivals and rituals, and proper dress.

The formation of Yoshida Shinto, with these particular features, can be likened to the development of Taoism in China. Its historical significance is apparent from the following two points:

(a) This was the first time "Shinto" appeared with a meaning of Japan's indigenous religion in contrast to other religions such as Confucianism and Buddhism.
(b) The ideological interpretation about the deities in light of imperial myths ("Shinto" teachings) also are called "Shinto" ("Yuiitsu Shinto," for example).

Kanetomo called his own interpretation "The way of the *kami* of heaven and earth or Shinto," which was in common with medieval Shinto doctrine. He considered, however, his interpretation to come from the Unity of the Three Teachings (Shinto, Confucianism, and Buddhism) and "the theory of the origins (Shinto), leaves and branches (Confucianism), flowers and fruit (Buddhism)" (*konpon shiyō kajitsu setsu*). Thus, the fundamental difference from the medieval Shinto doctrine is that he considers Shinto a single "independent religion" that competes with Buddhism. For Yoshida Kanetomo, "Shinto" came to include those two meanings that clearly distinguished it from what had preceded it.

* * *

Notes

1 A discourse dealing with Japanese cultural, national, and spiritual identity purporting to show Japanese uniqueness or distinctive essence compared to other nations and people. It refers especially to discourses that try to find the basic common characteristics of the Japanese culture under the surface of great diversity.
2 Mark Teeuwen, "From *Jindō* to Shinto: A Concept Takes Shape," *Japanese Journal of Religious Studies* 29 (Fall, 2002):233–64.
3 For more information on the concept of *shinkoku*, see Allan Grapard, "Flying Mountains and Walkers of Emptiness: Toward a Definition of Sacred Space in Japan's religions," *History of Religions* 21 (February, 1982):195–221; Kuroda Toshio, "The Discourse on the 'Land of Kami' (Shinkoku) in Medieval Japan: National Consciousness and International Awareness," *Japanese Journal of Religious Studies* 23 (Fall, 1996):353–85; and Fabio Rambelli, "Religion, Ideology of Domination, and Nationalism. Kuroda Toshio on the Discourse of Shinkoku," *Japanese Journal of Religious Studies* 23 (Fall, 1996):387–426.
4 A particular form of government during the Heian period where the emperor abdicated the throne, took monastic vows, but still retained political power and influence—hence the name "cloistered government."
5 The three stages of this process are as follows: Stage one took place in the Nara period when shrine-temples (*jingū-ji*) were developed, based on the idea that *kami* were suffering beings subject to karma and in need of Buddhist salvation. The second stage of the amalgamation occurred in the Nara period when *kami* were considered to be protector deities of Buddhist temples and

Buddhism per se. Temples enshrined tutelary *kami* for that purpose, for example the god Hachiman for Tōdaiji Temple. Stage three is marked by the emergence of *honji suijaku* thought in the Heian period (ninth century). See Mark Teeuwen and Fabio Rambelli eds. *Buddhas and Kami in Japan: Honji Suijaku as a Combinatory Paradigm* (London: RoutledgeCurzon, 2002); Susan Tyler, "Honji Suijaku Faith," *Japanese Journal of Religious Studies* 16 (1989):227–50.

6 For more, see Allan Grapard, "Institution, Ritual, and Ideology: The Twenty-Two Shrine-Temple Multiplexes of Heian Japan," *History of Religions* 27 (February, 1988):246–69.

7 In the original text, Inoue lists all *ichinomiya* shrines, but this has been cut out of this translation.

8 Klaus Antoni, "Izumo as the 'Other Japan': Construction vs Reality," *Japan's Religions* 30, Nos. 1–2 (2005):1–20.

9 The *Nippo jisho,* originally entitled in Portuguese, *Vocabvlario da Lingoa de Iapam,* literally, The Portuguese Japanese Dictionary, was published in Nagasaki by the Jesuits in 1603 to help their priest-missionaries learn spoken Japanese.

10 This quote comes from the beginning of the *Jinnō shōtōki* (The Chronicle of the Legitimate Succession of Divine Emperors), which is a history of imperial rule by Kitabatake Chikafusa (1293–1354) written in 1339 around the time of the death of Emperor Go Daigo at the end of the Kemmu restoration (1336) and the onset of the Southern and Northern Courts period (1334–92). A statesman and supporter of the Southern Court, Kitabatake argued for the legitimacy of sacred imperial rule based on the line of succession through the Southern Court. Imperial rule was a sacred political order that was the basis of a stable Japanese polity in contrast to the chaos of the times with the ascendency of samurai power by Ashikaga Takauji. On the concept of *shinkoku* in the *Jinnō shōtōki,* see Evelyn S. Raws, *Early Modern China and Northeast Asia: Cross Border Perspectives* (Cambridge, UK: Cambridge University Press, 2015), 211ff. For the modern use of the work, see also Michael Wachutka, "'A Living Past as the Nation's Personality': *Jinnō shōtōki,* Early Shōwa Nationalism, and Das Dritte Reich," *Japan Review* 24 (2012):127–50. A full translation is found in H. Paul Varley, trans., *A Chronicle of Gods and Sovereigns: Jinno shōtōki of Kitabatake Chikafusa* (New York: Columbia University Press, 1980).

11 This text purports to be written by Kanetomo's progenitor Kanenobu, although it was written by Kanetomo.

12 Or "Shinto of the two Mandalas" was a Buddhist-inspired theological movement that interpreted Ise Jingū cult and deities based on Esoteric Buddhism. See Inoue Nobutaka, et al., *Shinto: A Short History* (London: RoutledgeCurzon, 1988), 84–88.

13 Or "Shinto as the founding principle of the universe," this is the term Yoshida Kanetomo uses for his own brand of Shinto, which he distinguished from forms reflecting the Buddhist combinatory paradigm or shrine-based forms focusing on origins. True Shinto for him originated from the gods of the *Kojiki,* especially Kunitokotachi. See See Inoue et al., *Shinto: A Short History,* 111.

14 In Esoteric Buddhism, the womb and diamond mandalas depict respectively the active instantiation of Buddha Nature into the phenomenal world and the essence of Buddha nature as such. Their two realms offer visual pictures of the Buddha Dharma.

15 For a full translation, see Allan Grapard, trans., "Yuiitsu Shintō *Myōbōyōshū,*" *Monumenta Nipponica* 47, No. 2:137–61.

16 These two texts, along with the *Sendai kuji hongi* compiled by Prince Shōtoku, are classified by Kanetomo as the "three primordial texts," indicating that Yuiitsu Shinto had existed since the beginning of the nation of Japan revealed by the Urabe clan *kami,* Ame no Koyane. See Grapard, trans., "Yuiitsu Shinto *Myōbōyōshū,*" 139.

17 Ibid., 139

18 Kanetomo argues that each of the three foundations of heaven, earth, and humankind has "six Shinto," one that corresponds to their fundamental spiritual energy and the other five corresponding to their five aspects or phases, an idea that comes from Chinese five phases of five elements cosmology and is combined here with different kami. See Grapard, trans., "Yuiitsu Shinto *Myōbōyōshū,*" 146.

SUGGESTED READINGS

Allison, Anne. *Precarious Japan*. Durham, NC: Duke University Press, 2013.

Beckford, James. *Social Theory and Religion*. Cambridge: Cambridge University Press, 2003.

Breen, John. *Yasukuni, the War Dead, and the Struggle for Japan's Past*. Oxford: Oxford University Press, 2008.

———. "Resurrecting the Sacred Land of Japan: The State of Shinto in the 21st Century." *Japanese Journal of Religious Studies* 37, No.2 (2010):295–315.

Clammer, John. "The Politics of Animism." *Interculture* 137 (April, 2000):21–44.

Duss, Peter. "Shōwa-Era Japan and Beyond: From Imperial Japan to Japan Inc." In *The Routledge Handbook of Japanese Culture and Society*, edited by Victoria Lyon Bestor and Theodore C. Bestor, 13–28. New York: Routledge, 2011.

Fujitani, Takashi. *Splendid Monarchy: Power and Pageantry in Modern Japan*. Berkeley, CA: University of California Press, 1996.

Hardacre, Helen. "Japan." In *Encyclopedia of Politics and Religion*, 2nd edition, edited by Robert Wuthnow. Washington DC: CQ Press, 2007, 492–98.

Honda Sōichirō. "Shinto in Japanese Culture." *Nanzan Bulletin* 8 (1984):24–30.

Inoue Nobutaka and Sakamoto Koremaru. "Modern and Contemporary Shinto." *Encyclopedia of Shinto*, http://eos.kokugakuin.ac.jp/modules/xwords/entry.php?entryID=738.

Ishii Kenji. "The Secularization of Religion in the City." *Japanese Journal of Religious Studies* 13 (February–March, 1986):103–209.

Kamata Tōji. "Shinto Research and the Humanities in Japan." *Zygon* 51 (March, 2016):43–62.

———. *Myth and Deity in Japan: The Interplay of Kami and Buddhas*. Translated by Gaynor Sekimori. Tokyo: Japan Publishing Industry Foundation for Culture JPIC, 2017.

Mullins, Mark R. "Religion in Contemporary Japanese Lives." In *Routledge Companion of Japanese Culture and Society*, edited by Victoria Lyon Bestor and Theodore C. Bestor, 63–74. New York: Routledge, 2013.

———. "Secularization, Deprivatization, and the Reappearance of 'Public Religion' in Japanese Society." *Journal of Japanese Religion* 1 (2012):61–82.

Nelson, John. *Enduring Identities: The Guise of Shinto in Contemporary Japan*. Honolulu: University of Hawai'i Press, 2000.

———. "Freedom of Expression: The Very Modern Practice of Visiting a Shinto Shrine." *Japanese Journal of Religious Studies* 23 (Spring, 1996):117–53.

———. *A Year in the Life of a Shinto Shrine*. Seattle, WA: The University of Washington Press, 1996.

Okuyama, Michiaki. "The Yasukuni Shrine Problem in the East Asian Context: Religion and Politics in Modern Japan." *Politics and Religion Journal* 3 (2009): 235–50.

———. "Historicizing Modern Shinto: A New Tradition of Yasukuni Shrtine." In *Historicizing "Tradition" in the Study of Religion*, edited by Steven Engler and Gregory Grieve, 93–108. Berlin: Walter de Gruyter, 2005.

Porcu, Elisabetta. "Religion and State in Contemporary Japan." In *Religion and Politics,* edited by Johann P. Arnason and Ireneusz Karoleewski, 168–82. Edinburgh: Edinburgh University Press, 2014.

Reader, Ian. "Secularization, R.I.P.? Nonsense! The 'Rush Hour Away from the Gods' and the Decline of Religion in Contemporary Japan." *Journal of Religion in Japan* 1 (2012):7–36.

Roemer, Michael K. "Shinto Festival Involvement and a Sense of Self in Contemporary Japan." *Japan Forum* 22, No. 3–4 (2010):491–512.

Rots, Aike P. "Sacred Forests, Sacred Nation." *Japanese Journal of Religious Studies* 42 (2015):205–33.

———. "Shinto's Modern Transformations: From Imperial Cult to Nature Worship." In *Routledge Handbook of Religions in Asia*, edited by Bryan S. Turner and Oscar Salemink, 125–43. London: Routledge, 2015.

Saeki Shōichi. "Is a Shinto Renewal Possible?" *Nanzan Bulletin* 17 (1993):32–35.

Scheid, Bernard. "Shintō Shrines: Traditions and Transformations." In *Handbook of Contemporary Japanese Religions,* edited by Inken Prohl and John Nelson. Leiden: Brill, 2012.

Shimazono Susumu. "State Shinto and Religion in Post-War Japan." In *The SAGE Handbook of the Sociology of Religion,* edited by James A. Beckford and N.J. Demerath III, 697–709. London: Sage Publications, 2007.

Smyers, Karen. *The Fox and the Jewel: Shared and Private Meanings in Contemporary Inari Worship.* Honolulu: University of Hawai'i Press, 1999.

Sonoda Minoru. "The Traditional Festival in Urban Society." *Japanese Journal of Religious Studies* (June–September 1975):103–36.

———. "Shinto and the Natural Environment." In *Shinto in History: Ways of the Kami,* edited by John Breen and Mark Teeuwen. Honolulu: The University of Hawai'i Press, 2000.

Takenaka Akiko. *Yasukuni Shrine: History, Memory and Japan's Unending Postwar.* Honolulu: The University of Hawai'i Press, 2000.

Teeuwen, Mark. "Jinja Honchō and Shrine Shintō Policy." *Japan Forum* 8, No. 2 (1996):177–88.

Ueda Kenji. "Shinto." In *Japanese Religion: A Survey by the Agency for Cultural Affairs*, edited by Hori Ichirō et al. Tokyo: Kodansha International, 1972.

Yanagita Kunio. *About Our Ancestors: The Japanese Family System.* Translated by Fanny Hagin Mayer and Ishiwara Yasuyo. Westport, CT: Greenwood Press, 1970.

GLOSSARY

Akitsumikami   Manifest *kami* or divinity. *Akitsumikami* most often appears in imperial proclamations and is an honorific term for the emperor who rules this world. However, there are cases where it mainly denotes a *myōjin*, a deity with marvelous powers that manifests itself in a form. This term became a matter of some controversy in regard to the emperor's "Humanity Declaration" (Ningen Sengen).

Amaterasu Ōmikami   The sun goddess and ancestress of the imperial house.

Amenominakanushi   Literally, Heavenly Center Ruling Deity, is the first *kami* to come into being in the Plain of High Heaven as a "solitary *kami*" (*hitorigami*) and to hide his presence. The deity is also counted as one of the *zōka sanshin* ("three *kami* of creation") and one of the five *kotoamatsukami* ("separate heavenly deities").

Arahitogami   A *kami* who is manifest as a human being.

Ashihara no Nakatsukuni   The Central Land of the Reed Plains. A term used for the Japanese isles in the chronicle literature.

Bekkaku Kanpeisha   Exceptional official shrine ranked as a special category under the governmental jurisdiction. This category was added in 1872, with Minatogawa shrine as the first case.

Bushidō   The idealized "way of the warrior," a code of conduct for the samurai class. It was given its classic expression in such pre-modern texts as Yamamoto Tsunetomo's (1659–1719) eighteenth-century work, *Hagakure* ("Hidden Leaves"). The code stressed frugality, loyalty to one's master, mastery of the warrior arts, and upholding one's honor even if it meant performing ritual suicide (*seppuku*). Some famous examples were the ritual suicides of the forty-seven rōnin after avenging the honor of their lord, Asano Naganori, during the Tokugawa period in 1703, and the *junshi* (following one's lord after death) of General Nogi and his wife after the death of Emperor Meiji in 1912. In pre-war modern Japan, the Bushidō ethic became centered on loyalty to the emperor.

Chian Ijihō   The Public Security Preservation Law of 1925.

Chinkonsai (also Chinsai)   Rite for the Pacification of the Spirit/Soul. Performed during the Winter Solstice for the reinvigoration of the emperor's body and spirit as well as the spirit of the rice.

Chinzasai   A ceremony to enshrine or, in some cases, re-enshrine a *kami*.

Chokusaisha   A shrine that has an imperial envoy in attendance at its festival as a sign of imperial patronage.

Dai Nihon Jingikai   Greater Japan Council on Deities

Daijōsai   Great Harvest Festival. This is a festival of state that inaugurates a new emperor's accession to the throne.

Daikyōin Great Teaching Institute, a body to help run the Great Promulgation Campaign and its Three Great Teachings in 1872. The institute, centered at Zōjōji in the Shiba district of Tokyo, was charged with disseminating state propaganda known as "Great Teachings." While the group of public instructors (*kyōdōshoku*) was originally composed of Shintoists and Buddhist sects, the Buddhist groups began to resist cooperating until the Institute was forced to disband.

Dai Tōa Kyōeiken Greater East Asia Co-Prosperity Sphere. This term was key in the discourse that was used to justify Japan's military aggression and expansionist policies throughout Asia. Although only formally announced as an official policy in 1940, it was a key ideological slogan in propaganda from the 1930s onward, emphasizing that Japan's own colonial conquests were in fact triumphs for a free "Asia for the Asians" against imperial Western powers. As an official state policy, it assumed that imperial Japan should rule over East Asian nations.

Dajōkan Council of State.

Emperor Jinmu Legendary/mythical first emperor of the imperial house.

Emperor Kinmei The twenty-ninth emperor of Japan according to the traditional lists. He is a historical figure who reigned from 539 to 571.

Emperor Kōtoku The thirty-sixth emperor, who reigned from 645 to 654 during the time of the Taika reforms, when Buddhism had become established among the aristocracy.

Emperor Sujin The tenth emperor in the traditional imperial line.

Engishiki *Engishiki* are the Engi era rules for implementing the ancient Japanese legal and administrative system, which comprises the penal codes (*ritsu*), civil regulations (*ryō*), and additional laws (*kyaku*). It is a fifty-volume compendium compiled by the imperial state in the Heian period. Begun in 905 and completed in 927, it covers two principal bureaucratic divisions of the government: the Council of Divinities (Jingikan) and the eight ministries included within the Council of State. It includes ten chapters devoted to *kami* worship, with chapters 9 and 10, the *Jinmyōchō*, listing the 2,861 public shrines (*kansha*) that receive offerings from the imperial court.

Fukensha Regional and prefectural shrine.

Fukko Shintō Revival or Restoration Shinto. This is an eighteenth-century Shinto school that used philology and the study of ancient texts like the *Manyōshū*, the *Kojiki*, and so on to reject Buddhist and Confucian influenced forms of Shinto in order to uncover its original pure form. It advocated respect for the emperor and an active religious devotion to the *kami*. As a form of National Learning Shinto, it is associated with the nativist scholars Motoori Norinaga (1730–1801) and his disciple, Hirata Atsutane (1776–1843), and gained prominence at the end of the Tokugawa period.

Fusha Regional shrine.

Gongen Shinto *kami* that were believed to be avatars or incarnations of Buddhist divinities.

Gōshi In modern Japan, Gōshi as a general term basically has two different meanings. One is the process of consolidating two or more shrines into one. Especially in late Meiji and later, because of this Gōshi process, the number of shrines was largely decreased. See "Jinja Gōshi." The second meaning is the ceremonial enshrinement as kami a group of souls of those who died in battle, performed at Yasukuni and other shrines for protecting the nation.

Gunjin Chokuyu The Imperial Rescript to Soldiers and Sailors is the code of ethics for military personnel issued by Emperor Meiji on January 4, 1882.

Hakkō Ichiu "All the world under one roof." A political slogan, originally attributed to Emperor Jinmu was first mentioned by Prime Minister Konoe on August 1, 1940 in his address on "Basic Principles of National Policy." The term suggests imperial Japan's rightful supremacy over other nations, the first step of which was to establish a new order in Asia under Japanese suzerainty.

Hatsumōde Annual Japanese custom of visiting a shrine in the opening days of the Japanese new year.

Himorogi Simple altars with ancient origins for worshipping the *kami* marked with a sacred rope with *sakaki* branches at the corners.

Hirata Shinto A school of Shinto associated with Hirata Atsutane (1776–1843), a disciple of national learning scholar Motoori Norinaga. He deemphasized the literary critical, empirical, and analytical approach of Motoori's studies of the *Kojiki* to promote a Shinto creed about the gods, ancestor worship, and ritual life that was the origin of all religious truths including Buddhism and Christianity.

Honji Suijaku The "one manifesting the traces." The medieval theory that explains the kami as incarnations or manifestations of buddhas and bodhisattvas. This doctrine ultimately is based on a general Buddhist idea that Buddhist divinities have the power to manifest themselves in temporary forms (*keshin* or *gongen*).

Ichinomiya Literally meaning principal shrine or first shrine, this was a way of ranking provincial shrines dating from the late Heian period. The shrine enshrined a *kami* who protected and represented the province.

Ikigami A Japanese term that literally means a "living god." Typically, it refers to men and women with charismatic powers and deep spiritual wisdom who also serve as spiritual mediators between the divine and human worlds. In Kūkai's Shingon school of esoteric Buddhism, for example, the goal is to attain buddhahood in this very body (*sokushin jōbutsu*) which is a "living buddha" (*ikibotoke*). *Ikigami* have long been a feature of Japanese folk religion and often appear as well as founders of Japanese new religious movements. *Arahitogami* can be understood as one version of *ikigami*.

Ise Jingū Grand Shrine of Ise

Ise Shinto A form of medieval doctrinal Shinto developed by the Watarai priests of the Outer Shrine of Ise. They were influenced by Buddhist monks whose twelfth-century esoteric texts attempted to understand the *kami* in terms of Buddhist doctrines. Watarai sacred texts (*Shintō gobusho*) drew on Chinese *yin/yang* and five-elements theories to explain their shrine's sacred meaning and the nature of its enshrined deity, Toyouke no Ōkami, a tutelary *kami*.

Iwasaka Stone altars or "divine seats" used in ancient times as a ritual space for worshipping the *kami*.

Izumokyō A type of sect Shinto not included in the original thirteen sects of Shinto in the pre-war period. It was founded by Kitajima Naganori (1834–93), a member of a priestly family at Izumo Shrine, after his line lost control over the hereditary leadership of the shrine due to Meiji era reforms.

Jingiin Board of Divinities. This was the extra-ministerial government administrative agency of shrine affairs attached to the Home Ministry. It was created according to Imperial Rescript 736 on November 9, 1940 replacing the Bureau of Shrines (Jinjakyoku). It handled the *jingū* shrines, shrine administration, priests, and the proper promulgation of Shinto ideology. It was dissolved by the Allies in 1945 in accordance with the Shinto Directive.

Jingikan Council of Divinities (in contrast to Council of State (Dajōkan)). The administrative office first established in the *ritsu-ryō* codes for the administration of *kami* worship, most particularly carrying out the annual rites as prescribed by the *jingiryō* (codes regarding deities), such as the Prayers for the Year (Kinensai) and the New Tasting Festival (Niinamesai). The office was reestablished in 1869 as part of the Meiji era reforms and abolished soon thereafter.

Jingishō Ministry of Divinities.

Jingū Hōsaikai Association of Devotees of the Grand Shrine of Ise.

Jingū Kōgakkan A university founded in 1882 by order of Prince Asahiko, the chief priest of Ise. In 1903 it was put under government control for the training of shrine priests until it was closed after the war. It was reopened in 1962 as a private university.

Jinja Gōshi Shrine consolidation. This was a government-supported policy in the Meiji and Taishō periods to establish centralized governmental control over shrines, and to consolidate smaller shrines through reorganization that would provide better support both economically and spiritually. A special focus was on the great number of small village (*sonsha*) and undesignated shrines (*mukakusha*). The latter were the lowest level of shrines according to the Meiji government's ranking system and received no government financial support. There were over 59,900 (over half of the shrines in Japan) that were given this designation. As a new policy, the Japanese government developed a shrine-merger policy that would eliminate and consolidate shrines as village worship centers in a way that would improve their financial condition. While the new policy ostensibly was "to exalt the majesty of the shrines and deepen the people's spirit of reverence," it furthered the government's political goals to unify the country under its centralizing control.

Jinja Gōshirei The Ordinance for the Consolidation of Shinto Shrines.

Jinja Honchō The Association of Shinto Shrines. This is an independent organization that formed after World War II that serves as an umbrella organization to support its shrine members. Established in 1946, it now supervises over 80,000 shrines in Japan.

Jinja Honkyō The Shinto Shrine of Fundamental Teachings.

Jinjakyoku Bureau of Shrines. A department set up within the Home Ministry in 1900 that endured until 1940. It was created as part of the institutional reforms of April 26, 1900, when the Home Ministry's Department for Shrines and Temples (Shajikyoku) fragmented into a Bureau of Shrines and a Bureau of Religion (Shūkyōkyoku). The department was abolished in November 1940 following the creation of the Jingiin.

Jinmu Kōki In 1872, the Meiji government decided that 660 BCE was the year of Emperor Jinmu's enthronement, and designated the year as the first year of the Japanese imperial calender that is called "Kōki." 1940 was the 2,600th anniversary of this Kōki, and a number of celebrations were held nationwide.

Jin'nō Divine emperor.

Jōmon The period extends from 13,000 to 300 BCE, and is identified by archeologists as comprised of several sub-periods. As its name indicates, the period is noted for the cord-marked decorative patterns on its pottery

Kami no Yo The Age of the Gods. More specifically, the opening section of the ancient imperial chronicles, the *Kojiki* and *Nihonshoki.*

Kamiyo Nanayo "The seven generations of the Age of the Gods." According to the *Kojiki* and *Nihonshoki*, the seven generations of deities that appeared after the world was formed, culminating in the pair of Izanagi and Izanami, the creator deities responsible for giving birth to the Japanese isles.

Kanchō Seido Chief management system, or chief manager system.

Kankokuheisha Official and national shrines combining Kanpeisha and Kokuheisha in one word. After the modern re-establishement of the Council of Divinities in 1871, this shrine ranking system was instituted by the government. See "Kanpeisha" and "Kokuheisha." By the Shōwa period, what distinguished these two types of shrines was mainly the source of their financial support.

Kannagara (Also *Kaminagara, Kamunagara*). Literally "the way as it is with the gods," the *kami* as such, as a *kami,* due to being a *kami,* or the will or the nature of the gods as it is. The term appears in early texts like the *Manyōshū* and the *Nihonshoki.* As glossed in the *Nihonshoki,* it means "to follow *kami* and to possess *kami* for oneself." Exactly what the term meant was a subject of controversy from the early modern period.

Kannagara no Michi The way of the gods. Another word for Shinto that became widely used after the Meiji period, particularly by Shinto nationalists, instead of using the Chinese-style term Shinto, in order to emphasize Shinto's indigenous character. In this sense, it refers to following the unique way of the *kami* conveyed from the age of the gods, that is following the will of the *kami* without any addition of human artifice or self-interest.

Kan'namesai First Fruits Festival or Autumn Harvest Festival performed by Ise Jingū in honor of the imperial house divine ancestry from the sun goddess Amaterasu Ōmikami. It also includes a ceremony for the imperial ancestors and a "worship from afar" (*yōhai*) by the emperor at the Kashikodokoro in the imperial palace.

Kanpeisha Official shrines that were administered by the national government, whose rites were supported by the imperial house budget (through the Ministry of Imperial Household). They were subdivided into three categories—major, intermediate, and minor. *Kanpeisha* were so designated because they could welcome an imperial envoy at their rituals who would present offerings. Since the establishment of Minatogawa Shrine in 1872, the new category of *bekkaku kanpeisha* was invented to refer to Minatogawa and other shrines.

Kansha Public shrine. General term for state-sponsored shrines or official shrines during the Meiji period for those shrines originally listed in the "Names of Deities" (*Jinmyōchō*) section of the *Engishiki.* After 1871 until the end of World War II, public shrines were divided into two major categories, *kanpeisha* and *kokuheisha* (generally referred to as *kankokuheisha*), both under governmental jurisdiction. These shrines were identified as 97 shrines at the beginning of the Meiji period, espanding finally to 224.

Kashikodokoro "Place of Awe," an imperial sanctuary also known as the Naishidokoro at the imperial palaces. It is the place where the *mitamashiro* (the sacred mirror), a replica of the mirror representing the sun goddess, Amaterasu Ōmikami, is kept for worship.

Kazoku Kokka The family state. It was the ideology of the pre-war Japanese government. As promulgated in imperial edicts and decrees like the Imperial Rescript on Education, this ideology was based on a patriarchal hierarchy that united loyalty (*chū*) to the state with filial piety (*kō*) to the head of the family household (*ie*). The emperor as the head of the Japanese state deserved the unconditional respect and obedience of his subjects, just as inferiors did toward superiors in the traditional Japanese family.

Kigensetsu Foundation Day. The national holiday held annually on February 11, inaugurated in 1872 to commemorate the foundation of the nation by the first emperor, Jinmu. It was listed as one of the four major national holidays (*setsu*) along with New

Year, the emperor's birthday (Tenchōsetsu), and Emperor Meiji's birthday (Meijisetsu). Abolished in 1948, it was restored in 1966, renamed as Kenkoku Kinen no Hi.

Kimigayo   This is the national anthem of Japan with lyrics based on a poem from the classical period with a melody that was added in 1880. The lyrics are as follows: "May your reign [that is the emperor's reign, *kimi ga yo*], continue for a thousand, eight thousand generations, until the pebbles, grow into boulders, lush with moss." Currently, the mandatory government rules reintroducing the singing of it in schools have generated much controversy.

Kinensai   The Spring Harvest Festival. Also known as Toshigoi Festival. See "Toshigoi no Matsuri."

Kodō   The ancient way. Motoori Norinaga's term for the originally pure form of Shinto found in the "Age of the Gods" section of the *Kojiki*.

Kōdō   Imperial way or the way of the emperor.

Kogaku   Ancient learning. What later became the National Learning School of Motoori Norinaga and others took its cue from early Tokugawa Neo-Confucian scholars like Ogyū Sorai, among others, whose method of study relied on directly studying the ancient Confucian classics. Nativists like Motoori, however, studied the *Kojiki* and other ancient Japanese texts to find a distinctively pure Japanese way of aesthetics, polity, and spirituality that preceded Chinese and Buddhist influence.

Kōgaku   Emperor or imperial learning.

Kojiki   The "Chronicle of Ancient Matters"—an imperial chronicle dating from 712.

Kōkoku   Imperial country or government by a divine emperor.

Kokka no Sōshi   Core or main rituals of state

Kokkyō   State religion.

Kokugaku   National learning—an intellectual and literary movement dating from the seventeenth to nineteenth centuries. Major figures included Kamo no Mabuchi, Motoori Norinaga, and Hirata Atsutane who aimed to discover a pure and unadulterated ancient way of Japanese culture, language, literature, religion, etc. free form foreign influence.

Kokugakuin   Originally established in 1890 under Kōten Kōkyūjo for the scholarly study of the Japanese classics, particularly mythologies and the history of shrines. It became a private university in 1906, and in 1908 a seminary for Shinto priests was additionally established.

Kokuheisha   National shrines. These were government-supported regional or provincial shrines. (under the pre-war system dating from 1906 until 1945 in which national shrines were directly financed by the government). The term *kokuhei* means offerings provided by the state derives from the *Engishiki*. Provincial shrines called *ichinomiya* were ranked as *kokuheisha*. These had lower ranking compared to *kanpeisha* and were subdivided into major, intermediate, and minor ranks.

Kokutai   National polity. The fundamental or essential national character a country should have as a unified nation state.

Konkōkyō   A Japanese new religion founded by Konkō Daijin (Akazawa Bunji, 1814–83), and focused on a faith in the deity Tenchi Kane no Kami, and the religious practice called *toritsugi* (spiritual intercession).

Kōreiden   "Imperial ancestor's altar." One of the three shrines housed within the Tokyo imperial palace, housing the imperial ancestors. It dates from 1869 and did not exist in the original imperial residence, the Kyoto Palace (*gosho*). It housed over 2,200 imperial ancestors including emperors, empresses, imperial consorts (*kōhi*), and other members of the imperial family (*kōshin*).

Kōshitsu Tenpan Imperial House Law.

Kōten Kōkyūjo The Research Institute for the Study of Imperial Classics. It was an institute founded in 1882, with Prince Arisugawa Takahito as its first director, whose aim was to cultivate, through education, moral virtue, which was the basis of a strong state. Later, in 1890, it established Kokugakuin in Tokyo.

Kunaishō Imperial Household Ministry. The modern institution was established by the Meiji government on August 15, 1869 and harked back to its precursor, established in the Taihō period's *ritsuryō* code (701–2). In 1949 it was renamed the Imperial Household Agency (Kunaichō) after post-war reforms.

Kuninotokotachi no Mikoto The lord who permanently founded the land. This deity appears at the onset of the "seven generations of the *kami*" in the *Kojiki*. He emerges following Amenominakanushi and the four other "separate heavenly *kami*" (*koto amatsukami*). On the other hand, the *Nihonshoki* suggests that he was the first *kami* to appear out of the chaos following the separation of heaven and earth.

Kurozumikyō Japanese new religion founded by Kurozumi Munetada (1780–1850). It is considered one of the earliest of the new Shinto groups classified as sect Shinto. Munetada was the son of a senior Shinto priest who experienced a direct conversion based on a profound religious experience of "direct receipt of the heavenly mission" (*tenmei jikiju*). As a healer and a preacher, his sect's teachings were based upon what he described as the "seven principles of everyday household life."

Kyōbushō Ministry of Public Instruction. Established in 1872, this office was responsible for running a revamped evangelism program to instill ethical conduct in the masses based on the way of the *kami*. But it also had power to regulate all religious sects and to appoint Shinto priests and Buddhist clergy. It reflects a broader tendency for centralized governmental control over the priesthood, ritual activities, and doctrinal matters. Its program for public instruction soon turned out to be outdated, and this Ministry was abolished in 1877.

Kyōha Shintō Sect Shinto. It is a term dating from the pre-war period referring to the thirteen Shinto sects that were officially recognized by the Meiji government as religious organizations.

Kyōiku Chokugo The Imperial Rescript (meaning edict or decree) on Education. It was promulgated by Emperor Meiji on October 30, 1890 (Meiji 23). The rescript was created as a guide for inculcating the basic moral principles of Japanese subjects essential for a strong state. The following year, copies were distributed to all primary schools, and its ceremonial reading before a portrait of the emperor (*goshin'ei*) was made obligatory as a school ceremonial practice.

Kyūchū Sanden The three sacred halls or shrines of the Tokyo imperial palace, which include the Kashikodokoro, Kōreiden, and Shinden.

Manyōshū This is Japan's first anthology of poetry dating from the Asuka to Nara periods, that is, from the second quarter of the seventh century until the middle of the eighth. The 4,516 short (*tanka*) and long (*chōka*) poems it contains are collected in twenty scrolls and often touch on religious themes. A source for the new era name, Reiwa, is traced back to *Manyōshū*.

Minsha Local shrines. In the pre-war shrine system established after 1871, in addition to *kanpeisha*, *kokuheisha*, and *bekkaku kanpeisha*, all other shrines were lumped together, subdivided into hierarchical categories, and treated as national facilities, regardless of their size or importance, until the end of World War II.

Misogikyō Japanese new religion founded by Inoue Masakane, a Shinto priest. The group splintered into many factions but has as its focus the three-creator *kami* (*zōka sanshin*) and other important deities.

Mukakusha Unranked shrines in the Meiji shrine ranking system.

Musubi The creative or vitalistic power or life process.

Naishidokoro Also known as Kashikodokoro. See "Kashikodokoro."

Nenchū Gyōji Annual events. The yearly round of local festivals and events often associated with shrines and Buddhist temples.

Nihonshoki An ancient imperial chronicle dating from 720, also called the *Nihongi*.

Nijūnisha The twenty-two shrines dating from the mid-Heian period that were especially venerated by the imperial court. These shrines made offerings on special occasions, for example, to pray for rain or to pray for rain to stop.

Niinamesai New Tasting Festival in which the emperor partakes of the first fruits of the harvest in a shared meal with the deities, preparing the way ritually for the new growing season.

Ningen Sengen (of Emperor Shōwa) The "Humanity Declaration." A declaration by the Emperor Shōwa renouncing his divinity, promulgated on January 1, 1946.

Norito Liturgies or incantations to be read before the deities in certain rituals or festivals for the deities. Ancient examples are the twenty-seven *norito* included in Book Eight of *Engishiki*, compiled in the twelfth month of 927. These are *norito* used at various ceremonies and rituals of the court, called *Engishiki norito* or *Engi norito shiki*.

Obon Also called "Urabone-e." One etymology explains the word derives from a Sanskrit "ullambana." Another etymology refers to an Iranian Sogdic term. The three-day festival of the dead taking place annually in the summer (the exact dates differ by area) when people return to their ancestral homes to clean and pray at the family grave sites. Obon dancing occurs in the evening, and ancestral spirits are believed to return from the other world to visit the family altar.

Ohigan Buddhist holiday event during the autumn and spring equinoxes in which special services are held at temples, and families come to offer prayers for the ancestral dead.

Ōkuninushi no Kami Literally great land master, this deity is the lord of the Central Land of the Reed Plains in the *Kojiki*.

Ōmotokyō A new religion in the Shinto lineage with headquarters in Ayabe in the Kyoto metropolitan area, founded by Deguchi Nao (1836–1918) in 1892, and led by the charismatic Deguchi Onisaburō (1871–1948). It was suppressed by the government in the pre-war period.

Onmyōdō The "way of yin and yang," a syncretic system of divinatory practices, originally based on Chinese yin/yang philosophy introduced into Japan in the fifth and sixth centuries and combined with Esoteric Buddhism and Shinto to create an eclectic syncretic system of occult practices and belief.

Ontakekyō Shinto sect linked to belief in Mount Ontake on the border of Nagano and Gifu prefectures.

Rikkokushi   The six early Japanese histories sponsored by the imperial court that traced the history of Japan from its beginnings in the age of the gods. These include the *Nihonshoki* (720), *Shoku Nihongi* (797), *Nihon kōki* (840), *Shoku Nihon kōki* (869), *Nihon montoku tennō jitsuroku* (879), and the *Nihon sandai jitsuroku* (901).

Ritsuryōsei   Literally, the system of "codes and ordinances." A political system of administration and laws based on Chinese models, which relied on Confucian and legalistic principles. The system of civil and administrative codes borrowed from Tang China that formed the legal basis of the early Japanese imperial state. It was implemented by Emperor Kōtoku in 645 with the Taika reforms.

Ryōbu Shintō   Shinto of the Dual Mandalas. A medieval form of Shinto centered on Ise Shrine that was deeply influenced by Shingon Buddhist esotericism. Particularly, it identified a parallel between the Inner and Outer Shrines at Ise with the dual mandalas, and speculated about the nature of the *kami* at Ise Shrine in terms of *honji suijaku* theory. In particular, at the end of the Kamakura period, Shingon Buddhist temples of the Ono and Hirosawa branches were important sources of Ryōbu Shinto doctrine outside the Ise Jingū priestly lineages. The monk Eison (1201–90), for example, founded a temple in the Inner Shrine at Ise, and developed Miwaryū Shinto in which he identified Amaterasu and the deities at Ise and Miwa as manifestations of the cosmic Buddha Dainichi.

Saiden   Divine rice paddies especially reserved and dedicated to the production of sacred rice for use in offerings of grain and ritual sake (*miki*) to the *kami* and used in the imperial Grand Harvest Festival (Daijōsai).

Saisei Icchi (sometimes spelled as Itchi)   The unity of rites and governance. This was a basic principle underlying pre-war State Shinto. The "imperial way" (*kōdō*), that is, the emperor's worship of Amaterasu and state-supported rites at Shinto shrines, was an ideal way of governing because politics was conducted in accordance with the will of the gods, whose blessings ensured the people's happiness and the nation's prosperity.

Saigi   Festivals, and ceremonies or liturgy, and interchangeable with *saishi*.

Saijin   The main deity of a shrine.

Saishi   Festivals, and rites or rituals, and interchangeable with *saigi*.

Sannō Ichijitsu Shintō   A Tendai Buddhist form of Shinto originating from a mountain shrine called Hie Taisha near Enryakuji Temple in present day Ōtsu in Shiga prefecture, which enshrines the deity Hie Sannō. Ichijitsu Shinto thought, developing from the Kamakura period, envisaged Hie Sannō as a supreme deity..

Sanshu no Jingi   The three divine treasures or imperial regalia. These are the mirror (*yata no kagami*), sword (*kusanagi no tsurugi*), and jewel (*yasakani no magatama*); the three imperial regalia are the symbols of imperial status

Seikyō Bunri   Meiji government policy of 1882 after the failure of the Great Teaching Campaign. It marked the formal separation of government from religion, although the government kept the principle of *saisei icchi*. Shrine Shinto and its rituals were defined as a moral and patriotic "way" different from sectarian forms of Shinto and other religions.

Sekai Kyūseikyō   A new religion that emerged from the Ōmoto line, founded by Okada Mokichi (1882–1955).

Shichigosan   The 7-5-3 annual festival in November at Shinto shrines for young children.

Shikinensai Rites held at palaces and shrines. For those honoring previous emperors and empresses, rites are held one year after on the same day as his or her death, and successively at three, five, ten, twenty, thirty, forty, fifty, and one hundred yearsposthumously, with subsequent ceremonies at one-hundred-year intervals.

Shikinen Sengū The regular reconstruction of a new shrine and transfer of the enshrined object from the old to the new location. The famous case is at Ise Jingū to be held every twenty years. The last one at Ise was completed in 2013.

Shinbutsu Shūgō The "synthesis of *kami* and buddhas." The longstanding unification or syncretism of Buddhist ideas, deities, practices, and temple spaces with those related to *kami*. See "Honji Suijaku."

Shinden Also known as the Hasshinden, this shrine was established in 1869 to house the eight deities in the Council of Divinities, and then moved in 1872 to the Imperial Palace to house those eight with the deities of heaven and earth. One of the three shrines within the Imperial Palace for private rites involving the imperial family.

Shinkoku Divine state or nation.

Shintai An object of devotion enshrined in a shrine.

Shintō Honkyoku Originally an administrative bureau under the name of Shintō Jimukyoku in the Meiji period representing independent Shinto sects. It became an independent religion, Shinto Honkyoku, founded in 1885 by Inaba Masakuni (1834–98) and was later known as Shinto Taikyō. Inaba sought to propagate the "Great Teachings" after the Pantheon Dispute. Some of the most important so-called "new religions" (*shin shūkyō*), Tenrikyō, Konkōkyō, and Kurozumikyō were originally classified as its sub-sects.

Shintō Jimukyoku Office of Shinto Affairs. Government office established in 1875 after the formal separation of Buddhism and Shinto and as part of a government effort to guarantee religious freedom by separating Shinto state ritual from what it defined as explicitly Shinto-related religious groups. For a time, it supervised both government-supported shrines and Shinto sects and promoted the state-sponsored "Three Great Teachings." After 1882, with the official separation of the government from religion, the office was renamed the Shintō Honkyoku.

Shintō Shirei The Shinto Directive issued by the General Headquarters Supreme Commander for the Allied Powers on December 15, 1945, concerning the "Abolition of Governmental Sponsorship, Support, Perpetuation, Control, and Dissemination of State Shinto (Kokka Shintō, Jinja Shintō)."

Shintō Shūseiha One of the thirteen Shinto sects of the pre-war period. It was founded by Nitta Kuniteru (1829–1902), an Edo-period samurai nationalist who became an ardent Shinto proselytizer in the early Meiji period under the state-organized moral preceptors (*kyōdōshoku*). He later set up his own group with ties to confraternities associated with Mount Fuji and Ontake worship.

Shōkonsha A type of shrine set up in the early Meiji period that venerated the war dead as protecting spirits of the nation. The most famous of these is Yasukuni Shrine in Tokyo. All the others became regional Gokoku shrines in 1939.

Shosha All other shrines not included among the state-sponsored shrines in the shrine system dating from the Meiji period. Also known as *minsha*.

Shugendō "The way of discipline and testing," a form of Mountain asceticism that was highly syncretic, combining elements of folk belief, *kami* worship, esoteric meditative practices founded in legend by the seventh-century Buddhist ascetic En no Gyōja, also known as En no Ozunu, or Jinben Daibosatsu. The goal of practice is to obtain spiritual powers through an experience of unity with the *kami* in the mountains and the natural world.

Shūkyō Hōjinhō   Religious Corporations Act, passed in 1951.

Shūkyō Hōjinrei   Religious Corporations Ordinance, passed in 1945.

Shūkyōkyoku   Bureau of Religion. In 1900 the government reorganized the Bureau of Religion and Bureau of Shrines in the Home Ministry. In 1913, the Bureau of Religion moved to the Ministry of Education. After World War II, it was renamed the Shūmuka (Religious Affairs Division), which administered religious affairs including shrine matters.

Soshin (also pronounced as Sojin)   Ancestral *kami*, and the originator of a family or clan. This is based on the belief that all human beings are descendants of the *kami*, an example of which is Amaterasu, who in the chronicle literature is cited as the progenitor of the imperial line.

Suika Shintō   "Divine benefits and protection Shinto." A Confucian-influenced form of Shinto founded by Yamazaki Ansai (1616–82).

Taika Reforms   The Taika (literally "Great Change") reforms of 645–46 instituted by Prince Nakano Ōe (later the Emperor Tenji) and Nakatomi Kamatari (later Fujiwara Kamatari) modeled the Japanese imperial government (the *ritsuryō* state) after T'ang Chinese legal and institutional precedents. Reforms included mandatory public ownership of the land (by the emperor), a new administrative and military organizational framework, an equitable public taxation system based on a census, and the codification of laws.

Taihō Codes   Legal and governmental administrative codes introduced to the imperial court from the T'ang dynasty in China in the early Nara period.

Taikyō   The Great Teachings. The three basic tenets of the new national doctrine originally promulgated by the Meiji government. The experiment lasted between 1870 and 1884 through the government-supported Great Dissemination Campaign which attempted to instill the teachings in the wider public. Along with promulgating a state-sanctioned pantheon with Amaterasu Ōmikami at its head, the campaign distilled its teachings to, above all, love of country and devotion to the emperor.

Taisei Yokusankai   The Imperial Rule Assistance Organization, also known as the Imperial Aid Society, was a nationwide organization organized by Prime Minister Konoe Fumimaro in 1940 as part of his efforts to unite the nation by creating a united single-party totalitarian state. As part of those efforts, the association organized a nationwide system of neighborhood associations (*tonarigumi*) dedicated to supporting the state behind the war effort.

Takamagahara (Takamanohara)   The High Plain of High Heaven where the gods dwell found in the chronicle literature.

Tenjō Mukyū no Shinchoku   The divine edict on the eternal sovereignty of the imperial line. This occurs in the *Kojiki* when Amaterasu commands her grandson Ninigi to rule the Central Land of the Reed Plains.

Tenrikyō   A new religion founded by a humble illiterate villager, Nakayama Miki (1798–1887) after her experiences of spiritual possession by the god that she later identified as God the Parent (*Oyagami*), Tenri-Ō-no-Mikoto, who revealed teachings for living a joyous life. Headquartered in Nara prefecture at Tenri City, it was one of the largest new religions until the end of World War II.

Tenson Kōrin   The heavenly descent of the grandchild of the heavenly *kami*, Ninigi no Mikoto, from the Plain of High Heaven to the Central Land of the Reed Plains following the command of Amaterasu Ōmikami and Takamusubi no Mikoto as related in the *Kojiki* and *Nihonshoki*.

Toshigoi no Matsuri   The New Year festival traditionally celebrated in spring to pray for a good harvest. A prayer service performed every year on the fourth day of the second month, according to the lunar calendar; it is for good crops, the well-being of the emperor and the nation.

Toyouke no Ōkami   A great imperial deity of the Outer Shrine of Ise who was originally venerated as the *kami* in charge of foodstuffs (*miketsukami*) for the Inner Shrine. This deity, found in the *Kojiki*, was assigned to accompany Ninigi no Mikoto on his descent into this world. She is identified with other deities (e.g. Ukemochi) as a divinity of foodstuffs.

Tsukinamisai   Shrine monthly festival.

Ujigami   Originally means a "clan deity," that is, an ancestral divinity associated and therefore worshipped by specific clans (*uji*). However, early on in Japanese history, these *kami* became associated with areas in which they had settled and became worshipped by local people in villages or regions as local tutelary or chthonic divinities (*ubusunagami*). This shift accelerated in the middle ages as warrior clans increasingly identified themselves with the lands of the manorial estates (*shōen*) under their control; they adopted local divinities as their clan gods, and local people also came to adopt warrior clan gods as local tutelary spirits. In other words, clan and local divinities merged as a result of this process that created village "*ujigami*" worshipped by local people called the "*ujiko*" ("clan members").

Ujiko Shirabe   Shrine parishioner registration regulations that were put into law on July 4, 1871 and lasted two years. All newborn children were registered at their local Shinto shrine and obtained an amulet as proof of registration. So, everyone hypothetically was registered and belonged to a specific Shinto shrine throughout the country. This was an attempt to replace the Danka system of household registration at Buddhist temples, which was enforced during the Tokugawa period.

Yamabushi   "One who lies/hides in the mountains." They are Japanese mountain ascetics associated with Shugendō, a form of itinerant spiritual practice associated with Esoteric Buddhism.

Yamatodamashii   "The spirit of Yamato" or Japan.

Yamatohime no Mikoto   She was the daughter of Emperor Suinin who found the permanent location for the worship of the great imperial sun goddess, Amaterasu, at Ise Jingū. Her shrine (Yamatohime no Miya) remains today in the Inner Shrine (Naikū).

Yōrō Code   This was one of several codes governing all facets of government administrative rules including state-sponsored religious offices and services. It was compiled in 718. As such, it was important to the administration of the Council of Divinities (Jingikan), one of the two main governing departments instituted by the *ritsuryō* legal system of eighth-century Japan.

Yuiitsu Shintō   "Only-one Shintō." Also known as Yoshida Shinto, this was a major school of Shinto thought that developed in the Muromachi period and was prominent through pre-modern times. It was founded by Yoshida Kanetomo (1435–1511), whose family was tied to the Urabe clan of court tortoise-shell diviners. Kanetomo's Shinto doctrines and rituals, like those found in Ise Shinto and Ryōbu, were an electic mix of Taoism, Onmyōdō, and Esoteric Buddhism.

Zōka Sanshin   The three deities of creation or three demiurges who originally created the world as noted in the *Kojiki* and *Nihonshoki:* Amenominakanushi no Kami, Takamimusubi no Kami, and Kamimusubi no Kami.

Zoku Shintō   This term, used by Hirata Atsutane and other national learning scholars, distinguished the Shinto that was combined syncretically in Buddhism and Confucian-based Shinto sects from the "true Shinto" of the ancient classical texts. A classic example of this usage is Hirata Atsutane's *Zokushintōtaii* (The Great Meaning of Vulgar Shinto), published in 1860.

INDEX

Abe Shinzō 284, 288, 294
akitsumikami 7, 20, 34, 129, 145–146, 168, 172, 178, 254–255
Amaterasu Ōmikami 67, 70, 71, 72, 104, 108, 139, 141, 146, 164, 167, 168, 171, 172, 173, 174, 175, 176, 179, 182, 184, 213, 214, 265, 271, 278, 288, 340
Amenominakanushi 64, 213, 214, 223, 224, 312–314, 338
ancestor worship 6, 13, 17, 80, 89, 93, 100, 111, 150, 158, 226, 256, 272, 336–347
ancient way (*kodō*) 3, 12, 128, 148, 170, 311
arahitogami 7, 34, 129, 153, 178, 196, 204, 254–255, 257, 343
Asad, Talad 7, 9
Ashizu Uzuhiko 13–15, 34, 195, 204, 236–247, 288
Association of Shinto Shrines *see* Jinja Honchō
Aston, W.G. 2–3, 8, 62, 92, 99

Bekkaku Kanpeisha 49, 186, 305
Board of Divinities (Jingiin) 19, 20, 34, 57, 121, 126–127, 132, 171, 180–191, 200, 202, 208, 238, 240, 300
Buddhism: assimilation with Shinto 5–6, 13, 61–73,91–96, 103–104, 113, 146–147, 149–151, 158, 161–162, 163–164, 170, 213–214, 267–281, 286, 302, 311–312, 315, 326, 333, 341–343, 352, 354–362, 363–364; distinguished from Shinto 12, 13, 19, 32–33, 44, 61–62, 91–96, 100–102, 106–108, 113,148, 151, 163, 222–223, 267–281, 291, 303–304, 305–306, 309, 311, 315–316, 336, 341, 342, 343–344, 357, 365, 367
bunkateki shūkyō (cultural religion) 11, 19, 283, 291, 326, 327
Bureau of Religion (Shūkyōkyoku) 11, 33, 91, 92, 306
Bureau of Shrines (Jinjakyoku) 11, 33, 34, 91, 126, 169, 306, 343
Bushidō 12, 76, 131, 154, 163, 170, 199, 219, 222

Cardinal Principles of Shrines *see Jinja hongi*
Cardinal Principles of the National Polity *see Kokutai no hongi.*
Chamberlain, Basil Hall 5, 12–13, 32, 62
Christianity: contrasted to Shinto 3–4, 14, 15, 17, 19; missionaries to Japan 4
Confucianism: distinguished from Shinto 86, 90, 94, 103, 107, 148, 279, 311, 314, 341, 367; influence on Shinto 36, 109, 131, 147–149, 161, 219, 222–223, 256, 279, 342–343
Council of Divinities (Jingikan) 11, 43, 69, 93, 95, 177, 183, 185, 186, 303, 304, 306, 343
Council of State (Dajōkan) 44, 46, 47, 49, 183, 303, 304, 343
cultural religion *see* bunkateki shūkyō

Dai Tōa Kyōeiken *see* Greater East Asia Co-Prosperity Sphere
Daijōsai 62, 64, 66, 69, 238, 251, 258, 260, 261–262
Dajōkan *see* Council of State
Daikyōin (Great Teaching Institute) 32, 306
Daoism *see* Taoism
Deguchi, Onisaburō 36, 125, 345–346

Engishiki 69, 94, 95–96, 138, 181, 182, 185–186, 189, 330

funerals 35, 50, 202, 244, 246, 351, 366

General Headquarters, Supreme Commander for the Allied Powers (GHQ) 4, 7, 19, 198, 199, 206–210, 211, 237, 239, 240, 241, 244
Gunjin Chokuyu (Imperial Rescript to Soldiers and Sailors) 222, 253–254, 264
Great Harvest Festival *see* Daijōsai
Greater East Asia Co-Prosperity Sphere 122, 167

Hardacre, Helen 2, 10–11, 14, 35, 127
Hearn, Lafcadio 2, 8, 12, 17, 35, 102–103, 129, 290, 334, 335–337, 347

national learning 4, 6, 8, 12, 13, 28, 32, 36, 89–90, 94, 107, 109, 110, 114, 128, 137, 241, 242, 279 298, 303, 309, 310, 311, 316, 343–344; *see also kokugaku*
national polity 2, 5, 9, 18–21, 31, 34, 35, 36, 62, 63, 65, 78, 80, 90, 106, 121, 123, 126–129, 137, 150, 153–165, 166–170, 171–180, 182, 199–201, 217, 219, 222–223, 231, 241, 249, 252, 256, 264–265, 303; *see also kokutai*
nationalism 1, 5–6, 8, 13, 18, 20, 27, 31, 32, 36, 74–88, 122–132, 147, 199, 208, 238, 242, 249, 279, 280, 287, 288, 290, 344
Ningen Sengen (The Humanity Declaration) 7, 39, 201
Nihonjinron 8, 290
Nihonshoki 4, 12, 15, 16, 17, 62, 65, 67–68, 70, 72, 95, 96, 106, 107–108, 113–115, 123, 129, 136–139, 142, 146, 148, 149, 160, 172, 174, 181, 183, 184, 222, 226, 231, 254–255, 265, 309, 333, 336, 340, 342, 347, 354, 360, 366
Ninigi no Mikoto 72, 129, 168, 172, 174, 175, 178, 265, 321

Occupation, post-war 7, 19, 195–201, 202–204, 211, 217–218, 236–247, 267, 287, 288, 297, 299, 300, 303
Ōmotokyō 33, 36, 125–126
Orikuchi Shinobu 6, 15, 132, 195, 203, 211–216, 236, 242, 297, 347

Religious Corporations Act (Shūkyō Hōjinhō) 200, 241, 245, 326
Religious Corporations Ordinance (Shūkyō Hōjinrei) 201, 203, 240, 245
Research Institute for the Imperial Classics 137, 237
Rikkokushi 96, 178, 185
rituals 11, 13–16, 19, 27, 33, 34, 43, 44, 46, 56, 62, 65, 69, 93, 96, 109, 176, 182–184, 188, 202, 204, 222, 237–238, 241, 246, 254, 257–263, 268, 270–271, 274, 276, 285, 286–288, 289, 291, 299, 302–303, 305, 317, 319, 326, 330, 333–334, 336, 341, 345, 351–352, 366–367

saisei icchi, *see* Unity of rites and governance
shinkoku (divine land) 21, 79, 130, 145, 172, 196, 307, 355, 360–362
Shinmin no michi 2, 4, 16, 18, 121, 127–129, 131, 166–170, 198, 208
Shinto: Directive 4, 7, 18–20, 27, 34, 126, 131–132, 195, 199–200, 203–204, 207–210, 236–242, 245–246, 249, 287, 297–300, 303; folk, 20, 283, 285, 290–291, 297, 311; Restoration 4, 110, 180, 223, 279, 303, sect 19, 33–34, 52, 92–93, 109, 129, 184, 209,

211–212, 255, 298, 310–311, 345–346; shrine 3, 11, 13–15, 18–20, 33–34, 131–132, 200–201, 202, 209, 211, 236–240, 242, 244, 247, 249, 286–288, 297–299, 307, 309–311, 318–319, 324, 326–327, 329, 364, 366; State 2, 6, 13–15, 18–20, 27, 31–36, 122–133, 199–202, 207–210, 250–257, 269, 279, 286, 288, 291, 297–308, 346
Shinto Association of Spiritual Leadership *see* Shintō Seiji Renmei
Shintō Seiji Renmei 13, 288, 289, 300, 301
Shōwa, Emperor (Hirohito) 124, 195–196, 201, 203, 289
Shrines: *ichinomiya* 12, 185, 276, 292, 356–361, 363–364; national 121, 127, 183–189, 240, 258–259, 261, 305, 360, 362; official 36, 182, 185–187, 188–189; prefectural 187–189, 301; tutelary 90–91, 158, 188, 325, 331, 360–361; village 11, 89–90, 187–188, 301, 302, 304, 331–332, 361
Shūkyō Hōjinhō *see* Religious Corporations Act
Shūkyō Hōjinrei *see* Religious Corporations Ordinance
Shūkyōkyoku *see* Bureau of Religions
Suinin, Emperor 70, 175, 184
Sujin, Emperor 47, 70, 71, 145, 175, 183, 185, 320, 333
Supreme Commander for the Allied Powers (SCAP) 19, 28, 34, 126, 196, 199–200, 207–210, 249, 298

Taikyō (Great Teachings) 45, 47, 114, 129, 132, 173
Taosim 107, 112, 113, 115–116, 222–223, 269–271, 275, 278, 310–311, 340–341, 343, 366, 367
Teeuwen, Mark 2, 3, 4, 15, 202, 288, 354–355
Tenrikyō 33, 91, 95, 306, 345, 352
Tsuda Sōkichi 4, 6, 12, 13, 35–36, 106–118, 123, 138, 226, 269–270, 275, 278, 279

Ueda Kenji 15–16, 283, 285, 287–288, 290, 309–322
Unity of Rites and Governance 130, 176–178

Watsuji Tetsurō 7, 16, 195, 203–204, 217–235
Way of Subjects, *see Shinmin no michi*
weddings 243–244, 262–263, 351
World War II 4, 7, 20, 29, 34, 125, 127, 197–199, 203, 236–247, 283, 310, 329, 344, 352

Yamatodamashii 8, 102, 131, 146
Yanagita Kunio 3, 5, 11, 13, 18, 20, 28, 35, 89–98, 211, 236, 242, 286, 291, 297, 298–307, 323, 347
Yasukuni Shrine 33, 49, 87, 101, 186–188, 202–203, 240, 244–246, 249, 289, 298, 301, 305